EFFECTIVELY MANAGING HUMAN SERVICE ORGANIZATIONS

Third Edition

SAGE SOURCEBOOKS FOR
THE HUMAN SERVICES SERIES

Series Editors: ARMAND LAUFFER and CHARLES GARVIN

Recent Volumes in This Series

HEALTH PROMOTION AT THE COMMUNITY LEVEL edited by NEIL BRACHT

FAMILY POLICIES AND FAMILY WELL-BEING: The Role of Political Culture
by SHIRLEY L. ZIMMERMAN

FAMILY THERAPY WITH THE ELDERLY by ELIZABETH R. NEIDHARDT & JO ANN ALLEN

SINGLE-PARENT FAMILIES by KRIS KISSMAN & JO ANN ALLEN

SUBSTANCE ABUSE TREATMENT: A Family Systems Perspective edited by EDITH M. FREEMAN

SOCIAL COGNITION AND INDIVIDUAL CHANGE: Current Theory and Counseling Guidelines
by AARON M. BROWER & PAULA S. NURIUS

UNDERSTANDING AND TREATING ADOLESCENT SUBSTANCE ABUSE
by PHILIP P. MUISENER

EFFECTIVE EMPLOYEE ASSISTANCE PROGRAMS: A Guide for EAP Counselors and Managers
by GLORIA CUNNINGHAM

COUNSELING THE ADOLESCENT SUBSTANCE ABUSER: School-Based Intervention and
Prevention by MARLENE MIZIKER GONET

TASK GROUPS IN THE SOCIAL SERVICES by MARIAN FATOUT & STEVEN R. ROSE

NEW APPROACHES TO FAMILY PRACTICE: Confronting Economic Stress
by NANCY R. VOSLER

WHAT ABOUT AMERICA'S HOMELESS CHILDREN? Hide and Seek by PAUL G. SHANE

SOCIAL WORK IN HEALTH CARE IN THE 21st CENTURY by SURJIT SINGH DHOOPER

SELF-HELP AND SUPPORT GROUPS: A Handbook for Practitioners by LINDA FARRIS KURTZ

UNDERSTANDING DISABILITY: A Lifespan Approach by PEGGY QUINN

QUALITATIVE METHODS IN SOCIAL WORK RESEARCH: Challenges and Rewards
by DEBORAH K. PADGETT

LEGAL ISSUES IN SOCIALWORK, COUNSELING, AND MENTAL HEALTH:
Guidelines for Clinical Practice in Psychotherapy by ROBERT G. MADDEN

GROUPWORK WITH CHILDREN AND ADOLESCENTS: Prevention and Intervention in
School and Community Systems by STEVEN R. ROSE

SOCIALWORK PRACTICE WITH AFRICAN AMERICAN MEN: The Invisible Presence
by JANICE M. RASHEED & MIKAL N. RASHEED

DESIGNING AND MANAGING PROGRAMS: An Effectiveness-Based Approach (2nd edition)
by PETER M. KETTNER, ROBERT M. MORONEY, & LAWRENCE L. MARTIN

PROMOTING SUCCESSFUL ADOPTIONS: Practice With Troubled Families
by SUSAN LIVINGSTON SMITH & JEANNE A. HOWARD

CREATING AND MAINTAINING STRATEGIC ALLIANCES: From Affiliations to Consolidations
by DARLYNE BAILEY & KELLY McNALLY KONEY

STOPPING CHILD MALTREATMENT BEFORE IT STARTS by NEIL B. GUTERMAN

ORGANIZATIONAL CHANGE IN THE HUMAN SERVICES by REBECCA ANN PROEHL

FAMILY DIVERSITY: Continuity and Change in the Contemporary Family by PAULINE IRIT ERERA

EFFECTIVELY MANAGING HUMAN SERVICE ORGANIZATIONS (3rd edition) by RALPH BRODY

EFFECTIVELY MANAGING HUMAN SERVICE ORGANIZATIONS
Third Edition

Ralph Brody
Cleveland State University

Sage Sourcebooks for

the Human Services

SAGE Publications
Thousand Oaks ▪ London ▪ New Delhi

For information:

Sage Publications, Inc.
2455 Teller Road
Thousand Oaks, California 91320
E-mail: order@sagepub.com

Sage Publications Ltd.
1 Oliver's Yard
55 City Road
London EC1Y 1SP
United Kingdom

Sage Publications India Pvt. Ltd.
B-42 Panchsheel Enclave
Post Box 4109
New Delhi 110 017 India

Printed in the United States of America

Library of Congress Cataloging-in-Publication Data

This book is printed on acid-free paper.

Brody, Ralph.
Effectively managing human service organizations / by Ralph Brody.— 3rd ed.
 p. cm. – (Sage sourcebooks for the human services series)
Includes bibliographical references and index.
ISBN 1-4129-0420-X (pbk.)
 1. Human services—Management. I. Title. II. Series.
HV41.B689 2004
361′.0068—dc21   2004007221

04   05   06   07   08   10   9   8   7   6   5   4   3   2   1

Acquisitions Editor:	Arthur T. Pomponio
Editorial Assistant:	Veronica Novak
Production Editor:	Julia Parnell
Copy Editor:	Diana Breti
Typesetter:	C&M Digitals (P) Ltd.
Indexer:	Kay M. Dusheck
Cover Designer:	Glenn Vogel

Dedicated to
my wonderful family:
Phyllis
Lisa, David, Mike, and Tara
Heather, Alex, Shannon, Celena, and Jason

Contents

Preface   xi

Acknowledgments   xiii

PART I: Setting Organizational Directions   **1**

1. Leading the Organization   3
    Dynamic Interaction: Managers, Staff, and Situations   4
    Flawed Leadership Styles   6
    Leadership Competencies   8
    Attributes Contributing to Leadership   15
    Diagnosing Your Leadership Style   16
    Questions for Discussion   17

2. Strategic Planning   20
    Embracing Change   20
    Developing the Strategic Plan   23
    Summary of a Strategic Planning Process   35
    Questions for Discussion   36

3. Designing and Developing Consumer-Oriented Programs   39
    Designing a Logic Planning Model   39
    Designing a Marketing Planning Model   47
    Summary of Elements of Good Design   55
    Questions for Discussion   56

4. Implementing Action Plans   58
    Setting Objectives   58
    Anticipating Unintended Consequences   62
    Managing Change   64
    Working Out the Details of a Plan   71
    Questions for Discussion   74

5. Problem Solving   77
    Step 1: Analyzing the Problem   77
    Step 2: Considering Alternative Solutions   82
    Step 3: Making Decisions   84
    Step 4: Monitoring Results   91
    Step 5: Making Corrections   93
    Questions for Discussion   94

PART II: Increasing Productivity   **97**

6.   Time Management   99
    Factors Affecting Time Management   99
    Diagnosing the Time Problem   100
    Planning the Use of Time   101
    Combating Time Gobblers   106
    Procrastination   110
    Questions for Discussion   111

7.   Finding and Keeping Productive Employees   113
    Finding the Right People for the Job   113
    Conducting a Nondiscriminatory Interview   114
    Developing Staff   119
    Structuring the Organization to Be Productive   120
    Restructuring Jobs   122
    Dilemmas About Keeping Good People   127
    Questions for Discussion   129

8.   Managing Employment Challenges   132
    Diagnosing Employment Problems   132
    Dealing With Legally Protected Employees   135
    Taking Corrective Action to Change Behavior   139
    Progressive Discipline   140
    Handling the Incompetent Employee   142
    Questions for Discussion   147

9.   Humanizing the Organization   151
    Creating a Culture of Caring   151
    Managing Stress   155
    Fostering Diversity   159
    Harassment in the Workplace   162
    Addressing Complacency and Stagnation   165
    Being Sensitive to Inequities   166
    Questions for Discussion   168

10.   Supervising Staff   172
    The Pickle in the Middle   172
    The Supervisor's Multiple Roles   174
    Delegating Assignments   178
    Applying Motivational Theories to
      Improve Performance   180
    Elements of Good Supervision   182
    Supervising Volunteers   188
    Questions for Discussion   189

11.   Appraising and Compensating Performance   194
    Appraisal Methods   194
    Conducting an Appraisal Conference   200

Compensating Work   204
Symbolic Rewards   216
Questions for Discussion   218

PART III: Enhancing Agency Survivability   **223**

12. Managing Agency Finances   225
     Understanding the Budgeting Process   225
     Understanding Types of Income and Expenses   229
     Conducting the Budgeting Process   233
     Using the Budget as a Management Tool   237
     50 Considerations for Reducing Costs   243
     Achieving Long-Range Financial Stability   248
     Questions for Discussion   252

13. Strategic Resource Development I   254
     Developing an Integrated Fund Plan   255
     Preparing a Case Statement   257
     The Annual Campaign   258
     Capital Campaigns and Major Gifts   262
     Questions for Discussion   273

14. Strategic Resource Development II   276
     Planned Giving   276
     Seeking Corporate Contributions   283
     Electronic Philanthropy   285
     Business Ventures   286
     Conducting Fundraising Events   289
     Questions for Discussion   298

15. Preparing Effective Proposals   301
     Preliminary Considerations   301
     Preparing Proposals   304
     Approaching Foundations for Funding   315
     The Proposal Is One Part of the Process   317
     Criteria for Effective Proposals   318
     Questions for Discussion   321

16. Seeking Funding   324
     Types of Foundations   324
     Primary Source for Foundation Funding:
         The Foundation Center   326
     Using Foundation Directories   327
     Using Online Directories and the FC Search CD-ROM   331
     Federal Government Funding   334
     State and Local Government Funding   336
     Lobbying for Government Funding   339
     Questions for Discussion   341

PART IV: Interacting Effectively　　　**343**

17.　Making Meetings Productive　　345
　　　Considering Whether or Not to Hold a Meeting　　345
　　　Making the Best Use of Time　　346
　　　Functions of Meetings　　348
　　　Dealing with Meeting Problems　　348
　　　Questions that Facilitate Discussion　　350
　　　Reaching a Consensus　　351
　　　Using the Group Process to Generate Ideas　　352
　　　Recording the Meeting Process　　357
　　　Leading a Meeting　　358
　　　Questions for Discussion　　359

18.　Improving Communications and Handling Conflicts　　362
　　　Factors That Interfere With Good Communication　　363
　　　Conquering Writer's Block　　363
　　　Handling Conflicts　　368
　　　Persuasive Communication　　371
　　　Facilitating Internal Communication　　373
　　　Facilitating External Communication　　378
　　　Questions for Discussion　　380

19.　Team Building and Coalition Building　　384
　　　The Importance of Team Building　　384
　　　Task Forces　　392
　　　Coalition Building　　393
　　　Questions for Discussion　　399

20.　Working with a Board of Trustees　　402
　　　Distinguishing Governance From Management　　403
　　　Board Roles and Responsibilities　　406
　　　Board Structures and Processes　　413
　　　Addressing Special Board Issues　　415
　　　Summary: Elements of a Well-Functioning Board　　417
　　　Questions for Discussion　　421

Web Sites for Human Service Managers　　425

Bibliography　　429

Index　　447

About the Author　　461

Preface

Several experiences prompted me to invest in developing this third edition. First, using the book in graduate courses on administration provided me an opportunity to receive invaluable feedback from my students. In the classroom, their inquiries caused me to clarify points and add examples to this new edition. I am greatly indebted to their suggestions and ideas. As a result, I have made changes in every one of the chapters. Many of the questions for discussion at the end of the chapters are drawn directly from my classroom experience.

Second, as a result of conducting managerial training workshops in the United States and abroad, I have grown to appreciate some of the universal issues facing those who are in human service leadership roles. Facilitating strategic planning for community agencies in the United States (with both a local and national focus) made me aware of how committed managers are to developing outstanding programs. Conducting workshops for nongovernmental organizations (NGOs) on fundraising and board development for managers in Ghana, on organizational development for community leaders in Nigeria, on leadership issues for NGO managers affiliated with the Alliance for Arab Women in Egypt, and on fundraising for community leaders and professionals connected with Madrasa Pre-School Programs in Kenya and Uganda all have contributed to adding new elements to this edition. Because the issue of sustaining organizations looms as such a major concern in the United States and abroad, I have written a new chapter on resource development, added information relevant for middle managers on overseeing project budgets in the chapter on managing agency finances, and expanded the chapter on working with agency boards.

Third, since the last edition I became aware of new developments in the field that would be useful for managers. Developing and teaching a course on service delivery models for Ph.D. students, many of whom were seasoned administrators seeking to broaden their perspectives, stimulated my thinking about ways to enhance consumer-oriented services. As a result, I have added a chapter on designing consumer-oriented services to this new edition. In this chapter and others, I have given special attention to designing programs that can demonstrate tangible results because of the increasing importance that public and private funders give to evaluating performance.

This edition is divided into four sections. Part I sets the organizational direction by examining leadership issues, planning strategically, designing consumer-oriented services, implementing action plans, and conducting problem solving.

Part II focuses on increasing productivity by managing time, getting and keeping employees, addressing employee challenges (including motivating unproductive employees), developing important organizational values, providing highly competent supervision, and appraising and rewarding performance.

Part III concentrates on sustaining human service agencies. The first chapter in this section is devoted to fund management; the remaining chapters offer concrete directions on how organizations can sustain themselves through such diverse resource development strategies as annual campaigns, planned giving, special events, and proposal grants. Specific guidance is given for seeking private foundation funding and government grants and contracts.

The last section, Part IV, reviews ways to improve internal communications and external networking. It covers such topics as making meetings more productive, improving communications and resolving conflicts, building teams within the organization, and developing important networking opportunities. The final chapter provides specific suggestions for working with a board of trustees.

Throughout the book I note the interrelationship of ideas and information. For example, writing a proposal (Chapter 15) requires an understanding of designing consumer-oriented programs (Chapter 3), setting objectives (Chapter 4), and implementing a timeline chart (Chapter 4). Similarly, the discussion on resource development (Chapters 13 and 14) is linked to developing a strong mission statement as a key element in strategic planning (Chapter 2).

As I have stated in previous editions, I was motivated to write this book because of my own experiences as a supervisor, middle manager, and executive director. The book draws upon a vast amount of literature that is filtered through my own pragmatic experiences. Although I am no longer a professional manager, continuous consultation assignments and training workshops have kept me alert to the needs of human service managers. I hope that this new edition provides current and future managers with the understanding and the skills to make their organizations the very best that they can be. We owe no less than our best to the people we serve.

Ralph Brody

Cleveland, Ohio

Acknowledgments

In addition to the feedback of my graduate students and those whose suggestions influenced the development of the first and second editions, several people contributed to this edition. I especially appreciate the contributions of Paul Alandt; Cynthia G. Bailie; Deborah Beckwith; Michael Brody; Phyllis Brody; Al Klubert; Bernadette Kerrigan; Patricia Nash; Pat Reid, Ed.D.; Lisa Brody Ritchey; Shantanu Shaligram; J. Toth; Chris Trunk; Kate Wladyka; Portia Winston, Ph.D.; Achila Wali; Chris Winslow; and Tom Woll. Many helpful suggestions were made by Gary Bess, Ph.D. on resource development and strategic planning, Marcella Stahm on fund management, and Walter Zborowsky on government programs.

PART I

Setting Organizational Directions

Chapter 1: Leading the Organization

Chapter 2: Strategic Planning

Chapter 3: Designing and Developing Consumer-Oriented Programs

Chapter 4: Implementing Action Plans

Chapter 5: Problem Solving

In this part you will learn how to

❖ Identify leadership styles

❖ Discern how personal flaws can interfere with good leadership

❖ Value competencies that effective managers must have

❖ Understand the value of strategic planning

❖ Establish an inspiring mission statement

❖ Address critical issues to gain mastery over the future of the organization

❖ Take specific steps to implement an action plan

❖ Design a logic planning model using systems concepts

❖ Develop a client flow chart

❖ Prepare measurable objectives

- ❖ Evaluate service outcomes
- ❖ Develop a marketing plan responsive to consumers and stakeholders
- ❖ Handle resistance to change
- ❖ Initiate innovative projects that can be dispersed throughout the organization
- ❖ Conduct contingency planning
- ❖ Work out details of an action plan, including implementation of assignments
- ❖ Take corrective action based on feedback
- ❖ Make decisions by analyzing problems and considering alternatives
- ❖ Monitor results and take corrective action, if necessary

1

Leading the Organization

All organizations require effective managers who can inspire staff, set general directions, and be accountable for the organization's achievements. Because good staff management is so crucial, it is important to identify those special qualities that characterize an effective leader. Be aware, however, that no simple formula exists for the "perfect" manager in either profit or nonprofit organizations.

A managing partner of a leading management consulting firm, McKinsey and Co., observes that, in his work with more than 50 chief executive officers (CEOs), he has not found an "ideal" manager. The visionary leader may be poor at implementing plans; the superb implementer may have difficulty in setting directions for the organization; the stickler for getting results may have poor interpersonal skills.[1] Indeed, effective managers can come in all sizes and shapes: extroverted or shy, personable or aloof, colorless or charismatic, self-centered or altruistic, and highly logical or intuitive. The only thing these managers have in common is the ability to get things done.[2]

Furthermore, some would argue that a distinction should be made between a leader and a manager.[3] According to this view, a *leader* is an innovator, has a long-range perspective, challenges the status quo, and "does the right thing." By contrast, a *manager* "does things right," maintains the status quo, has a short-range perspective, and focuses on structures and systems. The thesis of this chapter is that effective managers must provide both visionary leadership and day-to-day administrative direction.

To gain a better understanding of the manager's role, this chapter probes the following issues: (a) What are the dynamic interactions among managers, staff, and situations? (b) What flaws can limit management effectiveness? (c) What special competencies do effective managers need to make their organizations more productive? (d) What attributes contribute to leadership? and (e) How can you diagnose your own leadership style?

Dynamic Interaction:
Managers, Staff, and Situations

In any organization, a dynamic interplay exists among management orientation, staff behaviors and attitudes, and situational factors.[4]

Leadership Styles

Depending on their personal predisposition, managers will reflect different leadership orientations. Some managers prefer *directive leadership*, feeling that they must assume personal responsibility for making major decisions and then act as a taskmaster to get things done. Although they may occasionally ask questions or allow limited dialogue, there is no doubt that the decision is essentially and primarily theirs. They prefer to "take charge." They see themselves functioning as an orchestra conductor, calling on staff to harmoniously achieve a desired result.

Other managers choose *participative leadership*, in which they present ideas and invite feedback from staff. They want to retain final decision-making authority, but they also want their employees to suggest alternative solutions.

Still others prefer *delegative leadership*. These managers derive considerable satisfaction from giving decision-making responsibilities to their staff. If they participate in the decision-making process, they are comfortable in assuming no more authority than other members of the group.

Managers have their own predisposition toward one or more of these three orientations. Which is best for effective management? It all depends on the nature of the staff and the external and internal situations.

Factors Operating Within Staff

Managerial leadership (directive, participative, or delegative) can be greatly influenced by the way staff respond to organizational tasks and decision making. For example, if employees are intelligent, educated, and experienced; if they are motivated to make decisions; if they identify with organizational goals; if they can manage unstructured work situations; if they have the self-confidence and self-reliance to work independently; and if they are truly invested in their work, then a manager would more likely delegate responsibilities and decision making to them.

If, however, staff are inexperienced, feel reluctant to take on additional responsibilities, require structured and unambiguous assignments, or resist making decisions, then a more directive management style may be required.[5] This kind of staff presents a challenge to managers who value staff participation in decision making.

Situational Factors

Certain outside forces can affect managerial style. The organization itself may perpetuate certain values, work habits, traditions, and expectations around managerial behavior. Some organizations, for example, operate under pressure and crisis, thereby requiring directive management. Moreover, an organization's size and structure can influence the choice of leadership styles. An agency with offices in different locations, for example, will tend toward autonomous decision making because of its decentralized operations.

The problems an organization deals with may affect leadership style. If a problem is complex and requires staff with different types of knowledge and experiences, then a participative leadership style is appropriate. If a problem requires the expertise of only the leader, however, then staff may be involved in more supportive functions.

Time pressure is another key ingredient affecting leadership style. The more immediately a decision must be made, the more difficult it is to involve other employees. Agencies operating under emergency conditions (e.g., handling housing needs in the aftermath of a flood) require expedited decision making involving fewer staff.

To be effective, managers must exercise flexible leadership.[6] At times, a directive approach may be more appropriate than a delegative or participative one because of organizational context or the nature of the situation. Where a crisis exists, where staff have become complacent, or where difficult budget or personnel decisions must be made, a "take charge" (directive) leadership style is appropriate. A delegative style works best when staff are highly self-motivated and need little direction. The leader sets the pace for high performance standards and then expects staff to carry out assignments competently. Working within a framework developed by the leader, staff members are allowed the freedom to innovate, experiment, and take calculated risks. This style works best with employees who want to develop professionally and are willing to take on challenging assignments. Some professional staff may feel excluded if the manager does not consult them about the overall plan.

Participative leaders emphasize relationships. They value staff as individuals, and they value workplace satisfaction and harmony. These leaders build strong emotional ties, foster loyalty, create a sense of belonging, provide continuous positive feedback, and build staff morale. At the same time, effective managers do not give praise indiscriminately when performance is poor because this can invite mediocrity. In situations where staff need direction, this style by itself is not sufficient.

Managers need to combine approaches based on circumstances and the skills of the staff. For example, in setting up a phone system, a manager might ask a staff committee to recommend a system. By alerting staff in advance that all recommendations will be seriously considered but that the final decision will be made by management, the manager conveys respect for the staff's thinking and at the same time establishes boundaries—reflecting both a delegative and a directive approach. Unless the manager is clear about the staff role, confusion and dissatisfaction might occur.

Leadership styles need not remain constant and can change as staff change. For example, at the beginning of a project the manager may need to be more direct, but as staff become more familiar with their tasks and more competent in performing them, the manager can delegate and take a less active role in providing guidance. Hence there is a certain ebb and flow in the management style, as managers become more active or less directive, based on the needs of the staff.[7]

Although flexible leadership is generally desirable, certain leadership styles are realistically more responsive to the needs of a highly trained professional staff and more conducive to productivity in human service organizations. Today's professional staff expects organizational managers to be participative, and staff want to be consulted and exert influence, especially on those areas that have a direct impact on their own work. Most want the manager to hear and consider their ideas. Indeed, leadership and a sense of accountability and empowerment in most human service organizations, as in most corporations, are being pushed down and distributed throughout the organization. In effect, everyone in the organization can have opportunities for exerting leadership.[8]

Flawed Leadership Styles

As human beings, leaders are not perfect; they do have flaws—some more than others. Do any of the following managerial profiles seem familiar?

The Oblivious Manager. For oblivious managers the best leadership is no leadership. They assume people always know what they should be doing, and these leaders are passive with regard to giving directions or creating a vision for the organization. Follow-through and monitoring are not part of their management framework. Although well intentioned, their lack of urgency and follow-through results in plans that either drift or become unraveled. They feel so self-defeated through years of bureaucratic frustration that they define success merely as avoidance of failure. As a consequence of their lackadaisical attitudes, they seldom encourage staff to excel, and their low expectations result in limited staff performance. These managers think that ignoring problems makes them go away. They are usually unaware of pending crises until, regrettably, the world crashes down upon them. Their passivity is reflected in the often-used expression, "Whatever you want to do is fine with me." They typically abdicate responsibility for making tough decisions.[9]

The Misleader. The problem with misleading managers is that they convey mixed or even incorrect messages. For example, they ask employees to make a decision about the most effective budget cuts and, on hearing their opinions, announce that the final decision will be made by the board of trustees.

What they meant to ask for were suggestions that would be subject to review. They use a participative style, although being directive is more appropriate for the situation.[10] On the other hand, situations calling for more participation from staff are responded to with "the boss knows best." The staff never knows what to expect or how the manager will react. After making a number of these misleading requests, these managers can expect little input from their employees.

The Put-Downer. Managers who humiliate employees by belittling their abilities can expect little or no investment from staff. This style creates a backlash of resentment that harms staff attitudes and performance. One manager, for example, calls his social service staff "brain dead" because he thinks they are not working as hard as they should; the response is not a commitment to work harder but a protest in the form of t-shirts that read "Staff of the Living Dead." Typically, these managers are not as obvious; their pervasive deprecation is more subtle, conveying in many small ways that they believe staff are incompetent.

The Micromanager. Managers can become so invested in the work of staff that they commit the error of over involvement. They fail to allow responsible people the freedom and autonomy to do their jobs. These managers constantly check on staff performance and attitudes because of their own insecurities. They take the role of monitor to its extreme by constantly checking on staff's whereabouts, reading all correspondence that emanates from their departments, and obsessively checking staff's opinion of them. As a consequence, staff do not have the opportunity to grow, develop skills and experience, or learn from their own mistakes. These managers may not believe that their staff have potential, and gain great satisfaction from delving into details better left to others.

The Arrogant Manager. Arrogant managers display the hubris of exaggerated pride, super self-confidence, and consummate self-importance.[11] Disregarding staff contributions, they think that positive results are due only to their own special performances. When they proclaim an idea for a project, they believe staff will automatically understand it and assent.[12] These managers do not take the time to clarify, discuss, and work through concerns. They later wonder why their requests, regulations, and policies are not carried out with enthusiasm. They never admit mistakes, even to themselves; consequently, they easily become victims of their own fallibilities. Because of a blinding sense of self-importance, they make miscalculations that may be catastrophic to the organization.

The Narcissist. Some managers manipulate people to achieve personal ambitions; staff become instruments for the manager's self-gratification. Their work and projects they carry out are not primarily for the good of the organization but for self-aggrandizement. They constantly connive to advance their own position of power, and they excessively control the organization's process to achieve predetermined personal goals. Narcissists are also egocentric, believing that employees are pawns used to fulfill personal goals.[13] Even when they use a participative leadership approach, they still strive to control the outcome. Staff go through the motions of making a decision but know that their own security in the organization depends on bending to the will of their manager. Narcissists promote themselves so much that those who have actually done the real work soon lose their commitment. Narcissists may even represent staff ideas as their own to curry favor with superiors.

The Loner. By keeping their office doors closed most of the day and seldom having contact with employees, loner managers are usually seen as aloof and unapproachable. Loners rarely consult with staff because they do not want to be bothered with delays or objections that may lead to modifications of their original ideas. They feel like supplicants when asking for colleagues' support.[14] Through this self-imposed isolation, they contribute to the low morale in the organization because staff eventually feel ignored and abandoned.

The Charmer. The primary purpose of charmer managers is gaining personal acceptance from staff. To them, popularity is far more important than substantial achievements, and their charm is a cover-up for not getting things done. Although well liked by staff because of the limited demands these managers make, they ultimately are ineffectual.

These leadership flaws are exaggerations, and few managers manifest these caricatures in their pure form. Any one of us, however, may lapse into some of these behaviors. Being mindful of these possibilities can minimize their destructive impact on an organization's productivity.

Leadership Competencies

It is not enough for managers to be constantly aware of possible flaws in personal behavior that could detract from their leadership effectiveness. They must also discern how their strengths can heighten the organization's performance. Previously, it was noted that leadership style should be matched to the needs of the organization and the situation. Assuming that this match exists, there are certain traits and competencies that are of value to managing human service organizations. Effective managers evidence an outstanding ability to get things done. The following are some thumbnail sketches based on the lives of exemplary leaders.

Waulina T. heads a suburban children's residential treatment center. Several years ago she decided that her agency must aggressively confront inner city problems even though the agency is located 12 miles away from downtown. She has worked hard to establish drug treatment programs in the city's school system. Her successful efforts to make her organization more relevant have earned her both great respect and an infusion of funds for her agency.

Tom L. has expanded a program of health care for homeless people to include a variety of services: drug treatment, a winter housing program, and a facility for mentally disabled women. In addition, he has organized the business and political leadership of the community to create adequate low-income housing.

Ambler M. directs a special organization designed to combat crime in the community. He saw that gangs were a growing concern and led school officials, police, and parents to help them address gang-related issues more appropriately.

Rothina D. infused a moribund organization with a new spirit when she became its director. Established to obtain jobs for public assistance recipients, the organization had not been able to convince the corporate community to accept its trainees until she developed an outstanding training and orientation program. She conveys high expectations to her staff and imbues them with sensitivity to the needs of the trainees.

Smitty C. heads the local YMCA. He sees his most important managerial role as helping staff develop their potential. He has initiated a number of staff training programs, encourages staff to follow through on their ideas, and emphasizes the importance of staff ownership of successful programs.

Jeraldine H. is the head of a large staff unit within a mammoth bureaucracy. Her paramount concern is to help staff feel invested in their work. She meets regularly with her supervisory personnel, and they in turn meet with their staff to develop a greater sense of unity and dedication toward their work. As a consequence of these meetings and a series of staff appreciation sessions, staff are beginning to rededicate themselves. Many of them are staying after 5:00 P.M. or working weekends to complete assignments. Work teams are developing innovative ideas for dealing with emergencies. Staff enthusiasm about their work has increased because Jeraldine conveys daily how important their contributions are to the community.

What do these effective managers have in common? What follows are those competencies they share that enable their organizations to perform at a highly productive level.

Articulating a Future Orientation

Effective managers are constantly seeking out trends—possible changes in demographics, funding, or political alignments—and determining how these trends might influence their organization. They formulate a vision of the future either within their own mind or by mobilizing the organization to think strategically (see Chapter 2). They encourage everyone who should be involved—staff, boards of trustees, or even public officials—to focus their attention on issues leaders consider significant.[15] Sometimes, their view of the future is influenced by a profound desire to improve performance.

Competent leaders are never fully satisfied. Even when staff are performing well and their units or the organization as a whole are accomplishing their goals, effective managers continually ask, "How can we improve? How can we do things better?" Of course, they enjoy and appreciate achievements, but they have a need to reassess the status quo. They are intolerant of complacency that comes from previous successes, and as they meet one objective they press on to another. In short, effective managers are continuously working to help their organizations grow and change to meet new situations and to focus their members on the most significant issues.[16] Ambler M. had the foresight and the understanding that gangs were using the school building walls, mailboxes, and even their school artwork to communicate gang messages. He convinced his organization to make reducing gang activity a priority long before other community youth organizations realized the need for it. As a result of his vision, his organization now has a unique niche and is looked to as the expert source on gangs by juvenile court judges, school administrators, and political leaders.

Waulina T. is continually thinking about the future of the organization. She says,

> My ultimate purpose is to leave the organization in better shape than when I became its director. That is what my predecessor did, and that is the position I hope my successor takes as well. I am always dreaming up projects for the following year. Right now I'm planning for a new building on our campus that will house adolescents referred by juvenile court. It may take four years to build, but we've got to begin to plan now.

Being a Social Entrepreneur

Social entrepreneurs are organizational leaders who are driven to pursue programs they consider vital to meeting needs, and feel a heightened sense of accountability to the constituencies they serve. They are innovative, bold, action-oriented, resourceful, and value-creating change agents. Leaders develop a vision of how to achieve their goals and are determined to make their vision work.[17]

Effective managers persist in accomplishing goals even in the face of setbacks. They take risks, knowing that failures may occur, and they learn from their mistakes.[18] They assume that if something does not work, they will try something else until they ultimately succeed. This perseverance and tenacity in the face of obstacles and adversity is what sets effective managers apart from their less intrepid counterparts. The leader who can articulate a vision, however inspiring and relevant, but who cannot implement it is only a prophet.[19] Effective managers proclaim, "Damn it! We're going to make this thing work one way or another!" As high achievers, human service entrepreneurs obtain satisfaction from successfully completing challenging tasks, obtaining standards of excellence, and developing better ways of doing things.[20] By committing to a project wholeheartedly—based on conviction, determination, persistence, and confidence—social entrepreneurs increase the likelihood that their projects will succeed. They believe deeply in what they are doing and are skilled at convincing everyone around them that the project is right.[21] Unlike the business entrepreneur, the social entrepreneur does not mainly seek the reward of financial gain but rather the joy of achieving significant results.

Rothina D. can be considered a human service entrepreneur. Her quest was to create an organization that would help unemployed persons and public assistance recipients become self-reliant through employment. To do this, she obtained commitments from more than 350 companies by assuring them her organization would provide reliable, competent, and highly motivated employees. She built a program and accomplished this goal by convincing state and local officials that their investment in her program would produce excellent dividends for the community.

Rothina doesn't go by the book. If state regulations are not supportive, then she works to change them. If her trainees need a place for their children in the summer, she establishes a summer camp program in a downtown office building. If her participants have legal problems that impede their ability to stay on the job, she establishes a legal assistance program customized to their needs. All of these programs entail risks and the possibility of failure, but her commitment and entrepreneurial drive make them succeed.

As another example, Tom L.'s work with the homeless requires him to persevere time and time again. Homeless people have profound problems and needs that cannot be met through usual channels. When the welfare department was unable to give homeless people temporary shelter in the winter months because of security problems, he aggressively pursued another building and obtained help from the sheriff's department. When the state mental health department denied funding for a program to house mentally ill homeless women, he obtained a federal grant. He has the drive to achieve what others might consider impossible.

Effective managers, then, are passionate entrepreneurs who continually seek ways to make a contribution. They thrive on the challenge of making things happen.

Treating Staff With Dignity

Effective managers minimize the use of command language and maximize the language of persuasion and request. They understand that they cannot coerce staff to excel; true motivation must come from within.[22] They create a climate in which staff feel so positive about how they are being treated that they willingly perform at their best. These managers show concern and treat staff with respect, not as "service delivery units." Jeraldine H. remarks,

I care about my staff. We are like one big family, and I encourage them to work together whenever possible. I show respect for them and they reciprocate. When I can manage to do so, I attend weddings and funerals of the families of my staff. But even as I strive to promote positive relationships, I maintain a degree of objectivity because ours must be a professional, not a personal, relationship.

Thus, effective managers truly care about their employees; they convey empathy and compassion to help foster a supportive work environment.

Communicating Significant Messages

Effective managers are able to articulate concepts, ideas, and philosophies in such a way that staff understand both intellectually and emotionally how they are involved. These messages are clear and uncomplicated; they speak to the heart as well as to the mind. Managers help staff see the relationship between what they are doing and the mission of the organization—how they are a part of the whole.[23] These managers work to shape ambiguous ideas into operational programs with clear guidelines, thereby providing structure and clarity. Without patronizing their staff, effective managers clarify what the work is intended to achieve, why it needs to be done in a particular manner, and what constitutes successful performance. One of their major messages is that everyone must work together to achieve the organization's goals.[24] Effective managers allocate significant time and effort to developing a network of cooperative relationships among the people they feel are needed to satisfy their agendas.[25]

Moreover, effective managers communicate with—not just to—staff by listening to and incorporating their ideas and concerns. Listening is an essential but undervalued managerial skill. Given that many managers have achieved their positions because of their ability to express their ideas, they often do not realize that communication is a two-way process. The difference between mediocre managers and outstanding ones is the ability to tune in to what staff are thinking and feeling. This includes the manager's ability to listen to criticism without becoming unduly defensive when mistakes are brought to his or her attention. Jeraldine H. reflects this attitude in this statement: "Like everyone else, I'm fallible and can make mistakes. But with staff input, I am confident we can get our efforts back on course." She knows that she plays a vital role in linking the organization's communications. Good communicators, therefore, have the ability to give and receive messages effectively.

Engendering Trust

Effective managers have a deep sense of integrity. They are honest with themselves and are aware of both their strengths and their limitations. Staff respect and trust effective managers who take steps either to address their own limitations or to find ways to compensate for them.[26] Staff know what values their leaders are committed to, what positions they stand for, and know they can count on these managers. Competent managers are careful to promise only what they can deliver, and they expect others to do the same.[27]

The trust that effective managers earn is not based on blind faith. It is built upon a give-and-take interaction, which might sometimes include some degree of doubt.[28] The manager and staff feel committed to each other, but they both can also raise questions and challenge issues while maintaining mutual respect. Maintaining this balance of respect and willingness to challenge is the essence of the implicit trust between the manager and staff.

Whether as a result of staff interaction or through their own introspective tendencies, effective managers are continuously conducting self-appraisals: "Could I have handled the situation differently?" They want to learn from their mistakes and can candidly admit they have made an error in judgment, thereby earning the respect of staff.

Effective managers with a strong sense of integrity lead by example. They know that, as role models, they set the pace for the rest of the organization. Their actions are far more significant than words. Effective managers honor requests that discussions be held confidential, give credit to employees for their good ideas, and use professional discretion in communicating employee mistakes.[29] Because managers are visible, their commitment to the tasks of the organization and their degree of investment in the staff are continually under scrutiny. Staff view effective managers as genuine and sincerely dedicated. They are the ultimate exemplars of their organizations.

Jeraldine H. exemplifies a leader who has earned the trust of her staff. She says of them,

> They know I would not ask them to do any task that wasn't in the best interest of the clients. When I meet with staff I try to be open-minded when they raise questions concerning programs I propose because their constructive criticisms improve the original idea. What's great is that we feel a genuine respect for each other.

Effective managers are well aware, therefore, that trust does not come automatically but must be earned over time and in many ways.

Inspiring Top-Level Performance

By establishing high, but achievable, expectations, successful managers infuse in their staff a standard of excellence.[30] They create a positive and productive working atmosphere within which staff are stimulated to perform their best.

Even as managers expect high performance, at the same time, they are realistic. They attempt to stretch people, not overwhelm them.[31] The words that best describe this kind of leadership are *elevating, uplifting,* and *cheerleading.* Their optimism, confidence, and can-do demeanor mobilize staff to take on the toughest challenges. They lead best by their personal example.

Effective managers convey a mind-set that staff members are "winners" by creating continuous opportunities for successful experiences, thereby instilling in them the confidence to seek even higher levels of achievement.[32] They allow their staff to make their own decisions whenever possible and strive to get things done through cooperation.[33] Staff respond positively to managers who delegate their authority, make their subordinates feel powerful and capable, and foster their creative abilities to do their job.[34] Encouraging people to assume greater responsibility is challenging, but the effective manager instills confidence in his or her staff by providing them with successful experiences in which they can take risks and even make mistakes.[35] As facilitators, these managers work to remove obstacles that interfere with the staff's success. They continually ask, "What can we do to help you do your job better?" and "What can we accomplish as a team?"[36]

Waulina T. expresses this idea of empowering staff when she states,

> I am a servant-leader, for I try to be responsive to what staff want me to do to help them do their jobs better. I am at my best when I can take the time to be involved with my staff, to hear them out, to figure out ways to give them the resources to do their job better. They are closer to their situation and problems than I am, and so a good part of my job is to help them fulfill their professional responsibilities.

Smitty C. inspires his staff with these comments: "We have a tough assignment to complete in seven days, and I know that you are up to the task. If we all pitch in, we can produce a document that we can all be proud of." Also, when the quality product is completed, he says, "I am proud of the fantastic job all of you have done. I am glad that you are the kind of group I can count on."

Waulina T. places the same emphasis on facilitating staff investment and growth with this observation:

> As a manager, it is important that I not become too possessive of the organization. The staff must feel a deep sense of pride in their work and a sense of ownership in the organization. Whatever credit comes to me is based on the commitment and performance of my staff. If I help them grow, we all benefit.

More than 2,500 years ago, Lao Tzu, a Chinese Taoist philosopher, observed:

> A leader is best
> When people barely know that he exists,
> Not so good when people obey and acclaim him,

Worst when they despise him.
"Fail to honor people, they fail to honor you";
But of a good leader, who talks little,
When his work is done, his aim fulfilled,
They will say, "We did this ourselves."[37]

Thus organizational administrators continually seek to harmonize their various strengths. As managers, they work to bring order and consistency to complex organizations. As leaders, they challenge the status quo and work to meet new demands.[38] They strive to achieve their visions and simultaneously facilitate the staff's input in the direction-setting process. They are oriented to accomplishing tasks and are sensitive to the needs of their staff. They set their sights on the future while making certain to give proper attention to everyday details. They are both conveyers of messages and consummate listeners. They engender trust by respecting their staff and treating them with dignity. This blend of vision, sensitivity, and high moral purpose results in inspiring leadership.

Attributes Contributing to Leadership

Research is beginning to emerge that effective leaders have certain attributes that enhance their ability to lead people. These attributes, referred to as *emotional intelligence,* are identified as self-awareness, self-regulation, motivation, empathy, and social skills.[39]

Self-awareness. Emotionally intelligent people are keenly aware of their strengths, weaknesses, and desires. Those with a strong self-awareness are able to be honest with both themselves and others. They are aware of how their feelings affect them, other people, and their job performance. Self-aware people know when to ask for help, are willing to admit their mistakes, and at the same time are confident about what they can do. By sharing their imperfections, they underscore their authenticity.[40]

Self-regulation. Operating in the midst of ambiguity and change, a self-regulated person is able to control impulses, suspend judgment, and seek out information before making decisions. These people are comfortable with ambiguity and open to change. They tend to be reflective and thoughtful.

Motivation. Highly motivated people want to achieve results because it is exciting and fun for its own sake. They desire to challenge the status quo rather than opt for power or money. They are energetic and persistent and generally optimistic even though they may fail sometimes. Even those who have a high degree of self-awareness of their limitations will work to stretch themselves. People who are high achievers are committed to the organization. They set high goals for both themselves and for their employees.

Empathy. Considering the staff's feelings is part of an effective manager's decision process. If staff are feeling anxious or angry, an empathetic manager can acknowledge these feelings. As a leader of a team, the effective manager recognizes that various members may have different emotional reactions, alliances, and even clashes of opinions. A leader must recognize and understand these different perspectives.

Social Skills. Effective managers focus on developing relationships with others. Being friendly allows managers to persuade people to fulfill organizational goals. By developing a positive rapport, being interested in employees as people, and building bonds, they help people deal with day-to-day frustrations. No leader can truly hope to function in isolation. The leader's job is to get work done through other people; social skills are the grease that makes this possible.

Thus effective managers have a high level of emotional intelligence, which is required to carry out their jobs.

Diagnosing Your Leadership Style

Awareness of how you function as a leader within your organization is critical to being effective.[41] The more insight you have into how you react in various situations, the more you can ensure a proper match between behavior and organizational contingencies. This chapter has described several key elements that can be used to diagnose your leadership behavior: (a) leadership styles, (b) influences over staff, (c) flaws and limitations, (d) competencies and strengths, and (e) emotional intelligence. To heighten your understanding of your own leadership role, consider the following questions:

1. What is my predominant style (directive, participative, or delegative) of leadership? Are there clear benefits from using this style? Are there negative side effects? Thinking back to particular instances, have I matched the right style with the situation at hand? In the future, should I consider testing other styles?

2. Of the possible managerial limitations or flaws, do I see myself manifesting any of them in my own leadership behavior? If so, should I make efforts to modify my attitudes or behavior to increase my effectiveness? Are there times when some of these limitations may actually be useful and necessary?

3. In the review of leadership competencies, which ones do I exhibit? Is it within my capacity to strive for others? If so, can I find some safe ways to test out an underdeveloped competency? If not, can I find others who can complement my strengths?

4. Which of the emotional intelligence attributes do I consider to be well developed? Which attributes do I need to develop further?

The exploration of these questions, either by thinking about them on your own or by obtaining feedback from others whom you trust, can be useful in considering ways to develop further as an effective manager.

Questions for Discussion

Note: You will see that in this list of questions for discussion, as well as the questions in subsequent chapters, reference is made to "your organization." This could refer to your current organization (if you are a graduate intern or an employed professional) or to another one with which you are familiar.

1. What qualities of leadership do you see in your organization?

2. What leadership flaws are manifested in your organization?

3. In your organization, what do you consider to be the most important leadership competencies?

4. What elements of emotional intelligence do you see operating among managerial staff in your organization?

5. In your organization, what has management done that was effective or ineffective?

6. How would you describe your own leadership style? Which ideas discussed in this chapter would you like to give more attention to further develop your own leadership qualities?

Notes

1. J. E. Bennett, Reflections on successful CEOs: The match is everything, *Cleveland Enterprise* (Winter 1991–1992), pp. 18–20.

2. P. Drucker, *The effective executive* (New York: Harper & Row, 1985), pp. 22–23.

3. W. Bennis, *On becoming a leader* (Wilmington, MA: Addison-Wesley, 1989), p. 45; L. H. Garner, Jr., *Leadership in human services: How to articulate a vision to achieve results* (San Francisco: Jossey-Bass, 1989), pp. 9–12; R. R. Middleman & G. B. Rhodes, *Competent supervision: Making imaginative judgments* (Englewood Cliffs, NJ: Prentice Hall, 1985), p. 78–81.

4. R. Tannenbaum & W. Schmidt, How to choose a leadership pattern, *Harvard Business Review* 52 (March/April 1973), pp. 162–180.

5. E. S. Stanton, A critical reevaluation of motivation, management, and productivity, *Personnel Journal* 3 (1983), pp. 5–6.

6. D. Goleman, Leadership that gets results, *Harvard Business review* 78 (March/April 2000), pp. 78–90.

7. K. Blanchard, J. P. Carlos, & A. Randolph, *The 3 keys to empowerment* (San Francisco: Berrett-Koehler, 1999), pp. 25–43.

8. L. J. McFarland, L. E. Senn, & J. R. Childress, Refining leadership in the next century, in *The leader's companion*, ed. J. T. Wren (New York: The Free Press, 1995), pp. 459–460.

9. H. Bruch & S. Ghoshal, Beware the busy manager, *Harvard Business Review 80* (February 2002), pp. 62–69.

10. M. Wadia, Participative management: Three common problems, *Personnel Journal 11* (1980), pp. 27–28.

11. R. Townsend, *Further up the organization* (New York: Alfred A. Knopf, 1984), p. 94.

12. P. F. Drucker, *Effective*, p. 25.

13. R. Hogan, R. Raskin, & D. Fazzini, How charisma cloaks incompetence, *Personnel Journal 5* (1990), p. 76.

14. T. Caplow, *How to run any organization* (Hinsdale, IL: Dryden, 1976), p. 55.

15. National Assembly of National Voluntary Health and Social Welfare Organizations, *A study in excellence: Management in the nonprofit human services* (Washington, DC: Author, 1985), pp. 36–44.

16. R. M. Cyert, Defining leadership and explicating the process, *Nonprofit Management and Leadership 1* (1990), pp. 29–37.

17. J. G. Dees, J. Emerson, & P. Economy, *Enterprising nonprofits: A toolkit for social entrepreneurs* (New York: John Wiley & Sons, 2001), pp. 3–4.

18. W. Bennis, pp. 95–96.

19. L. H. Garner, Jr., p. 9.

20. S. A. Kirkpatrick & E. A. Locke, Do traits matter? in *The leader's Companion*, ed. J. T. Wren (New York: The Free Press, 1995), p. 135.

21. R. I. Sutton, The world of creativity, *Harvard Business Review 79* (September 2001), pp. 96–103.

22. R. Townsend, p. 170.

23. National Assembly of National Voluntary Health And Social Welfare Organizations, pp. 36–44.

24. R. M. Cyert, p. 33.

25. J. Kotter, What leaders really do, *Harvard Business Review 68* (January/February 1990), pp. 103–111.

26. W. Bennis, pp. 40–41.

27. M. H. McCormack, *Mark H. McCormack on managing* (West Hollywood, CA: Dove Books, 1996), p. 9; S. A. Kirkpatrick & E. A. Locke, p. 138.

28. W. Bennis, p. 140.

29. Bureau of Business Practice, Building loyalty, *Front Line Supervisors Bulletin 146* (1990), pp. 1–3.

30. W. N. Schultz, What makes a good nonprofit manager? *Nonprofit World* (1984), p. 32; L. H. Garner, Jr., pp. 151–152.

31. W. Bennis, p. 198.

32. T. J. Peters & R. H. Waterman, *In search of excellence: Lessons from America's best run companies* (New York: Harper & Row, 1982), pp. 83–84.

33. P. Slater & W. Bennis, Democracy is inevitable, *Harvard Business Review* 68 (May/June 1990), p. 175.

34. T. Teal, The human side of management, *Harvard Business Review* 74 (November/December 1996), p. 39.

35. R. A. Heifetz & D. L. Laurie, The work of leadership, *Harvard Business Review* 75 (January/February 1997), p. 129.

36. P. F. Drucker, *Managing the nonprofit organization* (New York: HarperCollins, 1990), p. 44

37. L. Tzu, *The way of life according to Lao Tzu,* trans. W. Bynner (New York: Capricorn, 1944), p. 34.

38. W. Bennis, pp. 46–47; J. Kotter, pp. 103–111.

39. D. Goleman, What makes a leader? *Harvard Business Review* 76 (November/December 1998), pp. 93–102.

40. R. Goffee & G. Jones, Why should anyone be led by you? *Harvard Business Review* 78 (September/October 2000), pp. 63–70.

41. J. Seltzer, (1989). Developing an effective leadership style. In L. E. Miller (Ed.), *Managing human service organizations.* New York: Quorum. pp. 46–49.

2

Strategic Planning

Embracing Change

Human service organizations operate in a continually changing and even turbulent environment. The needs of clients change over time, funding patterns shift, staff come and go, and the attention of community leaders and the media move to different social issues. Social issues that momentarily capture the community's attention, such as homelessness, substance abuse, or teen pregnancy, can be replaced by other "social fads." Because of the inevitable and constant nature of change, both internal and external, effective human service managers must be prepared not only to cope with it, but also to initiate and embrace it.

Not all change is necessarily good, nor is all resistance to change necessarily inappropriate. Abrupt or too much change at once, the wrong kind of change, or change from one activity to another without clear purpose can create problems, be disorienting, and even threaten the organization's survival. Maintaining the status quo can keep an organization from being in constant flux.

Strategic planning describes the process of addressing change. It develops goals, accompanied by a set of actions to help achieve those goals.[1] Emerging from the organization's key stakeholders (board of directors, staff, clients or their families, and other constituencies considered important to the organization), it is a shared vision for the future. It is also a roadmap for achieving that vision, given known realities and facts.[2] Usually organizations conduct their strategic planning every three to five years. Many see this timeline as imperative so they can reenergize themselves. Certain circumstances, however, may prompt more frequent planning, including a significant change in organizational leadership, a financial crisis, new opportunities, or new mandates from public officials.

Strategic planning produces a product—the strategic plan—that is the result of a process in which key stakeholders fully engage. The product is a written plan that the organization can use as a blueprint for guiding future directions. Equally important is the process of engaging key stakeholders, because this builds commitment and teamwork among board and staff and better assures follow-through on the plan's anticipated results. It also helps participants reach a consensus on fundamental issues that require ongoing, concentrated attention. Through strategic planning, stakeholders stimulate their organization to move beyond doing business as usual, by considering innovative changes.[3] In the absence of strategic planning, the organization may unintentionally drift into new services or programs that are tangential to its core mission. The following are some examples of organizations that made changes without the benefit of a strategic plan:

> An organization established to advocate for women's issues shifts its focus over time to providing needed services—counseling, day care, and job referral. Its original reason for being, advocating on behalf of women, becomes increasingly difficult to sustain and is eventually discontinued as the organization gradually shifts to a service emphasis—to the dismay of the organization's founders, who think the organization's original priorities have been distorted.

> A service agency shifts its attention from providing free or low-cost counseling in the inner city to offering employee assistance programs for those who can pay a fee. Initially, funds increase, but two years later, its primary funding source drastically cuts its support because the organization has abandoned its original focus.

> Finally, consider the example of a health coalition that provides direct services to women with small children. In its quest to obtain additional money, it modifies its focus from direct service to collecting and analyzing health data—causing a schism among staff that support clinical care and those that value public health-related activities.

These examples describe organizations that altered their basic purposes—from advocacy to service, from serving inner-city residents to serving fee-paying employees, and from emphasis on health services to health data analysis. These changes are not inherently good or bad. They reflect responses to immediate situations, but they did not occur purposefully within the context of a strategic plan and with the active involvement of the organizations' stakeholders. Only when an organization gives a focused, long-term view to selected issues can it be said to be involved in strategic planning.

The previous examples describe how an organization can unknowingly drift into carrying out activities that may not be related to its primary reason for being. As Peter Drucker, a well-regarded organizational consultant, has proposed,

> Only when a nonprofit's key performance areas are defined can it really set goals. Only then can the nonprofit ask, "Are we doing what we are supposed to be doing? Is it still the right activity? Does it still serve a need?" And above all, "Do we still produce results that are sufficiently outstanding, sufficiently different for us to justify putting our talents to use in that area?" Then you can ask, "Are we still in the right areas? Should we change? Should we abandon?"[4]

The value of asking these fundamental questions is that they help an organization assess its current status so it can control its future. Probing these issues helps the organization gain greater mastery over inevitable internal and external changes. Hence an organization will be in a better position to determine where it is, where it wants to go, and how it wants to get there.

Two circumstances invite a strategic review. The first involves a threat to the organization. Funding cutbacks, legislation that is detrimental to the organization, competition from another human service organization that could lure clients away are the kinds of crises that compel a response. Business cannot go on as usual when the organization faces major difficulties; it must react to the crisis or face serious consequences. It is interesting to note that the Chinese symbol for *crisis* is a combination of two words: *danger* and *opportunity*. Crisis can galvanize a reactive response, stimulating the organization to reassess its strategic directions so that the danger may be turned into an opportunity for positive change.

The second circumstance is more subtle, and on the surface might not seem to prompt strategic planning. When everything is going *right*— when the organization is strong, when funding is ample, when clients are being well served, when staff and volunteers are feeling positive about the organization—introspection might seem unwarranted. It is at just such a time, however, that effective managers must discern whether there are dark clouds on the horizon in the form of staff and volunteer leader complacency, potential competition for funds, or possible change in community interest. Strategic planning disciplines managers to assess the organization and its environment even when things are going well.

If the normal pattern of the organization is to provide services without questioning whether they can be improved, there is little stimulus for change. A thought-provoking aphorism states: "If you always think what you've always thought, and you always do what you've always done, then you'll always get what you've always gotten." By proactively searching for new ways to improve programs or processes that develop staff, you invite the organization to reach higher levels of productivity. To counter *entropy*, the inevitable tendency of organizations to wind down, it is imperative that organizations use the strategic planning process to reenergize and reinvent themselves. You want to be able to slough off yesterday's less productive and less relevant programs and procedures, thus freeing staff and other resources to meet emerging needs and to better fulfill the organization's mission.[5]

For example, suppose your organization has been providing an adolescent counseling service for many years, but you now find that demand is waning, though not enough to discontinue the counseling program altogether. The situation is not yet at a crisis level, but it could be in a year or two. Your assessment of teenagers shows that they do want the opportunity to talk with someone, though in a more informal setting than is now provided by the agency. You decide to change your point of contact from in-office interviews to an unconventional new approach—crafts and sports facilities. Your willingness to restructure the program propels you to seek other ways to be responsive to adolescents.

Some organizations will even adopt the policy of *organized abandonment*. Every service, program, and client category is open to question. The organization asks, "If we were not already doing this, and based on the information we now have, would we be doing the same things?" Asking this question invites the organization to make changes.[6] Abandoning things that no longer work pushes the organization to constantly improve.[7] The organization develops the attitude of innovating to improve the quality of services. For example, an organization dealing with substance abuse clients would constantly be looking for successful interventions, and this organization would be willing to abandon interventions that do not produce results.

Hence by forecasting its future, setting goals, and considering emerging opportunities and threats, an organization can concentrate on its most critical problems and choices. Through strategic planning, it can engage key organizational members in communicating and reaching a consensus on significant decisions about their organization's future.[8]

There are barriers, however, that can impede effective strategic planning. The process may consume time and money that could be spent on more immediately compelling projects. Smoldering problems may surface that must be handled. Board and staff who rely on intuitive or "gut" feelings to determine how to operate may question a time-consuming, systematic planning approach. They may resist the sometimes difficult introspection of examining how their efforts contribute to—or detract from—the organization's mission. Also, organizations facing an immediate crisis (e.g., a severe decline in funding) may have to devote significant energies to the urgent current situation before taking time to think long term. If there is a lack of devotion to carrying out the plans, then strategic planning can only lead to frustration. Finally, if major decision makers lack the conviction to follow through or tend to arrive at poor decisions based on faulty assumptions or hastily completed processes, then strategic planning may result in more harm than good.

These limitations should serve as reminders that although strategic planning can be a powerful tool, it is not foolproof. Even so, effective managers must embark on strategic planning to improve performance, stimulate thinking about the future, encourage teamwork, handle organizational issues, and provide a sense of renewal. It thus positions the organization to respond to new opportunities, create a competitive advantage, and take action to reverse decline or to expand programs.[9]

Developing the Strategic Plan

Every organization must develop a strategic plan that is compatible with its own interests, strengths, and limitations. What works for one organization will not necessarily work for another. The format that follows has been used by several planning consultants and can be flexibly used by most organizations.[10]

Getting Organized

Before embarking on the strategic planning process, consider the following important points. First, effective managers are aware that although the trustees of their organizations must be involved in strategic planning, they must also engage staff to instill a sense of ownership of the eventual plan. Everyone must share a conviction that the hard work and time involved will be productive for the organization. Second, be realistic about the required time investment. Planning will require many hours from staff and volunteers. Anticipate the amount of time involved in meetings and the preparatory and follow-up work required between them. It is desirable to set aside one full day, or at a minimum part of a day, to give concentrated time to strategic plan formulation. Third, consider the broad participation of staff from all levels of the organization, along with board members, funders, government officials, and others involved with the organization, to avoid possible schisms. At a minimum, a committee should consist of key staff representatives (from major departments or the union) and leaders of the governing body of the organization (see Chapter 20). In addition, other participants could include clients (or family members) and respected leaders and representatives from collateral organizations. Persons from outside the organization could be asked for their ideas by participating directly in the process, contributing to focus group discussions, or answering survey questions. Finally, establish ground rules of participation that emphasize that decisions are made by consensus, unless otherwise agreed, and that even as differences are aired, members are to be respectful of each other.

The reason for emphasizing participation is that the process is as important as the resulting plan. Working together helps educate members inside and outside the organization, builds commitment, and mobilizes participants to take action.[11] Otherwise you risk creating a lifeless document, the result of ritual behavior, rather than a call to action.

Conducting an Analysis

In a nonprofit organization, a board member typically chairs the strategic planning committee, with significant input from staff. In public sector agencies, the director or a selected staff member usually takes leadership responsibility. Some organizations rely on an outside professional facilitator to provide neutrality to the process, keep the group focused on tasks, and be sensitive to group processes and interactions.[12] Using a neutral third party has merit in that it assures that all stakeholders have an equal voice without one or more engaged in dual roles of participant and facilitator.

To get everyone thinking as a team, it is important to lay a proper foundation. Provide the group with a common understanding of the organization's past, its current operations, and its values. Also, review the services of the organization, its staffing pattern, its current and projected financial situation, and other salient facts. In addition, gather relevant demographic, political, and economic data on the service area. Conduct a competitive analysis to determine how the organization compares with its peer organizations on service programs, clients served, service accessibility, reputation, and costs.[13] A good analysis requires a review of your mission statement; focusing on fundamental questions; conducting a resource audit; examining strengths, weaknesses (challenges), opportunities, and threats; and considering the organizational life cycle.

Developing a Mission Statement

The purpose of a human service organization is to meet a need; addressing that need is the mission of the organization. The mission provides a sense of purpose without which the organization would lose its direction, support, legitimacy, and needed resources.[14] A good mission statement should be lofty and inspiring, yet concise and capable of being easily understood and remembered.

The mission statement is the most enduring part of an organization. It should not be changed without extensive involvement of key stakeholders, including staff, board, key donors, and community representatives. For example, an agency offering substance abuse services may have a mission that states it will serve everyone who comes for help. Faced with severe public funding cutbacks and an inability to fundraise in the private sector, the agency decides to alter its mission and restrict whom it will serve.

In addition to describing their fundamental purpose, some human service organizations describe what services they will provide, to whom they will be offered, and their geographic area. The following are examples:

Our mission is to ensure that appropriate, timely, accessible, and effective mental health and substance abuse services are available to people of all ages. Highest priority is to be given to adults and children with severe mental health disabilities who live or work in our geographic area.

Our mission is to assist individuals with mental retardation and developmental disabilities in choosing and achieving a life of increasing capability such that they can live, learn, work, and play in the community, and to assist and support their families in achieving this objective.

Your mission statement should be visible in key areas—on the wall of the boardroom, in the reception room, in the annual report, on the flipside of business cards, and in the newsletter. In staff meetings, when a new program or policy is under consideration, ask, "Does this proposal relate to our mission?" Similarly, at board meetings when several proposals are under consideration, choose those more likely to further the organization's mission.[15] The mission establishes boundaries for organizational activity and guards against the tendency to chase unrelated opportunities or thoughtlessly diversify, thus siphoning resources from the organization's *raison d'être* (reason for being).[16]

Asking Fundamental Questions

Although organizations differ in relation to their mission, funding, and style of operating, all must grapple with four fundamental questions as part of the strategic planning process.

What business are we in? Most organizations provide several services and serve multiple populations. How the organization defines these services determines which services and clients it emphasizes. A child welfare agency, for example, could define its basic purpose as ensuring the well-being of children under its care or it could define its focus as keeping families intact. The former might involve long-term foster care; the latter, intensive family counseling.

What business should we be in now? The organization may have been formed 10 or 20 years ago with a mission to serve a particular target population, but now it serves different populations with different needs. Some staff or board members may mistakenly believe that the organization continues to provide services for those it no longer serves. One of the values of strategic planning is that it forces members to ask the question, "If our organization did not currently exist, would it be created to meet the needs we are now trying to meet?"

What business do we want to be in a few years down the road? As a strategic planning exercise, it is useful to imagine what the organization might be in three to five years. Are there new clients to be served or can the organization be prepared to serve current clients better in the future? Is there new legislation in the offing that could provide needed funding? To give shape to this "crystal ball" thinking, the strategic planning group may want to capture its ideas about the future in a *vision statement*. The group would project how clients, services, staff, funding, and other aspects of the organization might be the same or different in the future.[17]

In considering this vision statement, you could improve on what the organization is doing now, or you could change direction entirely. For example, your agency currently offers recreational activities and limited workshop experiences to the mentally and physically disabled. You could shift to advocating for legislation that helps disabled persons function better in the community. The vision statement would include adding job developers and group home staff so disabled persons might function more independently. Thus the vision statement encourages strategic planners to think about what the organization can become if it were to perform at its optimum. The vision is a dream that may never be realized, but the pursuit is reason enough to try.[18]

In visioning your future, examine the particular niche you will fill in the human services of the future. In the business world, the term *branding* connotes a certain reputation of the enterprise. A strong brand uniquely distinguishes one organization from another. Business enterprises work hard at establishing their brand. Similarly, human service agencies must strive to develop their brand—their reputation for unique and excellent services. In the quest for positioning themselves to meet the needs of the community, however, agencies should not rely solely on their good cause. Positioning must also be based on delivering results—changing lives and changing conditions as a result of the organization's effort.[19]

What will happen if we continue doing business in the same way? Continuing in the same direction could have negative consequences in a changing world. For example, with regard to your day care program you find that, because of a change in the law, teen mothers are returning to school. Not facing this reality could mean that in a few years your program, which is not affiliated with schools, could be greatly diminished, replaced by competitors who are willing to set up their day care programs in schools. By exploring the continuation of even those programs that are going well for the moment, you consider potential consequences. The strategic planning process therefore requires you to intensely examine not only the organization's current relevance, but also whether you need to make changes that will better position the organization for the future.[20]

Conducting a Resource Audit and Situational Analysis: the SWOT (SCOT) Process

The resource audit is an inventory of the organization's existing and available resources needed to achieve its mission. As part of its review, the strategic planning committee would do the following:

1. Review programs and services to determine whether each one can be justified in relation to the organization's mission.

2. Examine the structure at every level of the organization, including job descriptions, staff responsibilities, and formal processes.

3. Determine the organization's management of staff and funding.

4. Identify significant community trends and issues that might impinge on the organization's functioning.

5. Carefully examine the extent to which other organizations are duplicating services or competing for funding or clients.

Major organizational trends and their implications would be identified in this analysis. For example, it may be determined that proposed programs may require staff with different expertise and experience; the findings could have long-term implications for upgrading or hiring staff.

Include in the analysis a situational analysis of internal (organizational) and external (environmental) factors. The acronym SWOT is intended to convey that, for the internal analysis, you review *strengths* and *weaknesses* and, for the external analysis, *opportunities* and *threats*. (Some organizations prefer the acronym SCOT, the C standing for *challenge*s.)

In examining your organization's internal strengths, you would obviously want to continue doing the activities you do well. You would ask, "What are our staff and volunteers best able to do, and how can we build on these assets?" Examining internal weaknesses requires candid discussions about where things are falling short or, in the case of programs, what needs are beginning to wind down. Are staff not as prepared as they should be for doing their jobs? Is your organization encountering severe financial constraints? Are you losing clients because the program is no longer relevant, or for other reasons? Focusing on weaknesses or constraints directs new energies or redirects efforts to make needed changes.

A dilemma that organizations face is whether (and to what extent) they should divert resources from their strong areas to strengthen their weaknesses.[21] Suppose, for example, that a mental health organization's primary strength is in providing mental health counseling, but it has a weak job-finding unit. Should it divert its mental health resources to devote staff to finding jobs? Or should it eliminate the job finding unit and rely instead on other community organizations whose primary function is to find jobs?

Of course, internal weaknesses can be caused by external realities. For example, in a public agency, the lack of statutory authority and funding to carry out needed programs may limit the ability to serve some clients, even though they need the agency's services. Conversely, the legal requirement to process every client who walks into a public agency may limit the desired quality of service. These constraints suggest that focusing only on internal improvements may not be sufficient to improve services. By being aware of these external constraints, the strategic planning group can begin to consider ways to mitigate them. Instead of concentrating only on improving staff performance, for example, attention would be given to changing regulations or the law itself.

The term *scanning the environment* means looking at both *opportunities* and *threats*. Scanning involves selectively reviewing relevant economic, technological, social, and political trends that now or in the future could affect your organization. A change in local public administration, reduced federal funding, expansion of women in the work force, and many other factors can have a powerful impact on the directions of the organization. Some organizations prefer to conduct the scanning process prior to preparing the mission statement because the scan may influence the organization's essential emphasis. As an alternative, the strategic planning group can develop a tentative mission position and be prepared to modify it if the scanning process reveals insights.

Scanning the environment is no easy task. Thousands of dollars can be spent on perceptions. Most organizations have limited resources and so may have to rely on published secondary data sources, such as the United States Census or published studies and planning reports sponsored by advocacy groups, local universities, the United Way, or a local planning council.

In addition, the strategic planning group could compile its own list of major assumptions or *key realities* that could have an impact on the organization. An agency that serves adolescents, for example, might identify such key realities as the following:

1. Teen pregnancy, already at a high rate, will continue.

2. AIDS among heterosexual adolescents will reach epidemic proportions.

3. Teen unemployment is likely to decline for those who graduate from high school but increase for those who do not.

4. The school dropout rate will continue to increase unless steps can be taken at the elementary school level to keep students from failing.

These and other key realities would be based in part on quantitative data and in part on the general knowledge of professionals or community experts that are often referred to as "key informants." These perspectives should be considered to help determine the future focus of the organization.

Opportunities can be manifested in various ways. A possible new funding source, such as the United Way announcing a special grants program for children, may create new opportunities. A recently recognized community problem, such as a drastic reduction in welfare grants, severe overcrowding in detention home facilities, a tragic domestic homicide, or an increase in the high dropout rate, may offer opportunities for new services and special funding. In the human service field, community crises sometimes provide opportunities.

External threats or constraints can be obvious or subtle. A reduction in funding can obviously affect the effectiveness of programs and even whether the organization continues to exist. Subtle threats are often difficult to discern. For example, another organization beefs up its staff to compete for your clients or opens a satellite office in your service area, or a formerly successful camping program begins to lose participants because of the growing availability of other recreation options. Loss of funds, competition from other organizations, or declining community interest are ever-present threats that may—or may not—require special attention, depending on how events unfold. These threats could prove to be either bogus or genuine.

In the strategic planning process, consider specifying anticipated opportunities and threats, and assess whether your organization has the capacity to deal with them. Further, the staff must determine whether they have the requisite resources—time, funding, expertise, and experience—to address future needs. If not, are they prepared to do what is required to strengthen their capability, including new skill training, organizational restructuring, and possible reassignment of roles and responsibilities? A candid assessment of capabilities affects the planning process.

Examining Critical Issues

To keep the strategic planning process from becoming a perfunctory ritual in which participants go through superficial motions, you must focus on critical issues. Concentrating on critical issues is especially useful for those organizations seeking to update a current strategic plan in response to new developments.[22] You need to ponder what significant problems, what burning issues, cry out for resolution. If you are primarily concerned with how to attract clients to the organization, for example, you may need to focus your strategic planning on various ways to reach them. If your burning issue is poor staff morale, then you concentrate on how to improve it. If future funding is a concern, this becomes your focus of attention. Thus, a critical issue is an unsolved present or emerging problem requiring resolution because of its potential impact on the organization.

Critical issues become *strategic* when they (1) involve high stakes, such as dealing with new funding opportunities or serious decline in client attendance; (2) require intensive attention that cannot be left to routine planning, such as taking the initiative to form an association with other agencies; (3) cut across various operating units of the organization, such as developing a new service that involves the marketing, accounting, and program staff working together; and (4) delineate where the organization should be going.[23]

Suppose the critical issue at hand is how well the agency's services are designed to meet client needs. The following are examples of the kinds of questions the strategic planning group would consider in planning programs.[24]

1. What changing community needs are of special interest to the organization?

2. Should our program be improved by expanding our services (e.g., housing services for our mentally disabled clients)?

3. Should we phase out certain services or programs that are declining or are incompatible with other services?

4. Should our basic funding pattern be modified, diversified, or more focused?

5. Should we make major modifications in the organization by (a) replacing some staff with others having different skills, or (b) retraining staff to perform their functions differently?

6. Should we contract with others to provide services we currently offer?

These illustrate the kind of critical issues and questions that could be raised, depending on the organization's focus of interest. An essential part of the strategic plan is for each organization to identify its unique critical issues. Sometimes issues can seem mundane, though they are of critical importance, such as installing a new computer networking system or building a relationship with collateral organizations.[25] Identifying critical issues concentrates attention on areas that are either currently or potentially of greatest concern.

Because every organization has finite resources, it is not likely that more than a few critical issues can be addressed at any one time. Priority decisions must be based on the organization's ability to have an impact, its assessment of resource demands, and on the impact of not addressing the issue.[26] Attempting to be everything for everyone guarantees organizational ineffectiveness.[27] In determining whether an issue or program is highest priority, an organization must first and foremost ask, "How will this help us achieve our mission?" In the process it may determine not to work on some desirable programs or important issues because it cannot do everything simultaneously. Once you have selected a few critical issues, formulate actions appropriate for each. Then pinpoint accountability for follow-up and prepare a timetable.

These action plans are the blueprint for the staff to use to fulfill the strategic plan and for the board to use to monitor progress. Suppose the strategic planning committee of a family counseling agency is concerned about meeting the needs of its clients. Figure 2.1 shows how it might formulate a critical issue. The strategic planning process should take place over a period of several months rather than in a one- or two-day retreat, so that governing board members and staff have an opportunity to do the necessary homework of gathering facts and preparing action plans. Based on information and facts, the strategic planning committee can determine what the organization should do over the next few years to resolve critical issues.

Drafting the Strategic Plan

From your planning group, select one or two members to draft a strategic plan based upon the critical issues identified. The draft plan would likely include the following elements:

- Mission statement (revised if necessary)
- Vision of the organization in three to five years
- Goals to be accomplished in three to five years
- Internal strengths and weaknesses and external opportunities and threats (or internal and external key realities)
- Critical issues
- Actions for each critical issue
- Accountability and timetable for each critical issue

By incorporating implementation actions in the strategic plan, you ensure that the planning process leads to results.

In the process of drafting the plan, certain unanswered questions may emerge that require further deliberations. The value of calling the initial plan a "draft" is that it can be reviewed by a variety of constituents—clients, staff, funders, community leaders—to ensure that all elements of the plan properly fit and that

Critical Issue:

Funds are diminishing, preventing our hiring new staff at a time when client demands are increasing.

Key Realities: (partial listing)

Internal:

- Our staff is committed but overworked.
- Management strongly feels that client needs must be met, despite fiscal constraints.

External:

- Federal, state, and local business funding is not likely to expand.
- Other agencies offering similar services are few.

Actions:

1. Expand new funding sources, such as special events and Friends of the Agency Campaign.

2. Expand volunteer base from 10 to 50.

3. Hire and train three nonprofessionals.

4. Develop self-help groups.

Accountability:

Four agency task groups, each headed by management staff, will develop plans for each action. The team leaders will report monthly to the executive director on progress.

Timetable:

Each task group will establish a specific timetable for Year 1 and more general timetables for Years 2 and 3. (See Chapter 4 for work plan and timetable format.) First-round plans will be prepared within 2 months.

Figure 2.1   Strategic Planning Format

it is workable. Special attention should be paid to possible flaws or negative consequences. The final result should be a sound and viable plan acceptable to the major decision makers of the organization, including the executive director, the board of trustees or relevant public officials, and key staff.

Transforming plans into action requires that tactics be considered and assignments be made and monitored. (See Chapter 4 for implementing action plans.) A good feedback system must be in place to ensure that programs are kept on track.

Some organizations may become complacent after the strategic planning document is prepared because of overemphasis on preparing the plan at the expense of making needed changes and following through.[28] So much energy and effort may have gone into preparing the strategic plan that participants assume they have created a master plan that will guide them indefinitely. To counter this tendency toward complacency, the organization must develop an ongoing review process—at least annually—that tracks achievement of goals by identifying performance indicators focused on accomplishments.[29] The key to eventually being able to evaluate progress is to answer the question, "Did the organization achieve what it set out to accomplish?"

Dynamic Planning

To avoid ending up with an inflexible strategic plan, a counterpoint approach is sometimes proposed. This approach may be referred to as *dynamic planning,* meaning that strategies become clear over time and are based on modest attempts to deal with changing circumstances. Because of the heightened pace of change, strategies gradually emerge to deal with new situations. The emphasis is on bottom-up learning—encouraging staff to try new approaches and then see what happens. This impromptu decision-making process is continuously sensitive to change resulting from opportunities or setbacks. When changes occur (e.g., new technologies, legislation, or funding alterations), managers may find it beneficial to review mission statements, reformulate goals and objectives, and redraft action plans in an ongoing process. In contrast to a comprehensive plan that may attempt to accomplish too much in too little time, dynamic planning continually tests ideas, obtains feedback, and incrementally reshapes plans.[30]

For example, an opportunity may arise that allows the organization to implement services to an underserved population. This opportunity may, in turn, require reorienting the mission statement to encompass new programs and target populations. Thus dynamic planning helps the organization deal with political, social, and economic realities and also helps ensure that risks involved in embarking on new directions can realistically be undertaken.

Fundamental to dynamic planning is *opportunistic thinking.* Managers continually ask, "What new opportunities can we grasp?" This is part of a never-ending search for new possibilities. Risk taking is built into a trial-and-error process in which failure is always a realistic possibility.

In Chapter 1, effective managers were described as having a vision of where they want to take their organizations. In reality, through a dynamic strategic planning process, *smaller visions* frequently emerge. These are modest-scale ideas that, if worthwhile, develop into ambitious undertakings. Not all of these emerging ideas necessarily emanate from managerial staff.[31]Consider this example:

A counselor expressed concern that she could not address the psychological needs of her clients because they were so deeply concerned about keeping their children fed. Moved by the plight of her clients, the counselor asked her director to allocate space for agency volunteers to bring in bags of food. From this small beginning emerged a greatly expanded food bank, which now provides supplementary food for public assistance recipients seen by the agency.

To respond to today's ever-changing environment, managers must encourage their staff to acquire adaptive solutions and take responsibility for problematic situations. No longer can agencies rely only on leaders who have a vision and require staff to mechanically follow them. Dynamic planning thus requires the work and commitment of everyone in the organization, not just those in the managerial role.[32] Effective managers are aware that staff develop ideas that may provide exciting new opportunities for the organization. All staff must be encouraged to develop keen insights about the possibilities of innovative interventions to meet changing needs.[33]

Dynamic planning fosters an ability to seize the moment of opportunity, take corrective action, and reformulate plans. It prevents premature commitment to a rigid solution that may not allow the organization to be responsive to unpredictable events. If one thinks of a plan as a road map to a destination, there may be detours along the way that need to be considered and to which one needs to adjust.[34] The key elements of dynamic planning are flexibility and experimentation.

Effective managers recognize the importance of the dynamic process. A meaningful strategic plan, therefore, combines a comprehensive approach and a dynamic planning process that sensitizes the organization to changing circumstances. Strategic planning provides a general course—a direction with specific action steps focused on critical issues identified by participants at a particular point in time. However, as new events precipitate unforeseen changes (e.g., new agency competitors, shifts in funding, and client requests for new services), adjustments may be made to the very mission of the organization.

Incorporating dynamic planning into the strategic planning process can periodically affirm your current services or convince you to embark on new directions based upon contingent events. Through strategic planning, you try to anticipate the future of your organization, even when you know the future is uncertain. If an organization has taken two or three months to formulate a three- to five-year strategic plan, it may wish to conduct an annual *dynamic* review to determine whether modifications are necessary. The organization may also assign various strategies to staff and/or board members to follow through and monitor their development on an ongoing basis. The imperative in today's changing world is to continually seek relevance in relation to the needs of the consumer and the community. Being able to read the shifting political and market winds makes it possible to navigate a turbulent environment.[35]

In summary, strategic planning focuses attention on both the process and the content of ideas. But the planning process by itself is insufficient.

Without a plan of action even excellent ideas can easily end up as reports on a shelf.[36] By engaging significant constituencies (staff, board members, public officials, funders, clients, and representatives from other organizations) in the process, a common vision and direction emerges. Bringing various units of the organization together fosters a commitment to cooperate in implementing the plan. The planning process itself encourages various parts of the organization to mesh their efforts.

During strategic planning, the organization takes stock to determine how best to position itself to deal with its uncertain future. The process disciplines the organization to make tough decisions about priorities, because not everything it wants to do will be possible with the resources available. Strategic planning clarifies what must be pruned to take advantage of new growth opportunities.[37] It helps establish the boundaries of what the organization will do—and what it will not do. Through strategic planning, the organization also determines what special needs must be addressed to develop a plan that is comprehensive and capable of being modified in the ever-changing human service environment.

Summary of a Strategic Planning Process

1. Determine why you want to develop a plan for your organization's future. What benefits do you see from embarking on an intensive process? Do these clearly outweigh possible disadvantages?

2. Ensure that the organization's leadership is committed to the process.

3. Form a strategic planning group.

4. Analyze your situation, including strengths, weaknesses, opportunities, and threats.

5. Develop a vision of what the organization could be like.

6. Prepare (or revise) a tentative mission statement, which may be altered later in the strategic planning process.

7. Identify, after obtaining considerable input, the most critical issues facing the organization.

8. Prepare action plans containing three- to five-year goals, implementation activities for the first year, and names of those accountable for follow-through.

9. Draft a plan that is reviewed by a planning group, staff, board, and selected persons outside the organization.

10. Implement the plan with the intent of modifying it as circumstances change.

11. Update the plan annually, and at least every five years conduct another in-depth analysis.

Questions for Discussion

1. What are examples of strengths and weaknesses/opportunities or threats related to your organization ?

2. What are the key elements in your organization's mission statement? Can you and most of your agency colleagues recite your organization's mission? Is your organization's mission statement clear, compelling, inspirational, and concise? How does your organization communicate your mission to its various stakeholders?

3. What changes, if any, should be considered for your agency's mission statement?

4. What is the status of your organization's strategic plan?

5. How does your strategic plan reflect the underlying assumptions regarding the organization and its purpose?

6. What are the major priorities identified in your strategic plan?

7. Does your organization have a vision statement reflecting what the organization will be like and what it will be able to accomplish in the future? If your organization does have a vision statement, what modifications, if any, would you suggest? If your organization does not currently have a vision statement, how would you formulate such a statement?

8. You are an organization that provides socializing experiences for older persons who live in public housing. Recently the public housing authority has offered you a considerable amount of funding to include single, disabled adults who reside in public housing and who could benefit from your agency's services. Your mission statement focuses on senior citizens. What should you do?

9. Suppose your organization has been developing part-time jobs for high risk teenagers still in high school. In the past you have provided counseling and tutoring to students who have been involved in substance abuse as well as those who are performing sufficiently well in school to be likely to go on to college. Because of recent funding cutbacks, you must reduce the number of students in your program. You are now faced with the difficult decision of choosing which students you will serve—and which ones you will not—in order to be responsive to the companies that are committed to hiring these students. How would you determine priorities for which students you would serve in the program?

Notes

1. S. N. Espy, Planning for success: Strategic planning in nonprofits, *Nonprofit World* 5 (1988), pp. 23–24.

2. J. A. Yankey & A. McClellan, *The nonprofit board's role in planning and evaluation* (Washington DC: Boardsource, 2003), p. 1.

3. S. P. Joyaux, *Strategic fund development* (Gaithersburg, MD: Aspen, 1997), p. 31.

4. P. Drucker, *Managing the nonprofit organization* (New York: HarperCollins, 1990), p. 141.

5. P. Drucker, *The effective executive* (New York: Harper & Row, 1985), pp. 59–71.

6. P. Drucker, *Management challenges for the 21st century* (New York: HarperBusiness, 1999), p. 74

7. P. Drucker, *Managing the nonprofit organization,* p. 31; R. Foster & S. Kaplan, *Creative destruction* (New York: Currency, 2001), p. 60, 288–296.

8. C. McNamara, Strategic planning, retrieved May 6, 2003, from www.mapnp.org/library/plan_dec/str_plan/str_plan.htm

9. J. G. Dees, J. Emerson, & P. Economy, *Enterprising nonprofits: A toolkit for social entrepreneurs* (New York: John Wiley & Sons, 2001), p. 57.

10. B. W. Barry, *Strategic planning workbook for nonprofit organizations* (St. Paul, MN: Amherst H. Wilder Foundation, 1986), pp. 1–72; R. T. Crow & C. A. Odewahn, *Management for the human services* (Englewood Cliffs, NJ: Prentice Hall, 1987), pp. 118–125; F. Moon, Decade of transition: The strategic plan as action blueprint for the 1990s, *Management Issues* (August 1990), pp. 1–2; F. Moon, Step one of strategic planning: Discover your organization, inventory your resources, and identify issues, *Management Issues* (September 1990), pp. 1–3; F. Moon, Building a strategic plan: The second step toward an action blueprint for the future, *Management Issues* (October 1990), pp. 1–3; F. Moon, The annual operating plan: Converting long-term strategies to achievable tasks, *Management Issues* (November 1990), pp. 1–4.

11. D. C. Eadie, *Changing by design* (San Francisco: Jossey-Bass, 1997), p. 37.

12. A. M. Renauer, A trained facilitator can be instrumental in successful strategic planning, *Management Issues* (April 1990), pp. 2–3.

13. J. A. Yankey & A. McClellan, pp. 11–13.

14. R. C. Andringa & T. W. Engstrom, *Nonprofit board answer book* (Washington, DC: Boardsource, 2002), p. 24.

15. P. C. Brincherhoff, *Mission-based marketing* (New York: John Wiley & Sons, 2003), p. 37.

16. D. C. Eadie, p. 153.

17. P. Senge et al., *The fifth discipline fieldbook* (New York: Currency, 1994), pp. 208, 282–284, 427; D. D. Pointer & J. E. Orlikoff, *The high-performance board* (San Francisco: Jossey-Bass, 2002), p. 24–26.

18. C. F. Dambach, *Structures and practices of nonprofit boards* (Washington, DC: Boardsource, 2003), p. 9.

19. G. J. Stern, *Marketing workbook for nonprofit organizations Volume I: Development plan,* 2nd ed. (Saint Paul, MN: Amherst Wilder Foundation, 2001), pp. 37–38.

20. S. N. Espy, Where are you, and where do you think you're going? *Nonprofit World,* 6 (1988), pp. 19–20.

21. J. G. Dees, J. Emerson, & P. Economy, pp. 147–148.

22. J. A. Yankey & A. McClellan, p. 9.

23. B. W. Barry, p. 40; D. C. Eadie, *Changing by design*, pp. 160–161; W. Weber, B. Laws, & S. Weber, Real world planning: Fresh approaches to old problems, *Nonprofit World* 2 (1987), p. 25.

24. S. N. Espy, Putting your plan into action, *Nonprofit World* 1 (1989), pp. 27–28; S. P. Joyaux, pp. 53–54.

25. D. C. Eadie, *Changing by design*, pp. 144–145.

26. D. C. Eadie, *Planning and managing*, p. 294; D. C. Eadie, *Changing by design*, p. 163.

27. R. S. Kaplan, Strategic performance measurement in nonprofit organizations, *Nonprofit Management and Leadership* 11 (2001), pp. 353–369.

28. D. C. Eadie, *Planning and managing*, p. 286.

29. J. A. Yankey & A. McClellan, pp. 16–17.

30. S. Cohen, *The effective public manager: Achieving success in government* (San Francisco: Jossey-Bass, 1988), pp. 126–127; T. M. Hout, Are managers obsolete? *Harvard Business Review* 77 (March/April 1999), pp. 161–168; J. B. Quinn, Strategic change: Logical incrementalism, *Sloan Management Review* (Fall 1978), pp. 3–16; T. Wolf, *The nonprofit organization: An operating manual* (Englewood Cliffs, NJ: Prentice Hall, 1984), pp. 81–83.

31. A. Campbell & M. Alexander, What's wrong with strategy? *Harvard Business Review* 75 (November/December 1997), p. 46.

32. R. A. Heifetz & D. L. Laurie, The work of leadership, *Harvard Business Review* 75 (January/February 1997), p. 134.

33. A. Campbell & M. Alexander, *What's wrong*, pp. 50–51.

34. S. P. Joyaux, *Strategic fund*, p. 64.

35. J. G. Dees, J. Emerson, & P. Economy, p. 146.

36. P. Drucker, *Managing the nonprofit*, p. 59.

37. T. Caplow, *How to run any organization* (Hinsdale, IL: Dryden, 1976), p. 205; P. Drucker, *Managing the nonprofit*, pp. 46–48, 55, 102, 142.

3

Designing and Developing Consumer-Oriented Programs

The purpose of this chapter is to identify ways to design and develop programs that are both effective and responsive to client needs. Two different perspectives, when combined, provide managers with a conceptual framework for formulating program design: (1) the *logic planning model* is designed to plan for, achieve, and demonstrate program effectiveness with clients; (2) the *marketing planning model* provides a framework for responding to service consumers' wants and needs.

Designing a Logic Planning Model

Using Social Systems Analysis

In a *logic planning model,* a human service organization's various service delivery elements are related to each other to produce intended results. Social systems analysis is a useful analytical framework for understanding how various parts within organizations effectively interact. This planning model shows the logical relationship between the objectives to be achieved and the resources and activities that are involved in achieving them. Human service organizations can best be understood by breaking them into elements related to *inputs, throughputs, outputs, and outcomes.*[1]

Inputs are of two kinds: *client inputs* are people who need services to improve their conditions and achieve their objectives; *resource inputs* represent the elements (e.g., staff, funding, facilities, and equipment) in the human service system that combine to help clients change themselves from persons with problems and needs into persons whose problems have been resolved.

Throughputs (usually referred to as activities) are those interventions or processes that the agency provides for clients. The number of service units or interventions that they actually receive (e.g., counseling interviews or educational sessions) is referred to as *outputs.* The positive change that occurs as a result of the intervention is the *outcome.* In human service organizations, throughputs might include counseling, job training, day care, information referral, and housing services. To accomplish throughput, organizations identify and implement a variety of activities to enable clients to accomplish their objectives. These could include, for example, assessing clients, conducting transactions between staff and clients, negotiating with internal and external service providers, providing direct services, and altering the client or the environment in some significant way.[2]

To more clearly show the range of activities available during this throughput process, it is useful to design a client flowchart that tracks clients from beginning to end. The term *pathway* is sometimes used to describe this sequence of structured contacts with clients as they move through the service delivery system. Pathways can be either a single route or multiple routes. Different clients in the same organization might follow different pathways and, of course, different organizations vary in the way clients move through their systems.

The value of a client flowchart is that it depicts various pathways clients can take into, through, and out of an agency. It identifies various points along the process where crucial decisions have to be made, where activities need to be monitored for feedback, and where different alternatives might need to be considered. Symbols used to describe client pathways are shown in Figure 3.1.

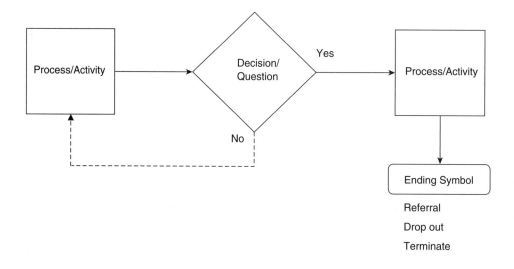

Figure 3.1   Client Pathway Symbols

- An arrow connects another process, question, or ending symbol.
- Dotted arrows reflect returning to a previous step.

- Three methods for closing a case are

1. the agency could make a referral to another agency;

2. the client could voluntarily discontinue because the problem is solved;

3. the agency could terminate the client.

Review of a Generic Client Flowchart Model

Figure 3.2, a Generic Client Flowchart, depicts a client moving through an agency that provides mental health counseling and that can also arrange for such outside services as housing, employment, or day care. Note that the client can be referred to the agency from several sources, such as self-referral, a family member, or the local school. During intake, staff determine whether the client is eligible for the service and meets appropriate requirements (e.g., income level, geographic location, and motivation for service). If the client

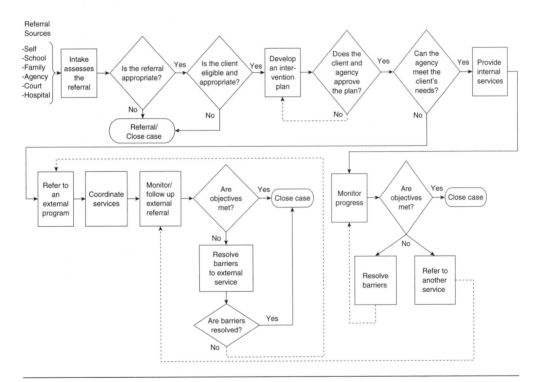

Figure 3.2   Generic Client Flowchart Model

is ineligible, the agency ends the contact with the client and, if appropriate, makes a referral elsewhere.

If the client continues, an intervention plan involving the achievement of specific objectives is mutually agreed upon between the agency and the client. Subsequently, the agency provides the agreed upon service(s). If the objectives are achieved, then the agency terminates the client as a successful case. During this process, the agency works to identify and remove barriers, either within the client or in the environment, that impede service delivery. For example, a client may be poorly motivated to work on his substance abuse problem, or he may be in a social environment that stimulates his drinking. Before treatment can proceed, the barriers that prevent him from working on his problems need to be addressed.

This generic flow chart reveals several instances of clients being at yes/no decision points that may involve their leaving the agency, returning to a previous process, or being referred to an outside agency. Client pathways should make these decision points clear, because they focus attention on those instances where clients' needs may require new or different ways of delivering services. In developing client pathways, be especially mindful of possible dropout points.

If Agency A determines that the client would benefit from Agency B's services, then a referral would be made, and Agency A may (or may not) monitor the delivery of services and the achievement of objectives. If barriers were encountered in Agency B, Agency A could pursue alternate referrals—or this could be the responsibility of Agency B. In examining client pathways through a particular service system or agency, consider the following questions:[3]

- Can there be multiple entry points?
- Is there only one or are there multiple pathways through the system?
- After going through intake, if the client is referred to a specialist, must the client return to a central point before going on to a second specialist or can the first specialist make a direct referral?
- Can a client go directly to a specialist, thus bypassing a central intake?
- How permeable are the agency's boundaries to admitting people (e.g., eligibility requirements, waiting lists, and bureaucratic "red tape")?
- What alternative pathways are open to clients if their conditions change or their objectives are not met?
- If certain objectives are met, but others are not, what does the agency do?
- Can clients who prematurely discontinue be recycled back into the agency's program at a later point?
- Does the agency attempt to re-engage and critically examine the reasons why clients drop out?
- Are those clients who need to be referred to outside agencies being assisted, and does staff follow up to determine whether the services were, in fact, provided and objectives achieved?
- Have proper forms (intake, screening and assessment, eligibility, admissions, case planning, evaluation, and termination) been developed to engage and track client progress through the service system?

The value of these questions is that they provide an analytic framework for viewing how clients are being treated as they are processed through the service delivery system.

Outputs are the direct products of program activities and usually measure volume of work accomplished.[4] The focus of an output performance measure is on the service. There are three types of output (units of service) performance measures:[5] (1) a material unit, such as one home-delivered meal; (2) an episode unit, such as one interview; and (3) a time unit, such as one hour for a home health aid program. An agency aggregates these performance measures across all clients receiving services, producing monthly or annual reports. The following are examples of output performance measurements:

- Number of counseling sessions
- Number of educational materials distributed
- Number of meals provided
- Number of community meetings held
- Number of clients completing a program
- Number of seniors completing prescribed, short-term treatment plans
- Number of children completing preschool education

In these examples, output units are shown as both units of service provided and units of service completed. Although most organizations are able to document their service units, by themselves these units are an insufficient measure of accomplishments. For that, *outcome measures* must be considered.

Outcome measures are defined as a measurable change in a client's life achieved between entry and exit of a program. The resulting accomplishments are attributable, at least partially, to a human service program.[6] In the absence of formal research, we can never be completely certain that the outcomes were the result of agency intervention. The fact that students are functioning at a higher grade level, or that people are able to get jobs, or recidivism rates are reduced may or may not be due to program interventions. Nevertheless, agencies can claim that client outcomes can be at least partially attributable to the service interventions. The following are examples of outcome measures:[7]

1. Service data
   - Job placements
   - Reduction in number of clients with arrests 90 days after completing treatment
   - Decline in child abuse
   - Performance at or above grade level
   - Discontinuance of drug use
   - Adults completing treatment reporting they are abstinent
   - Participants who receive a General Education Diploma (GED)
   - Participants retained in employment after one year
   - Homeless persons obtaining housing
   - Reduction in confirmed cases of abuse or neglect
   - Children placed with adoptive families within 180 days of the receipt of referral

2. Standards for measuring outcomes:
   - Preschool behavior rating scale
   - Parent attitude survey
   - Knowledge scales and aptitude tests

These scales document how people have changed after they have been involved in an intervention process.

3. Level of functioning scales that measure outcomes:
   - Rating of mentally ill on decision making and interpersonal interaction
   - Rating mentally disabled on daily living and communication

4. Client self-reported satisfaction as a measure of outcomes:
   - Satisfaction among clients who were treated or who were provided with services
   - In day care, percent of parents reporting their placement is safe, healthy, and nurturing
   - In a homemaker services program, consumers who feel that they have improved their functioning
   - In a nutrition program, consumers who feel that the meals program is an important source of nutritious meals

Note: Although client satisfaction can be useful, human service managers need to be cautious about overusing this scale as a substitute for more objective scales of outcomes.[8]

Establishing Initial, Intermediate, and Long-term Outcomes

For most clients, there is usually not one desired outcome, but rather a hierarchy of logically related benefits to be obtained from a program. This hierarchy is generally related to the length of time over which benefits can occur. *Initial outcomes* are the first benefits clients experience and are the ones most closely related to a program's outputs. These initial outcomes are immediate changes in participants' knowledge, attitudes, or skills, and they are necessary steps toward ultimate desired ends. In a school dropout prevention program, for example, an initial outcome would be students' active participation in a tutoring program and greater participation in school activities. In a job training program, an initial outcome would be learning a word processing skill or developing a better attitude about supervisors. Initial outcomes measure changes in program participants while they are still in the program.

Intermediate outcomes link the program's initial outcomes to long-term change in behavior that results from participants' new knowledge, attitudes, or skills. In a job training program, an intermediate outcome would be placement on a job. In a school dropout program, an intermediate objective would be regular attendance in school and passing to the next grade level. Intermediate objectives reflect participants' accomplishments at the end of the program or shortly thereafter (e.g., within three months of terminating the program).

Long-term outcomes are those changes in the client's quality of life (such as improved parenting or job stabilization) that are measured at a designated follow-up time.[9] These measurements can occur six months, one year, or even two years or more after the completion of the program to determine whether the initial gains were sustained. It would measure, for example, whether the person continued to be employed 12 months after completing training.

The reason to make this distinction is to acknowledge that achievements clients make at the end of the program may or may not be meaningfully sustained. Welfare recipients may be placed on jobs at the end of a training program, but they may not be employed 12 months later. Similarly, adolescents participating in a teen pregnancy prevention program may have increased their knowledge about using contraceptives, but their behavior may or may not have changed and they may become pregnant six months after they leave the program. Thus, the definition of *success* will vary depending on whether the focus is on initial, intermediate, or long-term outcomes.

In addition to considering the timeframe in determining outcomes, managers must also demonstrate the logical relationship between cause and effect, that is, how program interventions logically impact intended program results. This relationship can be thought of as an "If A, then B" chain of influences and benefits.[10] Consider the following:

> If the program can provide job training skills (throughput) for welfare recipients (input), and **if** clients complete the twelve-week training program (output), **then** they will be able to have more effective job interviews (initial outcome). **If** they have better job interviews, **then** they are more likely to find jobs that match their abilities and interests (intermediate outcome). And **if** they find suitable jobs, **then** they are more likely to become financially self-sufficient (long-term outcome).

By articulating these "if-then" statements, you make clear the assumptions for achieving desired outcomes. Subsequently, if that desired outcome is not in fact achieved, you may need to re-examine the assumptions upon which the program is based and consider making revisions. For example, if after the job interviewing training is completed people still do not obtain jobs, then you need to re-examine whether a program based on providing interviewing skills is the most appropriate means of achieving this objective.

To illustrate the relationship of inputs, throughputs (activities), outputs, and outcomes, consider how an employment training program would be designed to enable welfare recipients to obtain jobs:

> Long-term outcome: Participants remain on the job 12 months after completing the program.

Intermediate outcome: Participants are successfully placed in jobs.

Initial outcome: Participants learn how to conduct a job interview; they develop skills.

Outputs: Participants regularly attend 12 weeks of intensive training.

Throughput: Program provides classes on grooming, job interviewing, and word processing.

Inputs: Department of Human Services identifies participants for the program. Agency provides instructors, manuals, and other teaching tools.

Evaluating Outcomes

The logic planning model provides a way for both managers and outside funders to evaluate the extent to which the organization achieves its intended impact. By using measurement indicators attached to objectives, it is possible to determine the effectiveness of the organization. For example, you would indicate the percent of foster children projected to be placed in permanent families (their own or others) within one year. It is then easy to evaluate whether this was or was not achieved at the predicted, quantifiable level. Your decision about the level of expected achievement is based on your professional judgment and experience. Outcome projections are your best assessment of what will result from your intervention. For each expected outcome, you would determine how you would know that the outcome was achieved by providing quantitative indicators. This is how an agency providing transitional shelter for homeless families and children could evaluate itself in a given time period (e.g., one year).

Outcome 1: Families achieve residential stability.
    Indicator 1: 90% of families pay their rent on time.
    Indicator 2: 86% of families pay their utilities on time.

Outcome 2: Adults and families obtain job skills, education, and/or stable employment.
    Indicator 1: 88% of adult participants are employed full time.
    Indicator 2: 85% of adults are enrolled in GED classes, job training, or college.

Outcome 3: Families achieve greater self-determination.
    Indicator 1: 72% of adult participants attend post-treatment care group and maintain sobriety.
    Indicator 2: 90% of families complete their individual case plans.

At the end of the program period, the agency provides a report comparing the projected outcomes with actual outcomes in an evaluation review.

Ideally, before the end of the program period, if there are significant discrepancies emerging between projected and actual outcomes, agency management would have been asking, "What resources are necessary to make the program more successful? Should we alter our client input? Should our interventions be modified? Should the number of units be increased or decreased? Do we need to modify our outcome measures to make them more realistic?"

In summary, the logic planning model helps managers critically examine how inputs, throughputs, outputs, and outcomes are connected. The starting point in developing a logic planning model is with the desired end state or target. You ask the question, "What do we want to accomplish?" and then work backwards to figure out what needs to be done to achieve the target. This approach opens up the possibility of challenging the status quo and encourages "out of the box" thinking that could lead to more effective action planning. The kinds of questions that lead to action planning are as follows:[11]

- What program elements are critical to achieving what we want to accomplish?
- What program interventions need to be modified to achieve our objectives?
- What new program components should be considered to meet our objectives?
- How will we define success at initial, intermediate, and long-term intervals?

Designing a Marketing Planning Model

Determining the Consumer Service Market

As previously discussed, the logic planning model designs and measures programs based on their having an impact on service consumers. The *marketing planning model* provides a different perspective on developing effective service delivery programs. This approach focuses on determining what consumers of services (the market) want and then how the agency can meet those needs. A market-driven organization is one that understands its niche and works at how it can best meet the needs of its consumers.

After completing or revising its strategic plan (see Chapter 2), an organization has assessed its unique skills and competencies and can determine its niche—its place in the community for meeting an unmet need or responding to an opportunity for a new service that is within its mission. To better assess whether to modify an existing service or embark on a new one, an effective manager conducts a *competition analysis* to review whether other agencies are offering similar services or different services to the same clients. A neighborhood center, for example, offers recreation services to seniors and determines that seniors in nearby public housing do not make use of the center's programs. Although the local YMCA provides services for youth in public housing, it does not offer social and recreation programs for seniors. Based on a marketing analysis, the manager concludes that a need exists and that other agencies are not meeting it. The neighborhood center proceeds to develop a recreation program for seniors in public housing.

A focus on consumers of service (also conventionally referred to as *clients*) is at the heart of the market-driven approach. To convey this emphasis on meeting consumer needs, some organizations equate *service consumer* with *customer,* but this is an inaccurate application of terms. In private sector transactions, customers both pay for and receive the service. Private sellers of the service strive to preserve an ongoing relationship so that the customer will continue to buy their services. The word "customer" also implies that people have a choice to go somewhere else if they do not feel they are getting something of value in the transaction.

In the human services field, the person or entity paying for the service is usually not the consumer of the service (except in those few instances where clients pay full fee). Because many organizations experience more demand for their service than what their resources will allow, because dissatisfied clients who leave the agency can be replaced by someone else on a waiting list, and because funding limitations force agencies to reduce services, agency staff may tend to treat their consumers with less care and consideration. The term *customer* is used as a metaphorical expression to convey the importance of treating people with care and dignity. One should be cautious, however, about applying too literally the language of business in designing human service programs. Asking staff, for example, to refer to their homeless clients, or adolescent delinquents, or substance abusing service consumers as "customers" could feel awkward and insincere.

Offering the Consumer Outstanding Service

Because human service consumers rarely pay the full cost of service, some organizations may not feel the same obligation to respond to their needs as if they were full-paying customers. Human service organizations, however, must emphasize the primacy of the client. This sign was hung in the administrative offices of a public housing authority:

> We believe that our clients are not an interruption of our work; they are the very purpose of it. We are not doing them a favor by serving them; they are doing us a favor by giving us an opportunity to do so.

Even when a human service organization's staff believes that their clients are their reason for being, a number of factors can inhibit this from being their core purpose. If program funding is received from a third party, consumers may not have a direct way to express their concerns because they are not paying for the service. If consumers are considered fungible—that is, if there are so many people waiting to be served that dissatisfied ones can easily be replaced by others—then there may be little or no impetus to deal with client discontent. If too great an emphasis is placed on administrative or staff convenience, then meeting the needs of consumers becomes secondary. If the delivery of services involves more than one organization or more than one unit within an organization, their competitive, territorial attitudes can result in consumer services becoming fragmented and overly burdened with bureaucratic procedures.

The antidote for these inhibitive factors is a value commitment to—even an obsession with—meeting consumer needs. Effective managers must clarify to employees that this is fundamental. Organizations must develop a good feedback system and a method for reminding staff of the primacy of consumers. One major way to obtain feedback is through periodic, formal client satisfaction surveys. Just as hotels and car repair shops ask their customers regularly for suggestions on how to improve their services, human service organizations could benefit from such formal surveys of their constituents. Some organizations use a feedback device titled "Give Us a Grade," in which consumers are asked to answer questions or provide a rating regarding whether their expectations were met, how they were treated, and their level of satisfaction with the quality of care they received. Encouraging comment cards and letters—both positive and negative—helps staff understand how their services are perceived.

Some organizations even have management staff pretend they are consumers. They may call or visit an office where they are unrecognized to see firsthand how their concerns are handled. This is a common practice in retail stores that arrange for management, staff, or outside "professional shoppers" to experience what it is like to be treated as a customer. The purpose is not to evaluate specific individuals as much as it is to determine how responsive the system is to consumer needs. Experiencing the organization as a consumer can reveal discrepancies between how things should work and what actually takes place.

The message being promoted throughout the organization is that everyone serves clients directly or indirectly. If employees are not involved in direct service, they ought to be facilitating the work of those who are. This means that everyone in the organization has a client to serve: supervisors facilitate the work of their staff, accountants provide needed information to management, and support staff assist staff who work with clients. Consistency between rhetoric and action is vital if employees are to believe and accept that the organization sincerely cares about its consumers.

Many obvious clues indicate whether an organization is *consumer friendly*. Telephone calls are promptly answered. Staff parking is not any more convenient than client parking. The reception or waiting room is inviting, and the receptionist conveys a warm welcome to visitors. Intake and service staff genuinely convey positive acceptance and go the extra distance to be helpful to clients. Appointments are promptly kept; apologies are given if clients have to wait. Clients and volunteers are treated as genuine partners by engaging them in meaningful activities that assist the agency. They may, for example, be asked to serve on advisory committees, or on the board itself, to make suggestions to improve agency services.

These are small efforts, perhaps, but they project the organization's fundamental emphasis on the dignity and importance of the consumer. And they do not occur by happenstance. The culture of caring permeates the entire organization as it continually reinforces this primary value in new policies, staff meetings, annual reports, training programs, and documents describing particular programs. Effective managers do not tolerate denigrating comments about clients or coworkers. Through special training and supervision, staff learn how to treat clients with respect and dignity even when having to cope with hostility and complaints. By frequently stressing its commitment to caring and proving that commitment time and again, the organization develops a reputation for being responsive to the needs of the people it serves.

Three rules can be applied to good consumer service.[12] First, *the consumer is not always right, but the consumer is always the consumer, and therefore it is crucial to fix the problem.* Although consumers can be mistaken at times, their perspective is extremely important. Managers must infuse in their organizations an attitude of understanding and of trying to respond to consumers' perceived needs. For example, you have designed a program to provide substance abuse counseling, but a number of your clients express concern about the lack of adequate housing. Certainly they must deal with their substance abuse, but you also need to consider ways within the agency or through referral to respond to their housing needs.

Second, *consumers have crises, and it is therefore important to address their problems immediately.* From the perspective of the consumer, the problems need to be addressed with a sense of urgency. Programs need to be prepared to offer a compassionate response to what consumers feel is a crisis. Some agencies use this approach by providing *wrap-around services*—a range of services provided on a 24-hour basis, especially for adolescents who are likely to get into difficulty at times other than regular office hours.

Third, *seek total consumer satisfaction.* Never assume that clients, even those who evidence strengths and competencies, can automatically connect their problems to your solutions. Asking, listening, and responding are at the heart of providing outstanding consumer service. Solving consumer problems means that you need to understand their perspectives. Incredibly good consumer service starts with having insightful empathy for clients' problems and needs. Recognize, too, that though consumers come with their own strengths, they also are sometimes powerless and need an advocate to help them negotiate various community institutions for resources to sustain a decent quality of life.

Seeking Consumer Feedback

To understand better the special needs of their clients and also the interests of outside funders and public officials, agencies seek feedback to guide them in program development. To better understand consumer needs, organizations conduct focus group sessions, ask for consumer reactions through formal and informal surveys, and elicit client complaints.

Focus groups are useful ways to generate ideas about consumer needs and reactions to programs.[13] It is often a good idea to convene focus groups of similar consumers (e.g., separate meetings for Latinos or African-American consumers, or of teenagers and adults) because their perspectives may be influenced by cultural and other unique characteristics. Usually a focus group consists of eight to ten consumers and is guided by a facilitator who asks such open-ended questions as, "What appeals to you about the program? What aspects of the program turn you off? Who do you think would benefit from the program? How often should the program be offered? What would persuade you to try this program?" Responses to these questions can provide helpful directions for future programs.

Frequently, agencies survey current consumers about how they benefited from the service and what changes they would recommend. In conducting the survey, keep questions brief and focused, and be clear about what the specific value will be of each question. Surveys take time, financial commitment, and a degree of expertise. Have qualified researchers review questionnaires so as to avoid bias and potential distortion of results.[14] Consumers would rank services on the basis of accessibility, appropriateness of service, acceptability, recommendation of further service, and overall satisfaction.

A more open-ended approach is to use the Internet so that people can describe what they like if they are current consumers or what services they would like if they were to use your program in the future. Provide an easily accessible part of the Web site for people to request more information or for making suggestions about your services. Also, make sure that someone responds on a daily basis. A word of caution: do not over-rely on the Internet to obtain feedback on your services. Not all of your consumers can access the Internet, and be mindful that overusing Internet surveys can be perceived as pestering.

Everyone in the organization can be involved in a marketing effort to ascertain how consumers feel about their services and about the agency. The receptionist and intake worker can ask consumers how they learned about the organization. Board members and volunteers can ask people what they have heard about the organization. Feedback then needs to be channeled to staff who can respond. For example, if someone complains about the facility's physical appearance, that information has to be passed on to the maintenance staff. Continuous soliciting of opinions about the kind, quality, and level of service your organization provides shows that your staff care.[15]

To convey to consumers that they have basic rights, many human service agencies publicly post these rights at the agency or include them in intake handouts given to consumers. For example, consumers are informed that they have the right to obtain courteous and fair treatment and be treated with dignity, and information they give is confidential. Any state laws that limit confidentiality are explained. They also have an opportunity to communicate their concerns and obtain resolution of them. Some organizations create consumer relations teams whose job is to answer questions, resolve problems, and ensure that all clients receive prompt, courteous, and professional service. Clients have access to a conciliation procedure that invites them first to talk with the staff, then a supervisor, and then a customer relations specialist (also known as an ombudsman or a client advocate) who can meet with staff and clients in a conciliation process before they are carried to other county or state hearing levels. Consumers know that they can file an appeal without fear of repercussions, including interference, coercion, or loss of services.

Based on the feedback from its present and potential consumers, organizational managers are better prepared to consider both the services your agency could offer and your possible target markets.[16] Four fundamental questions could be explored:

1. How can we expand our existing services to our current customers? Example: A job training program contracts with the county commissioners to expand job training services to clients who live outside the central city.

2. How can we develop new services for current consumer segments? Example: Your program is designed to provide counseling and support for high-risk students who are in danger of dropping out of school. The teenagers seem resistant to talking directly about their problems, so you design a program where they can work on creative art projects while permitting informal discussions of issues that concern them.

3. How can we find new consumer segments for current services? Example: A neighborhood mental health counseling center contracts to develop a residential facility to house mentally ill women for whom they can provide ongoing counseling.

4. How can we develop new consumers and new service programs? Example: A family service agency contracts to develop a substance abuse prevention program in the elementary schools.

Being Responsive to External Markets

Effective managers rely on market planning as they consider the role of stakeholders—those who have a keen interest in the organization, though they do not receive direct service benefits. Stakeholders can be trustees, volunteers, family members, fund donors, service advocates, referral sources, elected officials, and community leaders who must all be satisfied with the effectiveness and efficiency of services delivered.

Three elements comprise the external market: referral sources, policymakers and administrators, and funders. Human service organizations need all three to survive. Referral sources, such as the courts, city or county department of human services, and nonprofit agencies, send consumers to agencies. Policymakers and administrators, such as elected and appointed officials, United Way leadership, and accreditation and credentialing professionals control resources and enact regulations that influence how your organization functions. Funders—federated campaigns (e.g., United Way, United Black Fund), foundations, insurance companies, individual donors, faith-based drives—provide needed resources. You need to be constantly tuned in to these external markets so you can then better serve your consumers. Trying to be responsive to these diverse external markets can be daunting. Effective managers must constantly strive to satisfy different and sometimes incompatible decision makers. The consumer, for example, may need extensive counseling service, but the insurance companies involved in managed care can restrict the number of interview sessions. Having multiple constituents presents an ongoing balancing act for most managers.

Effective managers are sometimes confronted with the dilemma of choosing between the organization's mission and what the market wants and needs. If you start with the premise that the market is always right, but that it may not be right for you or your organization, you have a choice not to meet the market's needs—as difficult a choice as this may be. So a good starting point in assessing whether to consider a new service project or major expansion is to determine the following:[17]

- Does the project support our mission?
- Does it support or conflict with our organizational values?
- Does it support our strategic plan, goals, and objectives?
- Does it result in net income or net loss? If it is a loss, can we afford it?
- Is this something we can do well?
- Is there evidence of user need and interest?
- Is there commitment to devote time and resources to the project?
- Does the organization have the capacity to carry out the project?

The point, then, is that you need to move with the external markets when you can, but you must be careful about being so opportunistic in your quest for new programs or new funds that you allow the organization to drift from its mission. Be wary of *mission drift*, for it can create confusion among the organization's key stakeholders and ultimately make the organization vulnerable. Sticking to the mission helps the organization resist chasing ideas and losing the organization's core reason for existing for the sake of money.[18] It may be difficult not to go after new sources of revenue, but this may be the best long-term decision for the organization.

It is crucial, however, that you tune in to what your external market determines and whether, in keeping with your mission, you need to provide a new program or redesign an existing one. When confronted with a situation in which consumers are not responding to your program, or public officials seem not to have an interest, or referring organizations are not making expected referrals, effective managers explore various avenues to determine what factors are preventing people from using their services. This is referred to as *strategic marketing* or as a *marketing audit*[19]—special efforts designed to uncover information that can help you create or refashion your service program.

This is what a faith-based organization did to be responsive to its external markets in designing services: Catholic Charities Services Corporation (CCSC) of the Cleveland Diocese was a collection of 24 separate agencies that were held together in a loose federation. Because services were poorly coordinated and highly fragmented, the parent organization decided to integrate services in the eight counties in which it operated. To determine ways to improve its services, CCSC embarked upon a strategic marketing program in which the directors went outside the security and certainty of their own buildings to consider a broad range of services. They needed to shift from thinking that they intuitively knew what was needed to actually finding out what human needs existed and devising ways to meet those needs.

In addition to conducting interviews with service recipients, the management staff interviewed leaders of the private sector, such as United Way, and public sector administrative staff responsible for planning, developing, and purchasing services. For example, managers learned that county commissioners were desperately looking for ways to keep foster children under their care in their communities rather than send them to other counties for residential treatment. This awareness eventually led to specially designed community-based services for foster children.

Through strategic marketing, managers made adjustments to current services. For example, adolescents involved in domestic violence were being detained unduly in the juvenile detention home for long periods without any meaningful plan. CCSC contracted with local juvenile courts to work out a joint custody program with the teens and their parents. Being responsive to the requirements of the public agency has become central to the CCSC service design. Sometimes this involved working out ways to directly communicate with the public agency should problems occur. Probations officers, for example, were to be informed immediately if a youngster missed more than one day of counseling or if there were any other departures from behavioral expectations.

The consequence of the strategic marketing endeavor was to identify, from the public sector's perspective, what populations were underserved because they cut across several different categories: juvenile offenders who are also substance abusers, disabled persons who also required employment opportunities, and substance abusing mothers who wanted their children returned to them. This comprehensive approach to people with multiple problems encouraged CCSC to develop combinations of services geared to meeting multiple needs of their clients. Hence chemical dependency counseling was made available to delinquent juveniles, employment counseling as well as case management was provided for persons with disabilities, and residential treatment and eventually job training were available for substance abusing mothers.

To carry out the strategic marketing, staff received cross training so that they could work with a variety of clients. Staff could function both as specialists and as generalists. In addition, CCSC developed a capacity to subcontract with other programs that were not under the sponsorship of CCSC. For example, two of its agencies contracted with other neighborhood-based agencies to provide after school programs. As a result of strategic marketing, CCSC staff shifted from being *service presenters* to becoming *service responders*. By being more responsive to the community needs, CCSC developed 111 new services totaling $8,000,000 in new revenues. This required a change in attitude from "what we have to offer to what the community needs."[20]

Summary of Elements of Good Design

By incorporating elements from both the *logic planning model* and the *marketing planning model,* effective managers can prepare a service delivery system that would include the following:

1. *Services are consumer oriented.* Staff have the authority to carry out meeting client needs or can refer clients elsewhere. Client pathways are clearly understood. If clients need to receive multiple services, the organization provides for this. Whether within the agency or outside, all staff working on a case interact with each other through the computer network, teleconferencing, or joint meetings.

2. *The design clearly spells out outputs and, more importantly, the outcomes to be achieved.* Special emphasis is given to demonstrating impacts at the conclusion of the program and, where feasible, at least six months or one year following termination.

3. *The design makes explicit assumptions and maintains a logical sequence of results if certain conditions are met.* This takes the form of a series of "if A, then B" events. For example, if clients were to attend a minimum of 10 substance abuse group sessions, and if they could test negatively for substance abuse for 10 weeks, and if they could become gainfully employed in a job paying at least 10% above the minimum wage, then they would be drug free for one year following completion of the program.

4. *The program is designed with a marketing perspective, with special emphasis on being responsive to consumer needs.* That is, the emphasis is on

providing outstanding consumer service, including meeting total needs, where possible.

5. *New programs fit the organization's mission and are feasible based on available or potential agency resources.*

6. *The organization has good feedback mechanisms in the form of focus groups, formal and informal surveys, and client complaint procedures.*

7. *The organization considers the needs of external markets including, for example, the needs of public officials and funders.* It would determine how best to balance the needs of the external markets with those of the consumers it is dedicated to serving.

Questions for Discussion

1. How does (could) your organization identify needs and opportunities for new services?

2. In what ways could your organization use market analysis to deliver better services?

3. A meeting has been called of representatives of United Way, the local mental health board, the developmental disabilities board, the county human services department, the local health department, the local substance abuse board, and the public schools. The intent is to explore whether to create a centralized intake system in several neighborhoods involving these organizations to serve multi-need families. What are the pros and cons of setting up a centralized office?

4. Your agency provides counseling services to mentally ill persons who are able to function in the community but who also need jobs. What are the pros and cons of (a) offering job counseling and job finding through your agency, or (b) arranging to refer clients to another organization that is in the business of job development? If you decide to work with the employment organization, what would you need to consider to make the program work for the benefit of your clients?

5. Develop a flowchart of clients going through your organization. Where are the dropout points likely to occur? What steps, if any, should your organization take to deter dropouts? At what critical points should the service consumers' experience be assessed?

6. How would you describe participants in your program? Are there any trends suggesting changes in the demographics of participants in the last few years?

7. Does your organization currently evaluate its programs in relation to its proposed outcomes?

Notes

1. P. M. Kettner, R. M. Moroney, & L. L. Martin, *Designing and managing programs* (Thousand Oaks, CA: Sage, 1999), pp. 111–138; M. Rosenburg & R. Brody, *Systems serving people* (Cleveland: Case Western Reserve University, 1974), pp. 9–17.

2. R. Brody & M. D. Nair, *Macro practice: A generalist approach* (Wheaton, IL: Gregory Publishing, 2003), p. 24.

3. R. Brody & M. D. Nair, p. 30.

4. United Way of America, *Measuring program outcomes: A practical approach* (Alexandria, VA: Author, 1996); M. Rosenburg & R. Brody, pp. 12–13; P. M. Kettner, R. M. Moroney, & L. L. Martin, p. 119.

5. L. L. Martin, *Financial management for human service administrators* (Boston: Allyn & Bacon, 2001), pp. 70–71.

6. R. Brody & H. Krailo, An approach to reviewing the effectiveness of programs, *Social Work* 3 (1978), pp. 38–43; P. M. Kettner, R. M. Moroney, & L. L. Martin, p. 128; L. L. Martin, *Financial management*, p. 71.

7. L. L. Martin, Budgeting for outcomes in state human service agencies, *Administration in Social Work* 3 (2000), pp. 71–88; L. L. Martin, Performance contracting in the human services: An analysis of selected state practices, *Administration in Social Work* 2 (2000), pp. 29–44.

8. P. M. Kettner, R. M. Moroney, & L. L. Martin, pp. 128–133.

9. P. M. Kettner, R. M. Moroney, & L. L. Martin, pp. 132–134.

10. United Way of America, pp. 32–33; P. M. Kettner, R. M. Moroney, & L. L. Martin, pp. 73–74; S. J. Wells & M. A. Johnson, Selecting outcome measures for child welfare settings: Lessons for use in performance management, *Child and Youth Services Review* 2 (2001), pp. 169–199.

11. A. Miller, R. S. Simeone, & J. T. Carneval, Logic models: A systems tool for performance management, *Evaluation and Program Planning* 24 (2001), pp. 73–81.

12. P. C. Brinckerhoff, *Mission-based marketing,* 2nd ed. (New York: John Wiley & Sons, 2003), pp. 197–207.

13. J. G. Dees, J. Emerson, & P. Economy, *Enterprising nonprofits: A toolkit for social entrepreneurs* (New York: John Wiley & Sons, 2001), p. 213.

14. P. C. Brinckerhoff, pp. 136–144.

15. P. C. Brinckerhoff, pp. 147–149.

16. J. G. Dees, J. Emerson, & P. Economy, p. 163.

17. P. C. Brinckerhoff, p. 33.

18. R. C. Andringa & T. W. Engstrom, *Nonprofit board answer book* (Washington DC: Boardsource, 2002), p. 245.

19. G. J. Stern, Marketing workbook for nonprofit organization volume I: Develop the plan, 2nd ed. (Saint Paul, MN: Amherst H. Wilder Foundation, 2001), p. 12.

20. R. Brody & T. Woll, *Toward developing an integrated service delivery system* (Cleveland, OH: Catholic Charities Services Corporation, 2001).

4

Implementing Action Plans

This chapter provides a framework and guiding principles for getting things done. Good strategic planning can easily go nowhere unless effective managers are astute about how to execute their plans. The best laid decisions can go astray unless managers develop a well-thought-out plan of action. Working with staff, effective managers establish annual objectives that contribute to the overall strategic plan. They involve staff in the decision-making process because by doing so they ensure proper implementation of plans. They anticipate that staff may be resistant to change, and they develop contingency plans to deal with possible unforeseen events.

In addition, effective managers consider small-scale pilot projects as effective means for implementing plans. To ensure that plans are carried out well, they develop mechanisms for handling details. Finally, effective managers monitor the implementation process to determine whether corrective actions must be taken to keep their plans on track.

Setting Objectives

To properly carry out plans, effective managers work with staff to establish objectives. In some organizations, the terms *goals* and *objectives* are used interchangeably, but it is useful to distinguish between the two.[1] Typically, goals represent long-term endeavors, sometimes as long as three to five years, and may even be timeless. Examples of these goal statements would be "improving access to health care services for low-income persons" or "reducing racism in our community." A goal statement containing a time horizon might be "increasing the financial resources of the organization by 30% within four years."

Objectives represent relevant, attainable, measurable, and time-limited ends to be achieved. They are relevant because they fit within the general mission and goals of the organization and because they relate to problems identified by the organization. They are attainable because they can be realized. They are measurable because achievement is based upon tangible, concrete, and usually quantifiable results. They are time limited (usually a year); this time frame helps the organization demonstrate concrete results within a specified period.

Kinds of Objectives

Organizations typically develop *impact, service, operational,* and *product* objectives. As discussed in Chapter 3, *impact objectives* specify outcomes to be achieved as a result of program activities. They detail the return expected on the organization's investment of time, personnel, and resources. The following are examples:

- To place 20 children in adoptive homes in one year
- To secure jobs for 35 juvenile delinquents in 5 months
- To increase the number of foster children reunited with their natural parents from 40 to 50 by June 30

In writing impact objective statements, consider the following criteria:

1. Use an action verb that describes an observable change in a condition—to *reduce, improve, strengthen, enhance.*

2. State only one specific result per objective. An objective that states two results may require two different implementations and could cause confusion about which of the two objectives was achieved. For instance, "to reduce the recidivism rate by 10% and obtain employment for 20 former delinquents" is a statement of two objectives and each should be stated separately.

3. Make objective statements realistic. Do not decide to decrease recidivism rates by 50% if staff and financial resources would at most likely allow you to reduce recidivism by 25%. On the other hand, do not set such unreasonably low objectives that the organization's credibility is called into question.

Service objectives are the organization's tally of activities provided or services rendered. Sometimes these are referred to as *activity* or *process* objectives. Examples include the following:

- To serve 300 clients in the program year
- To conduct 680 interviews
- To provide 17 neighborhood assemblies
- To interview 20 children needing foster homes

Operational objectives convey the intent to improve the general operation of the organization. Examples include the following:

- To sponsor 4 in-service training workshops for 40 staff
- To obtain a pilot project grant of $10,000 within 6 months
- To increase the number of volunteers by 150
- To reduce staff turnover from 20% to 10% annually

Operational objectives are essential to enhance the way an organization functions. They are a means to the end for which the organization was established. By providing in-service training, for example, an organization improves the way it serves its target populations.

Product objectives are designed to provide a tangible outcome to benefit a target population or a community. Sometimes these are referred to as *deliverables*. The following are examples of product objectives:

- To obtain passage of House Bill 41
- To develop a neighborhood family support system
- To review and critique a specific piece of legislation
- To open four schools in the evening for recreation
- To provide a media effort on teen pregnancy prevention
- To establish a weekly clinic
- To sponsor a community conference or a forum
- To coordinate a communitywide campaign on mental health
- To mobilize community support for Medigap legislation

Formatting Goals and Objectives

Which of these four types of objectives should an organization emphasize? The answer depends on the goals of the organization and its primary work efforts. Within the organization, different units may need to emphasize different types of objectives. For example, a unit dealing with clients likely uses service or activity objectives, as well as impact objectives; an administrative or planning unit likely develops product or operational objectives.

For most human service organizations, demonstrating and achieving impact objectives is of crucial importance. It is not enough for an organization to proclaim how well its processes are working and ignore whether it is having an impact on those it was established to serve. Because impact objectives emphasize measured outcomes, they should be the focal point for most service organizations. Agencies are in business to achieve results, which means they must demonstrate the impact they are having on clients. The following illustrates the relationship between an impact objective and other objectives that contribute to it:

Goal: To improve foster care services
  Impact objective: To decrease the number of children waiting each
  month for a foster home from an average of 150–170 to an average
  of 100–120
  Service objective: To conduct a recruitment campaign that will
  increase the pool of prospective foster parents from 10 to 60
  Product objective: To produce a training manual
  Operational objectives: To hire two additional recruitment staff
  To conduct an in-house training program on foster care

The advantage of this format is that it makes quite clear that the achievement of an interim activity or operating objective is not an end in itself but a means to an end. In the above example, the organization can only consider itself successful if it reduces the number of children waiting for foster homes. The interim objectives of conducting a recruitment campaign and convincing commissioners to hire additional staff, even if successful, are means to accomplishing the primary or impact objective of reducing the number of children waiting for foster homes.[2]

In establishing objectives for serving clients, the organization should clarify risk, target, and impact populations. The risk population is the total group in need of help. For example, in a certain community, there may be 800 ex-offenders who could potentially benefit from an employment service. A target population is the group toward which the program is focused. For example, only 70 out of 800 are employable and therefore qualify for services. The impact population is the group that actually benefits from the program. For example, of the 70 served, only 45 may actually find jobs (see Figure 4.1).

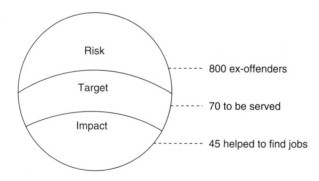

Figure 4.1   Risk, Target, and Impact Populations

Cautions About Objectives

Because managers in human service organizations are likely to be engaged in establishing objectives, it is important that these be developed with certain caveats in mind. Although a powerful tool, objective setting does have its limitations. Consider these cautions.

First, not all objectives lend themselves to quantifiable measurement. For example, counseling programs are more difficult to quantify than employment or housing programs, where results are more easily measured. Although human service organizations are under tremendous pressure to show measurable results, the quest to measure results, especially in prevention programs, is still underdeveloped. Be careful, however, not to select only those objectives that are measurable. Perhaps the most important things your organization does cannot be quantified.

Second, objectives should not conflict with each other. For example, the objective statement "to improve the recording of staff accomplishments" may actually reduce the effectiveness of the agency's services as staff devote more time to documenting services than to carrying them out. Achieving the objective "to reduce organizational costs" may result in serving fewer people, because part of the cost reduction may limit public information about the organization. Always be mindful of possible undesirable ramifications.

Third, because objectives may be in conflict with each other, and because overemphasis on one objective may have a detrimental effect on the achievement of others, managers must continually seek a proper balance and a way of integrating the organization's various objectives. There is always the danger that each unit in an organization may independently go about setting and achieving its own objectives, unmindful of its impact on the objectives of other units. For example, in striving to achieve the objective of making the organization better known in the community, the public information unit may be making such extensive demands on staff to handle speaking engagements that less time is available to achieve the objective of increasing client services.

Fourth, setting objectives requires everyone in the organization, including the board of trustees, management, and frontline staff, to be responsible for their work. Constituents of all parts of the organization should understand how they are contributing to the objectives and hence to achieving the organization's mission. This is risky, because when objectives are not achieved, there is a tendency to blame those who let the organization down. Insight that leads to further improvement in service delivery, not blame, must be the outgrowth of heightened accountability.

Finally, objectives should be designed to stretch, but not break, staff. The value of objectives is that they stimulate staff to extend themselves to reach a predetermined target. If the target is set too high and is virtually unachievable, the result will be a highly frustrated and even disgruntled staff. If set too low, objectives lose their potency to foster staff investment and productivity. Hence effective managers devote considerable thought to the objective-setting process.

Anticipating Unintended Consequences _____

Human service organizations experience unintended consequences either because members do not sufficiently do their homework, or because situations arise that nobody could have predicted. Obviously you can do little about unforeseen events, but with a little extra effort and disciplined thinking you can identify potential trouble spots.

Preparation is essential before taking action. Painters do not just start painting; they devote as much as 80% of their total time to preparing a job before ever making their first brush stroke. Similarly, it is important to think through in detail ahead of time what will happen as a result of a decision before you embark on it. Regrettably, many efforts fail because not enough time is spent making sure that those who will implement a decision are prepared to do so.[3]

Consider this example: In a juvenile court, a decision is made to provide intensive probation for delinquents who evidence high-risk behavior, such as repeated felony offenses. To carry out intensive probation, 10% of the probation officers are given a small caseload of clients to see frequently. The decision appears to be a good one because their clients begin to manifest a low rate of recidivism. A by-product, however, is that the remaining probation officers have to take on even larger caseloads, with unintended results of lower staff morale and less time available to work with clients, who then evidence an increase in recidivism. Had the focus of attention not been entirely upon the new program, perhaps the potential negative consequence of the decision could have been prevented.

In the medical field, the word *iatrogenic* is defined as an inadvertent, medically induced illness. No such word exists in the human service field, but there are certainly many instances where a particular decision, although beneficial in many ways, can produce negative side effects. Just as penicillin, prescribed to cure pneumonia, may cause patients who are allergic to it to go into shock, so too can specially created social programs have negative side effects. Subjecting unemployed persons to a job training program with no possibility of employment, placing clients in jobs without providing adequate day care, releasing mentally disabled patients in the absence of proper community supports, or incarcerating juveniles with no provision for rehabilitation are among many examples of plans that can produce negative results because managers did not adequately anticipate the negative consequences of the intervention.

Indeed, it is a common occurrence in agencies that well-intentioned interventions may negate the benefits of the intervention. Organizations, like individuals, tend to produce unintended compensatory responses when new efforts are tried.[4] A person stops smoking only to gain weight. An overprotective mother creates in her child the inability to resolve his or her own problems. At the organizational level, an agency that expands its volunteer activities may inadvertently reduce staff initiative. An overzealous manager who works to ensure that no mistakes are made reduces the ability of staff to grow and learn from experience.

Thus certain actions may possibly lead to a detrimental condition that is as bad as, or even worse than, the original problem. Carefully weigh whether implementing a particular course of action may be worse than the problem it is intended to solve.

Managing Change

Tipping Point Leadership

The theory of *tipping points,* which has its roots in epidemiology, is based on the idea that when the beliefs and energies of a critical mass of people are engaged in an organization, conversion to a new idea will spread like an epidemic, bringing about fundamental change quickly. To counter the natural inertia that exists in organizations, agency managers must be able to tip the scales from resistance to enthusiastic commitment. They can do so by making a strong case for change, concentrating resources on what really matters, and mobilizing the commitment of the organization's key players.[5]

A first step is getting staff to directly experience an issue or problem. For example, it is not enough for counselors in a school system to learn intellectually about the lives of their students. They need to be encouraged to make home visits so they can see firsthand what their students' lives are like. Providing a reality check is crucial to getting people to change their perceptions and engage in the issue.

A second step is to consider reallocating resources for an effective impact. For example, in a neighborhood center a decision is made to shift some staff from working with adults to concentrating on neighborhood gangs. The emphasis is on better targeting limited resources.

To motivate those in the organization that might be indecisive or resistant to change, a third step would be to identify key *influencer*s, that is, people inside or outside the organization who have the ability to persuade others or who have access to resources. Depending on the organization, these influencers could be a union organizer, a long time employee who is a relative of a local city council member, or a wealthy volunteer. By bringing these influencers on board, they can become engaged in stimulating a change in the mood and sentiment. Hence, effective managers consider carefully what must be done to influence change.

Initiating and Implementing Pilot Projects

Managers often must maintain current programs and services and, at the same time, develop innovative programs. The effective manager must determine how to generate projects without creating such great resistance and conflict that they are doomed before being tested or fully implemented. One way to deal with this is to create ad hoc temporary staff teams to work on pilot projects. The teams can try out new ideas and work out any project glitches before the projects are diffused through the rest of the organization. Often new ideas do not work out right the first time. Problems invariably occur that nobody even considered.[6] Through pilot projects, staff develop flexibility to experiment with new ventures. If the pilots fail, they can be aborted without serious consequence to the rest of the organization; if they succeed, they can be expanded.[7]

When staff embark on a small-scale, manageable undertaking, when they are committed to the task, and when they operate within a climate that favors innovation, pilot projects are more likely to succeed.[8] The pilot project must be conceived with a reasonable chance for success. By having a clear beginning and end, by having focus, and by achieving modest and measurable improvements, the pilot project team is spurred on to continue their efforts and, later, to spread the word about their success.

A project that focuses on achievable, short-term, and urgently needed results has the best chance of success. A task group can be quickly assembled to focus on problems requiring immediate and urgent resolution. Staff are assigned based on their expertise, experience, or other strengths. Their focus of attention should be on developing a breakthrough that can have great implications for the rest of the organization. They must strive for success in a few weeks (not months), be eager to tackle the challenge, and concentrate on achieving results with available resources.[9]

Pilot projects can involve a variety of efforts: reformulating the information flow of the organization, experimenting with new services, or developing new procedures. Whatever the project, its small-scale nature allows staff to try out ideas, be creative, and determine under what conditions the project works. By approaching the project on an incremental, trial-and-error basis, the organization avoids the possibility of a large-scale failure. If something does not work, the team can make corrections before implementing the project on a larger scale.[10]

All of us have had the experience in our personal lives of establishing achievable goals and, having achieved them, developing the confidence and the capacity to strive for more ambitious goals. This could apply to losing weight, managing finances better, or striving for a higher academic degree. Success builds on success. This is also true with organizations. When staff succeed with several phases of a pilot program they become more confident to tackle more challenging tasks. To achieve ultimate success, the original design of the pilot program may need to be revised as staff discover new and better ways to achieve their goals.[11]

Sometimes a crisis can lead to the creation of a pilot project that mobilizes special effort and attention. Staff are brought together with the expectation that they will be motivated to generate high energy and investment. The sense of urgency demands that the project receive the highest priority because an immediate resolution is required. Crisis projects could include (a) expanding outreach efforts to bring in more clients or face the consequence of immediate reduced funding, (b) improving safety procedures after a staff member was mugged leaving work, or (c) increasing client job placements by 20% in response to political pressures. Labeling the project a "crisis" focuses needed attention and rallies everyone to find a solution to a pressing problem. There is a danger, however, that must be noted: short-term successes from crisis management may become so intoxicating that they prevent the organization from adopting a long-range, strategic approach to resolving problems. Therefore be wary of overusing crisis management and having it become a way of life.

Unfortunately, even successful pilot projects may not spread throughout the organization. A project can collapse because of insufficient efforts to institutionalize it or because current policies and practices are not in harmony with it.[12] For example, a specially designed support program for school dropouts conducted outside of the schools may not be absorbed into the system because of such incompatible values and practices as the inability to give special attention to at-risk students or resistance to modifying the curriculum. In addition, some pilot projects tend to attract extra resources and highly motivated staff that are not available on an ongoing basis.

It is one thing to initiate change by engaging a small number of staff in a pilot project and dealing with their initial resistance; it is quite another to spread the change throughout the organization, to make it stick so that it becomes a permanent part of the way the organization operates. If the groundwork has been laid well, staff will be receptive to the change. Also if they have been involved in diagnosing needed improvements, and if they do not feel that change has been foisted upon them, staff are much more likely to accept the change. The key, then, is not to overmanage the change process, not to convey from on high, but to engage staff from all levels of the organization in thinking through and implementing the change.[13]

The same approach used in implementing a pilot project needs to be considered in expanding it throughout the organization. Other units need the opportunity to develop their own approaches to the change and to make suggestions that will mend possible flaws from their particular perspectives. The entire organization needs to feel the same excitement that occurred in creating the pilot project. Sometimes it is even better to let each unit "reinvent the wheel," that is, to discover its own way of implementing programs.[14] Those who were involved in the pilot project can be assigned to work with other units so they can seed the new ideas and spread their enthusiasm throughout the organization.

In addition, diffusing change throughout the organization requires continuous reinforcement and feedback. Frequent interaction needs to occur between management and staff. This ongoing interest and investment is communicated both formally and through the grapevine.[15]

Sometimes, for the change to take root, the organization must establish a parallel or alternative structure to carry out the new program while preserving the original one.[16] Suppose, for example, that the organization wants to reach out to a new clientele, such as an ethnic group that previously has not used the services of the organization. Instead of replacing the current outreach and intake services, the organization could establish a special unit to supplement the regular client access process. The new unit would link with the organization's basic services and still develop its own special style, its own consensus on operations, and its own value system. Eventually, the experiences of the parallel unit may result in the entire organization incorporating new ideas and behaviors.

To ensure expansion of a project, effective managers identify and select an enthusiastic, committed staff member to champion the assignment.[17] The term *intrapreneur* has been coined in the business world to reflect the idea that one person should be held accountable for developing products and services of the enterprise.[18] Human service organizations can adopt this same concept of a *social intrapreneur* or champion who zealously works to spread a successful project throughout the organization.[19]

Successful pilot projects can also be expanded through just-in-time training programs for staff. The purpose of the training is not to provide general information lectures but to offer specific skills training through role-playing or simulations for those who must learn new behavior patterns.[20] Frequently, the training is provided in a series of sessions over time so that staff can practice their new skills and share problems they are having in implementing the change.

As an effective manager, you should help staff invest in the new project by describing how services can be improved and, if appropriate, how the staff themselves can benefit. Then, too, in selling a new project or procedure, be careful not to disparage current methods, because to do so may discourage those who feel positively about the current mode of operation. Finally, allow time for people to adjust to the change. People have gotten comfortable with the status quo; they will need time to develop new attitudes and new patterns of behavior.[21]

In summary, initiating and expanding pilot projects in an organization requires an interesting balancing act. On the one hand, top management must be committed to change, for it is they who communicate the organization's values and set the implementation process in motion. On the other hand, expansion of the project must have the support of, and a sense of ownership by, those involved in implementing it. Both management and staff must be involved in the process of change in such a way that all staff feel dedicated to following through and implementing it.[22] The challenge, then, is to work at finding the right balance so that everyone feels a common commitment.

Handling Resistance to Change

Resistance to change in an organization alerts managers that a problem may exist. Even if staff are involved in the planning process, some may be reluctant to accept decisions that require them to change. The more fundamental and extensive the change, the greater the possibility that staff will lose something of value, such as stature, power, or employment. Moreover, if they misunderstand or misperceive change, they are likely to be resistant. A decision, for example, to allow staff to have flexible hours can cause them to become angry if they interpret it to mean they may be required to work weekends. Even positive and well-intentioned decisions for change can invite negative reactions if they are not fully explained.

Resistance is also likely to emerge because of differing perspectives of work demands. What management sees as a positive alteration in procedures may be considered by staff to be uprooting their current tasks and to be an intrusion into their work style. For example, a new administrative request for additional client information may be quite useful in documenting the need for expanded services. To management this makes sense, but to staff this request may be one more imposition on what they believe is an already overloaded schedule. If it is not possible to reprioritize their responsibilities, then management should at least acknowledge the new burden placed on staff.

In making a major decision, therefore, anticipate possible resistance so you can respond appropriately. Staff, for example, might feel ill-equipped to handle new data analysis responsibilities, and they may need special training before the decision is implemented. If the decision requires the development of different relationships or reassignment to new settings, then build in special support efforts to ease the transition. If the change will cause staff to lose status, then renewed efforts at building self-esteem, such as special recognition ceremonies, may be necessary.[23]

Before implementing change, ask: "How are staff likely to perceive the change, and how can we communicate our understanding of their situation during the change process?" In tuning in to staff concerns, it is important to identify who is complaining. Certain staff typically want to vent their concerns, in which case it is important to provide a sympathetic ear. There may, however, be appropriate and immediate cause for staff concern, requiring a special response.

In periods of austerity, when human service organizations are under severe budgetary constraints, tremendous demands are likely to be made on staff to "do more with less." Staff are being laid off, and the remaining staff are asked to assume more responsibilities, including conducting more billable interview hours and writing reports. In times of fiscal pressures, managers must step up their interactions with staff, provide them with more training, and help them reorient their priorities. It is also a time to express understanding for the new demands that staff experience, while simultaneously conveying that they have to meet production expectations.

Staff may certainly resist if they do not understand the purpose of the change. They must understand the rationale for the change and have confidence that the proposal is well thought out and that problems will be addressed. Staff need to know what will happen, who will do it, when it will take place, and how it will happen.[24] Be up front with them about any difficulties they are likely to encounter. A request to modify reporting procedures, for example, will receive more acceptance if staff understand that decision makers will be able to use the information to identify aggregate needs for funders.

The degree of organizational investment of time, energy, and personal commitment in the status quo will affect the extent to which staff may resist change. A new approach to treatment may be difficult to implement because much of the organization's funding and staff training have gone into current counseling approaches. Staff have a stake in preserving their investment. Of course, if the current mode of operation is not achieving positive results or is resulting in dissatisfaction on the part of clients or funding bodies, then staff may be more amenable to proposed changes. Effective managers spot when the forces pushing for change are stronger than those resisting change. Even when resistance is strong, however, effective managers are prepared to exert their influence based on the conviction that the current way of doing things is not producing sufficient results.

Sometimes it is wise *not* to implement a plan because staff strongly oppose it. Effective managers tune in to why staff are challenging the change. There is, to be sure, a certain timing to decisions, and the wisest course when in a quandary may be to delay until a more appropriate time. To use a football analogy, you would "punt." If staff are resisting a plan, there may be good reasons to delay implementation procedures. Rather than force a premature decision on them, allow enough time to pass so that new information surfaces or different circumstances arise that could soften their resistance.

Perhaps when you encounter strong resistance, instead of fighting it, you need to draw upon its energy source. In the sport of judo, you learn to use the strength of your opponent by taking advantage of a proper leverage point. In organizations you can ask complainers to come up with their own suggestions. Their negative energy can be turned into positive suggestions as they become partners in resolving the problem.

Assessing Risk Factors in New Projects

In the business world, before purchasers buy a business, they first examine in detail the performance and financial structure of the proposed deal. This is called conducting "due diligence." The same concept can apply to undertaking human service projects to determine the degree of exposure to risk and assessing the potential for success. Consider the following risk factors:[25]

- *Staff skills* include whether the staff have the proper skills to undertake the new project, how well the team works together, and their readiness to take on the new challenge.
- *The culture of the organization* fosters a high level of commitment to undertake projects designed to improve service to clients.
- *The feasibility of the project* is based on whether the conditions (e.g., funding, staff, skills, client needs) exist that would permit it to replicate a project that has been successful elsewhere.

- *Level of capitalization* includes both basic start-up funds and the ability to continue funding beyond the initial period.
- *Changes in the marketplace or in public policy* involve assessing shifts in clients' use of services or in the availability of funding through changes in legislation.
- *The risk of mission drift* can be of central concern for the organization that goes after funding regardless of whether the new project fits within the organization's mission. The organization must be mindful that the new project does not redirect the organization away from its central purpose.

Conducting a risk analysis may temper the initial enthusiasm for a project that the organization is contemplating. It is far better, however, to be aware of the downside risks before embarking on a program, than to discover them after the program is underway.

Contingency Planning

Effective managers assume that certain events can get in the way of implementing plans as originally conceived. Contingency planning imagines the unlikely. By thinking of the range of possibilities in advance, you may be able to gain mastery over them should they occur.

Suppose, for example, you are experiencing an influx of new clients needing service. Staff are already overtaxed. To meet your obligations, you have applied for additional funding and a decision is pending. Among your contingency plans could be the following:

Plan A: If you receive less funding than hoped for, you could consider hiring paraprofessionals working under close supervision.

Plan B: If the funding request is rejected, you could determine the reasons and be prepared to reapply.

Plan C: If expanded funding continues to be unavailable from this one source, you could consider an aggressive fundraising campaign.

Plan D: If, after reapplying, you are again rejected, you could consider either cutting staff or reducing salaries.

Plan E: If no funding is available, you could restrict the number of clients and redirect unserved persons to other agencies.

Plan F: If new funding is not possible, you could consider an innovative way of working with clients that achieves results at lower costs, such as group counseling sessions or telephone conferences.

As can be seen from this illustration, contingency planning helps managers develop a discipline for walking through a situation to prepare for possible events that could have an impact on the organization. In fact, a special form of contingency planning is called "fail-safe" analysis, in which you purposefully give attention to those possibilities that could cause your plan to fail.

Before you embark on your program, search for potential mine fields: What political leader or board member or staff could torpedo the idea? What staff or resource constraints could keep the program from getting off the ground? Which organizations must cooperate if the program is to succeed? Sometimes a colleague outside of the organization can be asked to give an objective critique or even serve as the "devil's advocate" to ferret out potentially explosive situations.

Decisions that do not allow for the possibility of glitches are dangerous ones because they give managers the false sense that nothing can go wrong. The reality is that plans have a low probability of succeeding unless major problems are anticipated and addressed. Fail-safe contingency planning focuses attention on possible problem areas and gets you to think about solving them before they occur.

Contingency planning is like a game of chess. You have to anticipate your opponent's moves and consider protecting your flank, even as you take the offensive. You cannot be so concentrated on moving ahead with your plans that you lose sight of where you might be vulnerable. As in chess, contingency planning requires your constant assessment of the potential consequences of every move. Unlike a game of chess, the forces that can unravel a plan may not reside in an "opponent" but in more amorphous forces, such as the lack of adequate staff training. The point of the chess metaphor is to encourage you to be on guard for unexpected possibilities even as you are moving forward.

Effective managers encourage contingency planning by stimulating "what if . . ." scenarios or questions. In a foster home recruitment drive, for example, you would ask, "What if recruitment materials don't come on time? What if it rains on the day of the promotional event? What if staff are unable to answer inquiries?" Of course, these things may not happen, but if they do, you will have thought about them in advance and taken the proper precautions.[26]

Thus contingency planning helps to anticipate and thus prevent problems before they occur; it is proactive. Obviously, not all events can be anticipated, and under some circumstances, you want to have the flexibility to respond to unexpected opportunities. The advantage of proactive planning, however, is that you can minimize or neutralize the possibility of downside risks by anticipating how you will deal with them.

Working Out the Details of a Plan

Attention to detail is a prerequisite for implementing a successful project. By anticipating specific outcomes as much as possible, you increase the likelihood that plans will be carried out properly. Even so, planning involves some degree of speculation; therefore, be prepared to revise even the most well-thought-out plans.[27]

To systematically structure the implementation phase, it is useful to think of major activities and specific tasks. Major activities can be completed within a specified time period and include the following elements:

- Those essential for achieving an objective
- Those that result in one identifiable product, such as a report, a meeting, or completion of a major assignment
- Those that occur either in sequence or simultaneously with other activities

Tasks are specific jobs required to accomplish a major activity. Feeding into a major activity, tasks are usually achievable over a few days or weeks by specified individuals or units of the organization. Although spelling out tasks can sometimes be time-consuming and tedious, the process more readily ensures completing major activities and implementing proper actions. Moreover, effective managers use the opportunity of programming the work plan to determine whether adequate resources are available to properly complete the job or whether resources should be redeployed from low- to high-priority endeavors. If there later appears to be a lack of progress in achieving a major activity, managers can more readily pinpoint the specific problem that led to the breakdown.

Implementing Task Assignments

Two approaches can be considered in specifying tasks: (a) reverse-order planning and (b) forward-sequence planning.[28]

Reverse Order Planning. In reverse-order planning, the organization begins with the final result to be achieved and identifies the tasks that feed into activities by reviewing the question, "What must we do just before reaching our final result, and then what needs to be done before that, and before that, and so forth?" until the beginning point is reached. For example, in organizing a staff speakers' bureau, the process of reverse order might include the following tasks:

Promote speaking engagements (last task)

Train speakers (fourth task)

Prepare speakers' kits (third task)

Recruit volunteer speakers (second task)

Plan training sessions (first task)

Forward Sequence Planning. In forward-sequence planning, the organization begins with what it considers to be the appropriate first set of tasks and then asks, "What should we do next, and what after that, and so forth?" until reaching the end result.

Whether an organization uses the reverse-order or forward-sequence planning approach, it is important to consider what preparation will be necessary to complete each task. In reality, an organization would combine reverse-order with forward-sequence planning. That is, the planning group would consider by what date they want to achieve a particular result and then review all the tasks they need to complete prior to that deadline. If the predominate approach is reverse-order planning, planners would employ forward-sequence planning (and vice versa) to double-check that no task has been omitted.

Timeline Chart. The implementation process requires that controls and reporting procedures be developed to determine the rate of progress compared with the original implementation schedule. The process pinpoints responsibility and identifies reporting dates. By establishing accountability for tasks within a time period, you develop a warning system that alerts you when you are not on schedule.

A timeline chart (sometimes referred to as a *Gantt chart*) is useful for implementing decisions and projects because it provides a visual overview of what needs to be done, who needs to do it, and within what specific time frame it should be accomplished.[29]

A timeline illustrates how various tasks should be subsumed under major activities in a comprehensible, easy-to-construct format. The chart clarifies the beginning and ending points projected for each task and shows at a glance what efforts must be made within a specific time period. For example, in Figure 4.2, certain major tasks in the public relations activity must be underway in July and August. The chart also pinpoints accountability by designating the person responsible and, if appropriate, members of the team. By referring to a timeline chart, you can determine on a continuous basis whether you are on schedule and reaching anticipated milestones.

By June, for example, were you able to formulate a plan? By September are public relations materials completed? By October are staff prepared? These milestones allow you to determine whether you are on course. If not, then you would modify your efforts to get back on course or consider making *go/no-go* decisions about whether to proceed with the project.[30]

The timeline chart also provides a visual sense of the efforts that must be undertaken in sequence and focuses attention on when organizational resources need to be expended. In the chart (Figure 4.2), it appears that the summer months will be demanding on certain staff. If this is normally a heavy vacation period, then seeing the demands of the project during June, July, and August may require adjustments in the schedule.

Campaign Plan

Objective: To recruit an additional 100 foster parents by the end of the year

	MAY	JUNE	JULY	AUGUST	SEPTEMBER	OCTOBER	PERSON IN CHARGE
Develop a plan and structure							
Appoint task force							Ahorn
Interview foster care agencies, parents, and staff							Slenk
Formulate foster care plan							Lapoor
Prepare public relations materials							
Identify profile of children							Meyers
Identify profile of potential foster parents							Botelli
Prepare PR campaign strategy							McVelan
Prepare bus posters							Madams
Prepare radio tapes							Jacob
Prepare TV ads							Hender
Prepare speakers' kit							Halligy
Contact public media							Gerdeim
Submit materials to media							Curl
Prepare foster care manual							
Prepare outline and drafts							Callder
Obtain foster parents' reactions							Bedford
Revise draft							Ponte
Prepare staff							
Plan processing procedures							Brode
Prepare phone instructions							Dunkin
Prepare follow-up materials							Serdan
Orient staff							Bosmy

Figure 4.2   Timeline Chart

Questions for Discussion

1. Create a hypothetical agency (e.g., working with high-risk adolescents or mentally challenged adults, or socialization for seniors). What would you determine to be the:
   - Mission statement?
   - Goals?
   - Objectives?
   - Programs?

2. How would you distinguish the risk, target, and impact populations in connection with your organization?

3. What examples can you give of impact, service, product, and operational objectives?

4. Suppose you were creating an agency that provides counseling services to substance abusing mothers who agree to discontinue drugs in order to keep their children from being taken from them. Create a goal statement and three objective statements related to the goal.

5. Consider developing plans for placing mentally ill persons in the job market. What kinds of problems could you anticipate and what contingency planning could you develop?

6. Suppose you were asked to implement a foster grandparents program. After identifying a dozen tasks, how would you organize them under activity categories and prepare a 12-week timeline?

7. Consider a past or potential project. What major activities and tasks could be prepared in a timeline chart?

8. What projects have been (or could be) implemented in your organization?

Notes

1. M. Schaefer, *Implementing change in service programs* (Newbury Park, CA: Sage, 1987), p. 31.

2. P. M. Kettner, R. M. Moroney, & L. L. Martin, *Designing and managing programs* (Newbury Park, CA: Sage, 1990), pp. 105–110.

3. P. Drucker, *Managing the nonprofit organization* (New York: HarperCollins, 1990), p. 32.

4. P. M. Senge, *The fifth discipline* (New York: Doubleday & Currency, 1990), pp. 59–60.

5. W. C. Kim & R. Mairborgne, Tipping point leadership, *Harvard Business Review* 81 (April 2003), pp. 60–69.

6. P. Drucker, *Management challenges for the 21st century* (New York: HarperBusiness, 1999), p. 87.

7. M. Schaefer, pp. 72–74.

8. Work in America Institute, Inc., *Productivity through work innovations* (New York: Pergamon, 1983), pp. 110–111.

9. R. H. Schaffer, Productivity improvement strategy: Make success the building block, *Management Review* (August 1981), pp. 46–52; R. H. Schaffer, *The breakthrough strategy* (Cambridge, MA: Ballinger, 1989), p. 5.

10. R. H. Schaffer & K. E. Michaelson, The incremental strategy for consulting success, *The Journal of Management Consulting* 2 (1989): pp. 1–5.

11. A. Etzioni, *The active society: A theory of society and political processes* (New York: Free Press, 1968), pp. 296–299; Work in America Institute, Inc., pp. 141–142.

12. E. E. Lawler, *High involvement management* (San Francisco: Jossey-Bass, 1986), p. 222.

13. M. Beer, R. A. Eisenstat, & B. Spector, Why change programs don't produce change, *Harvard Business Review* 6 (1990), pp. 158–166; Work in America Institute, Inc., p. 135.

14. M. Beer et al., pp. 158–166.

15. Work in America Institute, Inc., pp. 125–126.

16. Work in America Institute, Inc., pp. 120–135.

17. J. G. Dees, J. Emerson, & P. Economy, *Enterprising nonprofits: A toolkit for social entrepreneurs* (New York: John Wiley & Sons, 2001), pp. 183–184.

18. J. M. Newman, Compensation programs for special employee groups, in *Compensation and Benefits,* ed. L. Gomez-Mejia (Washington, DC: Bureau of National Affairs, 1989), p. 185.

19. P. Drucker, *Management challenges,* pp. 87–88; P. Drucker, *Managing the nonprofit,* p. 68.

20. R. H. Schaffer, Quality now!, *The Journal for Quality and Participation* (September 1989), pp. 22–27; Work in America Institute, Inc., p. 137.

21. Bureau of Business Practice, Inc., *Front line supervisor's standard manual* (Waterford, CT: Bureau of Business Practice, Inc., 1989).

22. E. E. Lawler, p. 219.

23. R. T. Crow & C. A. Odewahn, *Management for the human services* (Englewood Cliffs, NJ: Prentice-Hall, 1987), pp. 128–132; T. Kirby, *The can-do manager* (New York: AMACOM, 1989), pp. 55–58.

24. R. T. Crow & C. A. Odewahn, p. 132.

25. J. G. Dees, J. Emerson, & P. Economy, pp. 136–144.

26. R. von Oech, *A whack on the side of the head* (New York: Warner, 1983), p. 62.

27. S. N. Espy, Putting your plan into action, *Nonprofit World* 1 (1990), p. 28.

28. R. Brody, *Problem solving* (New York: Human Sciences Press, 1982), pp. 149–151.

29. M. Schaefer, pp. 88–89.

30. J. G. Dees, J. Emerson, & P. Economy, p. 80.

5

Problem Solving

Once an organization has determined its strategic plan, which includes its mission and goals, it can concentrate on daily administration (tactics). Much of this day-to-day management is focused on solving problems and making decisions. Often problems are complex, ambiguous, cumulative, and multifaceted. Sometimes their causes cannot be fully known and their resolutions may require the involvement of many different participants. Hence the problem-solving process requires an effective manager's keen judgment, intuition, and an understanding of the dynamics of a situation. Although there are no cookbook solutions, no simple formulas, it is useful to consider a series of steps to guide the problem-solving process, as summarized in Figure 5.1.

Step 1: Analyzing the Problem

The term *analysis* denotes separating a whole into its component parts. Problem analysis thus entails breaking generalized concerns into delineated segments. Good problem solving requires moving beyond such generalized statements as "staff morale is low," or "absenteeism is too high," or "there is poor communication between departments" to achieve greater clarity about the nature of the problem. It involves identifying and examining discrepancies between goals and actual results, specifying the problem as clearly as possible, determining the boundaries of the problem, clarifying different perspectives, and identifying insidious problems.

Identifying and Examining Discrepancies

A problem can be defined as a felt need or a discrepancy between an existing condition and one that is desired.[1] One of the major approaches managers can use to identify organizational problems is to determine

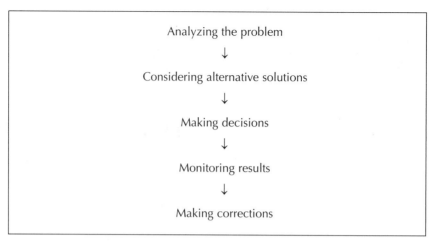

Analyzing the problem

↓

Considering alternative solutions

↓

Making decisions

↓

Monitoring results

↓

Making corrections

Figure 5.1   Steps to Guide the Problem-Solving Process

whether a situation or circumstance is preventing the organization from achieving its mission. Always focus on this first; otherwise, you may become trapped in a flurry of activities and problem-solving endeavors that may, in the long run, detract from your fundamental purpose. Effective managers give concentrated attention to those issues and problems that primarily affect the organization's mission and goals. Look for discrepancies between what the organization must achieve and what actually occurs.

Establishing measurable objectives and then determining later whether they have been achieved alerts managers to whether a problem exists. For example, in an adult training workshop for the disabled, if your objective of having 80% of clients function independently within one year is not met, you know a problem exists that must be addressed. Similarly, a problem becomes obvious, for example, when a unit of the organization does not meet its predetermined objective of contacting 125 clients in a given month. The fact that the unit is reaching only 85 clients should signal concern because of the gap between the predetermined benchmark and actual performance.

Specifying the Problem

Even if concrete objectives have not been established, staff or management may feel a vague sense of uneasiness. Something is wrong, but, at least initially, there is a lack of clarity about what the problem is. Someone might ask, for example, "Why aren't we serving more clients?" A general consensus might be that more clients could be served, but ambiguity exists about whether "the problem" is fewer clients in general or fewer clients from a particular geographic area or income level. Does "the problem" reside in the clients—something operating within them or their situation? Do they have difficulty in coming to the agency because of changes in public transportation, or have their perceptions changed about their safety in coming to the agency? By taking the time to obtain facts in any problem situation, you can avoid premature and impulsive solutions, or what is captured in the phrase *ready, shoot, aim.*

To analyze a generalized problem more specifically, be clear about exactly when the problem occurs, who is affected by it, and where it takes place. Furthermore, strive to understand the causes and underlying conditions of the problem. If, for example, you note that absenteeism among staff has increased, determine whether the problem is pervasive, and therefore indicative of a morale issue, or limited to a few staff, requiring disciplinary considerations.

Trying to identify the cause of a problem can be exceedingly difficult. In reality, a cause-effect chain of relationships can exist for any problem. One could analyze, for example, that absenteeism is caused by low morale, which is caused by feelings of being ignored, which in turn is caused by an organization that is built on an authoritarian structure in which little two-way communication occurs. To isolate one simple cause contributing to one single effect can be an oversimplification. You may not know until after you have attempted to diagnose a problem, formulated a response to it, and obtained feedback that your "solution" is not working. You then may need to concentrate on another possible solution.

In analyzing problems, an inductive approach of identifying concrete examples or critical incidents can be useful, especially if the nature of the problem is vague. By pinpointing under what specific situations the problem occurs, you begin to get a handle on it. You move from specific incidents to determining the nature of the problem.

Determining the Boundaries of the Problem

By defining the problem, you set boundaries around it; you determine what it is—and what it is not. Preparing a written problem statement is a good procedure. By putting your thoughts in writing, you develop more precise understanding of the problem and discipline your thinking. In addition, you have a statement that you can refer back to and revise if necessary. The danger of not putting your problem in writing is that your thoughts may remain vague and amorphous and hinder the problem-solving process.

In your problem statement, define key terms so that those also engaged in the problem-solving process have a common frame of reference. The simple question, "How can we reduce staff absenteeism?" requires defining precisely what is meant by the term *reduce—from* what to what—and what we mean by *absenteeism*—as it refers, for example, to sick leave, conference attendance, or unexcused absences.

Typically, problem descriptions tend to be narrowed too quickly, thereby cloaking the real problem. In conducting a problem analysis, determine whether a particular manifest problem is an exception or whether it reflects a larger issue. Does a particular problem reflect an idiosyncratic situation or a more general pattern? If it is unique, then pragmatic, expedient approaches may be used. If it is a general problem, then more fundamental change may be required. To treat a general situation as if it were a series of unique events can be a serious miscalculation.[2]

If you defined the problem, for example, as "staff are taking too many sick leave days," you limit your exploratory process and may not consider whether organizational policies may in fact be the real problem. "How can we deal with excessive absenteeism?" may be a better way to formulate the issue. In defining a problem, your goal should be to clarify what will be included in the problem's parameters and to decide, at least for the time being, what will *not* be part of your initial exploration. Determining the problem's boundaries moves it from an unfocused and ambiguous concern to a more targeted focus of attention.

In any process of formulating a problem, however, be aware that you may need to redefine it, depending on your focus. The reason for defining the boundaries of a problem and devoting so much time to its analysis is that by doing so you determine the nature of potential solutions. If you see the problem as absenteeism among many staff, that will lead you down one path. If you have narrowed it to unexcused absences on the part of a small number of staff who are unenthused by their work, that will lead you down another. Before you consider any solution, you will want to be quite certain that you have analyzed the problem properly.

Clarifying Different Perspectives

In any discussion, participants invariably come to the table with their own perspectives. There is an old fable of six blind men touching different parts of an elephant. Each one senses the elephant in a different way based on the part he touches. So too with problem analysis—people will sense a problem based on their individual experience with it.[3] Imagine this kind of group discussion on why an agency is not achieving its objective of reaching its predetermined quota of clients per month:

Employee A: "The problem is that I schedule appointments, but my clients continually cancel, and so I have time on my hands."

Employee B: "The problem is that clients do not find it easy to get to our agency from where they live. Public transportation has deteriorated, and unless clients have a car, they are not able to keep their appointments."

Supervisor: "The problem is that clients cannot schedule appointments when we're open. When I have followed up with people who have missed appointments, they tell me that if we were open evenings and weekends, they would find it easier to leave their children with someone."

Administrator: "The problem is that too many staff seem to be absent on Mondays or Fridays and this is affecting our client count. It would be higher if staff were more available on those days."

Each one has a different perspective of *the problem,* and therefore each has an approach about how it should be analyzed and eventually addressed. If, for example, Employee B's perspective is correct, then one solution may be to design ways to deliver services to clients outside the agency building. If, however, the focus turns to the administrator's perspective, then reducing staff absences becomes a priority. Because perspective is so influential in determining both problems and their solutions, it is crucial that the various perspectives be articulated as explicitly as possible. This should be done by asking participants to freely convey their different perspectives in an open discussion. As consensus on the problem develops, those with different views will decide whether or not to accept the problem as it is eventually defined.[4]

In all organizations, various individuals and groups are likely to have vested interests—that is, issues they consider vital to their own functioning. These vested interests certainly influence their perspectives. Managers, for example, are likely to focus on efficiency problems, whereas these may be of little concern to employees. Fringe benefits are likely to be of special concern to employees, whereas meeting legal requirements will be of paramount concern to management. Because of these different perspectives, it is always desirable in formulating the problem to ask, "Who owns which part of the problem?" The ownership of the problem greatly influences who wants to do something about it, that is, who owns the potential solution.

Identifying Insidious Problems

Sometimes problems lurk beneath the surface, accumulating and being ignored over time until finally they explode. We can use several analogies to describe this phenomenon: small waves forming in the distance, culminating in a tidal wave that capsizes the boat; or a small leak in the roof going undetected for many years, finally resulting in its collapse; or a symptomless cancer doing its damage to the body. These insidious problems are similar in that they seem too small to require attention, but unless detected early, they can cause great damage. In organizations insidious problems can also occur, as when, for example, staff who are treated like machines eventually find a way to communicate their grievances through strikes or disinvestment in their work.

Occasionally, a manifest problem identified initially may be a symptom of a much larger latent problem. The high rate of absenteeism involving a significant segment of the staff may, on further investigation, reflect a sense that staff feel exploited because they are not receiving their desired share of vacation days compared with the staff of other organizations. They may be using sick leave as a way of compensating for their feelings of exploitation. If this is so, then the more fundamental problem is how to deal with these feelings. Sometimes, too, it is the proverbial straw that breaks the camel's back; that is, something appears small and insignificant but inexplicably causes an outburst of negative feeling. Only on review might one be able to trace the series of earlier episodes that contributed to what appears to be an inappropriate reaction. Had the problem been identified while it was minor, the later, more damaging crisis might have been avoided. Clearly, "small" problems should be handled immediately.

Step 2: Considering Alternative Solutions _____

In any attempt to address a problem, it is important to develop and then critique alternative solutions. It is essential to realize that any action we take, any decision we make, is only one possibility out of a multitude of options.[5] This concept is especially useful for those managers who are prone to think their decision is the only pathway to a solution. In the event that one of the paths leads us astray, we have others on which to fall back. Considering alternatives also sharpens our thinking for the approach we finally select. Frequently, it is the second or third or tenth idea that can help solve the problem, not the first. In examining how to solve a problem, the following precepts can serve as a guide.

Developing Criteria

Problem-solving criteria should be established as *benchmarks* against which to compare alternatives. They should encompass the organization's limits and expectations and likely vary according to the problem under consideration. For example, with regard to a problem of staff going outside the building for lunch and thus taking extended lunch hours, the "solution" of in-house lunch arrangements might have to meet the following criteria: (a) annual cost to organization under $1,000, (b) tasty and well-prepared food, (c) cost to staff limited to the hourly rate of the lowest-paid employee, and (d) effective pest and insect control in new lunch area. The decision to use a lunch truck may emerge after comparing various alternatives.

Making Ideas Concrete

As you consider various possibilities, think in concrete, future-oriented terms by asking the question, "Suppose we were to select a particular approach, what would we expect one year from now?" By anticipating the future, you discipline your thinking to walk through one or more of the proposed ideas to see how they would play out in reality. Recall the in-house food service idea discussed above. Actually visualize the flow of traffic to and from workstations; imagine staff using the lunch area in the wintertime; consider the demands that would be made on your facility. By taking time to walk through the idea, you gain an appreciation of its possibilities and limitations prior to making a decision.

Making abstract ideas or plans concrete is especially important in considering alternatives for serving clients. By visualizing how clients would be served, you determine how they would be routed through your system and how the information flow should occur. One of the best antidotes to thinking too abstractly in the decision process is to go on the firing line for a period of time. Walk in the same door that your clients do and follow their path through your system. Sit where they sit for a while to get a feel for what it is like to linger in the waiting room. Hear their conversations and observe the professionals who serve them. Call the office as if you were a client to sense how the organization responds. Get out in the field and actually see how the operations are working. Through this kind of direct experience, you may be in a better position to judge the value of your current and proposed decisions.

Considering Trade-Offs

Every plan, however good, probably has inherent limitations. In your zeal to convince others of the efficacy of one approach over another, you may tend to overlook limitations or negative consequences. To combat these blind spots, build into your thinking the concept of trade-offs to identify the disadvantages as well as advantages of any course of action. For example, your plan to reach out to clients by sending staff to their homes can greatly improve contacts with those who formerly did not come in for interviews. But this plan may reduce the total number of clients served in a given period. The concept of trade-offs means accepting that every benefit has a cost. Considering alternatives is a matter of weighing whether the advantages or disadvantages of one are greater than those of other options. This probing injects a greater degree of reality into the problem-solving process and forces you to look at the downside of even a good idea before you make a final determination.

The word *satisficing* means there may be no one best solution to a given problem. The word was coined to convey the idea of finding solutions that both satisfy and suffice. Furthermore, it suggests that the search for an ideal but unattainable solution should be discontinued if a reasonable one— perhaps having some inherent limitations—can be found.[6]

The concept of *satisficing* decisions can help the effective manager make imperfect decisions in an imperfect world. An old axiom, "The ideal is the enemy of the good," conveys that waiting to arrive at a perfect solution may prevent us from considering other worthwhile ideas. We can accept the reality that even good decisions have their inherent limitations and therefore not be immobilized into thinking we have to make decisions that will have to satisfy everyone. For example, a decision to shift staffing to serve a selected group of clients means that others will receive less service. Moreover, if we know our decisions are satisficing, we can experiment with courses of action that, if they do not work out, can be abandoned and replaced by other alternatives under consideration.[7] Agonizing over alternatives can result in indecision, which can be worse than making a less than perfect decision.[8] In short, satisficing decisions help us to overcome paralysis by analysis.

Of course, in making satisficing decisions, effective managers should not be blinded to the possibility that a proposed plan may not fully or adequately solve a problem. Some decisions will provide only interim or ameliorative relief. Because of resource limitations or other constraints, they may not entirely correct or prevent problems.[9] Managers must live with this reality; by recognizing the temporary nature of the intervention, they can be prepared to seek more substantive solutions.

Step 3: Making Decisions

If problem solving encompasses formulating a problem statement and examining potential alternatives, then decision making is the process of choosing among alternatives and implementing an approach to deal with the problem. Perhaps this distinction between problem solving and decision making is artificial. If there is any value in the demarcation between them, it is that the former implies a probing phase; the latter, an action phase. Clearly, one flows into the other.

Making Risk-Taking Decisions Prudently

Most decisions involve some degree of risk because their impact cannot fully be appreciated until they are actually implemented and because no one can predict the future with complete accuracy. Given that uncertainty is inherent in risk-taking decisions, the possibility of failure always exists. The following questions can help minimize risk:

1. *Does your decision increase something of value?* Ask whether the service you are thinking of adding is available elsewhere in the community and therefore not needed. If it already exists, can you do it better and with fewer resources? If so, then the decision may be to go forward; if not, then the idea may need to be abandoned.

2. *Is the decision of such minimal consequence that it can be made quickly and at the lowest echelon possible within the organization?* Lightweight decisions should be made quickly so that staff can move on to more important issues. The effective manager helps staff take on small-scale, confidence-building decisions and allows them to make small mistakes. Staff can then grow in their capacity to deal with more significant decisions.[10]

3. *Can the decision be considered an experiment so that, if it works out, it can be developed and refined, but if not, it can be aborted?* For example, the organization makes a decision to provide services away from the main office, but you are not certain which locations clients are most likely to use even after you have conducted surveys. For a period of time, you might try using libraries, shopping malls, or religious facilities. After trying out different places, staff learn which are best—or whether none of them is suitable. The experimental approach allows staff to be open-minded before making a final decision.

4. *Are the potential negative consequences of a decision so great that such a decision should not be made?* Suppose productivity is being affected by interpersonal rivalry between two units in the organization. Should there be a major reorganization of staff and activities because supervisors are feuding with each other? A painful reorganization to accommodate a rivalry between two units may or may not relieve tensions. Once the reorganization has taken place, even if the results are much less than desired, the decision cannot easily be undone. In sum, you must weigh the benefits of a particular decision against its costs. Indeed, the costs may outweigh advantages and may therefore serve as a deterrent to making what seems like a more appropriate decision.

5. *Can commitments be made on an incremental basis?* By staging your commitments, you keep your options open as long as possible and allow making smaller, incremental investments over a long time frame. This avoids rushing into a process before you are certain whether or not it can succeed. Suppose, for example, you consider adding a day care program for 40 children to meet the needs of working mothers in your community. You would start off with, say, 10 to 15 children before determining whether to expand.

6. *Are you prepared to carry out the decision?* The most time-consuming step in the decision-making process is not making the decision, but implementing it. Unless a decision "degenerates into work" it is only a good intention. A good decision must be capable of being transformed into action.[11]

7. *Do you have a workable exit strategy in the event that the organization is exposed to intolerable risks?* It is useful to develop *go/no-go* points in the course of developing a project. An exit strategy allows you to assess your risk exposure and cut your losses. This requires being prepared to walk away from a previously desired project even after you have invested considerable resources.[12]

Risk taking could have both minor and major consequences. Some decisions can be reversed; that is, if something goes wrong you can shift to another course of action without the organization or the clients suffering. These are risks that you can afford to take. Some risks, however, have great significance, financially or otherwise, and the action may not be reversible; the consequences could be felt for years to come. These are the decisions you must weigh most heavily. In your analysis, therefore, ask whether the downside risks are such that the organization could withstand them if things went wrong. When making high-risk decisions, effective managers seek input from trusted colleagues both inside and outside the organization to gain objectivity and differing perspectives.

Being Boldly Tentative

If this statement sounds contradictory, it is because decision makers must be both courageous and flexible with their decisions. To be bold means to go forward with plans that do not necessarily please everyone but are nevertheless viewed as proper after all positive and negative aspects of the decision have been considered. Compromises and half measures will not do. Being tentative, however, means having an outlook that is experimental and trying out ideas on a provisional or temporary basis to see if they will truly work.

Suppose, for example, you want to mount a program that requires three full-time staff members to organize and work with the residents of the community. You determine that without these outreach staff you are not likely to fully engage the residents, which could negatively affect the overall program. You might decide that one staff member instead of the required three would result in frustration and a sense of failure. Your decision would therefore be based either on embarking on the program with the appropriate staff or on delaying implementation until the proper staff are available. Resist the temptation to make an administrative decision that, in your estimation, is eventually bound to fail. It is better not to have started than to arouse expectations, leading to more frustration.

To be sure, some decisions are inherently difficult. Cutting unproductive programs or removing inefficient but likeable staff can produce painful reactions, but to have staff linger and drain resources may be a worse alternative. In this context, "biting the bullet" has special meaning. During the Civil War, when anesthesia was often in short supply, wounded soldiers either had to undergo amputation or lose their lives to the gangrene that was spreading through their limbs. During the surgical procedure, biting a bullet was a way to endure this painful experience. Hence, symbolically, "biting the bullet" has come to mean making a painful choice to avoid an even more catastrophic consequence. Your decision to act is based on your assessment that the benefits outweigh the costs and risks. Your decision requires both intellectual judgment and courage.

Because of the fast pace of change, managers are forced to make decisions when complete information is not available or when there is uncertainty about the future. Under these circumstances, managers and staff still need to take calculated risks that may result in failure. The best approach is to recognize these failures, respond promptly, and move forward.

There is something to be said for making tentative or preliminary decisions that are subject to modification. Because any alternative can have negative consequences, and because it is often impossible to anticipate the negative effects of a decision, it is useful to allow time for modifications and challenges prior to making a final selection. This requires a willingness to experiment, to try things out, and to allow staff and clients to react to an idea before fully implementing it. There is an aphorism, "The map is not the territory," which can be translated to mean that a plan, however well thought out, may not fully encompass the reality that it intends to reflect. Trying out ideas on a small scale to "work out the bugs" may be necessary before embarking on a bold venture.

Involving Staff in Decision Making

An ancient Chinese proverb states, "Tell me, I forget; show me, I remember; involve me, I understand." Involving staff in organizational problems or decisions that affect them and their performance not only enhances their understanding but also engages them so they become invested in a positive outcome.

When staff are empowered to participate in making decisions, their sense of self-esteem and competence becomes linked to accomplishments. When they are involved and have a stake in their work, they tend to feel enthusiastic about and committed to it. Effective managers recognize that when staff have a say in decisions affecting the work environment in general and their jobs in particular, the result is greater job involvement and satisfaction.[13] In short, when staff have been part of the problem-solving process, the implementation process will flow quite naturally. Shared decisions work because of authentic collaboration.[14]

Every effective manager has had the experience of turning problems over to staff and seeing positive results emerge. For example, one manager concerned with the high rate of absenteeism asked the employee committee to wrestle with the issue. They came up with the idea of rewarding staff who had fewer than three absences a year with an extra day's vacation. The overall agency record improved by 10%. As another example, managers in one agency who were concerned that clients were missing scheduled appointments formed a task force of outreach staff to explore possible solutions. After many discussions, the staff concluded that the agency should borrow a vehicle to transport clients three mornings a week from a nearby agency that needed its minivan only in the afternoons. Staff also agreed to be available on a rotating basis two nights each week to see clients who found it difficult to make day appointments.

Genuine staff engagement can exact a price from both management and employees. Supervisors may feel that traditional prerogatives are being undermined and that greater staff involvement in decision making dilutes their authority. Effective managers accept the trade-off of diminished control for increased staff involvement because employee ideas are needed to improve the quality, service, productivity, and efficiency of the organization.[15] Another concern is that staff may have to invest considerable time in meetings that take them away from their regular assignments. In the long run, however, time invested in the process of work improvement can increase staff's ownership in the organization and commitment to be more productively engaged in their jobs. Japanese business managers have long been aware that the participatory decision-making process takes more time, but once decisions are made, implementation proceeds quickly because those who would carry out the decision have already been consulted.[16] In the United States, both profit and nonprofit organizations are relying increasingly on task forces for engaging staff and implementing plans.

The director of a $100 million organization whose mission is to improve the lives of those who are mentally challenged and have developmental disabilities has written this about the importance of staff involvement:

> Based on my years of experience, the single most important element in the success of any organization is gaining, maintaining, and enhancing the investment of the participants in the accomplishment of the mission, goals, and objectives of the organization. I have learned through often bitter experience that simply "being in charge" is no guarantee of success. What I have found to be most effective in gaining improvements in effectiveness and efficiency is placing a greater share of the burden of responsibility for success upon the individual members of the organization.
>
> The only way I know to accomplish this is to encourage people to "use their noodles" effectively by not presuming that either I or some other person in charge will have the right solution. In this way, everyone's hands are on the oars, so to speak, and our job as managers is to help guide the process by presenting enough valid information and support so that staff will raise pertinent questions and propose valid ideas. Of course, what one discovers along the way is that this requires

a rather high level of knowledge and intelligence among the members, so it is necessary to be much more selective in the appointment of staff.

What typically happens if the process works right is that the atmosphere created or "culture" is one of responsibility to each other, to the mission of the organization, and to the public. Malingerers typically do not last very long in such an environment.[17]

Watching Out for Decision-Making Pitfalls

Making tough decisions is undoubtedly one of the greatest challenges managers face. To improve their decision-making processes, managers should be aware of these flaws that may lead them astray: (1) clinging to the familiar, (2) overly justifying past decisions, (3) only seeking confirming evidence to support your case, and (4) framing issues poorly.[18]

Clinging to the Familiar. Managers, like most people, tend to base decisions on past information. For example, in estimating the number of clients to be served in the coming year, you may be unduly influenced by the number that you served the previous year, even though circumstances might have changed. Relying on old information may not necessarily be conducive to dealing with current realities. Therefore it is important to be open-minded in seeking information and opinions from a variety of sources to push your mind in fresh directions.

This flaw is also related to holding on to the status quo for decision making. It is safer to rely on the familiar than to take responsibility for trying something new that may be subject to criticism. In most organizations, particularly large bureaucratic ones, people are more likely to be sanctioned for doing something than for doing nothing. Omission is safer than commission. The consequence of standing still as the world moves forward is the cost of lost opportunities. Maintaining the status quo may be the best choice, but you do not want to choose it just because it is comfortable.

Defending Past Decisions. This flaw is based on making a choice and justifying it even when it is no longer valid. For example, you may have hired an employee and provided extensive training only to realize belatedly that you should not have hired that person in the first place. Making an investment of time and money in the incompetent employee is irrecoverable, but rather than dismiss the individual, you choose to live with your mistake. If you dismiss the poor performer, you may feel you will be perceived as having poor judgment. It may seem better to retain the employee, even though this decision compounds your earlier, faulty decision.

To deal with this mistake, it is helpful to accept that even the wisest of us makes errors in judgment. Develop the kind of organizational climate that allows people to acknowledge their mistakes and then move on. Identify situations that are not working out. Accept that decisions made earlier, based on the information then at hand, may now require a reassessment.

Seeking Confirming Evidence. Because managers all have biases, they may tend to seek out "facts" that confirm their point of view, while avoiding data that contradicts it. The tendency is then to decide on a course of action and be convinced the position is right, based on information that supports it, while ignoring data that may challenge it. The remedy is to develop a mindset of seeking out data from a variety of sources and to encourage counter arguments. For many managers, the idea of playing out "On the one hand . . .On the other hand . . ." may cause them to feel an uncomfortable degree of ambiguity before making a final decision. This honest exploration, however, sharpens one's thinking.

To understand better the tendency toward biased decision making, it is useful to distinguish two broad approaches involved in decision making: *advocacy* and *inquiry.*[19] When managers take an advocacy perspective, they view decision making as a contest. They are passionate about their preferred solution, strive to persuade others, and downplay their weaknesses. They present data selectively and withhold relevant, conflicting information. They are out to make a compelling case, not to seek a balanced view.

By contrast, inquiry-focused managers seek a variety of options and remain open to alternative possibilities. The goal is not to persuade others to adopt a given point of view, but rather to come to an agreement on the best course of action. They rigorously question proposals and assumptions so intellectual sparring may be intense. Through intense exploration, disagreements are based on reason and not predeveloped biases.

The Flaw of Too Narrowly Framing the Question. A poorly framed issue can greatly affect decision making. If you ask the question, "How can we improve transportation for our clients so that they can arrive for their appointments?" you invite discussions around transportation. If, however, you frame the issue as, "How can we make our services more accessible to our clients?" you open up a series of possibilities, including the hours that your agency is open, the possibility of using your van to go where your clients are, and even the idea of decentralizing services. To avoid adverse effects of improperly framing the problem, consider reframing it in different ways. Examine, especially at the end of your reframing process, whether you might have come to a different solution if you reframed the question. When others on your staff make recommendations, explore whether the issue should be framed differently.

These common flaws in decision making reveal that perceptions and biases can influence choices. Being aware of these tendencies can result in your being reflective about your assumptions and disciplining your thinking so as to reduce errors in judgment.

Step 4: Monitoring Results

The decision-making process is not complete until managers and staff review the results of their efforts. In the course of carrying out activities and tasks, you may find that some actions can result in partial or even complete failures. Staff can make mistakes, errors in judgment can occur, and something will inevitably go wrong. Monitoring results is the best way to assess how current reality compares with plans made earlier.

As discussed in Chapter 4, monitoring results should be based on written objectives. These should be quantifiable or measurable in some clear way so that their success or failure can be reviewed. This helps the organization compare intended results with actual outcomes.

To ensure accountability for results, organizations must determine standards for monitoring and controlling activities. As discussed in Chapter 3 with respect to designing programs, for every objective there should be a performance indicator that clearly demonstrates the extent to which the objective is being achieved.

This is no easy matter for many human service organizations because the outcomes of services are variable and do not easily lend themselves to quantifiable data analysis. It is difficult enough to determine in some quantifiable way the extent to which, for instance, a couple has improved their marital relationship through counseling; trying to aggregate in some reasonable format the progress made by the 220 couples seen in the course of a year is indeed formidable. Demands for increased accountability, however, make evaluation of results one of the major challenges human service organizations must address.

Recognizing the tremendous challenge involved in developing performance measures, agencies nevertheless have options for monitoring services. Among these options are the following:

1. Increasing the number of program participants

    Example: The number of persons who remain employed for six months

    Example: Reduction in the rate of recidivism among previously convicted drug addicts

    Example: The number of elderly persons in a nutrition program who maintain independent living

2. Satisfaction of program participants

    Example: The number of consumers who rate the counseling service as satisfactory

3. Improvement in service efficiency

    Example: Reduced waiting time

    Example: Shorter response time for emergency requests

Effective monitoring requires good input of information and proper packaging for decision makers. With computer software, reports can now be quickly generated to reveal deviations from targets. In this way, client information audits can reveal discrepancies between predetermined objectives and actual performance in much the same way that budget analyses are conducted to reveal variances in financial projections.

For information to be useful in the monitoring process, it must be timely and relevant. The information must be significant both for reporting to external funders and policymakers and for internal decision making. Reports must be user-friendly and not so complicated that staff are overwhelmed by them. Such information should not only be useful for analyzing the impact of services, as discussed above, but also for conducting analyses of the activities and work of the organization's units. A good information system should be able to answer questions like these:

- Are the activities of the unit contributing to the accomplishment of objectives?
- Are costs for conducting the work excessive in relation to meeting objectives?
- Are services provided in a timely manner?
- Is the level of service improving or declining?
- Are staffing levels appropriate for accomplishing objectives?

Work Quality

Through explicit policies and procedures, managers must devise ways to help staff become better oriented and more sensitive to work quality. Standards need to be established; if these are not met, a corrective response becomes necessary.

Quality control can determine that information errors on client eligibility have risen above a certain threshold, and this discovery could trigger specific responses, such as training or improved supervision. By establishing standards and developing mechanisms to measure them, the organization conveys that it means business about improving the quality of the work it does. The creation of a quality assurance committee can provide structure for implementing and evaluating quality standards.[20]

The following are some guiding concepts that should be considered in enhancing quality control:

Timeliness: How quickly can clients be seen after a request is made?

Correctness: How error-free is staff documentation?

Competence: How qualified are the staff?

Reliability: Does the agency deliver what it promises?

Accountability: Is the work properly reviewed? Are problems addressed?

Service demeanor: How pleasantly and courteously are clients treated?

Accessibility: How responsive is the organization to requests?

Handling complaints: To what extent does the organization react to client concerns?

Flexibility: Does the organization modify its services to meet special needs?

Step 5: Making Corrections

The purpose of monitoring is to identify performance deviations so that corrective action can be taken.[21] The value of identifying deviations from predetermined standards is to stimulate staff to think about how they could get back on course—or to revise the objectives so that they are more realistic. Self-correction is only possible if, as a result of the self-assessment process, the organization is prepared to ask hard questions. If the organization *does* achieve its objectives, the following questions could be asked:

- Given the nature of the problem and the resources that were available, were the objectives set too low?
- Was the cost worth the accomplishment?
- Even though you achieved the objectives, does the basic problem remain essentially unchanged?
- Does solving this particular problem create other problems?
- Has reaching these particular goals interfered with the achievement of other objectives; if so, do the balances have to be redressed?

If the organization *does not* achieve its objectives, the following questions could be asked:

- Were adequate resources (staff and funding) available to do the job?
- Were objectives set unreasonably high?
- Was the timetable appropriate?
- Given the time and financial constraints and other demands, should the organization redirect its energies to other broad problem areas?

The review of success, partial success, or failure of objectives provides a springboard for future decision making. Because organizations generally operate under less than ideal conditions, they may achieve some objectives partially and others not at all. Through the monitoring process, staff may become keenly aware that a discrepancy exists between their aspirations and actual outcomes. They may not have been able to select the optimum solution for a given problem because of inadequate resources, political constraints, time pressures, or finances. Not being able to provide the optimum solution, they may have to settle on a second- or third-best approach. Confronted with this reality, staff can either despair and do nothing, or they can use the opportunity to determine what changes need to be made in the problem-solving process.

This dynamic quality of decision making is evident, paradoxically, even if you succeed. Solving one problem sometimes creates or uncovers another. Suppose, for example, that, to encourage staff to develop more initiative and independence, you send them to special training programs. As a result, they are more prone to challenge supervisors and the organization's policies. This newly created problem may require supervisors to be trained in dealing with staff who raise provocative issues that challenge conventional ways of doing things. Thus the resolution of one problem may raise other issues that then must be dealt with, suggesting that the decision-making process is never ending. Obviously, this does not apply in all instances, but it may help to explain why one can never fully relax in terms of the affairs of an organization.

In summary, the problem-solving process is dynamic and subject to continuous revision. It involves analyzing problems, establishing objectives, developing alternatives through both rational and creative approaches, and designing and implementing action plans. Monitoring and assessing results promotes a review of whether to make changes at any point in the process. Perhaps the problems need to be redefined because their objectives are set too low and are unchallenging, or because they are set too high and are too difficult to achieve. It is possible that achieving the objectives did not solve the problem and that better targeting is needed. Perhaps you need to consider a different strategy that reflects changing circumstances. Finally, the activities and tasks you choose may require alteration if it becomes obvious that they are insufficient and will not achieve your desired objectives. It is through this continuous review and revision that an organization can take necessary corrective actions.

The willingness to base decisions on a critical review of changing circumstances is at the core of the problem-solving process. This attitude reflects a planning style that is open to constantly changing conditions, flexible in adapting to new needs, and capable of making modifications based on new situations.[22] By accompanying a built-in review with flexibility, an organization can avoid adhering to an approach that goes nowhere. It embraces the complex and kaleidoscopic nature of the real world in which everything is in constant flux. The problem-solving process is never ending and ever challenging.

Questions for Discussion

1. What might be an insidious problem in your organization?

2. Suppose you were considering three options for expanding programs for adolescent mentally challenged offenders: (a) develop group homes, (b) expand an institutional facility, or (c) provide in-home counseling. What are the criteria that could assist you in making a decision?

3. Suppose after applying the criteria, you decided on one of the options. What are the trade-offs involved in your decision? Would you consider your decision to be a *satisficing* one?

4. Develop a problem statement related to a population served by your agency. As an exercise, how would you redefine the problem more broadly or more narrowly?

5. How might a problem statement be defined by different stakeholders—administration, middle managers, staff, clients, board members, public officials—connected with your organization?

Notes

1. C. H. Kepner & B. B. Tregoe, *The rational manager* (New York: McGraw Hill, 1974), pp. 20, 44–47; R. G. Murdock & J. E. Ross, *Information systems for modern management* (Englewood Cliffs, NJ: Prentice Hall, 1975), p. 471.

2. P. Drucker, *The effective executive* (New York: Harper & Row, 1985), p. 125.

3. P. M. Kettner, R. M. Moroney, & L. L. Martin, *Designing and managing programs* (Newbury Park, CA: Sage, 1990), pp. 39–40.

4. R. Brody, *Problem solving* (New York: Human Sciences Press, 1982), p. 27.

5. V. Dishy, *Inner fitness* (New York: Doubleday, 1989), p. 75.

6. R. G. Murdock & J. E. Ross, p. 485.

7. T. J. Peters & R. H. Waterman, *In search of excellence: Lessons from America's best run companies* (New York: Harper & Row, 1982), pp. 134–135.

8. E. Bliss, *Getting things done* (New York: Bantam, 1976), p. 71.

9. C. H. Kepner & B. B. Tregoe, p. 132; H. Reynolds & M. E. Tramel, *Executive time management* (Englewood Cliffs, NJ: Prentice Hall, 1979), p. 164.

10. R. Townsend, *Further up the organization* (New York: Alfred A. Knopf, Inc., 1984), pp. 50–55.

11. P. Drucker, *The essential Drucker* (New York: HarperBusiness, 2001), pp. 241–242.

12. J. G. Dees, J. Emerson, & P. Economy, *Enterprising nonprofits: A toolkit for social entrepreneurs* (New York: John Wiley & Sons, 2001), pp. 149, 153.

13. R. S. Schuler, *Personnel and human resource management,* 3rd ed. (St. Paul, MN: West, 1987), p. 437.

14. M. Doyle & D. Strauss, *How to make meetings work* (New York: Doubleday, 1989), p. 243.

15. R. Stayer, How I learned to let my workers lead, *Harvard Business Review* 68 (June/July 1990), pp. 66–83.

16. W. Bowen, ed., Japanese managers tell how their system works, *Fortune* (November 1977), p. 131.

17. M. Donzela, personal communication, December, 1991.

18. J. S. Hammond, R. L. Keeney, & H. Raiffa, The hidden traps in decision making, *Harvard Business Review* 76 (September/October 1998), p. 47–58.

19. D. A. Garvin & M. A. Roberto, What you don't know about making decisions, *Harvard Business Review* 79 (August 2001), pp. 108–116.

20. C. Coulton, *Developing quality assurance programs: Managerial considerations and strategie*s (Unpublished Manuscript, 1990).

21. R. T. Crow & C. A. Odewahn, *Management for the human services* (Englewood Cliffs, NJ: Prentice Hall, 1987), p. 97.

22. R. Brody, p. 198.

PART II

Increasing Productivity

Chapter 6: Time Management

Chapter 7: Finding and Keeping Productive Employees

Chapter 8: Managing Employment Challenges

Chapter 9: Humanizing the Organization

Chapter 10: Supervising Staff

Chapter 11: Appraising and Compensating Performance

In this part you will learn how to

- ❖ Diagnose a time problem
- ❖ Make the best use of time to get things done
- ❖ Establish priorities
- ❖ Avoid time-wasting efforts
- ❖ Combat procrastination
- ❖ Recruit and match the right staff person to the job
- ❖ Conduct a nondiscriminatory interview
- ❖ Relate organizational structure to functions
- ❖ Respond appropriately to people who are covered by legal regulations
- ❖ Take corrective action to deal with unproductive employees
- ❖ Terminate employees properly

❖ Understand how organizational values impact staff attitudes and behavior

❖ Transmit such major values as job ownership, consumer satisfaction, work quality, and effectiveness and efficiency

❖ Appreciate the multiple roles of middle managers

❖ Delegate assignments effectively

❖ Apply motivational theories to influence performance

❖ Convey supervisory expectations

❖ Consider various ways of measuring performance

❖ Prepare for an appraisal conference

❖ Consider the advantages and disadvantages of job classification and skill-based pay systems

❖ Weigh the pros and cons of pay for performance

❖ Understand the use of bonuses and gain sharing

❖ Provide symbolic rewards and recognition as a way of influencing work performance

6 Time Management

Factors Affecting Time Management

Despite our best efforts to use time wisely, we tend to waste precious moments. Why do managers have such great difficulty gaining control over time? Many explanations can account for why managing time is such a problem.

First, managers' jobs are non-routine, and their days are filled with interruptions and unexpected requests: important phone calls that interrupt the flow of work, emergency conferences to deal with crises, correspondence needing immediate response, and staff complaints that require special attention. As a result of these constant interruptions, the attention span of most managers for any given task is quite limited. Human service managers, like those in the corporate world, often do not completely plan their days. They carry on brief and personal conversations with people outside their own immediate chain of command to feel the pulse of the organization. Even successful managers "waste" time walking through the halls of their organization engaged in random conversations that offer the opportunity to pick up ideas about what staff are thinking. They build strong human relationships and networks that may prove useful at a later time.[1]

Second, managers also have ancillary responsibilities. Not only are demands inherent in the job, but managers must be on committees for other organizations, attend ceremonial functions, and communicate with colleagues outside of their organizations. They live in an interdependent world that requires them to respond to colleagues' requests and agenda items as part of the give-and-take of professional relationships.

Third, natural time wasters are built into managers' jobs. Salespersons call and pitch the latest telephone or computer innovations. Colleagues ask if they can take time to talk with a friend who is exploring the job market. Managers spend time sorting through junk mail, e-mail, and returning phone calls to people who do not answer.

Finally, certain tasks have limited payoffs. Some assignments are risky because their outcomes are unpredictable and can result in failure. Taking

99

precious time to work on a proposal that may not get funded or advocating for legislation that may not be passed, however, is a necessary aspect of managers' work that, while frustrating and time-consuming, may lay the foundation for later success.

As a result of these and other demands on time, managers are unable to give concentrated attention to important priorities that could help them achieve their organization's mission and goals. They have a longer list of things to do than can ever be accomplished and therefore tend to finish each day feeling frustrated and overwhelmed. They have a gnawing and unproductive sense of frustration for having taken on too much and not accomplishing what they consider to be most important. Faced with this ongoing demand on time, effective managers should give special attention to time management. In the following sections, practical suggestions on diagnosing and planning time are discussed.

Diagnosing the Time Problem

To gain a better understanding of how your time is spent, try a self time study. Keep a time log of your activities in 15-minute segments and then review it after a few days to determine whether you are devoting time to low-priority items. Of course, the definition of what is a high or low priority is subjective, but certainly it should be based on expected accomplishments you have established for yourself and your unit. Identify which activities (e.g., lengthy phone conversations, drop-in visitors, and unproductive meetings) might be curtailed because they contribute little to your goals and objectives.

An alternative diagnosis method is to keep track of your time on a selective basis, focusing on those problem areas you feel are consuming an inordinate amount of time.[2] Selective record keeping can identify where your trouble spots are. Of those activities taking more than an hour per week, ask which ones could be eliminated, be done in half the time or less, or delegated to someone else in the organization. Asking these questions can help you determine where to focus your efforts and revise work patterns.[3]

Another approach would be to do what one director of a children's institution does with his employees. When staff complain about not having enough time to complete administrative responsibilities because of the daily demands of working with children, he helps them distinguish the urgent from the important, based on previously agreed upon priority objectives. He requests that they list their typical activities at the end of a given week and the amount of time devoted to each. Reviewing time logs in supervisory conferences helps to determine which activities can be given less time in order to free up time for higher priority activities, based on mutually determined objectives.

To conduct an employee time study,[4] summarize how everyone's time is spent. In a children's institute, for example, major categories could include direct contact with children, contacts with outside agencies, meetings within the agency, and administration reports. The major categories in your own work will differ, so modify them to fit your particular situation.

In examining the data, determine whether you are concentrating on the correct priorities designed to achieve your objectives and whether you are leaving sufficient time for long-range projects. Determine with your staff where time needs to be allocated.

Planning the Use of Time

Because employees typically feel they have too much to do in too little time, working harder or longer is not an answer. Effective staff limit the amount of unproductive time and place greater emphasis on those activities that have the greatest importance in relation to mutually developed objectives. It is easy to get caught in the "activity trap" where time is filled with busywork that is not focused on the highest priorities and is not goal directed.

The best advice is to plan your use of time. In so doing, however, you may experience a paradox: you may not have enough time to plan and yet you cannot get more time until you do. Certainly planning takes time, but planning also saves time. In general, those who do not plan sufficiently end up devoting too much time to correcting, controlling, and monitoring staff activities. A common mistake of some managers is to try to cram as many duties as possible into one day. The result is that that they have little time to prepare, and they are then caught off guard when something unexpected and urgent arises. Effective managers allow about 10–20% of their time as buffer periods for unexpected situations.[5] Hence take time to plan, but also provide flexibility in your schedule to deal with unexpected demands.

Determining Priorities

Priorities can be based on *urgency* or *importance*. Activities that are important but not urgent tend to be put aside. For instance, handling a staff complaint could take precedence over a report due next week even though you recognize the report may take 25 hours to accomplish. When your work is unstructured, open-ended, and you are able to function with considerable autonomy, you may experience little pressure to complete an assignment immediately. You might delay working on it. Because it is possible to wait, and because other matters always press for your attention, you ignore the task until suddenly it demands your attention. To avert disaster, you must give attention to important, though not necessarily urgent, matters.

Only by anticipating what you need to accomplish over a long period of time and preparing for these tasks can you avoid the possibility of constant turmoil—that is, handling a chain of crises. Of course, if you enjoy the sense of panic, the thrill of staying up all night, the rush of excitement that comes with handling last-minute crises, then you can ignore these suggestions. Most effective managers realize that over extended periods of time, self-made crises can be wearing and they therefore work at pacing themselves.

How does one determine priorities? First, identify those activities you judge to have the greatest return on your investment of time. An hour spent now on preparing a memo on an anticipated staff concern may save many hours of troubleshooting later. Because the effective use of staff time is typically a major responsibility, you should give staff-related issues prime consideration.

Whether you should give attention to the immediacy of a staff complaint or put that request off to concentrate on the report depends on your priorities. If your primary objective is to boost staff morale, then handling the staff complaint is imperative. On the other hand, if the report is essential to obtaining better services or funding for the agency's clients and this is your highest priority, then you would delay handling a staff complaint. The point, then, is that at the outset you must be quite clear and focused on what you must accomplish to achieve your primary objectives.

Second, determine your major responsibilities—those things you must do to carry out your job competently. These include prescribed tasks—work that is required by your own supervisor or by the organization's work flow, such as attending weekly staff meetings or completing monthly reports. An effective manager continuously asks whether particular time demands will help further the organization's mission and are related to agreed-upon goals.

A third priority consideration is whether someone else is depending on your activities—for example, a client waiting for your services, a colleague waiting for your analysis to incorporate it into a report, or your director waiting for a reply to an important question. Sometimes your administrator may ask you to take on additional projects and duties. Before accepting the assignment, you should discuss your general workload and determine whether the new project should take precedence over other pressing demands on you time. Together you may determine what makes sense to put aside when you take on the new assignment, or you may decide that the new assignment should be delayed because of current pressing matters.[6]

Setting priorities initially requires your making a random list of activities—some being more important than others. To establish *priorities* (most important), you must have *posteriorities* (least important). These are activities that need not be done immediately or items that should be done by others.

Setting priorities means making an ABCD list, broken down as follows:

A. (Highest Priority) An activity that is both important and urgent because it provides the best payoff in accomplishing the organization's mission

B. (Medium Priority) Important, though not urgent; it is necessary to achieve a significant objective

C. (Low Priority) An activity that contributes only marginally to the achievement of an important objective

D. (Posteriority) Neither important nor urgent; it could be delayed, minimized, delegated, or even eliminated

To refine further your priorities, assign numbers to each lettered category, such as A-1, A-2, A-3, B-1, B-2. By adding priority categories to your list of items, you can concentrate on the A and B items and minimize time spent on C and D items. If you have such items as "call back salesperson" or "straighten out files" on your C list and on your A list you have "write an introduction to a 30-page report due tomorrow," you know where to apply time and attention.[7]

To make time for priorities, you must give special attention to eliminating the not-to-do D items, or posteriorities. These are time wasters that detract from your ability to carry out major assignments. Some examples of posteriorities are going to meetings that have little relevance to your position, participating in unproductive committees, or working on tasks that can be delegated to others.[8] If you can answer the question, "What would happen if I did not undertake these activities?" with the reply, "Nothing of consequence," then you should not be doing them. Weed out D items.

It is possible that what was previously on a C or B list may, as time passes, become an item on your A list. The thank-you letter that should have been written 10 days ago now must be written. Be prepared, therefore, to reorder priorities each day. Constantly ask this question: *What is the best use of my time right now?*[9] By forcing yourself to ask this question, you will keep uppermost what your most important priorities are and you will discipline yourself to put aside less important (but perhaps more enjoyable) activities.

Writing priorities can be useful in structuring time, but particularly if your job is not routine, expect the unexpected. Leave room for emergencies requiring immediate attention. Assume that it is an imperfect world and give yourself a time cushion to deal with unforeseen events.[10] Troubleshooting may be a standard part of the position, because you may have to deal with the responsibilities of your subordinates in addition to your own. Their concerns become yours and therefore must be added to your A list.[11] The list is a tool to increase productivity, but it must be used flexibly.

Prepare a priority list each day, and as you complete tasks check them off. If you do not complete the major activities scheduled for the day, determine whether the time frames you have established for them are realistic. Ideally, you should feel a sense of accomplishment in completing the priorities you set for yourself. Some managers prefer to make a priority list the night before so that can they start with it each morning.

Preparing a Daily Work Plan

A daily work plan is another helpful format for prioritizing time commitments.[12] It could consist of the following categories: appointments, phone calls, tasks, and a follow-up list. This one-page format tells you what you need to concentrate on during the day.

Restructuring Time: the 80/20 Principle

The 80/20 time rule is derived from the principle developed by Vilfredo Pareto, a nineteenth-century Italian economist who analyzed the distribution of wealth in his time (80% of the wealth was held by 20% of the people). The concept has been applied to time management to mean that if all activities are arranged in order of their value, 80% of value would come from only 20% of the activities, while the remaining 20% of value would come from 80% of the activities.

The 80/20 rule suggests that out of ten things to do, doing the most important two will yield 80% of the value to you or your organization. The key to effective time management is to focus on the right 20% instead of on low-value activities where the payoff is small. In other words, do not become bogged down in low-value activities (priority Cs and Ds). Develop the ability to say "no" to organizational requests that are on your C and D lists. Of course, the 80/20 rule should not be taken too literally. Percentages are a way of conceptually illustrating that more time could profitably be spent on a few highly critical issues or activities.

The Exception Principle

To take advantage of precious time, managers must determine where to concentrate their energies in relation to their supervisory responsibilities. When managers establish a baseline with clear standards for staff to properly complete their activities, then any unacceptable work will be obvious. Managers do not need to review everything—only those activities with outcomes that deviate from predetermined standards. Observing *the exception principle* allows managers to give limited attention to reviewing ordinary, acceptable performance and concentrate instead on major deviations or unacceptable work patterns requiring a remedy.

Activities could include job performance, quality of written materials, and behavior of employees. These invite special scrutiny to spot exceptional behavior. For example, you have established that phones should be answered within four rings. As long as calls are answered promptly, attention to the phone answering system is not necessary. If staff do not answer within five or six rings, however, then the situation may require special attention. Hence comparing actual performance with expected performance helps the manager to identify the exceptions that require attention.[13]

Blocking Out Time

Occasionally, you need to find time to undertake long-range projects that require sustained periods of concentrated attention. One hour of uninterrupted time will be worth more than four 15-minute time slots scattered throughout the day. You should mark the time blocks on your calendar and generally try to protect them, making exceptions only for special situations or emergencies. Reserve the time block as if it were an important scheduled meeting, canceling it only as you would cancel the meeting.

Use your time block for these kinds of activities:

- Writing an outline or draft of a major report
- Thinking about a major problem
- Completing difficult assignments
- Taking the time to visit branch offices
- Developing better relationships with significant staff, inside or outside the organization
- Working on a major project, such as a fundraising campaign or legislation

To block out time, you must prune activities; some things have to be let go to make room for other activities. Also, in scheduling time blocks, determine the rhythm of the organization. If, for example, the organization annually requires a heavy investment of time to prepare the budget in November, this would not be an appropriate month to set aside a time block for a major new project.

If a project requires concentrated attention, schedule a time block in a quiet room away from the office to prevent telephone interruptions or unexpected visitors. You may have to use weekends, evenings, or early mornings to make time blocks available. You may not want to do this on a regular basis, but occasionally, to get the job done, you may have to work extra hours. An hour spent from 7:30 A.M. to 8:30 A.M. or from 5:00 P.M. to 6:00 P.M. may be far more valuable than small intervals snatched during a hectic day. You may also need to establish "availability hours" so that staff and others trying to reach you will not feel shortchanged. By making yourself available at certain times, you can more easily set aside a time block. Of course, this approach must fit your management style; some managers prefer an open-door approach, in which case they may need to block out evening or weekend time.

Set deadlines and subgoals within the period you have allocated for your time block. By setting these deadlines, you discipline yourself to complete discrete pieces of work. Subgoals provide a target and keep you on track. Thus within each block of time, you should achieve a specific subgoal—for example, complete an outline, write four pages of a report, or finish an analysis of a staff problem.

If the task is too large to complete within a limited time period, then segment the tasks into smaller, more manageable portions, and discipline yourself to complete action on one segment before stopping. This way, you avoid leaving loose ends when you put the task aside. You have completed one phase of the project and are ready to begin the next. The emphasis is not on putting in time but on completing tasks. Develop a compulsion for closure.[14]

Combating Time Gobblers

In the course of a given workday, certain endeavors tend to waste time and limit results. The ideas listed in the following sections are no doubt more than any one person can implement in trying to combat time gobblers. They would not work for every manager all the time. Consider the following items as a smorgasbord of suggestions from which you could select those that fit your working style.

Handling Incoming Work

- Never handle a piece of paper more than once. If it is paper that requires a reply, do it now. If a short report is required, do it now. The main objective is to get the report off the desk.
- To handle the tremendous flow of paper, discipline yourself to see that each piece of paper is handled by (a) acting on it immediately, (b) referring it to someone else, (c) filing it, (d) discarding it, or (e) under special circumstances, delaying action pending other necessary events.
- For all reports longer than five pages, request a summary sheet.
- Arrange to have a place (folder) for every piece of paper you save.
- Critically examine correspondence, especially intraorganizational letters and memoranda, to determine whether your response should be a phone call, a handwritten note, or an e-mail.
- Consider whether staff can handle communications through phone calls or face-to-face contact rather than through long written reports.
- Give a subordinate screening authority regarding fund solicitations and sales letters.
- Carry reading material with you to take advantage of "dead time," such as waiting for a meeting to begin, waiting for transportation to arrive, or sitting in a large meeting where some of the items do not require your attention.
- Respond to incoming correspondence by writing a reply directly on the letter or on the e-mail.
- Use computer networking to quickly exchange drafts with colleagues.
- Attach documents to e-mail for quicker review.

Organizing Paper and Computer Information Flow

- Clear your desk of clutter periodically so that you do not waste time trying to find materials. If necessary, arrange to work occasional evenings or weekends to clean up.

- Before designing a new form, consider whether it is truly necessary, what it accomplishes, and whether a current form can be simplified or eliminated. What effect would the new form have on other departments? How much money and time would it cost to process the form? How much training time would be required? Use the new form for a few days to make sure it works.
- Use stick-on note tags to indicate what needs to be done with each item, especially for considering for later filing. Stack items in priority piles to make sure you deal quickly with "A" items.
- Create a "next step" list that identifies the various steps required to accomplish a particular task.
- Develop a tickler file that sorts, by days or months, projects that must be accomplished in the future.
- Establish at your desk a few working files you are likely to need in the next few days. These are projects you are currently working on that require your continuous attention.
- Schedule time to clean out files once or twice a year.
- Divide incoming items into four categories: dump it, delegate it, delay it, or do it.
- Divide work that comes to your desk into four categories and color-code them, for example:

  red folder: mail/memos-primary, contains items for immediate attention;

  orange folder: mail/memos-secondary, contains items of lesser importance;

  green folder: contains items requiring signature;

  yellow folder: easy reading, contains everything that could be ignored for a week without causing problems.

- Remember that there is a place for everything and everything should be in its place. This will greatly reduce clutter.
- If you have many files to keep track of, use hanging folders in which you can put several file folders. For example, a hanging folder designated as "personnel" could contain individual file folders for people in your department. Then create a master list index of all your hanging folders. When it is time to file, you know exactly where to place paperwork. You know, too, where to retrieve needed information.
- Ask people to put their requests in writing. Keep them in a special place until you have answered them.
- Be choosy about what to read. Practice the art of skimming materials, looking for the most significant and relevant aspects. Concentrate on the introduction and conclusion.
- Keep uncomplicated paperwork handy so that you can work while waiting for people on the phone.
- Get off unnecessary mailing and circulation lists.

- When writing, use short and simple words.
- Take courses in word processing, using spreadsheets, making presentations, and computer scheduling. All managers must become proficient in the use of these time-saving tools.
- Organize your computer files by categories so materials can be easily found.
- Periodically purge computer files of outdated information. Store important information on a disk and store these disks in a fireproof cabinet for protection.
- Organize your e-mail files so that you can file messages in easily-found categories.

Managing Conversations

- Keep a small notebook to jot down names of people you meet and a brief record of issues discussed with them.
- Organize your thoughts before beginning a conversation or a phone call. Know what you want to say, say it, and omit everything else.[15]
- Although socializing is enjoyable, remember to limit it so you can get your tasks done.
- Drop-in visitors present a special problem. Although they are important for relationships in and outside the organization, they can detract from accomplishing certain responsibilities. Be courteous and friendly but also maintain control. Of course, some spontaneous conversations may prove to be highly productive, so be flexible about this guideline.
- If a staff member asks to meet with you, consider going to his or her office instead. It will be easier for you to leave when the business is concluded.
- If possible, meet drop-in visitors outside your office so that you can easily end the conversation.
- Request a brief summary of issues that you can review before a meeting or discussion.
- Encourage staff to prepare any necessary facts and figures for the discussion.
- Keep a clock in full view so you and visitors can be aware of the passing of time.
- Have a file card with agenda topics available for each person with whom you are likely to meet so that you are prepared to discuss specific items with them.
- Establish a time limit when the visitor arrives and be candid about the time pressure you are feeling. If your time is limited, ask the visitor to set up another appointment.
- To let the visitor know that you are ready to end the discussion, use such phrases as "before we finish" or "before we wrap this up."

- Stand up and move the visitor toward the door when you are ready to conclude the discussion.
- Allow time each day for interruptions and unscheduled events.
- Learn to say "no, sorry" if someone asks if you have time to discuss a matter.

Managing Telephone Calls

- Sometimes callers tend to ramble. They go into great detail about a situation before getting to the point. Encourage them to state the "bottom line" issue and then go back to fill in the details. This focuses the discussion.
- If most of your interruptions come from your boss, do not assume that you must put up with them. Pick a judicious time to explain that you are trying to get better control of your time and would appreciate scheduling a mutually agreeable time to discuss routine matters.
- To make a phone message brief: (a) tell the person in one sentence why you're calling, (b) explain it briefly, and (c) say what you plan to do or what action you want the other person to take.
- When you leave the office, indicate on your answering machine when you will return so callers know when to reach you.
- Indicate to the caller your time constraints: "I only have three minutes because of an important meeting I have to prepare for. Will our discussion take longer?" Usually it does not, and your announcement will push the caller to get to the point.
- Find out when a person you've missed will be in and call back at that time to avoid playing "telephone tag." When calling someone who is not in, indicate when you are available for a return call.
- Use a notebook to keep a log of your telephone messages rather than jotting them down on the nearest piece of paper, so you will be able to keep better track of calls.
- Send a fax or e-mail in advance of your telephone call when you need to communicate complex information.[16]
- Keep a list of frequently called numbers by your phone. If possible, program your phone for those you call often.
- Certain times are generally better for returning calls: early morning (8:00 A.M.-9:00 A.M.) and at closing (4:00 P.M.-5:00 P.M.).
- Establish quiet hours during which you do not accept calls except in an emergency or from special persons you designate.
- If you are in a tremendous time bind, try to limit the time you accept calls, such as from 2:30 P.M. to 3:00 P.M.
- Outline topics to discuss before calling.
- Set aside a particular time for calling and make as many calls as you can at one time.

Procrastination

Procrastination is the avoidance of starting or following through on a task that you have defined as important and necessary. The basis for procrastination is usually fear of failure, particularly when undertaking unfamiliar or complex assignments. This fear can be heightened if managers wonder whether the outcome will be as good as their own high expectations. Perfectionism can be paralyzing. To overcome this paralysis, develop more tolerance for your own frailties, at least enough to get started on the challenging assignment you face. You might even humorously say, "If a thing is worth doing, it's worth doing badly."[17]

To prepare yourself for the awesome assignment, ask, "What is the worst that could happen if I try and it does not work out as well as I hoped?" The "worst" may not be so terrible after all. Ask further, "What is the consequence of my delaying?" Because you are faced with the prospect of having to do it anyway, procrastinating only delays the inevitable.

A good rule of thumb is to do the unpleasant things first, not last. If you have a number of tasks to complete, you may naturally want to start with the least demanding. Perhaps this is why staff do not like to set priorities; the biggest, most frightening jobs having the most risk frequently turn up as the top priorities.[18] Instead of delaying, devote the first part of the day to dealing with uncomfortable issues. By concentrating on the onerous tasks first, you are free to enjoy the more pleasant ones later. Your attitude should be one of, "Let's handle the pain first and get it over with."[19] Try not to leave the office at the end of the day without resolving a vexing problem. Otherwise, the problem festers and preys on your mind during your off hours.

Give yourself deadlines on written assignments and make them known to others with whom you work closely. Your deadlines can be divided into immediate (this week), intermediate (in the next three weeks), and long term (what must be achieved in the last week of the project). Then, start long before the deadline so you can pace yourself accordingly. Admit to yourself that you are resorting to escapism when you catch yourself wasting time. Think, "I am wasting my time by not working on my 'A' project."

Be aware that an inability to say "no" can cause procrastination. You may overcommit yourself and then procrastinate because there are not enough hours in the day to get all the work done. Train yourself to ask how long projects may take to complete. Provide a list of your current responsibilities to your supervisor and then discuss which are high priority items and which might be set aside temporarily.

When faced with an overwhelming task, divide it into smaller parts. By doing one part at a time, you break the assignment into manageable pieces. For example, a large writing assignment can be divided into sections, each requiring concentrated attention. Reward yourself when you reach a milestone on a long project.

If you find you are putting off an assignment, it is helpful to analyze your mental blocks to determine whether you can come up with a new approach.

You may need more information to help you resolve the issue. Perhaps you lack conviction about the assignment and may need to confront your superiors with a recommendation for a different course of action.

To speed up the decision-making process you might ask, "What will I know in the future that I don't already know?" If your response is "nothing," then make the best decision you can and move on. If you need to obtain more information or confer with other staff members, put the document in a pending folder and use a date book to remind yourself when you must make the decision.[20]

In dealing with subordinates who tend to procrastinate, avoid giving orders that result in passive compliance and even resentment. Strive to foster commitment by asking, "When can you get started on the rough draft?" and "How much can you complete by X date?" Break long-term, amorphous, or complex tasks into short-term, well-defined projects.[21] By putting boundaries around them, you can reduce the anxiety that comes from open-ended, vague assignments.

The same fear of failure that may cause you to procrastinate can certainly affect the performance of your staff. If procrastination has been a staff problem in the past, make assignments that yield clear success and recognition. You can then build on these successes for more challenging work. You may need to help staff establish realistic timelines, assist them with the quality of their work, and pinpoint what needs to be done to finish on time.

If possible, provide choices for staff as to how they can implement the assignment. For example, ask them when they can reasonably complete an assignment, then come to a mutual agreement. Allow feedback if they think they might have trouble with the assignment. Help them determine a timetable for completing an outline, for example, or the first section of a report. Consider postponing other work to focus on the latest assignment. Encourage them and let them know that if procrastination is likely to be a problem, you are prepared to help them address it.

Effective managers are mindful of how people use their time differently. Be aware that both you and your staff have a life outside of work. Finding the right balance among different priorities is an ongoing challenge. Focusing on outcomes and developing a flexible work schedule may ease the pressure.[22] Do not become so efficient in the use of time that you neglect spontaneous or urgent assignments. Although allowances must be made for the unexpected, effective managers can still take action to be the masters of their time.

Questions for Discussion

1. Which of the time savers regarding incoming work, paper (e-mail) flow, conversations, and telephone calls identified in the text appeal to you most and why?

2. What are the ways staff could use time more productively?

3. In your organization, what are considered highest priorities? Posteriorities?

4. Give an example of a purposeful effort that was made to plan for a project in your organization. What made it succeed?

5. In your experience, what is the best way to block out time for a writing project?

6. How do you avoid procrastination on an important, time-consuming project?

Notes

1. J. P. Kotter, What effective general managers really do, *Harvard Business Review* 77 (March/April 1999), pp. 154–159.

2. A. Lakein, *How to get control of your time and your life* (New York: New American Library, 1973), p. 47.

3. R. N. Askenas & R. H. Schaffer, Managers can avoid wasting time, *Harvard Business Review* 60 (March/April 1982), pp. 98–104.

4. A. Uris, *101 of the greatest ideas in management* (New York: John Wiley, 1986), pp. 284–286.

5. Alexander Hamilton Institute, Inc., *Effective time management: Taking control of your workday* (Ramsey, NJ: Author, 1997), p. 12.

6. Alexander Hamilton Institute, Inc., *Effective time management*, pp. 8–9.

7. H. Smith, Hyrum Smith's simple steps to much better time management, *Bottom Line Personal* (March 1999), pp. 11–12.

8. Alexander Hamilton Institute, Inc., *Effective time management*, p. 16.

9. A. Lakein, p. 96.

10. M. H. McCormack, *Mark H. McCormack on managing* (West Hollywood, CA: Dove Books, 1996), pp. 45–46.

11. A. Uris, p. 292.

12. H. Reynolds & M. E. Tramel, *Executive time management* (Englewood Cliffs, NJ: Prentice Hall, 1979), pp. 15–17.

13. A. Uris, pp. 127–129.

14. E. Bliss, *Getting things done* (New York: Bantam, 1976), p. 180.

15. Alexander Hamilton Institute, Inc., *Effective time management*, p. 27.

16. Alexander Hamilton Institute, Inc., *Effective time management*, pp. 35–37.

17. A. Lakein, p. 96.

18. T. Kirby, *The can-do manager* (New York: AMACOM, 1989), p. 145.

19. M. S. Peck, *The road less traveled* (New York: Touchstone, Simon & Schuster, 1978), p. 19.

20. B. Hemphill, Organize your increasingly complex work life, *Bottom Line Personal* (June 1999), pp. 9–10.

21. R. N. Askenas & R. H. Schaffer, p. 101.

22. S. D. Friedman, P. Christensen, & J. DeGroot, Work & life: The end of the zero sum game, *Harvard Business Review* 76 (November/December 1998), p. 121.

7

Finding and Keeping Productive Employees

A skilled, committed, and caring staff is crucial for every productive human service organization. In addition to hiring and developing the right people, effective managers ensure that the organizational structure fosters productivity and that job tasks are reasonable and challenging. It is essential that employees are motivated, their jobs are made inherently satisfying, their workload balanced properly, and their physical environment is conducive to work. Your goal should be to keep the best qualified staff, even during periods of contraction. Attracting and retaining good employees require your constant attention to the work atmosphere.

Finding the Right People for the Job

Productive organizations require that competent staff be matched with the right jobs. When a vacancy occurs, often the reaction is to contemplate filling the position immediately. It may in fact be better to use the vacancy as an opportunity to assess the organization's staffing pattern and consider whether existing staff might be deployed differently. Reviewing the strengths and weaknesses of current staff in relation to the results you want to achieve is an ongoing process, but it should occur, especially at the time of a vacancy. Through this assessment, you can determine what specific expertise or competency would be needed to complement other staff skills.[1]

Because hiring new staff can commit an organization financially for many years, you should examine several options. Consider redeploying existing staff, as noted above. A second method is to hire temporary workers during critical work periods without assuming a long-term obligation.[2] A third approach is to borrow people from other organizations to take on special assignments. Temporary and borrowed workers provide the organization with flexibility, although there may be some loss of commitment.

One of the best sources for filling vacancies is from within your own organization. People who have demonstrated competency and improved skills are obvious recruits. The clear advantage of promoting from within is that you are obtaining a known entity, and staff feel positive that they might one day advance. Skills available in one role may not necessarily be suited for another, however. The human service counselor may or may not function well as a manager. Moreover, a policy of promoting from within invites staff to have expectations that could lead to disillusionment if they are not selected. This can be of even greater concern if job announcements or postings are listed to comply with the law and affirmative action policies but hiring decisions are made even before postings have been made public. This makes a sham of interviews with current employees. If internal recruitment is to be truly meaningful, sincere efforts must be made to review candidates and to take the time to explain to those rejected why they were not selected.[3]

Conducting a Nondiscriminatory Interview

The term *bona fide occupational qualifications* (BFOQ) describes those qualifications that are necessary to perform typical tasks of a position. In conducting an interview, it is important to keep in mind that if you have a legitimate concern about a candidate's ability to meet the job requirements, you should frame your questions accordingly. For example, if weekend and evening work is required, ask whether this presents a problem. If, however, you do not need the information for actual job-related reasons, do not ask. If you interview a woman who mentions that she has children, you should not ask her how old her children are, what child care arrangements she would make, or whether she has reservations about working alone at night. (Of course, if working alone at night is a requirement, safety issues could be discussed.) Similarly, you should not ask about a candidate's religious or civic affiliations.[4] Your focus is on essential job functions identified in the job description.

In interviewing potential staff for positions, special care must be taken to avoid illegal discrimination involving race, gender, age, place of origin, sexual orientation, and disability. If a person is otherwise qualified but rejected in preference for someone else, the organization may then be subject to a discrimination lawsuit.[5] It is not enough for the organization to proclaim that it has an affirmative action policy. Specific plans must be in place to demonstrate recruitment of minority employees, such as advertising in minority newspapers and contacting minority professional associations.

In conducting the interview, be especially mindful of how you document the following:

1. If the person does not meet the bona fide job requirements, state specifically what you mean by this. Never use language such as "overqualified," which could imply age discrimination.

2. If the person lacks the experience or education required, be sure to document this.

3. Avoid documenting marital status and dependents. Also, do not note whether a candidate owns a home or how long he or she has lived in it.

4. Do not document arrest records or military discharge. These questions have been removed from employment applications because they are viewed as discriminatory. Check your state laws regarding whether questions about felony convictions are permitted; some states require that references to convictions be accompanied by statements that convictions do not automatically disqualify job applicants.

5. Questions about health and disabilities must be related to job tasks. Do not document, for example, how a person with a disability would travel to work.[6]

Your written comments following the interview should explain exactly why the applicant is not qualified; they should be objective and based entirely on job requirements.[7]

The following is a list of questions designed to focus on job performance. Select from this list those questions that are relevant to the position under consideration:[8]

Background Relevancy

- What are your major qualifications for this kind of work?
- What in your educational background is relevant?
- In your previous work experiences, what projects or tasks relate to this work?
- What assignments do you think you are best (or least good) at?

Qualifications

- What are your best qualities as an employee aside from technical competence?
- What are your weakest qualities as an employee; what areas do you need to develop further?
- How do you keep informed of work-related issues in your field?

Expectations

- What are the major outcomes you expect from this job?
- What are your short- and long-range goals, if any, at this time?

- How does this job fit with your long-range plans, if any?
- What part of your work has given you the greatest satisfaction and the least satisfaction?

Work Pressure

- How do you determine which tasks have a priority?
- If you have ever had to change priorities, how did you handle the situation?
- How have you handled situations in which expenses threaten to exceed the budget for your unit?
- How have you dealt with unforeseen circumstances?
- How do you cope with pressures on the job?
- Can you describe a situation when you sought advice from your supervisor?
- What methods do you use to keep track of things that require your attention?

Accomplishments

- What were your objectives for last year and how did you go about achieving them?
- What are your two greatest accomplishments? How were these planned and implemented? What was your most difficult task and how did you deal with it?
- Would you give an example of when you did more than was required of you?
- What performance standards do you set for yourself? What do you do if you find yourself not meeting these standards?
- Describe an experience where initially you failed to gain acceptance of an idea and later succeeded. What made the difference?
- Can you give an example of surmounting an obstacle to reach an objective?

Analysis and Decision Making

- Describe a project or idea that you originated in the last two years.
- How do you keep informed about possible work-related problems?
- What was the best decision you ever made? How did you go about making it? What were the alternatives?
- What was the toughest decision you had to make last year?
- How have you gone about dealing with a work-related problem?

Supervision

- How do you normally assign work to employees?
- How did you handle a situation in which you helped a staff member solve a problem or meet an objective?
- How have you handled (or would you handle) supervising former peers?
- How would you deal with a situation in which you had delegated responsibility and the work was not done as expected?
- How would you handle poor performance or work attitude?
- As a supervisor, describe how you help make your subordinates' work easier and more fulfilling?

Cooperation and Independence

- How have you worked with staff in your unit, members of other units in your organization, or staff from other organizations?
- Can you describe a situation in which you expressed concern about or disagreement with your agency's policies?
- Can you give an example of consulting with your boss before proceeding and an example of acting independently?
- Have you ever undertaken a project that was not popular with some people in your organization? How did it work out?
- With what other departments did you normally work on your previous position?
- What are examples of how you solved or failed to solve problems?

Staffing decisions should be based on the competency and talents of staff matched to job requirements. A strong accountant may be reticent and shy in interpersonal relationships, but that may matter little as long as the books are in order. An outreach worker may use poor grammar but have the ability to establish excellent relationships with residents of the community. While writing skills are occasionally desirable, this talent is not a major factor in an outreach job. People with strong talents may also have weaknesses; only if these weaknesses could seriously affect job performance would an otherwise strong candidate be disqualified. Although you are seeking to understand weaknesses and flaws that may impact performance, your primary interest is in the strengths that recruits bring to the job.[9] A fundamental approach in hiring staff is to concentrate on strengths and not be unduly concerned about inconsequential weaknesses.

A major reason newly hired staff quit is that they have unmet expectations based on misinformation or lack of information the employer provided about the responsibilities and opportunities of a position. Sometimes during recruitment interviews, employers discuss only positive elements of the job while ignoring less attractive realities. This emphasis may depend on how eager the interviewer is to hire the recruit or because skilled staff are in short supply in the marketplace. The prospective employee, faced with limited options, may also overemphasize the job's positive aspects. In general, a preferred approach is to discuss candidly all elements of the job. Effective recruiting requires managers to clearly communicate such job qualifications as the education, skill, and experience needed for the job and the salary range for the position. The more definitive an interviewer is about the expectations and demands of a job, the more likely a suitable candidate will be identified.[10]

The recruitment process should be taken seriously because if it is not done well, you can create a "revolving door" leading to continuous processing of applicants. Employee turnover is both disruptive and costly. To reduce turnover, take the time to invest in recruiting so that you have a pool of the most qualified candidates.

Although checking references is an important part of the selection process, it has become a difficult legal problem because of lawsuits filed for illegal invasion of privacy and defamation. Before you check any references, obtain the written consent of the applicant. Specify that your reference check will ask questions about work experience, character, personal habits, and educational background.[11] Checking references requires collecting information without being discriminatory. Questions should be related to specific job skills. There is nothing wrong with asking general questions about an applicant's attitude or conscientiousness. Make sure to keep written documentation of every reference call you make. Be alert to the possibility that a glowing report can be a way for another employer to pawn off an undesirable employee on your organization.[12]

A telephone discussion is much more informative than a letter of reference because you can ask more specific questions. In the telephone interview, determine how the applicant performed on prior assignments because this, more than anything else, offers clues about how he or she will perform in the future.[13]

Sometimes former employers are reluctant to give information about a job applicant because they fear possible litigation. The following are questions that can prompt former employers to open up without their risking a lawsuit.

- Can you provide factual information, such as dates of employment, final salary, and titles?
- What responsibilities did the applicant have?
- Can you pinpoint professional decisions or behaviors that your former employee showed that might apply to this new position?
- How would you describe the way your former employee implemented work assignments?
- Were there any major problems that affected your former employee's performance?
- Would you rehire this person?[14]

Investing in the recruitment process helps ensure a proper match between applicant and job. There is an old saying that you should never try to teach a chicken to give milk; it wastes your time and annoys the chicken. Taking the time to hire the best person for the job saves considerable grief in the long run.

Developing Staff

As interest in improving productivity increases, organizations naturally want to improve staff capabilities. Training alone, however, has its limitations. Training programs to develop staff must build on the staff's internal desire to improve. Programs must also provide sufficient reinforcement and feedback to ensure significant positive impact.[15]

Good staff development must be built on both a *job-needs analysis* and a *person-needs analysis*. The tasks, information, and skills necessary to do the job can be determined from current employees and their supervisors. The person-needs analysis can be determined by comparing actual employee performance with predetermined performance standards. Those staff performing below proficiency level are candidates for staff development.[16] In addition, staff should be encouraged to take responsibility for performing their jobs properly. Do not guess at what people need—ask them.[17]

In considering how staff development can be used to enhance productivity, keep several points in mind:

1. Training should fit within the overall strategy of the organization. Staff development should assist the organization to deal with its future requirements. For example, if the organization intends to emphasize advocacy efforts, then staff should develop skills along those lines. If the organization needs better marketing, then staff development should stress this.

2. Because what staff learn in training sessions can sometimes elicit negative reactions from colleagues and supervisors back on the job, take certain steps to ensure a receptive climate. Trainers need to be mindful of the environment in which new skills are to be applied. Managers can often benefit from an orientation session that helps them prepare for staff returning from training.[18] Managers should not be caught off guard; in fact, they should encourage newly trained staff to implement new ideas and skills on the job. For example, after being in a training session, some staff may want to propose changes in the way communications are handled within their unit. By anticipating this in advance, the manager can receive these ideas more constructively and positively.

3. Probably the best training occurs on the job. Although one can gain knowledge in formal training, the development of long-term skills and behavioral changes are more likely to occur as part of a job experience. The

advantage of on-the-job training (OJT) is that it provides relevance and reinforcement for the actual work to be done. Small organizations with limited budgets for formal training typically rely on OJT and one-on-one monitoring. Some of the disadvantages of OJT are that it may require a prolonged trial-and-error period, and staff may need assistance in identifying patterns and general concepts that can be applied to other situations.

4. In addition to OJT, training that is anchored in reality provides good opportunities for growth. Special assignments can help develop skills. For example, staff may be asked to provide leadership to a team assignment, thus gaining leadership skills as part of the experience. Or staff may be rotated to a job in another unit for a three-month period as a means of developing new skills. Cross training helps staff better understand the organization and adapt more easily to changing job requirements. The organization thus becomes more responsive and flexible in meeting new demands.

5. A useful off-the-job development technique is the case method of training, which draws upon actual problems and situations experienced by staff. If done well, the case method (sometimes called *situational scenarios*) does not engender "correct" answers from experts but fosters considerable staff participation and encourages a high level of independent thinking. The training value of the case method is that it pushes participants to explore possibilities and to question assumptions.

All training should contain opportunities for feedback using multiple criteria that include the trainees' reactions to the sessions and materials as well as responses from their supervisors on how well staff are applying training to their jobs. In this way, the training itself is subject to continuous examination and revision.

Structuring the Organization to Be Productive

The quality of staff work and interactions can be influenced by the organization's structure, for structure helps determine who works with whom on what tasks. The following questions on structure pertain to increasing staff productivity.

How can structure relate to function? The purpose of structure is to allow the organization to divide its work into various units and then provide ways to integrate this work. No one structural format is appropriate for all organizations because structure should fit unique needs and should emerge from an organization's goals and objectives.

In his analysis of major corporations, Alfred Chandler showed how the form of the organization follows its function.[19] This same concept can be applied to human service organizations. For example, if the organization provides services over a large geographic area, it would likely decentralize its delivery of services. If agency services need to be coordinated with other programs, then staff teams could be established. Form should always follow function.

Structure also can be affected by the composition of the staff. In some instances, the structure emerges from special strengths or weaknesses that staff possess. For example, a manager with strong interpersonal skills may be weak in handling administrative details. Elaborate structures are sometimes built based on special qualities of the staff, and when certain staff leave, restructuring may be necessary. Hence structure takes into consideration both the organizational tasks and the attributes of staff available to fulfill them.[20]

What is the best way to structure staffing patterns? An organization can have a variety of staffing patterns on which to develop a structural framework. Jobs can be organized by (a) *specialization,* in which all similar jobs are placed in one department (e.g., financial activities); (b) *service programs,* with all positions clustering around a particular service (e.g., counseling); or (c) *site location,* with different positions coordinated at the site (e.g., outreach offices).[21] These different formats can be combined depending on what an organization must accomplish. Sometimes, only through a process of trial and error does the proper structure emerge, and even then there may be trade-offs because no structure is likely to work optimally under all conditions.

What structural formats can be used to coordinate the work of the organization? Each organization develops one or more structures to help carry out needed functions. Usually one structure is predominant, but it is possible that several coexist. Moreover, a structure suitable at one time may be altered to meet a special situation at another time. Effective managers continually assess their organization's structural emphasis to maximize the use of scarce resources and staff productivity.

The *bureaucratic* or *hierarchical format* is commonly used in large human service organizations. Staff have specialized jobs, are accountable to a higher authority, and are promoted on the basis of competence. Despite the negative connotation attributed to the term *bureaucracy,* the bureaucratic format persists because it helps coordinate the work of many people. In some organizations, standardizing procedures through a bureaucratic format helps reduce friction and ensures predictability of response.[22]

The *market format* allows staff to move in and out of assignments based on changing needs. High turnover is normal. Staff are attracted by either compensation or a particular assignment. Considerable negotiating and bargaining occur between the organization and employees. In human service organizations, an example of this approach would be staff brought on to fulfill the requirements of a two-year proposal, with no commitment for permanent employment.

A *matrix* or *team-based format* operates temporarily within an organization that is divided into functional areas (e.g., accounting, counseling, day care). Structuring an organization along departmental units generally works well, but such a structure could invite isolated thinking. The matrix approach is designed to offset a *silo mentality* in which staff operate within their own compartments or silos and are reluctant to collaborate with each other, thereby losing the opportunity to gain the knowledge and experience of others in the organization. By temporarily instituting the matrix format, staff continue to report to their unit supervisors for their normal job responsibilities, and also have the flexibility to function in time-limited, cross-functional teams to deal with specific tasks or problems. For example, staff from the mental health counseling unit, the day care unit, and the accounting department would come together as a team to work on how the organization can make its services more accessible.

The advantage of this approach is that it fosters coordination and stimulates staff to focus on problems from different perspectives. Of course, the fact that members of the team continue to have ongoing responsibilities within their own units and have dual lines of accountability can cause problems. By anticipating problems and yet making the expectations of a temporary or focus assignment clear, the matrix approach can be an effective way to deal with issues that cut across functional areas of responsibility.[23] Increasingly, organizations are relying on the matrix or cross-functional approach to heighten commitment, encourage collaboration, and engender creative thinking.[24]

Organizational structure may need to be modified with changing circumstances. During times of fiscal contractions or periods of innovation, the market approach may be suitable. If implementation of routine tasks is needed, then a hierarchical emphasis makes sense. On the other hand, certain structures can interfere with an organization's goals. For instance, a task force designed under the matrix plan for a particular purpose may strive to exist beyond its original intent because staff enjoy working together. What was once an asset to the organization becomes an impediment to the usual flow of work and should be abandoned. Obviously, the issue of structure should periodically be revisited to ensure that organizational needs are being met.

Restructuring Jobs

To meet changing needs, organizations have to reorganize periodically. Occasionally, management should consolidate the work of units to increase efficiencies, reduce duplication, improve the flow of work or communications, take advantage of new technologies, and respond to changing consumer patterns. Special circumstances may warrant organizational restructuring:

1. Funding reductions may require combining some tasks. Work formerly done by managers may either be discontinued or transferred to line staff during this downsizing.[25]

2. Office automation—word processing, electronic mail, audiovisual conferences, and information retrieval systems—allows organizations to redesign jobs so that more time can be spent providing direct service.

3. Alternative work schedules, including flextime, job sharing (involving staff willing to accept reduced hours and pay to preserve their jobs), permanent part-time employment, work-at-home schedules, and compressed work weeks are trends that require the organization to revise jobs.[26] Adjustments must be made in the need for colleague interaction, accountability to supervisors, and group decision making.

4. Competition for good staff may force an organization to restructure its jobs so that the best people are not lured away. If high-quality staff see little opportunity for promotion, or if they find their jobs inherently limiting, then the job structure may need to be refashioned to retain them. Perhaps paraprofessionals can be hired to perform less complex tasks while high-level staff are given more challenging assignments, with accompanying increases in salary. Of course, there is a limit on how far an organization can go with restructuring to keep good people. Staff do outgrow their jobs at times, and the preferred option may be to accept their moving on.

5. The need to reduce errors and achieve better results may require reengineering.[27] If an organization's multiple layers cause decision delays or improperly completed work, a radical restructuring of jobs may be necessary. For example, when a high degree of specialization requires clients to shift from one staff member to another, delays are inevitable, and accountability becomes blurred. Jobs may need to be redesigned for greater emphasis on achieving results and less emphasis on processing clients or paper.

Reorganization can produce negative side effects. It can disrupt informal patterns of communication that are so important for organizational functioning. It can be used by some managers to avoid dealing with problems that could be solved in less traumatic ways. It can create tremendous anxiety, suspicion, and insecurity for staff who become disoriented by the change of relationships.[28] One organization experienced so many alterations over the course of a year that staff coined the phrase "Etch-a-Sketch agency" to reflect the capricious nature of the structural changes. While reorganization should be considered an option in changing circumstances, an organization should not undertake it without considerable forethought and attention to possible repercussions.

Conducting Job and Workload Analyses

The design of jobs has a critical impact on organizational goals and employee performance. The way tasks and responsibilities are clustered can affect productivity. Unsatisfying or highly demanding jobs are difficult to fill and contribute to high turnover. Hence thoughtful job design benefits both the organization and the staff.[29]

Every organization should undertake a task analysis of its major jobs. This analysis provides clear job expectations, facilitates performance reviews, connects staff with the goals of the organization, provides continuity during staff turnover, ensures an evenhanded approach to compensation, helps in identifying training needs, and determines staff support required to perform certain activities.[30]

A job analysis can be similar to a job description or it can contain an even more detailed list of tasks for staff to carry out. If, for example, one of the major activities in a job description is to use a "client information system," a task analysis would spell out the kind of files staff should keep, the information they must provide to other organizations, and the information they must collect. Similarly, if another major activity is "participating as a member of a team," the detailed job analysis specifies expectations in relation to cooperative relationships outside the organization and responsibilities as a team member within it.

A thorough job analysis should be conducted by various people in the organization, and it should include discussions between supervisors and staff, an inventory of tasks, conferences with job analysts and experts, structured and unstructured questionnaires completed by current job incumbents or by supervisors, and documentation of critical tasks that reflect major aspects of the job. By negotiating between staff and administration, an organization clusters its inventory of tasks under major activities and scales them down to a manageable number.[31] The resulting job description includes the skills, knowledge, training, and experience required to perform each job.

A sufficiently detailed job description informs employees what their assignments are, to whom they report, what results they should generate from their work, and what quantity of work is expected of them. You might consider spelling out specific behaviors that are expected of them; for example, in a placement facility, children are not to be left unattended. A precise job analysis can provide, where appropriate, a high degree of staff autonomy and flexibility because staff know exactly what is expected of them.

An important purpose of job analysis is to ensure that staff have proper support. Staff are more productive when they have the proper tools, information, clerical backup, and support of colleagues whose jobs complement theirs. In a counseling agency, for example, counselors must feel that the intake staff are conducting thorough initial diagnoses and making proper referrals. Jobs should be designed so that all staff can fulfill their proper roles and so that the various organizational units are properly integrated.

Moreover, a proper job analysis ensures a balanced workload. Employees who are inundated with tasks or who have an inordinate number of clients are likely to feel overburdened and perhaps even exploited. Staff may make critical decisions that have tremendous impact on their clients based on inadequate information. A solution would be to base caseloads upon reasonable expectations of the time that it takes to complete various tasks. The next step would be to establish standards that reflect the staff's ability to deliver quality and timely services.[32]

Organizations are now beginning to analyze caseloads on the basis of the number of problems presented, their intensity, and the nature of the required intervention.[33] A systematic weighting process categorizes needed services by degree of severity: (a) slight (requiring little or no time investment), (b) moderate (requiring biweekly contact), (c) high (requiring considerable involvement, at least weekly), or (d) critical (requiring several hours each week and perhaps even daily contacts). One staff member might have 35 moderate cases and another might have 10 critical cases. The value, therefore, is in the organization's ability to shift service emphasis from less critical to higher risk subpopulations, thereby permitting a differential and more purposeful deployment of staff.[34]

Enriching Jobs

If at all possible, staff should experience inherent satisfaction in what they do. They must believe that their work is worthwhile if they are to feel truly committed. Peters and Waterman's observation that excellent companies tap the inherent worth of the task as a source of intrinsic motivation can certainly be applied to human service organizations.[35] In fact, human service organizations have an advantage over profit-making organizations in that many of the staff are attracted by the opportunity to enhance people's lives.

To increase job satisfaction, organizations can try a variety of approaches, of which job enrichment is the most appealing. Other approaches include work simplification, job rotation, and job enlargement.

Work simplification creates highly specialized jobs, each consisting of a few operations. This allows staff with limited training and experience to perform the work. An example would be the creation of a staff aide's position to conduct a limited form of interviewing. Job rotation permits staff to take turns performing several work-simplified jobs. It provides more flexible work assignments and reduces monotony. Job enlargement involves adding more components to a job so as to reduce boredom, add meaning and variety, and make the work more challenging. If this is accompanied by an increase in pay so that staff do not feel exploited, enlarging the job can be a positive step toward reducing stagnation.

While work simplification, rotation, and enlargement play important roles in fulfilling organizational needs, it is through job enrichment that staff are most likely to experience an increase in their work motivation. Job enrichment provides staff with an opportunity to experience an entirely new job requiring new skills and talents. Typically, job enrichment allows staff to discern outcomes of their work; they know they are having an impact. Also, staff experience a high level of independence, autonomy, and discretion in performing the work.[36]

For example, suppose that a veteran secretary has been performing her work competently but expresses concern about the routine nature of her work. She has been going to school at night and has a little less than a year to complete her undergraduate degree. Most of her clerical functions have been taken over by automated office systems. The solution may be to enrich her job by making her a paraprofessional with such new responsibilities as interviewing clients and making referrals to other agencies.

Certainly, for job enrichment to succeed, individuals must be able to expand their skills. Job enrichment should be influenced by a sense of individual accomplishment, achievement, and competence. Without developing proper skills, enriching jobs could overwhelm staff. When upgrading job responsibilities, do so initially on a trial basis before committing to a permanent assignment. This permits a careful review of the staff and the new job requirements.

Successful job enrichment may be affected by other aspects of the organization. Supervisors must be especially responsive to staff concerns. Staff may feel that they deserve higher pay, which must be taken into account. Special training may be required.[37] Staff whose jobs are not enriched may express resentment and jealousy. Despite these constraints, the requirements of an increasingly sophisticated work force and the quest for continuous job stimulation can propel you as a manager to concentrate attention on job enrichment programs.

Reducing Staff Turnover

Some agency managers experience high staff turnover. If you are faced with this challenge, you can consider a number of actions. Make sure that new staff have realistic expectations about what their jobs entail. Staff should have an orientation program that provides the skills and training they need to move into their jobs. You could provide a good support system, involving a "buddy" who looks out for the new employee. You could establish clear performance expectations and positive feedback, plus frequent information sessions that can help staff feel valued. Increasing job satisfaction can help reduce turnover. By providing changes in job responsibilities and increasing job autonomy, you can improve morale.[38]

Physical Environment and Staff Productivity

Certain aspects of office design can contribute to staff being unproductive. These concerns may be obvious, but because they happen frequently, management in all organizations must be prepared to address them.

Staff who are squeezed into close quarters and have no sense of privacy may spend an inordinate amount of time socializing. If space is at a premium, one method of dealing with this problem is to install wall dividers made of soundproofing materials designed to reduce the "bull pen" atmosphere.

Give immediate attention to uncomfortable staff environments created by such conditions as poor heating in the winter and poor air-conditioning in the summer. Expect staff to be distracted from their tasks if they are forced to work under poor environmental conditions. Money spent on refurbishing formerly gloomy surroundings is a good investment. People need to feel good about coming to work.

The traffic pattern can also have an impact on productivity. For example, as staff walk to and from the fax machine, the copier, and the water fountain, they can too easily socialize or disturb other staff whose offices are en route. Be mindful of how staff physically move through the workplace.

The location of the manager of a unit can have an impact on productivity. It is sometimes tempting to put managers together, removed from their respective staff. Although communication between managers is certainly desirable, this should not be at the expense of losing close contact with their staff.

Dilemmas About Keeping Good People

Effective managers must continuously work to keep good staff. But funding reductions and the natural desire of good staff to seek better opportunities elsewhere can present tremendous challenges to managers trying to keep the organization functioning at an optimal level.

When Funding Reductions Force Termination

Because of cutbacks at the federal, state, and local levels and increased competition for funding from foundations and localized funding drives such as the United Way, many human service organizations sooner or later must deal with funding cutbacks. This harsh reality requires managers to undergo considerable soul-searching about whether to freeze wages or reduce staff. The dilemma is that if you freeze wages or reduce the number of hours to avoid layoffs, you run the risk of raising the level of staff discontent and jeopardizing the organization's overall productivity. On the other hand, laying off staff could mean diminishing services. In general, effective managers opt to lay off unproductive staff while striving to keep the best. They use the cutbacks as an opportunity to communicate to the remaining staff their importance to the organization and their need to continually work for increased productivity—a painful but necessary decision. Here is how one manager described her soul-searching decision.

About two years ago, I saw my budget becoming tight. I was faced with a severe reduction from my governmental resource, and I had to begin figuring where I could make cutbacks without affecting my program. I trimmed telephone, supplies, and other costs, but 75% of my budget was in personnel. Faced with additional budget cuts, I had to make a wrenching decision to cut staff. I came to the difficult—but proper—conclusion that I should eliminate the educational director's position. Unless I did so, I would have to cut funding for other needed services. Although this decision caused me personal anguish since she was a long time, loyal employee, I knew I made the right decision.

Clearly, what influenced the painful decision to let go of a dedicated employee was the harsh reality of the budget. Had the budget continued to expand, it is possible that the employee might have been retained. Sometimes work expands to fill the staff time that is available, and budget cuts, as devastating as they are, forces the organization to become more efficient. Budget reductions in human service organizations, no less than their counterparts in profit-making companies, impose a sometimes necessary pruning process. Such decisions also can put extraordinary pressure on the remaining staff who must take on added responsibilities.

When employees must be let go, they can be given a longer-than-usual time period to look for other employment. Agencies sometimes tolerate one or two months of inefficiency to allow the person to look for another job. Some organizations prefer not to keep an unproductive employee on the job, preferring to provide severance pay for a limited time period. In addition, employees could be provided with outplacement counseling to assist in their job search. Recognize that there could be fallout from letting an employee go. Other employees begin to wonder, "Are we next?" There may be an undercurrent of resentment and hostility when a valued colleague has to be terminated. It is extremely important to clarify the status of the remaining employees to squelch rumors and offer assurances to the extent they can be offered.

When Good Staff Are Offered Better Pay Elsewhere

Sometimes valuable employees present a dilemma because they are offered more lucrative jobs elsewhere. The employee would prefer to remain, but the increased pay is just too enticing. As discussed earlier, one way of dealing with this problem is to restructure the employee's responsibilities to justify a competitive salary. If this is not possible and a slight increase in the current salary does not provide sufficient incentive, you are then faced with the dilemma of either increasing the salary significantly (assuming you have funding to do so) or accepting the employee's departure.

As a general rule, it is not a good idea to keep staff simply to avoid having to find a replacement. But more important, you should avoid consenting to excessive salary increases just to retain an employee because to do so may, in the long run, do more harm than good. Other staff will hear about the increased salary sooner or later, and they may resent the fact that one of their colleagues is receiving a salary far out of line with the organization's pay scale. They might feel the need to resort to a similar tactic to boost their own salaries.[39] The internal problems caused by avoiding the departure are likely to be far greater than the benefits of keeping the staff member. Keeping good people is a desirable objective, but not at all costs. It is best not to hold an employee back when better opportunities are available elsewhere. This positive attitude reflects well on you and the organization as a place to learn and grow.

Questions for Discussion

1. Under what circumstances would you organize your services by function, geography, service, or matrix?

2. Assume that you are interviewing someone for a position in your agency. What questions might you ask that could potentially invite legal troubles?

3. What are some questions that would qualify as bona fide job requirements?

4. Select several questions in the text that you might likely be asked in a future job interview. How would you answer them?

5. What does your agency do about job training? How effective is it in your estimation?

6. Does your organization provide opportunities for discussion of how you might respond to problem situations? Could you construct situational scenarios that would engender discussion?

7. Examine your job description. Does it accurately reflect what you do? What would you change? How are other jobs structured in your agency? In your opinion should they be modified?

8. In your agency, do you see possibilities of job rotation, enlargement, or enrichment? What are the advantages or disadvantages of considering your proposal?

Notes

1. S. Cohen, The effective public manager: Achieving success in government (San Francisco: Jossey-Bass, 1988), p. 32.

2. S. Cohen, p. 32.

3. M. Beer, B. Spector, P. R. Lawrence, D. Q. Mills, & R. E. Walton, Managing human assets (New York: Free Press, 1984), p. 91.

4. Alexander Hamilton Institute, Inc., Lawsuit-free documentation: A manager's guide to fair and legal recordkeeping (Ramsey, NJ: Author, 1997), p. 13; Alexander Hamilton Institute, Inc., Interviewing made easy: The right way to ask hiring questions (Ramsey, NJ: Author, 1999). pp. 4–7.

5. R. S. Schuler, Personnel and human resource management, 3rd ed. (St. Paul, MN: West, 1987), p. 169.

6. Alexander Hamilton Institute, Inc., A manager's guide to fair and legal, pp. 13–15.

7. Alexander Hamilton Institute, Inc., Lawsuit-free documentation, pp. 12–15.

8. Alexander Hamilton Institute, Inc., Interviewing made easy, pp. 8–23.

9. P. Drucker, Managing the nonprofit organization (New York: HarperCollins, 1990), p. 148.

10. R. S. Schuler, p. 127.

11. Alexander Hamilton Institute, Inc., A manager's guide to reviewing résumés and handling references (Ramsey, NJ: Author, 2001), pp. 16–21.

12. M. Beer et al., p. 75; T. Caplow, How to run any organization (Hinsdale, IL: Dryden, 1976), p. 134; R. E. Herman, Keeping good people: Strategies for solving the dilemma of the decade (Cleveland, OH: Oakhill, 1990), pp. 100–101; G. T. Milkovich & J. W. Boudreau, Personnel/human resource management, 5th ed. (Plano, TX: Business Publications, 1988), pp. 376–377.

13. P. Drucker, p. 146.

14. Alexander Hamilton Institute, Inc., Interviewing made easy, pp. 23–24.

15. R. S. Schuler, p. 427.

16. R. S. Schuler, p. 403.

17. P. Drucker, p. 153.

18. G. T. Milkovich & J.W. Boudreau, p. 550.

19. A. Chandler, Jr., Strategy and structure (Garden City, NY: Doubleday, 1966).

20. S. Cohen, p. 54.

21. R. T. Crow & C. A. Odewahn, Management for the human services (Englewood Cliffs, NJ: Prentice Hall, 1987), p. 10.

22. M. Beer et al., pp. 178–179; R. T. Crow & C. A. Odewahn, pp. 26–28.

23. R. T. Crow & C. A. Odewahn, pp. 28–29.

24. T. H. Peters & R. H. Waterman, In search of excellence: Lessons from America's best run companies (New York: Harper & Row, 1982), pp. 270–277.

25. R. S. Schuler, pp. 453–455.

26. R. S. Schuler, pp. 461–464.

27. M. Hammer, Reengineering work: Don't automate, obliterate, Harvard Business Review 68 (May/June 1990), pp. 104–112.

28. S. Cohen, pp. 60–61.

29. G. T. Milkovich & J. W. Boudreau, p. 125.

30. R. E. Herman, pp. 178–179; P. J. Pecora & M. J. Austin, Managing human services personnel (Newbury Park, CA: Sage, 1987), pp. 24–25.

31. G. T. Milkovich & J. W. Boudreau, pp. 135–144; P. J. Pecora & M. J. Austin, p. 25; R. S. Schuler, p. 98.

32. Public Children Services Association of Ohio, PCSAO Caseload Study (Columbus, OH: Author, 1988).

33. C. J. Coulton, S. Keller, & C. R. Boone, Predicting social workers' expenditures of time with hospital patients, *Health and Social Work 1* (1985), pp. 35–39.

34. C. Mills & C. Ivery, A strategy for workload management in child protective practice, *Child Welfare 1* (1991), pp. 35–43; L. Sametz & D. Hamparian, Innovating programs in Cuyahoga County Juvenile Court: Intensive probation supervision and probation classification (Cleveland, OH: Federation for Community Planning, 1990), pp. 1–48; R. G. Wiebush & D. Hamparian, Probation classification: Design and development of the Cuyahoga County Juvenile Court Model (Cleveland OH: Federation for Community Planning, 1986), pp. 1–20.

35. T. H. Peters & R. H. Waterman, p. 72.

36. M. Beer et al., p. 160; G. T. Milkovich & J. W. Boudreau, p. 127; R. S. Schuler, pp. 448–449.

37. E. E. Lawler, High involvement management (San Francisco: Jossey-Bass, 1986), pp. 95–100.

38. Nonprofit organization management (New York: Aspen, 2002), pp. 3:60–3:66.

39. S. Cohen, p. 42.

8

Managing Employment Challenges

No matter how well managed, every human service organization inevitably faces employee challenges. If they are handled well, managers can then concentrate on achieving the agency's mission. If they are handled poorly, however, managers can become consumed with people problems and the organization could be diverted from focusing on its mission. This chapter highlights some of the more common employment issues.

Diagnosing Employment Problems

Analyzing the Problem

Some employees perform poorly because management has not clarified organizational policies or because supervisors have not properly spelled out work priorities and expectations. Other employees may take advantage of lax office procedures by coming in late or socializing excessively. Still others may require more structured work assignments or may have been mismatched with their jobs.[1] These problems are generally correctable in supervisory discussions. Policies can be enunciated, work priorities delineated, expectations clarified, office procedures tightened, assignments structured, and reassignments (if feasible) made. Following corrective action, unproductive staff presumably can improve their job performance and functioning.

By discussing the problem directly with the employee, you can determine whether extenuating circumstances should be addressed. For example, you may discover that an otherwise productive employee is frequently late to work because he needs to take his child to day care in the morning. You could consider altering the rules about lateness so he can make up the time by working an extra half-hour at lunch. This is, of course, a judgment call based on your overall assessment of the situation. It is possible that providing flexible time for one employee could create problems with the rest of the staff. Hence in making your analysis, consider both the circumstances particular to the employee and the likely responses of the rest of the organization.

The next section identifies some common people problems and suggests ways managers can deal with them.

Dealing with Problem People

The Dead-ender. Staff at the top of their job classification with no place to advance can feel stymied and may need special motivation. To prevent their high motivation from deteriorating, consider the following:

- Seek their advice and suggestions on how they can continue as high performers even if they are at the top of their pay scale. By doing so, you demonstrate that you value their opinions.
- If possible, give them additional decision-making responsibilities.
- Assign trainees to them; they may gain satisfaction from serving as mentors.
- Provide out-of-the-ordinary assignments that offer challenge and a chance to shine. For example, put them on loan to another department where their talents and abilities can be appreciated.

Frequently, staff who feel they are at a dead end do not communicate their concerns directly but show their disinvestment with below-average performance. Excessive absences, increased socializing, or argumentative behavior may be symptoms, and they require corrective action. Convey your concerns and expectations before the behavior turns into complete indifference.[2] Spell out what has gone astray with the employee's performance and discuss what steps can be taken to turn the situation around. Ask the staff member to explain the reason for performance decline and determine together how to rearrange priorities. As with other employees who may be performing poorly, it is important to keep proper documentation to justify any action you take now or in the future.[3]

The Passed-over Employee. Being denied a promotion can be discouraging and frustrating and may result in staff disengaging from their work. The first step is to talk privately to explain why another person was selected. The emphasis here should be on what makes the other person more qualified, not what makes the employee less qualified. If the employee has shortcomings, you might suggest how these shortcomings might be addressed and improved. In addition, you could work out a plan for additional assignments or special studies that would enhance the employee's competitiveness for future job openings. By reinforcing employee self-esteem and providing practical assistance, you help them re-engage in their work.

The Technophobe. Sometimes an otherwise competent employee is unable to take on new assignments or deal with new technologies, especially involving the use of electronic devices. Frequently the employee fears failure, and moreover, experiences tremendous discomfort in having to be taught by younger staff who are more familiar with new technology. This could, after all, involve role reversal in which a subordinate becomes the leader, even the critic. If possible, select peers instead of junior staff to teach new technology. Even if this is not possible, supervisors must be clear and unequivocal: While accepting the resistance as an understandable temporary response, the organization is committed to having staff grow with the new technologies.

In addition to conveying clear expectations, the organization needs to show its support and recognize the anxiety of the technophobe. This supportive atmosphere can create a spirit of camaraderie wherein everyone participates in a "community of learning." Managers need to understand that staff productivity may be lower for a time while employees learn new skills. Staff may even need to be relieved of some duties to lessen overall work pressures. The organization must provide training—not only one-time workshops, but also ongoing consultation and troubleshooting.

The Mismatched Employee. Sometimes, employees are hired into jobs that subsequently prove to be a poor fit for them. Though mismatched, staff have other skills, talents, and commitments that warrant their being retained but perhaps not in the position for which they were hired. Rather than letting employees go, one option is to assign them to other positions for which they are better qualified, even if they are lower paying. Reducing salary is a calculated risk, but if the alternative is terminating a worthwhile employee, it is important to help the staff understand and accept the situation.

The Work Climate Spoiler. Some employees poison the work atmosphere with a sour demeanor. Their grumpy mood negatively affects the rest of the staff, though they may be quite competent in their main job responsibilities. If their work requires only minimal interaction with staff or clients, then some latitude can be allowed. An accountant in the back office with this attitude might be more tolerable than a counselor working directly with clients. Other work spoilers are employees who constantly gossip, spread malicious rumors, or seek gratification by pitting one employee against another. You need to convey the magnitude of your concern and your desire for a more constructive attitude; work spoilers cannot be tolerated. If all else fails, the disruptive staff member may need to be dismissed.

The Work Laggard. Sometimes, new staff who may not be used to the work ethic of the organization tend to slough off work or generally be unresponsive to requests to produce. They may be dilatory in carrying out work assignments. Ordinarily, these behaviors could be grounds for dismissal, but if you feel these employees can be turned around, you need to remind them in unambiguous terms of the consequences of indolent behavior. A good practice is to provide a handbook to all new employees that spells out work performance expectations. Sometimes you may need to allow a period of time for adjustment and a considerable amount of discussion regarding tardiness, absenteeism, excessive use of sick time, personal phone calls, or reading non work-related material on the job to allow staff to acclimate to the work ethic of the organization.

The Poorly Trained Employee. You may find some staff to be unproductive because no one has ever taken the time to fully explain their responsibilities and walk them through their assignments. They may be thrust into situations for which they are ill prepared because of poor hiring decisions. For these employees, training and supervision are key elements. They may need to be sent to a formal training program or at least be provided with a mentor who can work with and guide them during their learning period.

All of these "types" have two things in common: they are not performing up to the standards of the organization, and they could potentially be fired. In fact, some managers take the understandable position that the excessive concentration required to turn around unproductive employees presents a serious drain of time and energy and creates resentment among productive staff. You need to discern whether straightening out an unproductive employee is worth the effort. Yet there are few things more rewarding than salvaging a formerly unproductive employee and taking pride in his or her new and sustained achievements and contributions.

Dealing With Legally Protected Employees

In recent years employment law has been developed to protect staff of human service agencies. Effective managers must keep current with employment laws and regulations so that they can treat their employees responsibly and avoid expensive lawsuits. Consult legal counsel or your human resource department for possible changes in the law.

Older Persons

Covering all employers with 20 or more employees, the *Age Discrimination in Employment Act* (ADEA) prohibits discrimination against older workers. It generally eliminates mandatory retirement at any age, provides protection to any employee over the age of 40, and disallows denying promotion or transfer of anyone over 40 because of age. When hiring or promoting covered employees, you cannot hint at a preference for younger ones. You must also make sure that older workers receive the same training opportunities as do younger ones.

In terminating older workers, as with any employee, you must provide good documentation through written evaluations and disciplinary reports.

You must apply performance standards uniformly, and you cannot make subtle hints that the employee might be laid off if he or she does not take retirement. Your reason for terminating can never be age related; the reason has to be connected with inability to perform the job satisfactorily. If you need to reduce your workforce, avoid the trap of simply transferring duties from older, higher-paid employees to younger, lower-paid ones. Determine which functions—rather than people—need to be eliminated. In offering early retirement, make sure that the plans are completely voluntary.[4]

Persons With Substance Abuse Problems

Many human service agencies have adopted a drug and alcohol policy to educate their employees about the dangers of substance abuse and to take disciplinary action when it occurs. Any agency receiving federal grants must comply with the *Drug Free Work Act* of 1988, which requires agencies to make good faith efforts to maintain a drug-free workplace. Some agencies provide for alcohol and drug testing when there is reasonable suspicion through personal observation or from reports based on specific facts, symptoms, or observations of other persons believed to be reliable.[5] The employee remains on probation during treatment. Those who voluntarily choose treatment should, if at all possible, be provided with medical insurance benefits and counseling programs.[6]

The 1990 *Americans with Disabilities Act* (ADA) protects recovering drug users and alcoholics in organizations with 25 or more employees. The ADA makes it unlawful for employers to refuse employment, deny promotion, or otherwise discriminate against recovering drug abusers or alcoholics. Current abusers of alcohol or drugs are not protected by the ADA.[7] An appraisal record can document declining performance that may indicate a substance abuse problem and can give the employer "reasonable suspicion" required by many states to test and to take disciplinary action, including discharge.

The key to helping rehabilitate an employee is a fair, firm, and conscientious manager. Managers can help best by focusing on job performance, by following the discipline policy explicitly, and by periodically reviewing the employee's performance.[8] Develop a recovery plan with the employee that spells out how he or she will obtain help for the substance abuse problem.

Accommodating Employees With HIV Infection or AIDS

Applicants and employees with HIV or AIDS are protected by the ADA. Discrimination is prohibited in recruitment, hiring, promotion, training, job assignments, leave, and layoffs. Qualified individuals must be able to perform the essential functions of the job with or without reasonable accommodation, which is defined as a change or adjustment to a work environment that allows qualified individuals to perform the essential functions of the job. Examples include restructuring a job, changing work schedules, and modifying equipment. If the reasonable accommodation imposes an undue hardship (unduly costly, extensive, or disruptive) on the organization, it is not required. It is *not* considered an undue hardship if clients refuse to come to an agency knowing that someone with HIV/AIDS is either working in or being served by the organization.

Managers can not reject a qualified applicant because they fear the person may become too ill to work or incur high medical insurance in the future. The hiring decision must be based on how well the individual can currently perform. Managers must honor HIV/AIDS employees' requests for confidentiality, set clear job performance expectations, and hold employees accountable for their work.[9]

Managing Persons With Disabilities

The ADA makes it unlawful for employers to discriminate against individuals with disabilities in regard to hiring, firing, compensation, training, advancement, and all other conditions of employment. The ADA applies to all employers with 15 or more employees (except government agencies). It protects any individual with a "physical or mental impairment that substantially limits one or more major life activities." It protects people with hearing impairments, mental illness, learning disabilities (e.g., dyslexia), and severe obesity. It does not cover compulsive gambling, kleptomania, and transvestism.

The agency with responsibility for enforcing the ADA is the Equal Employment Opportunity Commission (EEOC). Employees have a right to a jury trial and punitive and compensatory damages after a finding of intentional discrimination.[10]

If the organization has a fair and rational appraisal system (see Chapter 11), actions taken by the organization can stand up in court. An employee with a disability who is not performing the job in spite of being given reasonable accommodation can be subject to disciplinary action, including termination. The EEOC expects to see a record of substandard performance appraisals. Further, the ADA does not require that an employee with a disability be promoted or offered training that would make advancement possible if either action would place undue hardship on the employer.[11]

An employer can hold staff with disabilities to the same standards of productivity and performance as other staff without disabilities. A double standard should not be applied in such a way that persons with disabilities receive less discipline than any other employee. Again, it is important that the appraisal process document poor performance in order to avoid claims of discrimination.

Persons with disabilities can provide an organization with challenges that must be addressed. For example, a person with epilepsy whose disease is under control because of medication does not necessarily present a risk to the children under her care. A person with a stuttering problem who meets the qualifications of being a counselor must be considered for that position. A person who is somewhat obese is not covered by the ADA, but one who is severely obese—more than 100% of the norm—is under its protection. This is the purpose of the ADA.[12]

In considering a person who might qualify under the ADA for a position in the organization, all questions must be focused on the job and not on the person. For example, you would not ask:

"Are you taking medications that would make you drowsy?"

"Have you ever been treated for mental health problems?"

"How did you become disabled?"

"Have you ever been treated for an inability to handle stress?"

"How often have you used illegal drugs in the past?"

These questions cannot be asked because they focus on the disability. The provisions of the ADA were designed to prevent discrimination against individuals with hidden disabilities.[13]

You could ask persons with disabilities, however, whether they could perform the functions of a particular job with or without reasonable accommodation. You could inquire about how they would perform particular job-related functions and whether they could meet job attendance requirements. You could ask whether they currently are using illegal drugs. These questions must be aimed at determining their ability to perform essential job functions, not at discovering the existence or severity of a disability.

Agencies may have to make reasonable accommodations, such as wheel-chair ramps for employees with physical handicaps, or telephone devices for the hearing impaired. If a supervisor receives a request from an individual with a disability, there should be an informal process to clarify what the individual needs and identify the appropriate reasonable accommodation. If there are two possible options and one costs more or is more difficult to provide, the supervisor may choose the one that is less expensive or easier to provide as long as it is effective.

Some jobs may need to be restructured. If an employee is unable to perform a minor job task, the supervisor can require the employee to do a different minor job function in its place. However, a supervisor does not have to eliminate a primary job responsibility, nor have to lower productivity standards that are applied to all employees. A supervisor never has to excuse a violation of a uniformly applied rule that is job related and consistent with business activity. Finally, a supervisor does not have to provide a reasonable accommodation that is significantly difficult or expensive. If employees with a disability are not able to perform their job despite being given reasonable accommodations, the organization has the right to terminate employment. To obtain assistance in accommodating workers with disabilities, check with the Job Accommodation Network (see Web Sites for Human Service Managers).[14]

Family and Medical Leave Act (FMLA)

Managers should review the agency's family and medical leave policy with legal counsel to make sure that it complies with the *Family and Medical Leave Act* (FMLA). The purpose of this law is to help employees balance their work and family lives by allowing them to take unpaid leave for illness, birth or adoption of a child, or care of a child, spouse, or parent who has a serious health condition. A full time employee is entitled to a total of 12 weeks of leave during any 12-month period. The employer must allow the employee to return to the same job or one of equal position with equal pay and benefits. The FMLA applies to any employer that has more than 50 employees.

Taking Corrective Action to Change Behavior

When employees manifest attitudes or behaviors that interfere with meeting performance standards, corrective action must be taken. Usually, the supervisor takes the initiative and formulates a performance plan that clarifies acceptable performance standards, identifies actions needed to meet those standards, spells out a specific timetable, and states consequences if improvement does not occur.

In preparation for the performance interview, the supervisor should document substandard performance and behaviors. The interview itself should be straightforward, firm, and non-threatening. The supervisor should convey that, although the organization values the staff member, there can be no compromise on job performance.

Confronting an unproductive employee can be a profound experience for both the supervisor and the employee. It requires a consistent and direct approach to help employees face issues they might want to deny or minimize. Ultimately, it should help unproductive employees accept responsibility for their behavior and implement specific steps to improve job performance.

In confronting an unproductive employee, the following are specific guidelines that are useful in most situations:

Document specific, concrete behaviors that reflect the deteriorating work performance or unacceptable behavior and the circumstances under which they occurred. Concentrate on the results of behavior rather than on the individual's shortcomings. For example, emphasize the lateness of reports rather than the employee's tendency to procrastinate. This approach helps diminish the employee's feelings of being personally attacked.

Discuss the unacceptable behavior as soon as possible after it occurs. Do not wait for the end-of-the-year evaluation to discuss events that happened four months earlier. Immediacy adds potency to the discussion.

Conduct the discussion in private. Public reprimands can embarrass staff, and their "losing face" makes them more resentful and resistant to change.

To emphasize the caring and supportive concern you have about the employee, identify strengths as well as limitations. Few people do everything wrong, and most do far more things right. By being positive, you provide a context within which the criticism can be tolerated more easily. When the employee does make progress, acknowledge the turnaround. Applaud the new behavior as a way of reinforcing it.

Avoid making value judgments and moralizing. If personal or emotional problems are offered as explanations, you can be sympathetic without abandoning your expectations of quality work performance. Employees must be seen as adults responsible for their own behavior, but you may need to encourage some to seek counseling with the understanding that doing so would not jeopardize job or promotion opportunities.[15] Because of the recognition that employees' personal lives can spill over into their work attitudes and behaviors, many organizations offer Employee Assistance Programs that provide confidential interviews to troubled staff.

Focus on changing behavior. Be clear about specific actions you want the staff to change. Furthermore, you should involve the employee in finding a solution, remembering that your purpose is not punishment but changing unacceptable behavior. Because the employee may feel defensive, it may be helpful to use "I statements," which indicate your point of view: "I am concerned about your attendance" or "I want you to make an effort to be more cooperative."[16]

Progressive Discipline

Many states follow the *employment at will* doctrine, which states that unless a definite period of service is specified in an employment contract, hiring is considered to be "at will." Subject to specific legal restrictions, an employer has the right to discharge an employee at any time without notice and for any reason or for no reason at all. This has been upheld by the United States Supreme Court as being constitutional.[17] Progressive discipline must be seen within the context of this *employment at will* doctrine.

In contrast to those affected by employment at will provisions, human service professionals are sometimes covered by collective bargaining agreements or civil service rules, which provide for due process and *just cause* standards. Normally, agency personnel practices provide for a grievance appeal process, usually limited to an internal appeal within the agency, with no opportunity for an impartial third party. Some unionized agencies, under their collective bargaining agreement, permit an employee to have representation at the point of discipline and throughout the grievance procedure. The grievance is submitted to arbitration if the management and the union cannot resolve the discharge grievance. This third party arbitrator is jointly selected by the parties and conducts an impartial hearing that is binding on both. Typically, selected arbitration agreements require progressive discipline—counseling, verbal warning, written warning, and suspension—prior to discharge. The value of voluntary arbitration is that it avoids wrongful discharge lawsuits and protects against abuse of managerial authority.[18]

Whether agencies operate under employment at will or just cause, they typically follow a set of procedures or deliberate steps in addressing performance problems or disciplining their employees, depending on the extent to which employees have violated the rules or exhibited unprofessional behavior. These explicit progressive discipline policies provide guidelines for both management and employees regarding expected staff behaviors and consequences for noncompliance. By observing the following five steps, you are fair to the employees, you avoid capricious actions, and your disciplinary process will hold up in court.[19]

1. Provide the employee with explicit expectations for behavior and performance. Generally, most problems can be solved by clarifying ambiguous expectations.

2. If the problem continues, convey a verbal warning specifying how expectations are not being met. Reach an agreement as to how the employee can correct the problem. Depending on the problem, you may wish to issue more than one verbal warning. During this phase, individual or group counseling may need to be provided to help the person correct the problem.

3. The next step is to send a written warning, including a description of the behavior that is expected of the employee and what the employee is perceived to be doing wrong. Convey how you expect the employee to correct the behavior or overcome the problem. Indicate what the consequences are if the employee does not correct the problem within a specified time period. It is possible that an employee may request a transfer to another unit. He or she may be in the wrong job, or chemistry between staff and supervisor may be affecting work performance. A change in position may therefore resolve the problem. Whether the employee remains or is transferred elsewhere, indicate, if appropriate, what kind of support will be given. Specify that further disciplinary action may be taken if the problem persists. If the employee refuses to sign the warning, another supervisor should immediately be brought in to sign the written document to acknowledge the employee's refusal.

4. If the problem persists, the next step is a consequence, often in the form of one to three days' suspension without pay, to convey how serious the problem has become. If you tell your employee that a suspension will result from repeating the problem, you have to follow through on it unless the staff member offers a reasonable explanation. Some organizations use a variation by providing a paid suspension, with the requirement that the employee return with a written plan on how he or she will correct the problem. To convey that employee attitudes and behavior will be closely scrutinized upon return, inform the employee that he or she is on probation.

The employee must understand that termination may result if performance problems continue.

5. The final step is termination. This will be discussed in more detail below.

Under some special circumstances, you may need to bypass the progressive approach outlined above. For example, in a children's residential treatment center, if staff have been irresponsible in monitoring children's behavior, several days' suspension may be necessary immediately to convey the severity of the situation.

Moving beyond the verbal warning to a more serious consequence should, if at all possible, be spelled out in advance.[20] In all the steps prior to termination, it is important to convey that you think that the employee is capable of changing behavior. In some instances, it may be better to place staff on probation, perhaps up to three months, to emphasize that there will be a period of close scrutiny. Some behaviors may be serious enough to warrant immediate termination, such as misusing or stealing agency property, sleeping on the job, or physically abusing a child. Each organization should determine its response to unprofessional behavior in its personnel practices.[21]

To protect employees from capricious, arbitrary acts, organizations should develop a grievance procedure that permits staff to appeal decisions. This procedure should be clearly spelled out in the organization's personnel practices manual.

Handling the Incompetent Employee

In some extraordinary situations, you may find it very difficult to fire an incompetent staff member. Requirements of civil service or union procedures may prevent this, and in the real world, political considerations may be a factor. These barriers do not automatically mean that you should not terminate an unproductive employee. Some effective managers confront obstacles to terminating an unsatisfactory employee with credible documentation and tremendous resolve and conviction even to the point of putting their own jobs on the line. Nevertheless, if termination is not possible, the manager must develop a strategy to ensure that the incompetent staff does not "contaminate" productive employees with his or her bad work habits and poor attitude.

Some organizations develop an unimportant special assignment for the unproductive employee that is unlikely to result in much damage to the organization if it is not performed competently. Some even go so far as to isolate the incompetent staff person in the least desirable physical space. These are "last resort" desperate actions, which should not continue indefinitely. Be aware that putting an employee in an undesirable situation can be construed as a *constructive discharge;* this could invite a lawsuit in which the employee charges that the new working conditions are so intolerable that the employee was forced to quit.[22]

Another approach is to assign the least essential function to a team of poor performers, sometimes called a "turkey farm."[23] This could, of course, backfire and create embarrassment for the organization. A variation of this idea is to loan an unproductive member who has some redeeming qualities to another unit or another organization, thereby removing the troublesome staff person and breaking up patterns of dysfunctional behavior. In some instances, this could be a positive move for both the employee and the organization. By placing the unproductive staff member in a new setting with different work relationships and job requirements, it is possible that improved performance can occur. Again, these suggestions are made with extreme caution; some managers have an unequivocal policy not to keep incompetent employees. Service to clients is their overriding concern.

Terminating Employees

Because human service organizations are in the business of rehabilitating people, there may be a tendency to hang on a little longer and hope the incompetent employee will improve. Recognizing that some circumstances make it exceedingly difficult to terminate employees, managers nevertheless must be willing to act with the conviction that terminating staff is a necessary and essential part of keeping an organization productive. The reality is that employees may be mismatched with their jobs, may lack motivation, may evidence behavior that warrants termination, or may be unwilling to carry out the tasks that help the organization achieve its mission. If attempts to improve performance seem to go nowhere, then termination is necessary for the continued health of the organization. Grounds for firing include the following:[24]

- Physical violence
- Sexual harassment or assault
- Gross insubordination
- Alcohol or drug use during work hours
- Repeated shirking of responsibilities
- Lack of skills to perform required tasks or to meet objectives
- Chronic or excessive absences
- Dishonesty, including falsification of employment records and expense accounts
- Carelessness that causes actual or potential harm
- Continued incompetence, despite training

Staff incompetence is not always easy to spot. A person may be generally destructive but may still perform an important function. An incompetent staff member may be a nice person. Termination should occur when the organization's work becomes threatened or when hanging on to a poor performer significantly affects the work of others or the organization's ability to function. Keeping unproductive staff members is unfair to others in the organization who must make up for their failures and untangle their messes.[25]

Legally Sound Disciplinary and Termination Processes

In taking disciplinary action or terminating employees, effective managers must carefully avoid the organization's becoming entangled in costly and time-consuming lawsuits. If employees feel that their employer does not adopt or enforce fair and consistent procedures, litigation alleging discrimination or violation of implied contractual obligations can occur. Watch for the following problems:

Lack of Clear and Consistent Policies. The absence of clear written policies can lead to the inconsistent treatment of employees. If staff feel they are treated differentially because of gender, race, ethnicity, sexual orientation, age, or physical or mental disability, they may resort to litigation. Policies should spell out conditions under which termination can occur. Supervisors must be instructed on the importance of impartially enforcing regulations; otherwise, staff could claim bias. Progressive discipline policies should be circulated so that all staff clearly understand the ground rules for professional behavior.

Inconsistent Evaluation History. Terminated employees may insist that their appraisal history be reviewed; therefore, you should avoid being trapped in the inexplicable situation of having given acceptable performance appraisals or merit salary increases to marginal employees. Consistently document unsatisfactory performance by providing a *paper trail* that records disciplinary actions and performance reviews. Indicate on the record where even small problems are occurring so that a pattern of marginal performance becomes clear. The best approach for dealing with unproductive employees is to keep extensive, fully documented records so you can establish just cause for any eventual terminations. Documentation is the single most effective weapon in any type of legal action.[26]

This record should be free of any statements mentioning age, race, sex, national origin, religion, or disability. It should also be free of derogatory statements and subjective descriptions. For example, instead of saying the employee has a "bad attitude," the employee's conduct should be specifically described. All previous written disciplinary warnings or performance reviews should have been signed by the employee, acknowledging awareness of supervisory concern.

Letting Subjective Biases Affect Termination Decisions. If supervisors show partiality in the enforcement of regulations by favoring one employee over others, the result could be a charge of bias. Be certain that you treat discipline and termination actions consistently by reviewing whether other employees in similar circumstances would be treated in the same way. Check potential biases with other members of the administrative staff to ensure you have followed correct procedures. By focusing on performance, supervisors reduce the risk of being accused of capricious and discriminatory behavior. Inform employees of performance criteria in advance, and clarify expectations in measurable and identifiable terms.[27]

Be aware that wrongful discharge lawsuits can be filed if discrimination can be shown regarding age, disability, race, religion, and sex discrimination. Firing or demoting someone over the age of 40 without documented proof, letting go an employee with a disability before exhausting all the accommodation efforts, discharging a minority person for an offense for which nonminority employees were not discharged, terminating an employee who has a sincerely held religious belief, and demoting a female employee because she did not get along with men in the organization are all situations that can result in challenges in the court.[28]

Failure to Inform Staff That Their Positions Are in Jeopardy. Litigation is likely to occur when employees can claim they were unaware that their performance could result in adverse consequences; they can say they were denied the opportunity to take corrective action.[29] Occasionally, a supervisor may place negative observations in an employee's files but then not share the information—a procedure that can backfire when a lawsuit is filed. Negative written reviews must include specific problem areas or mention of inadequate performance, ideas for improvement, and a stipulation that continued similar problems will result in adverse action. A good procedure provides the employee with the opportunity to comment on, or even dispute, the performance appraisal. At the very least, the employee should sign the appraisal form.

Discipline Documents

Most organizations have written policies and formal warning systems to address possible employee problems. Assuming that a progressive discipline system is in place, a supervisor should be able to provide documentation that lists both the positive and negative aspects of staff performance and behavior. If the employee's record includes previous favorable appraisals, then you would prepare a detailed description of the reasons performance is no longer considered satisfactory. Furthermore, the reports should be prepared on a regular basis and should avoid any bias.[30]

If an employee has received a final warning notice, the language should be clear and specific: termination will result from one more of the same infraction. It is a good idea to have all disciplinary documents signed by both you and the employee before a copy is put in the personnel file.[31]

To avoid being legally burned in a lawsuit, managers should observe the following:[32]

1. Initiate training or counseling to indicate that you have been fair in trying to improve performance.

2. Document verbal warnings and provide for the employee to sign off on your notes to indicate that he or she has been made aware of your concerns.

3. Make certain that the employee is aware of consequences should the situation be repeated.

4. Obtain a second opinion from upper management before you actually fire an employee to make sure your termination is based on concrete evidence and not subjective factors.

5. Provide the employee with a valid reason for termination and a copy of the rule that has been violated.

6. Consider having the employee voluntarily sign a release from future legal claims. This may require providing the employee with more than the normal severance pay. Encourage the employee to obtain legal advice before signing.

7. To avoid a potential defamation or slander lawsuit, indicate in response to a reference request only that the person worked for the organization in a given period of time.

In summary, check with an attorney regarding the possible charge of *unjust dismissal* if you have any doubts. Effective managers realize that although there is no absolute way to prevent lawsuits, by operating fairly, communicating frequently and candidly, and documenting thoroughly, litigation can be avoided.[33]

Conducting the Termination Interview

If you must terminate an employee, the following guidelines may assist you:

- Avoid poor timing of the termination: birthdays, anniversaries, holidays, or Fridays.
- Termination early in the week allows time to wrap up loose ends promptly instead of allowing the individual to "stew" over the weekend.
- Determine in advance the termination interview benefits that the person is entitled to, including unused vacation, pension disbursement, and severance pay.

- Arrange, if feasible, for outplacement counseling.
- Determine in advance exactly what you will say in the interview. Be specific about when the person is to leave the organization.
- Allot no more than 30 minutes for the interview to communicate and come to closure.
- Accept what the employee has to say in his or her defense but do not become argumentative. Anticipate and respond without being defensive to the question, "Why me?"
- Say something positive about the individual, but do not be excessive. Avoid transmitting "mixed messages" that may convey hope to the employee that something can be negotiated.
- Immediately following the meeting, contact all those persons who need to hear about your action firsthand.
- Minimize discussion with other staff about dismissed employees. Respect their dignity and the confidentiality of your decision. Discuss the situation only with those who absolutely need to know.
- Take pride in knowing that you acted constructively, honorably, courteously, and aboveboard.[34]

Under some circumstances, employees could be encouraged to resign. They benefit because they preserve their dignity in the outside world, and they improve their chances for reemployment. The organization benefits because it avoids potential legal battles.[35] Some organizations resort to a generous "severance" payment in exchange for a signed waiver indicating the resignation was voluntary and no lawsuit will be forthcoming. This should be considered with utmost caution, however, because of possible repercussions from staff who may resent the special consideration given to the departing, unproductive employee.

Questions for Discussion

1. Jane S. is a three-year, loyal, and competent staff member who has just returned from a 12-week family leave to care for her hospitalized child, who is now in day care. As a single mother, she indicates that she is exhausted and that she cannot continue to carry the full responsibilities of the job. As a supervisor of the unit, you have the responsibility to assign large caseloads to your staff. How would you handle the situation with her?

2. Carl M., a 55-year-old employee, has worked for your agency for the past 10 years. Within the past 10 months his work performance has begun to deteriorate: he is coming in late almost every day, he is consistently behind in his reports, and a few clients have called you to say that he seems disinterested in their problems. As his supervisor, how would you handle the situation?

3. You have just hired a recent honors graduate who had good references. Her reports are well written and she is obviously bright and intellectually well prepared. She seems to be doing well as a counselor. Her only problem is that she tends to be arrogant and supercilious with her colleagues, and they in turn are complaining to you about her superior attitude. How would you deal with this?

4. You know that Jim L. has had a problem with taking drugs, and you are also aware that he is covered under the ADA as long as he is in counseling and taking action to deal with his situation. One of the reasons you hired him is that he could be in a good position to provide counseling to homeless addicts who come to your agency for health services. Recently, a staff member has informed you that she has seen him drinking at lunch. You have no other corroborating evidence. You are concerned that if this situation is true, he could be impaired in performing his counseling responsibilities. What would you do?

Notes

1. P. J. Pecora & M. J. Austin, *Managing human services personnel* (Newbury Park, CA: Sage, 1987), p. 42.

2. Bureau of Business Practice, Inc., *Front line supervisor's standard manual* (Waterford, CT: Author, 1989), pp. 14–15.

3. Alexander Hamilton Institute, Inc., *Conducting successful appraisal interviews: The right way to discuss employee performance* (Ramsey, NJ: Author, 1998), pp. 25–26.

4. *The practical guide to employment law* (New York: Panel Publishers, 2001) in *Nonprofit organization management* (New York: Aspen, 2002), pp. 4:23–4:37.

5. *The practical guide to employment law,* pp. 4:23–4:37.

6. National Institute of Business Management, Inc., *Fire at will: Terminating your employees legally* (New York: Author, 1991), p. 13.

7. Alexander Hamilton Institute, Inc., *A manager's guide to preventing people problems* (Ramsey, NJ: Author, 2002), p. 5.

8. Alexander Hamilton Institute, Inc. *A manager's guide to creating a drug-and-alcohol-free workplace* (Maywood, NJ: Author, 1991).

9. *Nonprofit organization management* (New York: Aspen, 2002), p. 4:10.

10. Alexander Hamilton Institute, Inc., *What every manager should know about the Americans with Disabilities Act* (Ramsey, NJ: Author, 1997), p. 1.

11. Alexander Hamilton Institute, Inc., *Conducting successful appraisal interviews,* p. 32.

12. Alexander Hamilton Institute, Inc., *What every manager should know about the Americans with Disabilities Act,* pp. 6–9.

13. Alexander Hamilton Institute, Inc., *What every manager should know about the Americans with Disabilities Act,* pp. 28–30.

14. *The practical guide to employment law,* pp. 4:3–4:9, 4.11–4.12; Alexander Hamilton Institute, Inc., *A manager's guide to preventing people problems,* pp. 10–11.

15. T. K. Connellan, *How to grow people into self-starters* (Ann Arbor, MI: The Achievement Institute, 1980), pp. 141–143.

16. Alexander Hamilton Institute, Inc., *A manager's guide to the do's and don'ts of discipline* (Ramsey, NJ: Author, 1998), pp. 24–25.

17. S. C. Kahn, B. Berish Brown, M. Lanzarone, & B. E. Zepke, *Legal guide to human resources,* 3rd ed. (Boston: Warren, Gorham, & Lamont, 1994), p. 801.

18. M. Tambor, Employment-at-will or just cause: The right choice, *Administration in Social Work* 19, 3 (1995), pp. 45–57.

19. Alexander Hamilton Institute, Inc., *A manager's guide to conducting fair and legal discipline interviews* (Ramsey, NJ: Author, 2002).

20. T. K. Connellan, p. 132.

21. Alexander Hamilton Institute, Inc., *A manager's guide to the do's and don'ts,* pp. 10–11, 20–21; R. T. Crow & C. A. Odewahn, *Management for the human services* (Englewood Cliffs, NJ: Prentice Hall, 1987), pp. 612–613; R. E. Herman, *Keeping good people: Strategies for solving the dilemma of the decade* (Cleveland, OH: Oakhill, 1990), pp. 83–85; P. J. Pecora & M. J. Austin, pp. 93–97.

22. Alexander Hamilton Institute, Inc., *A manager's guide to avoiding termination lawsuits* (Ramsey, NJ: Author, 1997), p. 19; Alexander Hamilton Institute, Inc., *A manager's guide to the do's and don'ts,* pp. 28–29.

23. S. Cohen, *The effective public manager: Achieving success in government* (San Francisco: Jossey-Bass, 1988), pp. 48–50.

24. Alexander Hamilton Institute, Inc., *A manager's guide to avoiding termination lawsuits,* pp. 1–38.

25. R. Townsend, *Further up the organization* (New York: Alfred A. Knopf, 1984), p. 76.

26. National Institute of Business Management, Inc., p. 2; Alexander Hamilton Institute, Inc., *A manager's guide to avoiding termination lawsuits,* p. 18.

27. Alexander Hamilton Institute, Inc., *A manager's guide to avoiding termination lawsuits,* p. 18.

28. Alexander Hamilton Institute, Inc., *A manager's guide to avoiding termination lawsuits,* pp. 27–34.

29. S. D. Bruce, *Face to face: Every manager's guide to better appraisal and discipline interviewing* (Madison, CT: Business and Legal Reports, 1989), pp. 87–113; S. A Goering, Steps can protect company from ex-employee lawsuits, *The Plain Dealer* 21 (August 1990), p. F2; Alexander Hamilton Institute, Inc., *A manager's guide to avoiding termination lawsuits,* p. 19.

30. Alexander Hamilton Institute, Inc., *Lawsuit-free documentation: A manager's guide to fair and legal recordkeeping* (Ramsey, NJ: Author, 1997), p. 30.

31. Alexander Hamilton Institute, Inc., *Lawsuit-free documentation,* pp. 28–29.

32. Alexander Hamilton Institute, Inc., *A manager's guide to avoiding termination lawsuits,* pp. 19–24, 35–37.

33. Alexander Hamilton Institute, Inc., *Conducting successful appraisal interviews* (Maywood, NJ: Author, 1991); National Institute of Business Management, Inc., pp. 1–40.

34. R. L. Swain, 66 ways to avoid trouble when terminating the long-termer, *The Human Resources Professional* (September/October 1989), pp. 28–31; Alexander Hamilton Institute, Inc., *A manager's guide to avoiding termination lawsuits*, pp. 22–26.

35. T. Wolf, *The nonprofit organization: An operating manual* (Englewood Cliffs, NJ: Prentice Hall, 1984), pp. 61–62.

9

Humanizing the Organization

Setting the right tone in an organization by creating a positive, humanizing environment contributes immeasurably to staff effectiveness. Creating an organizational culture in which values are clearly stated and staff are encouraged to invest in achieving the agency's mission can have a significant impact on service consumers. Still, even though managers may mean to do the right thing, interpersonal and emotional problems affecting work performance are bound to occur. If not handled properly, these problems tend to fester until they cause great damage and require a tremendous investment of time and energy—efforts that could be better spent on achieving the agency's mission. By inspiring positive values, helping staff deal with stress, fostering diversity, minimizing harassment, and being sensitive to inequities, managers can make their agencies more humane and more productive.

Creating a Culture of Caring

Organizational culture is the operating style, traditions, rituals, beliefs, and fundamental values of the organization. This culture influences the way staff think and behave.[1] It is the system of values that a service organization has invented, discovered, or developed over time while learning to cope with its problems of external adaptation and internal integration.[2] *Culture* is the way staff perceive that there is a right way to do things in the organization.

Shared values give the organization a sense of direction so that staff see how to fulfill their professional goals in relation to the organization's goals. Above all, organizational values provide a profound sense of meaning to staff work. When influenced by a strong organizational culture, staff truly care about their work; they significantly invest themselves in what the organization represents. Where a strong culture exists, either people buy into organizational norms or they are encouraged to leave. Those who remain identify deeply with the organization's value system, and their professional lives have greater significance because of their affiliation.

Although managers in most organizations strive to develop a strong culture as a way of influencing staff performance, cultural strength may or may not be associated with effectiveness.[3] Sometimes an older organization with a strong culture benefits from having units with diverse perspectives that question the usual way of doing things, thereby allowing adaptation to environmental changes. The challenge for effective managers is to harness the organizational culture's benefits while staying in sync with the needs of the community. Enlightened managers can avoid cultural blind spots by accommodating selective nonconformity in their organizations and by themselves deviating from it when this makes sense.[4]

Effective managers serve as the primary shapers and communicators of organizational values. They influence the organizational culture by what they pay attention to, measure, and control; how they handle crises and critical episodes; how their own behavior serves as a role model; how they allocate rewards and status; and how they recruit, select, promote, and fire staff.[5] Do they tolerate or challenge criticism? Do they limit or make information available to staff? Do they control or empower staff to make decisions? Managers are frequently faced with these value choices.

Effective managers always play a key role during those times when the organization faces problems, external or internal. Indeed, one of the crucial functions of leadership is to provide guidance at precisely those times when habitual ways of thinking or doing things no longer work or when drastic environmental changes require fresh responses. It is during these transitional times, too, that effective managers provide staff with security to help them tolerate the anxiety of giving up old responses while new approaches are being tried.[6]

Clearly, effective managers play a significant role in influencing the culture by the messages they communicate and, more important, through their own behavior. They convey expectations, stress performance, and establish a reward and recognition system that embodies what the organization deems important. In human service organizations a number of key values highly influence staff attitudes and behavior.

Key Values Foster Job Ownership

Employees must care so much about their work and be so invested in it that they do whatever it takes to get the job done. This is *job ownership*. Staff own their jobs when they are committed to working extra hours because a special report has to get done, responding in special ways to the needs of the people they serve, or advocating changes in organizational procedures for the benefit of their clients. How does profound commitment to a job come about? The organizational culture can promote a climate that furthers job ownership by instilling in staff a sense of higher purpose, emotional bonding, trust, stakeholder involvement, and pride in their work.[7]

Higher Purpose. Fortunately, most staff who work in the human service field prefer an organizational culture where people want to make a contribution, serve others, and feel that they are a part of something larger than themselves. They typify the third worker in the following story: A traveler encounters three men at work. Each is asked what he is doing. The first says, "I am laying bricks." The second, "I am making a wall." The third replies, "I am building a cathedral." Staff who share a genuine vision want to grow and excel—not because they are told to do so but because they want to.[8] If staff believe the organization can make a difference, they can be inspired to invest themselves more fully.

In religious settings, the imperative to achieve a sense of higher purpose is referred to as a "calling." But one need not have a religious affiliation to feel a profound sense of dedication. As one manager expressed it, "We are absolutely committed to taking our clients out of poverty forever." She conveys her zeal to accomplish this overriding cultural value. Everyone—office staff, counselors, teachers, job finders, research analysts—can feel this deep commitment. The greater the belief in the significance of their work, the more likely staff invest in achieving results.

Emotional Bonding. An organization in which people deeply care about each other fosters strong allegiances and a powerful sense of togetherness. Their bonding produces feelings of comfort and security. Feeling wanted and cared about, they like to come to work because they find their relationships emotionally and intellectually fulfilling. Fellowship is particularly important in organizations where clients make high demands and work pressures are tremendous.

Trust. This value is not easily defined, but employees know it when they have it, and they also sense when it does not exist. Perhaps when trust exists we tend to take it for granted, but its absence can cause tremendous problems for an organization. If the organization's leadership conveys the expectation that everyone should work hard but managers are seen taking long lunch breaks and not investing time in their own work, mistrust grows. In contrast, a sense of fairness flows throughout the organization if, for example, *everyone*—including managerial staff—experiences a salary cut because of funding reductions.

Trust is built on honest interpersonal relationships. It is based on the assumption that staff are all working for the common good. Certainly, they may evidence self-interest at times, but they must also be willing to put aside their individual agendas for a greater benefit. This value encourages and promotes mutual commitment.

Pride in One's Work. Effective managers encourage staff to be the best they can be. Because of a collective sense of pride, each organizational member gains a reputation for providing a superior quality of service.

Periodically, effective managers ask staff, "What makes you most proud of the organization? What gives you the most satisfaction?" Professional growth contributes to pride. Effective managers present staff with high work standards that are attainable if they expend reasonable effort and if they are given the proper training and supervision. When staff feel proud of what they do, they become concerned if something goes wrong. They ask to be trained so they can improve their performance. They want their organization to invest in them so they can produce quality work.

Developing a Values Statement

Many organizations prepare a *Values Statement,* either as part of their strategic planning process or as a separate endeavor to reflect what they stand for. Each organization will determine what it wants to emphasize. Some will discuss core values. A children's counseling agency would express as one of its values that all children should have a safe and loving environment. A homeless shelter agency would discuss as one of its values the belief in treating all people with dignity. Some organizations express their values in the form of a Best Practices Format, as illustrated in Figure 9.1.

Best Practice Tenets for Working With Those We Serve

1. We build relationships through listening, meeting people where they are, and fully respecting them.

2. Those we serve are our partners; they have shared responsibility and ownership and bring resources to the change process.

3. We seek to create webs of connection for people, assisting those we serve in forming relationships with community supports.

4. We honor diversity, and we respect differences within communities.

5. We are family centered, however broadly "family" is defined.

6. We never give up! We seek to find—or if need be, create—the best options for the consumer of service, whatever and wherever that might be.

7. We start our work from the point of learning the strengths of an individual or family and developing services based on these strengths, skills, and talents.

8. Meeting the needs of those we serve requires the integration and use of a wide array of internal and external services and supports. There is no hierarchy of services—each is critical and equally important.

Figure 9.1   A Values Statement

Adapted from the Catholic Charities Services Corporation of the Catholic Diocese of Cleveland, (2004).

Figure 9.1 illustrates how the managers and staff of one organization became engaged in developing a *Values Statement*. Note the strong commitment this statement makes about being client—not institution—focused. Taking time to periodically revise values can serve to strengthen the organization's commitments and invite new initiatives.[9] Managers can also articulate their organization's values formally and informally at staff meetings, in orientation materials, or during ceremonies honoring staff for their commitment.[10] When staff behavior reflects important and positive organizational values, managers can take steps to expand it, improve it, and reinforce it.

In summary, managers are mindful that the organization's culture has a strong influence on staff behavior and performance. Cultural values are entrenched as traditional ways of thinking and doing and are developed over a long time period. Effective managers can influence the strength of staff values by stressing job ownership, by emphasizing the importance of meeting the needs of service consumers, and by ensuring that work quality encompasses both service delivery and outcome. Every organization would benefit from a periodic examination of its values to determine which need clarifying or modifying. Effective managers must periodically assess how they can help staff make the organization's values their own.

Managing Stress

Imagine seeing this ad in your local newspaper:

> Job opening for a committed professional willing to work long hours for low pay. You will experience many complaints, fatigue, and irritability that will likely result in emotional and physical exhaustion. You may be required to make painful decisions for which you no doubt will be criticized. You will be working with difficult clients who are victims of neglect, abuse, and exploitation and who are living under deplorable conditions. Your supervisors will be demanding and highly critical, and you will have limited opportunities to make decisions. You will never have the resources to do the job properly. You are more likely to experience failure than success. Moreover, because it will be so difficult to measure the results of your efforts, you may not even be aware of success when you do achieve it.

Of course, no such advertisement would ever appear, but the fact that such terms as *job stress* and *job burnout* have become so prevalent is a reflection of the tremendous pressure and demands that human service staff must endure. Stress can at times become so severe that it causes physical and emotional exhaustion.[11] Because stress has become an increasing concern, there may be a tendency to get rid of it altogether. This should not, however, be your objective. It is not only unrealistic, but some stress actually contributes to productivity.

Many employees do work well under pressure; anxiety and tension mobilize their energies. These staff experience "positive stress."[12] In high-performance organizations, staff are expected to function under pressure. They are held accountable for getting results and are constantly pushed to do better. Offsetting this pressure, however, is a sense of accomplishment and being part of a valued team. Hence the goal of service organizations is not to be stress free but to provide a work environment in which the pressures of the job are not so demanding that they immobilize staff.

Organizational Stress Factors

Certainly, the work of many human service organizations is inherently stressful. Staff who make critical decisions regarding whether children should be removed from their homes because of neglect or abuse experience tremendous stress. So do welfare or Red Cross staff who locate emergency housing or employment staff who are responsible for finding jobs for school dropouts. Frustration and tension are, unfortunately, an integral aspect of these jobs, and learning to manage stress is essential.

To be sure, some organizationally-caused stress can be controlled enough to reduce the harmful impact on staff.[13] Organizations should be aware of—and do something about—the following stressors.

Role Ambiguity. If objectives and tasks are unclear, staff may become confused about what is expected of them. Job descriptions and mutually agreed-upon objectives can reduce this uncertainty.[14]

Overload (or Underload) of Work. Some organizations are addicted to work. This is a particularly insidious problem because we value dedication so highly. But when the demands of the job regularly require 60 or 70 hours a week to complete assignments properly, the workload has gotten out of control, not unlike a disease. An organization fostering this problem needs to analyze and seek ways to address its unusual and continual heavy work-load demands. Conversely, an organization may provide professional staff with too little to do; the resultant underachievement engenders feelings of uselessness and boredom among those directly affected—and a sense of inequity among other staff members who resent the way work is distributed.

Contradictory Expectations. Some organizations state one kind of promise or expectation in their mission, but staff experience something quite different in their daily professional lives. The incongruity between the ideal and reality leads staff to become disillusioned and deflated. For example, an organization may espouse the ideal of wanting to improve the lives of poor people but then may require staff to impose layers of regulations on clients before they qualify for services. Contradictory expectations also create stress when staff have to report to multiple lines of authority and juggle the demands of different supervisors. This occurs especially when staff are encouraged to participate on ad hoc problem-solving teams while still maintaining home-base responsibilities. Under these circumstances, staff have the awesome responsibility of reconciling the different priorities of their managers.

Poor Planning. If the management of an organization does not prepare carefully, small problems can be exacerbated, eventually causing undue stress on staff. For example, because of inadequate preparation, a computer error in a public assistance agency results in clients receiving checks in the amount of $3 instead of $300. Because of the system foul-up, staff have an extra burden— on top of their already demanding schedules—of handling clients' understandable complaints. The tremendous feelings of frustration could have been avoided with better planning.

Laid-back Atmosphere. An overly permissive atmosphere can also cause undue stress. Consider, for example, an agency that provides outpatient counseling for teenagers. In its quest to establish a family feeling of warmth and informal relationships, the agency permits a two-hour lunch break, unfocused supervisory sessions in the park, and "shooting the breeze" with teenagers. Because of this commitment to an informal, relaxed atmosphere, however, clients are not required to notify the agency when they must miss their appointments. Moreover, staff are not held accountable for their work, nor do they set objectives. There are no guidelines for handling crises such as suicide attempts. The results: work does not get done, and staff feel that they are overworked because they have to put in 60 hours each week. The laissez-faire atmosphere, paradoxically, causes the staff to feel tremendously burdened and "burned out."

Poor Match Between Staff and Jobs. Stress can occur as a result of staff being assigned work that is beyond their abilities, as, for example, when an effective staff person promoted to a supervisory position finds himself unprepared for the new responsibilities and challenges. Conversely, stress can occur when employees are assigned jobs that only minimally use their skills—for example, highly motivated college graduates being assigned menial, routine work.[15]

The Supervisor's Role in Handling Stress

Staff may need assistance in understanding how their own attitudes can affect their propensity for stress. As supervisor, you should be aware of danger signals and be prepared to assist staff in dealing with job stress. You can anticipate, for example, that staff who start out with enthusiasm and seemingly inexhaustible, youthful energy are headed sooner or later for disillusionment. You know, too, that staff may experience exhaustion from always giving and never receiving.[16] These staff may feel unappreciated or experience excessive, unfulfillable client demands. At the same time, they may be unable to distance themselves sufficiently from work demands to return refreshed the next day. They need guidance to alter their habits that have trapped them in the exhaustion cycle.

The following are suggestions that may help staff manage personally stressful situations.

Help them reconnect with those aspects of their work they truly enjoy. In this way, they can balance problematic parts of the job with those that give them satisfaction. Encourage them to rediscover what attracted them to the job in the first place. Have them list their "sources of joy" and work together to help accentuate those activities.[17]

Put them in touch with a support group of staff who are having similar stress experiences. This could take the form of an informal communication network with colleagues who are experiencing similar kinds of stress or with others outside the organization who are good listeners.[18]

Help identify and change whatever is causing stress. If, for example, time pressures are becoming extraordinary, then develop methods for helping staff to manage time better (as discussed in Chapter 6). By identifying the causes of their stress, you help them take the first step to gain control of it. If they are experiencing stress because of personal problems (e.g., marital problems) or their own emotions, consider referring them to an Employee Assistance Program, if your organization has one. If not, put them in touch with a counseling program outside your agency where they can have confidential discussions.

Provide extra support when they are experiencing a crisis outside of work. As their supervisor, you must not become their therapist, a role that requires a different and special relationship. If your staff member is going through an especially difficult period because of a sick child, a divorce, or a major health problem, you can be available to be a good listener. Knowing that their supervisor cares about them can be of support during a particularly difficult period. Again, if a staff member requires more extensive discussions, referral out to a counseling program would be appropriate.

Recognize that some staff over-invest themselves in their work to the point of exhaustion. For some people, their passion for their work and commitment to their clients, while at first a blessing, can become a curse. For periods of time, they fly high with extraordinary energy and verve, but may eventually become worn out and crash to the ground. Supervisors could think with staff about developing outside interests, like sports, hobbies, or social activities, that could help put the problems of the job in perspective. Positive personal life experiences can greatly assist staff in facing on-the-job tensions.[19]

Assist staff in developing work habits that can help reduce unnecessary tension and anticipate crises. For example, help staff anticipate work assignments so that they do not experience last minute, extraordinary pressures on top of their already demanding schedules. If handling crises is a natural part of the workload, help them develop an "inoculation" to stress. By simulating difficult situations through role playing and by discussing a crisis plan with staff in advance, they learn to handle problems that arise with more skill and sensitivity.[20]

Develop realistic expectations with frustrated staff. Discuss the results of their work and their use of time.[21] Some staff demand more of themselves than the situation can ever allow. For example, given the nature of the particular target population of young cocaine addicts without family supports, recidivism rates are likely to be quite high. Staff need assistance in measuring "success" not in relation to "curing" their clientele but in helping achieve some limited progress with their clients' educational, employment, and social goals.

If all else fails, help them consider leaving the stressful situation. You could consider transferring them to another unit or changing their assignments to better suit their abilities and interests.

In summary, manageable stress is a natural part of a productive organization. It is only when staff find that they are unable to cope with the pressures of the job that negative stress becomes an issue. The best antidote for handling stress is to convey high expectations within a supportive organizational climate. Effective managers help staff address those factors that cause them stress and at the same time take pains to mitigate unnecessary organizational stressors.

Fostering Diversity

Almost half of the United States work force consists of minorities, immigrants, and women. In the human service field, effective managers must foster and nurture work force diversity.

Title VII of the *Civil Rights Act* prohibits discrimination on the basis of race, color, sex, national origin, and religion. The law's protection involves hiring, firing, promotion, compensation, and training. Employment decisions must be based on bona fide occupation qualifications and merits. Discrimination need not be intentional; policies that have discriminatory impact are prohibited. Agency supervisors must have zero tolerance of workplace language that indicates bias or actions that result in different treatment along race or gender lines. It is also considered discrimination to harass employees because of their religious beliefs. Agencies should have a clear, written policy that harassment in the form of slurs directed at an ethnic or religious group is prohibited. This includes harassment based on sexual orientation. For more information on ways to prevent discrimination, refer to the Equal Employment Opportunity Commission Web site: http://www.eeoc.gov.

Because the work force is not homogeneous, scenes like these are becoming more frequent:

A black female supervisor criticizes a white male subordinate for an error he committed on the job, and he feels she is throwing her weight around. . . . Two female colleagues complain about the "bitchiness" of their female supervisor (a term they would not use to describe a male supervisor). . . . A newly hired gay professional feels excluded when two of his heterosexual colleagues do not invite him to lunch. . . . A white supervisor is reluctant to challenge a Hispanic employee for not completing his work on time. . . . An African American male is criticized for being tardy for several consecutive days and feels that he is being singled out because of his race.

These instances involve perceptions and are not easy matters to resolve. They require great sensitivity and understanding. Some managers think that complying with affirmative action requirements is the end of their responsibility. Managers hire qualified minority and female applicants and then place the burden on these new staff members to make the necessary adjustments. But simply placing people of diverse backgrounds together does not necessarily create a positive, culturally rich work atmosphere. Employees naturally tend to cluster with people like themselves and with whom they feel comfortable. This can produce cultural misunderstandings and feelings of prejudice in other staff members. Moreover, as a result of the changing work force, managers find themselves dealing not just with diversity but with unassimilated diversity. People with different cultural backgrounds should not be expected to automatically assimilate.[22] Affirmative action is therefore a necessary, but not sufficient, means of addressing diversity.

To move beyond affirmative action, organizations need to manage diversity in a way that achieves the same productivity and quality from a heterogeneous workforce as from a formerly homogeneous workforce.[23] This should not require compromising standards nor even deny upward mobility to those who demonstrate merit. Rather, competence must count more than ever as each member of the organization is encouraged to perform at his or her fullest potential. The emphasis must be on creating an organizational climate in which all members of the staff are stimulated to do their best work.

Fostering diversity is not a single program for preventing discrimination. Rather, it is a process for developing an environment that works for *all* employees.[24] It involves a holistic approach of creating a cooperative environment in which all kinds of people can reach their full potential in pursuit of organizational objectives.[25] To take advantage of a heterogeneous workforce, effective managers can take such proactive measures as the following:[26]

Establish a baseline of data regarding the number of women and minorities in your organization. This "snapshot" is an essential first step against which future progress toward meeting affirmative action requirements can be assessed. Many government contracts stipulate that the organization must take affirmative action as a condition of receiving funds, and the baseline provides evidence that efforts are being made to hire women and minorities.

Establish guidelines and goals to help managers promote competent minorities and women (e.g., "Increase qualified women in upper level positions from 5% to 20% within the next three years"). Evaluate individual managers on their assigning high-potential minorities and women to pivotal jobs that could lead to upward mobility.

Develop policies to increase the gender diversity of the workforce. Some organizations provide for maternity, disability, and dependent care benefits. They also provide part-time work, flexible work hours, job sharing, work-at-home arrangements, paternity and maternity leaves.

Establish diversity awareness teams, headed by senior staff, to encourage progress for talented minorities and women. They could, for example, initiate mandatory gender and racial awareness training designed to identify practices, procedures, and individual behaviors that work against minorities and women.

Sponsor workplace celebrations of racial, gender, ethnic, and religious differences. Schedule celebration of holidays that are special for different religious and ethnic groups. Make sure all groups are represented, not just major religious ones. Also, be aware that some staff may not wish to participate in any religious holiday festivities.

Create a new paradigm that emphasizes a learning perspective. Establish a climate that encourages people to bring fresh ideas into the organization based on their life experiences. For example, a mental health agency would hire a former mental patient to provide services and to participate in discussions of ways to reach persons with emotional problems. An organization striving to reduce substance abuse in a community would hire a former substance abuser. An employment training program would seek the advice of former clients. Taking advantage of the insights and the skills of these persons greatly enriches the effectiveness of these organizations. (Be aware, however, that federal laws prohibit informing staff of a person's former medical or mental conditions.)

Encourage management staff to examine their assumptions and expectations regarding minority groups. Avoid putting persons in a second class status by expecting less of them in the way of attendance, punctuality, and performance than other people on the staff.[27] Be careful, however, not to establish unrealistically high or unattainable objectives that set up staff for failure. Selecting people to be in a position that they are not qualified for only to meet diversity goals can be harmful both to the people involved and the organization.[28]

Develop or expand summer intern programs with emphasis on minorities and women. Establish recruiting contacts with minority and women's organizations. Advertise in minority and cultural publications.

Conduct regular attitude surveys of the entire organization to determine how and in what ways women and minorities experience prejudicial attitudes. In exit interviews, include questions that determine whether discrimination was a factor in decisions to leave.

Establish "core groups" of 8 to 10 people led, if possible, by a skilled facilitator to stimulate informal discussion and self-development, and encourage staff to candidly express experiences with prejudice in the organization. Those who have concerns about their supervisors' perceived, subtle, prejudicial attitudes may be more likely to communicate directly with facilitators based on support and feedback from the group. The result is that both staff and managers can become more aware of their own biases where these exist.

Assign a mentor to promising persons who may be underrepresented in upper level positions, such as minorities and women, to help them move up the organizational ladder. Coaches should encourage those with whom they are working to ask for help, especially if roadblocks are encountered.

These measures are not intended to give special advantages to underrepresented groups but to ensure that those with talent have an opportunity to get ahead. They are based on the fundamental assumption that diversity is now a reality in the workplace requiring awareness, vigilance, and proactive efforts so that all staff can achieve their potential and contribute fully to the organization.

Harassment in the Workplace

Non-sexual Harassment

It is important to be aware that illegal hostile harassment or creating a hostile environment need not necessarily have anything to do with sexual advances or innuendo. If a supervisor creates a hostile environment for an employee, this may be considered harassment. If a female supervisor treats a male employee differently from the other female employees, then a court ruling could favor the employee. For example, a woman supervisor treats a man differently in her department by setting up unrealistic deadlines, or assigning him a heavier workload than she would female employees. The male employee may seek redress in the courts for sexual harassment on the basis that his supervisor created a hostile environment.

Based on a review of lawsuits in which the employee plaintiff has prevailed, the following are examples of illegal harassment:[29]

- Mimicking someone's speech or accent
- Imposing religious views on others
- Referring to a coworker by a derogatory name
- Singling out a coworker and subjecting him or her to ridicule
- Ostracizing an employee

Promoting a work atmosphere in which people are treated humanely is not only the decent thing to do, it is essential if the organization is to avoid possible lawsuits.

Dealing With Sexual Harassment

Although harassment can take different forms, the most common episodes involve sexual harassment. In many organizations, sexual harassment is grounds for disciplinary action, including dismissal. On the basis of accusations made by clients, any overt sexual advances made by staff to clients or pressuring of clients into sexual acts violate professional ethics and compel termination hearings. Supervisors who use their position to make demands for sex from subordinates abuse their power and should also be terminated.

At times, there can be ambiguity regarding what constitutes sexual harassment. Coworkers can mutually agree to engage in intimate relationships without harassment being a factor. When mutuality is absent, however, and when men and women have different perspectives about their relationships, personal and organizational turmoil can follow. For example, although some employees may think that sexual references or jokes are harmless amusement, others believe these comments are offensive. When an employee puts his or her arm around another employee's shoulder, is it a sign of friendly affection or a sexual overture? Is telling a person that she looks attractive a genuine compliment or a subtle come-on? These interactions between employees in the workplace can be fraught with ambiguities, reflecting signs of friendship or bordering on unwelcome advances. The courts have defined sexual harassment on the job as,

> any unwelcome sexually oriented behavior, demand, comment, or physical contact, initiated by an individual at the workplace, that is a term or condition of employment, a basis for employment decisions, or that interferes with the employee's work or creates a hostile or offensive working environment.[30]

Prohibited behaviors would include offensive sexual flirtation, continued verbal abuse of a sexual nature, graphic verbal commentaries about an individual's behavior, offensive jokes, and social invitations accompanied by discussion of employment conditions or evaluation. Same-sex harassment is prohibited by Title VII of the *Civil Rights Act,* and gender of the harasser and the victim are irrelevant. Supervisors should be aware that the agency can be held responsible if they knew or should have known of harassment of an employee by coworkers. If a staff member complains about being sexually harassed by a client, you should always take the complaint seriously and report it. Also, a person can be a victim even if not directly involved with the harasser. If an employee can prove, for example, that he or she was passed over for a promotion because the other candidate had a sexual relationship with the supervisor, the employee could be a victim of harassment.[31]

To prevent sexual harassment episodes from escalating to an illegal, hostile environment, effective managers can help employees use a variety of self-defense techniques. These techniques are designed to match the intensity of the offense. Through role playing, employees can become comfortable in asserting themselves to stop offensive behavior. For example, employees can ask offenders to refrain from engaging in mild forms of harassment: "Jack, those cartoons on your wall are offensive to me. Would you please remove them." A second technique is to tell the offender that the particular behavior is of concern: "Mary, your sex jokes are bothersome to me, and I would appreciate your stopping them." Another approach is a warning that unless the behavior discontinues, a complaint will be filed: "Bill, that gender slur is unprofessional, and if you do it again I will file a complaint against you." These various techniques are thus designed to help employees recognize when harassment crosses the line and to take action against it.[32]

Should employees feel that they must communicate their concerns beyond communicating with the offender, then agency management should consider the following procedures:[33]

- Make it easy for an employee to register a complaint by establishing clear, written policies and procedures describing how to file a complaint, with whom, and in what form.
- Appoint an investigator from outside the department. This is especially important when a supervisor is accused of harassment. Inform staff that complaints may be registered with the human resources professional, the supervisor's boss, or with top management.
- Ensure that the accuser and the accused understand that false statements can be grounds for discharge.
- Make clear that the accuser cannot withdraw a complaint. Once a charge has been initiated, it must be investigated for the sake of the employee and the protection of the agency.
- If a supervisor is accused of harassment, ensure that he or she understands that any form of retaliation will not be tolerated.
- Give the accused fair and objective consideration when obtaining his or her side of the story.
- Have witnesses sign statements.

In addition to these internal procedures, employees should be informed that if they wish to pursue a legal remedy outside the agency, they can contact their state discrimination agency or the federal Equal Employment Opportunity Commission. They need not have an attorney to file a claim, but they may wish to speak with one who specializes in employment discrimination. Under the *Civil Rights Act* of 1991, victims of sexual harassment are entitled to punitive and compensatory damages for pain and suffering as well as any lost pay.[34]

Because accusations of sexual harassment can be subjective, it is important that protocols be observed so as not to recklessly impugn the reputation of staff. In fact, the offender may not have ulterior motives and may not be aware that the remarks or behavior are offensive. Each situation must be assessed on its own merits, with both parties having an opportunity to resolve their concerns in a confidential manner. Dialogue should occur throughout the organization on possible misuses of power, misperceptions, and insensitivities. The goal should be an atmosphere in which staff operate on a cordial, professional basis.

Dating Policies

Office romances sometimes occur, and policies dealing with them have to be carefully formulated. You do not want to convey to staff that you plan to control their off-the-job activities. However, if such relationships interfere with job performance or create the possibility of a third-party sexual harassment lawsuit, then an organization has the right to enforce a "no dating" policy. This can be particularly troublesome when a supervisor is romantically involved with one of the employees and other employees complain of favored treatment. Your response has to be fair and consistent. You cannot fire an employee for dating the supervisor and then let the supervisor off without consequence. If the romance is causing a problem, document it before taking action in order to deal with a potential lawsuit.[35]

A "no dating" policy is difficult to enforce when coworkers are involved with each other. The focus has to be on whether the romance affects job behavior. For example, if coworkers are overtly romantic and this is causing agency clients to be concerned, or if they are involved in a lovers' quarrel that affects their ability to communicate, these behaviors must be dealt with directly.

_____ Addressing Complacency and Stagnation

Like all living systems, organizations have a tendency to wind down over time. Borrowing from the physical sciences, social systems theory uses the term _entropy_ to describe this tendency of organizations to move toward disintegration.[36] To offset this natural tendency to decline, organizations must be constantly infused with new ideas, new people, and new ways of doing things. Otherwise, individuals and the organization as a whole stagnate.

Sometimes members of the organization are not even aware of stagnation. Staff become entrenched and comfortable in performing the routines of the organization. Managers concentrate on preserving their position and power. Supervisors become complacent about the quality of the work performed by their staff. Successful organizations are especially prone to complacency because everyone rests on the good feelings that come from having achieved the organization's goals. Like a tree in full bloom that is suffering from dry rot, a successful organization can look good from the outside while experiencing inner decay.

As a manager, the antidote to becoming stale on a personal level involves self-renewal and revitalization. Sometimes this requires changing your routine, such as gathering data differently or experimenting with different approaches to carrying out your activities. Sometimes the process of self-examination stimulates you to ask such questions as these: "What have I learned from the past year's experience that I can apply to this year's goals?" "How can I make a special impact on the organization and the people I serve?" and "What skills do I need to truly improve my job performance?"

Sometimes seeking self-renewal by taking on a special assignment engenders new ways of performing your usual activities. The change of pace pushes you out of a rut. The key to this effort is that the responsibility for seeking change rests within you. Self-renewal must be seen as an important personal value that keeps you from retiring on the job.

Be cautious, however, in the quest for self-renewal. While personal growth or new experiences may contribute to the work of the organization, other efforts may be diversionary. Take, for example, the manager who attends more than five or six out-of-town meetings each year. Is the primary purpose to use these meetings as a perquisite ("perk") to get out of town or truly to add value to the work of the local organization? Both the individual and the organization need to scrutinize the self-renewal process to see if it adds value.

Just as individuals must change and adapt, so too must organizations. Both profit and nonprofit organizations can go out of business if they do not continually strive to be relevant to the changing needs of their customers and clients. Adaptation, innovation, and experimentation are ways that organizations evolve to meet changing conditions.

How can an organization keep from becoming unresponsive and inflexible? It can hire dedicated, motivated staff. It can promote qualified, high energy, enthusiastic, prudent risk takers, rather than tired, burnt-out staff (keeping in mind seniority rules). It can foster constructive competition among various units. It can establish a special unit designed to create innovative pilot projects without requiring the initial acceptance of other parts of the organization. It can create a climate of calculated risk taking in which failures are accepted and even honored as "good tries." It can seek partnerships or joint ventures with other organizations to tackle a new problem or deal with an old one in a different way. All these efforts are designed to counter organizational paralysis.

Being Sensitive to Inequities

One factor that distinguishes human service staff from their counterparts in private industry is that they are attracted to their work because of idealism—their desire to help improve the lives of vulnerable people. They expect that their organization will operate with integrity and high-mindedness. Many have had professional education and are imbued with values that may at times be in conflict with expedient measures taken by their organization.

When actions of the organization's management run counter to staff's professional values and expectations, the staff may become deflated, disillusioned, and hostile. This is especially likely to occur when management makes decisions not so much to benefit clients but to make their own jobs easier. Disgruntled staff become less invested in their work because they have lost the caring spirit that originally attracted them to the organization.

It is useful here to distinguish between staff dissatisfaction and low morale. Staff discontent and unhappiness can be based on a number of ongoing concerns: low wages, periodic conflicts, difficulties in working with clients with severe problems. This unhappiness usually results from conditions over which management has little control and is something to be endured equally by all who work in the organization. People can live with their unhappiness and still try to do the best they can.

Low morale, however, is based on a sense of injustice, whether perceived or real. Staff who think they are operating under inequitable conditions have an increased disaffection and even distrust of the organization. In this atmosphere, expect staff productivity to decline.[37]

It is not difficult to find examples of inequities. The following are a few actual examples drawn from several human service organizations:

- A staff committee goes to management requesting flextime. After considerable discussion, the management decides to provide this special arrangement for the managers but not counselors and support staff. The result: bitterness, jealousy, and divisiveness.

- Eleven staff are terminated, and their clients are reassigned to other already overburdened colleagues on the basis that a financial crisis needs to be averted. A month later, top managers are given raises from $2,000 to $5,000. The result: staff are bewildered and resentful at an apparently deceptive approach used to curtail client services.

- Staff in one agency complain that their furniture is old and dilapidated. They are told that no funds are available to buy new furniture. Several months later, a manager buys a $700 desk. The result: an anonymous staff memorandum is circulated throughout the organization detailing this inequitable action.

- Supervisors in one organization use support staff to type term papers for their children, pick up laundry, and bring in their lunches. Support staff are referred to as "girls." The result: staff feel exploited, and the organization is shortchanged because of time tied up in non work-related tasks.[38]

- In an organization dealing with delinquents, a special unit is established to provide intensive counseling to a caseload of no more than 30 juveniles. The remaining staff have to pick up their additional cases, bringing their caseloads to more than 200. The result: the overburdened staff feels resentful and demoralized.

- Job changes are fairly common in the organization, but a supervisor learns through the grapevine that she is being replaced by the director's longtime friend. The result: rumors of cronyism run rampant throughout the agency, and staff wonder whether competency counts.

- Two supervisors in a juvenile delinquency prevention unit decide to go into their own consulting business to deal with juvenile gangs. Staff become aware that they are using agency time to conduct their business. The result: staff are resentful about this conflict of interest and wonder if they should use agency time to pursue their own personal interests.

- Hoping to provide greater challenge to a select number of employees, one agency establishes a pilot program that gives increased autonomy and responsibility to the staff. No effort, however, is made to provide increased pay to accompany the increased responsibilities, nor is there any explanation given about whether increased pay would be forthcoming. The result: staff feel that they are being exploited, and their productivity declines.

These examples have in common a lack of evenhandedness in organizational decisions. Inappropriately favoring some staff over others, providing perquisites, treating staff unfairly, inappropriately discriminating, using agency time to conduct personal business, and exploiting staff may or may not be intentional. Either way, staff probably perceive that the organization is operating with diminished integrity, and this affects their own attitudes and professional performance. Because staff are acutely aware of possible injustices, effective managers must be sensitive to staff's perceptions of unequal treatment while doing all they can to prevent inequitable decision making.

Questions for Discussion _____

1. What values are explicitly expressed in writing by your organization?

2. What values, though not written, are nevertheless obvious? How did you learn about them?

3. Are there discrepancies between your organization's expressed values and actual practices? If there are, what do you think should be done?

4. What does your organization and your supervisor do to help staff deal with stress?

5. What procedures, if any, does your agency have to foster diversity? What do you think of diversity education programs?

6. Does your agency have a policy on sexual harassment? Does your agency provide procedures for dealing with it? Have you seen instances of harassment?

7. Are you aware of inequities occurring in your organization? What recommendations would you consider making to reflect equitable treatment?

Notes

1. T. E. Deal & A. Kennedy, Corporate cultures (Reading, MA: Addison-Wesley, 1982), p. 78; E. H. Schein, *Organizational culture and leadership* (San Francisco: Jossey-Bass, 1986), p. 9.

2. E. H. Schein, Coming to a new awareness of organizational culture, in *The great writings in management and organizational behavior,* ed. L. E. Boone & D. D. Bowen (New York: Random House, 1987), p. 445.

3. E. H. Schein, *Organizational culture*, pp. 450.

4. V. Sathe, Implications of corporate culture: A manager's guide to action, *Organizational Dynamics* (Autumn 1983), p. 22.

5. E. H. Schein, *Organizational culture,* pp. 224–225.

6 E. H. Schein, *Organizational culture,* pp. 451–452.

7. M. Beer, B. Spector, P. R. Lawrence, D. Q. Mills, & R. E. Walton, *Managing human assets* (New York: Free Press, 1984), pp. 81–83; J. H. Boyett & H. P. Conn, *Maximum performance management* (Macomb, IL: Glenridge, 1988), pp. 31–34; R. E. Herman, *Keeping good people: Strategies for solving the dilemma of the decade* (Cleveland, OH: Oakhill, 1990), pp. 74, 286; R. Howard, Values make the company: An interview with Robert Hass, *Harvard Business Review* 68 (May/June 1990), pp. 133–143; T. J. Peters & R. H. Waterman, *In search of excellence: Lessons from America's best run companies* (New York: Harper & Row, 1982), pp. 75–77, 319–325.

8. P. M. Senge, *The fifth discipline* (New York: Doubleday & Currency, 1990), p. 9.

9. D. R. Connor & B. Gold, Hospital corporate culture and its impact on strategic change, *Dimensions in Healthcare* (May 1993), p. 3.

10. D. C. Eadie, *Changing by design* (San Francisco: Jossey-Bass, 1997), pp. 146–148.

11. L. Moss, *Management stress* (Reading, MA: Addison-Wesley, 1981), pp. 94–95.

12. R. E. Herman, *Keeping good people: Strategies for solving the dilemma of the decade* (Cleveland, OH: Oakhill, 1990), pp. 160–162.

13. R. R. Middleman & G. B. Rhodes, *Competent supervision: Making imaginative judgments* (Englewood Cliffs, NJ: Prentice Hall, 1985), pp. 132–135;

A. W. Schaef & D. Fassel, *The addictive organization* (San Francisco: Harper & Row, 1990).

14. L. Moss, pp. 101–102.

15. R. T. Crow & C. A. Odewahn, *Management for the human services* (Englewood Cliffs, NJ: Prentice Hall, 1987), p. 144

16. M. Bramnall & S. Ezell, How burned are you? *Public Welfare* 1 (1981), p. 24.

17. M. L. Kaplan, Labor of love: The joys and stresses of nonprofit management, *Nonprofit World* 3 (1990), p. 28.

18. L. Moss, pp. 200–202.

19. R. B. Flannery, The stress resistant person, *HMS Health Letter* (February 1989), p. 6; J. S. Shepherd, Manage the 5 c's of stress, *Personnel Journal* 4 (1990), pp. 64–69.

20. R. B. Flannery, p. 7.

21. M. L. Kaplan, p. 28.

22. R. R. Thomas, *Beyond race and gender: Unleashing the power of your total workforce by managing diversity* (New York: AMACOM, 1991) p. 174.

23. R. R. Thomas, pp. 109.

24. R. R. Thomas, pp. 10–15.

25. R. R. Thomas, pp. 15, 167; D. A. Thomas & R. J. Ely, Making differences matter: A new paradigm for managing diversity, *Harvard Business Review* 74 (September/October 1996), p. 80.

26. L. Copeland, Learning to manage a multicultural work force, *Training* (May 1988), pp. 1–5; B. Geber, Managing diversity, *Training* (July 1990), pp. 23–30; C. M. Solomon, Careers under glass, *Personnel Journal* 4 (1990): pp. 96–105; R. R. Thomas, From affirmative action to affirming diversity, *Harvard Business Review* 68 (January/February 1990), pp. 107–117; K. Hildebrand, Use leadership training to increase diversity, *Harvard Business Review* 74 (July/August 1996), pp. 53–58.

27. D. A. Thomas & R. J. Ely, p. 90.

28. D. S. Evans & M. Y. Oh, A tailored approach to diversity planning, *Harvard Business Review* 74 (June/July 1996), p. 131.

29. Alexander Hamilton Institute, Inc., *What every manager must know to prevent sexual harassment* (Ramsey, NJ: Author, 1997), pp. 33–35.

30. K. L. Lloyd, *Sexual harassment: How to keep your company out of court* (New York: Panel Publishers, 1991), p. 7; Alexander Hamilton Institute, Inc., *What every manager must know*, pp. 9–10.

31. Alexander Hamilton Institute, Inc., *What every manager must know*, pp. 10–11.

32. R. B. McAfee & D. L. Deadrick, Teach employees to just say "no!", *Human Resource Management* 41, 2 (February 1996), pp. 86–89.

33. Alexander Hamilton Institute, Inc., *What every manager must know*, pp. 18–19; E. Cassedy & K. Nussbaum, *9 to 5: The working woman's guide to office survival* (New York: Penguin, 1983), p. 38; K. L. Lloyd, pp. 47–58; National Institute of Business Management, Inc., *Fire at will: Terminating your employees legally* (New York: Author, 1991), p. 29; *The practical guide to employment law* in *Nonprofit organization management* (New York: Aspen, 2002), p. 4:22.1, 4:27–4:28;

Alexander Hamilton Institute, Inc., *Conducting sexual harassment investigations* (Ramsey, NJ: Author, 2001), pp. 1–30.

34. 9 to 5, Sexual harassment [Brochure] (Cleveland, OH: Author, 1990); R. Sandroff, Sexual harassment: The inside story, *Working Woman* (June 1992), p. 51.

35. Alexander Hamilton Institute, Inc., *What every manager must know*, pp. 19–20.

36. F. K. Barrien, *General and social systems* (New Brunswick, NJ: Rutgers University Press, 1968), pp. 16–53.

37. T. Caplow, *How to run any organization* (Hinsdale, IL: Dryden, 1976), p. 157.

38. E. Cassedy & K. Nussbaum, p. 25.

10 Supervising Staff

anagers face tremendous challenges in dealing with different
supervisory aspects of their jobs. Among them are reconciling the
expectations of superiors with the needs of subordinates, integrating the
many roles they must play, and determining when and how to delegate
assignments. To help them supervise more effectively, managers should
consider applying motivational theories to staff behavior. These aspects will
be covered in this chapter, which concludes with a review of elements of
good supervisory practice.

The Pickle in the Middle

In a children's game, one player runs between two bases while trying not to
be tagged by the catchers on either side. That child is "the pickle in the middle." Managers are frequently the pickle in the middle, caught between the
conflicting expectations of their bosses and those who work under their
supervision. They are often called upon to reconcile the expectations and policies of the organization with the concerns and needs of their subordinates.[1]

Whether a supervisor in a local welfare office, a director in a mental health
clinic, or a unit head of a foster care program, the effective manager must deal
with value conflicts and differing perspectives. Middle managers must truly
understand and accept that there is validity in different points of view. If, for
example, as a middle manager you understand and are committed to the mission and goals of the organization, you can appreciate why it has regulations
that restrict some client services. Simultaneously, you understand that staff
may want to "bend the rules" to increase eligibility for those with whom they
come in contact.[2]

As a result of appreciating different perspectives, managerial loyalties can
be pulled in several directions. Managers' abilities to connect the needs and
requirements of one level of the organization to those of another ultimately
determine their effectiveness. Effective managers work to diminish a "we they"

atmosphere, replacing it with an emphasis on teamwork. Managers could explain to staff, for example, why they must complete the monthly reporting forms that the top administration requires, and also work with the administration to modify the report requirements so that staff can complete the forms with greater ease. At times, some may lean toward advocating for staff because most middle managers have moved up through the ranks and therefore naturally identify with their former peers. They may believe that to sustain staff loyalty they must be willing to advocate for staff concerns. As a result, managers may try to convince the administration to make changes based on the experiences of their staff.

Even if middle managers question a particular change made by top administrators, after making their case, however, they are obligated to help staff understand why the change is necessary and help them implement the new arrangements. Hence middle managers are the ultimate facilitators of communications between different staff levels of an organization.

For new supervisors, the transition from staff to administration can be especially difficult. The new assignment requires giving up roles to which you have become accustomed, learning new skills, and developing different attitudes. You must shift from being involved with clients to vicariously experiencing client progress through staff. You have to replace a narrow and limited perspective with one that is broad and organization-wide. You now have to think about such issues as funding and deployment of staff resources. You have to be willing to delegate and use power judiciously. The friendships you have had with staff need to become muted as you take on supervisory responsibilities.

Because middle managers themselves have to report to people above them, it is important that they tune in to their bosses. It is essential that middle managers determine their bosses' strengths, work performance, and values. This is the secret of "managing" the boss.[3] Middle mangers, however, need to watch the natural tendency to be so invested in their own advancement that they inordinately curry favor from administrative heads, even when they deem it appropriate to challenge positions.

Sometimes departmental staff may want to bypass their own supervisors to complain directly to their managers. Perhaps an immediate supervisor has a personality conflict or a work style that causes problems with a staff member. Under these circumstances, it is important to convey to employees that they need to respect the chain of command and try to work out their problems with their immediate supervisor. Simultaneously, the supervisor may need special coaching or training to build relationships with subordinates. The goal is to avoid undermining the supervisor's authority while working to resolve problems.[4]

Because they are close to day-to-day operations, middle managers typically have insights and creative ideas. Supervisors are in the best position to learn from their staff about what is actually happening at the operational level and therefore to make recommendations that are client friendly. Middle managers are also able to communicate proposed changes across an organization.

During major changes, such as absorbing new programs or working with a new and different cohort of clients, supervisors can help find the right balance between moving too quickly and succumbing to natural staff resistance. As problem solvers, they can figure out how to make the new situation work. As middle managers, supervisors are in the best position to help the organization hold onto its core values and capabilities while simultaneously helping to shift the organization in new strategic directions.[5]

The Supervisor's Multiple Roles

Imagine being in a play where you are the only actor. First, you are the mother, then the uncle, the hero, and finally the villain. Supervisors' daily performances are no less taxing. Each day, supervisors are called upon to play multiple roles. Just as they must reconcile working with different parts of the organization, so too must they reconcile major supervisory roles: coach, judge, explorer, warrior, treasure hunter, media expert, and advocate.

Coach/Counselor. One of the most demanding roles a manager has is that of coaching the staff. As a coach, a manager's primary responsibility is to train staff to attain the goals of both the organization and the unit. The coach must recognize that each employee has a different array of strengths and weaknesses. The manager/coach provides feedback to staff, encourages them to devise their own plans for performance and improvement, and supports their growth. As the situation demands, the coach may provide support and counseling or confront staff with the consequences of their behavior. Throughout all of these activities, the coach conveys a combination of genuine concern for the employee and an expectation that tasks be accomplished.[6]

Effective supervisors practice these coaching techniques:

- Actively listen to your staff so that they know you truly understand their ideas and concerns. Listening carefully enables you to clarify any misunderstandings.
- Help staff reflect on what is happening. In a coaching meeting, for example, you might ask, "What do you think happened and why? What feedback did you receive? Why do you think your reaction was different from others?"
- In helping staff to develop skills, start with those that are easy to master and proceed to those that are more difficult.
- Expect a certain amount of trial and error; if changes require several different behaviors, work on the easiest ones first.
- Set intermediate objectives that lead to an ultimate objective. For example, a staff member who needs to reduce controlling behavior might be encouraged to hold back opinions at meetings until others have had a chance to express their ideas.

- During times of major change, encourage open and honest communication and an understanding of how change will affect staff personally.[7]
- Practice role-playing situations that are particularly troublesome for staff. By walking through the situation and anticipating some of the problem areas, you can help staff gain greater confidence and mastery.

Behavioral change takes place in small increments, and people do not move forward in a straight line. Allow for occasional backsliding.[8]

Judge. As judge, the manager must evaluate the extent to which staff achieve their objectives. If they are not achieved, the manager must diagnose whether the problem lies with the staff, the work environment, or the nature of the task itself. Moreover, if the problem lies with staff, you must determine whether the solution involves skill training or other measures.

To carry out this role, staff should be monitored through formal review procedures (e.g., computerized data or evaluation sessions) or informal, but purposeful, direct contacts with staff. Closely linked to this judging role is the ability to evaluate and then influence the distribution of resources. Pay increases, promotions, or symbolic rewards are connected to employee assessments. In this role of judge, a manager may also be called upon to handle disturbances and resolve differences between staff or units of the organization.[9] The supervisor must also be willing to make difficult and often painful professional decisions. Committed to acting fairly and consistently, the middle manager embraces tough decisions and finds the right balancing points.[10]

Explorer. The manager frequently engages staff as partners in searching for solutions to problems. Involving employees in mutual problem solving, supervisors build the confidence and commitment of their staff. As a pathfinder, the supervisor seeks to understand the basis of the problem but resists jumping prematurely to final answers, encouraging staff to search out constructive options instead. By encouraging staff to develop their own ideas and communicating the genuine belief that staff can develop creative solutions, the supervisor fosters a commitment to exploration.[11] Because communication is so essential to discovering new paths, supervisors must seek out and disseminate information to staff. They must develop a network of contacts both within and outside of the organization.[12]

Competitor. As a person of action, the supervisor seeks higher performance levels. Decreasing levels of productivity galvanizes the supervisor to find ways to achieve better results by coaxing staff to do better. To be an effective competitor, the supervisor must persevere in the face of obstacles. If certain operations are inefficient or unproductive, the supervisor has to make the painful but necessary decision to discontinue them. If the organization or the unit experiences a crisis, the supervisor-as-competitor has the temperament to deal with it forthrightly and to prevail.[13]

Treasure Hunter. Effective supervisors must be ever mindful that the organization's survival depends on generating resources. Supervisors must devote a considerable amount of their time hunting ways to bring new support for their units. This could involve suggesting proposal ideas, identifying governmental funding possibilities, or encouraging volunteers to lend their time to projects. They must also work continuously to preserve the funding that they have previously garnered.

Public Relations Ambassador. As middle managers of their organizations, supervisors frequently have to obtain the support of the public for their programs. In turn, this need requires them to be knowledgeable about ways to communicate their messages in a way that is easily understood.[14] Effective supervisors know that working with the media involves

1. *gaining access* by developing newsworthy items that include sensation, conflict, mystery, celebrity, deviance, and tragedy. A story about middle-aged men teaching swimming at the YMCA is not news; a 92-year-old who rides his motorbike to provide swimming instruction is news.

2. *framing the issue* so that it can be easily understood by the public. Human service managers are well aware that their clients bring complex and interrelated problems. Supervisors recognize that the general public wants quick solutions. But reducing teen pregnancy, helping battered women, or assisting homeless persons to find independent living requires more than memorable slogans. These and other complex issues call for educating the public on factors that significantly contribute to the problem and using the media to communicate the right messages and stories that the public can relate to and understand.[15]

Advocate. To produce change, human service managers may need to engage in various forms of advocacy. Occasionally, management staff may need to be at the forefront of public controversy because this is one of the best ways to get the media to report on an issue. As a result of controversy, the people's level of awareness is raised.[16] Getting rid of alcohol advertisements on billboards in the inner city, challenging the school system to do a better job of educating students, and leading the effort to make agencies more culturally sensitive to the minority populations they serve all affect the lives of agency clients and must be confronted and addressed by both business leaders and policy makers.

These different roles are carried out by various levels of managerial staff. In large organizations, executive managers may concentrate their energies outside the organization—focusing on dealing with the legislature, communicating with the media, and working with publicly elected officials. At the supervisory level, middle managers ensure that staff are carrying out their role properly, see that clients are flowing through the system, check that referrals are being made properly, and that assignments are followed up. In smaller agencies, managers must continually juggle various roles, often simultaneously.

Handling Multiple Roles

Each of these roles must be handled judiciously and not be carried to such an extreme that it interferes or becomes incompatible with the other roles.[17] For example, supervisors should not be so focused on the encouraging and supportive functions of the coaching role that they are unable to fulfill the roles of objective judge and distributor of resources. When sorting out problems, the explorer role is appropriate, but when dealing with a crisis, a supervisor may need to become a competitor, able to implement intrepid decisions.

These different roles are sometimes incompatible because every supervisor has both strengths and limitations. Some are good at being evaluative, while others prefer to be supportive. It is important to assume the proper role as circumstances warrant. The inability to fire an incompetent bookkeeper whose error costs the agency $30,000 reflects a reluctance to carry out the major and necessary supervisory role of judge called for by the situation.

Supervisors need to understand these different roles, assess their own ability to carry them out, and obtain guidance where they need help. This counsel could be obtained either from a formal training program or, more likely, through a mentoring process in which a manager has an opportunity to associate with a role model from within or outside the organization. Handling various and complex roles is difficult; seeking guidance is not a sign of weakness but demonstrates true commitment to addressing concerns.

Although managers can do much to enhance their own productivity and job satisfaction, the organizations they work for must also be sensitive to the level of satisfaction that supervisors are deriving from their jobs. Administrators need to support supervisors who work with staff that provide direct service to the public. The following specific steps can be taken:

- Increasing the autonomy of managers so that they can have greater control and influence over their job tasks
- Increasing salary benefits, professional development, and opportunities for growth for all staff
- Providing adequate organization resources, including adequate support staff and professional backup staff
- Providing an organizational climate that visibly displays respect for direct services and supervisory staff

Clearly, the job satisfaction of supervisors plays an important role in a productive organization.[18] Agency administrators can enhance their sensitivity to line supervisors by periodically spending time in direct contact with those who provide direct service.

Delegating Assignments

If managing is the art of getting things done through working with others, then delegating is the process of giving staff assignments to complete. Delegation is no simple matter, however; it requires considerable planning and follow-through.

Both supervisors and staff can resist delegation. Some managers do not delegate because they fear that their subordinates may upstage them. These managers have an inordinate need to reap full credit. They may fear losing control, do not want to take the time to guide the process, prefer doing the assignment themselves (even when they are pressed for time), or perhaps do not want to invest in developing their subordinates. These problems reside in the delegator. On the other side, staff may resist responsibility because they lack the necessary experience or training, are overloaded with work, or are poorly organized.

These problems must be addressed if staff are to grow in their capabilities and if the work is to get done. By developing staff, effective managers increase the organization's flexibility. Also, by shifting responsibilities from one level of the organization to another, supervisors can free up staff to take on new assignments and expand their skills.

Of course, it is not desirable to delegate every task. Some responsibilities are simply too complicated, confidential, or controversial to pass along. Some tasks require such advanced technical knowledge and judgment that they cannot be easily delegated. And some are so sensitive, such as handling budget information or disciplining staff, that delegation may be inadvisable.

Therefore the issue of "when to delegate" is clearly a delicate one. Delegation must be used judiciously and with careful consideration of the following criteria:

- Select the right people. Delegate according to realistic assessments of strengths, limitations, and task preferences.[19]
- Ensure that assignments are fair and realistic by maintaining continuous communication with staff.
- Distinguish between delegating and dumping. If the assignment is boring, unpleasant, or exceedingly difficult, you could potentially cause ill will to give it to someone else. The best reason to delegate is because the delegatee can do the job better, and the assignment has the potential to spark interest and stimulate growth.[20]
- Make the assignments clear. Staff must understand what the organization expects of them. They should have a clearly spelled out work plan complete with deadlines.[21]

- Delegate tasks to the lowest possible level at which they can be performed satisfactorily to make the most efficient use of organizational resources.[22] Resist making a decision that your staff could make just as easily—even though it might be different than yours—if the result is likely to be a positive one.

- State the constraints (if any) within which staff must operate—for example, a budgetary constraint.

- Determine criteria for selecting employees to take responsibilities on the basis of who can best do the job, who can use time most productively, who wants more responsibility, and who would experience the most professional growth.

- Give staff a voice in the assignment. The delegation process should be a dialogue, not a monologue.[23] Being sensitive to staff preferences is more likely to ensure their completing assignments. Giving staff the opportunity to plan the project can make them feel accountable for its outcome.[24]

- Determine how thoroughly staff understand the task and, based on that understanding, communicate all necessary knowledge to assist them in completing it. Provide specific instructions about what the result should be, and clarify the limits of the employee's responsibility. Anticipate where problems are likely to occur, such as requests for more funding or more staff to carry out the assignment, and establish ground rules for what resources are available (or not) to carry out the project.

- Convey your expectation that if staff encounter problems, they should consider one or more solutions before coming to you. This communicates your confidence that they can work hard to resolve problems and will not become unduly dependent upon you as their ultimate problem solver. Some supervisors subscribe to the parachute principle of, "You pack it, you jump with it." On their own, people are forced to think like entrepreneurs and to implement the assignment without interference.

- Recognize that a fine line exists between no interference and lack of guidance. Occasionally, everyone needs some guidance and some support.[25] Alerting staff to potential problems is a necessary part of delegating as well as communicating where problems might arise. Make yourself available in the event they encounter particularly difficult challenges. Find the right balancing point between letting staff work out their problems and interceding when vexing problems arise.

- Grant authority to get the task done. Responsibility without authority never works. You may have to give your imprimatur to the employee who is carrying out the assignment so that others are aware of your backing.

The following is an example of a conversation in which a supervisor is effectively delegating an assignment to a staff member:

Maria: Ann, I am pleased that in our last two sessions together you have
          come in with good ideas about managing your new responsibili-
          ties. I'm also delighted that you are willing to meet the challenge
          of increasing the number of outreach contacts to women of child-
          bearing age. We have agreed that, within the next four months,
          your unit will reach a minimum of 350 women.

Ann: As we agreed, I am planning to hire two outreach staff, and I will
          be developing a reporting form within two weeks.

Maria: You have this assignment well under control. Can we meet every
          Tuesday, say at 10:00, to discuss any problems and your proposed
          alternatives? Do you have any questions about this assignment? If
          not, I'll send you a memo outlining our mutual decisions about
          this assignment.

Given that managers who delegate assignments are ultimately responsible
for the work of those under them, it is vitally important to maintain control
without limiting the freedom of staff to think and act. If you have made assignments clear and have mutually determined outcomes, then tracking progress
should be fairly easy. Moreover, if you have spelled out a method of feedback,
including a reporting schedule and checkpoints, then you help ensure proper
control of the project. On the one hand, you do not want to "micromanage"
the project or overindulge your own need for information and data. On the
other hand, you must not assume too passive a role so that needed information comes too late to take corrective action. You must clarify that staff must
tell you about any unexpected developments, delays, or problems.

Supervisors should be aware that even when staff members demonstrate
they can manage a situation on their own, they should not be abandoned to
figure out how to deal with discouragement that may be part of the process.
Not working with people as they encounter major challenges could potentially set them up for failure. Hence tracking people to determine appropriate times for providing guidance is essential.[26]

If done well, delegation can release a powerful force that may be latent
within staff. Through their new-found sense of challenge and freedom, staff
may invest as never before.

Applying Motivational
Theories to Improve Performance

Several theories can help explain what motivates people to work productively. If supervisors are familiar with them, these theories can be helpful
in improving job performance.[27] It is probably accurate to state that no one
theory can be used exclusively to explain how best to motivate work
performance. It may be more useful in working with staff to use an eclectic
approach that draws upon several motivational theories.

Maslow's Need Hierarchy

Maslow's Need Hierarchy theory postulates that individuals are motivated to satisfy the following needs: (a) physiological, (b) safety, (c) social, (d) esteem, and (e) self-actualization. The concept that an individual must fulfill the basic needs before a higher need is intuitively appealing, though not necessarily confirmed by empirical studies.[28] The value of the theory is that, for highly skilled professionals, self-actualization plays a significant role in motivating behavior—assuming that the other more basic needs have been satisfied.[29] Effective managers therefore strive to provide projects and activities that can enrich professional growth.

McGregor's Theory X and Theory Y

According to McGregor's Theory, two different assumptions may influence work behavior. Theory X assumes that unless managers are controlling and directive, staff tend to be passive and disinvested. Thus managerial tasks are to persuade, reward, and punish. Theory Y is based on the managerial assumption that staff are not basically passive or resistant but capable of and enthusiastic about assuming responsibility. Hence the managerial task is to engage staff in taking responsibility and initiative for their work performance. Most forward-looking organizations prefer Theory Y.[30]

McClelland's Need for Achievement Theory

McClelland's theory attempts to explain how employees differ in their desire for self-fulfillment. Some have a great need to achieve entrepreneurial success by accomplishing tasks and even keep score by how much money they make. They tend to be independent, high-risk takers. Others in the organization may have a strong need for affiliation—social relationships are more important to them than feelings of accomplishment. Still others have a strong need for power and control over others. McClelland's theory highlights the importance of matching individual needs to job roles. For example, achievement-oriented employees require extraordinary challenges and special recognition for success to sustain their work motivation.[31]

Vroom's Expectancy Theory

Vroom postulated that motivation is influenced by the individual's perception that better performance means greater rewards. Further, these rewards must hold value to the individual. The theory states that various outcomes are important to different employees. Levels of performance should be challenging, yet attainable, and the reward system should be accurate, prompt, visible, and significant.[32]

Herzberg's Hygiene-Motivator Theory

Herzberg's model is based on two frameworks that influence job behavior. The first involves hygiene (external) factors—supervision, salary, working conditions, job security, status, and fringe benefits. They are called "hygiene" factors because they represent preventive or maintenance needs. Their impact on motivation is minimal, but if absent, staff can become dissatisfied. The second framework involves motivational (intrinsic) factors and includes the actual work, growth, and responsibility. These are conditions that directly influence motivation. Unsatisfying work factors will also lead to general dissatisfaction but are not solely responsible for motivational loss.[33]

Empirical research conducted since Herzberg's theory was formulated has shown that certain external factors can indeed motivate behavior. Increases in pay, for example, do affect motivation.[34] The significance of the theory, however, is that it focuses attention on the importance of making the work itself more meaningful and more interesting. Job enrichment is viewed as a major motivator for employee behavior.[35]

These motivational theories offer helpful guidelines in working with staff:

- Expect staff to be genuinely motivated to do a good job. Assume they want to succeed and perform well—if they operate in an atmosphere that helps them succeed.
- Staff are more likely to be motivated toward those goals and objectives that are meaningful to them. The more they can participate in establishing their own goals and performance standards, the more likely they can carry them out.
- Staff should know what is expected of them. They need to understand how the organization in general, and their supervisors in particular, determine that a job is well done. Through expectations, staff gain clarity about the challenges they must meet.
- Staff are motivated in individual and unique ways. They all have different needs—status, affiliation, a sense of accomplishment, financial rewards, and praise. Therefore, it is important to tune in to their individual motivations to find out what they want, and if reasonable, do your best to help them achieve it.

Elements of Good Supervision

Chapter 1 discussed aspects of effective management and good leadership, which are qualities that could be applied to front-line supervisors. After all, they are on the firing line with their staff. These supervisors, however, also have the unique responsibility of dealing one-on-one with staff. To bring out the best in each employee, supervisors must focus on enhancing their supervisory relationships, providing constructive criticism in a non-threatening way, and clearly conveying expectations.

Enhancing the Supervisory Relationship

Effective supervisors follow the guidelines presented in the following paragraphs to help foster positive and productive relationships with staff.

Set and/or identify positive examples for others to follow. This enthusiasm and dedication can be contagious. Staff are keenly aware of whether the supervisor is committed to the work or is merely filling in time. The process of providing positive examples, sometimes known as *reflective modeling,* is based on setting a work ethic that employees can emulate. Give recognition to those who follow your example. Furthermore, communicate respect to your staff and colleagues, de-emphasize your own personal goals and individual recognition in the spirit of being a team player, and take on some of the less desirable assignments to convey that all employees have to pitch in.[36]

Sometimes, other staff convey behaviors and performance that you would like to see emulated. This is the process of identifying and praising the best behavior patterns in your organization. In industry, the term "benchmarking" has come to mean finding the best practices and emulating them. In effect, you are identifying individual performance as benchmarks. By praising those individuals who set high standards, you convey a strong message of what is important.[37] Be cautious, however, of focusing praise on only one or two people, so that an impression of favoritism does not develop.

Take time to know staff. Good supervisors meet with their staff both formally and informally on a regular basis. They take time to find out if staff are satisfied with their jobs and what gives them feelings of achievement. Strive to understand what staff are going through, either because you have been on the firing line like them, or because you have invested in finding out what staff is truly experiencing. If staff sense your empathy for them, they come to see you as responsive to their concerns.[38]

Give clear instructions. Supervisors need to convey specifically what needs to be done, within what time period, and what factors constitute success on a particular project.

"Sell" rather than "tell." To gain the enthusiastic support of staff, supervisors' requests should be accompanied by an explanation of potential benefits for the staff, the unit, or the organization as a whole. The staff should be persuaded, not ordered. In this sense, people are not managed, but rather they are led by capitalizing on their strengths and knowledge.[39]

Foster a collaborative spirit. Get used to saying, "We are on the same team, so when things go well, we share the credit and when problems occur, we work together to resolve them." Some organizations foster this spirit by referring to their staff as associates, not subordinates. This term conveys a respect for the knowledge and expertise that the staff member brings to the position.[40]

Draw the line between supervision and therapy. Being a good listener and being empathetic are important, as long as the focus remains on improving service to clients. An effective supervisor acknowledges, but does not take responsibility for, personal problems of the staff. If personal problems are interfering with job performance and are disruptive to other employees, supervisors must take action, such as referring the employee to a counseling agency or an employee assistance program.

Engage staff in problem solving. Good supervisors actively seek ideas and suggestions from staff to improve productivity. They understand, for example, that direct service staff can probably make helpful suggestions on how best to handle client complaints.[41] Convey that when a problem occurs, or when a mistake is made, everyone can learn from the experience, grow from it, and then move on.

Providing Constructive Criticism

One of the major responsibilities supervisors have is pointing out to staff when their performance is not measuring up to standards. It is tempting to confront staff with what they are doing wrong, but people do not easily change their behavior on the basis of explicit criticism. Sentences that begin with, "Do you realize that . . .," "You have a problem with . . .," or "What you are doing is unacceptable . . ." evoke defensive reactions rather than help staff improve performance. Unfortunately, some supervisors derive great personal satisfaction from putting staff down and being insensitive to their feelings and concerns. Such a self-serving attitude does little to change behavior but it does much to foster resentment and resistance. Certainly, the supervisor does have an obligation to engage staff in improving their performance. The best way to provide constructive criticism is to observe the following:[42]

- Criticism can best be tolerated within a trusting relationship. If the relationship is based on mutual respect, then your staff will know that you can accept mistakes, that criticism is not equated with failure, and that you expect people to learn from their mistakes and grow professionally.
- Provide feedback that is descriptive and specific rather than evaluative and vague. For example, instead of saying, "You have a reputation for being rude with other staff," you might point out specific instances when the staff member behaved inappropriately with coworkers. By being specific, you allow your subordinate to consider whether a destructive pattern is emerging.
- Concentrate on behavior the staff member can change. There is little value in criticizing abilities or behavior patterns over which staff have no control. It only increases their frustration and heightens insecurities about shortcomings.
- Use the "sandwich technique" to convey constructive criticism. Soften the impact of criticism by sandwiching it between appreciation for good work. Find a reason to acknowledge the positive contribution before expressing a concern. After expressing criticism, indicate that the employee may make an even greater contribution once the concern is corrected. (Be mindful, however, that if this approach is used repeatedly and indiscriminately, it can have a ring of insincerity.)[43]

- Time the criticism to be most effective. Usually, you should meet with the staff member as soon as possible after a given behavior occurs. Sometimes, however, you may decide to delay discussion to permit a cooling-off period. You might say, for example, "Our emotions are running high at the moment. Let's take a day to mull it over and then review it."
- Strive to understand what may be affecting poor performance. Could it be feelings of resentment for not having been promoted, fear of break up with a significant other, or an inordinate amount of stress on the job? Without turning the supervisory session into therapy, you could try to understand the problem so that staff can get back on track.[44] Be careful, however, about misinterpreting staff's motivation or intentions in the absence of dialogue because this can create resentment and distrust. It is the height of arrogance to assume that you know why a person said or did something. This may be a difficult suggestion to follow, particularly for those in the helping profession who spend their waking moments thinking about causes of behavior, but it can help you communicate more openly with your staff.
- Be aware that sentences that begin with "You should . . ." immediately cause staff to become defensive. For example, statements like "You shouldn't be so intolerant of your client's behavior," or "You should complete your assignments on time" may cause staff to feel they must defend their positions and deny the problem is theirs. Try, "I would suggest that . . ." as an alternative.
- Consider statements that convey how the staff's behavior affects you and the organization. You might say, for example, "When you do not complete your assignments on time, then I cannot be in a position to assist you" or "When you are intolerant of clients, this reflects badly on the organization, which is working to provide the best possible services to those who need them." You are challenging the behavior but in such a way as to reduce the employee's need to defend and justify it.

Avoiding Supervision Mistakes

There are some things that you should avoid in coaching your staff:

- Do not over control your staff, for this conveys little trust in them. By micro-managing your employees you deny them the opportunity to grow and develop.
- Do not set your employees up for failure by assigning them projects they may not be qualified to handle. Overestimating staff's experience and abilities and then letting them flounder leads to poor performance.
- Do not play with the truth. Even the smallest of lies can affect your credibility. Staff must be able to trust your integrity.

- Do not play favorites. If your staff thinks that you are not objective or that you value some more than others, they lose the team spirit you are trying to engender. Also, do not select some staff as your confidants. The word will get out.
- Do not encourage cliques to operate within the work setting. Yes, you can accept that after work, some staff gravitate to their friends. Cliques within the work setting, however, tend to exclude others, thus fostering anger and resentment.
- Do not create an environment where there is only one way to do things. Identify the unique perspective and skills of each of your staff and build on those.[45]

By avoiding these pitfalls you are more likely to ensure a positive work atmosphere.

Conveying Expectations

With so much emphasis on participation, decision making, and the need for diplomacy in conveying criticism, the reader might easily be misled to believe that supervisors should avoid making demands on staff. Some supervisors may be reluctant to push for growth, to make tough demands on their staff, and to request higher levels of performance. In fact, they may be asking too little from staff, out of fear of either inviting rejection or causing resistance. For some, a relaxed, congenial atmosphere with low expectations is a way to keep work life pleasant and anxiety-free. It is certainly not conducive to creating productive organizations, however.

To counteract complacency, supervisors must convey their expectations. The best way to approach this is to identify an urgent problem, one where it is imperative to obtain results. Is there a shortfall in the number of foster homes? Are staff conducting fewer interviews this month as compared with the last? These are questions that cry out for action, that demand urgently needed improvements. Supervisors, as leaders of their teams, have a responsibility to mobilize their staff to face tough, often frustrating challenges. Although sometimes it may be necessary to protect staff, at other times you may want to keep people in a productive growth mode even it causes some anxiety.[46] When holding discussions with staff, it is the supervisor's responsibility to communicate and agree upon expectations about the tasks at hand. In a climate of identifying and successfully meeting specific objectives, staff can expand their horizons to identify other issues and problems requiring their attention.[47]

The culture and climate of the organization may be such that staff tend to cover up problems with "persistent positiveness."[48] People try to be positive even though they are aware that issues exist, and they look to top management to take responsibility that they themselves should be handling. The consequence of this poor communication, of feigning positive thinking, is that staff do not take the opportunity to explore how their own actions may contribute to the problem. For example, employees may not be completing their record keeping on time, but they deny that this is a problem. When they feel pressured at the end of the month or quarter, they attribute the problem to management's not giving them sufficient time. Good communication could result in exploring why staff do not want to take the time to take on the arduous task of writing. Both management and staff have to admit together, in frank discussion, that a problem exists and needs to be addressed.

Poor performance could also be the result of poor communication between management and staff. If managers' expectations are vague and employees have to guess at what they are supposed to be doing, then their performance is likely to suffer. Clarifying expectations is not simply a matter of setting formal performance standards and measuring accomplishments. It requires extensive and continuous collaboration between management and staff to elicit staff ideas on reasonable performance expectations. The following six-part, mutual interaction process can help the supervisor convey expectations and monitor staff progress:

1. Determine what the staff member is capable of achieving.

2. Decide whether the staff person's abilities are sufficient to the task.

3. Define the work that must be performed.

4. Communicate the assignment.

5. Assess whether the performance matches ability.

6. Identify, where necessary, why the performance was inadequate.

Supervisors must convey their expectations because staff who understand precisely how they must perform tend to work better than those who do not. Managers should continually reinforce expectations in formal evaluations and in writing.

Management by expectations is a two-way street. Managers should not only convey expectations to staff but also understand what staff expect of them. By doing so, managers gain insights into what they need to do to improve overall performance. One interesting approach to obtaining staff feedback is called the "upward performance appraisal."[49] Here, managers provide employees with an anonymous questionnaire asking for ratings on managerial performance in such key areas as communication, team building, motivation, suitability of assignments, and support. In a climate of mutual trust and respect, personal discussions focusing on such questions as, "What am I doing that helps you with your work? What am I doing that hampers you?" can be enlightening.[50] On the manager's part, this requires a great deal of personal security and an ability to react positively to constructive criticism. Being open to ideas from staff brings new insights into improving productivity and helps managers develop closer relationships with their staff.

Supervising Volunteers

Human service organizations depend on volunteers to carry out important functions, and effective managers know that they must give special attention to attracting volunteers, work to retain their initial enthusiasm, and prevent them from drifting away. Because they are not being paid for their work, volunteers must find inherent satisfaction from their efforts, and they must be carefully nurtured if they are to continue to invest in the organization.

Volunteer involvement with agencies is changing from an emphasis on ongoing programs to more of a focus on short term projects. Accordingly, effective managers are making adjustments in the way they are organizing volunteer work. In the past, many volunteers were stay-at-home mothers or retirees who were loyal to one organization; they volunteered to work in programs that required regular attendance and ongoing dedication. Examples would be Big Brothers or ongoing tutoring programs. To continue to attract these kinds of volunteers, managers must recruit carefully and invest heavily in extensive training.

Currently, many volunteers are more oriented to short term projects. Their lives are so packed with obligations and plans that they cannot commit large amounts of time to volunteering. They are interested in having their work organized so that they have a beginning and ending date and specific outcomes. Bringing in accountants to volunteer to improve the agency's accounting system or having a church group take on a painting project are examples. These volunteers want a clear understanding of how many hours they have to devote, and they want to have flexibility. As a result of this change, effective managers must organize work with specific objectives in mind and identify specific tasks that volunteers can carry out.[51]

The following should be kept in mind to make the best use of volunteers:

1. Make sure volunteers find a good match in the organization. Find out why volunteers are interested in your organization, the kind of work they are interested in doing, the skills they bring to the organization, and their time commitment. Based on this information you would then tailor volunteer roles that interest them. Be sure to listen to what they want—and what they do not want—to do, even if they have skills in a particular area. A retired accountant may prefer volunteering with children over helping in the accounting department.

2. Help the volunteers feel connected to the organization by making clear how their activities contribute to the organization's mission and goals. For example, asking volunteers to organize a letter campaign on day care legislation would be much more meaningful if the volunteers understand the

significance of the legislation and how it will impact the community's children. Ask them to be ambassadors in the community to tell the good news of the agency's work.

3. Develop meaningful relationships with volunteers. Learn the names of regularly scheduled volunteers. Personally welcome them to the agency. Ask their opinions at special sessions and meet periodically with a selected group to obtain their ideas. They become even more committed if they sense they truly matter to the agency's managers.[52]

4. Provide social opportunities for volunteers to become acquainted with others in the organization, including other volunteers, staff, and board members. Opportunities to socialize are an important aspect in making the volunteer look forward to coming to the agency.

5. Identify tasks that meet both volunteers' and the agency's needs. Volunteers will accept a certain amount of menial work if they can have other activities that are satisfying. Getting out a fundraising mailing is more easily tolerated if volunteers can participate in fundraising strategy meetings. If they can learn and develop themselves, they will feel enriched and want to continue participating.

6. Make sure that you are well organized and prepared to make good use of volunteers' time. Nothing can be more frustrating than for volunteers to show up eager to contribute only to have to sit around waiting for an assignment. Provide an orientation with written materials covering job descriptions, expectations, duties, confidentiality, safety, major policies and where to seek assistance.

7. Determine the most meaningful form of recognition. It could be an appreciation note to the volunteer's employer, a listing in a program, a certificate, or a newsletter article. A few will not want to be publicly recognized, but most will.[53]

Volunteers can be a valuable resource for the organization, but they must be carefully nurtured and developed.

Questions for Discussion

1. You have just received word from top management that because of managed care you must reduce staff counseling time. The agency does not have sufficient funding to continue providing counseling sessions beyond those authorized by managed care. How would you work with staff to reduce average client sessions from 20 to 6?

2. If you have been motivated by a supervisor, what do you think he or she did? If you haven't been motivated, what could the supervisor have done differently?

3. How would you handle a resistant staff member who did not want to take on an assignment?

4. Normally your agency encourages a highly participative style in which staff come together to make decisions affecting the agency. Typically, staff participate in committees or let their views be known in staff meetings. Now the organization is faced with a crisis that it has never experienced before—a 25% reduction in funding and the likelihood that 20% of the staff must be laid off. Should the staff be involved in determining the criteria for who stays and who goes? What actions, if any, could staff take to soften the layoffs?

5. Ms. Headstrong acknowledges that she is a strong-willed person and this is reflected in her supervisory style. In fact, her leadership vision and track record of getting things done has catapulted her to being the director of the agency. But now she has come to the staff saying that the organization must develop a housing program for homeless persons. In the staff meeting she says, "I know I have been somewhat domineering in the past, but I recognize that for this project to be successful, I will need your support and cooperation." She has asked you to prepare suggestions on how this—and future projects—can be implemented with your enthusiastic participation. What are your suggestions?

6. In your organization, what different roles does your supervisor play?

7. In your organization, what situations have required supervisors to serve as intermediaries?

8. Which motivation theory makes most sense to you? Discuss your choice.

9. How are tasks delegated in your organization? Is the delegation process similar to or different from the one described in the text?

10. What has been your experience in having a supervisor critique your work or convey high expectations?

11. How have volunteers been supervised in your agency? How would you suggest the agency develop or expand a volunteer program?

Notes

1. H. M. Havassy, Effective second-story bureaucrats: Mastering the paradox of diversity, *Social Work* 2 (1990), pp. 103–109.

2. A. Kadushin, *Supervision in social work,* 2nd ed. (New York: Columbia University Press, 1985), pp. 117–333.

3. P. Drucker, *Management challenges for the 21st century* (New York: HarperBusiness, 1999), pp. 184–185.

4. Alexander Hamilton Institute, Inc., *Coaching & counseling: Managers' secrets for improving employee performance* (Ramsey, NJ: Author, 1998), pp. 3–7.

5. Q. N. Huy, In praise of middle managers, *Business Review* 79 (July 2001), pp. 73–79.

6. A. Kadushin, pp. 145–164; A. Lauffer, *Working in social work* (Newbury Park, CA: Sage, 1987), p. 278; R. R. Middleman & G. B. Rhodes, *Competent supervision: Making imaginative judgments* (Englewood Cliffs, NJ: Prentice Hall, 1985), p. 6.

7. Q. N. Huy, pp. 73–79.

8. J. Waldroop & T. Butler, The executive as coach, *Harvard Business Review* 74 (November/December 1996), pp. 111–117.

9. Bureau of Business Practice, *Front line supervisor's standard manual* (Waterford, CT: Bureau of Business Practice, 1989), p. 79; S. Cohen, *The effective public manager: Achieving success in government* (San Francisco: Jossey-Bass, 1988), p. 117; R. E. Herman, *Keeping good people: Strategies for solving the dilemma of the decade* (Cleveland, OH: Oakhill, 1990), p. 192; R. E. McCreight, A five role system for motivating improved performance, *Personnel Journal* 1 (1983), p. 24; H. Mintzberg, The manager's job: folklore and fact, *Business Review* 68 (March/April 1990), p. 171.

10. D. C. Martin, Performance appraisal, 2: Improving the rater's effectiveness, in *Performance appraisal* (New York: American Management Association, 1989), p. 25, pp. 28–33; M. S. Peck, *The road less traveled* (New York: Touchstone, Simon & Schuster, 1978), pp. 76–77.

11. T. Kirby, *The can-do manager* (New York: AMACOM, 1989), p. 49–54.

12. H. Mintzberg, p. 169.

13. R. Brown, *The practical manager's guide to excellence in management* (New York: AMACOM, 1979), p. 113; T. Caplow, *How to run any organization* (Hinsdale, IL: Dryden, 1976), p. 44; A. Lauffer, *Working in social work*, pp. 283–284; R. von Oech, *A kick in the seat of the pants* (New York: Harper & Row, 1986), pp. 115–135.

14. L. Wallack, L. Dorfman, D. Jernigan, & M. Themba, *Media advocacy and public health* (Newbury Park, CA: Sage, 1993), p. 47.

15. L. Wallack, et al., p. 80.

16. L. Wallack, et al., p. 121.

17. D. C. Martin, p. 25.

18. J. E. Poulin, Job satisfaction of social work supervisors and administrators, *Administration in Social Work* 19, 4 (1995), pp. 35–49.

19. S. Cohen, pp. 71–72.

20. M. McCormack, A fine line separates dumping & delegating tasks, *The Plain Dealer* (9 March 1999), p. 5C.

21. P. Drucker, *The effective executive* (New York: Harper & Row, 1985), p. 182; M. McCormack, Giving instructions that make things happen, *The Plain Dealer* (25 November 1997), p. 3C.

22. R. Brown, p. 11.

23. S. Cohen, p. 72.

24. Alexander Hamilton Institute, Inc., *Delegation: How to give it, how to accept it* (Ramsey, NJ: Author, 1997), p. 21.

25. M. McCormack, *Mark H. McCormack on Managing* (West Hollywood, CA: Dove Books, 1996), pp. 93–96; Alexander Hamilton Institute, Inc., *Delegation*, p. 31.

26. K. Blanchard, J. P. Carlos, & A. Randolph, *The 3 keys to empowerment* (San Francisco: Berrett-Koehler, 1999), p. 30.

27. R. T. Crow & C. A. Odewahn, *Management for the human services* (Englewood Cliffs, NJ: Prentice Hall, 1987), pp. 63–67; A. Lauffer, *Careers, colleagues, and conflicts: Understanding gender, race, and ethnicity in the workplace* (Beverly Hills, CA: Sage, 1985), pp. 21–32; G. T. Milkovich & J. W. Boudreau, *Personnel/human resource management*, 5th ed. (Plano, TX: Business Publications, 1988), pp. 167–172; D. Sanzotta, *Motivational theories and applications for managers* (New York: AMACOM, 1977), pp. 17–28; D. E. Terpstra, Theories of motivation: Borrowing the best, *Personnel Journal* 6 (1979), pp. 15–18.

28. E. Terpstra, p. 15.

29. A. H. Maslow, *Motivation and personality* (New York: Harper & Row, 1954).

30. D. McGregor, *The human side of enterprise* (New York: McGraw-Hill, 1960).

31. D. C. McClelland & D. Burnham, Power is the great motivator, *Harvard Business Review* 54 (January/February 1976), pp. 100–111.

32. V. H. Vroom, *Choosing a leadership style: Applying the Vroom & Yetton model* (New York: AMACOM, 1973).

33. F. Herzberg, B. Mausner, & B. Synderman, *The motivation to work* (New York: John Wiley, 1959).

34. D. E. Terpstra, p. 16.

35. F. Herzberg, One more time: How do you motivate employees? *Harvard Business Review* 81 (January 2003), pp. 87–96.

36. Alexander Hamilton Institute, Inc., *Coaching & counseling*, pp. 21–23.

37. M. McCormack, *On communicating* (Los Angeles: Dove Books, 1998), pp. 37–38.

38. R. Brown, p. 62.

39. P. Drucker, Management's new paradigms, *Forbes* (October 1998), p. 166.

40. P. Drucker, Management's new paradigms, p. 164.

41. Bureau of Business Practice, Get the best from your employees, *Front Line Supervisor's Bulletin* 157 (1991), pp. 1–2.

42. S. Ford, *The ABC's of managing with employee teams* (Campbell, CA: Sondra Ford & Associates, 1983), pp. 77–79; T. Gordon, *Leader effectiveness training* (New York: Bantam, 1977); M. S. Peck, pp. 150–153; R. S. Schuler, *Personnel and human resource management*, 3rd ed. (St. Paul, MN: West, 1987), pp. 261–262.

43. Alexander Hamilton Institute, Inc., *Feedback: How to give it, how to get it* (Ramsey, NJ: Author, 2000), p. 12.

44. N. Nicholson, How to motivate your problem people, *Harvard Business Review* 81 (January 2003), pp. 57–65.

45. Alexander Hamilton Institute, Inc., *Coaching & counseling*, pp. 29–31.

46. W. C. Taylor, The leader of the future, *Fast Company* (June 1999), p. 136.

47. R. H. Schaffer, Demand better results and get them, *Harvard Business Review* 69 (January/February 1991), pp. 145–149.

48. C. Argyris, Good communication that blocks learning, *Harvard Business Review* 72 (July/August 1994), p. 82.

49. Bureau of Business Practice, The performance appraisal: Yours, *Front Line Supervisor's Bulletin* 151 (1990), p. 1–3.

50. P. Drucker, *Managing the nonprofit organization* (New York: HarperCollins, 1990), p. 184.

51. W. Murray, Volunteers are changing: How volunteer programs can adapt, *Grassroots Fundraising Journal* 19, 2 (April 2000).

52. S. Ellis, On volunteers: Real motivation, *The Nonprofit Times* 17, 21 (1 November 2003).

53. A. Moore, The volunteer coordinator: Key to a successful volunteer program, *Strategic Governance* 3 (1998), in *Nonprofit organization management,* p. 3:68; R. Brody & M. Nair, *Community service: The art of volunteering and service learning,* 2nd ed. (Wheaton, IL: Gregory, 2000).

11 Appraising and Compensating Performance

E ffective managers in human service organizations, like their counterparts in profit-making enterprises, use performance appraisals as a means of accomplishing several objectives. Appraisals are an important means of connecting staff performance to the organization's mission and goals. They are helpful in focusing on areas requiring staff improvement and training. They contribute to decisions requiring disciplinary action or termination. They also provide feedback on performance that could result in salary increases or staff promotions.[1] It is difficult to imagine any effective organization not conducting performance appraisals of its staff. Because appraisals can have such a profound impact on staff performance, effective managers must periodically review the appraisal content and process to determine their usefulness and relevance to both staff and the organization.

Appraisal Methods

Because no universal appraisal format exists, each organization must develop a customized method to meet its special needs and circumstances. In establishing or revising a particular performance system, consider the following questions:

- Does it reflect organizational values and goals?
- Does it apply qualitative or quantitative standards, or both?
- Is it used primarily for analyzing performance or for such other purposes as salary determination, promotions, reassignments, disciplinary action, or layoffs?
- Are the performance standards acceptable to directors, supervisors, and staff?
- Is the method user-friendly?

- Is it both reliable (i.e., consistent over time and across the entire organization) and valid (i.e., does it actually measure what it is intended to measure)?
- Is it likely to motivate appropriate behavior?

Human service organizations face the continuous problem of whether to focus on behaviors (activities) or outcomes (results). Ideally, effective managers should focus on outcomes; in reality, these can be difficult to measure and can be contaminated by forces outside of staff's control. Frequently, organizations devise evaluation methods that review both behaviors and results.

Organizations typically use one or more of the following appraisal methods: graphic rating scales, critical incidents, behaviorally anchored rating scales, and management by objectives.

Graphic Rating Scale

The graphic rating scale appraisal method is used more frequently in evaluating performance than others. Organizations select those key characteristics—for example, initiative, creativity, job knowledge, dependability, cooperation, reliability, perseverance, and adaptability—that are identified as being most relevant to accomplishing their overall mission and goals.[2]

Ratings can be discrete, such as "outstanding," "good," "acceptable," or "unacceptable," or they can be scaled along a continuum from 1 (poor) to 10 (outstanding). Often scores are given without precise definitions, so that evaluators are able to rate results based on their own subjective interpretations. Sometimes, organizations define each characteristic. For example, the characteristic "takes initiative" might be defined as "carries out assignments with minimum instruction; willing to take risks and experiment with new ideas."

The advantage of graphic rating scales is their convenience and simplicity. If numerical values are given, they can be easily scored and are subject to statistical computations. Each employee can be scored against all others. The disadvantages include selecting inappropriate characteristics, incorrectly scaling them, and giving the illusion of precision when in reality the numbers reflect subjective opinions.[3]

Behaviorally Anchored Rating Scale (BARS)

The behaviorally anchored rating scale (BARS) is similar to the graphic rating scale, except that BARS is quite specific in defining behaviors. Each point along an evaluation continuum is defined in behavioral terms. For example, if one of the behaviors is "relationship to clients," then the rating of "excellent" is defined as "always responding appropriately and being helpful to clients." The rating of "poor" is defined as "acting with hostility and rejection toward clients." The organization determines how it defines "excellent," "competent," and "poor" for each of the qualities being evaluated.[4] Each organization selects those characteristics it considers crucial, such as a commitment to tasks, response to supervision, communication skills, initiative, and analytic ability.

For example, a manager might use the following criteria for evaluating an employee's "knowledge of job":

- *Outstanding:* Has exceptionally thorough knowledge about all facets of the job and its relationship to other jobs. Greatly exceeds job standards.
- *Good:* Has above-average knowledge about most aspects of the job; requires only limited supervision on complex tasks. Exceeds job standards.
- *Average:* Knows the necessary elements of the job to meet the requirements of the job; requires periodic supervision. Meets job standards.
- *Poor:* Knowledge of job is limited; needs additional training or experience in several phases; makes frequent mistakes and requires close supervision. Below job standards.

The advantage of BARS is that it reduces bias among evaluators because the ratings are related to behaviors established by the organization. Evaluators are still influenced by their subjective impressions, although presumably this subjectivity is reduced by their having specific behavioral definitions. Of course, the organization must devote considerable time and effort to developing a customized scale.

Critical Incidents

Critical incidents are descriptions by supervisors or other qualified observers of staff behaviors that are especially effective or ineffective. After the various accounts are recorded and studied, a group rates them on a scale in relation to contributions to the organization. In reality, few human service organizations go to the trouble of identifying a large number of critical incidents to form a scale. Instead, supervisors use this approach to record incidents of behavior that reflect a pattern. For example, the evaluator might note that a staff member met 12 times with various units to develop a workable referral system, or the evaluator would observe that "uncooperativeness" was reflected in the way the employee failed to respond to several staff's requests for information.[5] The greatest value of this method is that it highlights outstanding or poor performance and therefore it can be used to supplement other scales.

Management by Objectives (MBO)

Recall that in Chapter 4 organizational objectives were developed to hold the organization accountable for results. This same approach, usually referred to as management by objectives (MBO), can be used to guide individual staff performance and accountability. Preferably, individual performance objectives and their standards should be mutually developed by staff and their supervisors so that both have a clear idea of how the staff can work to achieve the organization's mission and goals. The advantage of MBO is its flexibility and adaptability in responding to different agency situations and individual staff circumstances over time.

Before evaluating individual employees, the organization should define those key results (or goals) it wants to accomplish for the coming year, such as providing information, increasing revenue, developing an XYZ system, recruiting foster parents, reuniting families, and serving X number of clients. Typically, individual objectives are then linked to selected key results. They can include both normal work expectations and innovations or special areas of improvement. Key results in a human service unit within a public housing authority, for example, could include increasing referrals to ancillary services, mobilizing community resources, counseling individuals, and preparing reports.

Attached to each key result would be specific performance objectives that staff are expected to accomplish annually to achieve results. For example, connected with the key result "increasing referrals to ancillary services" would be the following individual staff objectives:

- Make an average of 20 referrals each month
- Ensure that clients connect with a referral organization 60% of the time

Similarly, connected with the key result "preparing reports" would be the following individual staff objectives:

- Complete reports on clients within an average of five working days
- Complete all administrative report requirements within the schedule specified

Figure 11.1 illustrates examples of management and staff objectives.

The previously discussed objectives are illustrative; each organization and each job category requires careful examination to determine which results should be measured. Some organizations make a distinction between routine and exceptional or innovative objectives. Routine objectives usually remain the same from year to year and reflect the ongoing work expected of staff. Innovative objectives are set for new projects or programs to respond to new circumstances. Also, some effective managers make a distinction in a given job between the objectives established for experienced staff and novices.

To be useful, objectives should emerge from an interactive process in which managers, supervisors, and staff collectively decide on them. For example, in a children's institution, if management and staff mutually determine that monitoring the distribution of medication is an important objective,

Management Objectives

- Maintain an average program capacity of X consumers
- Implement X program
- Cross-train X staff
- Develop X objectives for each staff person
- Write X grants for Y funding during the course of the year
- Administer customer satisfaction surveys
- Reduce deficit in X program by Y amount
- Provide documentation that illustrates X cooperative arrangements with other units
- Reduce cost per unit of client service by X%
- Reduce staff absenteeism by X%
- Reduce staff grievances by X%
- Implement a plan for promoting the organization
- Increase gross operating income by X%
- Complete the quarter with no more than X audit exceptions to all contracts.

Staff Objectives

- Conduct X group activity sessions
- Increase number of clients served by X%
- Match X volunteers with clients
- Give X presentations during the course of the year
- Conduct X home visits
- Contact X service providers for progress reports each month
- Increase average starting wage of job program clients from X to Y
- Increase number of completed placements by X%
- Increase the number of clients completing the program from X% to Y%
- Increase acceptances of recommendations by referral source from X% to Y%
- Increase client satisfaction from X% to Y%

Figure 11.1   Examples of Management and Staff Objectives

they would establish quantifiable objectives for this activity. Because they created the process together (continually modifying it, if necessary), staff should deem it equitable. Staff involvement is essential because no appraisal system is completely objective, and everyone must live with the results.

The following guidelines can help to develop performance objectives:

- Use an achievement-oriented action verb (examples: *implement, complete, write*).
- Specify a target date or time period for each objective.

- State objectives that are realistically attainable and yet challenge staff to stretch themselves.
- Specify a single key result to be accomplished.
- Include a process that requires supervisors and their staffs to mutually agree on the objectives.
- Set objectives that are consistent with resources available, that provide the best return on the investment of time and resources, and that are clear and understandable to employees.
- Be certain that your objectives reflect what you truly want to accomplish. If, for example, "increasing job placements" is a key result your organization has selected, include in the objectives a performance criterion to secure jobs for clients, not just get them job interviews.[6]
- Prepare action plans that are sufficiently detailed to provide clear guidelines for staff behavior.
- Be prepared to renegotiate objectives if circumstances warrant.
- Record the objectives and periodically refer to them to assess progress.[7]

Because of the possibility that objectives may be vague and ambiguous, it is important to establish measurement indicators in advance. For example, if management is concerned about the lack of cooperation between units, then "enhancing cooperation" becomes a key result and would include such specific objectives as "conferring with other units before decisions are made," "holding joint meetings," and "obtaining feedback from colleagues."

Some organizations establish an elaborate point system to quantify how people are performing. For example, foster home placement staff may earn points for having returned children to their biological parents or arranging for permanent placement within a designated time. Case mangers may be given points based on the number of referrals they make and then bonus points for the number of referrals that actually become client contacts. By quantifying results, the organization can more systematically rank staff performance. The organization, however, has to be confident that an objective is truly measurable and does not force staff into being so concerned about achieving points that they ignore other important, but not easily measurable, activities.

Although MBO has the potential for distinguishing mediocre from outstanding employees, it is understandable that an organization may not want to rely solely on it as a means of appraising performance because of inherent measurement problems. Are measurement indicators true reflections of performance? What if an employee's performance is dependent on factors that may not be entirely controllable? These are questions that are often raised about MBO appraisal programs and for which there may not be ready answers.

Some organizations see value in combining a rating system that emphasizes such staff qualities as interpersonal relationships and knowledge with an

MBO appraisal system that emphasizes achievement of results. This provides an evaluation of both staff qualities and accomplishments. In addition, the organization may wish to provide a rating of the contribution the individual makes to the achievement of the department's or the organization's objectives that is above and beyond the individual's objectives. For example, a combined performance appraisal might include the supervisor's assessment of the individual staff member's (1) personal attributes (e.g., job knowledge, interpersonal relationships, work quality, analytical ability, initiative, and dependability); (2) achievement of individual objectives (e.g., make four agency visits to become more familiar with community resources); and (3) assistance in achieving department's objectives (e.g., helping to achieve the department's objective of permanent placements of 90% of children).

Use of Narrative

Regardless of the specific appraisal method an organization uses to obtain a more rounded assessment, it is also generally a good idea to encourage supervisors and staff to engage in discussions about staff performance. These questions might help to facilitate such a dialogue:

- What has the employee done to improve performance since the last evaluation?
- What performance areas should receive special attention in the year ahead?
- What can the employee do to strengthen job performance?
- What are the employee's highest priorities for the coming year?
- What career goals does the employee have?
- What additional training does the employee need to achieve these goals?
- What does the employee think the organization should do to improve?

By discussing these broader issues, staff have an opportunity to think about and articulate how they can enhance their own professional growth and contribute to the organization's productivity. These observations by both the staff member and the supervisor should be written out and become part of the employee's permanent record.

Conducting an Appraisal Conference

Prior to the appraisal conference, and even at the beginning of a staff member's probationary period, the staff member should be given a copy of the appraisal form that will be used to evaluate performance. In this way employees know, long before the appraisal session, what the specific expectations are regarding performance and what behavioral and attitudinal qualities will be reviewed.

Effective managers are aware that, regardless of the format used to evaluate staff, they must carefully prepare for appraisal conferences. They must gather relevant information about performance and compare it with objectives that have been established. Staff should be expected to come to the appraisal conference with information documenting their achievements. In addition, consider the following guidelines in conducting the appraisal conference:

Connect the employee's work to unit objectives and organizational values. Effective managers use the appraisal conference to transmit the values of the organization and what it is trying to achieve. Staff should understand how their efforts tie in with the mission of the organization and the objectives of their department. They need to see how their individual efforts relate to the agency's mission. The measures that apply to the individual must fit within the context of the unit.[8]

Conduct appraisals throughout the year. The end-of-year appraisal should provide an opportunity for reviewing previous discussions. Continuous appraisals are far better for changing behavior than a one-time, annual review session that may contain surprises. The annual review should be used to sum up performance, not shock the employee.[9] In fact, one of the best ways for staff to grow and develop is for the supervisor to take advantage of *teachable moments.* Immediately following a crisis, the supervisor would meet with staff to discuss what went wrong and what the staff member needs to consider doing if this, or a similar, situation were to occur again. It is wise to establish intermediate objectives that can be measured within the next few weeks or few months to determine whether progress has been made.[10] For example, if tardiness is a problem, establish objectives that can be met within the next month. In addition to conferences held throughout the year to deal with special problems, it is desirable that formal appraisal conferences occur at least twice annually to make certain that corrective measures are taken.

Determine desired outcomes in advance. Effective managers prepare for the interview by thinking through what they want to accomplish: What information do you want to impart? What objectives for the coming year do you want to see achieved? What skills do you want staff to develop and how will they develop them? What steps are you prepared to take if the employee does not agree with changing his or her performance? How is the employee likely to react, and how might you respond to that reaction? Always go into an appraisal session with an agenda and be clear on what you want to achieve.

Foster mutual problem solving. Staff should be encouraged to take an active role in the discussion. The atmosphere during the appraisal conference should be one of mutual problem solving. Before jumping to conclusions about the cause of a problem, ask open-ended questions to elicit ideas from the staff. For example, ask what the employee thinks is causing a downturn in performance.[11] Identify together what specific steps the staff member must take to improve performance. For instance, if you have conveyed concern about "lack of initiative," mutually develop specific actions the employee must take to foster more proactive work behavior.

In most performance reviews, encourage employees to do most of the talking. By asking open-ended questions that require thoughtful responses, you encourage the staff member to fully engage in thinking through issues. The following are examples of open-ended questions:

How would you describe your progress this past year?

Why do you think the problem is occurring?

What areas do you think need strengthening?

What concerns do you have about accomplishing your goals and objectives?

By actively listening, you convey respect for your staff's ideas. Only after you have heard what your staff has to say—fully and completely—would you begin to express your own thoughts.[12] It is appropriate for a manager to use the appraisal discussion to offer interpretations and judgments of the employee's performance. In this regard it is important to use "I statements" that are behaviorally specific. For example, instead of using the vague, judgmental term "You should be more responsible," you might say instead, "I'd like you to take more time preparing for your group counseling sessions each week."

Sometimes, staff use the appraisal interview to convey their concerns or complaints about other staff members or about policies and procedures of the organization that they perceive interfere with their work performance. The best approach is to let the staff discuss their concerns and to consider together what some options are to deal with the issue. Especially focus on those aspects that impinge upon the staff member's performance. Show your understanding and your empathy, seek out as many facts as possible, avoid snap decisions, and then determine together what steps might be taken.[13]

By the end of the session, supervisor and staff should develop an action plan with clear objectives, specific target dates, and plans for following up.[14] By emphasizing shared problem solving, you help staff maintain their sense of dignity and respect, thus reducing their defensiveness and making them more responsive to your suggestions for growth and improvement.[15]

Be aware of the following appraisal pitfalls that can creep into the appraisal process:[16]

1. The *recency tendency* focuses on the most recent performance rather than on behavior during the entire rating period.

2. The *halo effect* is based on one characteristic or performance rather than a complete view of the employee.

3. The *average tendency* results in supervisors assessing everyone toward the average as a way of avoiding exceptional ratings they may have to defend.

4. The *forced choice tendency* occurs when supervisors feel they must balance those staff given positive ratings with an equal number of staff given negative ones, whether deserved or not.

5. The *inflation tendency* occurs when supervisors give all their staff indiscriminately high ratings.

Provide meaningful feedback. Discussions about how an employee's personality characteristics negatively affect performance are usually not helpful because they are loaded with value judgments, probably make the employee feel defensive, and hardly ever result in personality change. The emphasis should be on improper behavior that affects the employee's performance.

The best feedback is clear and descriptive, not vague and judgmental. Back up general statements with concrete examples that illustrate thematic concerns. These descriptions, "Does not take sufficient initiative" or "Fails to follow agency procedures" are too vague, but "Needed constant supervision during X project" or "On three occasions, reports were submitted after the deadline" clearly define the problem. Set up a file folder for each staff member, and throughout the year when episodes occur, record information on special achievements or failures or evaluative comments made by other professionals. These data provide specific backup to general observations.

Put major points of the appraisal in writing. It is especially important to write out objectives for the following year, any changes in duties and expectations, and observations that relate to performance. Note particularly agreements and disagreements you as supervisor have with the staff member. Writing out these ideas greatly reduces misunderstandings later.

Some managers are especially uncomfortable about criticizing their subordinates, either verbally or in writing. Their written record of underperforming employees contains instead only positive or neutral observations. Then when the employee's performance deteriorates to the point where the person must be terminated, the supervisor belatedly writes up observations that had never been fully shared with the staff member. This process can surely backfire in court proceedings. It is therefore important to ensure that the written appraisal contains objective statements about performance and that employees are aware of everything that goes into their files.[17]

Mutually determine staff priorities. This is important if the supervisor or the organization wants to augment a staff member's responsibilities. Determine which assignments can be postponed if staff are overloaded. The appraisal conference offers the opportunity to assess how to balance multiple assignments.

Be positive and constructive, not negative and punitive. Be especially watchful regarding the way you express criticism; staff generally think they are performing at their best level. Convey, when it is meaningful to do so, improvements that staff are making or the positive results they are achieving as a prelude to constructive criticism. Be aware, however, that the "good news-bad news" approach can itself become ritualistic. Depending on the person, you may want to vary the pattern. The important thing is that staff are more amenable to criticism when you can genuinely recognize their positive attributes in the context of criticism.

The appraisal conference should provide a positive opportunity to assess past performance and future directions. Effective managers use the conference to provide a forward thrust, a sense that progress has been or can be made, and an affirmation that employees have been contributing and will continue to contribute positively to the goals of the organization. If staff performance has improved following the appraisal conference, then positive feedback—genuine and sincere praise—can be meaningful to your employee. Reinforcing good performance helps sustain improvement.

Compensating Work

In almost every study that asks employees about what is important to them, pay is at the top of the list. Pay and benefits ranked among the most important rewards for employees in different job classifications—managers, professionals, clerical staff, and hourly workers.[18] In human service organizations, pay as a reward for work is certainly an important factor. Although staff hold their jobs out of a deep sense of commitment and a desire to have an impact on the lives of other people, managers know that it is a mistake to take advantage of staff's goodwill by compensating them at a rate below what they are worth. The work must be inherently interesting, but staff must have extrinsic (pay) rewards as well. This section reviews various ways that salary can be used to compensate staff for work: pay based on job, on skills, and on performance. Because pay for performance is of particular interest to managers, it is given special attention. The importance of symbolic rewards will also be discussed.

Job Classification System

In most human service organizations, the usual method of determining pay level is to analyze the value of a job based upon such criteria as education required, technical knowledge, degree of autonomy, and importance of the job to the organization. A rating should be made for each factor, with jobs ranked in a hierarchy. A job salary survey could be conducted by the agency or by an outside organization to determine what other organizations are paying for similarly rated jobs. On the basis of this analysis, administrators can then develop pay ranges for job categories, which are then adjusted for inflation and other market factors.[19]

Organizations using the job classification system pay staff within an established salary range, usually on the basis of seniority. Typically, organizations bound by union agreement, or those that have difficulty in measuring performance, cannot objectively distinguish highly productive from average employees. They are likely to base salaries on length of service in classified jobs. Employees are slotted into specific classifications, each with its own salary range. More experienced staff tend to be at the middle to upper range of their classification; newer, less experienced staff tend to be at the lower end.

Pay based on job classification typically remunerates staff for their job responsibilities, taking into consideration the relationship of a particular job to others both within and outside the organization. The advantage of job classification is that it is a useful way of maintaining equity, because the relative value of the job can be established with some degree of objectivity.[20]

Increases in pay are often made uniform and are intended to keep pace with cost-of-living increases. Thus, if inflation is running at 3%, then pay increases are likely to average about the same. Consistency and equity are hallmarks of the job classification system, and the majority of staff are not likely to express dissatisfaction. Under this system, those who demonstrate outstanding performance may be promoted to supervisory positions.

One of the problems with the job classification system is that pay inequities can occur. Organizations may tend to reward seniority over merit so that longtime workers receive more pay even if they are less productive than their younger colleagues. Length of time on the job, not merit, becomes a primary criterion for pay level.

Another problem is that staff receive significant increases in pay primarily through promotions. A highly skilled counselor may not receive much more in pay than one less skilled because of his or her classification; only by moving up to supervisor can the counselor achieve a significant increase. Movement up the hierarchy, with accompanying responsibilities and increased compensation, is one way exemplary performance is rewarded.

By far the greatest problem associated with job classification systems is that they do not emphasize outstanding achievements. If you know you will receive a modest pay increase just by remaining on the job another year and there are no other values operating to stimulate excellent performance, what incentive is there for excelling in the job? High achievers can feel frustrated because monetary rewards ultimately do not reflect their accomplishments. In a few instances, agencies establish a two-track system so that highly skilled staff may be eligible for pay equal to that of supervisors.

Some organizations establish a culture of high performance expectations instead of relying upon financial incentives. They communicate to staff that they are special people hired to do a special job. Staff are expected to be dedicated to their work and have a strong service commitment. In organizations that are new, have charismatic leadership, promise future opportunities, or provide intrinsically satisfying jobs, this value orientation can be a significant incentive. Be mindful, however, of the inherent danger of relying on charisma, promises, and cheerleading as means of dealing with the absence of adequate financial compensation.

Effective managers work especially hard in a job classification system to change staff mentality from that of "I'm owed it" to that of "I've earned it."[21]

Skill-Based Pay System

Some organizations base pay ranges on a hierarchy of the least skilled to the most skilled. The skill-based evaluation system encourages staff to acquire new skills through on-the-job training or through special internal or external training programs. Staff can move upward through the hierarchy and thereby increase their pay based on increased talent rather than having to jump into a management position. Providing for growth in skills accompanied by pay increases allows upward mobility in organizations that want to reduce management hierarchy and maintain a flat structure. Staff grow within their current positions rather than having to move up the organizational ladder.

In addition to increasing skills in a single specialty area or job classification, some organizations provide opportunities to obtain skills in a number of different jobs across the organization. A secretary, for example, might be encouraged to obtain bookkeeping skills. A public relations representative may develop fundraising skills through a process of cross-training. By achieving these new skills, staff become more valuable to the organization. They are then able to fill in when needed, and the organization benefits further by having greater flexibility. Managers give increased pay to those employees who develop a breadth of skills useful to the organization.

Many human service organizations do not necessarily reward staff for obtaining new skills but expect them to grow on the job. Professional staff who attend training conferences or agency-sponsored workshops for continuing education credits do not receive extra pay because the organization distinguishes this expected professional growth from that which is extraordinary, demanding, and may require several years of specialized training. The latter is more likely to be financially rewarded. An example would be increasing the pay of an employee who attains a master's degree while maintaining regular duties.

One of the problems with a skill-based system is that some staff may reach the top of their skill level and find themselves with no place to go after several years in the same position. In addition, staff who obtain university degrees or special technical training may become more marketable and decide to leave, thereby causing a *brain drain* on the organization. Despite these problems, an organization that emphasizes a skill-based system can benefit from staff who seek constant upgrading of their technical skill levels.

Pay for Performance (PFP)

Pay for performance (PFP) systems adjust the salary based on appraisals of staff performance. Variations occur depending on the extent to which the organization emphasizes rewards. Some organizations, for example, provide across-the-board increases for union staff and PFP for nonunion management staff.

The fundamental purpose of PFP systems is to reward staff for their expenditure of effort, the quality of their work, and most importantly, the results they achieve. It provides special motivation to work hard because staff know that the highest financial rewards go to those whose performance is outstanding.[22] Particularly for achievement-oriented staff, PFP provides that extra incentive for them to function at their optimum level, whereas it conveys to unproductive employees that they will receive little or no financial gain.

PFP permits management to reward staff whose performance contributes to the achievement of the organization's goals and objectives, and helps staff to focus on management priorities. Staff have an incentive to give attention to activities (e.g., completing records) that may not be as appealing as others they might choose (e.g., working with clients). Financial incentives may motivate staff to perform boring or routine administrative chores they might otherwise delay.

Some organizations establish an elaborate point system based on well-defined appraisal measurements that provide for a range of percentage increases. These increases in pay are incorporated in the staff's base salary. An employee paid $30,000 who receives a 5% increase at the end of Year A will have a base salary of $31,500 in Year B. Specific expectations are defined for each position, and management makes weighted judgments based on points assigned to each work category. In a vocational employment program for disabled and disadvantaged persons, staff might be measured as shown in Figure 11.2.

Note in Figure 11.2 the vocational employment agency has developed objective and measurable standards to evaluate a vocational counselor. These standards include number of clients served, number placed, wage rates, and achievement of concrete objectives. A client satisfaction survey is also incorporated. The point system can result in 0–7% salary increases.

As another illustration, a mental health organization establishes PFP for its nonunion managerial staff. The executive staff establishes concrete objectives in discussion with each of the managers. Together they determine that staff performance is to be measured on the basis of achieving one of two major performance ratings: standard or outstanding. To be eligible for an outstanding performance rating, supervisory staff must meet superior performance objectives. Staff who achieve standard performance receive a 3% increase; those few who achieve a superior performance rating (e.g., by obtaining special funding or conducting two additional training programs) can receive a 6% increase. These merit increases are applicable until the base salary reaches the salary ceiling for that particular job classification.

Staff and management jointly develop measurable outcomes so that the definition of success is clear to everyone in advance. A combination of objective and subjective measures is used, although the key to success is the

KEY RESULT AREA	WEIGHT	POINTS EARNED
a. Number of Clients Served		8
1. 250–300	10	
2. 225–249	8	
3. 200–224	5	
4. Less than 200	2	
b. Number of Clients Placed		20
1. 150–175	20	
2. 125–149	15	
3. 100–124	10	
4. 75–99	5	
c. Average Starting Wage		15
1. $6.50 and up	15	
2. $6.25 – $6.49	10	
3. $6.00 – $6.24	7	
4. $5.25 – $5.99	5	
d. Supplementary Objectives		
1. Provide quality quarterly reports	5–15	12
2. Obtain additional funding ranging between $25,000–$100,000	5–15	11
3. Conduct four quality training programs	5–15	14
e. Consumer Satisfaction Survey Results		
1. Fully satisfied	10	
2. Highly satisfied	7	
3. Moderately satisfied	5	5
4. Poorly satisfied	0	
TOTAL		85

In this hypothetical example, the employee received 85 out of a possible 100 points. The employee would be eligible for a pay increase between 3.0% and 4.9%, based on a formula applied to a rating scale. 85 is 50% of the difference between 80% and 89%. The raise is therefore 50% of the difference between 3.0% and 4.9%, or 3.95%.

RATING	PERFORMANCE RATING	SALARY INCREASE
Exceptional	90% – 100%	5.0% – 7.0%
Highly Qualified	80% – 89%	3.0% – 4.9%
Competent	70% – 79%	1.0% – 2.9%
Conditional	60% – 69%	0%

Figure 11.2   Performance Rating Objectives: Vocational Placement Counselor

achievement of results. Consequently, staff buy into the prospect of earning a higher pay level based on their performance, and pay based on accomplishments ultimately becomes a highly regarded value of the organization's culture. Staff also accept that management may exercise a certain amount of judgment in their final decisions on salary increases.

Cautions About Pay for Performance

As increasingly more corporations develop PFP systems, volunteer business leaders will be encouraging human service organizations to follow suit. This pressure, along with the inherent appeal of rewarding outstanding performers and using pay as a primary motivator, may propel agencies to move prematurely without considering all the ramifications. Several caveats should be kept in mind.

There is a natural tendency for staff to overrate themselves and then feel upset when they are not evaluated in the highest category.[23] If the PFP focuses primarily on merit, it could cause all but the superstars to have negative reactions. Studies show that most employees rate their performance in the 80th percentile when they compare themselves with others in the organization. Given the fact that an organization cannot pay everyone in the 80th percentile, it is not surprising that many employees who work in organizations that provide differential pay rewards feel they are underpaid relative to their coworkers.[24]

One of the reasons employees tend to overrate themselves is because supervisors may not provide candid performance evaluations. Not wanting to confront staff with their shortcomings, and concerned that their assessments could have a direct impact on the pay of their subordinates, some supervisors may tend to inflate their evaluations. Consequently, staff develop unrealistic views of themselves and become dissatisfied with their pay.[25] Obviously, for PFP to succeed, employees must understand that they would most likely fall in the middle range of pay increases, with only a few receiving substantive increases. If objectives can be quantified, there is less possibility that employees can overrate themselves; the numbers speak for themselves.

A PFP program assumes that staff can have control over projected achievements, but in reality they may be dependent on factors beyond their control. There are few outcomes in human service organizations that are not subject to external variables.[26] For example, in a juvenile justice program, when probationers get jobs in a growing economy and stay out of jail, juvenile counselors understandably would want to take credit and be rewarded financially for success. But when recidivism is high, in part because probationers cannot find jobs, then staff must operate under a disincentive of no financial rewards. Staff would likely perceive the PFP as being unfair when factors beyond their control influence outcomes negatively.

PFP may not be flexible enough to respond to important changes. Staff evaluations and pay in some agencies are based on meeting predetermined objectives that, during the course of the year, may be put aside for other emerging priorities. The remedy for this situation is a flexible PFP that permits both employee and supervisor to negotiate objectives to be calculated into the PFP system.

If PFP becomes a primary motivator, it could subvert other important organizational values. If staff become psychologically consumed by the pay reward system, their self-worth and motivation may be based almost exclusively on this tangible measure. Consequently, monetary compensation becomes the central driving force for performance and tends to overshadow other desired values. Employees, for example, may become highly competitive and place their own interests over those of their team or unit.[27] In some instances, staff may be tempted to inflate client services because of the pressure to increase their productivity numbers and be eligible for bonuses.

Managers should take this caution seriously and work to keep PFP from becoming the dominant motivator. They need to give continuous attention to the importance of interpersonal relationships, job enrichment, and the significance of providing high-quality service to consumers. Managers need to carefully monitor staff records to ensure that they are accurate. Pay incentives cannot be a substitute for good employment practices; rather, they should be used to reinforce positive work behavior. PFP should be a secondary, not a primary, method of influencing behavior.[28]

Serious measurement problems can affect PFP systems. In the private sector, considerable evidence now exists that in most enterprises, merit pay systems fail to create a close relationship between pay and performance. As a result, these systems fail to motivate employees. In large part, this failure is due to the lack of credible, comprehensive measures of performance. By default the decisions rely on the subjective judgment of managers. These judgments are sometimes seen by subordinates as invalid, unfair, and discriminatory. In the eyes of some employees, merit pay is a fiction, a myth that managers try to perpetuate for the purpose of influencing behavior.[29] This concern about measurement limitations in the private sector needs to be considered by managers in human service organizations.

Objective measures, such as counting interviews or job placements, can appropriately be used in PFP. Organizations must give considerable thought to measuring more subjective accomplishments. This is especially true in organizations that provide some type of counseling as their primary service. It is difficult to measure the extent to which child-parent or marital relationships improve on an aggregated caseload basis. It is also difficult to measure the relative worth of various staff. Does the staff person who recruits the most volunteers deserve a merit increase over the accountant who competently keeps the agency's financial records?

As noted earlier in this chapter, methods of appraising staff may be subject to supervisory bias. When presented with a scale ranging from "poor" to "outstanding," some supervisors tend to rate staff at the upper end of the scale, others rate at the lower end. To avoid skewed ratings, the organization could set strict guidelines for rating staff—for example, only a certain percentage of staff are eligible for the highest pay increases. Even under this arrangement, however, it is possible that the best member of the worst group is given a higher pay increase than the worst member of the best group. If this is likely, top management must take responsibility for overseeing the totality of the PFP system to determine whether it is in fact identifying outstanding employees.

A PFP system is no insurance for continued high performance. Over time, previous pay increases based on high performance become a permanent part of the base pay and are paid in perpetuity.[30] But last year's outstanding performance gives no assurance that this year's will be equally outstanding. Previous high performers may tend to coast. Of course, this criticism also applies to job classification systems where seniority, rather than merit, is built into the base pay. At least the PFP system allows for limiting financial rewards for those who do not perform, even though they may have done so in the past. The disadvantages of building salary increases into the base pay under a PFP system could be mitigated through a one-time bonus system, which is discussed in the next section.

PFP places a strain on supervisors and managers because it is time-consuming and emotionally demanding. Preparation of evaluation materials can be challenging as both staff and management feel pressure to carefully document performance and productivity. Evaluation takes on even greater significance when increases (or decreases) depend on it. Staff would likely want to negotiate objectives and challenge those that their supervisors have established.

Moreover, staff may refuse to embark on a vital new activity during the course of the year, fearing that it could jeopardize other previously established objectives. Or staff may think that supervisors are not giving enough weight to their current activities. These complications mean that supervisors may need to invest themselves as never before in negotiating and renegotiating with their staff. This investment is not necessarily wrong and, in fact, may be essential to fulfill the supervisory role properly; it is listed here as a caveat to acknowledge that PFP can be quite a demanding challenge for supervisors.

In addition, supervisors must understand that if objective measures are limited, the PFP system thrusts them into a more judgmental role, which could affect their usual role as coach and supporter. This may place strains on the relationship with staff, who are well aware that their supervisors have the power to determine whether they receive a $200 or a $1,200 pay increase.

Sufficient funds may not be available to fulfill PFP goals. The PFP system may be appropriate when an organization has additional discretionary funds or when staff salaries lag behind those paid for comparable positions in other human service organizations. When funds are limited, or when long-time, high-achieving staff reach the highest level of their salary scales, however, then PFP becomes more difficult to carry out. When there is only a finite amount of money to distribute, such other demands on the pay system as cost-of-living increases and maintaining salary competitiveness may have to take precedence.[31]

One way to deal with these conflicting demands is to reduce across-the-board pay increases based on the conviction that poor performers should receive no or limited increases (or even layoffs), leaving additional funding available for high performers. The culture of the organization must clearly support this conviction. When top performers reach the maximum of their pay scales after several years of above-average increases, special arrangements must be made so that they do not lose their incentive, such as providing them with a bonus that allows them to be paid above the maximum of their classification.

Special organizational constraints may inhibit the development of PFP. In situations where unions work out contractual arrangements, PFP may be limited to managerial staff. In some instances, an organization may initiate special negotiations with a union. Dealing with the board of trustees presents another constraint. Many trustees appreciate improving productivity and increasing efficiency but balk at giving incentive pay. They think this detracts from the dedication of staff. Because board acceptance is usually required, it is advisable that trustees participate along with management in developing a PFP system.

The best advice for organizations considering PFP is to be prepared to invest a maximum degree of managerial, staff, and board time. While much can be learned from other organizations, each agency must go through its own intense process and prepare a customized program geared to its particular situation. At the very minimum, an incentive system can only be effective if managers assure their staffs that the organization has a clearly defined mission, long-range goals, carefully constructed objectives, good job designs, a performance appraisal system that clearly demonstrates individual accomplishments, and sufficient funds to provide financial rewards.[32]

Bonuses

The advantage of bonuses is that they do not automatically become part of the base pay the following year. Organizations award them only under special circumstances with no guarantee that they are to be repeated. One way of designing a bonus system is to pay a flat rate to everyone in a particular job category and then establish a merit bonus range and pool of money to raise some individuals substantially above that job rate. Each year, the system would require new appraisals and open the total bonus range to each individual, so that past performance gives no assurance of future total pay or bonus.[33]

Although bonuses are usually identified with profit-making organizations, a number of human service organizations (especially those that do not have unions or do not operate under civil service restrictions) have some flexibility in providing bonuses. For example, a career counselor might receive a bonus for placing an extraordinary number of clients in jobs.

A bonus sends a message that the salary an employee earns is based strictly on demonstrated competencies and effort in the current job.[34] It likely has more impact if it is given all at once; a lump sum of $500 has greater significance than $10 payments spread over 50 weeks. Increasingly, private sector companies are establishing bonus plans based on specific performance goals.[35] With the expansion of performance contracting, some human service organizations establish a base salary and one-time bonuses based on producing service units beyond a specified threshold.

Consider this variation on the use of a bonus that motivates staff to *sustain* positive work behavior. Staff receive a bonus in recognition of the work done in Year 1. Their base pay remains unchanged in Year 2, but at the beginning of Year 3, the Year 1 bonus is added to their base rate. Hence there is a one-year delay in increasing the base salary, although they are eligible for another year-end bonus. Of course, staff who do not perform satisfactorily in Year 2 do not have the bonus included in the following year's base rate.

Although there are advantages to giving bonuses, they can create problems. In the absence of clear and acceptable criteria, if only a few staff are awarded bonuses, the majority of staff who did not receive them may come to feel that a few privileged employees receive unwarranted, set-aside income that could have been spread throughout the staff. Perhaps for this reason, some organizations treat bonuses confidentially, though in doing so, run the risk of staff finding out anyway, thereby creating even more resentment.

Another potential problem is that if bonuses are perceived as a way an agency's administration can avoid paying adequate across-the-board annual increases, staff may become resentful. Staff soon catch on that their base pay rate is being manipulated. For example, instead of receiving a 4% increase, most staff in a mid-sized agency receive a 2% increase and also become eligible for a 2% performance bonus, which most receive. The next year, however, their base pay is built only on the 2% increase, and they resent that their base rate is not higher. Bonuses could paradoxically serve as a disincentive if staff sense they are being manipulated. This underscores the importance of investing considerable time with staff to clarify possible misinterpretations.

One additional concern: despite all the management disclaimers to the contrary, employees do expect bonuses to be repeated year after year. When they are not, either because of lack of discretionary money or because someone else is selected for it, staff feel let down. If they feel that they worked just as hard and were just as productive this year as previously, they may be offended by the "demotion."

A bonus plan can best function if it is clearly understood by staff, is easy to calculate, is based on definable results, involves staff in developing the plan, and results in a feeling of fairness among staff.[36] The bonus plan must operate within a context of trust between staff and management. It should be seen as an added incentive over and above an internalized commitment to providing good service.

Unit- and Organization-Wide Pay Plans (Gain-Sharing Plans)

Gain-sharing plans, which are being used more frequently in industry, provide extra funding for particular staff if a unit within the organization or the entire organization meets or exceeds its objectives. Occasionally, a human service organization may find that it has a positive fund balance (surplus) because of staff effort to keep down expenses or raise income. The extra proceeds are then distributed to the staff as a way of celebrating the organization's achievements. This special distribution might be especially welcome if staff have gone one or two years without salary increases. Staff receive this special compensation with the clear understanding that it is not likely to occur annually.

Gain-sharing can stimulate staff to work harder and cooperate with one another. It encourages staff to make suggestions on improving economies and to share ideas that can lead to more effective programs.[37] It works best in a climate of involvement among all levels of staff.[38] Some organizations encourage units to establish group objectives, and if these are met or exceeded, members of the unit receive funding. At a Veteran's Administration Hospital, for example, a unit decides to provide bus tickets for clients instead of having them rely on special transport service, thereby saving the VA thousands of dollars and earning the unit that suggested this idea a group bonus.

In some organizations, one or more units may generate income above and beyond the costs required to run the unit. By selling the organization's products or services or raising new endowment funds, staff may feel that they, and only they, should receive special financial rewards. This presents a dilemma that some organizations handle by stipulating a certain minimum income expectation; beyond that, members of the unit do receive rewards. Other organizations, in keeping with their culture, never provide special rewards based on the expectation that some units will produce income, while others produce non-monetary beneficial results.

The Impact of Monetary Rewards

In the absence of empirical evidence, it is difficult to know unequivocally the extent to which special monetary rewards motivate behavior. For those staff who are self-starting, achievement oriented, and willing to put in extra time, monetary rewards are appealing. For those who want to leave at 5:00 P.M., give a good day's work, not over-invest, and be valued for their seniority, financial incentives may not be significant motivators. What may be satisfying and motivating to one person may be stressful and discouraging to another.[39]

In some organizations, highly committed staff may claim they are not primarily motivated by the money incentive, although they like receiving the lump sum bonus. They strive for a good evaluation; for them money is a way of keeping score and a gauge of how well they are doing. What may be most important to committed staff is that they are paid fairly and are earning a competitive salary compared with others doing similar work.

Because research on the impact of using money as a reward for productivity is limited, organizations may need to consider experimenting with their compensation systems.[40] Using pay as an incentive requires thoughtful and deliberate examination of its potential positive impact on staff as well as its possible pernicious consequences.

The implication of this discussion is that financial rewards can work in certain human service organizations where the cultural values are conducive to it. Financial incentives can induce achievements where (a) staff have participated in their creation, (b) staff accept the idea that they can be rewarded on a graduated basis, (c) increased efforts can potentially be translated into higher income for the organization, and (d) objective measurements can distinguish staff performance.

A pay incentive system should not be used for every organization. It should not be undertaken if performance is difficult to measure in any objective way, if staff are likely to feel the payment system is unfair, if staff have limited control over outcomes, or if financial constraints limit the amount of money that is available.

Because the availability of funds is such an important factor in a PFP system, it warrants special attention. In for-profit organizations, if employees work harder, they presumably attract more customers, and consequently there are more profits to be shared. But in human service organizations, staff do not necessarily reap the rewards of hard work because "customers" often are not able to pay the full cost of services. The organization relies on third-party payments, usually in the form of public funds, insurance, and private donations.

Organizations receiving reimbursement from external funders that require results as a condition for payment (performance contracting) may find pay incentives to be a useful approach (see Chapter 12). Just as the organization itself can be rewarded for achievements by its funder under a performance contract, so too can those super-achievers be rewarded by the organization. For example, if an organization is in the business of placing low-income persons in jobs and its county department of human services provides funding on the basis of the number placed in a given quarter, then when the organization exceeds its goals and is funded at a higher amount, it can pass this extra funding on to staff. Of course, the reverse can be true as well: if the organization does not achieve its goals, then staff may have to face a cut in pay.

When an organization is committed to pay incentives but has only a limited pool of funds to distribute, then the actual amounts high-performing staff receive may be more symbolic than substantive. The pay difference could amount to only $200, hardly enough to be felt over a period of 50 paychecks. Some would argue that such increases are too small to have an impact on staff motivation, particularly given the potential of PFP to damage the self-esteem of those who do not receive a pay increase at all.[41]

Rather than thinking of pay incentives as an "either-or" system, consider their possible use on a continuum. For some organizations, rewarding a few outstanding individuals on an occasional, ad hoc basis may make sense within the context of a job classification system that provides most of the staff with across-the-board raises. For other organizations, an ongoing bonus program can provide lump sums to outstanding individuals without increasing base salaries. Still other organizations can establish a formal pay incentive system that applies to some, but not all, positions within the organization. Moreover, some organizations may develop an appraisal system that combines the subjective judgments of supervisors with the achievement of concrete, measurable objectives. Finally, some human service organizations could develop an elaborate point system that qualifies everyone for PFP on a graduated basis. There will no doubt continue to be considerable experimentation occurring in human service organizations. Effective managers must consider both positive and negative aspects of pay incentives before embarking on a course of action.

Symbolic Rewards

Because compensating staff for accomplishments may present special difficulties, human service organizations should consider other ways of rewarding staff for their performance. The values and the ethos of the organization may require it to use nonfinancial or symbolic methods of influencing employee behavior. Rewarding good performance increases the likelihood that it will continue and provides long-term benefits for the organization.[42]

Because feelings about rewards can be highly subjective, it is important to tune in to what is important to various staff. For instance, a "Worker of the Month" award may motivate paraprofessional staff but may be inappropriate for higher level program specialists in the same organization. Inviting staff to a dinner with the boss may cause some staff to feel anxious, whereas others may welcome it as a special opportunity.[43]

Of course, while employees' wishes are important, the reward system must also consider the needs of the organization. For example, staff may express a preference for time off as a reward for a job well done. But because productivity suffers when good people are given too much time off, staff and management may need to agree upon other rewards.

Rewarding productive behavior need not wait for final achievements, such as the completion of a project. People need to feel that they are making good progress toward achieving an objective. Celebrate milestones on the journey toward the major goal.[44] When acknowledging staff progress, observe more than just the superstars. There are plenty of people backstage—accountants, receptionists, support staff—whose daily acts are worthy of praise. Your attitude should be one of "let's catch people doing something right."[45] It is an unfortunate part of workday experiences that people receive little acknowledgment for doing a good job. Informal, ongoing pat-on-the-back expressions of appreciation can be done regularly and are always welcome.

Some organizations establish a "complimentary interview" procedure in which the employee receives formal commendation for superior performance.[46] Other organizations encourage the practice of sending thank-you notes. An especially good newsletter, an outstanding report, or the delivery of services under trying circumstances are the kind of events that warrant written notes of acknowledgment. Many organizations provide an annual awards program that acknowledges staff in various units for their work. Effective managers make these formal ceremonies a priority in their busy schedules to recognize those staff who have made special contributions. Whether structured or informal, if the appreciation is sincere and based on noteworthy achievement, then you cannot err by giving too much praise.

To avoid the monotony of providing rewards on a routine basis, consider altering the pattern by spontaneously and intermittently proffering symbolic rewards—taking a staff member to lunch, buying a small gift of appreciation, acknowledging their good performance to their peers in the next staff meeting. When staff are truly surprised by thanks, they appreciate it all the more.[47]

Sometimes, unfortunately, a meaningful acknowledgment practice dies out because of the lack of commitment to continuing it. Too many offices have half-filled Employee of the Month plaques adorning the walls because new administrations discontinued the practice.

One way to provide staff with formal public acknowledgment is to have them make a presentation of their work to the board of trustees or to public officials. Providing them with this audience allows them to gain recognition in the community because it broadens the circle of significant people who are aware of what they have done. Giving staff this opportunity assumes they have the confidence and communication skills to make a good presentation. If they do not, it could backfire.

Here are some other ways to recognize performance:[48]

- An important assignment
- A celebratory party for a department's accomplishment
- A gift certificate for merchandise
- Modest financial rewards (e.g., $50)
- An article about their accomplishments in the organization's newsletter
- A status symbol, such as a new title or a special parking spot

- Assignment to serve as acting head of a unit in the supervisor's temporary absence
- Opportunity to attend workshops and conferences
- A memo to your own boss citing your subordinate's accomplishment
- A move to a more prestigious office
- Appointment as chair of a special project
- An informal breakfast with the Executive Director and one or more staff members who have done something special
- Encouragement of coworkers to post congratulatory notes on a "thank you" bulletin board to acknowledge helpful deeds
- Provision of a "personal touch," such as bringing flowers from your garden or homemade cookies, which conveys special personalized appreciation
- Staff invitation to an important meeting

The issue of non-monetary rewards may seem to be a self-evident one, but unfortunately many organizations fail to regularly give any appreciation to staff for the work they do. Effective managers in highly productive organizations give considerable attention to this issue. As Peters and Waterman indicate in their study of profit-making organizations, "We were struck by the wealth of non-monetary incentives used by excellent companies. Nothing is more powerful than positive reinforcement. Everybody uses it. But top performers, almost alone, use it extensively."[49] Through explicit acknowledgment of successful performance, you reinforce the notion that staff are winners and, in all likelihood, this will enhance their sense of self-worth and encourage continued high performance.

Questions for Discussion

1. What kind of appraisal form (graphic rating scale, behaviorally anchored rating scale, critical incident report, or management by objectives) does your agency use? How would you modify it?

2. What has been your experience with appraisal conferences? What have you found to be most (or least) helpful?

3. How would you conduct an appraisal interview of a staff member who has been with the agency for two years and who does a generally good job but who rarely completes reports on time?

4. What compensation system is used in your agency—job classification, skill based, pay for performance, bonus and/or gain sharing? What do you see as the advantages or disadvantages of your organization's system?

5. Would you recommend pay for performance in your organization? Under what circumstances would it work?

6. Do you think bonuses would benefit your organization? How could they be set up?

7. In what non-monetary ways does your organization communicate its appreciation for staff accomplishments? What more could be done?

Notes

1. D. Cherrington, *Personnel management: The management of human resources,* 2nd ed. (Dubuque, IA: William C. Brown, 1987), pp. 237–238.

2. G. T. Milkovich & J. W. Boudreau, *Personnel/human resource management,* 5th ed. (Plano, TX: Business Publications, 1988), pp. 195–196.

3. D. Cherrington, pp. 248–249.

4. D. Cherrington, p. 252.

5. G. T. Milkovich & J. W. Boudreau, pp. 200–203; P. J. Pecora & M. J. Austin, *Managing human services personnel* (Newbury Park, CA: Sage, 1987), pp. 77–84; Alexander Hamilton Institute, Inc., *Lawsuit-free documentation: A manager's guide to fair and legal recordkeeping* (Ramsey, NJ: Author, 2001), pp. 12–21.

6. D. D. McConkey, *MBO for nonprofit organizations* (New York: AMACOM, 1975); P. J. Pecora & M. J. Austin, p. 75.

7. J. Stratton, ed. *Board and administrator* (New York: Aspen, 2001), in *Nonprofit organization management* (New York: Aspen, 2002), p. 3:32.

8. J. H. Boyett & H. P. Conn, Developing white-collar performance measurement, *National Productivity Review* (Summer 1988), pp. 209–218; Tarkenton Productivity Group, *Motivational theories and applications for managers* (New York: AMACOM, 1977), pp. 1–2.

9. D. Sanzotta, *Motivational theories and applications for managers* (New York: AMACOM, 1977), p. 89.

10. Alexander Hamilton Institute, Inc., *Conducting successful appraisal interviews* (Maywood, NJ: Author, 1991), p. 12.

11. Alexander Hamilton Institute, Inc., *Conducting successful appraisal interviews,* p. 16.

12. Alexander Hamilton Institute, Inc., *Conducting successful appraisal interviews: The right way to discuss employee performance* (Ramsey, NJ: Author, 1998), pp. 10–11.

13. Alexander Hamilton Institute Inc., *Conducting successful appraisal interviews: The right way,* pp. 13–17.

14. S. D. Bruce, *Every manager's guide to better appraisal and discipline interviewing* (Madison, CT: Business and Legal Reports, 1989), p. 223.

15. D. C. Martin, Performance appraisal, 2: Improving the rater's effectiveness, in *Performance Appraisal* (New York: American Management Association, 1989), pp. 26–28.

16. S. D. Bruce, pp. 16–17; D. Cherrington, pp. 238–239; R. I. Henderson, *Compensation management: Rewarding performance* (Englewood Cliffs, NJ: Prentice Hall, 1989), p. 318.

17. Alexander Hamilton Institute, Inc., *Conducting successful appraisal interviews: The right way*, pp. 30–31.

18. M. Beer, B. Spector, P. R. Lawrence, D. Q. Mills, & R. E. Walton, *Managing human assets* (New York: Free Press, 1984), p. 118.

19. M. Beer et al., pp. 131–132; J. H. Boyett & H. P. Conn, *Maximum performance management* (Macomb, IL: Glenbridge, 1988), p. 178; M. C. Haller, The new balancing act: Variable but equitable pay, *Human Resources Professional* (July/August 1989), p. 31.

20. G. T. Milkovich & J. W. Boudreau, pp. 716–717.

21. R. I. Henderson, p. 286

22. W. C. Nelson, Incentive based management for nonprofit organizations, *Nonprofit Management and Leadership* 1 (1991), pp. 59–69.

23. T. Caplow, *How to run any organization* (Hinsdale, IL: Dryden, 1976), pp. 153–156.

24. M. Beer et al., p. 119; T. Rollins, Pay for performance: Is it worth the trouble? in *Performance and Rewards: Linking Pay to Performance* (Alexandria, VA: Society for Human Resource Management, 1989), p. 12.

25. M. Beer et al., p. 120.

26. M. Beer et al., p. 141.

27. J. H. Boyett & H. P. Conn, p. 195; P. C. Jordan, Effects of an extrinsic reward on intrinsic motivation: A field experiment, *Academy of Management Journal* 29, 2 (1986), pp. 405–412; E. E. Lawler, III, Pay for performance: A strategic analysis, in *Compensation and Benefits,* ed. L. Gomez-Mejia (Washington, DC: Bureau of National Affairs, 1989), p. 150.

28. W. C. Nelson, p. 59–58; A. Pileggi & D. T. Hickey, Incentive pay plans, *Nonprofit Management Strategies* 6 (1991), pp. 1–3.

29. E. E. Lawler, III, p. 151.

30. B. P. Maclean, Value added pay beats traditional merit programs, *Personnel Journal* 9 (1990), p. 46.

31. W. L. Mihal, More research is needed: Goals may motivate better, *Personnel Administrator* (October 1983), pp. 63–68.

32. E. E. Lawler, III, p. 155; W. C. Nelson, pp. 59–69.

33. E. E. Lawler, III, p. 153.

34. B. P. Maclean, pp. 46–51.

35. R. I. Henderson, p. 298.

36. R. S. Schuler, *Personnel and human resource management,* 3rd ed. (St. Paul, MN: West, 1987), p. 349.

37. E. E. Lawler, III, p. 152.

38. M. Beer et al., p. 145; J. H. Boyett & H. P. Conn, p. 198.

39. R. I. Henderson, p. 292.

40. R. Steinberg, Profits and incentive compensation in nonprofit firms, *Nonprofit Management and Leadership* 2 (1990), pp. 137–149.

41. M. Beer et al., p. 143.

42. J. H. Boyett & H. P. Conn, pp. 144–170.

43. J. H. Boyett & H. P. Conn, p. 143.

44. Alexander Hamilton Institute, Inc., *A manager's guide to motivating without money* (Ramsey, NJ: Author, 1999), pp. 5–6.

45. R. E. Herman, *Keeping good people: Strategies for solving the dilemma of the decade* (Cleveland, OH: Oakhill, 1990), p. 132.

46. J. P. Cangemi & J. C. Claypool, Complimentary interviews: A system for rewarding outstanding employees, *Personnel Journal* 2 (1978), pp. 87–90.

47. Alexander Hamilton Institute, Inc., *A manager's guide to motivating without money,* p. 15.

48. S. Cohen, *The effective public manager: Achieving success in government* (San Francisco: Jossey-Bass, 1988), p. 41; R. E. Herman, pp. 134–135; W. Nord & J. L. McAdams, Performance-based reward systems: Which will work best for you? *Human Resources Professional* (May/June 1989), p. 32; Alexander Hamilton Institute, Inc., *A manager's guide to motivating without money,* pp. 9–38.

49. T. J. Peters & R. H. Waterman, *In search of excellence: Lessons from America's best run companies* (New York: Harper & Row, 1982), p. 269.

PART III

Enhancing Agency Survivability

Chapter 12: Managing Agency Finances

Chapter 13: Strategic Resource Development I

Chapter 14: Strategic Resource Development II

Chapter 15: Preparing Effective Proposals

Chapter 16: Seeking Funding

In this part you will learn how to

- ❖ Prepare a budget

- ❖ Monitor income and expenses

- ❖ Determine managerial budget decisions based on variances

- ❖ Consider a variety of cost-cutting measures

- ❖ Develop specific approaches to resource development, including writing a case statement, preparing an annual fund drive, working on a capital campaign, soliciting major gifts, raising funds from corporations, mounting a planned giving campaign, conducting special events, using the Internet to raise funds, and developing a business plan

- ❖ Write an effective funding proposal

- ❖ Review criteria that funders use to evaluate proposals

- ❖ Seek funding from foundations and government agencies

12 Managing Agency Finances

Understanding the Budgeting Process

No matter how well you perform your non-financial managerial responsibilities, if the "money is funny" and if the budget is off kilter, you are heading for trouble. In a turbulent economic environment, human service managers must develop a keen understanding of the budgeting process to manage their resources more effectively. This chapter reviews the budgeting process to help you provide better managerial oversight and gain managerial mastery over agency finances. Subsequent chapters focus on ways to increase revenues.

A *budget* is a plan for anticipating income and expenses to achieve specific objectives within a certain time period. To mount an effective budgeting process, you need to consider past financial experiences, be aware of current information about organizational programs, and identify future assumptions. Budgets guide you in implementing policies, allow you to determine the organization's financial health, give direction for acquiring and using resources, anticipate operational expenses and the income needed to pay for those expenses, and offer ways to control spending to avoid deficits.[1] A financial plan should be integrated into the overall strategic planning process undertaken by the organization.[2]

The budgeting process should involve the perspectives, priorities, and needs of several constituencies: the board of trustees, staff, donors, clients, and public officials. Budgeting is also an ongoing process; data are continuously being gathered and analyzed, and projections and assumptions are continually being revised. New information can lead to budget changes.

Human service agencies use several different budgeting formats to reflect projected income and expenses. These formats are not mutually exclusive and can be combined in various ways. The most commonly used budget formats are *line item, performance, program, support services (administrative), operating, incremental,* and *zero-based.* In addition, it is important to understand the categories *capital budgeting* and *cash flow budgeting* to be discussed subsequently.

The *line-item budget* is widely used in both public and voluntary human service agencies because of its simplicity in reporting. It allows for managerial oversight for the agency's overall income and expenses, but does not attempt to distinguish income and expenses related to specific programs. Nor does it provide sufficient information about how various programs are faring in relation to the intended objectives.

Performance budgeting relates agency expenses to program units of service.[3] For example, if the total program cost for counseling services for a fiscal year is $200,000, and the agency provides 5,000 counseling hours, then the cost per counseling unit hour is $40. Performance budgeting provides an understanding of the productivity and efficiency of a human service program. Calculating an agency's cost per unit of service helps an administrator better understand and control costs.

Program (outcome) budgeting systems require dividing the total cost for the fiscal year by the number of outcomes to achieve a cost per outcome.[4] For example, if the total cost for a homemakers' services program for the fiscal year is $50,000, and the agency maintains that 100 clients are able to remain in their own homes as a result of the program, then the cost per client outcome is $500. Through program budgeting, an agency can translate increases and decreases in agency funding to increases and decreases in its ability to impact the lives of clients. Many agencies strive to achieve outcome performance measures, but these are difficult to develop, and reporting performance outcomes continues to be an elusive goal. As noted in Chapter 3 on designing programs, some outcomes are long-term and not necessarily compatible with an annual budget timeline.[5]

The *support service (administrative) budget* involves expenditures required to administer agency services or to conduct fundraising activities for the entire organization. The *operating budget* is a composite of the program budget and the support services budget. The budget model shown in Table 12.1 reflects a combination of line item, program, and operating budgets.

Most of the organization's expenses should be related to program services. The agency's funders want assurance that by far the greater portion of the budget is devoted to programs rather than to support services. The operating budget of the Hypothetical Agency Inc. totals $1,176,600. Of this amount, $358,700 is devoted to support services, which represents 30.5% of the total budget ($358,700 ÷ $1,176,600). To some outside funders, devoting 30.5% of the total budget for support services may seem excessive unless it can be justified that extraordinary fundraising expenses are being incurred for future development of the agency. There is no magic formula for the proper balance between support services and program services, though many outside funders prefer that support services be under 20%. Whatever the percentage, managers need to make a case to justify the amount being spent on administration and fundraising. Both management and the board need to focus on this issue.[6]

Table 12.1   Hypothetical Agency, Inc. Operating Budget

Hypothetical Agency Inc.
Operating Budget - Expenditures 20XX

	Program Services ($)				Support Services ($)			Total Agency
	Day Care	Foster Home Care	Counseling	Total	Management & General	Fundraising	Total	
Salaries	$121,000	$73,300	$210,000	$404,300	$120,300	$87,400	$207,700	$612,000
Fringe Benefits & Payroll Taxes	34,100	18,600	57,600	110,300	28,300	24,100	52,400	162,700
Total Salaries & Fringe Benefits	$155,100	$91,900	$267,600	$514,600	$148,600	$111,500	$260,100	$774,700
Supplies	29,300	18,300	3,600	51,200	5,000	4,900	9,900	61,100
Telephone	19,600	2,900	3,500	26,000	4,000	10,100	14,100	40,100
Postage	7,000	3,700	9,700	20,400	2,100	21,200	23,300	43,700
Occupancy	47,100	17,800	25,700	90,600	4,400	3,500	7,900	98,500
Equipment	8,700	3,300	3,200	15,200	4,200	2,000	6,200	21,400
Printing	12,700	12,800	14,900	40,400	1,400	6,600	8,000	48,400
Travel	2,700	5,100	5,700	13,500	6,000	3,600	9,600	23,100
Conferences	1,400	2,400	7,100	10,900	11,000	1,900	12,900	23,800
Membership dues	700	400	0	1,100	0	0	0	1,100
Insurance	12,200	9,500	7,300	29,000	1,800	1,100	2,900	31,900
Depreciation	1,600	1,900	1,500	5,000	2,000	1,800	3,800	8,800
Total Nonsalary	$143,000	$78,100	$82,200	$303,300	$41,900	$56,700	$98,600	$401,900
Total Expenditures	$298,100	$170,000	$349,800	$817,900	$190,500	$168,200	$358,700	$1,176,600

An *incremental budget* involves increasing (or decreasing) the various budget items by a small amount year after year. Agencies with a fairly stable funding base typically practice incremental budgeting. For example, depending on inflationary or other circumstances, expenses such as salaries or utilities could increase (or decrease) 2 to 4% annually.

A *zero-based budget* (ZBB) is based on the premise that annually every program and every item starts from zero. It requires managers to assess whether each particular activity or unit should continue; they must justify each item, rather than merely build incrementally on the previous year's budget. Perhaps a particular unit should be discontinued, or at least modified in some major way. Nothing is taken for granted. If a program or item can be justified, however, it is included in the budget.

ZBB can be threatening to both managers and staff since it involves critical challenges to the budget and possible radical change. Moreover, cost calculations based on detailed information must be made available, which is not always possible. Despite these problems, ZBB disciplines managers to explore more options than they would if they limited themselves to incremental budgeting. Many managers use a modified form of ZBB: most of the budget is done on an incremental basis, but certain program expenses are identified for closer scrutiny and challenge.

Capital budgeting requires fairly large, one-time expenditures for such items as major building repairs, equipment purchases (e.g., computers or furniture replacement), or buying agency vehicles. Usually, capital projects entail making an expenditure in one year, though the income needed to support the expenditure may be set aside for several years either before or after the actual expenditure. For example, the organization might anticipate needing to set aside money for the next three years in order to pay for an expected major roof repair. The value of developing a capital budget is that it helps alert the organization to future major expenditures for which fundraising or long-term borrowing may be necessary.[7]

Cash flow budgeting records the difference in the amount of actual cash coming into the organization and the amount of cash expended. This kind of budgeting requires agencies to project the schedule of actual revenues and expenses and is essential to both the day-to-day and long-term fiscal health of an organization. When income lags behind expenditures, the agency could experience a crisis. For example, if an agency is not reimbursed for its contracted services for several months, it could experience a cash flow problem.[8] Under these circumstances staff salaries and other expenses need to be paid from some other sources while waiting for cash reimbursement. *Negative cash flow* occurs when a gap exists between projected disbursements and cash on hand. Conversely, when more cash is available than is needed, the agency experiences *positive cash flow*.

During those times when negative cash flow is expected, the organization needs to generate more cash, reduce cash outlays, or both. A projection may show, for example, that a negative cash flow will exist in the seventh and tenth months of the year. Knowing this, managers may delay purchases, move up the date for planned fundraising, consider short-term borrowing, or transfer funds from reserve accounts, if available. Suppose, for example, that managers anticipate a shortfall of $20,000 in July, but know that the August fundraising event will likely raise net income of $40,000. Managers could delay paying major vendors until September.[9] By having a cash flow projection, the agency has an early warning mechanism to prevent cash reserves from becoming too low to meet cash needs.

Obtaining credit from a bank to cover expenses should be a short-term measure of last resort and be based on the full confidence that funds will be forthcoming to cover expenses (plus interest on the loan).[10] A chronic cash flow problem indicates the organization is continuously spending more than it is raising—with no end in sight. This is irresponsible and could affect the agency's survival. Irresponsible managers sometimes finance their over all deficit with money earmarked for special programs. For example, they obtain a two-year foundation grant to provide a special counseling service, but then use that money to pay for current expenses in the hope that other money received later will provide funding for the foundation-supported program.[11] Sooner or later this "borrowing from Peter to pay Paul" gets the agency—and the managers—into serious trouble. Cash flow projections provide oversight for agency management so that it can avoid getting deep into debt and meet its contractual obligations. It is thus an effective procedure to conduct cash flow projections for the entire upcoming fiscal year and then update monthly projections throughout the year.[12]

Understanding Types of Income and Expenses

Managers should understand the following basic income and expense terms used in fiscal management:

Unrestricted funds are not tied to any specific purpose. A funding source permits the agency to use its funding in whatever way deemed appropriate, and the agency can make a decision about how and when to expend unrestricted income. For example, it can reallocate funding from one budget item to another. Money raised through the annual campaign or membership dues falls into this "no strings attached" category.

Donor restricted funding means donors have specified instructions on how the funding is to be used. For example, those setting aside money in their wills may restrict funding for certain purposes, such as a scholarship fund. Annual contributors may also designate that their pledges be used for specific programs. Cash-strapped organizations may be tempted to use restricted funds for current general operating purposes, but nothing is more likely to damage an organization's reputation than for it to use restricted funds for purposes other than those specified by the donor.[13]

Contract or *grant funding* also restricts funding for specific purposes. Those served by the program may have to meet eligibility requirements, expenses may be limited to those specifically identified in the budget proposal, and approvals may be required to modify the budget. The organization may be audited to ensure compliance with funding requirements. Sources may be public or private funding or agencies.

Income from service or business activities can involve fees charged for services rendered. Usually based on a sliding income scale, the aggregated income is calculated based on previous years' experience. A tax advisor may be necessary to determine whether taxes need to be paid on income derived from products or services that may be deemed to be unrelated to the main purpose of the agency (see Chapter 14). *Asset generated income* can come from existing assets, such as investments or rental income.

Endowment income could be unrestricted or restricted funding. These are funds established by donors in a specific name, for example, the Smith Family Endowment Fund. Funds may be designated in several ways: 1) endowment in perpetuity—the principal of the fund may never be expended; 2) time limited endowment—the principal may be expended after a given date or time period; 3) general endowment—the principal may be expended either upon passage of an event or at agency discretion (see Chapter 14).

Pledged income involves anticipated income over a period of time. People do not always pay what they have pledged, and therefore the budget must factor in a percentage of uncollectible pledges and periodically be updated based on an evaluation of whether pledges are being honored.

Cash or in-kind matching funds can take the form of a challenge grant, which requires the agency to raise a certain amount in order to be eligible for additional outside funding. A noncash or in-kind matching gift involves goods, facilities, services, or equipment worth a specified amount to support a program. This matching share would be included in the budget with the method of determining value indicated.

Accounts receivable are revenues earned by a human service agency but not yet received. For example, an organization provides mental health counseling and at the end of the month bills the mental health board. A receivable is recorded for the amount of the billing. When the actual cash is received, the accounts receivable item is removed. *Accounts payable* are moneys owed by the agency to a vendor but not yet paid.

Cash and *accrual accounting* are two different methods of financial bookkeeping. *Cash accounting* means that transactions are recorded only when cash is received and only when cash is paid out. The preferred method is *accrual accounting*, which means that transactions are recorded when revenues are earned (even though the money has not yet been received) and when expenses are incurred (even though they have yet to be paid). Accrual accounting provides a more complete financial picture, and the agency avoids being surprised about transactions that will not be discovered until funds are actually received or paid out.

Fixed revenues are based on a constant income flow, commonly referred to as "hard money." Examples include regularly received income from United Way or interest from an endowment fund. *Variable revenues* fluctuate from year to year. Revenue from special events, foundation grants, and annual pledges are considered variable or "soft money."[14]

Fixed expenses are calculated using recurring expenditures, for example, staff salaries, fringe benefits, payroll taxes, and rent. *Variable expenses* fluctuate, depending on the increases or decreases in services used. Changes in supplies and travel could depend, for example, on the kind and frequency of programs the agency provides.

It is a good idea that fixed expenses be funded by fixed income sources such as income from endowment or reasonably assured government funding. Similarly, variable expenses should be matched with variable revenues.[15] For example, if staff are hired to fulfill a two-year foundation grant, their salaries are tied to the length of the grant. When the grant runs out and there are no other sources of funding, these staff may need to be laid off.

An *indirect cost* is any cost in an agency's budget that benefits two or more programs. Sometimes an indirect cost is referred to as a *shared cost* or an *overhead cost* because the item is shared by two or more programs.[16] The process of assigning indirect costs to programs is called *cost allocation*. Three methods can be used to determine indirect costs. One method is based on tracking as precisely as possible the actual indirect costs of each program. For example, each program keeps track of its copying expenses. Timesheets used by the accountant and the executive director indicate the specific amount of staff time allocated to each program. The problem with this approach is that not all expenses are covered. For example, how would one allocate costs for the hallways, conference rooms, and local phone calls? Because it is difficult to track all expenses and because precise recordkeeping can be time consuming, most organizations prefer one of the two other methods.

The *total indirect costs* method uses a ratio of indirect costs to direct costs. For example, if the total indirect cost in an agency's budget is $20,000 and the agency's total budget is $100,000, then the indirect cost is 20%. If the homemakers' service program is $25,000, then the indirect costs attributed to this program is $5,000 ($25,000 x 20%).

The *salaries and wages* method is another common cost allocation method. This is because, in many agencies, about 80 percent of the total program cost relates to wage costs, which is an easy figure on which to determine indirect costs. Suppose that the agency determines that indirect costs should amount to 25% of salary costs. If the homemakers' service program salaries amount to $16,000, then the indirect costs attributed to this program is $4,000 ($16,000 X 25%).

The specific method used to determine indirect costs should be made after discussion with the agency's accountants, auditors, and funders. It is particularly important to obtain clarification from government agencies that might be funding the organization on their preferred or required method of cost accounting.

Break-even Points. Budgetary decisions related to one-time agency activities, such as workshops, special events, or training sessions, are concerned with establishing cut-off points. These involve go/no-go decisions in which a guaranteed minimum number of service units must occur or the activity is cancelled. For example, if an agency wants to provide a training session for 50 participants, and it needs a minimum of 25 participants in order not to lose money (break-even point), then if the count came in at 20 persons, it could decide to call off the session.[17]

Fund Balance (Reserves). In accounting terms, what you own are designated *assets.* Examples include cash, investments, and office furniture. What you owe are *liabilities.* Examples include the organization's debts, such as obligations due to creditors involving loans and accounts payable. The net worth of an organization is determined by subtracting its liabilities from its assets. At the end of a year if an organization has more assets than liabilities, this is referred to as *net assets, reserves,* or *fund balance.* (Note: In the profit-making world, this is referred to as a *surplus.*)

A more conservative and useful definition of fund balance is current liquid assets (cash and assets that can be readily converted into cash) minus current liabilities. Nonprofits usually express reserves or fund balances as a percentage of a fiscal year's total operating expenses. Thus if an organization has $12,000 in liquid reserves and its annual operating expenses are $300,000, it has reserves of about 4%. Each organization has to determine a reasonable amount to have in its reserves to meet unforeseen increased expenses or decreased revenues.

Internal Revenue Service (IRS) Form 990. Every 501(c)(3) private, nonprofit human service agency must file an IRS Form 990 annually showing its financial activities for the fiscal year. This same information can be found in an agency's statement of financial activities (profit and loss summary) and statement of financial position (balance sheet). Both the IRS and individual states furnish copies of an organization's Form 990 to anyone who asks. Form 990 has become the major information source for public accountability. Note that there are now Internet sites, for example www.guidestar.org, that distribute information submitted on the Form 990. The significance of this is that funders can easily learn about your organization's operations. Information on the Form 990 includes the roster of board members, sources of revenue, expenses by category, value of assets held, investment performance, fundraising costs, and compensation of the five highest-salaried employees.[18]

Conducting the Budgeting Process

Preparing an Organization-Wide Budget

Organizations with multiple programs require an organization-wide budget. This budget involves all income and expenses needed for the coming year, including the cost for employees, programs, facilities, and all other elements necessary to carry out the organization's activities.

The size and complexity of an organization determines the extent to which the budget resembles a pyramid with each level representing a budgeting unit or cost center. For example, the lowest level involves all agency programs. The second level involves the department budgets of which they are a part. Finally, the organization-wide budget is at the top of the pyramid. Each agency determines how many cost centers (i.e., primary fiscal units) it wants to keep track of. Each of these self-contained cost centers has an income and expense budget.

To establish an organization-wide budget, consider the following steps:

Step 1: Set organizational objectives. The fundamental purpose of an overall budget is to help the organization achieve its goals and objectives. The budget is a means to an end, not an end in itself. Hence the organization must first determine what it wants to accomplish and then build a budget to help achieve its objectives (see Chapters 2, 3, and 4).

Step 2: Establish organizational budgeting policies and procedures. Prior to setting income and expense targets, it is important to establish responsibilities and timetables in a budgeting schedule. Determine who is responsible for collecting data on income and expenses. Also discuss with the board of trustees or public officials what your overall budgeting parameters are. Develop guidelines about staff expansion or reduction, make estimates regarding inflation, and anticipate certain organization-wide extraordinary expenses.

You must also determine the dates of your *fiscal year*. Many organizations select a fiscal year that coincides with the receipt of major funding. For example, if major funding is from the federal government, the fiscal year might be from October through September. If the organization provides most of its programming during a certain part of the year, then it may select a fiscal year that closes after its busiest season. An agency providing a day care services program that ends in June might select a fiscal year that begins on July 1.

Step 3: Set annual income and expense targets for the entire organization. This initial calculation provides the units with an advance understanding of income that is either available or can be expected for the coming year. The projected expenses give guidance to the units on the upper limits of expenses that they may incur.

Step 4: Each unit establishes draft budgets that indicate its priorities. Reflecting an incremental budgeting process, some organizations require departmental units to prepare three variations of cost center budgets for review. Draft Budget A reflects no changes from the previous year's budget. (Such a remain-even budget, however, actually may experience reductions in some items to account for automatic inflationary increases in other items.) Draft Budget B represents an incremental increase (e.g., 5% increase). Draft Budget C represents a percent decrease (e.g., 5% decrease). This review of options allows managers to assess the consequences of budget variations. Unit managers relate their budget to program objectives and also supply a rationale for major changes in the projected budget compared to the current year's budget. For example, a program manager would justify significant changes in salaries, supplies, travel, and printing. Detailed information justifying projected costs for any new or expanded programs or positions must be provided. Hence unit managers must do considerable homework to justify expenses in their program budget.

Step 5: The management team proposes a budget for board approval. When all the program draft budgets are received, the finance staff prepares a summary for management staff so they have an idea of the resources needed for the total budget. The agency director then determines if the draft budgets must be trimmed prior to sending the budget to the board or public officials for approval. These recommendations are based on calculations of income and expenses, aggregated for each unit. If the organization is a nonprofit, the board's finance committee carefully scrutinizes this projected budget prior to making recommendations to the agency's board of directors. In the public sector, a budget officer examines the agency's budget prior to review by decision-making public officials. Where conflicts exist, the management team works with the finance committee to resolve them.

Developing Program or Unit Budgets

In some agencies financial statements are closely guarded secrets, with staff often being told mysteriously that a request cannot be honored because "it's not in the budget." Other organizations, however, place great emphasis on *bottom up* program budgeting based on the assumption that staff nearest to providing direct services can and should have a deep understanding of goals, objectives, policies, rules, and budgets that produce a defined product or service.[19] This approach is in contrast to the concept that top management always knows best.[20]

Four components are essential for "bottom up" budgeting to work:

1. Train staff to read financial statements. They may be puzzled at first about certain elements, but they can learn easily how the agency is working to balance its budget and remain financially viable.

2. Give staff responsibility to develop budgets and the authority to spend that budget. This assumes that people who provide services know what they need to do their jobs. Staff would feel more involved, experience ownership of their work, and be motivated to achieve their objectives. Over time, staff who might feel overwhelmed initially by the responsibility of proposing and managing a budget grow in their confidence to make the right decisions.

   Example: In a children's institution, staff assigned to cottages are given budget responsibility for such items as food, allowances, monthly personal needs shopping, weekend recreational activity money, clothing, and birthday celebrations. Over time, they begin to see where they need to adjust their spending patterns so that they can purchase high-priority items.

3. Base risk and reward on successful accomplishment (or failure). When staff spend less or bring in more income than was budgeted, they can use the additional net income for purposes they designate. Drawing from the previous children's institution example, net savings can be used for a special event, such as an amusement park outing. If, on the other hand, staff incur debts for a given month, they would have to make cuts to their plans for the coming month. Staff must then explain their decisions and may have to carry forward the deficit to the next year, resulting in a reduction for the following year. Establishing a risk and reward system encourages staff to put the extra effort in to save money or bring in new income.

4. Provide for regular monitoring and share information openly. Staff need to be informed about how they are doing. Where there are major deviations from the agreed-on budget, determine with staff why this is the case and what can be done about it.

These suggestions for involving staff in "bottom up" budget planning can be tried on an experimental basis with certain programs and, if successful, can be spread to other parts of the organization. Identify those units that are most likely to succeed before expanding to additional units.

Relating the Unit's Budget to Its Work Plan and Objectives

Whether organization-wide or related to a particular unit, a budget is a means by which the organization accomplishes its objectives, and therefore there must be a clear connection between the budget and a work plan. Recall the chapter on implementing objectives and the timeline chart on foster care recruitment (Chapter 4, Figure 4.2). In spelling out the details of activities to be carried out to achieve foster care placements, the manager and staff need to document expenses that may be involved, such as personnel, supplies, transportation, and equipment.

It is a good idea to provide a budget justification or documentation of costs, especially if the cost item is unusually large or may be open to question. For example, if travel expenses are high, you might need to indicate how staff mileage was derived and why out-of-town trips are essential to achieve program objectives. Personnel costs should be based on the going rate other agencies are paying for staff in those categories. This can be determined in consultation with other agencies, through the local governmental funding body, or the local United Way.

Prior to estimating budget expenses, a program manager would determine various policy decisions affecting these expenses. Is there to be an increase in salary for all positions or just designated ones? Is overtime permitted? Would part-time staff be brought on? Should all positions in a new program be budgeted for the entire year or just part of the year? Clarifying policy decisions and budget assumptions makes the budgetary process more efficient.

Projecting fringe benefits requires review of applicable state and local laws affecting minimum benefits. Use government publications to identify the employer's share of Social Security, Medicare, and unemployment insurance. Insurance carriers can provide estimated costs of health, life, and worker's compensation insurance.

Estimating other operating costs involves review of leases and contracts, estimated price changes in services and supplies, and estimated annual rate of inflation. If significant cost increases are projected (e.g., printing costs or travel expenses), obtain specific estimated increases. If a significant expansion is expected in a particular program, estimate the costs involved in that expansion. Prepare an annual summary of major changes.

In developing the budget, managers must pay attention to pricing services in order to assure proper reimbursement for actual costs. Because funders may not reimburse for overhead expenditures and instead only reimburse for costs directly related to the project, you may find that you are actually under-pricing your services. If you have no other means of subsidizing the service, then you may need to decline the project.[21] For example, an agency is offered the opportunity to provide counseling services to severely disturbed, substance-abusing youth. Each adolescent is to receive three intensive counseling sessions per week, which the agency estimates to cost a total of $150 ($120 direct costs + $30 indirect cost). The contracting agency, however, can only provide $100 per adolescent per week, $20 short of the direct costs and $30 short of the indirect costs. As much as the counseling agency wants to provide the service, it decides not to because of the discrepancy between cost of service and revenue. The agency does not have sufficient funds from other charitable contributions to make up for the shortfall.

Using the Budget as a Management Tool

Monitoring and Modifying Budgets

The best way to monitor a budget is to systematically compare the projected organization managers' budgets to actual financial reports. You must identify income shortfalls, expense overruns, or operational problems that require corrective action. By receiving reports on a monthly basis, you can focus on discrepancies or variances that invite closer scrutiny. If these variances are identified early enough, mild corrections, such as postponing filling a vacant position, deferring nonessential purchases, or looking for new sources of revenue, may be possible. If, however, the variance is large or discovered late in the year, more severe action may be required, such as reducing staff.[22] It is critical that the organization take action immediately when major variances between budgeted income and expenses are discovered. Most problems only worsen over time, and delays can lead to serious deficits and potential difficulties with funders. (See discussion at the end of this chapter on ideas for cost reductions.)

During the course of the year as you obtain new expenses and income information, you should revise your budget estimates. For example, if an anticipated program is not funded, then the income and expenses connected with that program would be eliminated from the budget. Similarly, if an unanticipated new program is acquired during the year, then the revised budget would contain new income and expenses. The organization should determine in advance how programs are to be modified and who has approving authority.

Managers need to guard against two dangers in reviewing the budget on a monthly or quarterly basis. The first is giving equal attention to all items, no matter how small the variances. This can be an overwhelming task. The second is not paying sufficient attention to the most important variances requiring managerial attention. The best way to manage a budget review is to conduct a *variance analysis* that helps you determine which variances require special attention. If you develop a percentage figure that indicates the degree of fluctuation you can tolerate, then reviewing income and expenses using that figure guides you in taking corrective action.[23] Using Excel, Peachtree, or other spreadsheet programs can assist in predetermining threshold percentages or dollar amounts requiring possible corrective action.

Closely examine the two tables that follow. Table 12.2 is based on a one-month comparison of actual income and expenses to budgeted income and expenses for a Family Counseling Program, which is one of five programs in the Hypothetical Agency. Table 12.3 is the Hypothetical Agency's Revenue and Expenditures Report for the month of March and the quarter ending March 31, 20XX.

Table 12.2   Family Counseling Program Budget

	Family Counseling Program Statement of Revenues and Expenditures (Budget to Actual) for the Month Ended January 31, 20XX			
	Actual	Budget for January	Variance Amount	Variance Percentage
Revenues				
Fees	$1,900	$2,500	($600)	(24.0)
Juvenile Court fees	6,100	8,100	(2,000)	(24.7)
Medicaid	12,000	15,000	(3,000)	(20.0)
United Way	2,000	2,000	0	0.0
Total Revenues	$22,000	$27,600	($5,600)	(20.3)
Expenditures				
Salaries	$14,000	$12,000	($2,000)	(16.7)
Fringe benefits	2,500	2,200	(300)	(13.6)
Supplies	400	360	(40)	(11.1)
Telephone	520	420	(100)	(23.8)
Occupancy	2,100	2,100	0	0.0
Equipment	290	320	30	9.4
Printing	1,100	900	(200)	(22.2)
Travel	850	650	(200)	(30.8)
Conferences	600	350	(250)	(71.4)
Membership dues	50	50	0	0.0
Insurance	700	700	0	0.0
Depreciation	200	200	0	0.0
Expenditures before overhead	$23,310	$20,250	($3,060)	(15.1)
Administration overhead	2,300	2,250	(50)	(2.2)
Total Expenditures	**$25,610**	**$22,500**	($3,110)	(13.8)
Excess (deficiency) Revenues over (under) expenses	**($3,610)**	**$5,100**	**$8,710**	

Note: Parentheses indicate a negative variance

The Family Counseling Program Budget in Table 12.2 is reviewed by the manager of that unit, which has one supervisor and five staff members. Note that the budget is for one month and that the variances between actual and projected budget are shown numerically and with percentages. An unfavorable variance on the income side means that less funds were received than had been anticipated when the budget was developed. An unfavorable variance of expenses means that higher-than-expected expenses were incurred. The manager must focus on those unfavorable variances even in this first reporting month.

To calculate the percentage variance, subtract the actual amount from the budgeted amount and divide this difference by that item's budgeted amount.

For example, in Table 12.2, the variance for salaries would be calculated as follows: a budgeted salary of $12,000, less actual salaries of $14,000, gives a negative variance of $2,000. To arrive at the percentage variance, divide the dollar variance ($2,000) by the budgeted amount ($12,000). The resulting percentage is negative (16.7%). The variance is negative because the agency overspent this line item by $2,000. Revenue variances are negative when the agency raises less money than it had budgeted.

In Table 12.2, the revenue category reveals that client fees, Juvenile Court fees, and Medicaid reimbursements are below budget, indicating negative variances must be reviewed to determine whether corrective steps should be taken. Also of concern, overall expenditures exceed the budget. The fact that staff salaries are higher than were budgeted could invite exploratory questions: Are there too many "no shows?" Are staff as productive as they could be? Can the program do with less supervisory time, thus freeing up supervisory staff to conduct billable interviews for which the Juvenile Court or Medicaid would provide reimbursement? Would special training help recently hired staff to be more efficient? Would working with the accounting department speed up Medicaid billing? Negative variances should trigger considerable managerial inquiry.

In addition, non-salary items that have out-of-the-ordinary variances must also be reviewed. Although the amounts involving supplies, telephone, printing, travel, and conferences are relatively small, this is only the first month of the fiscal year, and the manager had best review these costs before they get out of hand.

Note the item "administrative overhead," representing about 10% of expenses. Some agencies may choose not to include this as an identifiable expense; they may determine to subsidize administrative costs with endowment income, fundraising events, or annual campaigns (see Chapters 13 and 14). In this example, the Hypothetical Agency Inc. has determined that the Family Counseling Program, like all the other units, must contribute a portion of its budget to administrative overhead. In part, the overhead is covered by United Way funding. To meet agency requirements, the manager of this unit must exceed productivity standards and raise the amount generated from billable hours, discontinue non-fee generating staff (e.g., secretarial support staff), or consider other ways to work with the agency's management to help generate additional revenue.

Table 12.3 provides the Hypothetical Agency Inc. Statement of Revenues and Expenditures (Statement of Activities) for the month ended March 31, 20XX. This report also provides year to date (YTD) information. For both the month and YTD, a variance column indicates the difference between actual income and expenses and budgeted amounts. The percentage variance reflects the degree to which the actual amounts differ from the budgeted amounts. Note that a favorable variance on the income side reflects income received in excess of the budget. A favorable variance on the expense side reflects expenses incurred below budget. Unfavorable income, that is, income

Table 12.3 Hypothetical Agency Revenue and Expenditures Report

Hypothetical Agency Inc. Statement of Revenues and
Expenditures Month Ended March 31, 20XX

| | Monthly | | | | Quarterly | | | | |
	Monthly Actual ($)	Monthly Budget ($)	Variance ($)	Variance (%)	YTD Actual ($)	YTD Budget ($)	Variance ($)	Variance (%)	Annual Budget
Revenues									
United Way	$12,000	$12,000	$0	0.00	$36,000	$36,000	$0	0.00	$144,000
Government funding	50,000	43,000	7,000	16.28	136,200	129,000	7,200	5.58	516,000
Foundation grants	3,500	12,500	(9,000)	(72.00)	36,000	37,500	(1,500)	(4.00)	150,000
Contributions	3,400	11,300	(7,900)	(69.91)	14,800	34,000	(19,200)	(56.47)	136,000
Fees	18,500	19,500	(1,000)	(5.13)	57,700	58,500	(800)	(1.37)	234,000
Total Revenues	$87,400	$98,300	($10,900)	(11.09)	$280,700	$295,000	($14,300)	(4.85)	$1,180,000
Expenditures									
Salaries	$52,500	$51,000	(1,500)	(2.94)	187,500	153,000	($34,500)	(22.55)	$612,000
Fringes & Payroll Taxes	14,900	13,600	(1,300)	(9.56)	44,900	40,700	(4,200)	(10.32)	162,700
Tot. Salaries & Fringes	$67,400	$64,600	($2,800)	(4.33)	$232,400	$193,700	($38,700)	(19.98)	$774,700
Supplies	4,000	5,100	1,100	21.57	25,000	15,300	(9,700)	(63.40)	61,100
Telephone	4,300	3,300	(1,000)	(30.30)	9,900	10,000	100	1.00	40,100
Postage	3,700	3,600	(100)	(2.78)	10,000	10,900	900	8.26	43,700
Occupancy	9,900	8,200	(1,700)	(20.73)	30,300	24,600	(5,700)	(23.17)	98,500
Equipment	1,000	1,800	800	44.44	5,400	5,400	0	0.00	21,400
Printing	5,200	4,000	(1,200)	(30.00)	10,000	12,100	2,100	17.36	48,400
Travel	2,800	1,900	(900)	(47.37)	8,400	5,800	(2,600)	(44.83)	23,100
Conferences	2,100	2,000	(100)	(5.00)	5,700	5,900	200	3.39	23,800
Membership dues	100	100	0	0.00	600	300	(300)	(100.00)	1,100
Insurance	2,700	2,700	0	0.00	8,200	8,000	(200)	(2.50)	31,900
Depreciation	700	700	0	0.00	2,200	2,200	0	0.00	8,800
Total Nonsalary	$36,500	$33,400	($3,100)	(9.28)	$115,700	$100,500	($15,200)	(15.12)	$401,900
Total Expenditures	$103,900	$98,000	($5,900)	(6.02)	$348,100	$294,200	($53,900)	(18.32)	$1,176,600
Excess (Deficiency) Revenues Over (Under) Expenditures	($16,500)	$300	($16,800)		($67,400)	$800	($68,200)		$3,400

NOTE: Parentheses indicate a negative number or percentage

less than expected, is shown with amounts and percentages in parentheses; unfavorable expenses, that is, higher than budgeted are also shown in parentheses. For purposes of this example, the monthly budget is approximately 1/12 the annual, and the quarterly budget is approximately 3/12 the annual. In the real world, income and expense streams would be budgeted based on the best available information, rather than a mathematical formula. For example, printing expenses may be higher in certain months because of anticipated special annual report or brochure printing costs, and those months would be budgeted accordingly.

In Table 12.3 under the income category, United Way funds are being received by the agency as projected, and government funding is actually showing a favorable variance. Although fees are down by 5.13% in March, they are only down by 1.37% for YTD. Of greater concern is that both foundation grants and contributions are considerably down for the month. These losses should alert management that more effort is needed to secure grants. An aggressive contribution campaign must be mounted or else significant reductions in expenses would be required to keep the budget balanced.

For expenses, several line items do not require special attention because either the variance is favorable (i.e., the expenses incurred are below budget), or if there is a negative percentage variance, the dollar amount is low (e.g., postage, equipment, membership dues, insurance, and depreciation). Management can quickly determine which items do not require attention so that they can spend more time analyzing those items that are unfavorably out of line with expectations.

Managers should be alerted to specific items in this hypothetical budget. Although the supplies item is under budget for the month, it is considerably over budget for YTD and requires ongoing attention. Salaries and fringe benefits are only 4.33% over budget for the month, but for YTD they are nearly 20% over budget. This item should be of serious concern because of both the unfavorable percentage variance and the relatively high unfavorable dollar amount. Telephone expense for the month is considerably over budget and should require special attention even though YTD is on target. This may indicate the beginning of a negative trend. Occupancy costs are over budget for both the month and YTD, and should alert management that this is a problem that requires action. Staff travel is 47% above budget for the month and about 45% above budget for this first quarter, indicating that the allocation to this line item either has to be modified considerably or travel limitations need to be enacted.

In determining which items require special attention, you may establish certain threshold percentages, such as 5% or 10%, which would alert management and a board finance oversight committee that the budget is heading for trouble. Management could also identify certain dollar amounts (e.g., unfavorable variances that are above $1,000). Whether using percentages or dollar amounts, managers need to establish thresholds that require exploration, decision making, and corrective action.

In some instances there may be good reasons for unfavorable variances. As mentioned previously, certain costs may be unusually high and have to do with the timing and flow of program activities. A conference may be held during a particular month that may put pressure on the travel budget, but if possible, this strain should be anticipated in the budget. Backup worksheets for each month should allow managers to calculate more precisely when unusual expenses or revenues are expected.

Although there may be good reasons why income and expenses are worse than expected, it may also be that the agency is hemorrhaging and that management must take steps to reduce expenses or significantly increase income. At the very least, questions must be asked, and corrective action must be considered early in this fiscal year to avoid more severe measures later on. For example, it may be painful to lay off one staff member at the beginning of the year when it is apparent that salary costs are exceeding budget. But if a tough decision is not made then, a more difficult decision will have to be made later to lay off two or three employees because of budget overruns. The advantage, then, of having this income and expense report is that it provides an early warning of a problem that can become more serious.

Essential to the budget review process, especially during periods of austerity, is the importance of questioning everything that the organization does at all levels of expenditures. In reviewing costs, small changes can add up to big savings. In the past, for example, an organization may have sent five staff members to an out-of-town annual conference. As a way of reducing costs, it may determine that only one staff member should attend and report back to the rest of staff. Management needs to foster an organizational culture that encourages all employees to be on the lookout for new ways to manage money and to cut costs.

It is a good idea for managers to complete a *variance report* for the organization's governing body (board of trustees or public officials) that explains why variances are occurring and details the manager's action plan. Such a report gives decision makers and funders confidence that management is in control of the budget.

Because the budget represents an understanding between the agency's administration and its funders, board, or public officials to whom it is accountable, managers are obligated to work to keep the budget in balance. Managers get into trouble because, in their quest to meet the needs of their clients, they develop an overly optimistic attitude that somehow their board or public officials would find the money to meet necessary expenses. Certainly, hope and optimism have a place in the budgeting process, but if these are carried too far, managers can develop a reputation for being irresponsible.

The best course for managing the agency's finances is to make sure that policies and procedures are in compliance with the funders, whether foundations or public agencies. Funds should be expended in accordance with the latest approved budget, and any major adjustments require the board's finance committee to make recommendations to the board (see Chapter 20).

Management should account for all funds in compliance with the rules and regulations required by the applicable funding source, and delineate clearly all major grants in the budget. The agency should write procedures for handling money (e.g., the same person should not control receipts and disbursements of cash) and also specify the roles of executive, finance manager, and project manager. An annual audit is a must.

Although it is essential to strive for a balanced budget, it is also important to recognize that the budget should have some flexibility. After all, the budget is based on yearly estimates, which in turn are based on certain assumptions about inflation and other information available at the time the budget is prepared. During the course of the year you may need to revise the budget. For example, you obtain an unexpected grant, which requires budgeting new expenses as well. Be prepared to revise the budget as circumstances change. Using spreadsheet software makes it easy to adjust the budget on individual items that then alter totals.

50 Considerations for Reducing Costs

One of the most demanding and challenging responsibilities a manager faces is reducing costs to bring budget expenses in line with anticipated income. To reduce costs, managers can consider the following:[24]

1. Form a cost-cutting team to examine the options contained in this section and generate additional ideas. The team may develop enough austere measures that you can avoid more drastic measures—or they may not, in which case a proposal to cut staff may be justified.

2. Reward staff for cost-saving ideas. Staff are a good source for ways to save money. A $25 reward to a staff member for suggesting ways to recycle paper, for example, could save hundreds of dollars in paper costs.

3. Postpone filling new or vacant positions. If cuts require reducing current staff, anticipate expenses connected with terminating positions—for example, unemployment compensation, severance pay, or continuation of fringe benefits for a specified period. Be certain also that in reducing staff, the organization is able to meet its obligations. Also, be aware that reducing costs related to fee-for-service contracts may reduce the total amount of reimbursement an organization is eligible to receive. Reducing staff, for example, can have a detrimental impact on achieving the agency's targeted billable hours in Medicaid and other cost reimbursement programs. Carefully review contracts and grant agreements before making cuts.

4. Examine whether such needed services as payroll preparation or public information materials can be contracted with an outside vendor (called *outsourcing*) instead of using current staff or hiring additional staff.

5. Eliminating positions can provide a quick fix to balance a budget. Referred to euphemistically as "downsizing" or "organizational restructuring," the disadvantage is that scaling back employees can create more work for those remaining, which contributes to stress, resentment, and poor quality work. Downsizing should be related to those individuals and those units of the organization that are least productive. It is possible that you could be both "downsizing" and "upsizing" at the same time. It may be difficult, but nevertheless necessary, to lay off people in one section as you expand another, more productive unit of the organization.[25]

6. Use contract employees or consultants for specific projects. Working with a consultant on a specific project can help to match project and staffing needs. This may eliminate the need to reduce staff once a project is completed. Check with a tax expert regarding possible employee versus independent contractor issues for employment taxes.

7. Ask staff to consider working part time (especially during off-season periods, such as summer months). Some organizations have instituted voluntarily sharing positions, that is, two full-time staff agreeing to cut their work time in half to preserve jobs.

8. Delay starting new activities or expanding existing ones, such as buying new equipment. Prioritize requested purchases. Those designated low priority would either be postponed or not included in the budget.[26]

9. Reduce services and programs. For example, instead of providing individual counseling to 400 clients in a substance abuse reduction program, you could serve 220 individually and provide group counseling for the others. Be aware, however, that you may be shortchanging your clients.

10. Delay salary increases or reduce employee benefits. Personnel costs, including salaries and benefits, are usually the largest items in the budget (as much as 70–80%) and therefore are an understandable target for cost cutting. The disadvantage is that these measures can have serious effects on the morale of the organization and could increase staff turnover.

11. Restructure the organization with special emphasis on non-income-producing positions. To increase billable income, supervisory staff may have to devote a portion of their time to direct service. Certain support and administrative staff may have to be laid off.

12. Explore the advantage or disadvantage of leasing rather than purchasing equipment, such as a copying machine. In the long term you may be paying more, but leasing may help with cash flow and provide short-term budget relief.

13. Determine whether there are any ways departments can share resources. For example, can support staff or the copying machine be shared? Sharing facilities, such as conference rooms, with other agencies may be cost effective.

14. Create an in-house printing operation to produce stationery, newsletters, and other printed materials, thus reducing the expense of outside printing.

15. Obtain bids to produce competitive pricing on purchases, such as equipment, supplies, and other work-related materials. It is especially important to initiate a bidding process for vendors with whom you have been doing business for a long time. They may be willing to come down in price when they think you might buy from their competition.[27]

16. Ask your vendors if they provide discounts to nonprofit agencies. Request a discount on guaranteed purchases over an extended period of time. For example, your printer might quote a volume price for all stationery, newsletters, and forms that you might need for the next two years. Also, inquire whether your vendor could provide a discount when you pay in cash. Check with your phone company to see if it gives a discount to nonprofit organizations.

17. Take advantage of *economies of scale* by making bulk purchases. Bundling purchases, currently made separately, could result in lower prices. It may be possible to join with other agencies in contracting for a bulk purchase arrangement. Be aware, however, that a large amount of supplies can disappear quickly unless you have proper controls on distribution. Inquire if there are any purchasing "co-ops" in your area. Some co-ops offer opportunities for purchasing medical supplies and capital items as well as general items such as office supplies and paper disposables.

18. Give staff responsibility for site-based decision making. Staff responsible for department and program budgets can be more accountable for expenditures.

19. Use zero-based budgeting to determine whether programs should continue based on their demonstrated value and their contribution to the mission and goals of the organization. As discussed previously, ZBB requires you to justify expenses each year, rather than just build on last year's budget.

20. Seek donated items, such as furniture and equipment. Companies that are moving their offices are a good source of usable furniture and equipment.

21. Purchase items or services at the right time of year. For example, winter items can be purchased in early spring for the following winter.

22. Change the fiscal year from January–December to October–September to purchase auditing services at a reduced rate, because this is their slow period.

23. Use volunteers to provide services, perform clerical tasks, and assist in running programs. Companies sometimes "lend/lease" their staff for a specific time period or a specific purpose. For example, a company might release its controller to assist your bookkeeping department in setting up

a computerized accounting system. Many attorneys, business people, accountants, and carpenters donate their time to nonprofits. Also check with local universities that offer course credits for student service experience.

24. Check in your community whether the local criminal justice system can provide "volunteer" assistance. Instead of serving time in jail, persons convicted of nonviolent crimes have the option of providing community service. Services range from carpentry to computer programming and maintenance work. Also check into involving Welfare to Work participants and senior citizens participating in retraining programs.

25. Negotiate contracts carefully to determine whether there are any hidden costs. For example, foundation grants may not sufficiently cover administrative costs or overhead. A government contract might require financial reporting and have audit requirements. Preparing reports will require someone's time, and therefore assess whether this time can be fiscally justified and be included in the grant request.

26. Review personnel policies to ensure compliance with legal requirements and train staff to follow these policies with no exceptions. A wrongful termination or harassment judgment can be extremely expensive (see Chapter 8).

27. Hire staff carefully. This admonition is especially important when supervisors are tempted to hire staff out of desperation to fill a position. Having a mismatch between the person and the job can be very costly in the long run (see Chapter 7).

28. Reduce staff turnover. It is an expensive hidden cost because you have to devote time to hiring new staff and training them. Conduct exit interviews with staff to determine why they are leaving. It may be more cost efficient to increase salaries and benefits to stop employees from moving to more competitive agencies.

29. Invest cash in short-term instruments such as certificates of deposit, an interest-bearing checking account, or a savings account that is linked to a checking account. Many banks offer special interest-bearing accounts to nonprofit organizations that are not available to for-profit organizations.

30. Set up a system to track all equipment and building use. Examine whether moving to smaller offices can reduce expenses. You may need to consider the cost of breaking leases or renegotiating for space compared to the cost of moving.

31. Review current staff positions and assignments to determine whether all activities are essential, whether some assignments conducted by a highly paid employee can be delegated to a lesser paid staff member, or whether work can be performed by a part-time employee.

32. Review personnel practices to reduce carryover of unused vacation or sick leave time. Some agencies require staff to take all or most of their vacation each year.

33. Consider offering staff an improvement in their benefits (e.g., time off, health, dental, and life insurance) in lieu of cost-of-living pay increases. This idea requires considerable dialogue with staff.

34. Review unemployment compensation claims for those employees who quit your agency. Your state unemployment insurance office will request an explanation when former employees apply for funding. If employees have left voluntarily or have been fired for good cause, you should provide an explanation. If the unemployment office rules against your agency, your insurance costs could increase.

35. Convert fixed costs into variable costs. Instead of paying part-time staff on a salaried basis, pay them based on the number of clients that they interview.

36. Encourage employees to opt out of benefits when their spouses already have medical and dental benefits that could cover them. Offer incentives, such as cash or more vacation days.

37. Ask the landlord for a rent reduction by paying the rent in full but then requesting the landlord to donate back a portion of it. This exchange preserves the landlord's ability to show the property at its true market value based on rents collected and at the same time provides your organization with unrestricted funding.

38. Consolidate your office space and sublet unused space to a compatible group.

39. Negotiate free use of space for meetings and events. Sometimes banks, hotels, and corporations offer conference rooms for nonprofit meetings and special events.

40. Arrange to have an organizational supporter purchase equipment and then have it leased to your organization through an accounting method called "asset conversion." The supporter can depreciate the equipment and take a tax deduction, and the cost of leasing to the organization is less than the full cost of the equipment. At the end of the designated period, the organization can purchase the equipment at a nominal cost. Check with a tax advisor to determine compliance with tax laws.

41. Regarding your travel budget, determine whether hotels offer a discount. Some hotel chains offer a government discount; inquire whether they would provide a special discount for a nonprofit organization. Limit staff attendance only to trips that can truly add value to achieving your mission. Use the Internet to obtain the best travel deals.

42. Identify excess capacity or underutilized resources in the private sector. For example, a business that has moved to new offices may have excess space for your temporary staff needs. Recently laid-off or retired accountants may welcome the chance to volunteer until they find a full-time job.

43. Regarding insurance, negotiate a fee that is limited to about 15% and select an agent that works with nonprofits. Consider using the Nonprofit Insurance Alliance (www.niac.org).

44. Strongly encourage the board of directors to authorize purchase of officers' and directors' insurance, which would pay for the cost of defending a lawsuit and also the cost of any settlement.

45. Use e-mail instead of long distance phone calls or faxes. E-mail can also be used to obtain information about grants and other essential information. If you are planning to hook up to the Internet for e-mail communications, consider using an Internet access provider that gives you a free Web site. You can then create a Web page that can be viewed by those interested in your activities, including potential donors. In addition, newsletters can be sent via e-mail, thus saving printing and postage costs.

46. If you have a large mail volume, use discounted postage rates; contact the National Federation of Nonprofits in Washington, DC (202–628–4380) for more information.

47. Examine potential local tax savings. Check with your local tax authority to see if your agency qualifies for a tax exemption on all or a portion of the equipment and furnishings your organization owns. Check your lease to determine you are not paying this tax as part of your rental. Also, determine whether you are exempt from real estate taxes. Have a knowledgeable professional review whether you have possible tax overpayments. You should not be paying tax on any purchases (office supplies, etc.). Your accounting department should routinely be reviewing all invoices for possible erroneous taxes.

48. Periodically prune mailing lists and eliminate those whose mailing addresses are unknown or who are no longer part of your organization.

49. Manage cash flow by collecting early, paying only when bills are due, and earning interest on balances. This is particularly important for managing large grants at the beginning of the grant period.

50. Consider using service agreements for maintenance and repair of equipment instead of paying repair costs for each occurrence.

Achieving Long-Range Financial Stability

Effective managers are not only committed to the current economic health of their agencies but also to their long-term viability. To continually strengthen their organization, managers must (1) establish working capital or cash reserves, (2) assure cost effectiveness, and (3) seek diversified funding.

Establishing Working Capital

A few organizations make the mistake of hoarding resources for potential future use, thus denying benefits to those who currently need services. For example, an organization may choose not to expend the interest endowment funds received for a period of years so it can build up its principal. The more common problem, however, is that some agencies do not adequately prepare for the future because of their desire to provide for current service needs. They do not allow for future inflation adjustments. They put little value on building a financial base and erode their cash reserves, hoping that the future will take care of itself.

Understandably, human service organizations want to use all the money available to provide services rather than set aside funding for unknown future needs. Some go further in providing services (even though funding is not assured) in the hope that if the program is good enough, funders or their trustees will eventually bail out the agency. They would even argue that it is immoral to put aside cash when needs are so great. Unfortunately, organizations that live "hand-to-mouth" must spend an inordinate amount of time looking for the next bailout—not focusing on long-term issues. Trying to be all things to all people is a formula for eventual poor services and possible financial decline.

Generally, it is a good idea to have about 90 days of cash reserves or roughly 10% of the overall budget, depending on the organization's need. For example, if an organization provides counseling services, and a Medicaid contract delays payments for four months, then the organization must have sufficient working capital to meet its payroll while waiting for cost reimbursement.[28] An agency that has a regular income and predictable expenditures needs less reserves than one that experiences a continuous turnover of grants and has much more unpredictability connected to its income and expenditures. The greater the unpredictability, the greater the need for a large amount of cash reserves.

Another reason to develop working capital is the ability to respond quickly to unmet needs. Having this flexibility allows the agency to deal with changes in the environment and to avoid staying rooted in the present instead of moving into the future. As program trends change or funders convey new priorities, so too agencies must develop a flexible response. An effectively run agency must be able to take advantage of new opportunities to fulfill its goals. A well-developed strategic plan can anticipate how the agency might seek out opportunities for expansion and consider a budget that is practical and feasible. Some agencies even develop an "opportunity budget" that identifies where and when the agency needs to invest in new staff, training, and equipment. For example, in anticipation of new employment training legislation, an agency may want to invest in a six-month pilot training program that demonstrates its effectiveness in this area. It is now in a position to take advantage of new legislation. To create this desired cash reserve, an agency must have more years with positive revenue than it has years in which net revenue is negative.

While it is desirable to build up cash reserve, be mindful that some funders may have reservations about building up too large a cash reserve fund. For example, some United Way budget committees frown upon agency cash reserves, considering that United Way funding is supposed to be "last money in." They would prefer that United Way money not be used until an agency is without much cash reserves. Those agencies that have greatly fluctuating income and expenses must have a reserve fund to provide financial stability, and the United Way budget panel must be convinced this is necessary. On the other hand, budget panels may be justified in questioning when a reserve fund becomes inordinately large (however this is defined). Be prepared, therefore, to make your case for cash reserves.

Assuring Cost Effectiveness

An effectively run organization can further its long-term financial strength by demonstrating its ability to achieve its objectives at reasonable costs. Developing a cost-effective program is not the same as developing a program at minimum cost. Sometimes high costs are necessary to achieve sustained improvement. For example, one employment program may cost $1,000 per participant, but most participants are employed in a menial job for an average of only six months. Another employment program may require costs of $7,000 a participant, but because of extensive job training this would result in clients' keeping their jobs for over a year and being paid at a higher rate. Hence cost-effectiveness must be related to the desired objectives.[29]

Cost-effectiveness is defined as the measure of how effectively resources are used—results obtained for each unit of cost. To carry out cost-effectiveness analysis, organizations track the cost of a program and record its results; then they compare the two to determine whether the results justify the costs.[30]

Obviously a good accounting system would track actual costs, including both direct and indirect expenditures. For example, a calculation would be made in a tutoring program of the cost of administering volunteer tutors. Recording results may be much more difficult than recording costs. Most agencies can readily identify output results, namely, efforts expended on behalf of clients. These include the number of clients served, the number of training sessions provided, and the number of youth participating in a recreation program. Outcomes are more difficult to measure. We could more easily determine, for example, how many youngsters participated in a recreation program than how many we helped prevent going to jail. Measuring both costs and benefits remains a major challenge for human service managers.

To further the agency's cost effectiveness, managers must focus on agency productivity. Frequently, productivity indicators are expressed through the agency's quantitative objective statements. For example, an agency providing group counseling services would want to track the number of participants in each session on a weekly or monthly basis. An agency that provides recreation services for older persons would have a different set of numbers relevant to its services. These numbers should not be collected primarily as a public relations effort; rather, they should be relevant for managerial review of productivity.

Reviewing quantitative information allows managers to ask the following questions:

- How does the number of staff hours compare from one month to another?
- How many new clients does the agency have each month? How does this year's trend compare with last year's?
- How many clients are able to pay for services?
- How many billable hours do we have this month compared to the previous month?
- What is the cumulative total of different clients seen in the agency during this period?

Each organization must determine its own productivity standards against which monthly quantitative information can be assessed. Periodically, managers should report to their funders, public officials, or trustees regarding the productivity of agency operations.

Seeking Diversified Funding

Excessive dependence on a particular funding source is a major problem in sustaining any organization. Such concentration puts the organization unduly at risk, because if the funding resource dries up, the organization becomes highly vulnerable. An organization that has relied primarily on United Way funding may experience pressure to raise its own money or risk losing a portion of United Way funds. A mental health agency that has come to depend almost entirely on state mental health funding for its prevention services may find that its mental health board has shifted its priorities to other essential services not provided by the agency. A neighborhood organization that has received five years of foundation grant funding may belatedly realize that this funding cannot go on indefinitely and that it must seek other funding if it is to survive. These are among many examples of why it is important to diversify the organization's portfolio to diminish the risks of becoming too dependent on only one main source.[31] The next few chapters in Part III are devoted to exploring ways human service agencies can sustain themselves through a variety of fundraising options.

Questions for Discussion

Note: To answer these questions, take time to discuss your agency's budget with your supervisor, agency controller, or administrator.

1. What has your agency done about cutting costs? Which of the cost-cutting measures listed in the text might be considered by your organization?

2. How useful is the concept of zero-based budgeting for fiscal management?

3. How would you characterize your budgeting process (e.g., line item, program, incremental, zero-based)?

4. Can you identify restricted and unrestricted funds in your agency?

5. In your agency's budget, which income and expenses are fixed and which are variable?

6. How does your organization monitor current income and expenses? Are variances identified?

7. What strategies are in place to ensure long-term financial health of your organization?

8. What plan, if any, does your organization have for developing financial reserves?

9. What are the various cost centers (programs) in your organization's budget? What are their income sources?

10. Has your agency developed cash flow projections?

11. Are there internal controls in place to ensure that restricted funding is being appropriately spent and accurately accounted for?

Notes

1. M. Dropkin & B. LaTouche, *The budget-building book for nonprofits* (San Francisco: Jossey-Bass, 1998), pp. 3–5.

2. A. S. Lang, *Financial responsibilities of nonprofit boards* (Washington DC: Boardsource, 2003), p.1.

3. L. L. Martin, *Financial management for human service administration* (Boston: Allyn & Bacon, 2001), pp. 85–87; P. M. Kettner, R. M. Moroney, & L. L. Martin, *Designing and managing programs* (Thousand Oaks, CA: Sage, 1999), pp. 216–218.

4. L. L. Martin, *Financial management for human service administration*, p. 87.

5. R. L. Karski & R. P. Barth, Models of state budget allocation in child welfare services, *Administration in Social Work* 24 (2000), pp. 45–66; L. L. Martin,

Budgeting for outcomes in state human agencies, *Administration in Social Work* 24 (2000), pp. 71–88.

6. R. Herzlinger, Effective oversight: A guide for nonprofit directors, *Harvard Business Review* 72 (July/August 1994), p. 56.

7. P. C. Brinckerhoff, *Financial empowerment* (Dillon, CO: Alpine Guild, 1996), pp. 48–49.

8. M. Dropkin & B. LaTouche, pp. 8–9.

9. A. S. Lang, *Financial responsibilities of nonprofit boards*, p.19.

10. K. Klein, *Fundraising for social change*, 4th ed. (Oakland, CA: Chardon, 2001), p. 364.

11. R. L. Gale, *Leadership roles in nonprofit governance* (Washington DC: Boardsource, 2003), p. 2.

12. M. Dropkin & B. LaTouche, pp. 89–90.

13. A. S. Lang, *Financial responsibilities of nonprofit boards*, p. 6.

14. M. D. Feit & Peter Li, *Financial management in human services* (New York: Haworth Press, 1998), pp. 39–40.

15. R. Herzlinger, p. 57; M. D. Feit, pp. 39–40.

16. L. L. Martin, *Financial management for human service administration*, pp. 98–107.

17. L. L. Martin, *Financial management for human service administration*, p.153.

18. L. L. Martin, *Financial management for human service administration*, p. 35; J. M. Greenfield & R. F. Larkin, Public accountability, *New Directions for Philanthropic Fundraising* 2 (2000), pp. 51–71.

19. L. L. Martin, *Financial management for human service administration*, p. 11.

20. P. C. Brinckerhoff, pp. 120–125.

21. P. C. Brinckerhoff, p. 140.

22. M. Dropkin & B. LaTouche, pp. 86–89.

23. P. C. Brinckerhoff, pp. 92–94.

24. G. J. Dabel, *Saving money in nonprofit organizations* (San Francisco: Jossey-Bass, 1998); M. Dropkin & B. LaTouche, pp. 75, 84; M. H. McCormack, *Mark H. McCormack on managing* (West Hollywood, CA: Dove Books, 1996), pp. 192–200.

25. M. H. McCormack, pp. 193–194.

26. M. Dropkin & B. LaTouche, p. 74.

27. M. H. McCormack, pp. 199–200.

28. P. C. Brinckerhoff, pp. 49–50.

29. M. Browman, J. Baanante, T. Dichter, S. Londner, & P. Reiling, Measuring our impact: Determining cost-effectiveness of non-governmental organization development projects, in *Cost-effectiveness in the nonprofit sector,* ed. G. L. Schmaedick (Westport, CT: Quorom Books, 1993), pp. 93–118.

30. G. L. Schmaedick, ed., *Cost-effectiveness in the nonprofit sector* (Westport, CT: Quorum Books, 1993), pp. 3–15.

31. R. Herzlinger, p. 57.

13 Strategic Resource Development I

Increasingly, managers of human service organizations realize that they must provide leadership to raise funds strategically from a variety of sources. Strategic fundraising requires long-term planning that is diversified and builds a base of involved, supportive contributors. It is not based on a series of isolated, haphazard events. You will have limited success if you try to deal with a major budget deficit by making a last-minute appeal to unknown donors, hastily preparing a special event, or requesting foundations provide bailout funds. Begging and haphazard appeals for money are not ways to conduct fundraising.[1]

Some organizations that receive funding from several sources (that generate large amounts of income) hire part-time or full-time fund resource development staff. These development staff, however, cannot operate in isolation from the rest of the organization and must rely on board members, other staff, and volunteers to contribute ideas and make important contacts. Smaller organizations and those that look to only one or two income sources or rely on service fees require their management staff to be their principal fund developers. This is an inescapable role and an essential part of every effective manager's job in both large and small organizations.

Although the term *fundraising* still denotes an essential aspect of the manager's role, the more common term today is *resource development*. This suggests a broader focus, as resource acquisition can include, in addition to funds, the donation of property, services, and equipment, which otherwise would need to be purchased with raised funds. The use of the word *development* also emphasizes the role that relationships play in obtaining donations. Human service managers focus on developing relationships with donors that lead to their willingness to honor requests for donations.

This chapter provides a framework for fundraising activities by discussing the need for an integrated fundraising plan and the importance of preparing a case statement. The chapter also highlights two major fundraising endeavors: running an annual fund drive and soliciting major gifts. The next chapter reviews planned giving, corporate fundraising, special events, and business ventures. In a subsequent chapter, preparing proposals and searching for funding are discussed.

Developing an Integrated Fund Plan

All fundraising activities should fit within the organization's overall strategic plan and be related to its goals and objectives. The organization must first decide what it must do to achieve its goals and then determine how it would raise the necessary funds to achieve them. Moreover, as part of its strategic planning, an organization should examine various funding options to determine which ones are most suitable and how the various funding activities can build on each other.

Organizations must determine which funding approaches are best pursued. An organization established to provide innovative programs is continuously involved in writing proposals for government or foundation funding. Those agencies that receive the major source of their funding from a government agency, such as a mental health or substance abuse agency, need to develop close working relationships and be responsive to these government entities.

Even as managers give concentrated attention to their most likely source of funding, they must be careful not to concentrate only on this source, because if this funding stream declined, the organization's survival could be at stake. An organization, for example, that is entirely dependent on government contracts and grants is highly vulnerable during a period of federal or state cutbacks. If foundations that have been providing major funding decide to put their funding elsewhere, then an agency may be forced to discontinue its core programs. Also, corporate, private, and community foundations usually request a listing of various other sources of support as an indication that the organization can be sustained and that it has a broad base of support in the community. Diversity of funding can add to an agency's credibility, security, and sustainability.

Each organization must conduct a careful review of its funding options based on an in-depth understanding of its past performance in fundraising and its strengths and weaknesses. A grassroots organization, whose constituents have limited discretionary funds, might determine that a neighborhood carnival or bake sale is appropriate because of its ability to attract large numbers of people. In contrast, a hospital might offer a five-star cooking event and charge a limited number of patrons $300 a ticket because it can attract affluent people to this special event. Each approach is sound because each builds on the strengths of the organization and an assessment of its donors.

An effective fundraising campaign works to combine various fundraising endeavors so that they are part of a total integrated plan. For example, a special event might elicit the names of potential contributors to an annual campaign. An annual campaign can produce the names of those contributors who might be solicited for special, large contributions or for making gift commitments in their wills. Before submitting a funding request to a foundation, an organization may conduct a low-key internal fundraising campaign to demonstrate its own trustee commitment to a portion of the proposed project's cost. A commitment from board members and others close to the organization communicates to donors that personal involvement of members includes contributions of time and money. Hence it is crucial to determine how the various fundraising efforts interrelate and build on each other—and how they are packaged to donors.

If an organization is involved in several different kinds of fundraising activities, then it is desirable to establish a committee that gives general oversight and plans strategically to implement various funding endeavors. Typically, organizations appoint a resource development committee, often consisting of both trustees and other volunteers, to provide this oversight. Depending on the complexity of funding efforts, this committee could either be limited to planning, carrying out each fundraising activity itself (e.g., special event, annual donations, or capital campaign), or delegating each activity to special task groups. Though resource development committees can also tackle proposals, it is more common that the organization's management undertakes this form of fundraising.

Before a fundraising program is undertaken, an organization would do well to get its house in order by seeing that the following are in place:[2] First, the board and the staff must articulate their shared vision in a mission statement[3] (see Chapter 3). One of the dangers that organizations face is that the mission statement may become obsolete if it is not periodically reviewed and, if appropriate, revised. To determine if its mission is current and realistic, the organization must engage in ongoing market research to identify emerging issues or conditions to be addressed. Developed as part of the strategic planning process, the mission must be understandable to outsiders and potential funders, in addition to providing direction to board and staff.

Second, the organization's management and board must be able to demonstrate how they complement each other and work together. The organization's volunteers should be actively engaged and committed to raising funds and providing financial stewardship. Board members must feel a personal ownership for the organization's functioning (see Chapter 20).

Third, the organization must be able to articulate a meaningful and significant rationale for its fundraising. Its goals and objectives must be clearly defined so that the results of its interventions are readily apparent. It must show that its programs are responsive to community needs and document measurable outcomes (see Chapters 2, 3, and 4). Typically, a case statement will be the vehicle for communicating the rationale for fundraising because it links concern for an unmet need with a solution to be undertaken by the organization.

Clarity of mission, engaged staff and board members in a collaborative partnership, and a well-prepared case statement provide a powerful backdrop to any fundraising that is undertaken.

Preparing a Case Statement

Organizations prepare a case statement to articulate a clear and compelling reason why people should consider making a contribution.[4] The case statement expresses why the organization is important to the community, how the organization meets urgent community needs, how contributions makes a difference, how the agency measures outcomes, and how it responsibly manages its funds.

To attract community support, the case statement should express a powerful reason for contributing money. For example, the goal could be to reduce hunger, to help people become self-sufficient, to help children learn better, or to improve health care. It should be client-focused and contain an inspiring message, such as striving to achieve social justice or improving the quality of life of the agency's clients.[5] In addition to these lofty statements, it should describe and specify the number of people that it serves (or will serve) and the impact that the program has on them.

Effective managers will want to develop two parallel case statements. An *internal case statement* is the organization's planning document, and an *external case statement* informs outside constituencies. Through the internal planning document, the organization clarifies how the project would be staffed, what facilities are required, how finances would be managed, what target audiences you want to reach, how success is defined, and how the program is evaluated. By being clear about these programmatic issues, the organization is in a better position to respond to questions and concerns of potential donors. The internal document is generally not shared with donors. It is a primary resource document that helps the development campaign leadership create brochures, grants, and external documents for the campaign.

The external case statement focuses on how the organization clearly understands the problem and has a program to resolve it or is prepared to take advantage of new opportunities. Potential contributors tend to enthusiastically support programs that meet a compelling community—not agency—need. For example, expanding the number of offices is not in itself a sufficiently compelling case. The fact that this expansion would enable the organization to serve more people in its literacy program, however, provides an urgent rationale for financial support. The case statement is the organization's marketing tool.

The case appeal should be both rational and emotional, because people give with both their hearts and their minds. A quote from a satisfied client or an anecdote about how a child would benefit from a counseling service needs to be accompanied with an explanation about the organization's finances and accountability. In addition, the case needs to identify the variety of gift opportunities that are available, such as a donation to an equipment fund or a scholarship fund. Each donor could designate a specific category for giving (e.g., $50, $100, or $250). If a tax deduction is possible, this should also be made known, although tax deductibility has not been found to be a primary motivation for giving.

The case should offer a sense of the future, a confidence that the organization has accurately defined the problem and offers a compelling solution. You want to convey that your organization has a track record and a history that makes it competent to accomplish your intended objectives.[6] It should inspire and motivate constituencies to become engaged as partners in volunteering and contributing to your cause.

The form that the case takes is based on the particular audience you are trying to reach. It could be an annual report sent to the organization's members. Elements of it could be included in a speech to a service club where funds are being requested. It could be included in a brochure or in an annual campaign letter. Regardless of the form it takes, it is helpful to involve as many organization members, particularly from the board, as is feasible because people who have an opportunity to shape the case in the process learn more about the program and increase their sense of ownership. Of course, one or two people can be ultimately responsible for writing the case statement, since it is impossible for a committee to do so. After the case statement is prepared, use it to educate your trustees and volunteers.

The Annual Campaign

The primary purpose of an annual campaign is to raise money to support the organization's ongoing operations. Usually, the annual campaign is time limited (six weeks or less) and is held at the same time each year. Through the annual campaign, the organization identifies a base of donors to expand over time; it includes donors who may eventually make major gifts. First-time donors can be identified through direct mail or telephone solicitation. Renewed donors may receive telephone solicitation or personalized letters from board members. Some of these donors increase their donations from one year to the next through personal contact. The annual fund is thus designed to acquire, maintain, and upgrade a large number of committed donors, who give relatively small contributions.[7] These members become informed, and they develop a habit of giving to general operating funds. Because the annual campaign brings in unrestricted funds, it provides stability for the organization and should therefore never be canceled or deferred. It takes precedence if the organization does not have the resources to conduct other campaigns.[8] To make the campaign a success, consider the ideas proposed in the next section.

25 Ideas for Making the Annual Campaign a Success

1. Focus initially on those closest to the organization, meaning trustees, past donors, staff, consumers, and volunteers. Give special attention to trustee contributions. Their support sends a clear message to the community that they believe in the organization, and for this reason it is important to have their 100% participation. All trustees should be expected to make contributions at a leadership level, or within their ability to give.[9]

2. Obtain the largest gifts early to set the leadership pace for the annual campaign. Before beginning the formal annual campaign, solicit advance gifts from board members and major previous contributors.

3. Take advantage of enthusiastic volunteers by asking them to host small gatherings in their homes, at which time the director might give a brief fundraising pitch.[10]

4. Although personal contact puts a burden on volunteers who may not be comfortable asking for money, it is the primary way to raise money from the largest annual contributors.

5. Make telephone calls to those who already have a relationship with the organization. This provides an opportunity to raise money, and to communicate directly what the organization has been achieving. It is best to use volunteers who can convey their own commitment to the organization.[11] To ease their making calls, provide callers with a written presentation.

6. In phoning, convey briefly why you are calling and suggest a specific tax-deductible amount. If they turn down your first request (e.g., $100), ask for a smaller contribution (e.g., $50), and then an even smaller one (e.g., $25). If they are still uncertain about contributing, offer to send a brief description, plus a return envelope. If they definitely turn you down, indicate appreciation for taking their time and express hope that they might consider a gift in the future.

7. Some organizations phone prospects after an appeal has been made by mail. The letter might indicate that prospects would be called unless the organization receives a reply by a date prior to the phone-a-thon.[12]

8. In a direct mail campaign, express the case for contributing to the annual campaign. To increase the possibility of response, trustees can write a personal note to people they know, saying how valuable the organization's contribution is to the community.[13]

9. Because a direct mail campaign is expensive, particularly for acquiring new donors, it makes no financial sense to do it without a strong cultivation program so that you can eventually upgrade contributions.[14]

10. The annual campaign should provide for different giving levels, such as contributing friend, supporting friend, and president's circle. Then print contributors' names in the appropriate category in the annual report so that people are recognized each year for their level of support.[15]

11. Offer contributors the opportunity to designate their donations for specific purposes, such as to purchase supplies for clients or to support specific programs.

12. The annual fund letter should contain the following elements: (a) personalize the salutation; (b) select a signer who is known to the donor; (c) tell the reader how a gift can make a difference in achieving the organization's

mission; (d) ask the reader to consider upgrading the gift, citing a specific amount; (e) provide an emotional reason to contribute; (f) communicate your organization's track record for accomplishing results; and (g) provide a pre-addressed envelope.[16]

13. Ask contributors to make monthly installments. As a member of the "Donor's Club," a contributor who formerly gave $100 to the annual campaign can now be asked to give $25 monthly.

14. To encourage donors' contributing year after year, provide opportunities for involving them in your organization, such as volunteering with clients or serving on special committees.

15. Because of the likely fall-off of contributors each year, known as *shrinkage*, it is important to (a) renew as many contributors as possible, (b) work to upgrade current contributors, (c) acquire new contributors, and (d) recapture lapsed contributors.[17]

16. Obtain the names and addresses of people who attend your special events so you can add them to your mailing list. Create an annual fund category to honor a high profile business or civic leader who has been honored at your event.[18]

17. Provide for memorial gifts to honor deceased persons who have made a profound commitment to the organization or as a remembrance for someone who has died recently to express condolences to the family.

18. Use your Web site to attract potential donors to your annual campaign by providing a secured "return message link" to make inquiries or contributions.

19. Every letter or e-mail message can have a standard closing that invites people to join the organization or indicates where they can find out more about the organization through the agency's Web site.

20. In prospecting for potential annual contributors, consider the following: (a) vendors who do business with the organization; (b) friends, neighbors, and business associates of trustees and volunteers; and (c) families of those that the organization serves, provided that confidentiality is not an issue.

21. Reply immediately with a thank-you note, signed with an original signature by the board president or campaign chairperson. Keeping in touch with prospects can be done through newsletters, notes, periodic e-mails, and personal visits.

22. Develop a good tracking system to manage donor information. This information should reflect the relationship of the prospect to the organization and all previous contributions. The information should be kept confidential.[19]

23. Organize a campaign team that develops, implements, and evaluates the annual campaign.

24. The annual fund can be organized in the form of a volunteer solicitation pyramid. At the head is the chairperson, who in turn recruits campaign division captains, who in turn are responsible for division solicitors. This hierarchy of responsibility ensures good campaign follow-up and accountability.[20]

25. Crucial to the success of the annual campaign is the selection of a respected and enthusiastic chairperson who can motivate committee members and prospective donors.[21]

Constructing a Gift Chart

Planning the fundraising campaign requires establishing a reasonable goal based on evidence of recent fundraising experience and an understanding of the potential contributor pool.[22] Suppose you have decided on an annual goal of raising $50,000. To determine whether this is realistic, identify specific prospect names and consider how much money each one could contribute toward that goal. Note that the Gift Range Chart (Table 13.1) calculates the projected gift range categories, the number of actual gifts from expected contributors, the pool of prospects needed, and expected totals in each category. In this example, less than 10% of the contributors provide 60% of the projected funds raised. Note also that in order to obtain two gifts of $2,000 each, eight prospects would have been identified that are capable of making this kind of specific contribution, a ratio of 4 to 1. The organization anticipates that 4 prospects need to be contacted to achieve these major gifts. Similarly, 24 prospects would be contacted to achieve eight gifts of $1,000, a ratio of 3 to 1. At the lowest end of giving, a mailing to 1600 people is expected to achieve a return from 400 prospects.

Table 13.1   Gift Range Chart for a $50,000 Annual Fund Program

Gift Range	Number of Gifts	Pool of Prospects Needed	Expected Totals
$2,000	2	8 (4:1)	$4,000
1,500	3	12 (4:1)	4,500
1,000	8	24 (3:1)	8,000
500	12	36 (3:1)	6,000
250	30	90 (3:1)	7,500
100	50	200 (4:1)	5,000
50	100	400 (4:1)	5,000
25	400	1600 (4:1)	10,000
Total:	605	2,300	$50,000

Constructing a gift chart for both annual and major gifts programs helps the organization anticipate the challenge ahead and permits the organization to make a realistic assessment of whether it can achieve the anticipated fundraising goal. The development of the gift chart disciplines the organization's fundraisers to identify specific individuals who can make large gifts. It also fosters discussion about donors who might upgrade their gifts. Those who have given over a long period of time and have tended to upgrade their gifts are candidates for a larger solicitation—and for personal attention.[23]

Fundraisers have determined that certain solicitation activities are more effective than others:

1. A personal visit by one person or team involving a volunteer and a staff member (This is by far the most effective way of obtaining a large annual gift.)

2. Solicitation by personal letter with a follow-up telephone call

3. Solicitation by a personal note at the bottom of an annual form letter

4. A personal phone call followed by a letter with an enclosed self-addressed return envelope

5. Phone-a-thons in which volunteer solicitors conduct a telephone campaign

6. Door-to-door solicitations

7. Direct mail campaign

In general, emphasize personal contacts for those individuals identified as potential major contributors to the annual campaign. Referring to the above list, note that the broader the appeal, the more impersonal it becomes. In the first few years of developing an annual campaign, if you primarily solicit by mail, expect to raise only a minimal amount—maybe to only break even. As you expand to a phone-a-thon, you do better. Some businesses or law firms may be willing to let you use their phones if your own organization has limited capacity.[24] In some instances, you may be surprised to receive a larger-than-expected gift from a few people. These donors should be put on the list for major gift solicitation at another time. They may also be considered as a candidate for planned giving, to be discussed later.

Capital Campaigns and Major Gifts

Capital campaigns differ from annual fundraising in that they usually help an organization raise a significant amount of money in a limited time for a special project: building a new facility, adding major equipment, or launching a new program. Capital campaigns do not fund current operations. They have clearly defined timetables, occur less frequently than annual campaigns, and enable the organization to accomplish specific project goals.[25] You are asking that the donor make a one-time extra financial commitment, possibly a pledge over a period of several years, from their assets (e.g., stocks or bonds) or from their discretionary income.

Certain principles that apply to fundraising in general can be reiterated in regard to capital campaigns:

1. The organization should conduct a pre-campaign feasibility analysis to determine its readiness to ask and the community's willingness to give. Certain key people would be interviewed to determine whether the case for a capital campaign is sufficiently appealing and the needs sufficiently valid. During this feasibility phase, campaign leaders would be identified and proper timing is considered.[26]

2. During the planning phase, you would consider whether the organization has the resources to proceed with a capital campaign without diminishing the effort directed toward the annual fund campaign.[27]

3. The campaign should evoke an enthusiastic response. Successful campaigns build enthusiasm for the cause by initiating the solicitation process from the inside. People closest to the organization, especially board members, make the first contributions; their enthusiasm makes them good solicitors for later gifts. People give in order to make a difference to those programs that are particularly important to them. Make certain that your case statement provides a solid plan and an inspirational message to your potential contributors.

4. The personal relationship between solicitor and donor is extremely important. People give to those with whom they have a relationship, and so matching solicitors and donors is a critical consideration.

5. The more involved people are in the organization and the more they are interested in the organization, the more significant their gift.

6. As in an annual campaign, carefully select a chairperson who can attract high-level participation.[28] That person should make the first contribution.

7. The campaign must be built on a compelling need that benefits the community. Merely expressing the need to purchase a building is not enough. A campaign must be able to convey how the use of a building would contribute to meeting needs of those the agency serves. In addition, consider providing naming opportunities for those who would find it appealing to have their names or those they wish to honor on plaques in rooms, hallways, and offices.

8. The finance goal should include (a) the cost of running the campaign itself, (b) the project's cost (e.g., architecture and building construction) and the cost of the maintenance, (c) equipment and furnishings, (d) start-up and other initial service costs, (e) cost overruns, and (f) donor attrition.[29]

9. The campaign goal should be realistic and be based on previous fundraising experiences, the number of qualified prospects, and the commitment of volunteer and board leadership who are willing to make personal solicitations. The most common mistake in capital campaigns is setting an unreasonable goal. This mistake is influenced by the desire to meet a need rather than a realistic assessment of the ability to raise money to pay for it.[30] The goal is based upon the gift range chart previously discussed. This format emphasizes that a few people at the top provide the pace setting or lead gifts in order to obtain the highest percentage of the funding.[31]

Each organization would modify the chart based on its particular circumstances. For example, a small organization with a few potential committed wealthy donors could have a higher percentage of contributors at the top, in contrast to an organization with several thousand annual donors and no history of major gift funding. In the latter instance, a smaller percentage might be raised from a few major contributors. Although the gift range chart should be customized to the organization, lead ("pacesetter") gifts of approximately 25% should be raised in advance of the public campaign. Less than this means that the financial goal may not be attained, and the capital campaign may need to be delayed to allow time for cultivating a few crucial, high-contributing donors.[32] Their commitment must be secured before the campaign begins.

10. Although the campaign relies heavily on the contributions of top donors, these donors do not want to feel totally responsible for the success of the campaign. A broad based plan gives them confidence that they alone are not responsible for the success of the program and that they are contributing to a cause that has general commitment.[33]

Developing a Base of Loyal Donors

Developing a donor base profile is absolutely essential because it reveals trends on each person's contribution. With the use of a computer, the database can preserve information and provide feedback on which donors are repeating and even adding to their contributions. These people become good prospects for a major gift or upgrading.[34]

It is helpful to distinguish between a *genuine potential contributor* and a *vague prospect*. Someone who is well known in the community and who has considerable assets but is not connected with the organization is a vague prospect. Any attempt to secure a gift without personal access to that person is probably a wasted effort. Similarly, conducting a mail campaign or telephone solicitation campaign with the general public that has no awareness of the organization typically provides limited financial return for the amount of effort expended.

Potential contributors are those who have a good likelihood of donating funds to your organization. In this connection, it is helpful to draw upon the *linkage-ability-interest principle.* Fundraisers have long used this principal to distinguish potential contributors from vague prospects:

Linkage relates to having direct access or access through a peer to the potential donor.

Ability means that the potential donor has discretionary income and is committed to making a philanthropic contribution.

Interest is based on the potential contributor's having knowledge of and commitment to the organization's mission and accomplishments.

Without all these elements, it is difficult to secure a significant donor gift.[35]

Fundraisers face a major challenge of identifying donors with the ability to give a substantial gift and establishing proper linkages with them. Think of your major contributors being in the center of a circle and constituting those who are most strongly committed to the organization: members of the board, staff, management, founding members, and major past contributors. Outside this central ring, in the second ring, are those who are committed because they are annual contributors, employees, volunteers, clients, or those who have been directly affected by the need that you address. The third ring might consist of former board members, vendors, and people who have a general philanthropic interest and some awareness of the organization. The farther one moves out from the center, the less committed and the lower the potential for contributions. The task of the organization is to engage these various constituencies as much as possible and help them feel a connection to the work of the agency.

It is tempting to identify people of wealth in a community (those with ability) and try to determine how they can be induced to make substantial contributions. The wealthy widow with assets of more than $40 million, the CEO whose annual salary is more than $1 million, and the well-known celebrity may each be potentially capable of making a substantial contribution. Until a meaningful connection occurs, however, these hoped-for contributions will not happen. Therefore the challenge for a fundraiser is to identify ways to attract those with discretionary income to the organization.

For example, an organization providing research and planning on health and human service issues is interested in raising funds to provide ongoing staffing on health issues. The former director of the agency approaches a retired industrialist who had formerly chaired a health committee from the organization. Because of his past interest and because of the linkage with the former director, the industrialist agrees to fund a permanent position in health planning.

Contrast this approach with an organization that is interested in attracting a celebrity who would help raise money for its AIDS programs. The local organization is aware of the celebrity's commitment to AIDS research but recognizes that probably hundreds of AIDS organizations around the country are seeking this celebrity's donation. The odds of securing this donation through a mail solicitation and without linkages may be only slightly better than winning the lottery. The hour that it takes to compose and transmit the letter may not be much of an investment, but a big payoff without a linkage is highly unlikely. (Perhaps a more realistic request of a celebrity is to make a minimal request, such as acting as an honorary chairperson or providing autographs that could be auctioned off.)

The question still remains, "How can we create linkages to affluent donors?" Some organizations can more easily do this by their very nature. Typically, wealthy donors participate in organizations that attract their peers, such as boards of hospitals, universities, local United Ways, and museums. Therefore you might select people on your board who have relationships with those who serve on these elite boards. For example, one of your board members is involved in a university fundraising campaign, and through this involvement talks with new friends. It is fairly common that a *quid pro quo*, or exchange mentality, operates among those who are involved in different charitable organizations. Often, people phone each other saying, "I gave to your campaign last year, now I would appreciate you contributing to my campaign."

Sometimes the linkages are indirect but nevertheless significant. The head of the bank may not be on your board, but certainly a neighborhood bank manager could provide you linkage with the top management of the bank. The vice president of a major corporation may not show interest in your children's agency, but the spouse or adult child may become heavily committed and eventually obtain a donation from the vice president's company.

Of course, linkage alone is not sufficient. Affluent people have to be shown why they should be interested in donating to your organization. Your organization must have a credible mission and a track record to appeal to potential donors (case statement). For example, suppose your organization is working to reduce crime and drug activity in selected neighborhoods. Your approach to the head of the grocery chain is to convey how your work would make it safer for shoppers. Clearly, the self-interests of the head of the grocery chain can result in a significant contribution to your agency. Similarly, knowing that an affluent person has a mentally challenged grandchild can open up the possibility of a donation. In these two examples, the donor's having a direct link to your children's agency increases the odds of obtaining more than just a token donation. Furthermore, you need strong written communication that conveys what you are trying to achieve and your degree of success. Those with linkages to potential donors need to convey that an investment in your agency can produce valued results.

Soliciting Major Gifts

A major gift contribution is different for each organization. For those agencies that customarily do not receive more than a few hundred dollars from their loyal contributors, a gift of $5,000 would be considered major. A mega-institution, such as a hospital or university, would likely have its sights set much higher. In either case, organizations seek out those few people who have the ability and the commitment to make a difference. Here the *80/20 rule* can be applied and perhaps even modified. This rule posits that 80% of the dollars will come from 20% of the donors. For many organizations, a more likely scenario is that 90% of the money raised comes from 10% of the donors.[36]

Recognizing the importance of focusing on a few potential donors requires organizations to limit spending significant amounts of time and energy on reaching out to every potential contributor. The focus instead should be concentrating on those few who could make a substantial contribution. This means that someone—management, staff, volunteer, or professional fundraiser—must concentrate on cultivating those on the major donor list.

How does one identify potential major gift givers? Typically, they come from the inner circle: board members, alumni (former board members, former clients, and former employees), volunteers, and top contributors to the annual fund. In addition, major donors are also those with financial ability within the second or third circle—that is, vendors and those community leaders who have expressed an interest in your organization. Each organization has to identify and develop its own customized list of potential major givers.

One of the most important aspects of a fundraising campaign is to arrange a meeting of a few people who are comfortable with discussing the personal finances of others. It is extremely important that the ground rules for discussion be confidentiality, discretion, and respect as the group determines the expected ranges of giving for the individuals on their list. The rating is based on what individuals have given to other organizations, whether they have the kind of assets that can be tapped into for a sizable gift, and their involvement with the organization.[37] The committee would then screen prospects to determine which ones are ready to be asked for a gift and which ones might require more time for cultivation. This may be because their personal ability to make a substantial gift at the present time is questionable or they show limited interest in the organization.[38]

It is important to develop a file on each potential major contributor that identifies not only demographic information but also previous giving patterns and interests. The most effective way to reach major contributors is through face-to-face solicitation. The process may begin with a personal letter or a phone call asking for a meeting, at which time a personal solicitation occurs. The donor should be made aware prior to the meeting of your intention to discuss your organization's fundraising activities, though not the amount to be requested. Before the meeting, research the potential donor's interests related to your organization's activities. Someone on your solicitation team or board of trustees may be aware, for example, that the prospect has grandchildren the same age as those that are being tutored in your tutoring program. Or perhaps your prospective donor has contributed to organizations similar to yours and therefore may be receptive to your special project.

Assuming that you have done proper homework and that you know about the interest and commitment of the potential donor, use the meeting to discuss common interests, highlight the plans the organization has for the future, and then close the discussion with a request.[39] It is important that the discussion conclude with a specific request or a suggested contribution range: "Would you consider providing a leadership gift of $5,000 toward our new tutoring program?" Or the following statement could be made: "It is not our purpose to tell you what to do, but we had hoped you would consider a gift in the range of $5,000 a year for the next three years as your contribution."[40] After you convey the request, it is best not to say anything. Allow time for the potential contributor to consider the idea, but encourage making the decision during the time of the interview rather than at an indefinite later time.

Developing a Mindset for Soliciting Major Gifts

Usually volunteers or members of the board of trustees make the direct solicitation request. Their request for money is viewed as a genuine commitment to the organization. If, however, only a staff member is involved in soliciting, then the potential contributor might perceive the request as self-serving. Knowing that a volunteer is committed to raising funds sends a message that the organization is worthy of volunteer support. The job of the administrative staff is to help recruit these volunteer solicitors. Recruitment of volunteers is no easy matter, however, because those soliciting for money, even though they are committed to the work of the organization, may feel uncomfortable about asking their peers to make a contribution. Asking people for money is an acquired taste; few people enjoy doing it initially and most are afraid of being turned down. Staff need to help volunteers deal with their concerns and foster a positive—even joyful—experience. Keep volunteers focused on your main purpose and on seeing that rejections are only temporary obstacles on the route to the main goal.[41]

Several factors can contribute to successful solicitation. Volunteer solicitors must be enthused about advancing the agency's mission. They should have the opportunity to see firsthand the good work of the organization. To mentally prepare for soliciting others, solicitors themselves must make a contribution. Only by making their own contribution do solicitors convey their personal commitment. Encourage solicitors to believe that they are providing prospects with the opportunity to give a donation. Without the solicitation, that person is denied the privilege of making a contribution to a worthwhile cause. The best attitude is that giving is neither an obligation nor a responsibility. Nobody can be forced to give. Rather, it is a privilege. The focus is not on giving money so much as investing discretionary, philanthropic dollars in a special organization that is making a contribution to the community.[42]

Meeting with a prospect should involve a dialogue, which includes giving serious attention to an understanding of the prospect's interests, possible objections, and complaints. It means genuinely listening to what is important to the donors and their philanthropic giving. The art of soliciting involves both talking and listening.[43] In the solicitation process, you are not selling but instead conveying knowledge and personal interest. By being sensitive to the donors' views and attending to their concerns, the solicitor conveys great respect.

Emphasize with solicitors that they must strive to obtain a commitment from their prospects. Before concluding the discussion, the solicitor would ask, "Could you consider a gift between $3,000 and $5,000?" Then the solicitor would remain silent and let the prospect have the opportunity to speak. Sometimes the prospect will say, "I'd like to assist, but that amount is way out of my range." The response could be, "What would you feel comfortable in contributing?" You could ask for a donation at the moment, provide an envelope for returning a check, or suggest that they make a pledge over a period of time.[44] Obtaining a commitment during the face-to-face meeting or shortly thereafter is crucial.[45] If the prospect needs time to make a decision, you would offer an opportunity for a follow-up discussion.[46]

Provide solicitors with techniques that they can use with prospects. For example, offer role-playing opportunities. Anticipate how they might handle questions or concerns. Let them see firsthand the work of the agency so they can communicate their personal experience with those served by the organization.[47] Give them a campaign kit or information sheets that contain a case statement, information on the organization, suggestions for working with prospects, and a pledge card that indicates a date by which the prospect intends to pay.[48]

Advise solicitors not to convey being disappointed if the gift is not as high as they had expected; the donor may have perfectly good reasons for the decision. Because negative reactions likely damage the relationship to the organization, solicitors must express appreciation for whatever prospects offer.[49] Request that solicitors ask for the prospect's reason for not contributing. It may be that they can give at a later time, they do not have sufficient information about the organization, they do not have the funds at the present time, or that they have a misunderstanding that can be addressed.

Whatever the reason, it either may be within the control of the solicitor to do something about the concern (such as getting more information to the prospect), or it may be outside the control of the solicitor. If the prospect has a particular grievance, make sure to communicate this to the organization. At a later time, the prospect can be re-contacted to clarify that action was taken regarding the grievance. Remind solicitors that gifts at all levels are valued and that all donors at all levels should be respected. With this approach you lay the groundwork for continuing goodwill that could lead to future donations.

Continuously Cultivate Donors

Developing a significant relationship with prospects is fundamental to effective fundraising. It involves high quality, frequent communications—both formal and informal—between the organization and potential contributors. Newsletters, luncheons, field visits, and events allow people to understand firsthand the work of the agency and to begin to develop a pool of prospects from which potential contributors can be drawn. In addition, you could develop a deeper level of commitment among prospects by seeking their advice based on their areas of expertise, asking them to serve on a strategic advisory committee, or inviting them to see the organization at work.[50] Contact your major donors a minimum of two or three times a year in addition to the times you ask them for money. Put on your calendar when you need to be in touch with these special donors.[51] Send birthday and anniversary cards. Every organization has to consider whether to expend limited volunteer and staff resources in reaching out to large numbers of people who may provide only limited, nominal gifts in contrast to focusing on more committed and more affluent potential donors who could make substantial gifts.[52]

In the long term, a donor renewal program is more cost effective, efficient, and meaningful to an organization than short-term gains that might be obtained through extraordinary efforts of seeking new donor acquisition. In the commercial world, businesses have learned to cultivate their current customers. Airlines know, for example, that their best customers are repeat customers; hence the widespread use of frequent flyer mileage programs. It is more cost efficient and financially productive to actively retain a donor than to acquire a new one.[53] A renewal program should focus on those donors who have contributed for several years and who have been active participants in the work of the organization. They are the ones that would benefit from a peer volunteer soliciting an increased donation.[54]

To move from one level to the next in contributions, donors must feel that they are investing in something that provides large returns. They want to know whether their investment can truly make a difference and therefore are entitled to information about how their investment has paid off. How many books did the agency provide? How many children learned to swim? How many houses were rehabilitated? The more concrete and specific an organization can be about its results, the better. If an organization can establish some measurable baseline, then it can document more accurately for potential contributors exactly how much progress has been made or could be made with additional funding.

If the newspapers have a positive story about your program, send them a copy. They should be recipients of your newsletters and annual reports. They like to hear good news about your program. Even if the news is not good, however, your contributors need to know, preferably before anyone else. If your bookkeeper has embezzled funds or a staff member has committed a criminal act, communicate with your contributors to indicate how you are addressing the situation. Donors appreciate being informed promptly about this and learning what corrective actions you are taking.

Hiring a Fundraising Consultant

A fundraising consultant can provide expertise and experience, and many do have an excellent track record of helping organizations gain funding to reach goals. Be aware, however, that board members and volunteers may be tempted to disengage in fundraising after hiring a consultant. Board members should be forewarned that a fundraising consultant might put even more pressure on them to be actively involved in the fundraising process.

Another concern relates to compensating a fundraising consultant. Because organizations often lack funding to hire a consultant upfront, they may be tempted to make an arrangement that the consultant would receive a commission based on the amount of funds raised. However, the Association of Fundraising Professionals (AFP) considers commission-based fundraising to be unethical and requires that its members work for a salary or fee, not for a percentage of philanthropic funds raised.[55] This ethical requirement can clearly present a problem to those organizations that do not initially have funds to hire a consultant. Many organizations strive to obtain funding for a fundraiser from a foundation or from board donors who see their contribution as organizational capacity building.

Assessing the Major Gifts Program

After the fundraising campaign, your organization's fundraising committee and your board should conduct an assessment. This can be accomplished through a donor survey and with an internal evaluation.

To build donor loyalty you must have donors who know the organization, trust what you do, and feel that you use their contributions appropriately.[56] You need to know how your donors feel about your organization to communicate with them properly. An open-ended donor survey questionnaire can be customized to your organization's specific needs and would cover the following: (1) How well is the organization fulfilling its mission? (2) What programs do you consider to be most (and least) important and why? (3) How long have you supported the organization? (4) What information would you like about the organization's work? (5) What is the best way to contact you: phone, mail, or e-mail? (6) What improvements would you suggest for our newsletter? (7) Would you like to consider naming our organization in a will or trust? This kind of inquiry can be used either through a mail survey or in a face-to-face contact.

An internal evaluation process can help the organization determine the best use of limited resources, make sure that the fundraising effort furthers the organization's mission, and assess the extent to which the fundraising objectives are in fact being achieved. The following questions should be explored:

1. Compared to the objectives we have established, how many new donors did we acquire?

2. Compared to our objective, what was our rate of retention?

3. What percent of donors moved into a higher category of giving?

4. What was the total amount raised from individual donors?

5. How many donors did we have in the following categories: a) Less than $25, b) $25–49, c) $50–99, d) $100–249, e) $250–499, f) $500–999, g) $1000+?

6. In what specific ways did we keep in touch with our donors this past year?

7. How many board members were involved as donors and in at least one fundraising activity?

8. What percentage of our board made an annual contribution (according to their means)?

9. How did we involve volunteers in fundraising?

10. How did we involve staff in fundraising?

11. For each fundraising activity, what did we know about the following: (a) amount of money raised (gross and net)? (b) number of new donors? (c) total number of contributors? (d) range of gifts? (e) who was involved in the activity? (f) additional benefits from the activity? (g) what worked and what didn't?

Organizations typically bring together the group responsible for a particular activity to celebrate the results and identify areas of improvement for the following year. Keep a written record of the evaluations so that next year's group can have the benefit of your thinking.[57]

At a minimum, an evaluation should be done immediately after the close of the campaign. In the course of the campaign, if it begins to appear that you are not on track to meet your goal, then you must review the situation to determine what special actions need to be taken. For example, you may need to ask major contributors to consider increasing their gifts even more, or identify new prospects to be solicited. Sometimes solicitors express difficulty in reaching their prospects, and additional, more aggressive efforts may need to be taken, either by the solicitor or by assigning another one. Sometimes solicitors even need to be replaced. Whatever the problems, leaders of the campaign must try to deal with them.[58]

At the conclusion of the campaign, you will need to conduct an intensive review. You'll want to know, for example, whether the goal you set was realistic, whether the campaign structure and materials were effective, whether you were able to correct problems in a timely manner, and whether the volunteers and staff performed well or not. You are looking for patterns of underperformance and potential improvements. The best source of this information is the solicitors. They can tell you what worked best for them and what would be helpful for people to have in the next campaign.

Questions for Discussion

1. Does your organization have a comprehensive strategic fundraising plan? If so, what are its main features? If not, and you are required to develop one, what would it include?

2. You are an agency that provides counseling to high-risk elementary school children. Due to a lost grant, you need to raise $40,000 to continue providing part-time counselors to seven inner-city elementary schools, despite the clear success of the program. What ideas would you convey in a case statement?

3. Has your organization established quantifiable fundraising objectives? What are they?

4. What steps would you take to convince your organization to undertake an annual campaign?

5. Assume that you have been asked to construct a gift chart for an upcoming campaign. What would it look like?

6. You have been asked to serve as a fundraising consultant on a proposed capital campaign to raise money for a new addition for your agency costing $5,000,000. What do you want to know before you begin the campaign?

7. How would you go about cultivating a suburban wealthy widow to interest her in funding mental health counseling for inner-city residents?

8. You have been asked to accompany a solicitor to meet with a potential donor. How would you prepare the solicitor for the meeting?

Notes

1. H. A. Rosso, *Rosso on fundraising* (San Francisco: Jossey-Bass, 1996), pp. 17–18.

2. H. A. Rosso, *Achieving excellence in fundraising* (San Francisco: Jossey-Bass, 1991), pp. 289–293; W. E. Lindahl, *Strategic planning for fundraising* (San Francisco: Jossey-Bass, 1992), pp. 4–5.

3. K. A. Williams, *Donor focused strategies for annual giving* (Gaithersburg, MD: Aspen, 1997), pp. 47–50; T. Poderis, *It's a great day to fundraise!* (Cleveland, OH: FundAmerica, 1996), pp. 15–18.

4. A. Kihlstedt & C. P. Schwartz, *Capital campaigns: Strategies that work* (Gaithersburg, MD: Aspen, 1997), pp. 31–42; K. A. Williams, pp. 103–118; H. A. Rosso, *Achieving excellence*, pp. 39–47; R. L. Edwards & E. A. S. Benefield, *Building a strong foundation: Fundraising for nonprofits* (Washington DC: NASW, 1997), p. 43.

5. W. C. Mengerink, *Hand in hand* (Rockville, MD: Fundraising Institute, 1992), p. 8.

6. T. L. Seiler, *Developing your case for support* (San Francisco: Jossey-Bass, 2001), pp. 93–94; T. Poderis, *It's a great day to fund-raise!*, p. 61.

7. H. A. Rosso, *Achieving excellence*, pp. 51–64; K. A. Williams, pp. 33–43; K. A. Williams, Annual campaigns, in *Nonprofit organization management* (New York: Aspen, 1997), p. 9:19.

8. T. Poderis, Annual and capital campaigns, Retrieved May 6, 2003, from www/raise-funds.com/399forum.html

9. T. Poderis, *It's a great day to fundraise!*, p. 9; *Nonprofit organization management* (New York: Aspen, 2002), p. 9:76; K. Klein, 55 ways for boards to raise $500, Retrieved May 5, 2003, from www.allianceonline.org/FAQ; W. C. Menegerink, p. 18.

10. T. Poderis, Cultivate a "grass-roots" fundraising campaign for your organization, Retrieved May 6, 2003, from www.raise-funds.com/0301forum.html

11. K. Klein, *Fundraising for social change,* 4th ed. (Oakland, CA: Chardon, 2001), pp. 135–137; K. Owens, Annual fundraising workshop (Cleveland, OH: Resource Development Network, February 2003).

12. K. Klein, *Fundraising for social change,* 4th ed., pp. 145–149.

13. C. Horton, *Raising money & having fun (sort of): A "how to" book for small nonprofit groups* (Cleveland: May Dugan Center, 1991), p. 61.

14. O. Morgan, Creating a budget for fundraising, *Grassroots Fundraising Journal* 2 (2003), pp. 4–6.

15. T. Poderis, *It's a great day to fundraise!*, p. 41.

16. K. Owens; T. Poderis, *Its a great day to fundraise!*, p. 41; F. Handy, How we beg: An analysis of direct mail appeals, *Nonprofit and Voluntary Sector Quarterly* 3 (2000), pp. 439–453.

17. K. Owens.

18. K. Klein, How to create an effective acquisition strategy, *Grassroots Fundraising Journal* 20(1).

19. R. L. Edwards & E. A. S. Benefield, pp. 32–33.

20. K. A. Williams, Annual campaigns, p. 9:19-22.1.

21. K. A. Williams, Annual campaigns, p. 9:21.

22. H. A. Rosso, *Rosso on fundraising*, pp. 10–15.

23. K. A. Williams, *Donor focused strategies,* p. 40.

24. W. C. Mengerink, p. 32.

25. A. Kihlstedt & C. P. Schwartz, pp. 1–14.

26. H. A. Rosso, *Achieving excellence*, pp. 80–85; T. R. Sudow, Resource Development Network Workshop (February 2003).

27. T. Poderis, Annual and capital campaigns.

28. W. C. Mengerink, p. 85.

29. K. Klein, Planning a capital campaign, *Grassroots Fundraising Journal* 3 (2001), pp. 4–7.

30. T. Poderis, *It's a great day to fund-raise!*, p. 50.

31. K. Klein, Testing the feasibility of your capital campaign, *Grassroots Fundraising Journal* 5 (2001), pp. 8–10.

32. A. Lauffer, *Grants, etc.*, 2nd ed. (Thousand Oaks, CA: Sage, 1997), p. 213; K. Klein, The phases of a capital campaign, *Grassroots Fundraising Journal* 4 (2001), pp. 8–12.

33. A. Kihlstedt & C. P. Schwartz, pp. 98–108.

34. H. A. Rosso, *Rosso on fundraising*, pp. 12–15.

35. H. A. Rosso, *Achieving excellence*, pp. 28–35.

36. H. A. Rosso, *Achieving excellence*, p. 176.

37. T. Poderis, *It's a great day to fund-raise!*, p. 34.

38. *Nonprofit organization management*, pp. 9:60.6–9:60.7.

39. C. F. Mai, *Secrets of major gift fundraising* (Washington, DC: Taft Group, 1987), pp. 21–22.

40. A. Lauffer, pp. 240–243.

41. W. C. Mengerink, p. 95.

42. H. A. Rosso, *Rosso on fundraising*, pp. 41–45.

43. K. A. Williams, *Donor focused strategies*, pp. 195–198.

44. K. Klein, The fine art of asking for the gift, *Grassroots Fundraising Journal* 2, 3 Retrieved May 6, 2003, from www.allianceonline.org/FAQ

45. R. L. Edwards & E. A. S. Benefield, pp. 55–57.

46. H. A. Rosso, *Rosso on fundraising*, pp. 61–62.

47. A. Lauffer, p. 221.

48. T. Poderis, Campaign solicitation kits, Retrieved May 6, 2003, from www.raise-funds.com/899forum.html

49. T. Poderis, *It's a great day to fund-raise!*, p. 31; K. Klein, Getting over the fear of asking, *Grassroots Fundraising Journal* 2 (2001), pp. 4–8; R. L. Edwards & E. A. S. Benefield, pp. 57–58.

50. R. L. Edwards & E. A. S. Benefield, pp. 27–32; K. Klein, Maintaining relationships with donors; T. Poderis, *It's a great day to fundraise!*, p. 26.

51. K. Klein, Maintaining relationships with donors.

52. K. A. Williams, *Donor focused strategies*, pp. 149–181.

53. K. A. Williams, *Donor focused strategies*, p. 158; R. L. Edwards & E. A. S. Benefield, p. 27.

54. H. A. Rosso, *Rosso on fundraising*, p. 13.

55. R. L. Edwards & E. A. S. Benefield, pp. 19–20.

56. M. Farmelo, Getting to know your donors: The donor survey, *Grassroots Fundraising Journal* 1 (2001), pp. 8–11.

57. S. Roth, Evaluating your individual donor program, *Grassroots Fundraising Journal* 6 (2001), pp. 8–11.

58. T. Poderis, *It's a great day to fund-raise!*, pp. 89–91.

14 Strategic Resource Development II

T his chapter continues the discussion of strategic resource development and covers planned giving, corporate contributions, electronic philanthropy, business ventures, and fundraising events.

Planned Giving

Increasingly, human service organizations use *planned giving programs* (PGPs) (also known as endowments or bequests) to obtain additional resources for their programs and to ensure long-term stability. The primary purpose of planned giving is to help provide the organization with long-term financial security and survival. It helps the organization keep pace with inflation, compensates for funds lost from other sources, permits expansion of programs that otherwise could not be funded, and provides for unusual emergency situations for which other resources are not available. In general, planned giving is not designed to meet agency short-term, operational needs.

Planned giving refers to a gift arranged by donors that usually does not become available to the organization until some time in the future. The gift can be money, securities, or other property. Usually the gift occurs following the death of the contributor, the death of a surviving beneficiary, or at the end of a specific term. In some instances the gift can be used by the organization while the donor is still alive. The gift is made from a contributor's accumulated assets and is part of an overall estate plan. This is in contrast to annual gifts that are derived from current income.[1]

An organization should consider undertaking a PGP only when it has demonstrated its value to the community and has developed sufficient financial stability for donors to feel comfortable making a donation to yield income in perpetuity. Because an endowment gift is forever, the organization needs to be well-established to give assurances of a long life. Where potential donors may have doubts about the longevity of an organization, arrangements can be made for them to give to a community foundation (see Chapter 16) and designate that the interest (and possibly the asset itself) be used to benefit the particular organization. In the event that the organization ceases to exist, the foundation could be instructed to provide funds to a similar organization in the community.

Before undertaking a PGP, the organization should determine that it can cover its operational deficit through an annual campaign or other gifts and grants. It is not a good idea to expend limited resources on a PGP when those resources could be used to meet an operational deficit. Moreover, the organization should have the capability and the commitment to raise a substantial amount of endowment money. Because only the interest, not the principal, is generally used, the goal should be sufficiently large enough to warrant the investment in a major campaign. Typically, organizations determine that only modest interest on the endowed principal, usually in the range of 4% or 5% of PGP gifts, is used within the budget year. Raising $20,000, for example, only yields $1,000 annual income; Raising $1,000,000 yields $50,000 each year.

The goal of a PGP should be carefully determined based on the capability of prospects to make a commitment. Some argue that the PGP campaign should be time limited and be held periodically (e.g., every five or ten years).[2] Many organizations, however, promote a PGP on a continuing basis, making it known to their constituents that PGP is something to be always considered.[3]

Types of Gifts

Persons of even moderate means may wish to make a planned giving contribution to the charity of their choice, and they have a variety of approaches for doing so. It is generally advisable for these contributors to obtain legal and tax accounting advice before making their decisions.

Outright gifts of appreciated property permit donors to reduce taxes by making a gift of stocks or bonds that have increased in value since they were acquired. Donors who itemize deductions can achieve tax savings. Suppose the value of a stock or mutual fund has increased from $2,000 to $10,000. Instead of making a cash contribution of only $2,000, the donor can give $10,000 of appreciated stock shares and deduct the entire $10,000 from his or her income tax.

Bequests are commitments written in a will that provide a gift of money or property at the time of the testator's death, or death of a designated prior beneficiary. The bequest could be a specific dollar amount, a percentage of the entire estate, or specific items, such as shares of stock. It is deductible from estate taxes. If an *irrevocable plan* is selected (i.e., the contributor gives up ownership of the assets), then the donor receives an income tax deduction and any additional payments of premiums can be charitable income tax deductions.

Life income gifts provide financial and estate planning benefits and are increasingly popular. The donor makes an irrevocable gift of cash or property and yet retains a life income for one or more beneficiaries. When the last income beneficiary dies, the assets that produce the income go to the charity. The donor enjoys a charitable deduction in the year that the gift is made, or the deduction can be carried forward for several years.

Charitable remainder trusts entitle the donor or another named person to income for life (or for a period of years), at the end of which time the named charity can have the *remainder* of the original gift. Under this arrangement, the donor can receive either a variable amount of income based on increases or decreases in the market value of a percentage of the trust assets (*unitrust*) or a fixed income (*annuity trust*). The income can be specified for the lifetime of one or more individuals or it can be for a fixed period of years. This latter trust arrangement is particularly suitable to meet the income needs of elderly beneficiaries. The trust income is fully taxable to the beneficiary unless the trust is invested entirely in tax-exempt bonds.

Pooled income funds allow donors to join together and create a pool of investments similar to a mutual fund. The donor or his or her designee receives a regular pro rata share in interest payments based on the earnings of the pooled fund. After all the designated beneficiaries die, the organization receives the principal.

Charitable gift annuities are a combination of an income gift and an investment. The organization accepts the gift and agrees to pay a specified fixed amount (annuity) to the donor or another recipient. It is an irrevocable gift and immediately becomes the property of the organization, which is then legally responsible to pay income for the lifetime of the donor. The advantages to donors are that they obtain a charitable deduction for their gift and receive a fixed income, partly tax-free. The advantage to the organization is that it is assured of the principal sometime in the future. Gifts to a pooled income fund are irrevocable (cannot be changed) and donors receive an income tax charitable deduction. Income payments to beneficiaries are taxed as ordinary income.[4]

Charitable lead trusts are directed to the organization for a number of years, often 10 or more. At the end of this period, the principal reverts back to the donor or someone else who has been designated. The *lead trust* differs from the *unitrust* or *annuity trust* in that the charitable organization receives the income from the trust during the trust period rather than receiving the principal at the end of the trust period. Donors experience the satisfaction of giving cash donations during their lifetime. The organization has the advantage of an immediate income flow, but it has to be prepared to lose this income at the end of the designated period.

A *life insurance policy* allows the donor to incur a modest out-of-pocket cost while being able to provide a significant charitable gift. Donors have an opportunity to make a larger gift than would normally be possible and pay for it on an installment basis through annual premiums. If the donor assigns ownership of a policy to the organization, the donor receives an immediate federal income tax charitable deduction for the amount of the premium.

In summary, if donors have highly appreciated assets that provide little income, then they could consider outright gifts or pooled income funds. If they want to make a significant commitment to the organization but need to maintain a secure income for themselves, then they would consider a charitable remainder trust or charitable gift annuities. If they want to support the organization but not give up their assets, then they would consider a charitable lead trust. If they want to make a donation to the organization but do not want to shortchange their heirs, they could consider an insurance policy.[5]

Implementing a Planned Giving Program

The process of raising money through planned giving consists of five major components, summarized in the acronym "IMRIP": integration, motivation, relationships, innovation, and persistence.[6]

PGP must be *integrated* as part of the organization, not an isolated activity. It should emerge from an organization's strategic plan and be connected with other fundraising endeavors. If your organization has excellent management and outstanding services that meet significant community needs and is perceived positively for its ability to help people effectively, your efforts at planned giving will be much easier.

Motivation is heightened by your conviction that a PGP gift can truly benefit the community long into the future, providing sufficient reason for staff and volunteers to put in the time and effort needed to obtain the gift. The motivation of the contributors is also essential. The contributors' needs must always be highest priority. They may want to preserve their assets while providing their heirs or their own financial future. You must demonstrate how the PGP can benefit them as well as the organization that they care about. They must also be motivated to leave a legacy that links their family name with an important community benefit.

Developing positive *relationships* with potential donors is a key element in a successful PGP. Positive feelings about an organization do not automatically translate into significant donations. People generally give because someone they like and respect asks them about a gift.

Innovation is also important because there is usually no simple formula for working with people who may be potential contributors. You need to create fresh ways to reach them. After all, you are not only meeting the needs of the organization but also the needs of contributors; therefore, you must think constantly about how to respond.

Persistence is another key quality. Invariably, the things you predict will happen do not occur. People make commitments and then postpone their decisions. It is not unusual to devote between three months and two years to cultivating a potential contributor. Establishing a meaningful relationship, providing ongoing information, and making continuous contact are essential in effective planned giving. Because events occur that can sidetrack the attainment of your objectives, you must be persistent and resilient in your efforts to reach out to donors.

Identifying Potential Contributors

Meeting directly with prospective donors is at the heart of a successful PGP. Although general announcements in your newsletter or even target mailings may be useful to alert people to planned giving, the most effective way of reaching prospective donors is through individual contacts.[7]

Because the organization's management staff and trustees must devote considerable personal investment to making individual contacts, narrow a potential broad list of prospects to a manageable few. Suppose you have a potential pool of 1,000 people who are connected with your organization. Presumably, many of these people would have contributed to your annual campaign in the last few years. Without an annual campaign it is probably unrealistic to initiate a PGP; people must have demonstrated their commitment to the organization through a pattern of giving.

You narrow this list to a smaller number of about 100 who have made financial, time, or talent contributions to the organization by participating on committees or volunteering their services to the organization.[8] This list needs to be narrowed even further to perhaps 40 most likely prospects, based on your assessment of the prospect's commitment, age, resources, and family situation. For these 40 prospects, you need to conduct additional research and develop individual profiles. In each file, include such basic information as address, phone numbers, family members, birth date, marital status, donation history, estimated worth of the individual and perhaps of her business, names of friends, and space for notations regarding contacts or other special information. These data can be put into a computer file for easy reference and updating, but you must ensure the safety and confidentiality of this data. Your profile research should provide important information that indicates where to concentrate your efforts. For example, you may want to expend more effort on a wealthy retired couple than a young couple who have a growing family and a modest income.

Planned gifts likely come from those people who are connected with your agency over a long period of time. The person of modest means participating in a senior citizen program, the veteran staff member of a children's institution, and the agency secretary who has been with the agency for 30 years and has no heirs are potential candidates for planned giving. Those people who have contributed to the annual campaign and have upgraded their gifts over the years demonstrate a commitment through their habit of giving. They may be interested in a long-lasting gift.

Maintaining Ongoing Contact and Awareness

It is extremely important that you maintain ongoing contact with donors, because if you do not, they may lose interest or feel neglected and even resentful. If they have included your organization in their will and come to believe that they are seen as unimportant, they may reconsider their financial commitment to the organization. Continually seek ways to maintain relationships. Notes reminding donors of the power of their contributions are vital ways to show respect and keep donors aware of their legacy. Because of the demands of other responsibilities, it is easy to relegate keeping in touch with those who have made a planned giving commitment to a low priority. Establishing a schedule of contacting three or four donors or potential donors on a regular basis preserves these important relationships.[9]

To encourage planned giving, some organizations have developed a pre-will program (sometimes called a legacy program or society) in which board members and others close to the agency are encouraged to sign a nonbinding letter of intent, stating they plan to provide for the organization in their estate planning. This program helps create a climate that supports planned giving. Members of the legacy society have their name listed (with their permission) in organizational materials such as the annual report, and are given recognition at annual meetings.

Administering Planned Giving Programs

Income from planned giving can be developed into three kinds of reserve funds for your organization: beneficial trust income, board-designated fund, and endowment income.[10]

Beneficial trust income is distributed to the organization based on the donor's wish. The principal, however, is controlled not by the organization but by community foundations, banks, or attorneys. The advantage of this type of reserve fund is that it permits the principal to remain intact and at the same time allows the income to be shared among several organizations. The donor has the security of knowing that should one of the organizations go out of business, an alternate could be selected or the balance of funds could be redistributed among the remaining organizations.

Board-designated funds are unrestricted donations of both the principal and earned income. The donor places no limitations on the use of the gift, thus providing trustees complete flexibility in determining how to use the principal and interest income. Because the principal can be used as board members see fit, this is technically not an endowment fund. Many organizations, however, treat open-ended gifts as *quasi-endowments*. That is, they use the interest income from the gift and avoid drawing upon the principal in the same way they would treat true endowments. This requires discipline among board members not to spend the principal, even if this might mean delaying or foregoing desired expenditures, such as increasing salaries or avoiding layoffs. By being disciplined, the organization assures long-term availability of funds.

Some organizations decide to withdraw part of the investment income to meet operating expenses and to return a portion of the investment income to the principal, which helps it keep pace with inflation. For example, suppose the principal based on a portfolio of stocks and bonds grows at the rate of 8% a year and the organization determines it will use 5% for operating purposes. The remaining 3% is reinvested so that the principal becomes greater the following year. A $2,000,000 endowment then becomes $2,060,000 the following year and is added to each year thereafter.

Having developed board-designated funds, agencies seeking funds from other sources, such as United Way, may have to deal with the criticism that all or portions of board-designated funds should be used before they are eligible to receive outside funding. If this issue surfaces, it is imperative that the organization educate the outside funder that board-designated funds are not considered a part of the operating reserves but are *quasi-endowment funds;* that is, only the income is used. In the example given above, the $60,000 added to the board-designated funds is not to be used for operating purposes. Increasingly, this option is being adopted because of the recognition that an aggressive PGP benefits the organization in the long term, which then leads to less dependence on outside community funders.

Some donors, although not specifically prohibiting organizations from invading principal, may prefer the organization not do so. This must be respected. Others might not care about the principal being used. Indeed, knowing how much organizations change, they may find flexibility appealing. This point should be clarified at the time the gift is being considered and, when feasible, reviewed after it is received.

True (permanent) endowments are used to fund specific programs, and donors may require that the income (interest) from the principal be restricted for specific purposes. Or they may permit the organization's board to determine how the income is to be used. Restricted, permanent endowments cannot invade the principal. Donors make a permanent endowment gift because they want to keep the fund intact in perpetuity and to assure the human service organization has ongoing income.

Some organizations may assign planned giving a low priority because other approaches—annual giving, special events, or grant writing—can produce funding more quickly to meet the current needs of the organization. The efforts to expand the organization's income through planned giving may not begin to yield tangible results for 15–20 years—and even then a $200,000 gift may only translate into $10,000 annual income. Still, planned giving is a strategy for building a long-term, continuous, and sustained financial support. Over a period of 10 years, an aggressive planned giving program could grow from $200,000 to $2 million.

Seeking Corporate Contributions

Although general corporations contribute only a small percentage of the total funds raised by nonprofit organizations, at some point many organizations seek corporate contributions.[11] Corporate contributions can take several forms. *Company foundations* are established by large corporations to manage their charitable requests. By transferring profits in good years to the company's foundation, they can provide a continuous level of funding even when corporate profits decline in some later years. They must follow regulations governing private foundations, including filing a form 990-PF with the IRS.[12] *Corporate giving funds* are provided directly out of the corporation's profits to designated charities. Some companies match the charitable gifts of their employees based on a predetermined ratio. In addition to cash donations, companies can provide such in-kind support as office space, meeting facilities, printing, legal services, company volunteers, and office equipment.[13] *Executive discretionary funds* are available to the chief executives of a company for providing small grants to organizations with which they are actively involved. *Subsidiary funds* are available to local offices of a national corporation for funding local groups. *Marketing budgets* allow a company to compensate an organization based on perceived value in marketing the company's identity and promoting its products and services. These funds can also be used to promote the company at community events. Sometimes this is known as cause-related marketing, which is discussed later. Organizations can concurrently approach each of these distinctive sources without concern for being accused of making excessive requests.

Contacting Corporations

Because of the tremendous competition for corporate funding, many companies concentrate their giving on local United Way campaigns or prefer organizations in which they can make an identifiable impact. Giving has become more tied to company strategic objectives. Companies seek to be identified with organizations that make them look good in the eyes of their customers. In addition, companies seek ways to leverage their support by using challenge grants. That is, they require the nonprofit to raise an equivalent amount from other sources before the company provides its own support. In approaching a corporation for a contribution, keep the following considerations in mind:

First, provide a rationale for why a company should support the organization for a particular project. It is especially important to show a link between the contribution and the benefits to the company. Remember that company contributions are often not far removed from corporate self-interest, including the interest in improving the community in which it is located.

Second, conduct research on the most likely companies based on such criteria as location in relation to clients or facility, its services or products, or known interests of senior managers or employees. Consider what might motivate companies to make a contribution. If your agency provides tutoring, you would identify a CEO who is interested in education. If your agency helps abused women, you would seek out a top corporate manager who has shown a commitment to women's issues.

Third, learn as much as possible about the company's giving guidelines, priorities, and procedures. Some companies are beginning to concentrate on only a few organizations where the companies can see tangible results, instead of spreading their charitable dollars to a wide variety of organizations. Others concentrate their giving to agencies that are in the vicinity of their business. Some companies have decided to limit their contributions to organizations with which their employees are associated and are beefing up their matching contributions. Still other companies allow their employees to purchase company products at a fraction of the cost providing their employees use the purchase as a charitable contribution.[14] It is worth the time and effort to determine what companies are doing in your community and consider engaging key employees in the work of the organization as volunteers and board members before pursuing corporate solicitations. (See Chapter 16 on seeking corporate contributions.)

Fourth, cultivate a relationship with an appropriate corporate executive by making a personal visit with those in charge of corporate philanthropy. These personal pre-solicitation visits provide helpful information in understanding the interest of the corporation. One of the most effective cultivation approaches is to involve the business's employees in the organization. Many corporations provide funds to match their employees' charitable contributions. Employees appreciate that their companies increase support for their favorite causes and companies themselves enjoy the goodwill their tax deductible donations provide.

Cause-Related Marketing

Cause-related marketing (CRM) is defined as the public relationship of a for-profit company with a nonprofit organization, intended to promote the company's products or services while raising money for the nonprofit organization. CRM is different from corporate philanthropy because the money involved is not actually a gift. Rather, it serves the purpose of reaching new or critical markets and of providing the company with positive publicity.[15] Corporations and nonprofit organizations can enter into several kinds of marketing alliances:[16]

1. In *transaction-based promotions* the corporation donates a specific amount of cash or equipment in direct proportion to sales revenue—often up to some limit—to one or more nonprofits. A local grocery chain, for example, would contribute a percentage of its sales from November 1 to December 31 to a hunger-prevention program.

2. In *joint issue promotions* the company and a nonprofit agree to deal with a social problem through distributing products and promotional materials. An example would be a clothing manufacturer distributing red ribbons as part of a promotion campaign against drug abuse.

3. In *licensing the name or logo* of a nonprofit to a corporation, the nonprofit receives a fee or a percentage of revenues. This is more likely to occur at a national level. For example, the Heart Association logo appears on many food products.

4. In a *partnership arrangement* the company agrees to provide funds and even employees to volunteer at a public or nonprofit agency. As part of the arrangement the company receives a considerable amount of good will publicity. For example, companies may join in an Adopt-a-School program or a mentoring project.[17]

5. In an *event sponsorship*, the company agrees to provide funding in exchange for having its name prominently displayed as part of the event.

Although CRM is tempting for nonprofits because of the infusion of funding, there are also risks. Major funders may reduce donations if they think the nonprofit appears to be obtaining sufficient money from a corporate sponsor. A second problem is that the nonprofit may come to unduly rely on corporate funding and then be devastated when the corporation decides to spend its marketing budget in a different manner. Program discontinuation is an inherent risk that organizations assume when they become involved with CRM.[18] A third risk relates to having the nonprofit linked to a company that might harm its image in the community (e.g., a beer company).

Despite these risks, cause-related marketing can be a win-win for both partners. The corporation enhances its image and increases sales, whereas the nonprofit obtains crucial funding. Both parties also focus attention on social issues that might otherwise be neglected.

Electronic Philanthropy

Some organizations are beginning to test electronic philanthropy by requesting Internet donations. Such national organizations as the American Red Cross, the Salvation Army, and the Heart Association are among those that solicit on-line contributions. Although many local organizations have yet to try this, the Internet does allow potential donors to educate themselves about the organization as they consider making decisions about where to give their money.

To determine whether to undertake on-line solicitations, it is important to know who among your potential donors uses this medium. You need to ask their permission to keep them informed about the organization's progress via e-mail; if they don't give you permission, do not communicate with them. Requesting e-mail addresses as part of the personal data updates can reveal how many donors have access. Conducting surveys or using focus groups can be other ways of determining whether to seek out on-line contributions.[19]

If the decision is made to solicit donations online, the organization must determine how the gifts would be processed. One option is to develop a customized processing system. A second option is to work with companies that accept, process, and acknowledge online contributions. A third option is to encourage donors to use philanthropy portals. (For more information about online services, see www.rdnonline.com and also the Web sites listed at the end of this book.)

Many agencies now use Web sites to educate people navigating the Internet about their organization. An appealing Web site can provide excellent publicity for an agency and also encourage people to enroll in an e-mail newsletter to receive material immediately. Agency Web sites can also feature a donor solicitation page. Potential donors are offered the opportunity to give directly, call a toll-free number, or even use their credit cards to make a donation. You must provide donors using a credit card a secure method of payment through encryption, which codes the transaction so that only the intended recipient can unscramble it.[20]

Some organizations use the Internet to directly conduct special events. For example, an Internet auction can sell products such as candy or CDs, or seek corporate sponsors for events. Organizations also use the Internet to participate in cause-related marketing, discussed earlier in this chapter. Persons committed to a particular agency are more likely to buy a company's product if they know that a percentage of the profits would be returned to the agency.[21] To be effective, the Web site must be kept current and you must respond to inquiries promptly.

Business Ventures

If successful, a venture can provide a stable source of income, increase the visibility of the organization, and potentially provide skills for the agency's clients. For these reasons, starting an income-generating business is appealing, but realistically most agencies should be cautious because of inherent risks. Even in the private sector where individuals are highly motivated to run their own business, many businesses fail within the first five years because of lack of expertise or capital. Because your business venture could lose money and drain resources, you must carefully weigh whether the financial risks outweigh the possibility of financial success.[22] You must also make sure that the venture can further the agency's mission.

Before considering whether to embark on a business venture, make sure that your other fundraising strategies are sufficient to provide necessary current income. Business ventures typically take several years to provide a profit and likely require upfront resources (staff time and capital) that can detract from current organizational operations.

To develop a business venture, consider taking the following actions. First, identify someone who can take primary responsibility as the *venture entrepreneur*. Second, develop a *brain trust* or *venture committee* that would plan, implement, and evaluate ventures. Third, draw upon outside help that could include a local business college, a local or regional community loan fund, business people, a local development agency, and business consultants.

Conducting a Venture Audit

Exploring a possible product or service venture should be done systematically to increase the chances of success. Conduct a *venture audit* before selecting a particular business to determine whether there is potential interest in, and marketability for, your business.[23] For example, a neighborhood center, serving a multi-ethnic community of African Americans, Appalachians, Italian Americans, and Hispanics wants to consider a possible business. The organization brings together a group of neighborhood leaders and business people for a brainstorming session to consider the following ideas: (1) distributing multicultural literature, (2) publishing an ethnic cookbook, (3) hosting an ethnic food fair, (4) assembling and distributing gift baskets for corporate use, or (5) distributing a household product, such as garbage bags or plastic containers.

As part of its venture audit, the committee explores (1) whether neighborhood centers elsewhere in the country have tried to produce and sell the ventures under consideration, (2) what a focus group representing potential customers (individuals and corporations) could reveal about potential interest, (3) what a survey of potential customers indicates, and (4) what insights might be gained from using prototypes to test consumer reactions.

Developing a Business Plan

A good business plan provides a snapshot of an organization's market, clients, competition, finances, and key personnel required to do the work within a given time frame. To undertake a business venture, effective managers should develop a business plan that includes the following elements:[24]

1. Linking the organization's strategic plan to the venture to test appropriateness for achieving the organization's mission

2. The nature of the business, including an understanding of how the product fits into the marketplace

3. The management of the venture, including the expertise required, legal liabilities, staff qualifications, information system requirements, and exposure to risk

4. Customer analysis, including total size of the market, what appeals to potential customers, market segmentation, and distribution methods

5. Market analysis, including competitors and uniqueness of the venture

6. Pricing, including pricing methods and comparison with competition

7. Product quality, including development and testing

8. Anticipated risks related to economic, technological, legal, and seasonal factors

9. Growth potential, including projected growth and revenue, net income, number of customers served, number of units sold, and number of years until profitability is realized

10. Finances, including income statement, balance sheet, and cash flow analysis. Also includes start-up costs and sources of capital

11. Assumptions about the future, including any issues not covered related to opportunities or risks

As with any new venture, a number of guesses need to be made, but by explicitly stating these planning assumptions, you can determine whether to pursue the venture or abort it when expectations prove to be incorrect.

Unrelated Business Income Tax (UBIT)

If the venture is successful, then you must consider tax consequences. Under current tax law, if a nonprofit organization creates a *related business,* profits from the business are exempt from income tax. The business must contribute importantly to the accomplishment of the organization's mission and help promote its work; for example, a vocational rehabilitation program's clients could assemble products for local businesses. If these clients learn employable skills that are central to the agency's mission, it would not be taxed.

Unrelated business income is generated from a commercial venture that is not substantially related to the agency's mission and is similar to activities conducted by for-profit ventures in the community. This could subject the organization to corporate tax rates on the unrelated business income.[25] Income tax is not collected even from unrelated businesses in a few situations, such as the following: (1) most of the work is done by unpaid volunteers, (2) the products sold have been donated to the nonprofit, (3) revenue is derived from rental property for which few management services are provided, and (4) revenue is derived from investment income.[26] Because an organization may be accused of engaging in unfair competition (in that for-profit businesses do not benefit from volunteers, donations, or tax relief), always consult an attorney before pursuing a commercial venture.

Some agencies create a for-profit corporate subsidiary to avoid placing its IRS 501(c)(3) designation in jeopardy. The board of directors of the nonprofit can also be the board of directors of the for-profit corporation. The profits of the for-profit entity are taxed, and profits not needed for the for-profit business can be transferred to the nonprofit agency.[27]

Conducting Fundraising Events

Considering an Event

There are several compelling reasons for implementing a fundraising event:[28]

- It can generate much needed income for the organization.
- It provides an opportunity to communicate with your constituencies and donors; staff, board members, and donors have an opportunity to interact in an informal way and celebrate the work of the organization.
- It can bring in new donors, especially those who had little previous relationship to the organization. The publicity generated from an event can increase awareness of the organization in the community.
- It is a less intimidating way to fundraise for board members and others who may be squeamish about asking people for money. Having a good experience allows them to take on new challenges in asking for funds.
- Finally, it fosters leadership opportunities for committed volunteers who can develop skills in organizing and implementing an event.[29]

Before undertaking a fundraising event, two fundamental questions should be asked. First, "How do fundraising events fit within the overall strategic fundraising needs of the organization?" Before focusing on any particular event, you should have determined a budget for the year, including how much you intend to raise from each event. If your budget calls for raising $4,000 from an event, that suggests one kind of activity; if it calls for $40,000, you must consider a different kind of activity. If one event is not sufficient, then you need to plan for several to achieve your financial objective.

Second, "Do you have the volunteers to undertake a fundraising event?" One of the most essential elements of any event is committed, hardworking, creative, talented, and experienced people. Determine if you have people who are willing to invest in making an event a success. Also, look inward to your members and constituency groups for special talent and experience. Examine your group's connections, such as theater owners, party hall proprietors, country club members, owners of mansions or townhouses, or hotel managers. Compile a list of resources within the organization and those to which your members have access.

Generating Ideas for an Event

In considering event possibilities, strive to think creatively; people are attracted to events that are special and unusual. If you have been offering an event for several years, be aware that people can become tired of repeating the same program in the same way. Volunteers become stale, and the audience becomes bored unless you provide something fresh. Developing a distinctive and original event in the charitable marketplace can help attract a following.

Another reason to be creative is competition. In the long run, whatever niche or special advantage you create for your event, there is a tendency for decline, due to others copying your idea. You may enjoy the advantage of uniqueness for a while, but expect this to be only temporary. Add innovation to your program or undertaking with different, imaginative events to stay ahead of your competition.

To think creatively, you must first develop an attitude of exploring different ideas. Assume that nothing is fixed and that any fundraising event is open to change. Even though previous events may have been successful, circumstances may have changed or there may be better and different ways to continue the event. You must be open to challenging familiar formats. If necessary, you must be willing to fall out of love with a cherished tradition or program. This openness to ideas involves taking risks. Remember that you are not seeking the unique for the sake of just being different. What matters most in this exploratory process is the willingness to look for worthwhile ideas.

Conducting a Feasibility Analysis

Before you select from the array of possible ideas, you need to critically review whether each one on your list is feasible. Every fresh, imaginative proposal needs to be scrutinized from a variety of angles through a feasibility analysis. Your goal is to narrow the list so you can select the right event. Certainly the possibility always exists that an excellent idea may be dropped. Equally problematic, however, is pursuing an event that should have been dropped but was not, due to inadequate screening. It is better to abort early than continue with an idea that could result in a dud. The screening process should eliminate all but the most desirable and feasible project ideas.

The following major questions should be considered in making a selection: (1) Is the event appropriate for our organization and community? (2) Does the event appeal to our members and to our target audience? (3) Do we have the capacity to undertake the event? (4) Would the event generate sufficient funds to warrant the effort? (5) Can the event accomplish objectives beyond raising funds? (6) Are we prepared to build up the event over a period of several years? (7) Can the event compete successfully with those of other organizations?

Initially, consider as many ideas as possible. Asking fundamental questions, using your imagination to brainstorm ideas, and uncritically considering diverse suggestions helps expand the range of possibilities. Following this creative period, narrow the list of ideas through a series of feasibility questions into a few selected ones from which you can make your final decision. During this exploratory period set a *go/no-go* date to discipline your committee to make a timely decision. Generally, you may want to allot about two months for selecting an event.

Setting Objectives

Every fundraising event should have objectives that are relevant, tangible, attainable, and measurable (see Chapter 4). Financial objectives can be more easily measured than non-financial ones, for example, to sell 350 tickets, obtain underwriting support of $2,000, and raise a net income of $15,000. In establishing financial objectives, be as realistic as possible. If you strive for a net income objective that is too high, volunteers may feel unduly pressured. If the objective is not achieved, they can experience defeat—even if more money is raised than ever before. Setting too low a financial objective, however, might result in volunteers not working hard enough. A financial objective that is within reach, reasonable, and achievable, even though it involves tremendous work, gives everyone a sense of accomplishment.

If possible, net income objectives should be related to a specific cause or project. Participants in an event like to feel that their donations are going for something concrete. Money raised at a special event should not be lost in the basic operating budget of the organization. Ideally, these funds should be segregated from the base budget and earmarked for a specific purpose in which volunteers and donors can take pride.

Non-financial objectives could include increasing the number of volunteers, increasing membership, heightening community awareness, and generating goodwill. In fact, one of the most important reasons for conducting an event is not so much to *fundraise* as it is to *friend raise*—that is, to offer a social experience for people who are part of your organization and to attract new people. Defining non-financial objectives and indicators of success in advance can benefit the organization—independent of financial objectives. By establishing these objectives, you sharpen thinking about events and activities you do *not* want to undertake, as well as those that you do. For example, if your primary objective is to improve goodwill within our community, you should obviously think twice about sponsoring a booth at another community's festival.

Planning an Event

Paying attention to details is crucial to the success of a fundraising event. In any one event there are many details to master, and the omission of one or several can make the difference between a smoothly run event and a failure.

Comprehensive, detailed planning can prevent cost overruns, volunteer burnout, and other losses. An activities list and a timeline chart facilitates attention to details.

Preparing an Activities List

An activities list can be produced through *reverse-order planning* or *forward-sequence planning* (see Chapter 4). To briefly review, in *reverse-order planning*, the event's planning committee begins with the final result to be accomplished and identifies the tasks that feed into the activities. This is achieved by asking the questions, "What must we do just before reaching our final result? "What needs to be done before that, and before that, and so forth?" In this way, you eventually arrive at the beginning point. In *forward-sequence planning*, the group begins with what it considers to be the appropriate set of tasks and then asks, "What should be done next, and what after that, and so forth?" until the actual event occurs.

Few event planning groups can compile a complete activities list in their first round of discussions. Whether forward-sequence or reverse-order planning is used, a review of the list of tasks reveals the need to omit some unnecessary tasks, reschedule some tasks to prevent overload, and add some tasks initially omitted. After you have prepared an activities list, you list the activities and tasks on a *timeline chart* (see Chapter 4), to visually display all that you need to do sequentially within a particular time period.

Analyzing Potential Customers

If your membership is too small to support a large event, you may have to recruit people from outside your organization. Your core members must mobilize and encourage outsiders to participate. By reaching beyond your limited membership, you spread the base of commitment. Your planning group's challenge is to analyze your market segments and then conduct target marketing.

Market Segmentation. As you implement your event, ask this important question: "To whom is this event likely to appeal?" One major way to identify potential customers is to divide them into constituencies based on how they relate to the organization. These can include a core constituency of persons closest to the organization, such as board members, volunteers, and clients. It could also involve a second circle of constituents, including families, friends, vendors, and inactive members. A third constituency comes from the general community. Although not directly involved with your organization, community members may choose to participate because they believe in your cause or find the event particularly appealing.

Target Marketing. It is usually helpful to target your event to particular persons or groups in the community. Although some organizations try to develop an event that appeals to everyone, you run the risk of attracting a limited response if only a few consider the event especially related to them. By pinpointing segments, you develop an event that directly appeals to a particular group or groups. If you identify a fairly homogeneous group that would naturally respond, or if competition is fairly intense in all but a few segments of the market, you may want to concentrate on a narrow segment.

For example, if you are a free clinic offering health services to older teenagers and young adults, your natural constituency is your clients and their friends. You determine that a rock concert at a farm outside of the city would be appealing. As another example, your health organization is planning to sponsor a golf tournament for business people. You would most likely try to obtain mailing lists from country clubs and public golf courses to increase attendance at the event. Or suppose you are a family planning association organizing a boutique that has special appeal to young, single adults. To reach this population, you would promote the event among singles clubs and young adult groups.

With differentiated marketing, you concentrate on several specific marketing segments, tailoring an effective activity for each of them. For instance, you may decide to host an event appealing to multiple market segments. Also, in the course of a year, you could purposefully decide to hold several different events, each appealing to different market segments, thus increasing attendance and income.

Managing Finances

Budgeting for an event is an ongoing process that requires estimating and tracking income and expenses. Often you must deal with uncertain projections that need to be revised as you obtain more information. Consider dividing the budget process into four phases: (1) Prepare an initial budget to determine whether the event has the potential for sufficient profit; be conservative by estimating expenses on the high side and income on the low side. (2) Prepare a detailed budget after you have decided to proceed with the event. (3) Monitor income and expenses and compare actual with budgeted amounts (see Chapter 12). (4) After the event, review income and expenses to determine whether to repeat it.

As part of the budgeting process, you need to become familiar with certain key terms. Estimate *gross profit*, the amount needed to cover all costs as well as your net profit. Also estimate *net profit*, the amount left over after all costs are deducted from income. Identify *fixed costs*, expenses you incur no matter how many people come to the event. For example, the fixed costs of a dinner include the cost of hall rental, the band, and promotional materials—no matter how many people attend. *Variable costs* are related to per person units. For instance, the cost of souvenirs for a swim-a-thon varies with the number of entrants.

Break-even point is the number of sales needed to equal expenses. After that point, all sales are net profit. If your costs are primarily fixed, then you can simply divide the total cost of the event by the cost of each ticket to determine your break-even point. For example, if your costs are $2,200 and you charge $10 per ticket, you must sell 220 tickets to cover the costs to break even. Any ticket sales above 220 are profits.

If, in addition to fixed costs, you are likely to incur variable costs, then these must be subtracted from the projected per-ticket income before dividing by the cost per ticket. For example, assume that the fixed costs of a dinner dance (band, hall rental, promotion) equal $4,200, and that each meal has a variable cost of $40. You think $100 would be an appropriate price for each ticket. To calculate the break-even point, use this formula:

fixed costs ÷ (ticket price − variable costs) = break-even point
$4,200 ÷ ($100 − $40) = 70

In this example, assuming that the variable costs of the dinner will be covered by matching variable income, you must sell 70 tickets to break even.

In setting up a budget, you should determine a net profit objective that is achievable. It is better to set a $1,500 net profit objective for a raffle and raise $1,800 than to establish a $2,500 objective and raise only $1,800. If you do not reach your objective, you risk volunteers becoming discouraged and unwilling to repeat an event that is identified as a partial failure. You may hope to eventually achieve $2,500 for this annual event as your ultimate financial objective, but expect to raise less than your optimum objective the first year of an event. Consider it a "dry-run" as you work to establish a procedure and preparation for your volunteers. In subsequent years, expect to exceed your first year's performance, but be mindful that events do plateau and even decline. If you are uncertain about establishing a specific net profit objective, consider a range (e.g., $2,000–$2,500).

Maximizing Profits

It is important always to be on the lookout for ways to maximize profits from fundraising events, whether they are new, successful, at a plateau, or declining. To do so, you need to develop marketing strategies, which can be divided into five major approaches: (1) penetrating existing markets, (2) developing new markets, (3) expanding or developing events for the existing customer base, (4) diversifying to different events and markets, and (5) promoting sales.

Penetrating existing markets consists of enhancing income through increasing sales from your current event. The event remains essentially the same, but you present it to your customers in more attractive ways or you promote your efforts more aggressively. Use a market penetration approach to increase the number of people attending an event. For instance, to increase income from your already popular dinner dance, consider ways to attract more people through more aggressive advertising or arranging for a discount for advance purchase of tickets.

Developing new markets consists of seeking increased sales by attracting new customer segments to the event. You could expand your customer base by holding the event in a different geographic location, appeal to a younger audience with a lower-priced ticket for attending the dance but not the dinner, or attract newcomers by each year honoring different community leaders who encourage their friends to attend.

Expanding or developing events consists of seeking increased income by significantly improving the event for current market segments. You could, for example, add income- producing aspects, such as a raffle or a silent auction, to the dinner. You could alter the basic character of the event, in this example, making the dinner dance more formal (black tie) or more informal (square dance).

Diversifying to different events and markets consists of developing an entirely new event for a completely new audience. This strategy makes sense when the organization thinks that its present event is waning or if other opportunities appear to offer a better financial return. If possible, this change should be focused on areas in which members have skills and interests. They could consider changing the event from a dinner dance to an entirely different event such as a decorator's home showcase tour or a crafts sale, thus drawing in an entirely new source of income.

These four strategies can help event planners think purposefully about current and potential events in relation to current and potential markets. Whatever the event being planned, *promoting sales* has to be the highest priority. Selling is what you think about first. This is how most successful event leaders proceed. They know that to raise money for their events, they must wage a tremendous selling campaign.

A few events may be so popular that they sell themselves, and for these events, publicity, invitations, and word-of mouth may be sufficient. Generally, however, these approaches do not bring people to an event. You must build a sales force of people to reach out aggressively to convince others to attend.

Some organizations make selling tickets mandatory. Unsold tickets must be purchased by the members, an approach that requires a high degree of loyalty and commitment. Other organizations rely on the voluntary participation of their sales force. Consider forming a special ticket selling committee consisting of people who can contact large numbers of friends. A well-observed axiom in event planning is this: *people sell to people.*

A good idea is to focus on group sales. For example, ask people to commit to selling two or three tables to an event or set a number, such as thirty tickets. Encourage friends to come as a group to the event. Identify table hosts and hostesses who commit to selling tables and are listed on the invitation or in the program book. Prepare a selling kit for sellers that gives details of the event, who would benefit from the event, and a description of the work of the organization. Hold a kick-off party for ticket sellers to generate enthusiasm. Keep in continuous contact with your sales force, preferably in person or by telephone. Consider offering premiums for those who sell the most tickets. In summary, convey to your sellers that personal contact and continuous follow-up is the best way to sell tickets.

Reducing Expenses

There are several ways to reduce expenses, which in turn can maximize profits. First, assign at least one volunteer the task of purchasing items for the event at the lowest possible price. The shopper should ask for a donation or at least a discount on items. Second, where possible, buy large quantities so you can obtain a discount. Perhaps you could consider joint purchasing with another local organization. Third, consider bartering by exchanging your services with those of another organization or business. For example, if you are sponsoring a concert, you could give free admission tickets to the printing company that provides your promotional materials. Fourth, ask your volunteers to absorb some of the costs of the event in return for their listing expenses as tax deductible donations. Finally, wherever possible, try to obtain free gifts and services, such as an accounting firm providing a free audit or a grocery chain contributing food items. Some companies are willing to cover costs, such as printing, in return for publicizing their name.

Companies sponsor events when they think they would benefit from the visibility of their participation. Seek out corporate sponsors who can underwrite major costs of the event in exchange for providing high visibility. Corporations become involved because they (1) believe in your organization and its cause, (2) view the event as a means of providing benefits to their employees, (3) become more visible to current and potential customers throughout the community, and (4) want to respond positively to a request from a special customer. In considering corporate sponsorship, focus on those companies that have a natural relationship to the organization. This relationship can include company employees on your board of trustees, an honoree who is a company employee, or a company that connects with the type of event you are offering. For example, if your event is a chili cook-off, you might interest a company that produces spices.

Contact the appropriate person that handles requests in advance of the normal annual budgeting process so that the event can be considered. After transmitting your letter, it is important to follow up with phone calls if you do not receive a response, because you may gain insights that can guide you next year. In seeking corporate sponsorship, be forewarned about the following: (1) Do not expect support to continue indefinitely and beware of becoming too dependent on any one source of funds. (2) Watch that your expenses do not become so high that questions are raised about how much funding is actually available for direct services. (3) Be careful not to make excessive demands from the same company. If, for example, you ask for a major underwriting gift, do not then ask for a direct corporate contribution a few months later.

Tax Considerations in Fundraising Events

It is advisable to seek professional counsel regarding current IRS rules and regulations. Consider the following as you plan events: (1) Donors should receive written acknowledgment of gifts over $250 that are given as straight donations and for which the donor receives nothing of value in return. (2) The IRS requires that charities provide donors with written documentation when they have donated more than $75 and have received some type of goods or services in return (e.g., attendance at a dinner event). The letter to donors must convey that only a part of the money they contributed is tax deductible. The deductible amount is the total amount given minus the value of the goods or services received.[30] (3) At an auction, the donor can take a charitable deduction only for the excess of the amount paid over the fair market value of the item purchased. Donors who contribute items may take a full charitable deduction for the value of the items. Organizations should keep accurate records of the values of services and goods provided and of donors who supply them or who purchase them.[31]

Evaluating Results

Review the event as soon as possible after it is over in an objective, frank manner, but avoid individual accusations. Invite ideas on how problems can be dealt with the next time. Your primary approach should be to elicit ideas for improvement and determine if mistakes or miscalculations are correctable. Ask for ideas for new activities. If the organization has previously laid the groundwork by setting objectives and developing action plans, then evaluating results is easier. The evaluation process should consist of two parts: monitoring tasks and assessing the achievement of objectives.

Through a monitoring process you can determine whether, and to what extent, tasks were carried out as planned. The following are questions to ask:

- Should the timetable have been altered to permit an earlier start and better sequencing of tasks?
- Were there sufficient funding resources and volunteers to do the job?
- Did the expected expenditures for tasks match the budget planning? If not, what are explanations for the discrepancies?
- Was there a proper number of volunteers assigned to tasks? Can imbalances (e.g., too many tasks for some persons and too few for others) be identified?

These questions help you review how well you implemented the activities and tasks. If you detect deficiencies, you can determine the remedies to consider for next year. If your event does not achieve its financial objectives, the following questions should be asked:

- Was the financial objective unreasonably high? Perhaps this was a first-time event, and you guessed incorrectly. Perhaps there were unforeseen and unique circumstances that were unpredictable.
- Were adequate resources available to accomplish the event? Was the number of ticket sellers and backup staff sufficient? Was there enough up-front money?
- Was the timetable appropriate? Would an earlier start-up time ensure better results? Could the tasks be scheduled better?
- Although the financial objectives were not achieved, were other equally important, non-financial objectives accomplished?

This last question is perhaps the most difficult assessment to make. Frequently, groups that do not achieve their financial objectives decide that such benefits as good public relations, esprit de corps of volunteers, identification of new members, or leadership development compensate for poor financial results. In fact, the achievement of these and other objectives may be sufficient to overcome the limited financial results. Only your organization can make that highly subjective assessment.

Questions for Discussion

1. You have been asked to accompany a board member to make a call on an elderly widow of moderate means who has no children. She is a longtime supporter of your agency. How would you go about discussing a planned giving gift with her?

2. Suppose she says that she would like to think about a gift. What would you do to maintain ongoing contact with her?

3. You have several large companies in the area served by your agency. What are some of the ways you might connect them with the work of your organization?

4. Suppose you wanted to take advantage of *cause-related marketing* with one or more of these companies. What are some possibilities you would consider?

5. What are the pros and cons of developing electronic philanthropy for your agency?

6. You have been asked by your agency director to convene a few staff for a brainstorming session for a business venture your agency could consider. What creative ideas might you consider? Select one of these

ideas for further consideration. What questions would you need to explore to determine if the idea were feasible? What would you consider in developing a business plan?

7. You have been asked to staff a meeting of a board committee charged with preparing a fundraising event. How would you go about helping them consider event possibilities?

Notes

1. C. Dolan & R. Brody, *Planned giving* (Cleveland, OH: Federation for Community Planning, 1991), pp. 2–3; R. D. Barrett & M. E. Ware, *Planned giving essentials* (Gaithersburg, MD: Aspen, 1997), pp. 35–50; H. A. Rosso, *Achieving excellence*, pp. 97–99; A. Lauffer, pp. 214–216.

2. T. Poderis, *It's a great day to fund-raise!*, pp. 44–45.

3. C. Horton, *Raising money & having fun (sort of): A "how-to" book for small nonprofit groups* (Cleveland: May Dugan Center, 1991), p. 52.

4. J. Steel, Fundamentals of planned giving, in R. L. Edwards & E. A. S. Benefield, *Building a strong foundation: Fundraising for nonprofits* (Washington D.C.: NASW, 1997), pp. 79–80.

5. B. Bonde, Planned giving communications, in *Nonprofit organization management* (New York: Aspen, 2002).

6. C. Dolan & R. Brody, pp. 3–4.

7. C. Dolan & R. Brody, pp. 13–16.

8. W. C. Mengerink, *Hand in hand* (Rockville, MD: Fundraising Institute, 1992), p. 64.

9. C. Dolan & R. Brody, pp. 19–22.

10. C. Dolan & R. Brody, pp. 9–12.

11. K. S. Sheldon, Corporations as a gift market, in H. A. Rosso, *Achieving excellence in fundraising* (San Francisco: Jossey-Bass, 1991), pp. 229–242.

12. The Foundation Center, A fresh look at corporate giving *The Foundation Center Newsletter* (May 2000).

13. E. A. Scanlan, Corporate and foundation fundraising: A complete guide from the inside (1997), in *Nonprofit organization management* (New York: Aspen, 2002), pp. 9:44–48.

14. C. H. Deutsch, A much-loved concept gets a few new twists, *The New York Times* (17 November 2003), p. 6.

15. W. C. Mengerink, p. 59.

16. A. R. Andreasen, Profits for nonprofits: Find a corporate partner, *Harvard Business Review* 74 (November/December 1996), pp. 47–49.

17. J. D. Marx, Strategic philanthropy: An opportunity for partnership between corporations and health/human service agencies, *Administration in Social Work* 20, 3 (1996), pp. 57–73.

18. A. R. Andreasen, pp. 47–59; J. P. Shannon, ed., *The corporate contributions handbook* (San Francisco: Jossey-Bass, 1991), pp. 139–151; R. L. Edwards & E. A. S. Benefield, pp. 120–121.

19. B. L. Ciconte & J. G. Jacob, *Fundraising basics: A complete guide,* 2nd ed. (2001), in *Nonprofit organization management,* pp. 10:15–10:19.

20. M. Johnston, *The nonprofit guide to the Internet,* 2nd ed. (New York: John Wiley & Sons, 1999), pp. 101–107.

21. M. Johnston, pp. 120–124.

22. R. Larson, *Venture forth! The essential guide to starting a moneymaking business in your nonprofit organization* (St. Paul, MN: Amherst H. Wilder Foundation, 2002), pp. 10–14.

23. R. Larson, pp. 14–17.

24. J. G. Dees et al., (2001). *Enterprising nonprofits: A toolkit for social entrepreneurs.* (New York: John Wiley & Sons), p. 274–297; Women's Business Center & Women's Business Institute, The essential elements of a good business plan, retrieved May 6, 2003, from www.onlinewbc.gov/docs/starting/bp_essentials.html

25. G. M. Grobman, *The nonprofit handbook,* 2nd ed. (Harrisburg, PA: White Hat Communications, 1999), p. 183.

26. K. Klein, *Fundraising for social change,* 4th ed. (Oakland, CA: Chardon Press, 2001), p. 274.

27. L. L. Martin, Management for human service administrators (Boston: Allyn & Bacon, 2001), pp. 185–186.

28. The ideas in this section are developed in R. Brody & M. Goodman, *Fundraising events: strategies and programs for success* (New York: Human Sciences Press, 1988). A revised shorter version was published in 1993 by the Federation for Community Planning.

29. S. Roth, Making special events work for you, *Grassroots Fundraising Journal* 6 (2002), pp. 4–6.

30. G. M. Grobman, *The nonprofit's guide to e-commerce* (Harrisburg, PA: White Hat Communications, 2001), p. 64.

31. R. L. Edwards & E. A. S. Benefield, *Building a strong foundation: Fundraising for nonprofits* (Washington, DC: NASW, 1997), pp. 112–112.

15

Preparing Effective Proposals

Preliminary Considerations

Raising funds through grants for important projects or programs can be both enriching and daunting. Preparing proposals disciplines thinking and stimulates more purposeful fund seeking endeavors. But the process can also be challenging because of the many details to focus on and the many decisions you have to make. The purpose of this chapter is to identify those aspects of proposal preparation that can make your grant seeking activities more effective. Chapter 16 discusses various specific requirements that certain funders may impose on grant submissions; this chapter provides a general overview of proposal writing that can be applied to private and public funding bodies.

Conducting a Preliminary Assessment

Because you will be investing a considerable amount of time, energy, and organizational resources in a proposal, you should conduct a preliminary assessment. During this pre-proposal phase, review the following fundamental questions:

First, do you have the right reason for raising program funds through a grant request? Seeking foundation funding can be habit forming, especially for organizations in which the trustees do not want to take major responsibility for raising funds. Staff, too, find the foundation option attractive because they do not have to push or cajole board members into asking for money. The danger is that foundation funding is usually time-limited, and when staff and board have become overly dependent on this as a primary source, they discover they can't sustain themselves beyond the foundation grant.[1] Moreover, foundation staff are vigilant about not wanting to fund ongoing programs that are artificially reshaped just to attract foundation dollars.

Second, is the project idea desirable and feasible? Conduct a preliminary review of the literature and contact people who have undertaken similar projects. Determine whether the project idea is unique. If a similar project has been done elsewhere, are there compelling reasons to duplicate it or are there aspects that are unique (i.e., different target populations or cultural or community considerations)? Assess the urgency of addressing the needs of the target population at this time. Make an initial assessment about the feasibility of the project, including a preliminary judgment of implementation difficulties.[2]

Third, is your organization able to carry the project forward? Analyze the project in relation to the mission, goals, and strategic plan of the organization. Review whether there is sufficient organizational will and staff capability to take on a new endeavor. Examine your competitive position in relation to other potential applicants if they are known. Determine whether your proposal is a top priority of your agency, since other projects under consideration may preclude your request for funding at this time. Assess your ability to take on the demands of the project, considering other pressing priorities. Would taking on a new project divert funds and staff time away from ongoing projects?

Fourth, are there funders who might be interested in the project idea? Determine through preliminary direct contacts or through descriptions of funding sources whether their priorities match your proposal idea[3] (see Chapter 16).

Finally, what are the potential financial consequences of obtaining funding? Examine whether the likelihood of a new funding source limits your autonomy and curbs your decision making regarding how you provide services to your clients. Consider the impact of discontinued funding at the end of the grant period. Review whether the funding you are seeking is likely to be sufficient to carry out the program adequately.[4]

The exploration of these fundamental issues suggests caution in seeking foundation or government funding for new projects. Anticipate possible consequences before moving too quickly to write your proposal. Do your homework!

Prior to Writing the Proposal

Because foundations give grants only to organizations that are incorporated as nonprofit agencies, you will need to obtain this designation from the Internal Revenue Service. An attorney can help you obtain the designation of 501(c)(3) status. To achieve this status, you will need to have a board of trustees and prepare bylaws. The 501(c)(3) status is a Federal tax exemption, and forms are filed with the IRS. Individual states may also require filings to comply with state regulations. The Secretary of State or the Attorney General's office in your state can provide you with the appropriate forms. Once the application is approved, your organization receives a tax number and you are registered with the Secretary of State as a nonprofit agency. You are then eligible to receive tax deductible gifts. While you are waiting for approval, it is still possible to receive tax deductible gifts if you have made arrangements with another nonprofit organization to serve as your *fiscal agent*. This organization serves as a *conduit of funds* (intermediary between the funder and the applying agency) and gives assurances to the grantor that expenses will be properly monitored.[5]

Assuming that you have either 501(c)(3) status or a creditable fiscal agent, you should strive to assure the funder that you have a worthy organization. In some instances, funders may be willing to take a chance on an unknown organization if they are excited about the idea and have confidence in the leadership. Your strategic plan should convey a sense of direction and an ability to implement programs. By being clear about your priorities, you can be proactive in searching out funding. This approach is far better than selecting programs that fit priorities of funders but are not in keeping with the mission of your organization. Do not create programs merely because a funding opportunity exists.[6]

When you are about to write the actual proposal, make certain that you have gathered all the information you need to document your case. Invest time and thought in designing your program, as discussed in Chapter 3. Effective managers know that the most challenging part of the proposal writing is not the writing itself, but conceptualizing the proposal project. Because you are only at the beginning of the process, details around the budget may have yet to be worked out. You should have some general idea of the expenses involved, however, so that you can consider whether to reduce the magnitude of your program. To add human interest to your document, have in mind actual situations of need and how people would benefit.

How Fundable Is Your Project?

If your idea is a new one and your organization is not well known, do not expect foundations to be immediately receptive. Although foundations are in the business of providing risk capital, they nevertheless like to know that your organization has experience or a track record that indicates project feasibility. If you start your program on a small-scale pilot project before requesting funds, you considerably increase the chances of funding. At the very least, in a funding climate that emphasizes evidence-based practice, identify programs similar to yours that have succeeded elsewhere.

Generally, foundation and corporate funders prefer specific projects over general operating requests. Grantors prefer to know exactly how their money would be used and the specific impact it could have. Because foundations are generally reluctant to fund agency operations, it is important to develop diverse sources of funding (see Chapter 13). Consider seeking funding for general operating purposes from non-foundation sources, such as the local United Way, fundraising events, or annual campaigns. Requests for foundation money can then be concentrated on program support.

To increase your chances of funding, demonstrate to potential funders that you have developed ways to raise your own resources. Funders are impressed to learn that 100% of your trustees contribute to your annual fundraising campaign. Knowing that you are raising money in various ways gives them confidence that your organization's proposed project can be sustained.

Preparing Proposals

Proposal formats and lengths vary depending on the requirements of funders. Government proposals use a highly structured, prescriptive format that designates points for covering each of the required topics. Proposals for foundations are not usually as structured, but generally all want to know what you intend to accomplish and how you propose accomplishing your objectives. Larger foundations provide a format for application; others may require a letter of inquiry. The following format is offered as a guide, which can be modified if the funder requests a different outline:

Summary Statement

Statement of Need

Goals, Objectives

Program Components

Evaluation

Organizational Capability

Program Continuation

Budget

Appendices

Summary Statement

Typically a summary statement appears first because readers need an overview to orient them to the project and to prepare them for the details that are to follow.[7] The summary should be less than one page and contain the following elements:

- What the need is
- What will be accomplished
- Who you are and why you are qualified
- What activities you will perform
- What it will cost
- How long it will take

The summary should be prepared after the full proposal is written because it should accurately reflect its major elements.

Although funders may not request a cover letter, it is a good idea to include one, even though it may cover some of the same points as your summary statement. In the cover letter, indicate the size of your request, explain why the organization is applying to this foundation, and describe the program briefly. Indicate why the program fits within the foundation's guidelines. If there has been any previous discussion with the foundation, mention this. Offer to schedule a meeting to obtain valuable feedback and develop a relationship.[8]

Statement of Need

The purpose of the statement of need is to define a problem and to explain precisely what your organization wants to change. Focusing on local conditions would likely appeal to a local foundation. Dealing with an issue that has implications beyond your own community may appeal to a large national foundation or a federal agency. Whether you approach a local or a national foundation, focus on the people who would be served, not on how funding would benefit the organization.[9] Specify the target population to be helped, the specific problem to be addressed, the problem's geographic location, its origin and causes, and why it continues to exist. If the problem is multifaceted, then all the significant aspects need to be identified, though not all need to be impacted by your proposal. For example, a problem statement about out-of-school, unemployed, adolescent ex-offenders living in poverty would describe the clients' lifestyle, educational lags, and need for income.

Within the statement of need, distinguish between *risk*, *target*, and *impact* populations (see Chapter 4).[10] The risk population is the total group needing help or at risk. For example, there are 800 ex-offenders in the community. The target population is that subset toward whom the program is aimed; for example, 70 ex-offenders are to be served. The impact population is the subset likely to benefit from the program; for instance, 45 of those served would obtain jobs. If possible, the theoretical basis for the problem should also be discussed. You should review the literature on the target population's needs to develop a conceptual understanding of the factors causing the problem. In discussing the problem, avoid circular reasoning. It is not enough, for example, to say that the problem is the lack of the service you intend to provide.[11]

To demonstrate your grasp of the problem, provide prospective funders with current data from a variety of sources: national studies and their local implications, testimony from congressional records, surveys, news media articles, or quotes from authorities. Document as best you can through data obtained through local sources (e.g., United Way, local planning council, department of human services, juvenile court, and the local urban college). Be as specific as possible when describing the need, and do not assume that a funder will readily understand the meaning of a statistic you cite. Make sure that you interpret the data you present.

Unless a funder requests detailed information in the narrative, do not inundate it with pages of statistics; rather, summarize the data and place detailed, statistical tables in an appendix. Because many problems are chronic, the statement of need should convey why there is a special urgency to seek funding now. For example, are the kinds of crimes being committed by adolescents more serious than before? Does new state legislation place a special burden on the local community to deal with delinquency? A description of special circumstance makes the importance of funding the project more compelling. Potential funders must see the problem as both critical and timely.

Where feasible, indicate how a community constituency or client group has been involved in defining the problem. Such involvement is especially desirable if the proposal relates to community improvements, because clients are in the best position to comment on their special needs. Even those who normally do not participate, such as mentally ill offenders, can be consulted through their families. Their participation conveys a commitment to understanding the problem in depth.

Although the statement of need is presented before the section on goals and objectives, it should be written with objectives clearly in mind. Because needs and objectives must be consistent with each other, it might even be desirable to write the latter section first. This would be especially necessary if the prospective funder has specified what the proposal should accomplish, which is usually the case with federal grants.[12]

If your program is to be considered a model, show how it can be replicated. If, however, your own program is itself a replica of another project done elsewhere, document the success of that program and show how it can directly benefit your community.[13]

Goals and Objectives

As discussed in Chapter 4, organizational or program goals should represent broad statements of what the organization wants to accomplish. They provide a general direction for commitment to action. They are global descriptions of a long-term condition toward which the organization's efforts are directed. Goals are idealistic, timeless, and rarely achieved. Goals should inspire all those associated with the organization to want to move towards a desired end point.[14] The following are examples of goal statements: *Reduce crime in the community. Upgrade housing. Improve interracial relations. End homelessness. Prevent teenage illegitimate births.*

Although goal statements are inspiring, they are not easily amenable to clear definition and measurement. (Some organizations delineate *subgoals,* that is, statements about what a project expects to accomplish in the future, say in 5 or 10 years: *to reduce juvenile recidivism by 30% in 5 years*). In contrast to goals, objectives represent relevant, attainable, measurable, and time-limited ends to be achieved. They are relevant because they fit within the general mission and goals of the organization and because they relate to problems identified in the proposal. They are attainable because they can be realized. They are measurable because achievements are based upon tangible, concrete, and quantifiable results. They are time-limited because the proposal specifies the time frame within which results can be achieved (typically within 12 months or less, though the timeline should be based on programmatic considerations). Objectives provide the funder with clear-cut targets for organizational accountability. Be aware that while objectives are intended to be realistic and achievable, their accomplishment may not necessarily eliminate a problem described earlier in the proposal. Obtaining jobs for 45 ex-offenders will not solve the goal of reducing the high rate of recidivism in the community.

Four kinds of objectives are typically stated in proposals: operating, service, product, and impact objectives.[15] *Operating objectives* convey the intent to improve the general operation of the organization. The organization is then in a better position to help its clients. Funds designed to enhance the organization could include sponsoring in-service training workshops for 40 staff, increasing the membership base, or hiring a fund developer so that the organization can become self-sustaining.

Service objectives (sometimes called activity objectives) are based on the organization's quantifying units of service rendered: to serve 300 clients in the program year, to conduct 680 interviews, to provide 17 neighborhood assemblies, or to refer 125 clients to agencies in a year.

Product objectives relate to a tangible piece of work to be delivered at the end of the funded period: to prepare a resource directory, to create a case management system, to produce a videotape that provides clients with information. Sometimes these are referred to as *deliverables,* that is, products to be delivered.

Impact objectives specify outcomes to be achieved as a result of process activities (see Chapters 3 and 4). Whereas activity objectives reflect the amount of effort to be expended, impact objectives detail the return expected on the investment of time, personnel, and resources. Impact objectives focus on results. Examples include the following:

- to place 50 percent of the youth enrolled in the vocational training program in full-time jobs within 18 months
- to increase educational attainment of a school's 200 entering students, 80 percent of whom will complete at least one full year of school

The advantage of each of these objectives is that they make the grantee accountable for attaining clear-cut project outcomes. Stating objectives in measurable terms disciplines you to set realistic achievements, not ideal ones. While considerable flexibility can be used to prepare impact objective statements, the following criteria are suggested:

1. Generally use a strong verb that describes an observable change in a condition. "To reduce," "to improve," "to strengthen," and "to enhance" are examples.

2. State only one aim with one specific result. An objective that states two aims may require two different implementations, and confusion could later occur about which of the two objectives was achieved. "To reduce the recidivism rate by 10 percent and obtain employment for 20 former delinquents" is an example of an objective with two aims.

3. Be certain that the objective is realistic. For example, do not promise to significantly reduce unwed teenage pregnancies through a program designed to work with 100 youngsters in a community that experiences 2,000 unwed births a year. Furthermore, although the format presented here separates goals and objectives from program components (the next section), they may be combined so that specific activities and tasks are listed under each objective.

Program Components: Activities and Tasks

The program component section of the proposal presents a work plan of how the organization intends to accomplish its objectives. To convey the logic and continuity of the project, the proposal should describe, in relation to each objective, what will be done, by whom, and by when. In planning the work that needs to be accomplished, undertake reverse-order and forward-sequence planning, as discussed in Chapter 5. For a project designed for ex-delinquents in which one of the objectives is to obtain jobs, a simplified work plan would be formatted as follows:

Objective: To place 50 percent of previously delinquent youth in the vocational training program in full-time jobs within 18 months.

Activity #1: Develop a pool of not less than 40 potential jobs.
Tasks:

1. Screen potential job developers

2. Hire job developers

3. Train job developers

4. Contact prospective employers

5. Place participants on jobs

6. Monitor progress after six months

In addition to creating a visual timeline chart (see Chapter 5), describe in detail how the program would actually function. For example, if you were creating a training program for placing ex-offenders in jobs, you would provide a training schedule and describe what they would be expected to learn. Detailed material could be included in the appendices. When relevant, state in the narrative such details as how the proposed work has been successfully used elsewhere, how it will relate to existing programs in the community, and what current organizational resources will be used. The determination of activities and tasks typically involves several agency people because knowledge is not usually concentrated in one person. Consensus may be needed if organizational members are to be involved in implementing the proposal. But a committee itself cannot do the actual proposal writing; one or two people have to take primary responsibility. The group can react to drafts as they are developed and refined, and their suggestions can then be incorporated.

Evaluation

For most proposals, worthwhile evaluation compares intended results with actual outcomes. Objective statements should be written to foster subsequent evaluation by incorporating measurement indicators, as indicated by the following examples:

- To improve school performance of past offenders in 50 percent of the cases served in one program year. (Teachers make school performance evaluations.)
- To improve personal adjustment in 75 percent of those served during one program year. (Specifically constructed psychological tests of former mental hospital patients determine personal adjustment.)
- To reduce the rate of recidivism of juvenile offenders by 50 percent during the next program year. (Official police re-arrest data measure recidivism.)
- To develop ongoing funding for the innovative delinquency prevention project by the end of the second year. (Letters of commitment from the Youth Commission and the United Way indicate funding.)

In some instances, it is necessary to devise instruments, called *performance indicators*, to measure results. In the objective statements illustrated previously, these might be teacher assessment forms or psychological tests. Each organization determines whether to create its own or adopt existing performance indicators. When the information has been collected, the organization can compare its planned performance with the actual outcome. *Process evaluation* (sometimes referred to as monitoring) examines the internal processes and structure of the program to determine whether it is functioning as planned. Is it achieving its objectives in a timely manner? Is it keeping an accurate record of who is being served and under what conditions? Are clients being processed as expected? What administrative problems are being encountered? The major value of process evaluation is that it helps the program staff review whether they are going off course and allows them to take corrective action before the end of the funding period.[16] It also informs similar projects about likely pitfalls they may encounter at similar stages of development, and it assures funders that proper feedback is being built into the project.

To carry out process evaluation, a local advisory committee could be appointed to judge the effectiveness of the effort and report back to the funder. Another possibility is to identify an evaluation expert in the field to visit the project periodically and furnish reports to the donor. A third possibility is for the project staff itself to monitor the project and report the results, particularly when objectives are measurable. Regardless of the design model, the proposal should explain the questions to be answered and the details of the evaluation plan, including who performs it, how evaluators are to be chosen, and what instruments are to be used.

Capability of the Organization

Funders want to know that the organization is capable of implementing the project.[17] Because they must be convinced of your ability to accomplish what you promise, you must demonstrate credibility in undertaking the project. Describe briefly how and why the organization was formed, past and current activities, the support you receive from other organizations, and your significant accomplishments. Especially if your organization is unknown to funders, provide evidence of your involvement and competency in the area in which you are requesting funds. Indicate what financial or other resources are available. Letters of endorsement are desirable, but letters committing actual resources (staff, equipment, funding) are even more impressive. (Note: You have the option of discussing the organization's capability as part of a general introduction or in a separate section after discussing program evaluation. Review the funder's guidelines for the specific format.)

Because the proposal itself must be concise, refer to staff qualifications in the appendices and provide a list of positions, titles, qualifications, salary levels, an organization chart, and specific responsibilities related to your proposal. If appropriate, describe the qualifications and selection process for key personnel assigned to the project. Funders appreciate knowing that your board of trustees is actively involved in policy-related decisions and fully supports the proposal. List trustees and their identifying information in the appendices. Testimony from key figures in the community is also useful if their endorsement letters are sincere and reflect genuine support. Indicate the role and names of an advisory committee, if appropriate. If requested, include in the appendices an annual report, documentation of your organization's IRS nonprofit status, latest independent audit statement, your agency's 990 tax return, and a copy of your agency's affirmative action policy.

Program Continuation

In this section of your proposal, which is sometimes referred to as the *sustainability section,* indicate whether and how the organization would continue the program beyond the grant period. Foundations that give time-limited funding want assurance that the project will be sustained if it proves successful. Among the options for continued revenue are the organization's core operating budget; revenue from client fees; third-party payments, such as insurance; special fundraising drives; or application for membership in or special funding from the United Way or other federated fundraising programs.

Although it may be difficult to anticipate sources of funding two or three years hence, funders find this point so crucial that you should make a concerted effort to explore other funding options as part of the proposal preparation process. If you intend to have a scaled-down version of your program absorbed by other community agencies, indicate how you plan to have your program incorporated into their agencies. Be prepared to answer the inevitable question funders always ask: "How will you sustain your program when our funding stops?" If you have no idea how you can sustain the program, you decrease your chances of attracting foundation seed money. Even if you succeed in obtaining an additional grant, you are heading for trouble if you cannot maintain the program. Both your clients and your organization's reputation will suffer.

The Budget

Funders often consider a budget to be the best way to understand a project. Upon receiving a budget request, some funding decision makers immediately examine the budget to determine if income and expenses are realistic, accurate, and creditable. Be careful not to overinflate the budget, and be prepared to defend line items that the funder could question.

Your search process (see Chapter 16) should reveal whether your funding request is within the funder's contribution range—or whether your budget requires you to seek funding from several sources. Consider the following general guidelines in preparing the budget.[18]

Different funders require varying degrees of detail in the budget. Most government agencies require a great deal of detail and usually provide budget forms and completion instructions. Some government agencies have regulations listing special instructions for preparing the budget. These instructions are continually being revised. Use the most recent instructions available rather than delay budget preparation. Allow time to make necessary changes if you find that a new set of instructions is to be issued shortly before the final application is due. Grant application instructions generally include information regarding budget forms, examples of how to calculate specific budget items, agency formulas for determining the maximum allowance in major budgetary categories, and allowable rates for consulting fees, per diem expenses, and travel. Be prepared to defend your needs when costs exceed the agency formula. Foundations and corporations are less structured in their requirements, but they require a budget that is well thought out and complete.

As an aid in developing the budget, prepare worksheets. They provide a structure for budget planning so that no type of expense is overlooked. Make detailed records of each budgeted item, and be prepared to discuss the potential impact of budget cuts during negotiations. The worksheets provide a plan to use when the project is actually in operation. A well-prepared budget relates directly to the project's objectives and activities, and it should enable a reviewer to understand key aspects of the program. Each budget item should be justified on the basis of its potential contribution to the project.

Remember, the budget is an estimate of the program's revenues and expenses. With regard to projected revenues, foundations want to understand both committed and anticipated revenues for your particular project. You are wise to identify a portion of project revenues, either in-kind or cash, as being contributed by your organization. There are always some expenses that can be covered by your agency, and this makes the point that the organization is financially committed to the project's success. When applying for a grant, determine if a match is required so that the agency will be in compliance if the grant is awarded.

Adapt Figure 15.1 to your situation to provide information that you have obtained—or anticipate obtaining—funding from various sources inside and outside your organization.

	Committed	Requested	Total
Government Sources (e.g., city, county, state)			
Foundations (list)			
Income from the Organization Events Fees Other			
Total Projected Income			
- -			
In-Kind Contributions (list)			

Figure 15.1   Projected Revenues

Completing this form will clarify for the foundation how their contribution relates to other possible funding sources and documents agency in-kind contributions.

Figure 15.2 provides a format for indicating project expenses. The budget lists direct costs related specifically to the program, e.g., personnel, furnishings, office space, equipment, supplies, and travel. Note that the columns provide an overview of the amount being requested of the grantor, as well as what the agency itself would contribute to the projects (in cash or in-kind) and what other funding sources are being asked to fund. You should be aware that many government grants require matching funds, which can come from other non-government sources or the agency's own operations. Depending on the grant specifics, the match may be either in-kind, cash, or a combination of both.

Attach a budget narrative in which you discuss line items. Give special attention to line items that are out of the ordinary or about which the funder might have questions. You would discuss, for example, why you must purchase, rather than rent, furniture; why you need postage for more than routine mailing; and why your consultant costs are high. Regarding salaries, provide a detailed breakdown of each position and the percentage of the employee's time allocated to the program. Fringe benefits can include worker's compensation, state unemployment insurance, social security, medical insurance, retirement, and other such items. Document exact costs for each major item. If you include items in the budget that you cannot fully support, the integrity of your project may be questioned. All major elements described in your proposal narrative need to be reflected in the budget.

Indirect costs are more difficult to determine than direct costs, but they are important to the financial well-being of your organization. Indirect expenses relate to any item involving more than one program unit. They can include estimated time spent on the project by the agency's director, accountant, and maintenance personnel. Indirect costs can also encompass expenses that are difficult to account for with precision, such as the depreciation of office equipment and the sharing of common spaces (see Chapter 12).

Some grantors will permit indirect costs to be included in the budget as a percentage of total direct costs of the grant.[19] That percentage is usually determined after an analysis of your overall financial operations by an experienced accountant (see Chapter 12). Many organizations that frequently receive grants from federal agencies negotiate an acceptable percentage with one government agency and are then able to use the same rate in contracts with other government agencies. The federal government allows indirect expenses arrived at either as a percentage of total salaries involved in the project, or as a percentage (much lower) of the total direct costs of the grant. Some foundations are becoming more accepting about including indirect costs, but depending upon the policies of a particular foundation, you may have to absorb indirect costs in other parts of your budget. Check with your funder on its policies on indirect costs.

Expenses					
Personnel Costs	% on Project	Agency Contribution	Other Funding Sources	Foundation Request	Total
Position A					
Position B					
Subtotal					
Fringe Benefits					
Subtotal Personnel					
Non-personnel costs					
Audit					
Consultants					
Rent					
Utilities					
Furnishings					
Maintenance					
Insurance					
Office					
Office Supplies					
Printing					
Postage					
Copier Rental					
Telephone					
Computer Supplies					
Out-of-town Travel					
In-town Travel					
Conference Fees					
Indirect Costs					
Other Costs					
Subtotal Non-personnel					
Total Projected Expenses					

Figure 15.2   Projected Expenses

Generally, you would have some flexibility in spending, as long as you do not exceed the total amount of the grant. Requests for budgetary changes should be made in writing to the funding source and, if approved, become formal budget modifications that change the conditions of your grant. Adequately planning your budget reduces the number of changes that may be required and also establishes the credibility necessary to obtain permission for needed modifications. Usually, if the grant is to cover more than one year, funders want a breakdown of the year-by-year budget and then a total amount. Be prepared to have your program reviewed each year in a multi-year funding request. Furthermore, if more than one funder is being asked to contribute to the costs, indicate the expected income from each source.

If you intend the program to serve a certain number of people, divide this number into the costs to see if the cost of service per client is reasonable. Funders often calculate this figure; so if you have not provided it in the proposal, be prepared to defend the program's per capita cost. Do not accept less money than is needed for a successful effort just to obtain the grant. You receive no credit for good intentions if the program is not accomplished. If you decide to accept fewer dollars, be sure you revise your anticipated achievements.

Any earned income anticipated (e.g., fees, special events, use of endowment income) should be included in the budget. The funder will appreciate your acknowledgment of anticipated revenues that would offset anticipated expenses.[20] Government grants may require an estimate of related revenues as part of the budget form.

Appendices

The proposal appendices provide information that is not essential to making the case but lends reliability and understanding to the organization and its request.[21] Include the following items: mission statement, a list of your board of trustees, documentation of your agency's 501(c)(3) tax-exempt letter from the IRS, independent audit report, job descriptions, résumés of key staff, your agency's 990 tax return, agency operating budget, affirmative action policy, statistical data on services provided, letters of support or agreement, evaluation instruments, and other items that bolster your proposal or that may be required by the funder.

Approaching Foundations for Funding

After identifying a list of foundations whose funding patterns appear to match your interests, the next step is to determine how to approach them. Before submitting a proposal to a foundation, determine exactly how the grant maker wants to be approached by accessing information supplied through the foundation's Web site, in a foundation directory (see Chapter 16), or call or write the foundation. Many foundations have Web sites where you can download their guidelines for funding and application forms.

There is no universal rule of operation; each foundation has its own style. Increasingly, however, funders are requesting *letters of interest* as a precursor to a complete proposal submission. In general, small private foundations require a brief (two or three page) letter telling who you are, what your concern is, what you propose to do, and how much funding you seek. Letters to small private foundations suffice because such organizations rarely have full-time staff and have limited funds and scope; they can more quickly indicate whether the proposal is within their area of interest.[22]

This same procedure can be used when approaching corporate-sponsored foundations. After sending a letter, it is important to make a personal contact with the person responsible for the corporate foundation (sometimes the president of the company, a person in public relations, or a specially designated program officer). In considering corporate support, ask the following questions: Does the firm have significant business or employees in the community? Is the business related in any way to the type of project you are developing? Does your organization deal with issues that are of unique importance to the firm? Can the firm gain special benefit for being associated with the project, including publicity or visibility with key consumers? Does the firm sell substantial products or services to your primary constituents? Positive answers to these questions enhance your chances of securing funding.[23] Besides providing grants, corporations can give other valuable resources, including the expertise of their personnel, gifts from their inventory, company facilities, and released time of employees.

Program officers of community foundations are typically inundated with many proposals each year. They must screen these to determine which ones to submit to their distribution committee for final approval. Some community foundations prefer that you first submit a proposal to determine if it has merit before considering meeting in person. Then the program officer can advise you on how to refine the proposal for maximum impact. Others encourage you to discuss a proposal in person or by phone with the program officer before investing considerable time and energy in proposal development. If you submit a proposal several weeks ahead of the deadline, you may have the opportunity to meet with the program officer in advance to make helpful revisions. Meeting with staff is crucial, because although not everything they recommend to the board of the foundation passes, their opinions and recommendations are highly regarded.

A general rule, offered by the Foundation Center, is to approach three funders for every grant you need. Because competition for funding is so great, be prepared to be turned down by several foundations before finally succeeding. If you send your proposal to more than one funder, be sure to indicate in the cover letter where else you are requesting funds.[24]

Using the Internet to Apply for Funds

Expect that in the future foundations will accept applications over the Internet. The first step in this process is for foundations to accept grant applications as transferred files. Your proposal can be sent as an e-mail attachment. Another possibility is for foundations to provide online grant applications, thus allowing for instant submission.

Using the Internet can provide innovative ways for an agency to convey its range of activities to a potential funder. The grant application could involve a combination of text, graphics, and links to give the program officer an in-depth understanding of your organization. Video and audio clips could demonstrate agency activities and provide powerful testimonials. A community organization could, for example, demonstrate how it participates in community partnerships by linking with its partner organizations. These virtual documentations could also be employed to meet the funders reporting requirements.[25] Before submitting electronic files, make sure the foundation wants to receive this information and has the software needed to open and view them.

The Proposal Is One Part of the Process

Proposals by themselves—even well written ones—do not necessarily ensure that funding is guaranteed. To maximize a grant request's chances, you must make a meaningful connection with a potential funder.

Those who give away money want to be inspired and feel that their funds are going to a good cause that will result in meaningful impact. Funders want their grants to be used by an organization that can implement a worthwhile program. Expect, therefore, that some grantors will be interested in your program if you provide them with an opportunity to collaborate.[26]

Ideally, the proposer should develop a partnership with the potential donor. Building a relationship is an essential part of the funding process. Although it is true that funders look to the track record and the reputation of the organization, they are investing in people, not the organization as an abstract entity. When developing a relationship with potential funders, it is generally a good idea to contact a foundation staff person to determine whether there is a good fit between your proposed ideas and the foundation's priorities. This contact provides an additional opportunity to obtain input from the funder about the criteria to be considered.

Depending on the initial interest of the foundation and its style of operating, you can phone or arrange an in-office interview with the staff member. In some instances it may be useful to ask one of your board members who knows a foundation trustee to contact that person, but recognize that you risk having the contact interpreted as exerting undue influence in the foundation decision-making process.

If your proposal is not accepted, it is a good idea to make a call thanking the funder for the time spent reviewing your proposal. Ask about any shortcomings in the application so that you might revise it when applying in the future.[27] You lay the groundwork for succeeding with future proposals.

Criteria for Effective Proposals

Funders obviously vary in the criteria they use for judging a proposal. As indicated previously, government agencies have specific and unique criteria for each grant. Foundation funders tend to be more flexible in using criteria to judge proposals. The following criteria should be kept in mind when preparing your proposal:

Competency of the Individuals Involved

Are those who have prepared the proposal competent?

Are they dedicated to making their ideas a reality?

Do they have a successful track record?

Do they demonstrate a depth of knowledge about the problem they are addressing?

Participation of the Organization's Membership

Are your board members familiar with the proposal? Have they approved it?

Is the board composed of the best possible combination of members of the community, client representatives, and others who can be effective resources for the organization?

Is the board willing to provide some of the organization's own resources?

If appropriate, are clients participating in the design and implementation of the project?

Desirability of the Project

Does the proposal make a strong case for the urgency of funding?

Is it clearly a high priority for the requesting organization and for the community?

If similar programs already exist, does the proposal acknowledge this and strongly convey why one more program is necessary?

Is the project creative in proposing an innovative approach to dealing with a community problem?

If asking for a grant renewal, has the project adequately demonstrated accomplishments?

If the project has fallen short of its accomplishments, does the proposal adequately explain why and what the organization intends to do about it?

Is the proposal consistent with the funder's own priorities?

Feasibility of the Project

Does the proposal illustrate how it would adequately cope with the identified problem, neither being too limited in its objectives nor too grandiose in its claims?

If it proposes to meet a long-standing problem, does the proposal have a well-conceived rationale for success?

Does the proposal demonstrate an understanding about what is happening in their community and across the country?

Does the proposal show sufficient awareness of the complexity of the problem?

On the basis of research of programs in other communities, does the proposal indicate why it can succeed in the same way as others have?

If others have failed, what modifications are proposed to ensure success?

Possibility of Leveraging Funds

Will the project draw on other private or public funding?

If the funding request is large, has the organization explored combining this request with requests to other funding organizations?

If several funders are involved, can each funder's contribution be separately identified?

Continuity of the Project

If funds are being requested for a startup project, what are assurances that the requesting organization or another group would continue it?

If the proposal is a demonstration project, what is the likelihood it might be replicated if it proves successful?

Impact Potential

Are the results likely to be transferable to other programs and other communities?

Would the results have a significant impact on the community?

Does the organization have a record of being able to involve other organizations and outside individuals to work together to achieve objectives?

If the proposal purports to make institutional or systemic change, can it assure success?

Dedication

If the proposal was previously rejected, has it been resubmitted with necessary modifications made?

Does the organization demonstrate a willingness and ability to obtain resources from its own community or constituency?

Clarity of Proposal

Is the proposal clearly written with limited use of professional jargon?

Are subheadings used to guide the reader?

Is the proposal concise?

Fiscal Soundness

Is the budget adequate to do the job, but not wasteful?

Does the operational budget of the organization appear sound?

Does the organization have a 501(c)(3) tax-exempt status with the IRS?

Have all budget requirements specified by the funder (e.g., indirect costs, agency match) been addressed?

Record of Results

How will results be accurately recorded to demonstrate the project's success?

Has appropriate evaluation advice been considered?

How would the funder be kept informed through written or verbal reports?

Following these guidelines can both enhance your competitiveness and provide a basis for a well thought-out plan that can be implemented effectively to achieve your objectives.

Questions for Discussion

1. Assuming that your organization currently or in the past has prepared proposals for funding, (a) what prompted the use of this method for raising funds over other options, and (b) what preparation was essential for developing the proposal?

2. Examine a past proposal developed by your organization.

   How was the proposal organized?

   How was need documented?

   What kinds of objectives were proposed?

   How measurable were the objectives?

   How detailed were the activities and tasks?

   Was a timeline prepared?

   Was an evaluation undertaken?

   Was the organization's capability documented?

   How was the program to continue the project at the end of foundation funding?

3. How detailed was the project's budget?

   How were indirect costs handled?

   Was there a budget narrative?

4. Reviewing the criteria at the end of the chapter, which ones apply to your agency's proposal—and which ones need to be developed further?

5. Consider preparing a proposal for a program related to your agency.

   How would you establish a need for the program?

   What would be your goals and objectives?

   What specific interventions would you develop?

   What would be your timeline?

   How would you document your various budget items?

   How would you demonstrate the effectiveness of your program?

   Which of the criteria at the end of the chapter would you address?

Notes

1. K. Klein, *Fundraising for the long haul* (Oakland, CA: Chardon Press, 2000), pp. 7–75.

2. R. Brody, *Guide for applying for federal funds for human services* (Cleveland, OH: School of Applied Social Sciences, Case Western Reserve University,

1974); R. Brody, *Problem solving: Concepts and methods for community organizations* (New York: Human Sciences Press, 1982), pp. 170–172; M. S. Hall, *Getting funded: A complete guide to proposal writing* (Portland, OR: Portland State University, 1988), pp. 15–20.

3. M. S. Hall, pp. 15–20.

4. R. Brody, *Problem solving*, pp. 170–172.

5. J. C. Geever & P. McNeill, eds., *The Foundation Center's guide to proposal writing,* revised ed. (Washington, DC: The Foundation Center, 1997), pp. 1–4.

6. P. Martin, Preparation before proposal writing, *New Directions for Philanthropic Fundraising* 28 (Summer 2000), pp. 85–95.

7. L. F. Jacquette & B. I. Jacquette, *What makes a good proposal* (Washington, DC: The Foundation Center, Aug 1977), pp. 1–7.

8. E. A. Scanlan, *Corporate and foundation fundraising: A complete guide from the inside,* in *Nonprofit organization management* (New York: Aspen, 2002), pp. 9:4.9–5.1.

9. J. Gooch, *Writing winning proposals* (Washington, DC: Council for the Advancement of Education, 1987).

10. R. Brody, *Problem solving*, pp. 41–42.

11. N. J. Kiritz, *Program planning & proposal writing* (Los Angeles: The Grantsmanship Center, 1980), p. 15.

12. R. Brody, *Problem solving*, p. 179.

13. J. C. Geever & P. McNeil, *The Foundation Center's guide*, pp. 111–120.

14. L. Lauffer, *Grants, etc.*, 2nd ed. (Thousand Oaks, CA: Sage, 1997), pp. 272–275.

15. P. F. Drucker, What results should you expect? A users' guide to MBO, *Public Administration Review* (January/February 1976), pp. 12–39; R. Elkin & D. J. Vorvaller, Evaluating the effectiveness of social services, *Management Controls* (May 1972), pp. 104–111; A. P. Raia, *Managing by objectives* (Glenview, IL: Scott Foresman, 1974), p. 24.

16. H. Rossi & H. E. Freeman, *Evaluation: A systematic approach* (Newbury Park, CA: Sage, 1989), p. 141.

17. R. Steiner, *Total proposal building* (Albany, NY: Trestletree, 1988), pp. 121–122.

18. R. Brody, *Problem solving*, pp. 185–187.

19. L. E. Decker & V. A. Decker, Grantseeking: How to find a funder and write a winning proposal (Charlottesville, VA: Community Collaborators, 1993), p. 71.

20. J. C. Geever & P. McNeil, *The Foundation Center's guide*, pp. 111–120.

21. M. E. Burns, *Proposal writer's guide* (Hartford, CT: Development & Technical Assistance Center, 1989), p. 18.

22. J. C. Geever & P. McNeil, *Guide to proposal writing* (New York: The Foundation Center, 1997).

23. J. C. Geever & P. McNeil, *Guide to proposal writing*, p.140.

24. M. Morth & S. Collins, eds., *The Foundation Center's user friendly guide: A grantseeker's guide to resources* (New York: The Foundation Center, 1996).

25. M. Johnston, *The nonprofit guide to the Internet,* 2nd ed. (New York: John Wiley & Sons, 1999), pp. 129–130.

26. J. C. Geever & P. McNeil, *The Foundation Center's guide,* pp. 111–120.

27. M. M. Goddard, Ten tips grant writers should commit to memory, *Foundation and Corporate Grants Alert 10, 12* in *Nonprofit organization management* (New York: Aspen, 2002).

16

Seeking Funding

B ecause there are potentially thousands of funders, you must be highly selective in finding those most appropriate for your organization and your proposal. Initially, you may have to identify many funding sources and then eliminate some to determine which ones are right for you. To avoid a time-consuming and often futile approach, it is best to initially select a core of foundations that match your interests. The ease of word processing might tempt you to send out non-customized proposals indiscriminately, but this kind of diffused distribution is generally ineffective. Through research, you can pinpoint those foundations whose patterns of giving over the past several years reflect a potential interest in your area.

In addition to discussing the search process involved in foundation grants, this chapter also reviews how human service managers can seek public funding through federal, state, and local grant requests, contracts, and block grants. Moreover, in seeking public funding, advocacy is a key factor.

Types of Foundations

Human service organizations are likely to request funds from three types of foundations: community, independent, and corporate.

Community foundations are publicly supported organizations that receive donations and make grants for social, religious, educational, or other charitable purposes. They are supported by, and operated for, the benefit of a specific community or region. They receive their funds from a variety of donors, both living and those who have made bequests in their wills to establish endowments. Their endowments are frequently composed of a number of different trust funds. Their grant-making activities are administered by a governing body or distribution committee. They typically have staff (called *program officers*) that review grants before they are submitted to a community foundation distribution committee.

Community foundations generally respond to a broad range of community concerns, and many of your programs may fit within their charge. Still, even community foundations have priorities. You can determine what they are through their 990 tax returns, their annual reports, foundation directories, or the CD-ROM which is discussed later. For best results, concentrate on the community foundation that serves your geographic area.[1]

Private, independent foundations are established to provide funds for community, educational, religious, or other charitable purposes. They derive funds from individuals, families, or groups of individuals. They may be operated under the direction of the donor or members of the donor's family and close friends, a type often referred to as family foundations, or they may have an independent board of trustees or directors that manages the foundation's program. A number of people can make decisions in these foundations: the donor, members of the donor's family, independent directors, or a trust official acting on the donor's behalf. They may or may not have staff. Many of the largest independent foundations have specific guidelines and well-defined priorities. Frequently, they limit their giving to the local area, but many of the largest foundations fund nationally and even internationally. In some instances, they are established to fund only one organization, in which case do not bother submitting an application to these operating foundations.

You can find information about independent foundations by contacting them directly. Only a small percentage issue separately printed annual reports. Annual information can be obtained from the IRS tax returns (990-PF) that must be made available to the public. Use the Foundation Center's Web site to go to links to grant maker Web sites: www.fdncenter.org/grantmaker/. If you have the name of a foundation, all you need is its address, contact name, or basic fiscal information. The Foundation Center's Foundation Web site can provide this: www.fdncenter.org/funders.

Corporate foundations, also called company-sponsored foundations, are created and funded by businesses for the purpose of making grants and performing other philanthropic activities, which they do as separate legal entities. Generally, they are managed by a separate board of directors composed of corporate officials, although the board may also include individuals with no corporate affiliation. (In some company-sponsored foundations, local plant managers and senior officials are also involved in grant-making and policy decisions.) Their giving programs usually focus on communities where the company has operations that are aligned with company interests. A corporate foundation makes it possible for a company to set aside funds in years when the company is doing well for use in years when earnings may be reduced and the needs of charitable organizations may be greater.

Company-sponsored foundations should not be confused with *direct corporate giving programs* that are under the full control of the corporation, with funds drawn solely from the corporation's pretax earnings.[2] In addition to monetary grants, direct-giving programs may also encompass non-cash, in-kind contributions, such as donations of equipment, office space, supplies, or the labor of volunteer employees. In contrast, a company-sponsored foundation, despite its close ties to the parent company, is legally an independent organization. It is classified as a *private foundation* by the IRS and is subject to the same regulations as any other private foundation.

In some instances, a corporation may choose to make charitable contributions to the same nonprofit organization through both its foundation and its direct-giving program. There may be little difference in the giving interests and procedures of the two vehicles, and the same staff and board may administer them. There are significant differences, however, in the type and amount of information available to the public about these two funding vehicles.

By law, corporate foundations must report annually on their activities and grant programs to the IRS on the same Form 990-PF used by all private foundations. Many corporate foundations also issue annual reports or brochures detailing their program interests and application procedures. Corporations are not required, however, to inform the public about contributions and grants made directly through the corporation. As a result, even with a growing number of corporations choosing to publicize their giving interests, restrictions, and application procedures, it is generally much more difficult to research direct corporate giving programs.

Faced with justifying philanthropy, corporate decision makers are increasingly expecting grant recipients to provide measurable program results. Corporate contributions must result in direct and tangible benefits to strategic business objectives. Programs that can document success in improving community services and racial harmony, for example, are attractive to corporate donors because they benefit community relations.[3]

Primary Source for Foundation Funding: The Foundation Center

The best source of information on foundations is The Foundation Center, 79 Fifth Avenue, NY, NY 10003. Its Web site is www.fdncenter.org, where you can find a wealth of information, including grant maker information and funding trends, a short course in proposal writing, and summaries of recent newspaper articles about philanthropy. To aid in the search for potential grant makers, the Foundation Center's site provides links to more than 2,000 funders that currently have Web sites. These sites often include guidelines for submitting proposals and the requirements for financial documentation. The Foundation Center's Web site is updated and expanded on a daily basis and provides a wide range of philanthropic resource information. For weekly information about new requests for proposals (RFPs) from grant makers, use this Web site: www.fdncenter.org/pnd/rfp.

The Foundation Center offers both an online subscription plan and CD-ROMs that provide a wealth of information on thousands of foundations. The following are among the data you could obtain:

- Name, address, phone number, e-mail, and Web site information
- Financial data, including assets and past grant amounts (high and low)
- Purpose and activities, including goals
- Fields of interest, such as education, substance abuse
- Limitations—what each foundation does not fund
- Application information
- Donors, officers, and trustees
- IRS identification number (for researching the 990)
- Selected grants, usually the amounts and grantees most recently reported

In addition to its main office in New York, The Foundation Center has field offices in Atlanta; Washington, DC; Cleveland; and San Francisco. If you live near these library/learning centers, it is worth making a visit to review their training materials, directories, and database on CD-ROM. If you do not have access to The Foundation Center libraries, you can obtain free information on foundations from the more than 220 Cooperating Collections that are located in all states. Visitors to the Cooperating Collection can acquire much of the information available electronically, including 990-PFs and The Foundation Center's database on CD-ROM. For a national listing of the Center's Cooperating Collections, visit www.fdncenter.org/collections.[4]

Using Foundation Directories

The following directories are available at The Foundation Center field office locations and at many of the Cooperating Collections:[5]

The *National Directory of Corporate Giving* gives reliable, up-to-date entries on more than 3,600 foundations and 1,300 direct giving programs. Corporate funders often make grants that reflect the priority interests of their parent companies. It features application procedures, key personnel, types of support awarded, giving limitations, financial data, and the average size of grants.

The *Foundation Grants Index on CD-ROM* contains information about foundations' recently awarded grants. The Grants Index covers the grant-making programs of more than 1,000 of the largest independent, corporate, and community foundations in the United States and features approximately 125,000 grant descriptions of $10,000 or greater. Designed for quick, grants-based research, its descriptions are divided into 28 broad subject areas, such as health and social services. Within each of these broad fields, the grants are listed geographically by state and alphabetically by name. The Index provides information on subjects funded, geographic areas, and former grant recipients.

The *Foundation 1000* provides the most comprehensive information available on the 1,000 largest foundations in the country. This directory describes which major foundations support projects like yours in your geographic area, what projects they have recently funded, how much of their budget is earmarked for your subject of interest, and the names and affiliations of the foundations' key personnel.

The Foundation Directory features current data on more than 10,000 of the top grant makers. The Directory provides fundraisers with insight into foundation giving priorities by describing more than 41,000 recently awarded grants.

The Foundation Directory Part 2 is designed specifically for nonprofit organizations seeking to broaden their base. It includes more than 10,000 mid-sized foundations that hold assets between $1 and $2 million or that have annual grant programs from $50,000 to $200,000. It includes more than 20,000 grant descriptions.

Guide to U.S. Foundations, Their Officers, Donors, and Trustees provides current information on more than 65,000 foundations. The comprehensive trustee, officer, and donor index is useful for determining possible foundation affiliations of your own organization's board members, donors, and volunteers. This is a helpful guide for identifying smaller foundations. Arranged by state and total giving, it can assist in pinpointing where to concentrate your search for local grant dollars. The Guide uses codes to show if another Foundation Center reference book includes more detailed information on the grant maker you are researching.

The Grant Guides Series provide current information on the grants recently awarded in 12 subject fields, including children and youth, mental health, addictions, crisis services, and the physically and mentally disabled. Each guide gives descriptions of hundreds of recently awarded foundation grants of at least $10,000. The subject index lets you search for grant makers by hundreds of key words. The geographic index directs you to foundations that have funded projects in your state or county. The recipient index lets you track grants awarded to similar organizations in your field.

Conducting the Search Process

To better manage your search for funding through one or more of the previously discussed directories, consider conducting your search in several phases:

Phase I. Begin with your own strategic plan. Focus on activities that help you achieve your mission. Do not create programs merely because a funding opportunity exists.[6] Prior to beginning your search, write two or three pages about what you want to accomplish, including the problem you plan to address, your target population, and specific outcomes. The more focused you are, the easier your grant seeking search.

Phase II. In phase two, develop a broad list of potential supporters. Think of the search process as an inverted pyramid. Identify as many possibilities as you can and then refine the list to a few, most appropriate candidates. For example, start with a broad area of social service counseling. This could yield hundreds of possible funders. Then narrow your search to counseling teenagers who are involved with substance abuse. The search process involves a truly creative exploration of different topics. In this example, possible categories could include adolescents, alcoholism, mental health, drugs, suicide, and pregnancy prevention.

By scanning the subject indexes in *The Foundation Directory* and *The Foundation Grants Index,* you develop some ideas of relevant subjects for your grant proposal. During this phase, it is important not to focus your search too narrowly, because, on the one hand, it is possible that those funders who have previously funded projects identical to yours may not want to repeat their funding. On the other hand, you may be able to locate funders who have similar, though not identical, interests to yours. They may be looking for fresh ideas.

Phase III. In phase three, you narrow down your broad list of possibilities to as many as 10 or 20 potential funders. Assuming you have access to various previously discussed directories, consider using one or more of the following: If you are seeking a grant over $10,000, consider going to *The Foundation Grants Index,* which provides information on actual grants of $10,000 or greater by the largest foundations, and also *The Grant Guides,* which identify foundations in other states that might fund organizations in your specific subject area and geographic location. In addition, review *The Foundation 1000* for detailed information on major foundations in your state or nationally. Also review *The Foundation Directory* for foundations that give out sizable grants.

If your grant is likely to be less than $10,000, *The Foundation Directory* and *The Foundation Directory Part 2* are good sources of information. If you are interested in applying for a corporate foundation grant, *The National Directory of Corporate Giving* is an essential resource.

Phase IV. In phase four, narrow the list of approximately 20 possible foundations down to 3 to 5. Accomplish this by identifying various criteria: the geographic focus, contact information, limitations (what foundations do not fund), range of donations, trustees, and pertinent information contained in the 990 Forms. You can find out most of this information from the directories or the FC Search CD-ROM (discussed below). You may wish to keep a worksheet of your findings, as shown in Figure 16.1.

Focus primarily on those foundations located in your local area and others in your state that have funded programs in your local community. If you are seeking corporate support, it is a good idea to obtain an annual report or printed guidelines that contain the company's philosophy and its

Information Source:
  Name
  Address

Contact Person   **Phone Number**

Financial Data:
  Total Assets
  Grant Ranges
  Single Year   Multi Year

Subject Focus Priorities:

Target Populations:

Special Limitations:
  Geographic
  Funding Restrictions

Types of Support:
  Program Development
  Ongoing Support
  Other

Trustees:

Application Information:
  Printed Guidelines
  Application forms

Initial Approach (letter of inquiry, formal proposal, phone call)

Deadlines:
  Proposal submission dates
  Trustee decision times

Follow-up Notes

Figure 16.1   Worksheet on Potential Funders

Source: The Foundation Center, Prospect worksheet, in *The Foundation Center's user-friendly guide*, rev. ed. (New York: Author, 1994).

plans for the future.[7] Determine whether you need to send a letter of inquiry or a full proposal. Some corporations have separate foundation offices; others may implement giving programs through their marketing department, in which case their corporate giving is more closely tied to marketing company products. Always determine in advance where your proposal letter should be sent.

Typically, foundation descriptions, located in the various directories, indicate limitations. Read this section carefully to determine what the specific foundation does not fund. Some foundations do not provide funds for ongoing operations, new projects, capital campaigns, or certain subject categories, equipment, or conferences.

Scan the list of trustees connected to the foundation to consider whether members of your board have a relationship with them. For corporate foundations, accessing trustees employed by a corporation that could fund your project might just give you an advantage.

Using Online Directories and the FC Search CD-ROM

Foundation Directory Online is available by subscription at four different price points. For example, Foundation Directory Online Platinum contains information on about 76,000 grant makers and over 350,000 grants. Information is updated biweekly. Check The Foundation Center's catalog to determine the best plan for your organization. These resources are available free of charge at The Foundation Center libraries and may also be available at the Cooperating Collections. To locate the 220 Cooperating Collections that have the CD-ROM available, use the Web site for The Foundation Center (www.fdncenter.org). Click on "Cooperating Collections," and note which ones nearest you have the CD icon next to their names.

FC Search: The Foundation Center's Database on CD-ROM gives you access to all known foundations, corporate givers, and grant-making public charities, as well as their associated grants. Choosing from 21 search criteria generates targeted lists of funding prospects in a matter of seconds. The Foundation Center offers a variety of CD-ROMs. The least expensive covers the largest 10,000 foundations. The most comprehensive, *FC Search*, details information on more than 76,000 U.S. foundations and corporate givers. This one disc also provides about 355,000 associated grants and identifies more than 324,000 trustees and donors.

FC Search includes data found in previously described sources: *The Foundation Directory, The Foundation Directory Part 2, The Foundation Directory Supplement, The Guide to U.S. Foundations: Their Trustees, Officers and Donors, The National Directory of Corporate Giving, The Foundation Grants Index,* and *The Foundation Grants Index Quarterly.*

The *FC Search CD-ROM* is a powerful tool for efficiently gaining information about foundations. It provides comprehensive information on both grant makers and grant files. By browsing through these two files you can determine the kinds of grants awarded by different grant makers and then obtain more detailed information on the grants themselves.

FC Search has a browse function that allows you to review lists of records in each database. You can browse the entire list or concentrate on specific states. By browsing the grant maker file, you can quickly locate a specific grant maker and then go directly to a list of grants previously made by that foundation. Browsing the grant file lets you scan a list of grants given to organizations, and then you can review the individual grants given to each organization.

The search function lets you pinpoint grant makers or grants meeting your specific criteria. Such criteria can include the following: geographic focus (national, state, or local), fields of interest (e.g., social services), types of support (capital, seed money, etc.), total assets, total giving, subjects, and annual dollar amount.

In the *Advanced Grants* mode you can conduct an in-depth search of grants, the grant makers that awarded them, and the specific organizations that received them. This is especially helpful if you want to determine which grant makers provide grants in a specific subject area for a specific population group in a specific locality. One of the benefits of this search process is that it contains an especially helpful index for guiding your search. Among the general fields of interest appropriate for health and human service agencies are the following: civil rights, community development, crime/law enforcement, education, employment, environment, health care, health organization, housing/shelter, human services, mental health/crisis services, mutual aid societies, philanthropy/volunteerism, recreation, social sciences, social services, and youth development.

Within each field of interest is a list of subject categories. Become familiar with these categories, since your search can be matched more directly with key words from the index. For example, if you are searching for fund programs for ex-offenders, you could search for this subject under the crime/law field of interest.[8]

The following items illustrate some of the searches you could undertake with *FC Search*:

- The address and telephone number of specific foundations
- An alphabetical listing of all nonprofit organizations in your state or community
- All the grant makers in your state that fund social services
- Foundations in your state that have given grants relating to aging and Alzheimer disease (as an example)
- Names of the trustees of a particular foundation
- Foundations that give more than $100,000 for capital grants
- Corporate foundations in your state that have given funds for specific purposes, such as building equipment
- Foundations that provide basic operating funds in your local community
- Foundations that have given money for specific purposes such as workshops or technical assistance
- Foundations that have given to organizations similar to yours (e.g., Boy Scouts, YMCAs, Red Cross)

Suggested Strategies Using FC Search

The search strategies described earlier also apply to the *FC Search*. The obvious advantage in using the CD-ROM instead of the directories is the speed with which you can conduct your search. If you plan on using the CD-ROM, the following suggestions may prove useful:

1. Your primary objective is to locate foundations that are amenable to funding your project, based on past giving patterns. For example, you assume that a particular foundation that previously funded a foster care recruitment program would be receptive to your foster care recruitment proposal. This may or may not be the case; having funded a previous foster care program, the foundation may be looking for other kinds of programs to help vulnerable children. Through an inquiry letter or a phone call, you can determine whether your proposal is still a priority for the foundations you have identified.

2. Conversely, foundations that may not have previously funded a program similar to what you have in mind may now be open to considering an innovative foster care recruitment effort. Knowing that these foundations are interested in vulnerable children in general is a good starting point for exploration.

3. The search process can be too broad or too narrow. For this reason, use the *FC Search* as a tool for exploration. The search process can involve a certain amount of trial and error. Suppose, for example, you are interested in establishing drug-free zones in your community. Perhaps very few foundations have funded such an effort. That need not deter you from exploring foundations that have an interest in substance abuse, prevention, alcoholism, or neighborhood development. You can explore all of these categories to determine your initial list of subjects. Be prepared to broaden your search if you identify too few "hits"; be prepared, on the other hand, to narrow your search if you identify too many "hits."

4. You need to learn specific techniques for using the *FC Search*. It is worth your time to take a workshop if your Cooperating Collection offers one, or at least to study the manual that is available with the CD-ROM. You can learn specific techniques and vocabulary for expanding or narrowing your search.

5. Assume you have a particular topic in mind. In conducting a search you can either (1) scroll through a field of interest with a pre-selected index or (2) use *Text Search*, which searches for words appearing anywhere within the grant maker records. Using text search requires some experimenting and time to understand the rules, but mastering it allows you to explore vast amounts of data. Studying the manual can show you how to focus your query. For example, putting quotes around the first three letters of a local zip

code would narrow the list to local foundations that fund grants in your community and nearby suburbs. Another example: by typing in "applications not accepted" you would eliminate from the search process those foundations that do not accept outside grant requests. There are a number of other techniques discussed in the manual that can greatly enhance your search process.

6. Check the Types of Support Index to limit your search to the types of support various grant makers make. The following list can be useful in determining how foundations categorize their support:

Annual campaigns	Equipment
Building/renovation	General/operating support
Capital campaigns	In-kind gifts
Conferences/seminars	Internships
Consulting services	Loaned talent
Continuing support	Matching funds
Debt reduction	Program development
Donated equipment	Public relations services
Donated products	Publication
Emergency funds	Research
Employee volunteer services	Seed money
Endowment funds	Technical Assistance

7. In considering foundations that might give funding to your community, focus not only on those foundations located in your community or your state but also those located elsewhere that have given grants to your area.

8. With *FC Search* you can print or save to a disk the search result lists or the grant maker records you have specifically marked for later examination.

Searching for funds requires a considerable amount of ingenuity, patience, persistence, and focus. The availability of directories, Internet subscriptions and CD-ROMs now makes it possible to explore a wide variety of possibilities in a fairly short time. Expect to experiment and go through much trial and error. The payoff in finding the right foundations can be enormous.

Federal Government Funding

The best source of information on grants at the federal level is the Web site for *The Catalog of Federal Domestic Assistance* at www.cfda.gov. A print version is also available (Superintendent of Documents, U.S. Printing Office, Washington, DC 20402), but the Web site provides easy access to a comprehensive listing of all human service programs sponsored by federal departments. The catalog is cross-referenced by type of program and by federal department or agency responsible for its issuance. It describes each program with funding levels and information about eligibility. It is also a portal to a number of useful links, including steps to take to obtain assistance, how to write a federal proposal, and availability of funding for all domestic grants. An especially useful link is www.grants.gov, which allows organizations to find and apply for competitive grants from all federal grant-making agencies.

For background information, the U.S. General Accounting Office (www.gao.gov) provides free publications on evaluation of government grants. At this Web site click the *search* button, then type in the specific subject for which you want information (e.g., substance abuse adolescent pregnant). To obtain information on specific topics prepared by the federal government, go to the Government Printing Office Web site: www. gpoaccess.gov. Refer to "A-Z Resource List" for a comprehensive list of titles. Browse through the list to locate a topic of interest (e.g., National Council on Disabilities). Then conduct further research for current publications and grants. At this Web site you can also obtain a record of all current grant opportunities and new federal regulations published in the *Federal Register,* which is issued daily (www.gpoaccess.gov/fr/index.html). You will find current grant requests if you search by department (e.g., Health and Human Services).

All federal agencies have Web sites that provide information on programs they are currently funding, suggestions on how to conduct your search, and current federal thinking on best practices. Many of these Web sites can provide you with free information if you register your e-mail, name, and address. By registering you can be informed of the availability of new grants and application kits that you can download. Also, be aware that many policy organizations have Web sites that are excellent resources for current legislative and policy initiatives. (See Web Sites for Human Service Managers for selected government Web sites and national organizations.)

In preparing a federal grant proposal, consider the following:

1. Become familiar with pertinent program criteria to make sure that the proposal relates to that criteria, because grant reviewers will likely apply a point scale to evaluate your proposal against the criteria.

2. Check to see if the program already exists in your locale, and explain why your program is unique.

3. Obtain letters of support, especially from local government agencies and officials and other grantees if service areas are in common.

4. Where appropriate, obtain in writing affiliation agreements to demonstrate community support. Two or three organizations working together usually have a better chance of funding than if each were to go it alone.

5. After you have identified the grant or agency, call to ask for a grant application kit. If it is appropriate, request that your contact person review your proposed project and offer suggestions and criticisms.

6. Most proposals require a proposal summary, a problem statement, project objectives, program methods and design, timelines, project outcome measures, evaluation, future funding plan, organizational qualifications and experience, endorsements, project budget, and budget narrative. Of course, you should observe the protocol developed in each application kit. (See Chapter 15 for discussion on proposal writing.)

State and Local Government Funding

Ascertaining the availability of human service contracts and grants from state and local government can usually be accomplished by signing on to a bidder's list, which involves contacting a government's procurement office or human service agency. In addition, one can review the legal advertisement section of the daily newspaper.[9]

State and local governments tend to prefer contracts to funding grants. Contracts are awarded in two ways: a *request for proposals* (RFP) or *invitation for bids* (IFB). In the RFP approach, human service agencies, as prospective contractors, prepare a proposal with an operating budget as specified in the government's RFP package. In general, RFP's are for soft services, that is, services directed at clients, such as counseling or adoption services. In the proposal narrative, the agency specifies how it intends to provide the services, indicates the qualifications of staff, discusses the impact it intends, and describes evaluation procedures. In the budget section it describes all cost items.

Although criteria vary from one RFP to another, they generally reflect the following: (1) proper completion of the proposal with a final budget, (2) demonstrated competency and track record of the agency to provide a service, (3) the feasibility of the proposal and the ability to acquire the necessary resources (staff, equipment, etc.) to provide the services, (4) reasonable costs.[10] The invitation for bids (IFB) is generally used when the government department specifies exactly what it wants. It more generally applies to providing tangible services for such projects as specialized transportation or home-delivered meals.

Local or Regional RFPs

Because much of the funding for human services is awarded through county or regional boards, it is crucial for agencies submitting RFPs to be clear about the criteria to be used. This is particularly true of the mental health and substance abuse field, where local mental health and substance abuse boards make funding decisions. For example, in an RFP for prevention services, these are the kinds of questions that are used to judge proposals:

1. Does the proposal include the relationship of the program to the agency's mission?

2. Is the problem statement well defined?

3. Does the problem statement include statistical data that supports the problem?

4. Does the proposal provide baseline data for measuring program effectiveness?

5. Does the agency provide prevention models on which the program is based?

6. Does the agency have experience with service delivery to the target population?

7. Is there an accurate description of the target population?

8. Does program staff have credentials and experience for delivering service?

9. Does the proposal include a well-defined set of milestones and timetable for completion?

10. Does the proposal describe scheduled activities?

Governmental Contracting

When contracting for human services, state and local government tend to use (1) *cost reimbursement contracts,* (2) *performance contracts,* and (3) *capitated (managed care) contracts.* Under a *cost reimbursement contract,* an agency contractor is reimbursed only for actual, allowable expenses incurred in providing the service, typically related to the approved line-item operating budget in the contract. If the agency has an expense that is not allowed, it is not reimbursed for it. Because cost reimbursement contracts do not relate to performance accomplishments, governments are moving away from this approach.

Performance contracts require designation of outputs and outcomes of service to compensate agencies and renew contracts. Examples of payments based on outputs are reimbursement of cost per hour of counseling or cost per hour of home-delivered meals. Examples of payments based on outcomes are reimbursement for clients' completing training programs and obtaining jobs or clients' finishing drug treatment programs and remaining drug free.[11] If the contractor provides the contracted amount of outputs and outcomes, the revenues earned could be equal to or greater than expenses incurred. But if the contractor's performance falls short of that stipulated in the contract, revenues received could be less than actual expenses, and the agency could lose money.

In a *capitated (managed care) contract*, the agency receives a fixed payment to provide services to clients for a fixed period of time. For example, an agency providing foster care services might receive a one-time payment for each child in its care. The payment is the only compensation the agency receives no matter how long the child remains in care. If the agency makes a timely placement, it could make money; however, if it is delayed in making placements, the agency could lose money.

A major caution that effective managers must be concerned about is contracting at low cost-reimbursement rates. Clearly, it is preferable that an organization strive to at least break even and, if possible, add to the fund balance. In the eagerness to obtain contracts, agencies may contract at rates below their actual service costs and then hope that they can subsidize these losses by applying for United Way support, using their endowment funds, or diverting funds from other funding sources. In the short term, this may be manageable, but in the long term, unless an organization has an ability to sustain the subsidy, the organization is headed for trouble. If the actual cost of providing a unit of counseling service is, say, $60, and the government contractor only pays $35, then the other $25 has to come from some subsidy. This reality may mean turning down contracts that do not fully reimburse for services rendered.

Government Block Grants

A *block grant* allows the government to pay an agency for services provided to accomplish a public purpose authorized by legislation. Grants provide support for an activity without specifying any product or service and thus encourage innovation. The advantage of block grants is that federal monies can be brought closer to state and local officials who have the flexibility to respond to local needs.[12] Federal block grant money is also given to cities to distribute to nonprofits for capital programs of major significance to human services, such as the rehabilitation of urban housing. Most cities provide a person in the mayor's office who deals with community development block grants.[13]

Depending on one's perspective, being able to find and influence expenditures at the local level can either be an advantage or a disadvantage for local organizations. Not surprisingly, politics play a role in determining disbursement of funding. Local politicians want to get mileage out of funds that are distributed so that they can influence people to vote for them at the next election. In community block grants, for example, you have a better chance of obtaining funding if you can demonstrate that many councilpersons' wards will benefit from the project. You both need to tune into the agendas of the politicians and be prepared to influence their decision making.

Lobbying for Government Funding

Some human service managers are uneasy about advocating for public funding, mainly out of concern that they might lose their 501(c)(3) Internal Revenue status. This is the key aspect of the tax code that describes what organizations must do to maintain the ability to offer tax deductions to their donors. In part the uneasiness is understandable, because the law is confusing in that it prohibits charities from conducting a "substantial" amount of lobbying, which is quite ambiguous. Your organization should seek legal counsel to clarify restrictions.

Certain restrictions do apply to charitable organizations. For example, you cannot endorse or oppose any political campaign. But you can sponsor a forum or candidate debate, and you can support or oppose federal or state legislation. Volunteers and agency staff have the same First Amendment right as anyone else. Regulations do not prohibit persons making political contributions or volunteering to work on a campaign, so long as reference to organizational affiliation clearly indicates that the reference is for identification purposes only. The organization's offices cannot be turned into a quasi-campaign office even during non-business hours. Financial penalties can be imposed on the organization and the managers.

For those organizations that are concerned about whether they could be penalized under the ambiguous rules governing 501(c)(3), they can elect to operate under 501(h), which provides clear-cut rules governing lobbying. This little-known option is simply an alternative accounting mechanism, not a different tax status. The organization does not lose the ability to offer tax deductibility to its donors.[14]

IRS 501(h) regulations permit organizations to spend on lobbying on a sliding scale—up to 20% of their first $500,000 in expenditures and up to 5% of expenditures over $1.5 million, with a $1 million ceiling in each year. Organizations can spend no more than a quarter of their lobbying expenses on grassroots lobbying (communications to the general public that attempt to influence legislation through changing public opinion). All 501(c)(3)s must report the amount they spend on lobbying on their 990 tax returns.[15] Charities that follow the alternative approach can lobby virtually all they want and not have to worry about the IRS.[16] Form 5768 can be downloaded from the IRS at www.irs.gov.

County Funding of Human Services

The process of shifting funding and programmatic decision making from the federal to the state and then to the county levels is called *devolution*.

Because of devolution, effective human service managers should give increased attention to local government spending, particularly to county budgets, to ensure that human services receive and are spending their funds effectively.

Counties are geographical units established solely to administer state law, and are instruments of state government. Although some states directly administer health and human services programs, other states give counties considerable discretion in determining how these programs are to be administered. Most of the funding that counties spend on health and human services is derived either from the state or federal government, although in some localities, county governments raise additional local funds through real estate levies. These levies can be single purpose: mental health, substance abuse, senior services, child welfare—or they can be comprehensive health and human service levies that cover multiple purposes.

The budgeting process within county governments is adversarial in that departments are required to defend their prior and current spending and be accountable for the use of public funds. At the county level, hearings are scheduled for interested parties to offer testimony on how public funds should be spent. Agency administrative staff, both within the government and from the outside, as well as clients, are invited to make statements. Although county commissioners by law must hold public hearings on the budget, significant changes are not frequently made as a result of these hearings, presumably because such changes would be a criticism of their own county department administrators. Hence to be effective it is essential to work closely with county departments as budgets are being prepared.

In some states' counties, independent governing bodies channel and monitor funding to deliver mental health, mental retardation, developmental disability, drug and alcohol, and children's services. Counties have responsibility for approving their budgets, but to the extent that they are separately funded through state money allocated directly to them, or by separate tax monies, the process of approving these budgets is more form than substance. Some counties may subsidize their human services, in which case the county commissioners have greater control over the approval of budgets.[17]

The significance of this funding pattern for administrators of human services is that there can be opportunities to influence funding at the local level for needed services. Here is an example from one county:

Local directors of services to seniors approach the county's Director of Senior and Adult Services because low-income, frail elderly need more extensive at-home services to keep them out of nursing homes. These services include case management, home delivered meals, medical transportation, personal care, and chore services. The commissioners in this large urban county are reluctant to undertake a major commitment without having a pilot program demonstrate the value of the services.

Commissioners lack, however, sufficient monies in the budget to cover a pilot program entirely. An advisory committee is established, consisting of key civic leaders and directors of major services for the elderly. A grant is obtained from a local community foundation, which is matched by the county for a three-year pilot program. Another local private foundation agrees to fund for three years the evaluation of the program. In the course of the three-year pilot program, 3,700 seniors are served from 46 different communities in the county. The evaluation documents the cost of providing the service as well as specific benefits to the recipients.

Reluctant to consider expending local dollars until all other options are considered, the commissioners request that the advisory committee explore state funding. The state legislature, however, is strapped for funds, and in the budgeting negotiations, legislators reject the request for earmarking additional monies for one county, fearing there would be demands made from the other counties. Because the commissioners are continually apprised of efforts to secure funding elsewhere and also of the success of the pilot program, they agree to raise money locally if the voters approve a local health and human services levy. Having worked on the project for over four years, an enthusiastic ad hoc group of seniors and service managers agrees to give several dozen presentations to local groups. Their dedication pays off and the levy passes.

Hard work, persistence, continuous communication with local officials, passionate commitment to a cause, and an understanding of the political process are ingredients needed to obtain local funding. After five years the program, which began as a small pilot program, is now a permanent community institution.[18]

Questions for Discussion

1. Identify community, private, and corporate foundations in your community. How can you determine how much some of them donate annually and examples of what they fund?

2. Using the Internet to find www.fdncenter.org, can you determine (a) the location of Cooperating Collections in your state? (b) examples of foundations that might be a source of funding for your organization?

3. If you have access to Foundation Center libraries or Cooperating Collections, what information could you obtain on selected foundations?

4. If you were to go online for the *Catalog of Federal Domestic Assistance*, what funding sources could you locate? If this approach might not apply to your organization, select a human service topic. How would you search for possible government funding?

5. What government contracts, if any, has your organization been involved in obtaining? How did the organization go about securing funding?

6. What block grants, if any, has your organization been involved in obtaining?

7. With what state or local advocacy fundraising efforts has your agency been engaged?

Notes

1. M. F. Nauffts, ed., *Foundation fundamentals: A guide for grantseekers,* 5th ed. (New York: The Foundation Center, 1994).

2. M. F. Nauffts, p. 3.

3. J. D. Marx, Corporate strategic philanthropy: Implications for social work, *Social Work* (January 1988), pp. 35–41.

4. The Foundation Center, *Fundraising & nonprofit development resources catalog* (New York: Author, Fall 2003).

5. The Foundation Center, *Catalog of fundraising and nonprofit development resources* (New York: Author, Fall 2003).

6. P. Martin, Preparation before proposal writing, *New Directions for Philanthropic Fundraising* 28 (Summer 2000), pp. 85–95.

7. P. Martin, pp. 85–95.

8. The Foundation Center, *FC Search Manual* (New York: Author, 1997), p. 27.

9. L. L. Martin, *Financial management for human service administrators* (Boston: Allyn & Bacon, 2001), p. 165.

10. L. L. Martin, p. 168.

11. L. L. Martin, p. 171.

12. R. Brody, M. Goodman, & J. Ferrante, *The legislative process: An action handbook for Ohio citizen's groups,* 3rd ed. (Cleveland, OH: Federation for Community Planning, 1985).

13. C. E. Henry, Effective proposal writing, in *Skills for effective management of nonprofit organizations,* ed. R. Edwards (Washington DC: National Association of Social Workers, 1998).

14. J. M. Berry, Nonprofit groups shouldn't be afraid to lobby, *The Chronicle of Philanthropy* (27 November 2003), pp. 33, 34.

15. G. M. Grobman, *Lobbying,* in *The nonprofit handbook* (Harrisburg PA: White Hat Communications, 1999), pp. 127–138.

16. J. M. Berry, p. 34.

17. R. G. Sheridan & D. A. Ellis, County budgeting is unique, *Planning and action: The journal of the federation for community planning* 9 (2000), pp. 1–5.

18. R. Brody, Letter to the Cuyahoga County Commissioners (June 6, 2003).

PART IV

Interacting Effectively

Chapter 17: Making Meetings Productive

Chapter 18: Improving Communications and Handling Conflicts

Chapter 19: Team Building and Coalition Building

Chapter 20: Working with a Board of Trustees

In this part you will learn how to

❖ Decide when a meeting is needed

❖ Improve the way meetings are conducted

❖ Ask the right questions to facilitate ideas

❖ Use consensus to make decisions—and challenge over-conformity

❖ Use creative techniques to stimulate fresh thinking

❖ Initiate task forces to achieve action

❖ Overcome problem communications

❖ Foster top-down and bottom-up communications

❖ Listen more effectively

❖ Reconcile conflicting expectations of supervisors and staff

❖ Develop well-functioning teams

❖ Facilitate alliances with other agencies

❖ Identify different collaborative structures

❖ Distinguish between governance and management in working with a board of trustees

❖ Help make a board of trustees and its committees function optimally

❖ Evaluate executive performance and board functioning

17

Making Meetings Productive

Poorly planned and poorly managed meetings waste staff time and can cost the organization a great deal of money. Think of the value of meeting time in dollars and cents: Suppose a staff meeting is held once weekly for two hours. Suppose, further, that the average hourly wage of the 12 professional staff who attend is $17.50. This translates to $420 per meeting (12 staff x $15 x 2 hours). During a 40-week period, the cost for this two-hour weekly meeting is $16,800. The cost to the organization could be half that amount if the meeting were reduced to one hour per week, held biweekly, or involved half the number of staff. Because managers spend a great portion of their time leading or participating in meetings, they should be purposeful and productive.

Considering Whether or Not to Hold a Meeting

Meetings should be called to deal with essential important matters that cannot be handled on a one-to-one basis.[1] Do not use them to conduct individual supervisory conferences while others in the group are passive observers.[2] In addition, it is generally not a good idea to hold a meeting when one or more of the following situations exists:

- You can communicate better by telephone, memo, fax, or e-mail.
- The issue is confidential, such as hiring, firing, or negotiating salaries.
- There are inadequate data or poor preparation.
- There is no compelling reason to hold a regularly scheduled meeting.

Holding a meeting, however, is a good idea when these conditions exist:

- You want to reinforce the organization's essential values (e.g., emphasizing cooperative efforts) or relate staff efforts to the organization's mission, goals, or objectives.

- You are dealing with a complex problem involving several options, and staff can help solve the problem or make a decision.
- You need the expertise or advice of selected individuals.
- You need to share concerns or clarify an organizational issue.
- You want to share with or obtain information from group members about a current project or event, and you want to ensure that everyone receives the same data in the same way.
- You want to coordinate activities of various units.
- You want to provide training or use the session for questions and answers.
- You want to publicly recognize an achievement, build morale, or encourage teamwork.
- You expect resistance from some individuals and think a meeting will ameliorate their concerns.

To enhance the effectiveness of meetings, consider these questions:

- What do you want to accomplish by the end of the meeting?
- Based on your expectations, who should attend and what kind of involvement do you want from them?
- What should be on the agenda? How much time should be allowed for each item?
- What specific tasks, deadlines, and responsibilities would you need to communicate?
- Who is responsible for decisions?
- With whom should you meet before the meeting?
- What materials must be prepared in advance of the meeting?[3]

Making the Best Use of Time

You cannot control the outcome of a meeting without being perceived as manipulative. You can guide possible outcomes and plan accordingly, however. Have a definite reason for every meeting. Think *reason* first, and then *meeting*. By doing this, you can avoid the malady of *meetingitis*—the tendency to have regularly scheduled meetings whether they are necessary or not. By letting participants know up front what you are hoping to achieve by the end of the meeting, you can facilitate discussion more easily.

You should also plan the meeting in detail. Think in advance about *why* the meeting is being held, *what* you want to accomplish, and *who* specifically should attend. Send out any pertinent reading materials in advance, such as minutes of previous meetings or special reports. Print out the agenda so everyone knows what will be discussed. Set a specific ending time and violate it only under extraordinary circumstances. Normally, meetings should last no longer than one to two hours. If a meeting is extended beyond that, the group runs the risk of cutting into others' schedules. As a result, staff who must leave before the meeting ends may feel that their departure prevents them from participating in significant decisions.

Set a time limit for each topic on the agenda and stick to it. Under exceptional circumstances, the group could agree to extend the time period of one item by subtracting time from another. Appoint a timekeeper (or let the chairperson retain the role) if the group tends to wander and needs the discipline of being reminded about time. To keep meetings on target, the leader should establish the ground rule that the group must avoid distracting and irrelevant ideas so that they can conduct the main business of the meeting within the agreed-upon time limit.

If the meeting has a function other than providing information, such as coordinating work or solving problems, select participants on the basis of their potential for contributions. Limit attendance to those directly involved with topics on the agenda to make the best use of everyone's time. The larger the group, the more discussion you may have, and the longer the meeting may run. Schedule some participants to attend only that part of the meeting to which they can contribute. When they complete their item, they may leave the meeting.[4]

It is better to delay a proposed agenda topic until you have the appropriate staff to deal with the issue. For example, in a children's treatment center, a meeting is called to handle discipline problems among the children, but the group inadvertently excludes the recreation counselor and the night supervisor—so not all of the appropriate staff are present to address the concern.

Always begin a meeting on time, regardless of late arrivals. If at every meeting you wait until latecomers arrive, those who do arrive on time develop the habit of tardiness, and the late ones become even tardier. There is an old saying, "People do not miss trains that leave on time."

Send out a meeting notice well in advance with background material related to items on the agenda so that participants come well prepared. Indicate under each agenda item whether it is for information sharing, discussion, or decision making.[5] This procedure avoids the time-consuming distribution of documents at a meeting and encourages group members to do their homework. By specifying each agenda item in advance, you create a working structure for the meeting. To make the best use of meeting time, you could hold a pre-meeting with two or three people to analyze the issues in depth and determine a proposed course of action based on their review of several options. The larger group should have an opportunity to examine the options and to understand the rationale for the option being proposed.

Some organizations provide an annotated meeting agenda called a "docket." Not only does a docket list the items to be discussed, it also gives a paragraph or two of explanation after each item to save time during the meeting itself. The docket is a useful technique for covering many items in a short time.

Functions of Meetings

It is critical that both the chairperson and the group understand the central function of a group session. Among the functions are the following:

Coordinating: Gather several participants to work on the same issue and develop ways to complement their efforts.

Distributing work: Clarify and distribute assignments to group members.

Team building: Establish an esprit de corps and mutual support among participants. Emphasize working cooperatively.

Reporting information: Provide the necessary background that later may become the basis for decision making. Reports can include facts and other findings gathered in recent studies.

Studying a problem: Undertake precise problem analyses.

Making decisions: Make a decision or recommendation from among alternatives. Group members may or may not be the same as those who study the problem.

Ratifying decisions: Propose a recommendation to a decision-making body.

Monitoring: Review progress toward resolving the problem.

A group can be established to undertake only one of these primary functions, but most carry out more than one, although not necessarily at the same time. That is, a group may study a problem, gather facts, consider alternate recommendations, act on a decision, and then finally monitor results. Moreover, identifying, analyzing, and solving problems can take several weeks or even months. In the meeting itself, it is important that the group always be aware of its primary function(s), because by doing so, discussions can be kept on track with irrelevant or peripheral issues handled in an objective manner.

Dealing With Meeting Problems

Whether a meeting fails or succeeds can be highly subjective. Some would consider a meeting a failure if considerable conflict took place without resolution. Others at the same meeting might say that the meeting was productive because participants aired long-festering concerns. Some might be concerned that the group did not accomplish specific objectives, while others might see the session as a first step in an extended process that eventually leads to results. Hence the success or failure of a meeting is in the eyes of the beholder. There are times, however, when there is a clear sense that a meeting was a waste of time. The following are some reasons that meetings can be unsuccessful and result in frustration.

Group Size. There is value in mass meetings that announce new developments or provide information to a large number of people. If, however, the purpose of the meeting is to engage in problem solving, limit the number to 6 to 10 people to allow for maximum participation. Only use mass meetings to make announcements or communicate quickly to the entire organization.

One-person Domination. When a high-level executive takes over a meeting, there can be trouble. He or she may exert influence by sending messages—subtle or otherwise—to members of the group about what should and should not be discussed. When, as a result, members "clam up," their withdrawal is seen as assent. Afterward, participants may express disgruntlement and frustration to each other. If members of the group are uncomfortable communicating that they wish to participate more, they may need to designate a spokesperson either from within or outside the group to clarify differing expectations.[6]

Pulling in Different Directions. Sometimes, leadership passivity results in members' competing for control of the meeting. Lack of leadership creates a void that is filled by more active, powerful participants, and the session may end in confusion or unresolved conflict. In this situation, stronger leadership is necessary to clarify where discrepancies and differences exist and to inspire resolution. In addition, if discussions drift from one topic to another without resolution, the leader must focus the group on one issue at a time.[7]

Problem Participants. The free flow of ideas in meetings may be hampered by the attitudes and behaviors of some participants. Some people, for example, have something to say about every topic, whether their statements are relevant or not. You may need to remind everyone to remain on topic and suggest that others need to be heard from. Other people may go through an entire meeting without saying anything, and the group misses possible valuable input. You may need to call on individuals to seek new insights. Some participants may appear condescending and even hostile toward other people's ideas. If they do not respond to the ground rules that "putdowns" are out of bounds, you may need to take them aside and discuss how their behavior is disruptive. Ask them to work on searching for constructive suggestions that build on other's ideas. The chair of the meeting must be ever mindful of how participants contribute to or distract from the flow of the meeting.[8]

Conformity Through Groupthink. Some members of a group feel they must show loyalty by agreeing with the group's position even though they inwardly have serious concerns with the direction of the meeting. This *groupthink* occurs when members want to avoid what they fear would be harsh judgments by their peers. Consequently, they keep criticism of a position to themselves—choosing acceptance and conformity over their need to express fundamental differences. *Groupthink* is most likely to occur in strongly cohesive groups where criticism is not the norm. Members suppress their differences of opinion and may minimize, even to themselves, their own misgivings. As a result, the group develops the illusion of unanimity.[9]

One danger of *groupthink* is that when members are pressured to give in, the resulting diluted decision greatly weakens what might otherwise have been a strong stand, position, or program. Another danger is that unvoiced criticisms may subsequently result in sabotage because of some members' deep-rooted reservations. A third danger is that the desire for conformity may squelch a valid criticism that could prevent a poor decision. Ways to prevent *groupthink* include the following:

- Encourage considering several options before the group makes a decision.
- Establish the ground rule that ideas are to be based on their merit, not on who presents them.
- Recognize there are many appropriate paths that can lead to desired results. Encourage members to play "devil's advocate" to ensure positions are defensible from a variety of angles.
- To examine positions from different perspectives, divide the group into two subgroups, with subgroup A presenting a proposal and subgroup B critiquing assumptions and recommending alternatives. The subgroups then work together to form a common set of recommendations.[10]
- To prevent premature closure and too quick an agreement, encourage members to ask hard questions and offer fresh perspectives about the limitations of the proposed program.
- Talk with people who are not part of the deliberations, including knowledgeable people outside the organization who can suggest other options and ideas.
- Think through scenarios about how different people would probably react to the ideas under discussion.
- Encourage members to express reservations if they have them.[11]

Questions That Facilitate Discussion

If participants feel their ideas and thinking contribute to common objectives, they are more likely to address the problem at hand and participate in its solution. One of the most useful techniques to enrich discussions is to elicit responses through targeted questions. Although the group facilitator is primarily responsible for directing the flow of ideas through questions, any member of a group can ask questions. The following questions in Table 17.1 can stimulate discussion:

Table 17.1

If you want to:	Then ask:
Focus the group on an issue	What information do we need to explore the problem?
Redirect the group's thinking	Are there other ways we can go about this?
Stimulate the group and bolster their arguments	What will make this work?
Inject your own ideas	What do you think would happen if we. . .?
Encourage alternative solutions	What are other options to consider?
Focus on one idea	Which is the best approach?
Clarify an issue	Could you explain further?
Make an abstract idea more understandable	Would you walk us through this?
Shift from the details to the essence of an idea	Before we get into the details, shouldn't we consider our main objective?
Stimulate new ideas	Are there new approaches we can consider?
Encourage participation	What does each of you think about this idea?
Consider next steps	Where do we go from here?
Come to closure	Do we agree on the following. . .?
Assist the group in assessing itself	How can we improve our decision making?

These questions do not exhaust all the possibilities. They illustrate that through the questioning process, you can guide the discussion without being perceived as manipulative. One of the main attributes of a good discussion leader is the ability to continuously pose questions that help the group with its decision-making process.

Reaching a Consensus

A consensus is a solution that everyone can live with—one that does not violate any strong convictions or needs. The process of arriving at a consensus is a free and open exchange of ideas that continues until the group reaches a decision. This process ensures that individual concerns are heard and understood and that the group will make a sincere attempt to take everyone's ideas into consideration while searching for a solution. The final resolution may not reflect the exact wishes of every member, but because it does not violate the concerns of any one participant it can be agreed on by all.[12] In fact, some members may even "agree to disagree" and be willing to cooperate because their differences are not tremendously deep and they are committed to the spirit of working together.

Consensus, then, is a cooperative effort to find a sound solution acceptable to everyone. It is not a voting process or a competitive struggle in which an unacceptable solution is forced upon a minority. Usually, those who initially express disagreement finally consent to go along with the prevailing viewpoint even though they may not fully endorse it. With consensus as the pattern of interaction, members need not fear being outsmarted or outmaneuvered. They can be frank in the decision-making process, knowing that different viewpoints can be expressed.[13]

In some cases, decisions are postponed until there is a "Quaker consensus," where not even one member of the group vetoes the action. If someone dissents, discussion continues until he or she acquiesces or the group delays its action. Typically, however, complete unanimity of opinion is not absolutely essential and is rarely achieved when seeking consensus.

In some staff situations, however, even when decisions do not have to be unanimous, there still exists the ground rule that supervisors or managers must approve decisions. Their vetoes can block action. If this criterion for accepting or rejecting a plan is understood in advance, staff may more easily accept that a manager may not approve of some staff decisions.

If the group cannot come to a mutually acceptable solution, then the decision may be placed in the hands of a manager to make an executive "win/lose" decision. If the group understands that a manager makes the final decision if consensus cannot be reached within a time limit, participants may work harder to develop a decision that all can accept.

Decision making by consensus works best when members of a group trust each other. In a trusting climate, disagreements are a natural and acceptable means of fostering opinions and ideas rather than a reflection of interpersonal hostility or rivalry.

In summary, consensus encourages group members to listen to each other and try to understand viewpoints that may differ from their own. It also encourages people who disagree to continue hammering out their differences. A consensus discourages an "I win—you lose" mentality and promotes a climate that benefits everyone.

Using the Group Process to Generate Ideas

Occasionally, group meetings may become mired in ritualistic patterns. Problems persist because fresh perspectives and new ideas are absent. Conventional solutions seem inadequate to address unfamiliar or complex issues. The challenge facing the group is to break out of the mold, explore new paths, and see problems and possible resolutions from different perspectives. Taking risks, exploring unusual connections, and taking nothing for granted are ways of generating fresh approaches.[14] To foster this kind of thinking, groups can use several techniques: brainstorming, nominal group technique (NGT), pro-con discussions, creative questioning, and analogous thinking.

Brainstorming

Brainstorming encourages creativity by generating ideas while suspending judgment. Nothing is too strange or funny to say; the goal is to express as many ideas as possible within a short time. Participants are encouraged to build on previous ideas. The theory behind brainstorming is that by discouraging evaluation the group expands the number and quality of ideas.

Groups should consider brainstorming when (a) conventional discussions lack fresh ideas or approaches, (b) individuals working independently need the stimulation of other people's ideas, (c) a group has become so hypercritical that ideas are being stifled, or (d) information needed for solving a problem is scattered among different people. Brainstorming does not help solve all problems. It works best for those issues that require new ideas because current modes of thinking are not sufficient. A problem best solved through a brainstorming session should hold the potential for many alternative solutions.

Participants who have practical experience with or knowledge of the issue should be engaged in brainstorming. In addition, you may purposefully include some people unfamiliar with the topic based on the premise that they may offer fresh perspectives. The size of the group should range from 4 to 12; groups greater than 12 are too large for meaningful exchange. The group facilitator should define the problem, stimulate ideas, prevent evaluative comments, keep the group on the subject, and end the discussion after an appropriate period of time (usually 15 to 30 minutes). A recorder should write all ideas on a chalkboard or on chart paper taped to a wall for easy viewing.[15] Remind the group that only a small percentage of the ideas is likely to be accepted.

Following this idea-generating session, the next phase of idea evaluation occurs. An evaluation panel can consist of everyone in the brainstorming session, a mix of brainstorming members and nonmembers, or a completely different group of people. Those involved in the evaluation and selection of ideas should be those who deal directly with the problem or who would implement suggested solutions. This panel must establish standards or criteria by which they would evaluate ideas, such as financial constraints, political acceptability, and staff availability. The panel would also rate the brainstormed ideas as immediately applicable, worthy of further exploration, or not useful. Considerable follow-up of the ideas generated from brainstorming is necessary to achieve practical application.

Nominal Group Technique (NGT)

The term *nominal group* means that it is a group in name only. It is a form of silent brainstorming in which members submit their ideas in round-robin fashion to the leader and have minimal interaction among group members. The purpose of this approach is to deter aggressive members from dominating the discussion and to elicit a wide variety of ideas from all participants.

Ask each member to generate as many ideas as possible on a given subject. For example, participants might be asked to consider ways to improve clients showing up for their appointments. Each group member contributes one idea over several rounds until there are no more ideas. After all ideas are presented and listed, the group pursues a discussion to clarify, defend, or challenge ideas. "Hitchhiking" is encouraged: When an idea mentioned by one member inspires someone else to come up with another idea, then that new idea is presented at the end of the round-robin round. Through voting, the group narrows the list to three or four ideas to pursue.

The advantage of NGT is that it draws out everyone's ideas. As with brainstorming, the initial list probably requires further evaluation. Some of the most creative ideas may later prove too difficult to implement or may require more resources than feasible. Hence ideas generated by NGT should be subject to further, careful analysis.[16]

Pro-Con Discussions

To stimulate good thinking and prevent premature emphasis on any one idea, use a pro-con approach. Ask the group to generate alternative ideas for a particular problem. For example, a staff group concerned with how to reduce "client no-shows" might generate the following possibilities:

- Send outreach staff to the homes of clients who are habitual no-shows.
- Telephone each client before their scheduled appointment to encourage attendance.
- Always send an appointment reminder letter.
- Discontinue clients after three no-shows.

For each suggestion, the group would be divided into four task groups, each one debating the pros and cons and summarizing their ideas before the plenary discussion.

Creative Questioning

Another method designed to generate creative ideas is to use a checklist similar to the following:

1. Can the idea be copied?
   - What other organization is doing something like this?
   - Has this been done before?

2. How can the idea be modified?
   - Should we try a new twist?
   - Should we change the format?
   - Should we develop new procedures?

3. Can the idea be expanded?
   - What can we add?
   - What can be done more frequently?

- Can it be strengthened?
- Can it be multiplied?

4. Can the idea be reduced?
   - Can elements be subtracted, condensed, made shorter, streamlined, split up?

5. What can be substituted for the idea?
   - Who else could do it?
   - In what other place or time could it be conducted?
   - Could different resources be used?
   - What other approaches could be considered in its place?

6. Can the idea be rearranged?
   - Are components interchangeable?
   - Can the sequence be altered?
   - Is the pace or schedule flexible?

7. Can the idea be reversed?
   - Can roles be reversed?
   - Can potentially negative aspects be turned into positive ones?

8. Can ideas be combined?
   - Can units be combined?
   - Can purposes be joined?

The following are some examples of how the checklist can be used to stimulate different approaches:

An organization wants to reach out to older people in the community but realizes that its limited staff resources prevent it from doing so. It considers the following alternative methods of expanding its resources: (a) hire neighborhood people to reach out, (b) arrange for elderly volunteers to provide current in-home services in exchange for future home services, and (c) expand volunteer participation through a "Volunteers of Distinction" campaign.

An organization is concerned that junior high school students who have failed more than one grade are potential dropouts. They can, however, read and do math problems at a sixth-grade level. Considering the idea of reversal, the organization devises a program in which these adolescents become "big buddies" to elementary school students who require tutoring and companionship. The tutors now experience elevated self-esteem.

Analogous Thinking

When an organization is bogged down with a problem and is seeking fresh perspectives, thinking with analogies can be useful. Analogies compare one situation with another where the similarities are much more substantial than the differences. By comparing a problem situation with something similar, you begin to see the problem from a different perspective. For example, you notice at the airport how passengers are processed when their flights are canceled. Are there not similarities in processing clients when a service breakdown occurs, such as approaches to handling inconveniences or developing alternative routing? Also, you might think of combining chemotherapy and radiology treatment for their cumulative effect on cancer cells and then ask, "Are there similar combined treatment programs for dealing with drug addicts, where cumulative effects might also be effective?" Analogies can be drawn from sports, gardening, astronomy, cooking, machine functioning, and so on. The analogies may seem farfetched and may not in themselves directly lead to a solution, but they are mind stretching and offer new perspectives that can ultimately yield results.

The value of being creative, then, is to encourage fresh perspectives. In doing so, some ideas may initially seem zany but may contain elements to build upon. In some instances, the group may become quite enthused about a brainstorming suggestion or an analogous idea. Now that you have adopted a new approach, it is time to apply critical thinking. Suppose, for example, the group considers tutoring for elementary school students an appealing and fresh approach to dealing with the high school dropout problem. The group must critically analyze who would benefit from the project, under what circumstances, with what backup support, and at what cost. To be truly effective, creative thinking must always be accompanied by critical assessment. This avoids the danger of sharing ignorance and implementing superficial ideas. Creative ideas, especially those you are enamored with, must be subject to analytic scrutiny.

Scenarios

Because the world is filled with uncertainties and the future cannot accurately be predicted, some organizations envision *scenarios* to identify a range of plausible situations. A group of stakeholders is convened to explore forces that could affect the community and the organization. It develops stories based on different assumptions about how the situation could be played out in the future. Creating scenarios requires the group to question their assumptions about the potential service consumers, the ability of the organization to intervene, and the community context, so they can anticipate the impact of their decisions. The scenarios provide a starting point to react to and build upon, and they can portray a future that the organization could either want to create or avoid.

When the group of stakeholders is convened, they are asked to break into smaller brainstorming subgroups of three or four people who identify forces they think would affect the future. Participants then create scenario themes or story plots that are relevant, provocative, and divergent. For example, one scenario might identify potential reduction in government funding. Another scenario might be a shift in consumer interest from current programs. A third theme could be a tremendous increase in public funding which could result in competing with the organization's own privately funded programs. These alternative futures are then presented for consideration and could influence steps the organization might take now in anticipation of possible future changes.[17]

Recording the Meeting Process

Meetings rich in information that present many facts and ideas can cause groups to experience data overload. A powerful tool for keeping track of ideas and assisting the collective memory of the group is to use a chalkboard or an easel with a large newsprint pad. A recorder writes down key words or basic ideas. As sheets fill up, they are taped around the room. These sheets allow the group to recall what has transpired. The advantage of this technique is that the group can (a) communicate many ideas at the same time; (b) visualize all the ideas at all times; (c) change the wording of ideas; (d) easily determine gaps in, and overlap of, ideas; (e) focus, if the group wishes, on one idea at a time; and (f) prevent the same idea from being repeated.[18] Sustaining group memory helps keep the meeting on track.[19]

Groups often take minutes as a way of preserving the ideas and actions agreed upon during the meeting. At the next meeting, the chairperson ensures that the minutes accurately reflect the essence of the previous session by providing an opportunity for corrections. Sometimes the actions taken by the group can be lost in the verbiage of the text. For clarity, some groups highlight each decision. Alternatively, minutes can use a format that distinguishes discussion from action, as shown below:

Discussion: Juvenile court staff expressed interest in developing formal procedures for addressing the special needs of mentally retarded offenders.

Action: Mental retardation staff agreed to prepare, in writing, procedures by April 15.

An alternative to minutes is a group action report, used only when one or two major topics are discussed. It contains three sections:

1. the issue, that is, how participants analyzed it and what alternatives they considered;

2. the group's decision;

3. who is assigned which tasks and within what time period.

Figure 17.1 illustrates a group action report. The special advantage of this kind of recording is that it captures the essence of the meeting and pinpoints responsibilities for follow-up, without requiring people to read extensive narrative.

NAME OF GROUP: Day Care Coalition DATE: May 25		
CHAIRPERSON: Fred Heim		
PRESENT:	Ahom, Botelli, Callder, Slenk, McVelan	
MEETING PURPOSE:	To consider ways of passing legislation in the state assembly on funding for day care for mentally and physically disabled children.	
PROBLEM/ISSUE:	Legislation on special-needs day care is encountering considerable resistance in the Human Resources Committee of the House.	
MAJOR POINTS OF THE DISCUSSION:	Major opposition appears to be those legislators who are pressing to keep a lid on spending for human services.	
DECISION:	The group agreed that committee members must undertake a vigorous advocacy campaign between now and June 12, when public hearings will be held.	
ACTION STEPS:	Divide into task forces.	
Assignments	**Responsible Person**	**By When**
1. Undertake letter writing campaign	Morris Dale	June 2
2. Obtain editorial support of local papers	Murry Niar	June 5
3. Have a newspaper reporter write a human interest story	Bill Michael	June 7
4. Have a busload of people appear before hearings	Walter Zoboro	June 12
5. Day Care Coalition to meet	Jack Magy	June 20

Figure 17.1   Group Action Report

Leading a Meeting

Whether the chairperson of a meeting is a supervisor or manager, or has been specially designated by the supervisor to lead the group, he or she should assume the following responsibilities:

State the purpose of the meeting. It is helpful for the chairperson to establish the goal of a meeting or series of meetings by articulating expectations. These expectations may be formulated by the organization's management, or the group may be given discretion to formulate its own charge. An example follows:

The charge to the personnel committee is to formulate a recommendation on a drug policy for the agency's staff. To achieve this objective, you will examine what similar organizations have adopted and engage in discussions with key staff and board members. The policy must be non-punitive and reflect the organization's mission to provide the highest quality services to our clients.

Prepare the agenda for the meeting. It is preferable to put this in writing and submit it in advance, as discussed previously.

Clarify ground rules. The chairperson identifies expectations on how members are to interact with each other and how the business of the meeting would be conducted. This includes clarifying the process for decision making.

Make assignments. Assignments should specify what is to be done, by whom, and within what time frame.

Deal with conflict. Conflicts sometimes surface at staff meetings as participants express differences about priorities and use of resources. The chairperson must work to keep competing forces under control by exploring ways in which staff members can reconcile their different interests. The chairperson can neither ignore these battles nor take sides without jeopardizing the leadership role. The primary recourse is to seek a genuine compromise based on a synthesis of positions.

Summarize discussion. The group leader should continually review the points that have been covered, identifying where there are differences of opinion and where there are agreements. By synthesizing different views, the chairperson suggests where there is consensus. Summarizing is especially important at the end of a meeting, when the chairperson should clarify what decisions were made and what the next steps are.[20]

In summary, effective managers are keenly aware that staff meetings are the place where the organization's domestic commerce occurs. They can be either a waste of time or highly productive. If they are conducted with good preparation and considerable purpose, they can contribute to the productivity of the group and the organization as a whole.

Questions for Discussion

1. In what ways, if any, could meetings be improved in your organization?

2. What are examples of the predominant function(s) of meetings in your organization?

3. What kinds of problems have you experienced in meetings? Have you seen examples of *groupthink?*

4. In groups of five or six, conduct a meeting on how to improve services to clients in a selected agency. Drawing upon the *Questions That Facilitate Discussion,* which questions did your group use to facilitate your discussion?

5. Which of the creative approaches suggested in the text—brainstorming, nominal group technique, pro/con discussion, creative questioning, analogous thinking, and generating scenarios—are used or could be used in your organization?

6. Identify an agency issue that requires creative thinking. How might you apply the various approaches suggested in the text (refer to question 3) to generate ideas?

Notes

1. R. Brody, *Problem solving: Concepts and methods for community organizations* (New York: Human Sciences Press, 1982), p. 51; M. Doyle & D. Straus, *How to make meetings work* (New York: Berkley, 1976), p. 158; Alexander Hamilton Institute, Inc., *A manager's guide to productive meetings* (Ramsey, NJ: Author, 1997), pp. 1–5.

2. H. Reynolds & M. E. Tramel, *Executive time management* (Englewood Cliffs, NJ: Prentice Hall, 1979), pp. 115–117.

3. M. Doyle & D. Straus, p. 84; Alexander Hamilton Institute, Inc., p. 7.

4. Alexander Hamilton Institute, Inc., p. 4.

5. S. Albert, Eight steps to productive committees, *Nonprofit World* 4 (1988), p. 25.

6. J. D. Jorgenson, I. H. Scheier, & T. F. Fautsko, *Solving problems in meetings* (Chicago: Nelson-Hall, 1981), pp. 9–17.

7. F. Pryor, Manage your meetings effectively, *The Nonprofit Executive* (March 1985), p. 7.

8. Alexander Hamilton Institute, Inc., pp. 21–24.

9. I. L. Janis, Groupthink, *Psychology Today* (November 1971), pp. 43–46, 74–76.

10. D. A. Garvin & M. A. Roberto, What you don't know about making decisions, *Harvard Business Review* 79 (August 2001), pp. 108–116.

11. R. Brody, pp. 68–69.

12. E. H. Schein, *Organizational psychology* (New York: Prentice Hall, 1970).

13. T. Caplow, *How to run any organization* (Hinsdale, IL: Dryden, 1976), p. 58.

14. E. de Bono, *Lateral thinking* (New York: Harper Colophon, 1973), pp. 21–22; A. T. Hollingsworth, Creativity in nonprofit organizations: Preparing for the future, *Nonprofit World* 3 (1989), pp. 21–22.

15. A. E. Schwartz, When good ideas are needed fast, *Nonprofit World* 6 (1989), pp. 22–23.

16. A. L. Delbecq, A. Van de Ven, & D. H. Gustafson, *Group techniques for program planning* (Glenview, IL: Scott Foresman, 1976); A. Lauffer, *Assessment tools for practitioners, managers, and trainers* (Beverly Hills, CA: Sage, 1982), pp. 63–89; C. M. Moore, *Group techniques for idea building* (Newbury Park, CA: Sage, 1987), pp. 24–36.

17. D. D. Chrislip, *The collaborative leadership fieldbook: A guide for citizens and civic leaders* (San Francisco: Jossey-Bass, 2002), pp. 104–106.

18. R. Brody, p. 81.

19. M. Doyle & D. Straus, pp. 40–44.

20. J. E. Tropman, *Effective meetings: Improving group decision-making* (Beverly Hills, CA: Sage, 1980), pp. 39–42.

18

Improving Communications and Handling Conflicts

When agency staff are adequately informed about their organization and have opportunities to convey their ideas, they are likely to be more involved and invested in their work. This chapter discusses ways effective managers can improve communication and resolve conflicts to heighten staff's commitment to their agencies.

Good communication occurs when staff feel their concerns are listened to and dealt with promptly, when mistakes can be quickly identified and corrected, and when staff understand what is taking place in the organization that might affect their work. In other words, communication involves upward, downward, and across movement of ideas, suggestions, and values. It is a process of continuously sharing and transmitting important information throughout the organization. A positive flow of information is the result of an attitude that respects people for their ideas and that views information not as a source of power but as a tool for accomplishing the organization's important work.

Although communication is generally desirable, under certain circumstances it is absolutely essential. When an organization is considering changes in strategy or structure, communication takes on special significance. The greater the change, the greater the need for communication.[1] Even when the basic structure of the organization is not changing, the tendency for organizations to delegate responsibilities to the lowest practical level means that every staff member is involved in making choices. To make good decisions, staff must share in the basic understanding and purpose of the organization.

In a time of crisis, communication is absolutely essential. For example, when an organization goes through a period of severe retrenchment, discussions must be held openly with staff to encourage expression of their concerns and to respond candidly to them. To do otherwise runs the risk of creating latent discontent in employees who remain with the organization but who feel that management cannot be trusted.[2]

Communication is also vitally important when staff are expected to implement important projects. The more they understand the significance of the project to the organization and to the community, the more likely they are to dedicate themselves to it.

Finally, communication is essential in enhancing staff loyalty to the organization. Staff may appreciate the work of their own unit but may not be aware of how it must mesh with other parts of the organization to accomplish the overall mission. By understanding their part in the whole picture, they come to feel pride in their organization. Proud people are committed people.

Factors That Interfere With Good Communication

Because communications are so significant in the organization's life, effective managers must be alert to situations that inhibit the positive flow of information.

Poor Use of Written Documents

Communicating to staff through memos and written announcements is a valuable tool for managers. First, the process of writing forces disciplined thinking. By putting messages on paper, you clarify your own thoughts and become aware of gaps in what you want to say. Second, written material has the power to focus attention on a single issue, more so than verbal communication. By putting your inquiry or request in a memo, you encourage the recipient to give the matter special attention. Moreover, memos are useful to disseminate easily understood and non-controversial information. If you want staff to remember your message, use written communication. (Because the process of writing can be an arduous task, the boxed text contains a discussion on overcoming writer's block.)

Conquering Writer's Block

Every manager is faced with communicating through the arduous task of writing reports. For some, this can cause overwhelming anxiety, causing writer's block. This is a malady that must be addressed, because writing is an essential aspect of professional work.

There are a number of factors that directly affect our ability to complete a writing assignment. If we expect it would produce anxiety and frustration, or if we feel insecure about it, we may complete it late, if at all. On the other hand, if the results of the writing process

---

lead to a sense of pride and are rewarding, we look forward to the undertaking. Hence our attitude about success or failure can greatly influence the degree to which we experience writer's block. The following are suggestions of ways to get out of the writer's rut:[3]

1. Approach the task with expectations of success. Accentuate the positive by stressing that you can give the time and effort to complete the assignment.

2. Visualize what you want to have happen as a result of the writing. By specifying what you want to achieve (e.g., more funds for your organization, motivating your staff, developing new procedures), your clarity of purpose is a powerful motivator.

3. Be clear about your audience. Form a profile in your mind of the readers so that you are communicating directly to them. Your writing must be geared to their level of understanding and to meeting their needs.

4. Have a quiet place and adequate time to write. This involves writing in an area that is comfortable for you at a time that permits uninterrupted thinking. If your day is filled with interruptions, you may need to find a "hideaway" to allow time for concentration. Try to block out at least 60-minute segments.

5. Become proficient in using the word processor so that you can easily and quickly make changes in your drafts; this technology is a tremendous time saver.

6. Organize your material. Usually, prepare an outline, but consider it tentative and modify it as your writing proceeds.

7. Keep a note pad or 3 x 5 cards in your car or on your nightstand at home to jot down ideas at odd times.

8. Prepare a "zero draft." If you are having a difficult time getting started, force yourself to write nonstop to get the words on paper. Known as "free writing," the purpose of this train-of-thought writing pushes you to get words on paper (or in the computer) without concern for spelling, clarity, or even coherence. This is not the time to be critical but to generate ideas to use later in preparing your first draft. The value of this "zero draft" exercise is to loosen you up and reduce your perfectionist tendencies.

9. Begin your writing project wherever you feel like starting. This may mean commencing in the middle rather than at the beginning. The actual process of writing itself allows you to determine what you want to say. Consider writing just the introduction.

10. If you feel confident enough in where you want to end up, write the conclusion first. By doing so, you are guided in preparing the rest of your writing assignment.

11. Talk out your writing. By reading it out loud, your ear helps make adjustments. Phrases that are trite, awkward, or filled with jargon are more easily discovered when spoken aloud.

12. When you have a hard time expressing your thoughts in writing, pause for a moment and ask yourself, "What am I really trying to say?" Think through what your point is and then work to get it on paper.

13. Put space between yourself and your first draft. Take a break of hours or preferably days so that you develop detachment and can come back to the assignment refreshed and ready to be critical. Knowing up front that you have time for revision can allow you to be less self-demanding when you prepare the early drafts.

14. Before you go public with a report, show it to one or more trusted persons for their critique. The advantage of this step is that outsiders may alert you to ambiguous ideas or poorly stated ideas. You may assume that you have stated something clearly, but the words themselves may not communicate precisely what you had in mind.

15. If, after the first or second draft, you still have some discomfort about sharing it, even to obtain preliminary criticism, you might try splattering coffee or stamping heel marks on the paper to emphasize that the writing is truly a draft, or mark "DRAFT" on the paper to convey that you expect it to be revised. Knowing in advance that your intent is not to present a perfect and final piece of writing may help lighten your burden. (Interestingly, some readers give more attention to a document stamped "DRAFT" than they do to a final document, so be mindful of this possibility.)

16. Because of time pressures, you may sometimes have to forego massaging a document until it is perfect. Of course, you do not want shoddy work going out under your name, but you may have to decide that the press of other important work keeps you from achieving a perfect document. You may have to reconsider which writing tasks require close attention to detail and which do not.[4]

17. During the revision process, keep uppermost in mind that good communication is your primary objective. Ask whether the writing is clear, well organized, and easy to follow. An important part of the editing process is eliminating wordiness.

Hence dealing with writer's block requires time and effort. Writing requires disciplined thinking, which is inherently hard work. For most people, writing always involves a degree of struggle and challenge, but like all other challenges, writer's block can be overcome by following the above suggestions and being willing to commit to the process.

If you want the reader to pay attention to your written message, announce in the first sentence what you want to communicate. If you are asking for a new computer, want to draw your reader's attention to a special problem, or have a request to make, say so up front. Also, keep your memos short and to the point. The reader does not need to know all your thought processes. Short words, short sentences, and short paragraphs work.[5]

Even a well-written message, however, can have its drawbacks. Because it is a one-way message, you are unable to obtain the immediate feedback you need—the reaction and questions that ensure that your ideas are understood.[6] Merely making written pronouncements does not guarantee that staff will understand issues or policies—particularly complex ones. For this reason, you may need to follow up written documents with opportunities for interaction.

Some managers resort to memos to protect themselves. They want to be on record as having taken a position so they are not blamed if something goes wrong. This is a poor way of handling the negotiating process; it is far better to engage in face-to-face discussions. Other managers are afflicted with "memo-itis," not an uncommon disease among those who desire minimal contact with staff. Still others write memos on unimportant, even trivial, matters so that staff, buried in paper, eventually view the paper that comes across their desk as meaningless. If you want staff to pay attention to your memos, make each one significant.

Moreover, some managers use paper as a way of exchanging barbs. They resort to arguing by memo. Such paper grenades serve to intensify hostilities, with each side working hard to cleverly defend a position while attacking the other.[7] The paper exchange serves to impede, rather than facilitate, the resolution of differences. Again, a face-to-face exchange is superior to the written word.

With the availability of faxes and e-mail, communication has become much faster and easier. New communication technology, however, can have its own special issues. A main concern is confidentiality. A sensitive fax message can be read by others; e-mails can be stored and retrieved. Therefore, make certain that your system guarantees a high degree of privacy, or caution staff about how confidentiality can be compromised with new communication technologies.

Because e-mail and voice mail are so easily available, staff may not take the time for face-to-face contacts when dealing with highly sensitive issues.

Like a memo, an e-mail is unambiguous and may be more harsh and more blunt than might be conveyed when people get together and look into each other's eyes.[8] Similarly, voice mail provides a medium for angry people to conduct a one-way diatribe. Hostile monologues are not conducive to working out problems.

As a general rule, when you have to explain ideas, when hostility may exist, when you want to influence behavior, or when you need to negotiate, arrange to communicate directly rather than send a piece of paper, an e-mail, or voice mail.

Misperceptions

The possibility always exists that staff may misinterpret what you intend to communicate. For example, you offer to meet with administrative support staff to discuss agency policies. They, however, resent that you are dealing with them separately from the rest of the staff and feel they are being treated as "second-class citizens." As another example, without conferring with staff, you temporarily hire a consultant, and staff misinterpret this as dissatisfaction with their performance. In these instances, staff perception is quite different from your intention.

In addition, nonverbal communications can have special meaning. Rolling your eyes, reading a report when an employee is speaking, failing to make eye contact, and ignoring a greeting are cues that convey lack of interest or even disapproval. Be aware that your reactions are constantly being observed and interpreted by each member of the staff in a very personal way. To avoid misperceptions, take careful note of how your nonverbal messages could be perceived by others. You need this sensitivity and empathy to ensure that people do not read more into what you are saying or doing than you intend. Take the time to obtain feedback from staff so you can counter any misinterpreted reactions.

The problem with communication is the illusion that what you convey has been received by the other party. You have said one thing, but they have heard quite another. That is why it is important to ask for feedback by requesting their response and their understanding of what you have conveyed. Sometimes, for example, a supervisor may request that an activity be accomplished but fail to indicate a specific time frame and a specific course of action.

Sometimes failure of communication occurs because silence gives the illusion of agreement. This is referred to as *the disagreement fallacy*. Just because people do not express their disagreement does not mean they automatically agree with you. The opposite can also be true: just because someone argues with some aspects of your position does not mean that they are opposed to the fundamental idea—or to the person proposing it. Arguments can take place within an atmosphere of people respecting each other and afterward going out to lunch.[9]

In summary, insufficient attention to communicating with staff may result in rumors, low morale, and even antagonism. Because managers can so easily take the communication process for granted, the likelihood of poor communications occurring is an ever-present danger that can quickly spoil a positive organizational climate. Once that happens, tremendous energy has to be spent undoing the unintended harm. Be aware that every major organizational action gives fodder to the rumor mill, and be prepared to continually focus on the interactions between you and the staff.

Handling Conflicts

In every organization, staff interactions produce inevitable conflict; there is just no way of avoiding it. Most of the conflicts do not threaten productivity and are not very painful to the people involved. In fact, constructive conflict can bring about genuine growth as participants gain new insights and perspectives different from their own. Positive conflict can be used to explore opposing thoughts so that outmoded ideas can be challenged and the organization can discover new ways of working.[10] In many instances, disagreements should be encouraged if they provide alternatives that ought to be examined before decisions are made.[11]

If, however, conflicts get out of hand, they can be devastating and tie up huge amounts of the organization's energy. The normal pattern of cooperation is disrupted, the organization may even undergo a great loss of resources, and its own survival may be at stake. Those who are forced to concede in a conflict situation are not inclined to remain or, if they do, are not as committed to the organization as before. Morale is likely to deteriorate throughout the organization. For these reasons, it is much better to address conflicts before they escalate to the point of being destructive.

Types of Conflict

In most human service organizations, certain conflict situations commonly occur: personal feuds, the alleged persecution of a subordinate by a superior, and struggles between two units of the organization.

Personal feuds between key members of an organization usually occur when they have mutual grievances, and the feuds can lead to suspicion and hostility. Each party pressures others in the organization to take sides. Under some circumstances involving low-level conflicts, it may be desirable for the manager to take one side or the other to quickly resolve an issue so that staff can get back to work.[12] Because arbitrarily taking sides can produce long-term animosities, however, an even better approach is to meet with the participants, individually and together, to sort out their grievances and reach a mutually agreeable resolution.[13]

The alleged persecution of a subordinate by a supervisor presents a special dilemma. If the manager sides with the supervisor, there appears to be unjust bias, whereas if the manager sides with the subordinate, there is a risk of losing the loyalty of not only the supervisor involved in the incident but also other supervisors. Some managers have an open-door policy that allows anyone in the organization to communicate a grievance. Because this can be a time-consuming process, and because of the possibility of perceived bias, some organizations arrange for impartial third parties to handle grievances in a reasonable, objective manner.

In the private sector, delegating the responsibility for investigating and settling a complaint to an impartial agent is a common practice. At IBM, for example, employees can take their grievances to any manager who must take time to investigate the problem. Another alternative is to have a committee of peers review grievances. At General Electric, a five-member panel of both management and hourly employees is available to investigate grievances. Some organizations use an *ombudsperson* who investigates complaints, listens to all sides, and works with participants to arrive at a solution they all can accept. Regardless of whether managers, peers, or an ombudsperson is used to resolve conflict, employees must feel they are treated fairly, that the resolution is reached in a timely manner, and that they are protected from recrimination.[14]

Struggles between two units of an organization occur when one feels the other is encroaching upon its sphere of responsibility. This is commonly known as a "turf battle." Unit A refuses to cooperate with Unit B as a way of protesting or even stopping the intrusion into its territory or functions. When such a rivalry occurs, the best approach is to clarify roles and assignments. If this is not successful, it may be necessary to reorganize the functions of each unit so that their boundaries are quite clear. This is not a time for indecisiveness or ambiguity.

Units within an organization can conflict with each other in different ways: they fight because the staff perceive different objectives to be achieved, compete for scarce resources, or believe other units are being treated more favorably.[15] In general, these conflicts are best handled by the feuding units or parties working out their own solutions. If this is not possible, effective managers must play a more vigorous role in helping the units come to a resolution, particularly if the conflict becomes highly disruptive.

The Manager's Response to Conflict

Basic differences involving major organizational change are, by their very nature, controversial. Honest disagreements emerge because well-intentioned staff feel strongly about fundamental directions.[16] For example, expect disagreements to occur among staff about whether to serve primarily paying or nonpaying clients. Why shouldn't there be controversy over such a profound difference in emphasis? In keeping their eyes on the larger picture, managers welcome these major debates as a means of stimulating the organization to come to terms with significantly different directions. Such controversy is healthy for the organization and must be worked out before final decisions are made. A key role that a manager can play is to manage staff's passionate differences in a way that diminishes destructive possibilities and constructively harnesses energy. By establishing ground rules that allow different people to voice their opinions respectfully, a manager provides an outlet for staff's emotions.[17]

Because each conflict has its own unique characteristics and nuances, effective managers must be cautious about responding in a set pattern, as if following a prescription. Even so, the following suggestions may be useful whether a conflict occurs between individuals, between staff and their superiors, or between units.

Confront conflicts as soon as they emerge. Immediate response is especially important in dealing with office politics; people are inclined to take sides, and political intrigue disrupts the work of the organization. If conflicts are allowed to fester, you can only expect more severe problems later. The best approach is to bring them out in the open and deal with them directly.[18] Discourage cliques from forming because a "we-they" atmosphere can poison professional relationships.

Accept the reality that there are two sides to every issue. It is important that all parties involved in a conflict feel that they will have their "day in court" and a fair and impartial hearing of their concerns.

Be aware that conflict resolution takes time and thought. Whoever is assigned to examine a conflict must be willing to invest in the process. Conflict resolution should not be viewed as an appendage to managers' duties but as an integral part of their responsibilities.

Expect that knowledge of most incidents will eventually spread to various parts of the organization. Although some conflicts may prove embarrassing to the parties involved, and confidentiality must be respected, news tends to travel among staff. For this reason, once a controversy is out in the open, do not attempt to cover it up.

Promote an atmosphere of decorum. Set explicit ground rules so there is a clear sense of fairness perceived by the parties involved.[19] If emotions are running exceedingly high, call for a "cooling off period" (e.g., overnight) before attempting to resolve matters. Insist that staff treat each other with dignity and respect, even if they have strong differences.

Establish a collaborative problem-solving process in which the conflicting parties seek a mutually beneficial resolution. Both parties strive to work through their differences by engaging in a *win-win* strategy. Both should feel that resolving the conflict would benefit them, the agency, and ultimately their clients. If this is not possible, then a compromise strategy involving some form of exchange (*quid pro quo*—this for that) may be needed. A problem-solving mode may entail both sides making compromises to seek resolution.

Persuasive Communication

Selling ideas and persuading people occur continuously in organizations. Supervisors frequently try to convince their superiors, colleagues, or staff of their opinions. Persuading and being persuaded are the vital commerce of every organization.

The following is one example of the selling process. You have received an invitation to an out-of-town professional conference, but you know that the agency's budget is tight and the conference occurs two weeks before a major budget must be prepared. It is not a good time to be traveling. As a middle manager in your agency, you consider the conference a unique opportunity to enhance your managerial skills, but you realize you must be very persuasive with the organization's executive in order to attend. What are some of the approaches you can consider? To answer this question, consider techniques used by good salespeople in selling their products.[20] In the business world, the term *customer* is used to describe someone who is on the receiving end of a sales presentation. For our purposes, the term *customer* is the person you are trying to persuade.

Preparation is the key to making a persuasive case. Every good salesperson takes time before making a call to become highly knowledgeable about the product and potential customer. In the case of the conference, you would gather details about costs and benefits to the organization prior to meeting with your executive. There is no substitute for knowing your facts and doing your homework. Moreover, as part of your preparation you should think through what is central to your concerns and what is secondary, or even peripheral. In advance of the negotiating session, learn as much as you can about the position of the person with whom you are dealing. For example, in this situation, develop an understanding of what your boss's position is regarding staff development and conferences.[21]

Assert your position in a clear, succinct, and unequivocal manner. You need to communicate what you want and why you think it makes good sense. Convey your own conviction about the value of the conference. In any proposal, your belief in the product and your enthusiasm for how it can benefit the other party (your supervisor or your organization) can be a deciding factor in making a convincing case. Certainly, any uncertainty or feelings of ambiguity can detract from being persuasive. You have to be convinced that your project is worthwhile before you can convince others.

Convey both data and an emotional story to get across your point. If you are proposing a new plan, provide evidence of how it can cut costs or add clients. Supplement numerical data with examples, stories, and analogies to make your story come alive. Paint a vivid picture to give compelling credibility and to make an emotional impact.[22] Document how going to the conference would produce tangible payoff to the agency and clients you serve.

Tune in with genuine empathy to your audience by understanding what is important and of high priority. Is staff development of major importance to your superior? If the answer is yes, you still must realize that the budget needs to be completed on time and financial constraints must be addressed. Having empathy for the executive's concerns about completing the budget can help you present your case. As a result of careful listening to what your audience is thinking, you may be willing to alter or compromise your own plans, which in turn makes your case more appealing to the other side.

Anticipate and deal with objections by engaging in a mutual problem-solving approach. For example, if your executive states that your being away would keep you from completing your part of the budget assignment, then you could ask, "Could we together figure out a way that I could complete my assignment in time for me to attend the conference?"

Sometimes, it is better to anticipate objections in advance of their being voiced by your audience. Suppose you anticipate two possible objections: the added costs to the agency in a period of austerity and the time pressures for completing your part of the budget preparation. You might say, for example, "Although I see major advantages to attending the conference, I also recognize that my going at this time may put demands on our budget and could affect completing next year's budget on time." By acknowledging the objection in advance, you gain the opportunity to defang it.

In responding to an objection, it is generally a good idea to cushion your response with such comments as, "I can appreciate and understand why you might feel this way, but I would like you to consider . . ." You can disagree without being disagreeable. Your objective is to remove or neutralize the roadblock without making your audience feel defensive.

Be specific about the advantages of your proposal to your audience. You would not give as a reason for going to the conference, for example, that you need a break from your daily work. The needs of the organization, not your own, must be paramount. Also, be specific in conveying how you would meet those needs. Describe, for example, which particular workshops would be helpful. You might even offer to train other staff upon your return. The point, then, is that your proposal should demonstrate in concrete terms how attending the conference would add value to the organization.

To gain closure, provide options for your audience to consider. Having tuned in to your audience and heard some of their objections, offer alternatives or even compromises that can help you "close the deal." If cost is a factor in your attending the workshop, you might offer to pay for half or arrange for out-of-town housing with a friend. If time away from the office is a factor, you may need to work weekends to complete your part of the budget assignment or take work with you and complete it by the time you return.

These options can generate a *win-win* decision: you get what you want, and more importantly, the agency gains. Your willingness to make adjustments shows your commitment to the organization. In conveying options, you provide your executive with choices: "Would you prefer that I attend two days instead of five to keep the costs down?" By using the choice format, you encourage your audience to make a decision rather than let it hang in the air. Of course, providing options requires a degree of flexibility and a willingness to make adjustments in your original proposal. The most effective persuaders seem to share common traits: they are open-minded, never dogmatic, and they begin the persuasion process prepared to adjust their views and incorporate others' ideas. When your colleagues (or your manager) realize that you want to understand their views and are willing to make changes in response to their concerns, they won't feel manipulated.[23]

This is an example of attending a conference, but the same approach could be used in considering whether to buy an additional computer or embark on a new program. In all instances, you are identifying a gap between what exists now and what could be accomplished as a result of your proposal.

In the final analysis, persuasive communication satisfies a need; it solves a problem. You should first crystallize what that need is and then show how your proposal answers that need. You must either neutralize objections or show how your solution provides overwhelming benefits. Persuading people to your point of view is not so much a matter of selling them but of tuning in to their issues and negotiating constructive solutions.

Facilitating Internal Communication

No single method of communication is useful for all situations. If staff number in the hundreds, formal written communications may be necessary, but this would likely be inappropriate in communicating to a staff of 10. In a large organization, the chief executive communicates through a network of key staff people, who in turn communicate with their staff. In a small agency, a more informal network of communication occurs. To enhance information exchange, consider various methods to enhance communication in the following sections.

Top-Down Communications

A common complaint among staff is that they lack information about developments in their organization. This can demoralize staff who want to think they are a part of, and contribute to, the organization. Communication must be given high priority if staff are to believe that everyone is important and plays a significant role in accomplishing the organization's mission.

In large organizations, communication flows down from the top of the structure. Usually, the agency is organized so that top management is responsible for formulating positions or carrying out policies of outside funders or policymakers. Typically, the *span of control* (supervision) involves four to seven managers who then meet with division heads under them. This hierarchy can be quite extensive, depending on the size of the organization. The more complex the structure, the more each manager is a key link in the communication network. Breakdowns in communication can easily occur when messages are lost or poorly conveyed, especially when middle managers feel free to add their subjective interpretations, which can engender problematic reactions. The results can be disastrous for the organization.

Communiqués to staff about a change in assignments or procedures should always be accompanied by clear explanations of the reasons for the change. Staff should understand the rationale behind the change; otherwise, they may resent what appears to be an arbitrary and capricious decision, ultimately affecting their carrying out the request. They need to have clear, candid explanations about how the change would benefit them, their clients, or the organization.

For example, suppose that management decides that staff who work with foster children must see the children at least once a week. Managers should communicate to staff that children would benefit from increased continuity resulting from these visits. To ensure that staff understand and accept the top-down communication, a monitoring system should be established so that supervisors can determine whether children are actually being seen once a week.

In addition to this hierarchical network, there are other ways of communicating from the top of the organization. Organizational newsletters, public announcements, e-mails, bulletin boards, and large staff meetings are among the ways that staff can learn about the latest developments.

Bottom-Up Communications

Staff should have ample opportunity to communicate ideas and give reactions to their immediate supervisors and top management. This upward communication network can help managers determine whether staff understand and accept requests or whether they have concerns or problems. Furthermore, a bottom-up approach can solicit valuable suggestions and provide information from those directly on the firing line. Most important, when staff are encouraged to send information to top management, they feel better about their own role in the organization.

Unfortunately, some organizations give the illusion of being an information network while treating staff ideas in a cavalier fashion or ignoring them altogether. If staff members believe that attempts at communication are insincere gestures, expect an even more demoralizing atmosphere than if no effort was made in the first place.[24] If you cannot carry forward staff ideas, at least make certain that you give them an explanation. Nothing is more frustrating to staff than when management claims their ideas will be taken seriously but then does not follow through.

Obtaining Key Information

Certain events and activities demand information that can impact decisions. For example, the information may deal with a project's progress, a new service, or staff performance. Certain activities or events become particularly crucial when they go beyond a particular threshold. For example, if there has been a substantial increase in client no-shows, it is important to understand the reason for this trend. Similarly, if there is a major decrease in client participation in group counseling sessions, this information must be shared. If there is a reduction in an expected income stream, this information should also be made clear. Managers seek to know if something unusual, unexpected, or exceptional is taking place. It is important to obtain data about emerging trends before they turn into major problems. To foster managerial decisions, weekly and monthly reports should distinguish general information from that which is key and exceptional. The term *management by exception* conveys the idea of concentrating on out-of-the-ordinary events.[25] If, for example, staff fail to meet their monthly interview targets, management would want to focus on this issue.

Employee Surveys

One way to encourage good communication is to have an opinion survey when a new policy is under consideration or a program needs to be implemented. Staff can be of particular help in identifying problems as they arise in a new program. Staff may not have the answers, but their ability to articulate problems can be invaluable to management.

Surveys are commonly used because they are inexpensive, collect information from everyone in the organization, and identify trends. Management could ask staff such questions as these: "What in this organization would you retain? What would you want to see discontinued? What do you think the organization expects of you? What do you expect of the organization?" Answers to these questions can provide insight about what is uppermost on the minds of the staff and permit management to consider new directions. Surveys, however, have the disadvantage of inviting bias in the way they are worded and of causing staff to become disenchanted if they see little response to their feedback.[26]

Suggestion Systems

To identify concerns from the entire staff, try the old-fashioned suggestion box. This permits people to communicate their concerns anonymously and could reveal festering problems. The suggestion box allows staff to present their complaints and concerns without feeling intimidated. Perhaps clients in the waiting room are not being treated courteously. Perhaps there is concern about the inconsistency of a staff dress code. Normally, without a suggestion box, these concerns might go undetected and therefore not be addressed. Through the anonymity of the suggestion box, everyone—professional staff, administrative assistants, and accountants—can express concerns or make suggestions.

Managers, of course, should determine whether the suggestions are helpful or are so vague and undeveloped that they cannot be addressed. As with surveys, respond to the entire staff so that employees know management hears and values their suggestions. Otherwise, the box becomes a receptacle for gum wrappers.

Another way to encourage communication is to have an open-door policy in which top management is available either on a continuous basis or for scheduled appointments. Some managers, for example, schedule an "open house" regularly each week. Staff welcome the opportunity to talk with top managers on matters that bother them. This approach can create problems for supervisors who feel that their subordinates bypass them, and it may tempt top management to try to resolve matters that are better left within the units. Still, safeguards can be implemented so that staff do not inappropriately circumvent supervisors. For instance, a manager could suggest that employees follow up the issue with their supervisors, or that supervisors form ad hoc task groups to address staff concerns. Furthermore, discussion could be limited to systemic (organizational) issues rather than interpersonal or individual matters.

Active, one-on-one consultation with subordinates is another way to foster good communication. Individual consultation with several staff, however, can result in delays between the formulation and execution of a top management idea, sometimes elicits irrelevant suggestions, and even invites criticism. The advantage of actively soliciting advice and information is that you can determine if there are mistakes in the management- formulated plan as well as gain insights from staff about whether and how well a decision might work.[27] If you are particularly interested in staff productivity, then supervisors can individually determine what makes staff feel productive by asking them such questions as, "When do you work at your peak? What do you like most about your job? What bothers you about your work? What resources do you need to be more productive? What policies and procedures should be modified so you can be more productive?" Based on staff responses, you can determine what is highly individualized and idiosyncratic and what concerns are held in common.

A variation of one-on-one consultation is for management to meet with small groups of employees. These face-to-face meetings, sometimes comprising staff from several different sections, can provide helpful responses to policies under consideration. These meetings can be time-consuming but worthwhile, not only for obtaining valuable input but also for squelching rumors.[28]

Informal Communication

One of the best ways to keep in touch with staff is through informal contacts. In the hallways, on the elevator, in the lunchroom, you can take a few moments to ask how a project is going, how the copy machine is working, or how a spouse is recuperating. Sometimes these spontaneous communications take place right after a formal meeting, and interestingly, can be even more important than the meeting itself. By asking people about their jobs as you walk through the building, you pick up ideas and suggestions that you would never obtain by sitting at your desk. The tag name for this is MBWA—*management by walking around.*[29] Some managers make a point of regularly scheduling time to walk through their unit so they can obtain feedback from their staff. Be careful, however, because when you make a daily walk you may be perceived as a prison guard making rounds. An alternative is to engage in impromptu discussions to and from your office.

If your schedule is too demanding during the workday, arrange to greet people as they arrive at work or go home. Informal staff functions, such as picnics, provide a chance to get to know staff on a more personal level.

Good Feedback

At the heart of any communication is feedback, a process that requires a reaction to actions or situations in the organization. High reliance must be placed on good feedback because it is the basis for taking necessary, corrective actions. To encourage good feedback, the ability and the commitment to listen are absolutely essential.

Unfortunately, meaningful listening, though subscribed to, is often breached. We all have a tendency to concentrate on our own agendas and thoughts so that we resort at times to "pretend" or selectively listen. Meaningful listening requires tremendous effort and total concentration.[30]

It is quite human for all of us to want to hear only compliments and to avoid criticisms. Some supervisors, for example, avoid listening to employees complain because it spoils their own good moods. Yet by taking time to listen, a minor complaint can be handled with minimal energy or a hidden problem can surface. In addition, listening to staff complaints, even though you may be limited in making changes, offers at least some solace that staff can feel free to express themselves.

On some occasions, Employee A may complain about Employee B: "He's goofing off on the job." "She offended a client." But then Employee A requests that the information be kept confidential, thus making it difficult to communicate directly to Employee B without divulging the source of information. Confronting Employee B with a rumor has elements of a witch hunt and usually results in defensive denials. This sensitive communication issue can be dealt with in one of three ways. Either ask Employee A to communicate the concerns directly to Employee B, or request that Employee A give permission to give the source of information. If neither of these first two options is agreeable, you may be forced to communicate with Employee B that this matter has been brought to your attention in confidence.

In summary, effective managers must ensure good communication to convey the organization's values, promote staff commitment, and handle conflict. Be mindful that communicating is a two-way process of transmitting ideas and tuning in to staff's thinking and feelings. Good communicators are good listeners.

Facilitating External Communication

Keeping in touch with important outside constituencies is vitally important for your organization's long term viability. Through continuous communication, you can gain the support needed to sustain your efforts and expand your organization's influence. This section highlights three useful ways of communicating to the outside world: using personal networking, electronic technologies, and the media to transmit your message.

Importance of Networking

To strengthen your organization's position in the community, you need to expand the number of people in your network and deepen the bonds with key persons. Consider the following activities:

• *Broaden your network.* Take the time to go to meetings and conferences. Join civic activities or leadership organizations where you can meet community leaders and develop relationships that could have significance. For example, assisting the county commissioners on a local levy campaign can put you on a first-name basis when you later appear before them at a budget hearing.

• *Identify "connectors"* who can introduce you to other key leaders in your community. These are persons who have extensive social networks and enjoy putting people together. Your board members or advisory committee members can help you gain access to other significant people in the community.[31]

• *Strengthen social bonds with key people.* Without being intrusive, you can stay in touch with people through frequent communications and informal contacts. Make a point of being in touch with key people, even when you are not making a request of them. For example, you need to be in touch with key donors, even when you are not asking for money.

Be mindful of distinguishing between building a beneficial network and engaging in self-serving contacts. Be prepared to reciprocate when they may call you for assistance.[32]

Using Electronic Technology

Web Sites. Many human service agencies have by now developed Web sites so that people can easily access information about an organization. It is important that the Web site be regularly updated because this encourages other organizations to link to your site and generates more traffic. Many reporters do much of their story research online, so if your site is not up-to-date, they are unlikely to feature your program. Also, it is useful to track the number of visitors to the Web site and encourage their registering by completing a guest book or a survey for other information. Offering incentives, such as recent publications or placement on the newsletter mailing list, can be effective. Web sites can also provide a way for visitors to volunteer or contribute.

Among the items that can be included on a Web site are the organization's mission and vision, staff information, board of directors, current programs, ways to get involved, procedures for contributing, calendar of upcoming events, how to contact the organization, and links to other Web sites.[33] Your Web site should disseminate information that your clients want, support your mission, generate contributions, and provide links to other Web sites.[34]

Your Web site could also include an *intranet* component that can be used by staff or board members only so that volunteers and staff can send documents to each other, keep a calendar of project meetings or deadlines, and even provide discussion space for long distance meetings. There are many "portals" that provide intranet-like features. One portal that provides group e-mail distribution and document-posting features on the Web is www.egroups.com.[35] You must maintain and update the Web site and arrange to register with all major search engines by providing key words related to your work.[36]

E-mail. Some organizations provide an e-mail newsletter instead of, or in addition to, a paper newsletter. By building a list of subscribers to the e-mail newsletter, you save on the cost of mailing and printing. Through a private access code, e-mail is an excellent way to keep board members and volunteers informed of matters that are of special interest to them but would not go in the general newsletter. Some organizations have a member listserv where any member can ask questions or discuss upcoming events. Someone needs to moderate the listserv to make sure that one or two people do not dominate and that the content stays focused. A few organizations use e-mail to encourage subscribers to contribute money directly and donate online by credit card.[37]

Involving the Media

Human service organizations typically become involved with the media under three circumstances: (1) to highlight an aspect of the organization, (2) to address a crisis, and (3) to influence public policy.

To get your story heard in the public media, you need to communicate to a reporter, editor, or television or radio producer an idea that will appeal to people's emotions or be unusual.[38] The greater number of people affected by the subject, the more likely your story would receive attention. The fact that your organization supports legislation to increase services for seniors in your community may not attract media attention. But if you were to arrange for four buses of seniors to go to your state capital, this event ("happening") stirs media interest. Your local newspaper is likely to have a photo of the seniors entering the bus, and the television reporters may interview seniors who are affected by the legislation.

When your agency faces a crisis, you can be certain that the media would be interested. When a staff member sexually abuses a client or an accountant embezzles agency funds, you do not have to worry about attracting media attention. The media would pounce on your organization. In a crisis, expect hard-hitting, often negative, questions from the media and subsequent panic from the organization. The best approach is to be proactive. After obtaining legal advice, set the record straight before inaccurate information has an opportunity to spread. If news is bad, the quicker accurate information is out in full, the better. Your main objective is to convey that your organization is honest, open, and willing to provide accurate information. Never lie.

Agencies often use the media to influence public policy. Media advocacy can be used to pressure political and business decision makers to make desired changes. For example, if your agency is involved in preventing substance abuse, you might take advantage of a tragic event involving a drunken driver killing a child to challenge the use of billboards marketing alcoholic beverages in your inner city community. You might organize a community vigil in front of the billboards, and then send information packets to a journalist about the extent of alcoholism among young people in the community. Further, you could write letters to the editor, or arrange to meet with the editorial staff to alert them to the nature of the problem. Thus the value of media advocacy is that it amplifies the agency's voice. It takes advantage of situations and uses them as an opportunity to dramatize an issue related to the organization's mission.[39]

In summary, good communication is proactive and constantly seeks ways to keep important stakeholders—inside and outside—in touch with organizational developments. Being proactive means anticipating who needs to know what information in a timely manner. By doing so, you engender goodwill and support.

Questions for Discussion

1. What factors, if any, inhibit the positive flow of information in your organization?

2. Can you identify instances of misperceptions occurring in your organization? How were they dealt with?

3. What are examples of top-down or bottom-up communications in your organization?

4. What are some ideas for improving communication in your organization?

5. As a middle manager, you ask staff to use the suggestion box to offer ideas to improve agency functioning. In the past, staff have not taken the suggestion box seriously, mostly using it to discard gum wrappers. How do you convince staff to take the suggestion box more seriously?

6. You have two weeks to prepare a major ten-page report for your agency. How would you approach completing the assignment? In the past, how have you dealt with writer's bloc?

7. How does your agency get its message out? To what extent is it using electronic technology described in the chapter?

6. In groups of three or four, discuss conflicts between units that have occurred in your organizations. How did you recommend problems be worked out?

7. Suppose you wanted to encourage the media to highlight the work of your agency. How would you generate a story featuring one of your clients (being mindful that client confidentiality and privacy must be respected)? What do you hope to accomplish by having a feature presented in the media?

8. Consider a situation in your agency in which you wanted to persuade other staff or your manager. How would you go about presenting your case?

Notes

1. D. H. Gaylin, Break down barriers by communicating your company's strategy, *The Human Resources Professional* (Summer 1990), pp. 20–21.

2. G. M. Barton, Manage words effectively, *Personnel Journal* 1 (1990), pp. 32–33.

3. B. Joseph, Writer's block: Is there a cure? *Nonprofit World* 3 (1986), pp. 27–28.

4. M. McCormack, *Mark H. McCormack on managing* (West Hollywood, CA: Dove Books, 1996), pp. 47–48.

5. M. H. McCormack, *On communicating* (Los Angeles: Dove Books, 1998), pp. 142–143.

6. E. Bliss, *Getting things done* (New York: Bantam, 1976), p. 93.

7. R. Townsend, *Further up the organization* (New York: Alfred A. Knopf, 1984), p. 134.

8. M. McCormack, Reliance on e-mail may erode the quality of communication, *The Plain Dealer* (3 August 1999), p. 8C.

9. M. McCormack, *On communicating*, pp. 15–28.

10. D. Tjosvold, *The conflict-positive organization* (Reading, MA: Addison-Wesley, 1991), p. 11.

11. P. Drucker, *The effective executive* (New York: Harper & Row, 1985), pp. 150–153; A. Lauffer, *Careers, colleagues, and conflicts: Understanding gender, race, and ethnicity in the workplace* (Beverly Hills, CA: Sage, 1985), pp. 145–146.

12. T. Caplow, *How to run any organization* (Hinsdale, IL: Dryden, 1976), p. 170.

13. H. Bisno, *Managing conflict* (Newbury Park, CA: Sage, 1988), p. 66.

14. G. T. Milkovich & J. W. Boudreau, *Personnel/human resource management,* 5th ed. (Plano, TX: Business Publications, 1988), pp. 614–617.

15. R. T. Crow & C. A. Odewahn, *Management for the human services* (Englewood Cliffs, NJ: Prentice Hall, 1987), pp. 145–146.

16. P. Drucker, pp. 122–123.

17. R. Heifetz & M. Linsky, A survival guide for leaders, *Harvard Business Review* 80 (June 2002), pp. 65–74.

18. D. Tjosvold, p. 4.

19. H. Bisno, p. 56.

20. J. Carew, *You'll never get no for an answer* (New York: Simon & Schuster, 1987); J. Gubkin, *Persuasive communication* (Cleveland, OH: Jack Gubkin & Associates, 1985), pp. 1–82.

21. R. N. Haas, *The power to persuade* (New York: Houghton Mifflin, 1994), pp. 171–174.

22. J. A. Conger, The necessary art of persuasion, *Harvard Business Review* 76 (May/June 1998), pp. 92.

23. J. A. Conger, p. 87.

24. A. Zaremba, Communication: The upward network, *Personnel Journal* 3 (1989), p. 36.

25. P. Drucker, *Management challenges for the 21st century* (New York: HarperBusiness, 1999), pp. 127–130.

26. J. H. Boyett & H. P. Conn, *Maximum performance measurement* (Macomb, IL; Glenbridge, 1988), pp. 256–256.

27. T. Caplow, p. 55.

28. G. M. Barton, p. 32.

29. R. E. Herman, *Keeping good people: Strategies for solving the dilemma of the decade* (Cleveland, OH: Oakhill, 1990), p. 140.

30. M. S. Peck, *The road less traveled* (New York: Touchstone, Simon & Schuster, 1978), p. 125.

31. M. Gladwell, *The tipping point* (Boston: Little Brown and Company, 2002), pp. 38–74.

32. J. G. Dees, J. Emerson, & P. Economy, *Enterprising nonprofits: A toolkit for social entrepreneurs* (New York: John Wiley & Sons, 2001), pp. 96–97.

33. B. L. Ciconte & J. Jacob, *Fundraising basics, a complete guide,* 2nd ed. (New York: Aspen, 2001), in *Nonprofit organization management* (New York: Aspen, 2002), p. 10:14.7.

34. C. Gable, Tech tips: How technology can support your organization, *Grassroots Fundraising Journal* 1 (2000), pp. 12–14.

35. C. Gable, pp. 12–14.

36. K. Klein, *Fundraising for social change,* 4th ed. (Oakland, CA: Chardon Press, 2001), pp. 285–290.

37. K. Klein, p. 287.

38. Federation for Community Planning, *2000 greater Cleveland media guide, 45th ed.* (Cleveland: Author, 2000).

39. R. Brody & M. Nair, *Macro practice: A generalist approach,* 6th ed. (Wheaton, IL: Gregory Publishing, 2003), pp. 342–344.

19 Team Building And Coalition Building

Managers of human service organizations must continuously work with others, both inside and outside their agencies. These collaborative relationships involve achieving mutual goals while respecting separate identities and different roles. In working together with others, managers seek common ground, but they can appreciate when it is appropriate for colleagues to take separate paths. This chapter explores how managers can work collaboratively with individuals and groups—internally and externally—to further the goals of their organization. Specifically, this chapter focuses on (1) building teams and task forces within the agency, and (2) working with collateral organizations.

The Importance of Team Building

Increasingly, organizations—whether corporations, voluntary agencies, or government bodies—are moving away from hierarchical, top-down to bottom-up decision making to better involve their staff members. This trend is especially true in the human service field, where many staff members actively participate in the operation of the agency. Effective administrators turn to staff members at all levels for information, for opinions, and for carrying out administrative decisions. Because those who are actively involved in decision making are most likely to have the enthusiasm for implementing those decisions, agency managers should seek meaningful ways to foster staff participation. Forming staff into teams is one of the most effective methods of developing staff commitment.

Merely putting a group of people together in the same room does not guarantee a team. As distinct from a group of individuals who may lack a common purpose, a team strives for unified goals. Team members use the group process to generate a diversity of ideas and experiences that can address organizational problems. The combined contributions of members equals more than the sum of their individual efforts. This group synergy results from staff members' working cooperatively to produce results that are qualitatively better than what each individual member could produce alone.[1]

Teams can be manager-led or self-managing.[2] Typically, manager-led teams are responsible for implementing assigned work. For example, in a children's institution, staff assigned to individual cottages work as a team under a supervisor. In turn, each cottage team is part of a larger residential unit team that meets periodically to work on problems. Under this format the supervisor assumes the role of team leader, and the individual members work together on common concerns.

Under a self-managing team, members assume responsibility for determining their own process and monitoring results. They select their own team leader, who may or may not be a manager. The team deemphasizes formal supervisory roles and encourages members to substitute group decision making and consensus for the direction of a supervisor. Management, however, can still retain responsibility for the overall direction and provide some coaching as needed. Self-managing teams may be ongoing or operate as task forces with a time limited schedule (to be discussed).

Responding to Circumstances

To borrow a sports analogy, different circumstances promote greater or lesser team interaction. A basketball, football, or hockey team may require much interaction and interdependence among its members. A singles tennis team, and to even a greater extent a golf team, requires its players to function relatively independently of each other. So too, in providing human services, circumstances may dictate the need for different degrees of independence and interdependence. For example, a counseling agency requires its practitioners to perform most of their activities in separate offices with individual clients. As a result of their isolated activities, staff rarely come in contact with each other. But under special circumstances, for example when the agency is being reviewed for reaccreditation, the agency may provide for numerous opportunities for staff to meet.

Creating Team Spirit

Highly productive teams share the following characteristics:[3]

1. They develop and communicate a shared vision and work toward common goals.

2. They deemphasize hierarchy, as every team member works to make the idea or plan succeed. With few exceptions, no one pulls rank.

3. The most important factors in selecting team members are their credibility, expertise, and the ability to connect to important constituencies within the organization.[4]

4. They encourage open communication. Although they may discuss complaints openly among themselves, they are discreet about what they share with those outside the team.

5. They develop trust in each other and respect their teammates both for their skills and as people.

6. They are comfortable with each other and enjoy playing and working together.

7. They are task oriented and focus on producing results. They are not just a discussion group; rather, they have identifiable objectives that they want to accomplish. They establish specific performance objectives, for example, developing a new service or responding to client requests within 24 hours.

8. They establish clear rules and behavior, such as attendance requirements, confidentiality, respect for each other, constructive confrontation, and full participation. These rules promote focus, openness, commitment, and trust.[5]

9. Team members are interdependent. They try to achieve something that would not be possible for them to do as individuals. Team members build on each other's contributions instead of duplicating or interfering with them. They are willing to sacrifice their own interests for the good of the whole team.

10. Team members are constantly aware of the team's performance. Based on continual feedback, they make self-correcting adjustments to improve performance.

11. They are highly committed to, and own, the team's work. They do whatever it takes to complete tasks, which sometimes means working hours beyond the usual work week.

12. Depending on the team assignment, members take responsibility for areas outside their immediate sphere. Working as a team member, a counselor may have suggestions for the marketing department; a support staff may have thoughts on how maintenance can be improved.

13. They make decisions by consensus, which is made possible because of agreed-upon goals. Generally, votes are not taken, and majority rule is not applied. The consensus is not based on the need to conform; rather, people argue, debate, and work their way to a common decision.

14. Training is provided, especially if members are new at working on a team. This training could include team problem solving, managing meetings, and conflict management. Team training helps people understand that consensus decision making means people might have

different opinions about the best solution to a problem, even after considerable discussion. Everyone is willing to get behind one option to make it work, however.

Overcoming Barriers to Winning Teams

Initially, not all participants on the team may be good team players. Even those who lack traits that would make them effective team members, however, may eventually become team contributors if they are given the right motivation and training. For example, some may want to work independently, preferring to receive credit or even criticism for their own individual efforts. They may believe that being part of the team interferes with their ability to complete individual work. They may need time to adjust to the team. Encourage their participation in meetings so that other members of the team can appreciate how their expertise can contribute to achieving team goals. An effective approach in team building is to have the group develop its own ground rules of operating, which has the effect of empowering team members.

Two other problems can occur among members of a team. First, one or more members may tend to dominate meetings, attempting to dictate directions and unduly influence the thinking of the group. Other team members can then become dissatisfied and frustrated. The leader needs to communicate with these "prima donnas" that their personal attitude is disrupting the team spirit, and that their overall work performance is measured by the extent to which they participate as a team member. A second, and opposite, problem is the tendency for some members to disengage. An effective team leader understands that disengaged team members may feel insecure and may be afraid to say something which might make them look foolish or turn out to be wrong. In both instances, the team leader needs to take members aside to talk about how their behaviors need to change for the benefit of the organization.[6]

Occasionally, you may encounter a member who is unwilling to respond to training and who is unable to work with other team members. Their mistrust is so profound that they poison the ability of the team to work together. If these staff members do not respond to coaching, they should be transferred off the team.

Becoming an Effective Team Leader

Not all team leaders are inherently effective. Their own personal style can negatively affect the team, or the atmosphere of the organization may not truly support team efforts. Team leadership, however, can be enhanced in several ways. First, team leaders need clear directives from senior managers regarding their role. At the very least, their roles should be legitimized with a formal title and job description that clarifies how this differs from usual supervisory roles. Team leaders must also understand the boundaries of their decision making as well as the parameters within which their team can function. How much initiative can they take? How innovative can their team be? These are questions that must be understood at the beginning of the team process. Second, team leaders should develop leadership skills that can enhance the functioning of their team. These include negotiating, communicating, agenda setting, goal development, and action planning skills. Third, a team leader creates a safe environment where people can communicate whatever needs to be said without fear of reprisal. In the course of discussions, a team leader pulls together divergent ideas and identifies themes that may show connections.[7]

Handling Conflict

Conflict can significantly affect a team's decision-making effectiveness. Inevitably, team members can have incompatible wishes or irreconcilable desires. Two kinds of conflict can occur in teams. *Relationship conflict* can involve tension and even dislike among group members. This form of conflict is detrimental to group performance and member satisfaction. Because relationship conflicts distract people from their tasks, both leaders and group members must work hard at controlling personal animosities. Team leaders must bring the antagonistic parties together to resolve their concerns—or help them work together as professionals despite their personal animosities.

Task conflict involves differences of viewpoints and opinions related to how the group is to accomplish tasks. Moderate levels of conflict over tasks can enhance group performance and further the development of new perspectives.[8] Teams whose members challenge each other's thinking develop a more in-depth awareness of choices, create a rich range of alternatives, and ultimately make the kinds of effective decisions required in today's turbulent environment.[9] Task conflicts can reduce apathy and generate a higher level of team investment. Managers can ask members to take opposing viewpoints. Members who come up with different and useful ideas should be given special acknowledgment. Debate within the team can reduce the dangers of *groupthink* (discussed in Chapter 17).

The key to managing conflict is to encourage people to debate their ideas, to have strong differences of opinions, and at the same time maintain a high level of civility. Team members must know that they can feel strongly about an issue and fight hard for it without questioning the competence or integrity of those with opposing views.[10] They avoid becoming personally hostile or angry with their colleagues. When conflict is managed well it becomes an effective tool for exchanging ideas and making better organizational decisions.

The most common type of conflict relates to work problems. One faction, for example, may want to change to a whole new procedure while the other opposes major change. Another kind of conflict occurs when some members feel that they have to carry the load of others. This kind of conflict can destroy a team if it is not resolved quickly. Pinpoint whether the persons not carrying their load lack skills or need additional training or coaching. A more serious problem would be apathy in relation to achieving the team's goals. Still another problem relates to individuals forming cliques within their teams. By excluding others, they invite hostility that can interfere with team functioning. These issues must be dealt with quickly if the team is to continue working together.

In all of these conflict situations, team leaders must determine the source of the conflict and then take proactive steps to deal with it. Initially, the team leader may wish to meet with those who are complaining to determine the nature of their concerns and then meet individually with those who are the target of their annoyances. It is important, however, that the team leader air these concerns before the full team.[11] If conflict is not discussed candidly, upset members can corrode the team process. Moreover, the team leader must help those who are in conflict to listen to each other, especially if each side is intent only on winning its own point. Asking key members to paraphrase what the other is saying is one way of opening up their minds. It is also helpful that each faction convey how its position could help the team achieve its goals. If both can see that everybody is working toward the same goal, there may be room for flexibility and compromise.

The team leader must encourage differences while discouraging interpersonal hostility. Ground rules for discussion must be established clearly in advance: no personal attacks, no disparaging comments, no personalizing of the issue. Another helpful ground rule is that changing a position is not a sign of weakness but of strength. Finally, people can express their feelings because positions are usually a combination of both intellectual thought and emotional reactions. Understanding how other people feel about an issue, and the depth of their feelings, is an important part of teamwork.

One approach a team leader can use to foster a more open negotiating process is to have each faction prepare a list of what it feels the other side should do, and then have the parties exchange lists to determine the compromises to which they might agree. Another approach is to ask the conflicting members to write questions that require answers from the other side. Out of this process can come a mutually agreed-on position.

Having a Good Fight While Getting Along

Understanding how group members can have fundamental disagreements and still get along without resorting to destructive conflicts with one another is vital. It is instructive to understand the specific tactics that can be taken to achieve this goal:[12]

- *Frame the choice as a collaborative, rather than a competitive, effort.* Successful teams believe that collaboration works to everybody's best interest. Having a shared vision and working toward a common goal furthers the team process.
- *Obtain facts.* The more current data that can be made available, the more likely team members can focus on issues, not personalities. In the absence of good data, a tendency is to debate opinions—some ill formed. Facts allow people to move quickly to the central issues and reduce reliance on guesses or self-serving desires. Therefore, it is important that preparation for team meetings be devoted to getting good information.
- *Develop multiple alternatives.* Having many options before the group encourages creative thinking and allows participants to consider combining elements from each of the choices. Sometimes members are encouraged to present a range of options just to have more choices before the group.
- *Put people in a positive mood.* It helps to have people loosen up before embarking on the seriousness of the team's agenda. Maybe they can tell some humorous episode that happened to them during the week or describe some positive personal experience. Good humor helps lighten the atmosphere and provides a psychological mood for blunting the threatening edge of criticisms or negative information.
- *Seek consensus with qualification.* This particular tactic may be more suitable in manager-led teams. It involves a two-step process in which team members talk over an issue and try to reach a consensus. If they cannot, the most senior manager makes the decision.

For example, a children's institution staff team may have different opinions about whether an adolescent is ready for discharge. The residential director in these special circumstances makes the ultimate decision with the guidance of various members' input. The other members of the team accept this decision as long as they believe the process is a fair one and that they have had ample opportunity to express their ideas. Most people want their opinions to be considered seriously, but accept that these opinions cannot always prevail. The key is that the ultimate decision is based upon open and honest communication and not on some hidden agenda known only to the team leader. This approach permits decisions to be made fairly quickly.

Interactive Team Exercises

Learning to be an effective team member takes work and a considerable amount of introspection. Team members need to be aware of how they are doing as a member of a team and be able to help their fellow team members function appropriately. One way of fostering this understanding and enhancing team skills is to ask team members to participate in preliminary exercises that allow them to simulate roles in a non-threatening manner. Here are three exercises team leaders can use to stimulate team understanding:

1. Ask two factions to debate an issue relevant to your agency. For example, a neighborhood center could debate the question, "Should we take youngsters to an outside playground?" Give each group starting arguments for their position for and against. Provide members of each group with disparaging remarks they might convey in regard to the other group's position. Discuss afterwards how the designated leader and other group members might have better resolved their differences. Also identify some of the positive ideas that were conveyed and how these might be replicated in regular team meetings.

2. Divide the group into those who wear blindfolds and those who lead others around obstacles and down stairs. Discuss afterwards how supportive (or not) the coaches were to those who had to wear the blindfolds. Discuss further what would foster trust or lack of trust in team discussions.

3. Ask people to take 30 minutes to draw together on a large roll of paper their individual thoughts about how they perceive their team functioning and their role in the team. Obviously, artistic talent is not the essential aspect of this exercise, so stick figures or use of color may be ways of expressing people's thoughts. For example, one person might draw a swing without ropes, indicating their feelings of lack of support. Another might draw an octopus, conveying concerns about the team going off in lots of different directions and lacking central focus. No one is to talk during the drawing, but afterward each uses the drawing to reflect on his or her position. This becomes an opportunity for people to examine what procedures need to be altered for team members to believe that they can contribute more.

Aside from the fun of doing these exercises, their value is for staff to take time to consider how their team is functioning and what they can do to improve it. Once people feel more comfortable, time can be set aside periodically for team members to reflect on how their team is working. Among the questions members can ask are the following:[13]

- Are members contributing suggestions about how the group can improve?
- How well do members of the team understand problems?
- How often do members ask for—and give—support to each other?
- How willing are members to finish the work that was assigned to individuals?
- Do group members respect each other's ideas?
- Is everyone pulling his or her weight?
- Is there a strong sense of collaboration, even in the face of differences?
- Is there a tolerance for individuals occasionally functioning independently, when this seems a good idea?

- Are innovative ideas encouraged?
- Are people encouraged to try out new roles and grow into them?

Positive answers to these questions indicate teams are working constructively and collaboratively to resolve issues.

Task Forces

Sometimes teams are designated as task forces, which implies carrying out a specific assignment on a time-limited basis. The term *ad hoc task force* suggests that when the group accomplishes its purpose, it disbands. The advantage of an ad hoc task force (sometimes known as an *action team*) is that it has a clear mandate to handle a particular problem and is terminated once the problem is solved. Usually, members are asked to participate voluntarily, based on their experience and expertise.[14] The group may establish its own timetable and set its own pace, or management may convey expectations. The supervisor can be team leader, or the role may be assigned to different members of the staff for different issues. To foster different perspectives, task force members may be drawn from different units of the organization.[15] Moreover, there is the possibility of developing a network as task force members communicate back to their home base units.

Five caveats should be kept in mind to keep task forces from becoming counterproductive. First, the staff who develop an action plan may not necessarily implement it. The group formed to carry out the plan may need to be reconstituted with management and participants from other units. Because newcomers may not have participated in the planning process, they typically need time to develop ownership of the undertaking.

Second, it is possible that staff may identify so much with their task force that they become elitist and exclusionary in their outlook. Others in the organization may become resentful because they perceive this task force to be a clique. Members of the group must understand that they have a responsibility to share their experiences with others. Time limits and rotation to different groups help diminish cliques.

Third, in establishing the task force, it is important to clarify roles, responsibilities, and ground rules under which it functions. Otherwise, the group may not understand its function and decision-making boundaries. Is it only advisory? Is it responsible for executing its own recommendations? Is it designed to initiate ideas or react passively to ideas being generated by management? Can its decisions be overridden and, if so, by whom? It is also important to clarify the role of the team leader. Is the chairperson responsible for following through, or only for facilitating the group discussion process? Thus, the task force must be given clear and detailed guidance about the job it is to carry out.[16]

Fourth, staff involvement on task forces must be meaningful. Unfortunately, it can be superficial when staff appear to have input into the organization's decision-making process but management ultimately ignores or belittles their ideas. If staff are limited to making trivial decisions, they do not invest in the process.[17] People sense when their ideas are genuinely desired and when the organization is resorting to gimmickry.

Finally, if several task groups are organized simultaneously around different issues, they must be coordinated. Unless the various parts of the organization coalesce on issues, serious problems can result. For example, if one part of the team is working to change the reward system, while another studies personnel practices, and a third group considers the organization's tasks, much confusion can result if there is no attempt to unify these group's efforts and findings. Hence, task groups must keep lines of communication open and work to achieve a collaborative effort. It may be helpful to appoint a "traffic cop" to oversee the various task forces.

Coalition Building

If team building requires that effective managers focus on developing strong internal staff relationships, coalition building requires managers to look outward to build collateral relationships and to partner with other agencies. To maximize the impact of their organization in the community, effective managers periodically join with collateral organizations in forming strategic alliances. This collaboration occurs when two or more organizations perceive that their own goals can be achieved most effectively and efficiently with the assistance and the resources of others. Collaboration emerges from a commitment to a common cause that involves assuming joint responsibilities, developing mutual accountability, combining resources, and sharing rewards.[18] Thus collaboration is a mutually beneficial and well-defined relationship that two or more organizations enter into to achieve better results than they are likely to achieve on their own.[19]

Alliances of organizations offer the possibility of pooling funds, sharing staff and volunteer time, and involving talent and expertise that may not be available in one group.[20] The term *synergy* conveys that the sum is greater than the parts, meaning that more clout and power can emerge when groups work together than when they work alone. By forming alliances, they increase the availability of people power. Not surprisingly, politicians and other public officials discern the difference between a group of fifty and one that represents a coalition of five thousand.[21]

Forming a coalition does not necessarily occur easily. Members of organizations generally want to control their own destiny and decision-making process, develop a sense of identity, and convey to the world their particular efforts and accomplishments. This need for autonomy and identity can be so profound that some organizations purposefully avoid interaction. They want to preserve their independence and think they can achieve their goals without relating to others. They want to be unencumbered, free to pursue their objectives without compromising. A child advocacy organization, for example, may decide not to participate in a cooperative community effort to improve foster care because it wants to preserve its advocacy "gadfly" role in relation to human service agencies.

Despite this tendency to be independent, organizations that work on complex community problems find it necessary—even essential—to deal with other organizations. A collaborative approach requires organizations to harmonize ways of working together on many community problems—such as unemployment, inadequate housing, and delinquency—that are complex and interrelated. Often organizations become highly specialized and concentrate on a given aspect of a problem. As specialization has increased, so too has the need for interaction among organizations. For example, establishing an employment program requires more than setting up training programs: health services, transportation, day care, counseling, and housing services all become necessary components. Hence, while many organizations seek to preserve a high degree of decision-making authority and power, the complexity of problems and the need for funds, skills, staff, community support, and other resources compel them to interact cooperatively to form strategic alliances.[22]

Factors Facilitating Strategic Alliances

Certain key capabilities should exist for strategic alliances to function successfully.

Goal Compatibility. Organizations forming an alliance should share a clear vision of what they want to accomplish. Through this common vision, organizations can maximize the chances of meeting their respective goals. Different organizations can have similar goals, such as when several decide to work together to reduce crime in a neighborhood. Goals also can be complementary, as when one agency decides to serve clients it ordinarily would not serve, because it would be paid by another agency for doing so. Sometimes goals can even be dissimilar, as "strange bedfellow" organizations harmonize their efforts to achieve their respective goals.[23]

Development of Resources. Organizations collaborate when sufficient resources exist to reduce competition or when they can agree on how resources are to be divided. Collaboration is less likely to occur when organizations must compete for scarce resources. Organizations can exchange tangible resources (involving funding, facilities, personnel, clients, and services) or they can be intangible (involving prestige and good will). Sometimes the exchange is immediately reciprocal: Organization A agrees to serve the clients of Organization B in exchange for funding. At other times, the exchange is sequential: Organization A agrees to assist Organization B on child welfare legislation in anticipation of Organization B assisting Organization A in passing a mental health levy the following year. Organizations thus weigh anticipated costs of the exchange against present or future benefits.

Role of Higher Authority. When state or national organizations encourage coordination of their local units, they are likely to work together. Similarly, foundations sometimes require (as a condition of a local grant) that agencies demonstrate that they would work together to achieve joint program goals. For example, Salvation Army, Catholic Charities Services, Neighborhood Family Center, and Hispanic Drug Prevention Program may join together in a community proposal to provide comprehensive services to a target population at the request of a community foundation.

Governance. Organizations tend to collaborate successfully when they agree about who would make decisions and what type of decisions can be made. A written protocol defines (a) when Organization A can make a decision independent of other organizations, (b) when it must consult with the others but not require their approval, and (c) when Organization A can act only with the consensus of its collaborating partners.[24] Furthermore, the decision-making process should include procedures for resolving conflict. For example, suppose a mental health agency and a substance abuse agency are working together to address the needs of homeless persons. What procedures might they develop should individual staff members disagree on how they should work with a particular mentally ill, substance-abusing client? These conflict-resolving procedures need to be clarified up front to avoid later inter-organizational problems.

Domain of Activities and Target Population. Organizations need to come to terms with how they would work with their client base. When roles are complementary, as when an employment organization provides different activities from those of a day care agency, then collaboration is facilitated. However, when a substance abuse agency decides to find jobs for its clients, then its participation in an employment alliance may come into question. When one agency begins to encroach on another's activities or their target population, collaboration will be impeded.

Cultural Compatibility. Although each organization in an alliance may have its own culture, these cultures should be compatible enough to develop a distinct culture within the alliance to support their mutual mission.[25] This development requires thinking through how individual organizations can affect other members of the alliance. Furthermore, it requires a mindset of negotiating and cooperating. Also, it means thinking about what is best for the alliance and the community, not just one agency.[26]

Power and Prestige. When an organization perceives that it can influence changes it thinks are important, and when it senses that others are not over-bearing, then it is more likely to collaborate. Further, when this organization and its partners perceive that their prestige is enhanced and others are not gaining prestige at their expense, they tend to continue collaborating. When parties have equal status and respect for each other, their relationships are likely to be more effective than when they do not have equal status or respect for each other.[27] People involved in successful collaborative ventures find ways to balance the unequal positions among all members.[28]

Communication Infrastructure. Open, consistent communication can lead to clear expectations of performance. By determining specific objectives for the alliance with a clear timetable, organizations can avoid problems of ambiguity. Information systems and up-to-date technologies (e.g., conference calls, faxes, and e-mail) can facilitate communication.

Trust. Perhaps the most intangible factor, but the one that is most indispensable, is that members of the respective organizations trust that others would honor their commitments. Over time, this trust is most likely to increase. As organizations have opportunities for successfully conducting joint programs, greater willingness develops to accept new forms of interdependence.

In summary, whether or not two or more organizations collaborate depends on how committed they are to working together to achieve their common goals.

Collaborative Structures

Structures developed as a result of collaborative efforts can vary, depending on the desired ends. Where the situation requires autonomous agencies to retain a high degree of independence while linking temporarily on a specific issue or situation, the collaborative process is ad hoc and limited. A special crisis (e.g., a hurricane) may require organizations to temporarily mesh their programs, but once the crisis recedes and in the absence of provisions for an ongoing structure, organizational relationships can evaporate as autonomous groups return to their independent activities.

Sometimes organizations with different goals work together informally through a loose coalition on a temporary basis. Coalitions emerge from the joining of two or more organizations that discover they have more to gain by collaboration on an issue or activity than by pursuing independent courses of action. When the project is completed, the coalition is dissolved. For example, ten mental health agencies form a coalition to pass a mental health levy. For a period of three months these mental health agencies send representatives to meet weekly to develop strategies for the campaign. When the campaign is concluded, the group dismantles. Four years later, a new coalition is formed for the next levy campaign.

Organizations may also establish a formal, ongoing relationship through a federation. Each organization is self-directing; none is entirely dependent on or completely responsible to the federated body. Each organization within the federation remains primarily accountable to itself and only in a limited way to the federation. Usually actions proposed by a federation must be approved by each of its constituency groups. Because a major purpose of the federation is to harmonize and integrate different groups, controversial issues that might cause the coalition to break up are avoided.

A good collaborative process builds a series of progressively deeper and more comprehensive agreements among the participants. Initially, they agree that common problems exist and should be addressed. Then they determine how they can best work together. They share relevant information, develop a common vision, and strategies of implementation. Finally, they take action steps to implement the strategies.[29]

If a collaborative organization is ongoing, then as it resolves one problem or issue, it prepares to move on to the next. For example, suppose that organizations form a coalition to combat neighborhood crime; they decide that their first project would be to secure better street lighting for various neighborhoods. Succeeding with this first project, the group then moves on to other compelling issues, such as gaining speedier police response to neighborhood crime.

Organizations may also form a consortium—a formal partnership to undertake joint activities or programs. The following are ways two or more organizations can coordinate their efforts:[30]

Joint Planning

- Planning coordinated delivery of services
- Information sharing of resources or policies
- Joint evaluation of program effectiveness
- Joint program design

Example: The County Department of Human Services and the local mental health board coordinate efforts to assist families with special mental health needs.

Administrative Services

- Central recordkeeping on clients seen in more than one organization
- Centralized purchasing and equipment use
- Joint advertising
- Sharing facilities and equipment

Example: Two agencies in the same building form an interagency committee to purchase supplies together, thus reducing administrative costs and taking advantage of bulk discounts.

Service Coordination

– Joint outreach to clients
– Common intake and diagnosis
– Formal referral patterns
– Follow-up with clients receiving common services
– Combined transportation
– Combined case conferences on families seen by different organizations
– Case management to coordinate services by different agencies

Example: A children's services cluster is formed consisting of the alcohol and drug addiction board, juvenile court, mental retardation and disabilities board, public schools, and youth services. The purpose is to assure service for children who have multiple needs and for whom appropriate local services are not accessible. The organization develops individual service plans, assures proper management, and arranges for shared funding for multiple-needs children.

Personnel Coordination

– Co-location of staff in a commonly shared facility
– Out-stationing of staff by one organization to that of another
– Lend-lease of staff from one organization to function under the administration of another organization for a specified time
– Joint training
– Interagency staff teams
– Compacts involving formal staff cooperative agreements, though no funds are exchanged

Example: An elementary school arranges for a mental health agency to co-locate a staff member in the school. The counselor meets with students referred by teachers in a group counseling session and works with them to improve their school performance. The counselor is accountable to both the principal and a mental health agency supervisor.

Financial Coordination

– Joint fundraising
– Purchase of service to provide a specified service in exchange for funds
– Joint project funding

Example: Three organizations in the local community related to day care, youth counseling, and vocational training sponsor a community event designed to publicize their services and raise money for their respective organizations.

The previous examples illustrate that the structural format of the coalition can vary depending on the nature of the task to be accomplished. Similarly, structural format can be customized in relation to various participants. In some instances, coalition leadership would rotate over time from one organization to another, or various tasks may be rotated among members. One agency may be designated to take fiscal responsibility, another might be responsible for intake, and a third for marketing the services of the coalition. Finally, an organization may be designated as the lead organization to ensure that services are completed, evaluated, and supported.[31]

Whatever the structural arrangement, collaborative alliances leverage resources to accomplish member agency goals. The synergy that is created by joining together with others results in a greater impact on the clients of the respective agencies.

Questions for Discussion

1. Working in groups of three or four, select an organizational issue, such as how to deal with clients not showing up for their appointments. What ground rules for developing a team spirit could you agree on? Then engage in a heated discussion about proposed solutions. How would you handle violations of your ground rules and conflicts? On reflection, what approaches could be taken to facilitate the team's deliberations?

2. Consider the drawing exercise described in the chapter. How would you characterize how teams function in your organization?

3. If you were to form a task force in your organization, what issue might it focus on?

4. Under what circumstances would your agency *not* join a coalition?

5. Assuming your organization participates in one or more coalitions, what were the factors that induced them to join? What were the benefits to your organization?

6. You are a neighborhood grassroots advocacy organization dedicated to changing living conditions in your community. Typically, you do not affiliate with other organizations because you prefer not to have your advocacy efforts diluted or be encumbered with extensive interorganizational discussions. Recently you have been invited to join a coalition of organizations from the broader community to address the problem of lead poisoning in homes. What are the pros and cons of joining this proposed coalition? If you do decide to join, how would you preserve your autonomy?

7. What kinds of collaborative structures has your organization participated in? Which ones identified in the chapter might be explored by your agency?

8. Several business and community leaders connected with United Way have proposed creating a community coalition to conduct a community needs assessment. Based on the results, the coalition would develop the community's agenda for addressing the highest priorities. What are the pros and cons of participating in a process that determines the community's focus and resources?

Notes

1. K. Blanchard, *The 3 keys to empowerment* (San Francisco: Berrett-Koehler, 1999), pp. 103–104; R. Skidmore, *Social Work Administration* (Boston: Allyn & Bacon, 1995), p. 169.

2. A. Seers, M. M. Petty, & J. F. Cashman, Team-member exchange under team & traditional management, *Group & Organizational Management* 20, 1 (March 1995), p. 19.

3. H. A. Rosso, *Achieving excellence in fund raising* (San Francisco: Jossey-Bass, 1991); Alexander Hamilton Institute, Inc., *Making teams succeed at work* (Ramsey, NJ: Author, 1997), p. 1–38; C. Joinson, Getting the best results from teams requires work on the teams themselves, *Human Resource Management* 44, 5 (May 1999), pp. 30–36.

4. M. H. McCormack, *Mark H. McCormack on managing* (West Hollywood, CA: Dove Books, 1996), p. 185.

5. J. R. Katzenbach & D. K. Smith, *The wisdom of teams* (New York: HarperCollins, 1993), p. 123.

6. Alexander Hamilton Institute, Inc., pp. 6–8.

7. B. Gummer, Go team go! The growing importance of teamwork in organizational life, *Administration in Social Work* 19, 4 (1995), pp. 93–94.

8. R. Wageman & E. A. Mannix, *Power & influence in organizations,* eds. R. M. Kramer & M. A. Neale (Thousand Oaks, CA: Sage, 1998), pp. 270–271.

9. K. M. Eisenhardt, J. L. Kahwajy, & L. J. Bourgeois III, How management teams can have a good fight, *Harvard Business Review* 75 (July/August 1997), p. 77.

10. Alexander Hamilton Institute, Inc., p. 21.

11. Alexander Hamilton Institute, Inc., pp. 23–27.

12. K. M. Eisenhardt et al., pp. 77–85.

13. A. Seers et al., p. 37.

14. R. B. Campbell, *The process.* Speech given at Higbee's Annual Meeting, Cleveland, OH, May 1982.

15. D. C. Eadie, *Changing by design* (San Francisco: Jossey-Bass, 1997), p. 165.

16. D. C. Eadie, p. 167.

17. E. E. Lawler, *High involvement management* (San Francisco: Jossey-Bass, 1986), pp. 53–59.

18. P. W. Mattessich & B. R. Monsey, *Collaboration: What makes it work* (Saint Paul, MN: Wilder Research, 1993), p. 7; See also D. D. Chrislip, *The collaborative leadership fieldbook: A guide for citizens and civic leaders* (San Francisco: Jossey-Bass, 2002), p. 41.

19. M. Winer & K. Roy, *Collaboration handbook* (Saint Paul, MN: Amherst H. Wilder Foundation, 1997), p. 24.

20. J. Rothman, J. L. Erlich, & J. G. Teresa, *Promoting innovation and change in organizations and communities* (New York: Macmillan, 1976), p. 314.

21. R. Brody & M. D. Nair, *Macro practice: A generalist approach,* 6th ed. (Wheaton, IL: Gregory, 2003), p. 325.

22. R. Brody & M. D. Nair, p. 324.

23. R. Brody & M. D. Nair, p. 325.

24. M. Winer & K. Roy, pp. 88–89.

25. PricewaterhouseCoopers, Building high-performing strategic alliances, *Growing Your Business* (July/August 1999), p. 3.

26. M. Winer & K. Roy, pp. 99–100.

27. J. K. Butler, Jr., Behaviors, trust, & goal achievement in a win-win negotiating role play, *Group & Organizational Management* 20, 4 (December 1995), p. 499.

28. M. Winer & K. Roy, p. 25.

29. D. D. Chrislip, p. 54.

30. R. Brody & M. D. Nair, pp. 328–330; A. Lauffer, *Grantsmanship and fund raising* (Beverly Hills, CA: Sage, 1984), pp. 62–71.

31. M. Winer & K. Roy, pp. 102–104.

20

Working With a Board of Trustees

A well-managed human service organization requires a governing body that actively works with the executive director and management team to provide organizational stewardship. By developing a collaborative partnership and by fulfilling their complementary roles, executive staff and board can work together to achieve the organization's mission.

Two major problems can cause confusion about the respective roles and responsibilities of executive staff and board that can hamper a true collaborative partnership between them. At one extreme, an executive director can use the board of trustees to affirm decisions and policies that staff have predetermined. Staff may screen out important information, offer limited or no options for decision making, use board meetings to report only how well they are doing, and have the expectation that the board would not challenge or question policies or programs. In this scenario the board chairperson is weak and malleable; trustees are passive and disengaged. A passive board tends to slide into a mode of neglecting to provide proper oversight. Directors fail in their collective legal and ethical duty to govern and abdicate their responsibility by delegating their obligation for oversight to the executive director.[1] Because of trustee disengagement, their financial support is limited. The board becomes incapable of achieving its proper governing role.

At the other extreme, a board can micromanage by becoming excessively involved in day-to-day operations, making decisions about hiring and firing staff, and becoming overly direct in telling staff how to administer programs. These interventions undermine professional staff and can result in a less effectively run organization. Board intervention conveys serious warning signals that the board lacks sufficient confidence in professional decision making or the ability of the executive director to properly carry out the executive functions. In this scenario, the executive director and the board experience considerable tension, and the executive director is reduced to an ineffectual administrator.

To achieve a high-level working relationship, both executive director and board need to understand clearly (1) the distinction between board governance and executive management, (2) the various roles and responsibilities that a board must fulfill, (3) the dynamic relationship between executive director and board, and (4) ways to improve board management and functioning.

Distinguishing

Governance From Management

Because the board bears ultimate fiduciary responsibility, authority, and accountability for the organization, trustees must be willing to devote the necessary time and energy to governing.[2] The board assumes this governing responsibility by concentrating on the future, carrying out strategic thinking, providing oversight of the organization's finances and operations, and being accountable for contractual, programmatic, and strategic outcomes.[3] In human service organizations, the emphasis on accountability means focusing on those policies that address consumer results, agency target population(s), and expenses necessary to carry out agency interventions. The board delegates to executive management decisions and actions that can achieve its desired ends.

The board's governing role should be distinguished from the executive director's management role. As the chief manager, the executive director is responsible for implementing board policies to carry out the primary mission of the organization. In a smoothly functioning organization these roles are complementary. The board and the executive director each conveys mutual respect for the other and supports their organizational partner without intruding on the role of the other. The executive director may, for example, assist the board chair in developing a board agenda, but the chair, not the executive director, ultimately determines board agenda and activities. Similarly, the executive director would not ask the board for management guidance or use board meetings to review detailed managerial reports, although individual board members might be consulted for advice because of their managerial experience.

In making this distinction between governance and management, some have argued that the lines should be rigidly drawn. Under this framework, the board focuses strictly on ends and develops only policies that limit or prohibit certain executive actions. These proscriptive polices convey to the CEO that the board considers certain managerial activities and decisions unacceptable, and the executive director is prohibited from doing them. Examples include prohibitions against overspending on budgeted items, spending on unbudgeted items, hiring unqualified staff, and using funds for personal benefit. These policies, called *executive limitations,* convey that as long as a particular means is *not* prohibited, management has wide latitude to implement board policies in whatever way is deemed necessary. The board establishes the boundaries of acceptability on operations instead of prescribing how operations are to be carried out.[4] By limiting the executive director in specific areas, the board also frees the director to do anything that is not unacceptable that could achieve the results determined by the board.[5]

Although it is important that the board and executive director observe their distinctive roles, this should not be done as if there were a wall between them; an effective working relationship requires that the two dynamically interact. At times, the executive director facilitates the chair's role by proposing policies for board consideration, by anticipating future directions that require board decision making, and by supporting the board's fundraising responsibilities. The conventional formulation (i.e., the board enacts policy, and the executive director and staff carry it out) is replaced by a dynamic partnership requiring flexible interactions between board and executive— and even between board and staff. At times, too, trustees become engaged in operations because it makes sense to do so.[6] For example, if an organization plans to make an addition to its nursing home facility, board members may become involved in selecting architectural plans and working out loan arrangements because they have the expertise in these areas.

In organizations where the staff is small, board members sometimes pitch in by volunteering for assignments, such as mentoring or writing newsletter articles. In their volunteer role of helping the staff complete the organization's mission, however, board members are clear that they are not functioning in their board role.[7]

Just as the relationship between the executive director and the board is becoming more flexible, so too the conventional approach of keeping staff at a distance from the board is changing. For example, staff members responsible for fundraising may work closely with the board's development committee. Finance staff must work with the board's treasurer, and program staff need to be in close communication with the board's program committee. When the organization undertakes a strategic plan review, staff members provide a valuable perspective and are in a position to make significant contributions. Thus while the board maintains its principle focus on policy, staff input is essential in helping the board make good decisions.

In furthering a positive working relationship, both the executive director and the board always must structure meetings to avoid the board's dealing with low-level staff decisions. A board's contribution should be strategic—the talented product of high-achieving people who bring their collective knowledge to address the major challenges facing the organization's clients. In reality, board members often feel discouraged and underused. Board members lose their energy and commitment when they focus on such mundane management issues as selecting carpeting, buying equipment, choosing vendors, hiring direct service staff, and approving individual staff salaries.[8]

The primary criterion applied to board deliberations is whether or not it relates to board policy and strategy. By consistently placing before the board issues of true consequence and significance, the chief executive prevents micromanagement. Boards that focus on management details usually do so because the chief executive fails to work with the board president to focus on policy and strategy and to equip members with the knowledge and ability to monitor organizational performance and progress. To avoid a natural drifting toward dealing with day-to-day operations, board members might periodically be asked to deal with this question: "What policy issue is our discussion attempting to address?"[9]

Facilitating the Board's Governance Role

To help the board fulfill its governance role, the organization's executive director should conscientiously observe the following actions and behavior:[10]

1. Maintain continuous communication with the board chair to clarify roles and discuss joint or separate responsibilities. Clarifying the respective roles up front prevents later misunderstandings.[11] Continuous and informal meetings are essential for ensuring viable organizational leadership.[12]

2. Prevent staff, including the chief executive, from dominating discussions at board meetings.[13]

3. Work with the board chair to make certain that the board committees and task groups relate their agendas to the organization's strategic plan and that they develop clear objectives for the coming year. Also, facilitate committee functioning by providing staff support (where feasible) to assist with preparing meeting notices, drafting agendas, taking minutes, and writing reports.

4. Work with the board chair to focus on substantive, policy-related issues by seeing that necessary materials are sent out before the meeting, and work with the board chair to set the agenda. In some organizations, the executive director or another staff member (instead of the volunteer board secretary) prepares minutes of meetings.

5. Work with the board to hold an annual retreat involving the management team and the board. Use this opportunity to review the strategic plan, discuss major initiatives, and articulate key issues. Apprise the board of changes in the environment and of new opportunities or crises that require organizational response.

6. Encourage the board or its finance committee to provide strong fiscal stewardship. See that the chair of the finance committee, who is often the board treasurer, has all the necessary information to review and report the organization's finances status.

7. In concert with the chairperson, compile a list of board policies that have been enacted over the years so that all board members become

aware of board positions. Also, assist the board chair in setting up a proper orientation for new board members.

8. Keep a pool of potential candidates for the nominating (governance) committee (if requested).

9. Work with the board chair and resource development committee on such fundraising activities as identifying and meeting with potential contributors and authorizing preparation of proposals for funding.

10. Prepare reports for the board, including budget reports, program service data reports, newly released information on the community and unmet needs for services, and non-service activity reports (e.g., invited presentations, audits, and honors and recognition). The executive director should shape this information so that the board is properly informed and can make decisions that are relevant and timely.

Board Roles and Responsibilities _____

Determining the Organization's Mission and Goals

As part of their governance responsibilities, board members are the challengers, revisers, and champions of the organization's mission.[14] While the staff may have input in developing and implementing the mission, the board is ultimately responsible for it. In determining whether to implement new programs or discard current ones, the board's responsibility is to make certain that the primary mission is considered foremost. Periodically—at least every three years—the board should take time to review the mission statement to assess its continued relevancy, adequacy, and validity in relation to its service offerings.[15]

Understanding the Organization

Members of the board must become knowledgeable about the organization so that they can become effective decision makers, communicators, and fundraisers. Initially, they should receive a thorough board orientation and continue to become informed throughout their tenure. It is a good idea to provide new trustees a board manual that includes the organization's mission, history, programs and services, finances and audit, guiding values, bylaws, committee structure, and current board and financial management policies. In addition, each member should receive a trustee job description.

Being Responsive to Stakeholders

The obligation of the board is ensuring that an organization's resources and capacities are deployed in ways that are responsive to its various stakeholders. In the human services field, stakeholders include clients, individual contributors, foundations staff, government officials, and even the community at large or segments of the community—all those that the organization is intended to benefit and whose interests the board must represent.

For these stakeholders the board must be able to answer the following questions:[16] (1) How is each stakeholder group dependent on the organization and how is the organization's success dependent on various stakeholders? (2) What does each stakeholder group expect the organization to accomplish on its behalf? (3) From each stakeholder's perspective, how is the organization's success defined? (4) What specific steps must the organization take to sustain stakeholder interest?

In some instances, the board may have to reconcile different stakeholders' interests and make priority decisions. For example, if the governor and state assembly reduce state substance abuse funding, thereby affecting services to clients, the organization's board has to determine whether it must cut services in response to the public stakeholder's will (or lack thereof), or generate new funding in response to local stakeholders' commitment.

Selecting, Supporting and Evaluating the Executive Director

Selecting an executive director is undoubtedly one of the most important functions of a board. Because conducting a good search process may take several months, the board may designate a search committee to identify and consider candidates, but the final choice rests with the board as a whole. As part of this process, the board would prepare a comprehensive job description, including clarity about the distinctive roles between the professional head and the volunteer chair. Sometimes a board and executive director sign an employment contract that articulates the board's expectations of the director and states clearly that the executive director has exclusive responsibility to select and supervise a management team and staff without board interference.[17]

Either the board as a whole or a designated committee is responsible for providing frequent and constructive feedback to the executive director. Both the board and executive director should agree on the process under which an evaluation occurs. Properly done, the performance evaluation should be equally beneficial to the executive director and the board. It should be an opportunity for constructive criticism and for praise for exceptional initiatives and performance. Board and executive director should understand that the organization's effectiveness depends on their mutual efforts. The appraisal process should provide an opportunity for the executive director to indicate how the board can be more useful in accomplishing the organization's mission.[18]

Performance evaluation should be based on a mutually agreed upon job description and on objectives that the executive director is responsible for achieving. A useful approach is that at the beginning of each fiscal year the executive director identifies program and administrative objectives for approval by the board. At the end of the fiscal year, the executive director documents the extent to which each of these objectives has or has not been achieved. For example, the executive director might include the following objectives: (1) update the computer system by establishing an office network, (2) develop a new agency brochure, (3) obtain two foundation grants of $30,000 each, and (4) increase the annual membership by 10%. Objectives can be specific to the executive director's performance (e.g., securing new grants or contracts or upgrading staff professionalism) or relate to the agency's overall achievement (e.g., serving a targeted number of clients).

The extent to which these objectives are achieved—fully, partially, or not at all—would be reported to the board with an explanation as part of the executive director's assessment. The board would provide explicit feedback, either concurring with or challenging the executive director's assertions, and work with the executive director to develop actions plans to continually improve performance.[19] (See Figure 20.1, Agency Executive Director Performance Review, at the end of this chapter.[20])

Some boards tend not to conduct an annual evaluation, either because members are reluctant to be put in a position of criticizing a well-regarded executive director, or because conducting an evaluation takes more time than board members want to commit. Effective executive directors understand the value and benefits of a regular performance review that sets specific perfor-mance objectives and measurable benchmarks, in the interest of personal and professional growth and to further the organization's mission.[21]

Providing Financial Oversight

The board treasurer or finance committee should carefully scrutinize financial statements and the organization's balance sheets. An accounting should be made of assets and liabilities each month, or quarterly if the budget is small. The board also monitors compliance with cash-management controls, ensures the purchase of adequate liability insurance (e.g., directors' and officers' liability insurance), develops policies around financial manage-ment, oversees investment activities, and watches that the organization makes timely reports required by federal, state, and local government agencies, including IRS form 990.[22] Although the responsibility for preparing and managing the organization's annual budget rests with the executive director, it is the board's responsibility, usually on the recommendation of its finance committee, to approve the budget.

In reviewing financial reports, a board may determine changes in policy, suggest new ways of presenting financial information, or request additional reports. Board policies should be developed for (1) how much money should be in reserves (e.g., a percentage of the operating budget), depreciation expenses (e.g., replacement of a roof), and reasonable costs per person served based on services received (e.g., group or individual counseling); (2) staff salary schedules and adjustments; (3) reasonable percent of variance between expense and revenues for each major budget item (see Chapter 12); and (4) approval procedures for expenditures over a certain amount or outside the approved budget.[23]

Some boards permit the executive director considerable discretion in spending money without board approval. Having provided general guidelines for the expenditure of funds and having approved a budget, these boards give the executive director autonomy in financial decision making. Other boards place constraints on the executive director by requiring that any expenditure over a certain amount (for example, $1,000) requires board approval through co-signature of the board chairperson or treasurer. Also, boards may require that no check be written unless monies are available from the appropriate fund for that specific expense. To reduce any appearance of impropriety, some boards request their finance committees be aware of all disbursements made directly to the executive director. Finally, the board must ensure that funds (specifically grant or designated funds) are spent in accordance with the approved budget of the funding body.

Assisting With Public Information

The board is responsible for building the organization's image in the community, for trustees promote and interpret the agency's mission and explain its functions both in informal conversations and formal presentations. Trustees are ambassadors in interpreting the mission of the institution, defending it when it is under pressure, and representing it to their and the agency's constituencies.[24] As advocates for the organization, trustees make presentations to United Way budget committees or give testimony at public hearings on behalf of the clients served by the agency.

Board members and executive staff play different roles in disseminating public information. Although on the one hand board members convey credibility as uncompensated representatives and spokespersons, on the other hand, the executive director is seen as the chief professional officer, is closest to the action, and is often better prepared to explain complex service and funding arrangements. Decisions as to who should speak for the organization should be made based on the issue and the audience. In formal presentations, board members and the executive director may jointly represent the organization.

Making Organizational
Plans and Evaluating Decisions

Board members must participate extensively in strategic planning so that they can feel ownership and commitment in helping the organization achieve its mission.[25] In regard to ongoing programs, their role in the planning process is to ask good questions, expect good answers, and serve as resources in their own individual areas of expertise. In making policy decisions, the trustees cannot be absorbed with details of operations; they should concentrate on reviewing agency results. To fulfill its stewardship responsibility, the board determines whether programs are departing from the organization's mission or whether the organization should be moving in new directions.[26]

In reviewing programs, the board can responsibly inquire into the following:

1. How do the costs of the program compare with its benefits?

2. Which programs are so central that they must be retained, and which are peripheral to accomplishing the organization's mission?[27]

3. How can the organization reach more clients?

4. Are the programs adequately staffed?

5. Can the quality of the programs be improved?

6. What kind of resources are necessary to sustain current programs or mount new ones?

7. Are performance targets being achieved, and if not, why not?

8. Are finance targets being met, and if not, what plan does management have to deal with the discrepancies?[28]

9. Should programs identified by certain stakeholders be explored as possible additions to, or replacements for, existing programs?

Policies involve three aspects where the management staff and the board intersect. First, formulating the policy can involve a series of suggestions or recommendations and can be initiated either by the staff or the board. Second, policy determination usually resides with the board. Although staff may have input into board deliberations, the board, not staff, ultimately determines policies. As part of policy determination, the board would set standards against which progress would be measured. Third, policy implementation typically is a responsibility of staff, though not always so. When an organization lacks adequate staff, it may rely on trustees to carry out certain activities. It is typically useful for the board, working with the executive, to make clear who is responsible for implementing the decision within a given time frame.[29] In its stewardship role, the board can request that corrective actions be taken when program objectives are not being achieved as planned.

Developing Personnel Policies

It is the responsibility of the executive director and senior management to hire, supervise, evaluate, make compensation decisions within the parameters set by the board, and (if necessary) terminate employees. The board is responsible for approving such personnel policies as wage scale ranges, health and retirement benefits, vacations, paid leave (holidays and personal time), and sick leave. The board also makes sure that a staff grievance procedure is in place. Although many boards purposefully avoid becoming entangled in specific issues involving personnel, on rare occasions a personnel committee of the board may provide a grievance process for an employee who has an unresolved dispute with the executive director and who seeks relief from some higher authority. Personnel practices should spell out this possibility.[30]

Although the executive director has responsibility for hiring staff, it may be necessary to consult with the board before hiring those staff that may have direct working involvement with the board. For example, the hiring of a development director or a chief financial officer might benefit from board committee consultation. Sometimes a board member would seek out the executive with a suggestion for hiring a friend or relative. Such efforts, if intended to put pressure on the executive director, should be discouraged by the chair of the board.

Conducting Fundraising

Whether the board or the staff takes primary responsibility for fundraising depends in large part on the nature of funding. If most of an organization's financial support is derived from foundation grants or state or federal subsidies, management staff are likely to have primary responsibility. Under these circumstances, the board serves in a supportive or oversight role.

If, however, the organization relies on community support through annual campaigns, United Way funding, regular donor appeals, or endowment funding, then the board of trustees must provide leadership and carry most of the load, with staff serving in a supportive role. This active approach is needed because effective fundraising is usually best implemented through trustees' communicating with their peers. If occasionally the organization must seek community support to supplement public or foundation grants, then board members are needed to raise funds or to have linkages to those who can provide funding. Even if most of the organization's support is raised through public funding, foundation grants, or United Way, these funding entities want assurances that the organization has a board of trustees that is well regarded and that shows evidence of genuine commitment to the organization through participating in agency fund drives.[31] Each board member should also contribute annually, according to each individual's means, and attend fundraising events, because funders expect the board to financially support the organization.

Ensuring Proper Legal and Financial Obligations

Under certain circumstances, and depending on the particular laws of the state, trustees can be held legally accountable for actions of their nonprofit organization. Organizations are vulnerable to being sued regarding the following issues: (1) employment claims around hiring, firing, and discrimination; (2) contract claims related to work specifications and payment; (3) negligence; (4) unauthorized release of records; and (5) defamation. Generally, the organizations themselves are defendants in lawsuits; seldom are charges made against individuals, but this can occur. For example, if trustees expend funds in excess of expected income and without proper cost controls, they could be sued.[32] If a board has not adequately carried out its oversight duties, it may be implicated in a lawsuit due to negligence of its duty of care. The reason boards incorporate is that this provides limited liability protection for board members and managers. In general, however, board members are *indemnified* (protected) by the organization against judgments incurred while they are carrying out the service of the organization. It is rare that a judgment is rendered against a trustee, but insurance is necessary to defray the expense of defending lawsuits.[33] Since indemnification is as good as the organization's capacity to pay, most organizations purchase insurance, called *directors' and officers' insurance,* to cover their defense.[34]

Because the integrity of the board is so important, board members must continually watch that behavior is of the highest ethical standards and that conflicts of interest do not creep into their decision making. The term *conflict of interest* refers to any situation in which a board member (or staff) is influenced in an organizational decision by personal or financial concerns unrelated to the organization's best interests.[35] A related term, *private inurement,* is used to indicate that a board member (or staff) may benefit financially from the organization. If the IRS audits the organization and it finds an appreciable amount of private inurement, it can revoke the organization's tax-exempt status.[36] Boards should prepare a written policy that deals with actual and perceived conflict of interest.[37]

Buying office supplies from a board member's company may not necessarily be considered improper if the price is as low as or lower than the competition, if the board member abstains from discussing and voting on the issue, and if the transaction is transparent to the entire board.[38] Transactions involving board members are allowable if the organization does not pay more than the service or product is worth. However, some boards may determine that under no circumstances should board members conduct business with the agency. The presumption is that the media or the general public might misconstrue their involvement and that if something should go awry, then this could result in embarrassment and awkwardness. All boards should develop a conflict of interest policy that provides for *transparency,* that is, revealing business and other affiliations that are related to potential transactions. The board would carefully scrutinize to determine that the transactions are in the best interest of the organization and document their decisions.[39]

Board Structures and Processes

To carry out the board's many functions it typically organizes into committees. Standing committees are usually established through the organization's bylaws and are ongoing units established year after year to carry out major board functions. These committees may tend to continue because of tradition rather than because they perform a useful function. It is a good idea to periodically review whether a standing committee should continue to exist, and whether time-limited (ad hoc) task forces with clearly defined responsibilities could do the work better.

Government agencies sometimes establish advisory committees to provide oversight and recommendations for public service departments. Nonprofit boards also establish advisory committees that can be a sounding board for the board or management, serve as an advocate in the community, recommend strategic directions, and assist in fundraising. These advisory groups can help the organization bring in expertise that might not otherwise be available to the board. For example, a small group of financial experts could advise the board on its investment policies. Or corporate managers might meet periodically to discuss strategic directions.[40]

While each organization forms its committee structure based on its own unique functions, the following are fairly common:[41]

An *executive committee* may be necessary if a board consists of more than 20 members; a board of less than 10 or 12 does not need one. The executive committee must be careful not to usurp board decision making, resulting in board involvement withering away.[42] To avoid delegating essential powers away from the full board, the executive committee should not make final decisions regarding hiring or firing the chief executive, changing the budget, or adding or eliminating programs.[43] It can be designated to act for the full board in emergencies and work with the chief executive to formulate annual personnel performance expectations.

The *finance committee* ensures that accurate financial records are maintained, oversees budget and financial planning, analyzes management financial proposals and makes recommendations to the board, recommends quantitative measures to be employed by the board in assessing the financial health of the organization, reviews the audit and auditor's management letter, and makes recommendations on changes in financial procedures.

The *resource development committee* develops the financial resources of the organization. It can give strategic directions to annual campaigns, capital campaigns, fundraising events, and soliciting government and foundation grants—or it can take on these efforts itself.

The *human resources committee,* sometimes referred to as the personnel committee, develops the personnel policies, reviews and recommends salary scale adjustments and employee benefits, and promotes staff development and training.

The *public information committee* promotes the agency through oversight of annual reports, newsletters, and other public information. It may also organize speakers for public functions and develop relationships with public officials at the local and state level.

The *governance committee* (also known as committee on trustees or nominating committee) defines board membership needs and membership responsibilities (attendance, contributions, and committee participation), recommends members and officers for election, identifies and cultivates nominees, oversees the orientation program, and designs board self-assessment.[44]

The *program committee* works with management to develop an annual analysis of consumer needs for board review. It recommends quantitative measures to be employed by the board in assessing program impact on clients. It also makes recommendations to the board about whether to add new programs or discontinue existing ones.

To guide committee deliberations, the board chair (in consultation with the executive director and each committee chair) should formulate a charge that states committee assignments for the year. For example, the governance committee might be charged with cultivating fifteen people from whom five would be ultimately selected to serve on the board. The finance committee might be charged with responding to concerns raised in the previous year's management letter regarding how cash is received and handled. Each committee would establish its annual work plan with a timetable that the board agrees upon.[45]

Board committees could function with or without staff support. If the chair of the board and the executive director determine that staff support is needed and could be made available, the following functions would be appropriate: (1) Give advice and information based on expertise, but do not participate as committee members and do not influence the discussion. (2) Work with the committee chair to formulate committee goals and objectives. (3) Serve as a liaison to other parts of the organization, especially staff units. (4) Assist the committee chair in constructing an agenda that provides ample opportunity for committee discussion and decision making. (5) Take minutes of the meeting if volunteers are unable to do so. (6) Work with the committee chair to prepare committee reports.

In summary, the staff liaisons work closely with the committee chair to ensure that the committee understands its functions, has the right information with which to make its decisions, and has a process that fosters full participation.

Addressing Special Board Issues

Dealing With Inactive Board Members

Trustees sometimes become inactive because they either have demands on their time that prevent them from engaging in board activities or they lose interest in the organization. To encourage continuous commitment, boards can ask their members to annually sign an affirmation statement that expresses their intention to attend a minimum number of meetings each year and participate on board committees. Some boards have an attendance rule that automatically terminates persons who miss two or three board meetings. For those who have a history of contributing financially or otherwise, but who no longer wish to regularly attend meetings, the board could create an honorary alumni group.[46] The best approach is for the board chairperson or chair of the governance committee to personally call those whose attendance has been poor to determine whether they wish to continue on the board.

Improving Board Meetings

The worst form of board meeting is the one where the executive director drones on about the work of the organization in the preceding month and members are passive listeners. They wonder what value they are adding as board members. The best board meetings are ones in which members interact—where they discuss, deliberate, clarify assumptions, and consider alternative new directions. Such meetings are stimulating, and members feel that they are contributing to the organization. The primary focus of board meetings is to make policy-level decisions that assist the organization in achieving its mission, and all board discussions and decisions should be directed to this purpose.

To make more effective use of meeting time, some boards devote a part of their meeting to a *consent agenda,* which is a collection of items that need board action but limited, if any, board discussion. Approval of the minutes and routine reports can be given with minimal debate. Any member may request that an item be removed from the consent agenda if a separate discussion seems warranted.[47] By sending out materials in advance of the meeting, less time is spent on hearing reports and more time can be devoted to discussion and decision making. Items on the agenda are identified on the basis of the following categories:[48]

1. Executive director and committee reports. (Questions may be asked, but discussion is kept to a minimum.)

2. Discussion of issues that are in progress but no action is to be taken.

3. Action items that require discussion, deliberation, and a vote.

This approach of delineating agenda items expedites processing committee reports and non-controversial issues, leaving more time to devote to major policy issues.[49] Also, it is helpful to allocate specific time to each item so that board members are aware of the time constraints under which they must function. Of course, the board may decide to alter the anticipated time devoted to agenda items if members wish to do so. If the board is to be an optimum-performing governing unit, it must be a body that deliberates.

The frequency of board meetings depends on several factors, including how far people have to travel and what functions need to be carried out. Some boards are opting for meeting bimonthly or even quarterly so that members have more time to work on committees. Other boards may be required by public regulations to meet monthly. Through e-mail, Web site access, and written reports, members are kept up to date. If board members live in the same community, board meetings can be held monthly, with time off during vacation periods. Considerable time is devoted to preparing proposals for action that are submitted in advance of the meeting. The meeting agenda should be developed by the board's chair with input from the executive director, though any board member should be able to recommend topics.[50]

Board meetings can be an opportunity for board member learning and development. Board members could be provided with information on specific programs by introducing them, for example, to a service consumer or a member of the community who has been impacted by the organization.

Some boards have found it useful to monitor a *vital signs report* at each meeting. Through graphs and tables, the board can quickly discern trends by comparing this month's data with the previous month's (or quarter's or year's) report on such categories as donations received, rates of consumer participation, and key expense items.[51] Some organizations also have adopted a reporting procedure in which at each board meeting staff present a brief write-up about a typical and an unusual case. Moreover, some board meetings are devoted to having members learn directly from clients or community representatives how much they have benefited from the organization's services. In these *mission interaction sessions*, board members can become energized knowing that what they are working on truly makes an impact on the lives of those the organization serves. [52]

Board Size

The number of trustees on a board varies from as few as 5 to as many as 80 or more. In general, it is a good idea for board size to range from 9 to 19 members, small enough to function as a cohesive, focused, and deliberative body, and large enough to disperse assignments. Although large boards have the advantage of assisting in fundraising, reflecting community participation, and sharing a burdensome workload, large boards have a number of disadvantages. They are a more cumbersome decision-making body than smaller ones, they tend to create powerful executive committees where the major work of the organization is done, and they reduce involvement and commitment of individual members.[53] Smaller boards invite good participation and engender a sense of genuine ownership by individual members.[54]

Board Tenure

Some boards are in a quandary regarding the length of time a trustee may serve. A few human service boards of trustees permit their members to stay on indefinitely. These are usually highly dedicated people who feel strongly about the organization and are willing to devote a significant portion of their time and money to it. A more typical pattern is for organizations to provide for term limits with an initial term of either two or three years, followed by a second, equal term. The member is required to discontinue for a minimum of one year following the second term before being re-nominated.[55] This approach allows a board to rejuvenate—to painlessly move people off the board who are not contributing and to bring new members with fresh ideas.[56]

Board Self-Assessment

Board members infrequently conduct their own self-review, but they should do so because self-assessment can help them meet the obligation to be the best they can be to fulfill the organization's mission. By better understanding their strengths and limitations, members can take self-corrective action to improve the functioning of their boards. Self-assessments need not be carried out annually, nor do they necessarily require outside evaluation.[57]

To ensure that the governance structure is effective, the board should address issues related to its ability to achieve the organization's mission, strategic planning, and committee task functioning.[58] The governance committee, working with the board chair, could construct a questionnaire that invites confidential or anonymous responses from board members, requesting that they identify issues and consider where improvements need to be made. (See Figure 20.2, Board Self-Assessment, at the end of this chapter.[59]) It is sometimes instructive to have management and board members each complete the survey so that the responses can be compared and contrasted.

Summary: Elements of a Well-Functioning Board

The following can serve as a checklist for whether a board is functioning properly:[60]

- Are board members recruited on the basis of their (a) commitment to the organization; (b) ability to meet organizational requirements, including board and committee meeting times; (c) likeliness to add representative diversity and balance; (d) experience and expertise and (e) ability to aid in the organization's resource development?[61]

- In the orientation of new board members, is supporting information (e.g., a board manual) provided? Does this information contain the history of the organization, mission, guiding values, evaluation procedures of the executive, description of current programs, fiscal data, bylaws, committee assignments, trustee job descriptions, and major board policies?[62]
- Are the expectations of being a trustee, including a job description, conveyed?
- Does the governance committee work throughout the year to identify and cultivate candidates for consideration?
- Are board meetings well organized and focused on priority issues? Are routine matters handled quickly and is major emphasis given to strategic issues and trends?
- Does the chair (assisted by the executive) develop annual plans with specific objectives for the board?
- Does the board monitor agency progress in relation to goals and objectives?
- Does the board receive periodic reports about agency progress (and sufficient data) prior to meetings?
- Are minutes of meetings concise and distributed following each meeting?
- Does the board have active committees for which responsibilities are clearly articulated and that develop an annual work plan based on strategic planning with specific assignments and a timetable?
- Does the board evaluate its own procedures, attendance, and participation?
- Do trustees recognize that they are expected annually to provide a financial gift to the best of their personal ability and to participate in fundraising activities?
- Does the board receive periodic financial reports that indicate whether the agency is meeting its budgetary targets? Does the board formally approve an annual operating budget and monitor the organization's ability to adhere to this budget?
- Does the board undergo a periodic review of its governance structure and roles?
- Do board members ask good, timely questions at board meetings?
- Does the board set aside time to learn about important matters of substance related to the organization's mission?[63]

Pursuing answers to these questions can result in an empowered board, which in turn ensures a viable organization.

Figure 20.1

Agency Executive Director Performance Review

After each item, provide a rating of High (H), Medium (M), Low (L), Not Applicable (NA), or Not Sure (NS). Modify this document based on mutually agreed criteria established between the executive director and the board. Use the results as a basis for dialogue.

The Agency Executive Director:

1. Works with the board to fulfill the agency's mission and goals. ____

2. Works with the board to develop and update strategic plans. ____

3. Works to achieve the organization's annual objectives. ____

4. Maintains a working relationship with the board that reflects open communication, respect, and trust. ____

5. Develops a positive atmosphere that reflects the agency's values ____

6. Ensures that appropriate systems are in place to facilitate day-to-day operations for programs, fiscal operations, and fundraising. ____

7. Works with the board to set high standards of program quality. ____

8. Prepares reports that help the board monitor programs. ____

9. Recommends new programs and the modification or termination of existing programs, as appropriate, to the board. ____

10. Works with the board to implement a fundraising strategy in line with agency goals. ____

11. Provides leadership for revenue-generating efforts. ____

12. Is knowledgeable about financial planning and budgeting. ____

13. Submits an annual budget for the board's possible revision and approval. ____

14. Oversees a clear and accurate accounting system so the board can monitor the agency's finances in relation to the approved budget. ____

15. Ensures that the agency has adequate insurance coverage. ____

16. Ensures compliance with all legal and regulatory requirements. ____

17. Ensures compliance with funder (public and private) requirements. ____

18. Actively engages in the annual performance review. ____

19. Arranges, where appropriate, for relevant staff to relate to board committees in their areas of mutual responsibilities (e.g., finance, program, fundraising). ____

20. Is an articulate and knowledgeable spokesperson for the organization. ____

Figure 20.2

Board Self-Assessment

After each item indicate a rating of High (H), Medium (M), Low (L), Not Applicable (NA), or Not Sure (NS.) Modify this Self-Assessment to fit the circumstances of your agency, and use the results as the basis of board discussion.

1. Board members understand and support the mission statement.   ____

2. The board's policy decisions appropriately reflect the agency's mission.   ____

3. The board gives concentrated attention to long-term, major policies.   ____

4. The board has developed a strategic vision of how the organization should be developing over the next two to five years.   ____

5. Periodically the board reviews the strategic plan and considers how the agency should meet new opportunities and challenges.   ____

6. The agency has a written job description of members' roles and responsibilities.   ____

7. The roles and responsibilities are clear between the board and executive director.   ____

8. The board regularly assesses the executive director's performance.   ____

9. The board is knowledgeable about the agency's programs and monitors program objectives.   ____

10. The board periodically considers adopting new programs and changing or terminating current programs.   ____

11. The board has developed a fundraising strategy for the agency.   ____

12. Board members carry out board policy to actively assist in providing and developing fundraising support.   ____

13. The board carefully reviews the annual operating budget before approving it.   ____

14. The board regularly receives accurate financial reports so that it can ensure that the agency meets its budgetary targets.   ____

15. The board contains a range of expertise, diversity, experience, and consumer advocacy to make it an effective governing body.   ____

16. The board identifies and cultivates candidates throughout the year who could strengthen the board's composition.   ____

17. The board orientation for new members includes their
    responsibilities, agency information, and a review of
    previous board policies.   ___

18. Prior to meetings, board members receive an agenda, minutes of
    the previous meeting, and relevant materials.   ___

19. Board members participate actively on board committees and
    task forces.   ___

20. Board meetings are well organized, make good use of board
    members' time, and are productive.   ___

21. Each board committee has a statement of purpose (charge),
    is clear about its objectives, and periodically makes
    recommendations for board approval.   ___

22. The agency has adequate directors' and officers' insurance and
    general liability insurance.   ___

23. Board members advocate for the agency's services and are
    ambassadors to the community on behalf of the agency.   ___

24. Board members avoid conflicts of interest.   ___

25. The board regularly assesses its own performance.   ___

General comments about what more the board can do to help the agency achieve its
mission:

_____

_____

_____

Questions for Discussion

1. What are the areas covered in the board orientation for new board
   members?

2. Does your board have a compendium of policies? What are some
   examples of board policies?

3. After attending a meeting of your organization's board or some other
   board:
   a. How would you assess the performance of the board?
   b. Does the board have procedures for ensuring turnover and renewal?

     c. Do board discussions keep the mission in the forefront?

     d. Does the size of the board seem appropriate?

     e. Do board members appear to be actively engaged in meetings and committees?

     f. Do board members receive the agenda and adequate information prior to the meeting?

     g. Is the board discussion focused, with minimal diversionary comments?

4. Is the board provided with indicators of organizational performance?

5. Does the board have a policy defining under which circumstances a board member may or may not do business with the organization (conflict of interest policy)?

6. Does the board of your organization focus on its governing role and not engage in micromanaging operational issues?

7. How does your board appear to avoid problems of either micromanagement or detachment?

8. Does the size and structure of the board and committees contribute to effective governance?

Notes

1. M. Gibelman, S. R. Gelman, & D. Pollack, The credibility of nonprofit boards: A view from the 1990s and beyond, *Administration in Social Work* 21, 2 (1997), pp. 21–40.

2. D. D. Pointer & J. E. Orlikoff, *The high performance board* (San Francisco: Jossey-Bass, 2002), p. 5.

3. J. A. Yankey & A. McClellan, *The nonprofit board's role in planning and evaluation* (Washington, DC: Boardsource, 2003), p. 38.

4. J. Carver, *On board leadership* (San Francisco: Jossey-Bass, 2002), p. 592.

5. J. Carver, pp. 586–587.

6. D. C. Eadie, *Extraordinary board leadership: The seven keys to high impact governance* (Gaithersburg, MD: Aspen, 2001), p. 30; B. E. Taylor, R. P. Chait, & T. P. Holland, The new work of the nonprofit board, *Harvard Business Review* 74 (September/October 1996), p. 42.

7. R. C. Andringa & T. W. Engstrom, *Nonprofit board answer book* (Washington, D C: Boardsource, 2002), p. 10.

8. K. S. Grace, *The nonprofit board's role in setting and advancing the mission* (Washington, DC: Boardsource, 2003), pp. 38–39.

9. R. P. Chait, *How to help your board govern more and manage less* (Washington, DC: Boardsource, 2003), p. 11.

10. B. E. Taylor et al., pp. 36–46; D. C. Eadie, pp. 30, 72–95; R. D. Herman & R. D. Heimovics, The effective nonprofit executive: Leader of the board, *Nonprofit Management & Leadership* 1, 2 (Winter 1990), pp. 167–180; R. L. Gale, *Leadership roles in nonprofit governance* (Washington, DC: Boardsource, 2003), pp. 11–17.

11. J. E. Tropman & E. J. Tropman, *Nonprofit boards: What to do and how to do it* (Washington, DC: CWLA Press, 1999), p. 130.

12. R. L. Gale, *Leadership roles in nonprofit governance* (Washington, DC: Boardsource, 2003), p. 11.

13. R. P. Chait, pp. 6–7; B. M. Lakey, *Nonprofit governance: Steering your organization with authority and accountability* (Washington, DC: National Center for Nonprofit Boards, 2000), p. 29.

14. K. S. Grace, p. 1.

15. R. T. Ingram, *Ten basic responsibilities of nonprofit boards* [booklet] (Washington, DC: National Center for Nonprofit Boards, 1995), pp. 1–7.

16. D. D. Pointer & J. E. Orlikoff, pp. 9–15.

17. R. T. Ingram, pp. 1–7.

18. R. T. Ingram, pp. 1–7; A. Swanson, Who's in charge here? *Nonprofit World* 4, 4 (July/August 1986), p. 18.

19. D. D. Pointer & J. E. Orlikoff, pp. 34–37; D. Eadie, *Extraordinary board leadership: The 7 keys to high-impact governance* (New York: Aspen, 2001) in *Nonprofit organization management* (New York: Aspen, 2002), p. 7:19.

20. Adapted from J. Pierson & J. Mintz, *Assessment of the chief executive* (Washington, DC: National Center for Nonprofit Boards, 1999).

21. S. Frey, What's love got to do with it? *Grassroots Fundraising Journal* 4 (2001), pp. 4–7.

22. R. T. Ingram, pp. 4–5.

23. R. C. Andringa & T. D. Engstrom, p. 241.

24. P. F. Drucker, *Managing the nonprofit organization* (New York: HarperCollins, 1990); A. Swanson, p. 16; R. T. Ingram, p. 15.

25. R. T. Ingram, p. 10.

26. R. T. Ingram, p. 9.

27. R. T. Ingram, p. 1.

28. D. D. Pointer & J. E. Orlikoff, pp. 69–73; J. M. Greenfield, *Fundraising responsibilities of nonprofit boards* (Washington, DC: Boardsource, 2003), pp. 1–4.

29. A. Swanson, pp. 16–18.

30. R. T. Ingram, p. 8.

31. A. Swanson, pp. 15–16.

32. T. A. Croxton, Liability & risk management, in *Nonprofit boards,* eds. J. E. Tropman & E. J. Tropman (Washington, DC: CWLA Press, 1999), pp. 225–233.

33. W. R. Joseph, Trustee liability: A practical view, *Weston Hurd Fallon Paisley & Howley LLP,* (1998), pp. 1–4.

34. B. R. Hopkins, *Legal responsibilities of nonprofit boards* (Washington, DC: Boardsource, 2003), pp. 12–15.

35. D. L. Kurtz, *Managing conflicts of interest* (Washington, DC: National Center for Nonprofit Boards, 2001), p. 5.

36. A. S. Lang, *Financial responsibilities of nonprofit boards* (Washington, DC: Boardsource, 2002), pp. 22, 33.

37. R. C. Andringa & T. W. Engstrom, pp. 272–273; A. S. Lang, p. 7.

38. A. S. Lang, p. 33.

39. D. L. Kurtz, p. 21.

40. R. C. Andringa & T. W. Engstrom, pp. 265–268; K. Klein, *Fundraising for social change,* 4th ed. (Oakland, CA: Chardon, 2001), pp. 49–50; C. F. Dambach, *Structures and practices of nonprofit boards* (Washington, DC: Boardsource, 2003), p. 19.

41. J. E. Tropman & E. J. Tropman, pp. 96–99.

42. J. Carver, pp. 135–155; R. C. Andringa & T. W. Engstrom, pp. 50–51, 58; J. E. Tropman & E. J. Tropman, p. 96.

43. M. J. Bobowick, S. R. Hughes, & B. M. Lakey, *Transforming board structure* (Washington, DC: National Center for Nonprofit Boards, 2001), p. 14.

44. R. T. Ingram, p. 13; C. F. Dambach, p. 14.

45. D. D. Pointer & J. E. Orlikoff, p. 43.

46. R. C. Andringa & T. D. Engstrom, pp. 134–137; K. Klein, p. 39.

47. B. M. Lakey, p. 32.

48. D. D. Pointer & J. E. Orlikoff, pp. 127–133.

49. C. F. Dambach, pp. 7, 19; M. J. Bobowick, S. R. Hughes, & B. M. Lakey, p. 5.

50. R. L. Gale, pp. 2, 5.

51. C. F. Dambach, p. 26.

52. K. S. Grace, pp. 19–23.

53. D. D. Pointer & J. E. Orlikoff, p. 85.

54. C. F. Dambach, p. 18.

55. R. C. Andringa & T. W. Engstrom, p. 135.

56. C. F. Dambach, p. 16.

57. C. F. Dambach, pp. 31–32.

58. D. D. Pointer & J. E. Orlikoff, pp. 93–96.

59. Adapted from L. Slesinger, *Self assessment for nonprofit governing boards* (Washington, DC: National Center for Nonprofit Boards, 1991). pp. 21–23.

60. S. P. Joyaux, *Strategic fund development* (Gaithersburg, MD: Aspen, 1997), pp. 85–89.

61. D. D. Pointer & J. E. Orlikoff, pp. 199–202; R. C. Andringa & T. D. Engstrom, pp. 103–107; D. Eadie, p. 54; C. F. Dambach, p. 5.

62. K. S. Grace, pp. 38–39.

63. R. P. Chait, p. 15.

Web Sites for Human Service Managers

Advocacy and Analysis Organizations:

Children's Defense Fund: www.childrensdefense.org
The Center on Budget and Policy Priorities: www.cbpp.org
National Association of Social Workers: www.socialworkers.org

Board of Trustees

BoardSource: www.boardsource.org
Internet Nonprofit Center: www.nonprofit-info.org/npofaq
CompassPoint Nonprofit Services: www.compasspoint.org

Business Venture Resources

National Community Capital Association: www.communitycapital.org
Community Wealth Ventures: www.communitywealth.com
Social Entrepreneurs Alliance for Change (SEA): www.se-alliance.org
Tax on Unrelated Business Income: www.irs.ustreas.gov/pub/irs-pdf/
    p598.pdf
The Institute for Social Entrepreneurs: www.socialent.org

Companies That Provide Donors
With Contribution Options

4Charity.com: www.4charity.com
BuyDomains.com: www.allcharities.com
Independent Givers of America: www.givedirect.org
Working for Change: www.giveforchange.com

Companies That Customize Web sites for Organizations

www.givingcapital.com
www.contribute.com

Corporate Contributions

The Conference Board: www.conference-board.org
Edgar Online-People: http://people.edgar-online.com/people/
CEO Express: www.ceoexpress.com
The Foundation Center: www.fdncenter.org
The Foundation Center's Cooperating Collections: www.fdncenter.org/
   collections
Council on Foundations: www.cof.org
Grantsmanship Center: www.tgci.com

Fundraising Resources

Association of Fundraising Professionals (formerly The National Society
   of Fund Raising Executives): www.nsfre.org
Association of Fundraising Professionals: www.afpnet.org
Charity Channel: www.charitychannel.com
Chronicle of Philanthropy: http://philanthropy.com
Fund-Raising Resources on the Internet: www.agrm.org/dev-trak/links.
   html
Fund-Raising.com: www.fund-raising.com
Grantwriters.COM: www.grantwriters.com
GuideStar Donor's Guide of Nonprofit Organizations National Database:
   www.guidestar.com
Internet Nonprofit Center: www.nonprofits.org
Links to grant maker Web sites: www.fdncenter.org/funders
Locating foundations: www.inp.fdncenter.org/finder.html
National Committee on Planned Giving: www.ncpg.org
Nonprofit Resource Center: www.not-for-profit.org
Resource Development Network, Inc.: www.rdnonline.com
Requests for proposals: http://fdncenter.org/pnd/rfp//
Sharing ideas on grants: charitychannel.com
Tony Poderis Non-Profit Fund-Raising: www.raise-funds.com

Government Information

Administration for Children and Families: www.acf.dhhs.gov
Catalog of Federal Domestic Assistance: www.cfda.gov
Centers for Medicare and Medicaid Services: www.cms.gov

Council of State Governments: www.csg.org

Department of Education: www.ed.gov/legislation/Fedregister

Department of Health and Human Services–Administration for Children and Families: www.acf.hhs.gov

Department of Health and Human Services: www.os.dhhs.gov

Department of Housing and Urban Development:www.hud.gov

Department of Labor: www.dol.gov

Drug Enforcement Administration: www.usdoj.gov/dea

Equal Employment Opportunity Commission: http://www.eeoc.gov

Federal government grant opportunities: www.grants.gov

Federal Register Online via the Government Printing Office (GPO): www.gpoaccess.gov/index.html

General Accounting Office: www.gao.gov

Government Printing Office and Catalog of U.S. Government Publications: http://www.gpoaccess.gov/index.html

Health Administration: www.samhsa.gov

National Council on Disability: www.ncd.gov

National Criminal Justice Reference Service: www.ncjrs.org

National Governors Association: www.nga.org

National Institutes of Health: www.nih.gov

Office of National Aids Policy: www.whitehouse.gov/onap/aids.html

Social Security Administration: www.ssa.gov

U.S. Census Bureau: www.census.gov

U.S. Administration on Aging: www.aoa.gov

U.S. Center for Medicare and Medicaid Services: www.cms.gov

Management Information

Alliance for Nonprofit Management: www.genie.org

American Society of Association Executives (ASAE): www.asaenet.org

Internet Nonprofit Center: www.nonprofit-info.org/npofaq

Job Accommodation Network: http://janweb.icdi.wvu.edu

Management Support Organizations: www.idealist.org/support_states. html

Peter Drucker Foundation for Nonprofit Management: www.pfdf.org/

Professional Support Software: http://fundraiser-software.com

Small Employers and Reasonable Accommodation: http://www.eeoc.gov/facts/accomodation.html

Technical Assistance for Community Organizations (TACS): www.tacs.org

Managing Donor Data

www.officeupdate.com

www.organizenow.net

Nonprofit Resources

Chronicle of Philanthropy: www.philanthropy.com
E-mail distribution: www.egroups.com
Free Management Library: www.mapnp.org/library/mrktng.htm
Fund-Raising Resources on the Web: www.agrm.org/dev-trak/links.html
Independent Sector: www.indepsec.org
National Committee for Responsive Philanthropy: www.ncrp.org
Nonprofit Resource Center: www.not-for-profit.org
Philanthropy Journal On-line: www.philanthropy-journal.org
Society for Nonprofits: www.danenet.wicip.org/snpo/index.html
National Council of Nonprofit Associations: www.ncna.org
National Assembly (Health and Welfare): www.nassembly.org/html/search.html

Search Engines

Alta Vista: http://altavista.digital.com/
Dogpile: www.dogpile.com
Excite: www.excite.com
Google: www.google.com
HotBot: www.hotbot.com
InfoSeek: www.infoseek.com
Liszt Directory: www.liszt.com
Lycos: www.lycos.com
Magellan: www.mckinley.com
TILE.NET/Lists: http://tile.net/listserv/
Yahoo!: www.yahoo.com

Volunteer Opportunities

Action Without Borders: www.idealist.org
Corporation for National Service: www.cns.gov
ServeNet: www.servenet.org
Americorps: www.americorps.org

Bibliography

Albert, S. (1998). Eight steps to productive committees. *Nonprofit World, 4,* 25.

Alexander Hamilton Institute, Inc. (1991). *Conducting successful appraisal interviews.* Maywood, NJ: Author.

Alexander Hamilton Institute, Inc. (1991). *A manager's guide to creating a drug-and-alcohol-free workplace.* Maywood, NJ: Author.

Alexander Hamilton Institute, Inc. (1997). *Lawsuit-free documentation: A manager's guide to fair and legal recordkeeping.* Ramsey, NJ: Author.

Alexander Hamilton Institute, Inc. (1997). *Making teams succeed at work.* Ramsey, NJ: Author.

Alexander Hamilton Institute, Inc. (1997). *A manager's guide to avoiding termination lawsuits.* Ramsey, NJ: Author.

Alexander Hamilton Institute, Inc. (1997). *A manager's guide to productive meetings.* Ramsey, NJ: Author.

Alexander Hamilton Institute, Inc. (1997). *What every manager must know to prevent sexual harassment.* Ramsey, NJ: Author.

Alexander Hamilton Institute, Inc. (1997). *What every manager should know about the Americans with Disabilities Act.* Ramsey, NJ: Author.

Alexander Hamilton Institute, Inc. (1998). *Coaching & counseling: Managers' secrets for improving employee performance.* Ramsey, NJ: Author.

Alexander Hamilton Institute, Inc. (1998). *Conducting successful appraisal interviews: The right way to discuss employee performance.* Ramsey, NJ: Author.

Alexander Hamilton Institute, Inc. (1998). *A manager's guide to the do's and don'ts of discipline.* Ramsey, NJ: Author.

Alexander Hamilton Institute, Inc. (1999). *Interviewing made easy: The right way to ask hiring questions.* Ramsey, NJ: Author.

Alexander Hamilton Institute Inc. (1999). *A manager's guide to motivating without money.* Ramsey, NJ: Author.

Alexander Hamilton Institute, Inc. (2001). *A manager's guide to reviewing résumés and handling references.* Ramsey, NJ: Author.

Alexander Hamilton Institute, Inc. (2002) *A manager's guide to conducting fair and legal discipline interviews.* Ramsey, NJ: Author.

Alexander Hamilton Institute, Inc. (2002). *A manager's guide to preventing people problems.* Ramsey, NJ: Author.

Alliance for Nonprofit Management. (n.d.). How can we allocate indirect costs to programs. Retrieved May 6, 2003, from www.allianceonline.org/FAQ

Andreasen, A. R. (1996, November/December). Profits for nonprofits: Find a corporate partner. *Harvard Business Review, 74,* 47–59.

Andringa, R. C., & Engstrom, T. W. (2002). *Nonprofit board answer book.* Washington DC: Boardsource.

Andringa, R., Flynn, O., & Sabo, S. R. (2002). *Nonprofit board answer book II: Beyond the basics.* Washington DC: Boardsource.

Argyris, C. (1994, July/August). Good communication that blocks learning. *Harvard Business Review, 72,* 77–85.

Askenas, R. N., & Schaffer, R. H. (1982). Managers can avoid wasting time. *Harvard Business Review, 60,* 98–104.

Badaracco, J. L., Jr. (1998, March/April). The discipline of building character. *Harvard Business Review, 76,* 115–124.

Barrett, R. D., & Ware, M. E. (1997). *Planned giving essentials.* Gaithersberg, MD: Aspen.

Barrien, F. K. (1968). *General and social systems.* New Brunswick, NJ: Rutgers University Press.

Barry, B. W. (1986). *Strategic planning workbook for nonprofit organizations.* St. Paul, MN: Amherst H. Wilder Foundation.

Barton, G. M. (1990). Manage words effectively. *Personnel Journal, 1,* 32–33.

Beer, M., Eisenstat, R. A., & Spector, B. (1990). Why change programs don't produce change. *Harvard Business Review, 6,* 158–166.

Beer, M., Spector, B., Lawrence, P. R., Mills, D. Q., & Walton, R. E. (1984). *Managing human assets.* New York: Free Press.

Bennett, J. E. (1991-1992, Winter). Reflections on successful CEOs: The match is everything. *Cleveland Enterprise,* 18–20.

Bennis,W. (1989). *On becoming a leader.* Wilmington, MA: Addison-Wesley.

Berry, J. M. (2003, November 27). Nonprofit groups shouldn't be afraid to lobby. *The Chronicle of Philanthropy, 33,* 34.

Bisno, H. (1988). *Managing conflict.* Newbury Park, CA: Sage.

Blanchard, K. J., Carlos, P., & Randolph, A. (1999). *The 3 keys to empowerment.* San Francisco: Berrett-Koehler.

Bliss, E. (1976). *Getting things done.* New York: Bantam.

Bonde, B. (2003). Planned giving communications. In *Nonprofit organization management.* New York: Aspen.

Borden, K. (1978). *Dear uncle: Please send money—A guide for proposal writers.* Pocatello, ID: Auger Associates.

Bowen, W. (Ed.). (1977, November). Japanese managers tell how their system works. *Fortune,* 127–138.

Boyett, J. H., & Conn, H. P. (1988, Summer). Developing white-collar performance measurement. *National Productivity Review,* 209–218.

Boyett, J. H., & Conn, H. P. (1988). *Maximum performance management.* Macomb, IL: Glenbridge.

Bramnall, M., & Ezell, S. (1981). How burned are you? *Public Welfare, 1,* 23–27.

Brinckerhoff, P. C. (1996). *Financial empowerment.* Dillon, CO: Alpine Guild.

Brinckerhoff, P. C. (2003). *Mission-based marketing* (2nd ed.). New York: John Wiley & Sons.

Brody, R. (1974). *Guide for applying for federal funds for human services.* Cleveland, OH: Case Western Reserve University, School of Applied Social Sciences.

Brody, R. (1982). *Problem solving: Concepts and methods for community organizations.* New York: Human Sciences Press.

Brody, R., Goodman, M., & Ferrante, J. (1985). *The legislative process: An action handbook for Ohio citizens' groups* (3rd ed.). Cleveland, OH: Federation for Community Planning.

Brody, R., & Krailo, H. (1978). An approach to reviewing the effectiveness of programs. *Social Work, 23*(3), 38–43.

Brody, R., & Nair, M. D. (2000). *Community service: The art of volunteering and service learning* (2nd ed.). Wheaton, IL: Gregory Publishing.

Brody, R., & Nair, M. D. (2003). *Macro practice: A generalist approach* (6th ed.).Wheaton, IL: Gregory Publishing.

Brody, R., & Woll, T. (2001). *Towards developing an integrated service delivery system.* Cleveland, OH: Catholic Charities Services Corporation.

Browman, M., Baanante, J., Dichter, T., Londner, S., & Reiling, P. (1993). Measuring our impact: Determining cost-effectiveness of non-governmental organization development projects. In G. L. Schmaedick (Ed.), *Cost-effectiveness in the nonprofit sector* (pp. 93-118). Westport, CT: Quorum.

Brown, R. (1979). *The practical manager's guide to excellence in management.* New York: AMACOM.

Bruce, S. D. (1989). *Face to face: Every manager's guide to better appraisal and discipline interviewing.* Madison, CT: Business and Legal Reports.

Bruch, H., & Ghoshal, S. (2002, February). Beware the busy manager. *Harvard Business Review, 80,* 62–69.

Bryson, J. M., Gibbons, M. J., & Shay, G. (2001). Enterprise schemes for nonprofit survival, growth, and effectiveness. *Nonprofit Management and Leadership 11*(3), 271–288.

Bureau of Business Practice. (1989). *Front line supervisor's standard manual.* Waterford, CT: Author.

Bureau of Business Practice. (1990). Building loyalty. *Front Line Supervisor's Bulletin, 146,* 1–3.

Bureau of Business Practice. (1990). The performance appraisal: Yours. *Front Line Supervisor's Bulletin, 151,* 1–3.

Bureau of Business Practice. (1991). Get the best from your employees. *Front Line Supervisor's Bulletin, 157,* 1–2.

Burns, M. E. (1989). *Proposal writer's guide.* Hartford, CT: Development & Technical Assistance Center.

Butler, J. K., Jr. (1995, December). Behaviors, trust, & goal achievement in a win-win negotiating role play. *Group & Organizational Management, 20*(4), 486–501.

Campbell, A., & Alexander, M. (1997, November/December). What's wrong with strategy? *Harvard Business Review, 75,* 42–51.

Campbell, R. B. (1982, May). *The process.* Speech given at Higbee's Annual Meeting. Cleveland, OH.

Cangemi, J. P., & Claypool, J. C. (1978). Complimentary interviews: A system for rewarding outstanding employees. *Personnel Journal, 2,* 87–90.

Caplow, T. (1976). *How to run any organization.* Hinsdale, IL: Dryden.

Carcer, J. (2002). *On board leadership.* San Francisco: Jossey-Bass.

Carew, J. (1987). *You'll never get no for an answer.* New York: Simon & Schuster.

Carl, J., & Stokes, G. (1991). Seven keys to an excellent organization: Fostering innovation and respect. *Nonprofit World, 5,* 18–22.

Cassedy, E., & Nussbaum, K. (1983). *9 to 5: The working woman's guide to office survival.* New York: Penguin.

The Catalog of Federal Domestic Assistance. (2003). Retrieved May 6, 2003, from www.cfda.gov/public/cat-writing.htm

Center on Philanthropy at Indiana University. (2002). Bequests and other forms of planned giving. *Giving USA Update, 2.*

Chandler, A., Jr. (1966). *Strategy and structure*. Garden City, NY: Doubleday.

Cherrington, D. (1987). *Personnel management: The management of human resources* (2nd ed.). Dubuque, IA: William C. Brown.

Chrislip, D. D. (2002). *The collaborative leadership field book: A guide for citizens and civic leaders*. San Francisco: Jossey-Bass.

Ciconte, B. L., & Jacob, J. G. (2002). *Fundraising basics: A complete guide* (2nd ed.). In *Nonprofit organization management* (pp. 10:15–10:19). New York: Aspen. (Original work published 2001)

Cohen, S. (1988). *The effective public manager: Achieving success in government*. San Francisco: Jossey-Bass.

Community Wealth Ventures. (2002). *Unlocking the profit potential*. Washington DC: Boardsource.

Conger, J. A. (1998, May/June). The necessary art of persuasion. *Harvard Business Review, 76*, 84–95.

Connellan, T. K. (1980). *How to grow people into self-starters*. Ann Arbor, MI: The Achievement Institute.

Conner, D. R., & Gold, B. (1993, May). Hospital corporate culture and its impact on strategic change. *Dimensions in Health Care, 3*.

Copeland, L. (1988, May). Learning to manage a multicultural work force. *Training*, 1–5.

Corporate engagement: Involving for-profit business in work of nonprofits. (2003, July/August). *The Foundation Center Newsletter*, pp. 1–2.

Coulton, C. (1990). *Developing quality assurance programs: Managerial considerations and strategies*. Unpublished manuscript.

Coulton, C. J., Keller, S., & Boone, C. R. (1985). Predicting social workers' expenditures of time with hospital patients. *Health and Social Work, 1*, 35–39.

Crow R. T., & Odewahn, C. A. (1987). *Management for the human services*. Englewood Cliffs, NJ: Prentice Hall.

Croxton, T. A. (1999). Liability & risk management. In J. E. Tropman & E. J. Tropman (Eds.), *Nonprofit boards*. Washington, DC: CWLA Press.

Cyert, R. M. (1990). Defining leadership and explicating the process. *Nonprofit Management and Leadership, 1*, 29–37.

Dabel, G. J. (1998). *Saving money in nonprofit organizations*. San Francisco: Jossey-Bass.

Deal, T. E., & Kennedy, A. A. (1982). *Corporate cultures*. Reading, MA: Addison-Wesley.

de Bono, E. (1973). *Lateral thinking*. New York: Harper Colophon.

Decker, L. E., & Decker, V. A. (1993). *Grantseeking: How to find a funder and write a winning proposal*. Charlottesville, VA: Community Collaborators.

Dees, J. G., Emerson, J., & Economy, P. (2001). *Enterprising nonprofits: A toolkit for social entrepreneurs*. New York: John Wiley & Sons.

Delbecq, A. L., Van de Ven, A., & Gustafson, D. H. (1976). *Group techniques for program planning*. Glenview, IL: Scott Foresman.

Deutsch, C. H. (2003, November 17). A much-loved concept gets a few new twists. *New York Times*, p. 6.

Dishy, V. (1989). *Inner fitness*. New York: Doubleday.

Dolan, C., & Brody, R. (1991). *Planned giving*. Cleveland, OH: Federation for Community Planning.

Doyle, M., & Straus, D. (1976). *How to make meetings work*. New York: Berkley.

Dropkin, M., & LaTouche, B. (1998). *The budget-building book for nonprofits.* San Francisco: Jossey-Bass.

Drucker, P. (1976, January/February) What results should you expect? A users' guide to MBO. *Public Administration Review,* 12–39.

Drucker, P. (1985). *The effective executive.* New York: Harper & Row.

Drucker, P. (1989). What business can learn from nonprofits. *Harvard Business Review, 67,* 89–93.

Drucker, P. (1990). *Managing the nonprofit organization.* New York: Harper Collins.

Drucker, P. (1998, October). Management's new paradigms. *Forbes,* 152–176.

Drucker, P. (1999). *Management challenges for the 21st century.* New York: HarperBusiness.

Drucker, P. (2001). The essential Drucker. New York: HarperBusiness.

Eadie, D. C. (1997). *Changing by design.* San Francisco: Jossey-Bass.

Eadie, D. (2001). *Extraordinary board leadership: The seven keys to high-impact governance.* Gaithersburg, MD: Aspen.

Edwards, R. L., & Benefield, E. A. S. (1997). *Building a strong foundation: Fundraising for nonprofits.* Washington DC: NASW Press.

Eisenhardt, K. M., Kahwajy, J. L., & Bourgeois, L. J. III. (1997, July/August). How management teams can have a good fight. *Harvard Business Review, 75,* 77–85.

Elkin, R., & Vorvaller, D. J. (1972, May). Evaluating the effectiveness of social services. *Management Controls,* 104–111.

Ellis, R. J. (1992, Spring). Centel Corporation: Using human resources programs to support cultural change. *Wyatt Communicator,* 4–9.

Ellis, S. (2003, November 1). On volunteers: Real motivation. *The Nonprofit Times, 17,* 21, 41.

Espy, S. N. (1988). Planning for success: Strategic planning in nonprofits. *Nonprofit World, 5,* 23–24.

Espy, S. N. (1988). Where are you, and where do you think you're going? *Nonprofit World, 6,* 19–20.

Espy, S. N. (1989). Putting your plan into action. *Nonprofit World, 1,* 27–28.

Etzioni, A. (1968). *The active society: A theory of society and political processes.* New York: Free Press.

Evans, D. S., & Oh, M. Y. (1996, June). A tailored approach to diversity planning. *Harvard Business Review, 74,* 127–134.

Farmelo, M. (2001). Getting to know your donors: The donor survey. *Grassroots Fundraising Journal, 21*(1), 8–11.

Federation for Community Planning. (2000). *2000 greater Cleveland media guide* (45th ed.). Cleveland: Author.

Federation for Community Planning. (2002). *2003 northeast Ohio media guide* (47th ed.). Cleveland: Author.

Feit, M. D., & Li, P. (1998). *Financial management in human services.* New York: Haworth.

Flannery, R. B. (1989, February). The stress resistant person. *HMS Health Letter, 6.*

Ford, S. (1983). *The ABC's of managing with employee teams.* Campbell, CA: Sondra Ford & Associates.

Foster, R., & Kaplan, S. (2001). *Creative destruction.* New York: Currency/Doubleday.

The Foundation Center. (1994). Prospect worksheet. In *The Foundation Center's User-Friendly Guide* (Rev. ed.). New York: Author.

The Foundation Center. (1997). *FC search manual.* New York: Author.

The Foundation Center. (1997, Fall). *Fundraising & nonprofit development resources catalog.* New York: Author.

The Foundation Center. (2001). Proposal budgeting basics. Retrieved May 6, 2003, from www.fdncenter.org/learn/classroom/prop_budgt/index.html

The Foundation Center. (2003). Grantseeking basics: Glossary of terms. Retrieved March, 2003, from www.fdncenter.org/learn/ufg/glossary.html

A Fresh Look at Corporate Giving. (2000, May). *The Foundation Center Newsletter,* 1–2.

Frey, S. (2001). What's love got to do with it? *Grassroots Fundraising Journal, 20*(4), 4–7.

Friedman, S. D., Christensen, P., & DeGroot, J. (1998, November/December). Work & life: The end of the zero sum game. *Harvard Business Review, 76,* 119–129.

Frumkin, P., & Andre-Clark, A. (2000). When missions, markets, and politics collide: Values and strategy in the nonprofit human services. *Nonprofit and Voluntary Sector Quarterly, 29*(1), 141–163.

Gable, C. (2001). Tech tips: How technology can support your organization. *Grassroots Fundraising Journal, 20*(1), 12–14.

Garford, R., & Drapeau, A. S. (2003, February). The enemy of trust. *Harvard Business Review, 81,* 89–95.

Garner, L. H., Jr. (1989). *Leadership in human services: How to articulate a vision to achieve results.* San Francisco: Jossey-Bass.

Garvin, D. A., & Roberto, M. A. (2001). What you don't know about making decisions. *Harvard Business Review, 79,* 108–116.

Gaylin, D. H. (1990, Summer). Break down barriers by communicating your company's strategy. *The Human Resources Professional,* 20–21.

Geber, B. (1990, July). Managing diversity. *Training,* 23–30.

Geever, J. C., & McNeil, P. (1997). *Guide to proposal writing.* New York: The Foundation Center.

Getting better at what we do: Is direct mail working? (2002, July/August). *Advancing Philanthropy,* 21–23.

Gibelman, M., Gelman, S. R., & Pollack, D. (1997). The credibility of nonprofit boards: A view from the 1990's and beyond. *Administration in Social Work, 21*(2), 21–40.

Gladwell, M. (2002). *The tipping point.* Boston: Little, Brown and Company.

Goddard, M. M. (2002). Ten tips grant writers should commit to memory. In *Nonprofit organization management* (p. 1). New York: Aspen. First published in *Foundation and Corporate Grants Alert 10*(12) (2001): 1.

Goering, S. A. (1990, August 21). Steps can protect company from ex-employee lawsuits. *The Plain Dealer,* p. F2.

Goffee, R., & Jones, G. (2000, September/October). Why should anyone be led by you? *Harvard Business Review, 78,* 63–70.

Goleman, D. (1998, November/December). What makes a leader? *Harvard Business Review, 76,* 93–102.

Goleman, D. (2000, March/April). Leadership that gets results. *Harvard Business Review, 78,* 78–90.

Gooch, J. (1987). *Writing winning proposals.* Washington, DC: Council for the Advancement of Education.

Gordon, T. (1977). *Leader effectiveness training.* New York: Bantam.

Grace, K. (1991). Leadership & team building. In H. A. Rosso (Ed.), *Achieving excellence in fund raising*. San Francisco: Jossey-Bass.

Greenfield, J. M., & Larkin, R. F. (2000). Public accountability. *New Directions for Philanthropic Fundraising, 2*(27), 51–71.

Grobman, G. M. (1999). *The nonprofit handbook* (2nd ed.). Harrisburg, PA: White Hat Communications.

Grobman, G. M. (2001). *The nonprofit's guide to e-commerce*. Harrisburg, PA: White Hat Communications.

Gubkin, J. (1985). *Persuasive communication*. Cleveland, OH: Jack Gubkin & Associates.

Gummer, B. (1995). Go team go! The growing importance of teamwork in organizational life. *Administration in Social Work, 19*(4), 93–94.

Haas, R. N. (1994). *The power to persuade*. New York: Houghton Mifflin.

Hall, M. S. (1988). *Getting funded: A complete guide to proposal writing*. Portland, OR: Portland State University.

Haller, M. C. (1989, July/August). The new balancing act: Variable but equitable pay. *Human Resources Professional*, 31.

Hammer, M. (1990). Reengineering work: Don't automate, obliterate. *Harvard Business Review, 68*, 104–112.

Hammond, J. S., Keeney, R. L., & Raiffa, H. (1998, September/October). The hidden traps in decision making. *Harvard Business Review, 76*, 47–58.

Handy, F. (2000). How we beg: The analysis of direct mail appeals. *Nonprofit and Voluntary Sector Quarterly, 29*(3), 439–453.

Havassy, H. M. (1990). Effective second-story bureaucrats: Mastering the paradox of diversity. *Social Work, 2*, 103–109.

Heifetz, R. A., & Laurie, D. L. (1997, January/February). The work of leadership. *Harvard Business Review, 75*, 123–134.

Heifetz, R., & Linsky, M. (2002, June). A survival guide for leaders. *Harvard Business Review, 80*, 65–74.

Hemphill, B. (1999, June). Organize your increasingly complex work life. *Bottom Line Personal*, 9–10.

Henderson, R. I. (1989). *Compensation management: Rewarding performance*. Englewood Cliffs, NJ: Prentice Hall.

Henry, C. (1998). Effective proposal writing. In R. L. Edwards (Ed.), *Skills for effective management of nonprofit organizations*. Washington DC: National Association of Social Workers.

Herman, R. D., & Heimovics, R. D. (1990, Winter). The effective nonprofit executive: Leader of the board. *Nonprofit Management & Leadership, 1*(2), 167–180.

Herman, R. E. (1990). *Keeping good people: Strategies for solving the dilemma of the decade*. Cleveland, OH: Oakhill.

Herzberg, F. (2003, January). One more time: How do you motivate employees? *Harvard Business Review, 81*, 87–96. (Original work published 1968)

Herzberg, F., Mausner, B., & Synderman, B. (1959). *The motivation to work*. New York: John Wiley.

Herzlinger, R. (1994, July/August). Effective oversight: A guide for nonprofit directors. *Harvard Business Review, 72*, 56–64.

Hildebrand, K. (1996, August). Use leadership training to increase diversity. *Harvard Business Review, 74*, 53–60.

Hitchcock, S. (2002). Direct mail techniques that smaller organizations should avoid. *Grassroots Fundraising Journal, 21*(5), 10–11.

Hogan, R., Raskin, R., & Fazzini, D. (1990). How charisma cloaks incompetence. *Personnel Journal, 5,* 73–76.

Hollingsworth, A. T. (1989). Creativity in nonprofit organizations: Preparing for the future. *Nonprofit World, 3,* 21–22.

Horton, C. (1991). *Raising money & having fun (sort of): A "how to" book for small non-profit groups.* Cleveland, OH: May Dugan Center.

Hout, T. M. (1999, March/April). Are managers obsolete? *Harvard Business Review, 77,* 161–168.

Howard, R. (1990). Values make the company: An interview with Robert Hass. *Harvard Business Review, 5,* 133–143.

Huy, Q. N. (2001, September). In praise of middle managers. *Harvard Business Review, 79,* 73–79.

Ingram, R. T. (1995). *Ten basic responsibilities of nonprofit boards* [Governance series booklet]. Washington, DC: National Center for Nonprofit Boards.

Jacquette, L. F., & Jacquette, B. I. (1977, August). *What makes a good proposal.* Washington, DC: The Foundation Center.

Janis, I. L. (1971, November). Groupthink. *Psychology Today,* 43–46, 74–76.

Johnston, M. (1999). *The nonprofit guide to the internet* (2nd ed.). New York: John Wiley.

Joinson, C. (1999, May). Getting the best results from teams requires work on the teams themselves. *Human Resource Management, 44*(5), 30–36.

Jordan, P. C. (1986). Effects of an extrinsic reward on intrinsic motivation: A field experiment. *Academy of Management Journal, 29*(2), 405–412.

Jorgenson, J. D., Scheier, I. H., & Fautsko, T. F. (1981). *Solving problems in meetings.* Chicago: Nelson-Hall.

Joseph, B. (1986). Writer's block: Is there a cure? *NonProfit World, 3,* 27–28.

Joseph, W. R. (1998). Trustee liability: A practical view. *Weston Hurd Fallon Paisley & Howley LLP,* 1–4.

Joyaux, S. P. (1997). *Strategic fund development.* Gaithersburg, MD: Aspen.

Kadushin, A. (1985). *Supervision in social work* (2nd ed.). New York: Columbia University Press.

Kahn, S. C., Berish Brown, B., Lanzarone, M., & Zepke, B. E. (1994). *Legal guide to human resources* (3rd ed.). Boston: Warren, Gorham, & Lamont.

Kaplan, M. L. (1990). Labor of love: The joys and stresses of nonprofit management. *Nonprofit World, 3,* 28.

Kaplan, R. S. (2001). Strategic performance measurement in nonprofit organizations. *Nonprofit Management and Leadership, 11*(3), 353–369.

Karski, R. L., & Barth, R. P. (2000). Models of state budget allocation in child welfare services. *Administration in Social Work, 24*(2), 45–66.

Katzenbach, J. R., & Smith, D. K. (1993). *The wisdom of teams.* New York: HarperCollins.

Kepner, C. H., & Tregoe, B. B. (1974). *The rational manager.* New York: McGraw Hill.

Kettner, P. M, Moroney, R. M., & Martin, L. L. (1990). *Designing and managing programs.* Newbury Park, CA: Sage.

Kettner, P. M., Moroney, R. M., & Martin, L. L. (1999). *Designing and managing programs* (2nd ed.). Thousand Oaks, CA: Sage.

Kihlstedt, A., & Schwartz, C. P. (1997). *Capital campaigns: Strategies that work.* Gaithersburg, MD: Aspen.

Kim, W. C., & Mairborgne, R. (2003, April). Tipping point leadership. *Harvard Business Review, 81,* 60–69.

Kirby, T. (1989). *The can-do manager.* New York: AMACOM.

Kiritz, N. J. (1980). *Program planning & proposal writing.* Los Angeles: The Grantsmanship Center.

Kirkpatrick, S. A., & Locke, E. A. (1995). Do traits matter? In J. T. Wren (Ed.), *The Leader's Companion.* New York: The Free Press.

Klein, K. (2000). *Fundraising for the long haul.* Oakland, CA: Chardon Press.

Klein, K. (2001). *Fundraising for social change* (4th ed.). Oakland, CA: Chardon Press.

Klein, K. (2001). Getting over the fear of asking. *Grassroots Fundraising Journal, 20*(2), 4–8.

Klein, K. (2001). How to create an effective acquisition strategy. *Grassroots Fundraising Journal, 20*(1), 3–7.

Klein, K. (2001). The phases of a capital campaign. *Grassroots Fundraising Journal, 20*(4), 8–12.

Klein, K. (2001). Planning a capital campaign. *Grassroots Fundraising Journal, 20*(3), 4–7.

Klein, K. (2001). Testing the feasibility of your capital campaign. *Grassroots Fundraising Journal, 20*(5), 8–10.

Klein, K. (2002). Asking current donors for money: Why, how and how often. *Grassroots Fundraising Journal, 19*(3), 3–6.

Klein, K. (n.d.). *55 ways for boards to raise $500. Grassroots Fundraising Journal.* Retrieved May 5, 2003, from www.allianceonline.org/FAQ

Klein, K. (n.d.). The fine art of asking for the gift. *Grassroots Fundraising Journal, 2*(3). Retrieved May 6, 2003, from www.allianceonline.org/FAQ

Kotter, J. (1990). What leaders really do. *Harvard Business Review, 68,* 103–111.

Kotter, J. P. (1999, March/April). What effective general managers really do. *Harvard Business Review, 77,* 145–159.

Lakein, A. (1973). *How to get control of your time and your life.* New York: New American Library.

Lang, A. S. (2003). *Financial responsibilities of nonprofit boards.* Washington, DC: Boardsource.

Larson, R. (2002). *Venture forth! The essential guide to starting a moneymaking business in your nonprofit organization.* St. Paul, MN: Amherst H. Wilder Foundation.

Lauffer, A. (1982). *Assessment tools for practitioners, managers, and trainers.* Beverly Hills, CA: Sage.

Lauffer, A. (1984). *Grantsmanship and fund raising.* Beverly Hills, CA: Sage.

Lauffer, A. (1985). *Careers, colleagues, and conflicts: Understanding gender, race, and ethnicity in the workplace.* Beverly Hills, CA: Sage.

Lauffer, A. (1987). *Working in social work.* Newbury Park, CA: Sage.

Lauffer, A. (1997). *Grants, etc.* (2nd ed.). Thousand Oaks, CA: Sage.

Lawler, E. E. (1986). *High involvement management.* San Francisco: Jossey-Bass.

Lawler, E. E. III. (1989). Pay for performance: A strategic analysis. In L. Gomez-Mejia (Ed.), *Compensation and benefits.* Washington, DC: Bureau of National Affairs.

Leavitt, H. (2003, March). Why hierarchies thrive. *Harvard Business Review, 81,* 96–102.

Lindahl, W. E. (1992). *Strategic planning for fund raising.* San Francisco: Jossey-Bass.

Lipman, H. (2001). Calling solicitors to account. *The Chronicle of Philanthropy, XIII*(12), 1, 24–27.

Lipscomb, W. (2001). *Philanthropic market study report and recommendations.* Cleveland, OH: El Barro.

Lloyd, K. L. (1991). *Sexual harassment: How to keep your company out of court.* New York: Panel.

Maclean, B. P. (1990). Value added pay beats traditional merit programs. *Personnel Journal, 9,* 46.

Mai, C. F. (1987). *Secrets of major gift fund raising.* Washington, DC: Taft Group.

Management Library Portal. (1999). Retrieved May 7, 2003, from www.mapnet.org/library/varietyofmanagement

Marash, S. (1989). Blueprint for quality improvement. *Personnel Journal, 3,* 122.

Marray, W. (2000, April). Volunteers are changing: How volunteer programs can adapt. *Grassroots Fundraising Journal, 19,* 2, 7–8.

Martin, D. C. (1989). Performance appraisal 2: Improving the rater's effectiveness. In M. Sahkin (Ed.), *Performance Appraisal.* New York: American Management Association.

Martin, L. L. (2000). Budgeting for outcomes in state human agencies. *Administration in Social Work, 24*(3), 71–88.

Martin, L. L. (2000). Performance contracting in the human services: An analysis of selected state practices. *Administration in Social Work, 24*(2), 29–44.

Martin, L. L. (2001). *Financial management for human service administration.* Boston: Allyn & Bacon.

Martin, P. (2000). Preparation before proposal writing. *New Directions for Philanthropic Fundraising, 28,* 85–95.

Marx, J. D. (1988, January). Corporate strategic philanthropy: Implications for social work. *Social Work,* 35–41.

Marx, J. D. (1996). Strategic philanthropy: An opportunity for partnership between corporations and health/human service agencies. *Administration in Social Work, 20*(3), 57–73.

Maslow, A. H. (1954). *Motivation and personality.* New York: Harper & Row.

Mattessich, P. W., & Monsey, B. R. (1993). *Collaboration: What makes it work.* Saint Paul, MN: Wilder Research.

McAfee, R. B., & Deadrick, D. L. (1996, February). Teach employees to just say "no!" *Human Resource Management, 41*(2), 86–89.

McClelland, D. C., & Burnham, D. (1976). Power is the great motivator. *Harvard Business Review, 54,* 100–111.

McClelland, D. C., & Burnham, D. H. (2003, January). Power is the great motivator. *Harvard Business Review, 81,* 117–126.

McConkey, D. D. (1975). *MBO for nonprofit organizations.* New York: AMA-COM.

McCormack, M. (1997, November 25). Giving instructions that make things happen. *The Plain Dealer,* p. 3C.

McCormack, M. (1998). *On communicating.* Los Angeles: Dove.

McCormack, M. (1999, March 9). A fine line separates dumping & delegating tasks. *The Plain Dealer,* p. 5C.

McCormack, M. (1999, August 3). Reliance on e-mail may erode the quality of communication. *The Plain Dealer*, p. 8C.

McCormack, M. H. (1996). *Mark H. McCormack on managing*. West Hollywood, CA: Dove.

McCreight, R. E. (1983). A five role system for motivating improved performance. *Personnel Journal, 1,* 22–26.

McFarland, L. J., Senn, L. E., & Childress, J. R. (1995). Refining leadership in the next century. In J. T. Wren (Ed.), *The leader's companion*. New York: Free Press.

McGregor, D. (1960). *The human side of enterprise*. New York: McGraw-Hill.

McNamara, C. (1999). Strategic planning. Retrieved May 6, 2003, from www.mapnp.org/library/plan_dec/str_plan/str_plan.htm

Mengerink, W. C. (1992). *Hand in hand*. Rockville, MD: Fund Raising Institute.

Mersha, S. (2000). Membership pays: The role of members in grassroots fundraising. *Grassroots Fundraising Journal, 19*(4), 3–5.

Middleman, R. R., & Rhodes, G. B. (1985). *Competent supervision: Making imaginative judgments*. Englewood Cliffs, NJ: Prentice Hall.

Mihal, W. L. (1983, October). More research is needed: Goals may motivate better. *Personnel Administrator,* 63–68.

Milkovich, G. T., & Boudreau, J. W. (1988). *Personnel/human resource management* (5th ed.). Plano, TX: Business Publications.

Miller, A., Simeone, R. S., & Carneval, J. T. (2001). Logic models: A systems tool for performance management. *Evaluation and Program Planning, 24,* 73–81.

Mills, C., & Ivery, C. (1991). A strategy for workload management in child protective practice. *Child Welfare, 1,* 35–43.

Mintzberg, H. (1990). The manager's job: Folklore and fact. *Harvard Business Review, 68,* 163–176.

Moon, F. (1990, November). The annual operating plan: Converting long-term strategies to achievable tasks. *Management Issues,* 1–4.

Moon, F. (1990, October). Building a strategic plan: The second step toward an action blueprint for the future. *Management Issues,* 1–3.

Moon, F. (1990, August). Decade of transition: The strategic plan as action blueprint for the 1990s. *Management Issues,* 1–2.

Moon, F. (1990, September). Step one of strategic planning: Discover your organization, inventory your resources, and identify issues. *Management Issues,* 1–3.

Moore, A. (2002). The volunteer coordinator: Key to a successful volunteer program. In *Nonprofit organization management* (p. 3:68). New York: Aspen. First published in *Strategic Governance 3*(9) (1998).

Moore, C. M. (1987). *Group techniques for idea building*. Newbury Park, CA: Sage.

Morgan, O. (2003). Creating a budget for fundraising. *Grassroots Fundraising Journal, 22*(3), 4–6.

Morth, M., & Collins, S. (Eds.). (1996). *The Foundation Center's user friendly guide: A grantseeker's guide to resources*. New York: Foundation Center.

Moss, L. (1981). *Management stress*. Reading, MA: Addison-Wesley.

Murdock, R. G., & Ross, J. E. (1975). *Information systems for modern management*. Englewood Cliffs, NJ: Prentice Hall.

Murphy, J. C. (2000). Foundation fundraising for new organizations. *New Direction for Philanthropic Fundraising, 28,* 5–17.

Murray, W. (2000, April). Volunteers are changing: How volunteer programs can adapt. *Grassroots Fundraising Journal, 19*(2).

Myerson, D. (2001). Radical change, the quiet way. *Harvard Business Review, 79,* 92–100.

National Assembly of National Voluntary Health and Social Welfare Organizations. (1985). *A study in excellence: Management in the nonprofit human services.* Washington, DC: Author.

National Institute of Business Management. (1991). *Fire at will: Terminating your employees legally.* New York: Author.

National Leadership Coalition on AIDS. (1991). *Small business and AIDS: How AIDS can affect your business.* Washington DC: Author.

Nauffts, M. F. (Ed.). (1994). *Foundation fundamentals: A guide for grantseekers* (5th ed.). New York: Foundation Center.

Nelson, W. C. (1991). Incentive based management for nonprofit organizations. *Nonprofit Management and Leadership, 1,* 59–69.

Newman, J. M. (1989). Compensation programs for special employee groups. In L. Gomez-Mejia (Ed.), *Compensation and benefits.* Washington, DC: Bureau of National Affairs.

Nicholson, N. (2003, January). How to motivate your problem people. *Harvard Business Review, 81,* 57–65.

Nickols, F. (2000). Three forms of strategy: Corporate, competitive, and strategy in general. Retrieved May 6, 2003, from home.att.net/~nickols/three_forms_of_strategy.htm

9 to 5. (1990). *Sexual harassment* [Brochure]. Cleveland, OH: Author.

Nonprofit organization management: Forms, checklists & guidelines (2nd ed.). (2002). New York: Aspen.

Nord, W., & McAdams, J. L. (1989, May/June). Performance-based reward systems: Which will work best for you? *Human Resources Professional,* 27–32.

Owens, K. (2003, February). Resource Development Network, Inc. Annual Fundraising Workshop, Cleveland, OH.

Panel Publishers. (2002). The practical guide to employment law. In *Nonprofit organization management* (pp. 4:23–37). New York: Aspen.

Parmadale Children's Village. (1991). *Value statement.* Parma, OH: Author.

Peck, M. S. (1978). *The road less traveled.* New York: Touchstone, Simon & Schuster.

Pecora, P. J., & Austin, M. J. (1987). *Managing human services personnel.* Newbury Park, CA: Sage.

Peters T. H., & Waterman, R. H. (1982). *In search of excellence: Lessons from America's best run companies.* New York: Harper & Row.

Petrock, F. (1991). Corporate culture and productivity. *Nonprofit Management Strategies, 7,* 13–14.

Pileggi, A., & Hickey, D. T. (1991). Incentive pay plans. *Nonprofit Management Strategies, 6,* 1–3.

Poderis, T. (1996). *It's a great day to fund-raise!* Cleveland, OH: Fund America Press.

Poderis, T. (2003). Annual and capital campaigns. Retrieved May 6, 2003, from www.raise-funds.com/399forum.html

Poderis, T. (2003). Asking for the money: If you don't ask you don't get. Retrieved May 6, 2003, from www.raise-funds.com/299forum.html

Poderis, T. (2003). Campaign solicitation kits. Retrieved May 6, 2003, from www.raise-funds.com/899forum.html

Poderis, T. (2003). Cultivate a "grassroots" fundraising campaign for your organization. Retrieved May 6, 2003, from www.raise-funds.com/0301forum.html

Poderis, T. (2003). Know your organization. Retrieved May 6, 2003, from www.raise-funds.com/1199forum.html

Poderis, T. (2003). Your organization's next special event: Fund-raiser or friend-raiser. Retrieved May 6, 2003, from www.raise-funds.com/112601forum.html

Pointer, D. D., & Orlikoff, J. E. (2002). *The high-performance board*. San Francisco: Jossey-Bass.

Poulin, J. E. (1995). Job satisfaction of social work supervisors and administrators. *Administration in Social Work, 19*(4), 35–49.

PricewaterhouseCoopers. (1999, July/August). Building high-performing strategic alliances. *Growing Your Business*, 3.

Pryor, F. (1985, March). Manage your meetings effectively. *The Nonprofit Executive*, 7.

Public Children Services Association of Ohio. (1988). *PCSAO caseload study*. Columbus, OH: Author.

Quinn, J. B. (1978, Fall). Strategic change: Logical incrementalism. *Sloan Management Review*, 3–16.

Raia, A. P. (1974). *Managing by objectives*. Glenview, IL: Scott Foresman.

Renauer, A. M. (1990, April). A trained facilitator can be instrumental in successful strategic planning. *Management Issues*, 2–3.

Reynolds, H., & Tramel, M. E. (1979). *Executive time management*. Englewood Cliffs, NJ: Prentice Hall.

Robinson, A. (2002). Business planning for enterprising nonprofits. *Grassroots Fundraising Journal, 21*(4), 11–15.

Robinson, E. M. M. (2003). Making the most of in-house prospects. *Grassroots Fundraising Journal, 22*(3), 10–15.

Rollins, T. (1989). Pay for performance: Is it worth the trouble? In *Performance and rewards: Linking pay to performance* [The HR Magazine Series] (pp. 10–15). Alexandria, VA: Society for Human Resource Management.

Rosa, P. (2003). In-kind gifts: Legal, financial, and matching considerations. *Grassroots Fundraising Journal, 19*(1), 11–12.

Rosenburg, M., & Brody, R. (1974). *Systems serving people*. Cleveland, OH: Case Western Reserve University.

Rossi, H., & Freeman, H. E. (1989). *Evaluation: A systematic approach*. Newbury Park, CA: Sage.

Rosso, H. A. (1991). *Achieving excellence in fund raising*. San Francisco: Jossey-Bass.

Rosso, H. A. (1996). *Rosso on fund raising*. San Francisco: Jossey-Bass.

Roth, S. (2001). Evaluating your individual donor program. *Grassroots Fundraising Journal, 20*(6), 8–11.

Roth, S. (2003). Building self-sufficiency: Grassroots fundraising success story in Brazil. *Grassroots Fundraising Journal, 22*(3), 7–9.

Roth, S. (2003). Making special events work for you. *Grassroots Fundraising Journal, 21*(6), 4–6.

Roth, S. (2003). Systemic record-keeping makes a difference. In K. Klein, Maintaining relationships with donors all year long. *Grassroots Fundraising Journal, 22*(2), 10.

Rothman, J., Erlich, J. L., & Teresa, J. G. (1976). *Promoting innovation and change in organizations and communities*. New York: MacMillan.

Rubright, R., & MacDonald, D. (1981). *Marketing health and human services.* Rockville, MD: Aspen Systems Corporation.

Ruderman, S. (2002, July/August). Planning for gold. *Contributions,* 19–20.

Sametz, L., & Hamparian, D. (1990). *Innovating programs in Cuyahoga County Juvenile Court: Intensive probation supervision and probation classification.* Cleveland, OH: Federation for Community Planning.

Sandroff, R. (1992, June). Sexual harassment: The inside story. *Working Woman,* 47–51.

Sanzotta, D. (1977). *Motivational theories and applications for managers.* New York: AMACOM.

Sathe, V. (1983, Autumn). Implications of corporate culture: A manager's guide to action. *Organizational Dynamics,* 5–23.

Scanlan, E. A. (2002). Corporate and foundation fundraising: A complete guide from the inside. In *Nonprofit organization management* (pp. 9:44–48). New York: Aspen. (Original work published 1997)

Schaef, A. W., & Fassel, D. (1990). *The addictive organization.* San Francisco: Harper & Row.

Schaefer, M. (1987). *Implementing change in service programs.* Newbury Park, CA: Sage.

Schaffer, R. H. (1981, August). Productivity improvement strategy: Make success the building block. *Management Review,* 46–52.

Schaffer, R. H. (1989). *The breakthrough strategy.* Cambridge, MA: Ballinger.

Schaffer, R. H. (1989, September). Quality now! *The Journal for Quality and Participation,* 22–27.

Schaffer, R. H. (1991, February/March). Demand better results and get them. *Harvard Business Review, 69,* 145–149.

Schaffer, R. H., & Michaelson, K. E. (1989). The incremental strategy for consulting success. *The Journal of Management Consulting, 2,* 1–5.

Schein, E. H. (1970). *Organizational psychology.* New York: Prentice Hall.

Schein, E. H. (1986). *Organizational culture and leadership.* San Francisco: Jossey-Bass.

Schein, E. H. (1987). Coming to a new awareness of organizational culture. In L. E. Boone & D. D. Bowen (Eds.), *The great writings in management and orga-nizational behavior* (pp. 442–451). New York: Random House.

Schmaedick, G. L. (Ed.). (1993). *Cost-effectiveness in the nonprofit sector.* Westport, CT: Quorum.

Schuler, R. S. (1987). *Personnel and human resource management* (3rd ed.). St. Paul, MN: West.

Schultz, W. N. (1984). What makes a good nonprofit manager? *Nonprofit World,* 32.

Schwartz, A. E. (1989). When good ideas are needed fast. *Nonprofit World, 6,* 22–23.

Seers, A., Petty, M. M., & Cashman, J. F. (1995, March). Team-member exchange under team & traditional management. *Group & Organizational Management, 20*(1), 19.

Seiler, T. L. (2001). *Developing your case for support.* San Francisco: Jossey-Bass.

Seltzer, J. (1989). *Developing an effective leadership style.* In L. E. Miller (Ed.), Managing human service organizations. New York: Quorum.

Senge, P. M. (1990). *The fifth discipline.* New York: Doubleday Currency.

Senge, P., Kliener A., Roberts, C., Ross, R. B., & Smith, B. J. (1994). *The fifth discipline fieldbook.* New York: Currency.

Senger, A. (2003, February). Resource Development Network, Inc. Workshop Materials.

Shannon, J. P. (Ed.). *The corporate contributions handbook*. San Francisco: Jossey-Bass.

Sheldon, K. S. (1991). Corporations as a gift market. In H. A. Rosso (Ed.), *Achieving excellence in fund raising* (pp. 229–242). San Francisco: Jossey-Bass.

Shepherd, J. S. (1990). Manage the 5 C's of stress. *Personnel Journal, 4,* 64–69.

Sheridan, R. G., & Ellis, D. A. (2000). County budgeting is unique. *Planning and Action: The Journal of the Federation for Community, 53*(9), 1–5.

Simmons, K. (1997, May). Your advisory boards: Don't let them do fundraising. *The Nonprofit Times,* 26–27.

Skidmore, R. (1995). *Social work administration.* Boston: Allyn & Bacon.

Slater, P., & Bennis, W. (1990, May/June). Democracy is inevitable. *Harvard Business Review, 68,* 175–185.

Slesinger, L. (1991). *Self assessment for nonprofit governing boards.* Washington, DC: National Center for Nonprofit Boards.

Smith, H. (1999, March). Hyrum Smith's simple steps to much better time management. *Bottom Line Personal,* 11–12.

Solomon, C. M. (1990). Careers under glass. *Personnel Journal, 4,* 96–105.

Stanton, E. S. (1983). A critical reevaluation of motivation, management, and productivity. *Personnel Journal, 3,* 5–6.

Stayer, R. (1990, June/July). How I learned to let my workers lead. *Harvard Business Review, 68,* 66–83.

Steel, J. (1997). Fundamentals of planned giving. In R. L. Edwards & E. A. S. Benefield (Eds.), *Building a strong foundation: Fundraising for nonprofits* (pp. 75–87). Washington, DC: NASW.

Steinberg, R. (1990). Profits and incentive compensation in nonprofit firms. *Nonprofit Management and Leadership, 2,* 137–149.

Steiner, R. (1988). *Total proposal building.* Albany, NY: Trestletree.

Stern, G. J. (2001). *Marketing workbook for nonprofit organizations Volume I: Development plan* (2nd ed.). Saint Paul, MN: Amherst H. Wilder Foundation.

Straton, J. (Ed.). (2002). Board and administration. In *Nonprofit organization management* (p. 7:1–51). New York: Aspen. (Original work published 2001)

Sudow, T. R. (2003, February). Resource Development Network, Inc. Workshop Materials.

Sutton, R. I. (2001, August). The weird rules of creativity. *Harvard Business Review, 79,* 96–103.

Swain, R. L. (1989, September/October). 66 ways to avoid trouble when terminating the long-termer. *The Human Resources Professional,* 28–31.

Swanson, A. (1986, July/August). Who's in charge here? *Nonprofit World, 4*(4), 14–18.

Tambor, M. (1995). Employment-at-will or just cause: The right choice. *Administration in Social Work, 19*(3), 45–57.

Tannenbaum, R., & Schmidt, W. (1973 March/April). How to choose a leadership pattern. *Harvard Business Review, 52,* 162–180.

Tarkenton Productivity Group. (1977). *Motivational theories and applications for managers.* New York: AMACOM.

Taylor, B. E., Chait, R. P., & Holland, T. P. (1996, September/October). The new work of the nonprofit board. *Harvard Business Review, 74,* 36–42.

Taylor, W. C. (1999, June). The leader of the future. *Fast Company,* 132–138.

Teal, T. (1996, November/December). The human side of management. *Harvard Business Review, 74,* 35–44.

Terpstra, D. E. (1979). Theories of motivation: Borrowing the best. *Personnel Journal, 6,* 15–18.

Thomas, D. A., & Ely, R. J. (1996, September/October). Making differences matter: A new paradigm for managing diversity. *Harvard Business Review, 74,* 79–90.

Thomas, R. R. (1990 January/February). From affirmative action to affirming diversity. *Harvard Business Review, 68,* 107–117.

Thomas, R. R. (1991). *Beyond race and gender: Unleashing the power of your total workforce by managing diversity.* New York: AMACOM.

Tjosvold, D. (1991). *The conflict-positive organization.* Reading, MA: Addison-Wesley.

Townsend, R. (1984). *Further up the organization.* New York: Knopf.

Tropman, J. E. (1980). *Effective meetings: Improving group decision-making.* Beverly Hills, CA: Sage.

Tropman, J. E., & Tropman, E. J. (1999). *Nonprofit boards: What to do and how to do it.* Washington, DC: CWLA.

Tzu, L. (1944). *The way of life according to Lao Tzu* (W. Bynner, Trans.). New York: Capricorn.

United States Equal Employment Opportunity Commission. (2002). Small employers and reasonable accommodations. In *Nonprofit organization management* (pp. 4:1–26). New York: Aspen. (Original work published 1999)

United Way of America. (1996). *Measuring program outcomes: A practical approach.* Alexandria, VA: Author.

Uris, A. (1986). *101 of the greatest ideas in management.* New York: John Wiley.

von Oech, R.(1983). *A whack on the side of the head.* New York: Warner.

von Oech, R. (1986). *A kick in the seat of the pants.* New York: Harper & Row.

Vroom, V. H. (1973). *Choosing a leadership style: Applying the Vroom & Yetton model.* New York: AMACOM.

Wadia, M. (1980). Participative management: Three common problems. *Personnel Journal, 11,* 27–28.

Wageman, R., & Mannix, E. A. (1998). Uses and misuses of power in task performing teams. In R. M. Kramer & M. A. Neale (Eds.), *Power & influence in organizations.* Thousand Oaks, CA: Sage.

Waldroop, J., & Butler, T. (1996, November/December). The executive as coach. *Harvard Business Review, 74,* 111–117.

Wallack, L., Dorfman, L., Jernigan, D., & Themba, M. (1993). *Media advocacy and public health.* Newbury Park, CA: Sage.

Weber, W., Laws, B., & Weber, S. (1987). Real world planning: Fresh approaches to old problems. *Nonprofit World, 2,* 25–27.

Wells, S. J., & Johnson, M. A. (2001). Selecting outcome measures for child welfare settings: Lessons for use in performance management. *Children and Youth Services, 23*(2), 169–199.

Wiebush, R. G., & Hamparian, D. (1986). *Probation classification: Design and development of the Cuyahoga County Juvenile Court model.* Cleveland, OH: Federation for Community Planning.

Williams, G. (2001, November 1). Turmoil at the Red Cross. *The Chronicle of Philanthropy,* 71–73.

Williams, K. A. (1997). *Donor focused strategies for annual giving.* Gaithersburg, MD: Aspen.

Williams, K. A. (2002). Annual campaigns. In *Nonprofit organization management* (pp. 9:19–21). New York: Aspen. (Original work published 1997)

Winer, M., & Roy, K. (1997). *Collaboration handbook*. Saint Paul, MN: Amherst H. Wilder Foundation.

Wolf, T. (1984). *The nonprofit organization: An operating manual*. Englewood Cliffs, NJ: Prentice Hall.

Women's Business Center & Women's Business Institute. (2001). The essential elements of a good business plan. Retrieved May 6, 2003, from www.onlinewbc.gov/docs/starting/bp_essentials.html

Work in America Institute, Inc. (1983). *Productivity through work innovations*. New York: Pergamon.

Zaremba, A. (1989). Communication: The upward network. *Personnel Journal, 3*, 34–39.

Index

Absenteeism
  decision-making and, 87–88
  problem solving and, 80–82
Abstract ideas made concrete, 82–83
Accessibility of organization, 93
Accountability
  objectives and, 62
  quality control and, 92
  strategic planning and, 31–32
Accounts receivable/payable, 230
Accrual accounting, 230
Action plan implementation
  anticipating consequences and,
    62–64
  contingency planning and, 70–71
  pilot projects and, 64–67
  resistance to change and, 67–69
  risk factor assessment and, 69–70
  setting objectives for, 58–62
  tipping point leadership and, 64
Action team, 392
Activity objectives, 59
Ad hoc task force, 392
Administrative budget, 226
Administrators, 53
Advocacy, 176–177
Age Discrimination in Employment
  (ADEA), 135
Alliances. *See* Coalition building
Americans with Disabilities Act
  (ADA), 136–138
Analysis of problems, 77–82
Annual campaign, 258–262
Annual campaigns, 258–262, 304
Annuity trust, 278
Appraisal of performance. *See*
  Performance appraisal
Arrogant manager, 7
Assessments. *See also* Performance
  appraisal
  of board of trustees, 417, 420–421
  corrections and, 93–94
  discrimination surveys, 161

employee evaluations and, 144
of executive director of board of
  trustees, 407–408, 419
expectations and, 187
job/workload analyses, 123–125
of major gifts program, 271–273
pre-proposal, 301–304
and results monitoring of problem
  solving, 91–93
Asset Generated Income, 230
Association of Fundraising
  Professionals (AFP), 271
Attitudes of problem people, 134
Authority
  board of trustees and, 403
  strategic alliances and, 395
Average tendency, 202

Behaviorally anchored rating scale
  (BARS), 195–196
Benchmarks and problem solving, 82
Beneficial trust income, 281
Bequests. *See* Planned giving programs
  (PGPs)
Block grant, 338
Board of trustees
  agency executive director
    performance review, 419
  checklist for well-functioning,
    417–418
  distinguishing governance from
    management and, 403–406
  inactive members and, 415
  meeting improvement and, 415–416
  roles/responsibilities of, 406–413
  self-assessment of, 417, 420–421
  size of, 416–417
  structures/processes of, 413–414
  tenure of, 417
Board-designated funds, 281
Bona fide occupational qualifications
  (BFOQ), 114
Bonuses, 212–214

Bottom-up budgeting, 234–235
Bottom-up communications, 374
Brain trusts, 287
Brainstorming, 352–353
Break-even points, 232, 293–294
Budgets. *See also* Finance management;
    Foundations; Funding
  board of trustees and, 408–409
  proposals and, 311–315
Bureaucratic structural
    organization, 121
Business ventures as income, 286–289

Campaigns
  annual, 258–262, 304
  capital, 262–273
Capital budget, 228
Capital campaigns, 262–264
Capitated contracts, 337–338
Case statements, 257–258
Cash accounting, 230
Cash flow budget, 228–229
Casual atmosphere, 157
*The Catalog of Federal Domestic
    Assistance*, 334–335
Catholic Charities Services
    Corporation (CCSC), 54–55
Cause-related marketing (CRM),
    284–285
Change. *See also* Action plan
    implementation
  dynamic planning and, 33
  organized abandonment and, 23
  pilot projects and, 64–67
  resistance to, 67–69, 346, 387
  strategic planning and, 20, 35
  tipping point leadership and, 64
Charitable gift annuities, 278
Charitable lead trusts, 278
Charitable remainder trusts, 278
Charmer manager, 8
Civil Rights Act, 159, 163–164
Coalition building, 393–399
Collaborative efforts/structures,
    396–399
Command language and dignity
    towards staff, 11
Commercial ventures, 286–289
Commission-based fundraising, 271
Communication. *See also* Harassment
  annual campaign and, 259–260
  appraisal conference and, 200–204
  appraisal methods and, 200

during change processes, 68
constructive criticism and, 184–185
conveying expectations and, 186–188
cost reduction considerations
    and, 248
decision to hold meetings and, 345
effective proposals and, 317–320
external, 378–380
facilitation of internal, 372–378
feedback and, 377–378
handling conflicts and, 368–370
informal, 376–377
managing conversations, 108–109
and media involvement, 379–380
misperceptions and, 367–368
of organizational values, 152
persuasive, 371–373
poor use of written documents and,
    363–367
with prospective donors,
    270–271, 281
roles of supervisor and, 174–175
of significant message, 12
strategic alliances and, 396
strategic resource development
    and, 271
team building and, 386
telephone calls and, 109, 262, 286
Community foundations, 324
Company foundations, 283
Company-sponsored foundations, 325
Compensation of work. *See also*
    Salary bonuses as, 212–214
gain-sharing plans and, 214
and impact of monetary rewards,
    214–216
job classification system and,
    204–206
pay for performance (PFP) and,
    206–212
salary and, 128–129, 212–214, 231,
    244, 271
skill-based pay system and, 206
symbolic rewards and, 216–218
Competence and quality control, 92
Competition analysis, 47–48
Complacency in organizations,
    165–166
Complaint-handling, 93
Conduit of funds, 303
Confidentiality
  employees with HIV/AIDS and, 137
  termination and, 147

Conflicts in organizations
  consensus and, 386
  of interest, 412
  manager dealing with, 369–370
  team handling of, 388–389
  types of, 368–369
Consensus. *See* Meetings
Consent agenda, 415
Consortiums, 397
Constructive criticism, 184–185
Constructive discharge, 142–143
Consumer needs, 49
Consumer service market, 47–48, 50
Consumer-oriented programs, 55–56.
  See also Logic planning model;
  Marketing planning model
Contingency planning, 70–71
Contract funding, 230, 244
Contradictory expectations of work,
  156–157, 159
Contributions. *See* Foundations;
  Funding
Control. *See* Self-regulation as
  leadership attribute
Conversations and time management,
  108–109
Coordinated efforts. *See* Coalition
  building; Team building
Corporate foundations, 325
Corporate giving funds, 283, 316
Cost allocation, 231, 263
Cost effectiveness, 250–251
Cost reduction considerations,
  243–248
Cost reimbursement contracts, 337–338
Counseling
  objectives and, 62
  program budget example for,
    237–239
  termination interview and, 147
  as throughputs, 39–40
County funding of human services,
  339–341
Crisis situations
  appraisal methods and, 196
  communication during, 362
  consumers and, 50
  and handling of stress, 158–159
  and media involvement, 379–380
  pilot projects and, 65–66
  strategic planning and, 22–23
Culture. *See* Organizational culture
Customers/clients, 48, 50

Daily work plan, 103–104
Dating policies, 165
Day care as throughputs, 40
Decentralized operations, 5
Decision-making
  board of trustees and, 409–410
  dynamic quality of, 94
  flaws of, 89–90
  meetings and, 352
  obtaining key information for,
    374–375
  problem people and, 133
  procrastination and, 111
  prudent use of, 84–89
  results monitoring and, 91–93
  task forces and, 393
  team building and, 386
Delegative leadership, 4–6, 177–178
Deliverables, 60, 307
Details and success, 71–74
Development of new procedures, 65
Devolution, 339–340
Dignity
  leadership competencies
    and, 11–12
  termination and, 147
Direct corporate giving programs,
  325–326
Direct mail campaign, 262
Directive leadership, 4–6
Disabilities. *See* Employees
Discharge. *See* Termination
Discrepancies. *See* Problem analysis
Discrimination
  age, 135–136
  diversity and, 159–162
  interviews and, 114–119
  termination and, 145–146
Diversified funding, 251
Diversity, 159–162
Docket, 347
Documentation. *See also*
  Policies/procedures
  budgeting and, 236
  corrective action towards employees
    and, 139, 141
  of meetings, 357–358
  solicitors of major gifts and, 267
  variance report as, 242
  of verbal warnings, 146
Donations. *See* Strategic resource
  development
Donor restricted funds, 229

Drucker, Peter, 20. *See also* Strategic planning
Drug Free Work Act of 1988, 136
Dynamic planning, 33–35

Economies of scale, 245
80/20 principle
   solicitation of major gifts and, 267
   time management and, 104
Electronic philanthropy, 285–286
E-mail, 379. *See also* Communication
Emotional attributes. *See* Leadership attributes
Empathy as leadership attribute, 16
Employees. *See also* Compensation of work; Organizational culture; Performance appraisal
   conduction of interviews for, 114–119
   corrective action towards, 139–140
   with disabilities, 137–138
   disciplinary action towards, 140–142
   filling vacancies, 113–114
   with HIV/AIDS, 136–137
   incompetent, 142–147
   job enrichment and, 125–126
   job ownership and, 152–154
   older, 135–136
   and restructuring jobs, 122–127
   stress and, 155–159
   with substance abuse problems, 136
   training of, 119–120
   types of problem people, 133–136
   use of time log for, 100–101
Employment at will doctrine, 140
Employment challenges, 132–135
Endowment income, 230, 281–282, 338. *See also* Planned giving programs (PGPs)
Entropy in organizations, 166
Environment, 126–127, 186
Equal Employment Opportunity Commission (EEOC), 137, 159
Evaluations. *See also* Assessments
   of fundraising efforts, 272–273
   of fundraising event, 297–298
   of proposals, 309–310
   supervisors and, 175
   termination and, 144
Event sponsorships, 285
Exception principle, 104
Executive committee of board of trustees, 413
Executive discretionary funds, 283

Executive limitations, 403–404
Expectancy Theory, 181
Expectations of work, 156–157, 159
Expense. *See* Income/expense
External case statement, 257–258
External communication, 378–380
External markets, 52–56

Faith-based drives, 53–54
Familiarity and decision-making, 89
Family and Medical Leave Act (FMLA), 139
FC Search: The Foundation Center's Database on CD-ROM, 331–334
Federal government funding, 334–336
Federal Register, 335
Federations, 397
Feedback system
   appraisal methods and, 203
   communication and, 377–378
   consumer-oriented programs and, 56
   from consumers, 51–52
   job training and, 120
   strategic planning and, 32
Finance committe of board of trustees, 413
Finance management. *See also* Proposals; Strategic resource development
   achievement of financial stability, 248–251
   the budgeting process and, 225–229
   cost reduction, 243–248
   fundraising events and, 293–294
   income/expense types and, 229–232
   monitoring/modifying budgets, 237–243
   organization-wide budgets and, 233–234
   program budgets and, 234–236
   revenue/expenditures report (example), 239–241
Fiscal agent, 303
Fixed expenses, 231, 247, 293
Fixed revenues, 231
Flexibility
   in budgets, 243
   leadership styles and, 5–6
   quality control and, 93
   resistance to change and, 67–68
   spending of grants and, 315
Flextime, 123
Flowcharts for logic planning, 40–42

Focus groups for consumer feedback, 51
Forced choice tendency, 203
Forward sequence planning, 73
The Foundation 1000, 327–329
The Foundation Center, 325–327
The Foundation Directory, 328–329, 331
Foundation Directory Online, 331
The Foundation Directory/Part 2, 328–329, 331
The Foundation Grants Index on CD-ROM, 327, 329, 331
Foundations
  directories of, 327–331
  external markets and, 53
  funding from, 315–317
  search process for funding and, 328–331
  types of, 324–326
Fund balance (reserves), 232
Funding. *See also* Compensation of work; Finance management; Strategic resource development
  external markets and, 53
  federal government, 334–336
  financial coordination and, 398–399
  The Foundation Center and, 325–327
  foundation directories and, 327–331
  income/expense types and, 229–232
  lobbying for, 339–341
  online directories, 331–334
  performance contracting as, 215
  restructuring jobs due to, 122
  as risk factor, 70
  state/local government, 336–339
  terminations due to, 127–128
  types of foundations, 324–326
  web site resources for, 426
Fundraising event. *See also* Proposals
  board of trustees and, 411
  considerations of, 289–290
  evaluation of, 297–298
  expense reduction of, 296–297
  feasibility analysis and, 290–292
  maximizing profits of, 294–296
  objectives and, 291, 298
  planning of, 291–294
  tax considerations of, 297
Future trends of leadership competencies, 9–10

Gain-sharing plans, 214
Gender. *See* Diversity
Gifts. *See also* Strategic resource development
  assessment of program of, 271–273
  and gift chart, 261–262
  life insurance policy as, 278–279
  planned giving programs (PGPs) as, 276–282
  solicitation of major, 266–269
Goals/objectives
  appraisal methods and, 194
  coalition building and, 393–394, 396
  complacency/stagnation and, 166
  diversity and, 161
  executive director of board of trustees and, 407–408
  external markets and, 53
  formatting of, 60–61
  fundraising event feasibility analysis and, 291
  fundraising events and, 298
  integrated fund plan development and, 255–256
  kinds of, 59–60
  limitations of, 61–62
  management by objectives (MBO) and, 196–200
  organization-wide budgets and, 233
  priorities and, 102–103
  procrastination and, 110–111
  of proposals, 306–308
  team building and, 384
  termination due to not meeting, 143
  tracking of, 33
  unit's budget and, 235–236
  volunteers and, 188–189
Go-no/go points, 86
Governance committee of board of trustees, 414
Governing bodies. *See* Board of trustees
Government funding, 334–339
Grant funding, 230, 248. *See also* Foundations; Funding
The Grant Guides Series, 328
Graphic rating scale appraisal method, 195
Grievances, 140–142
Gross profits, 293
Group sales and fundraising events, 295–296

Groupthink and meetings,
    349–350, 388
*Guide to U.S. Foundations, Their
    Trustees, Officers, and Donors,*
    328, 331

Halo effect, 202
Harassment
    dating policies and, 165
    non-sexual, 162
    sexual, 163–165
Herzberg's Hygiene-Motivator
    Theory, 182
Hierarchical structural
    organization, 121
Higher purpose of workjob ownership
    and, 153
HIV/AIDS, 136–137
Housing services as throughputs, 40
Human resources committee of board
    of trustees, 414
Humiliation, 7
Hygiene-Motivator Theory, 182

Idealism, 166–168
Impact objectives, 59, 307. *See also*
    Goals/objectives
Incentives. *See* Compensation of work
Income tax
    Form 990 and, 232, 283
    fundraising events and, 297
    nonprofit designation and, 302–303
    unrelated business income tax
        (UBIT), 288–289
Income/expense
    fundraising events and, 296–297
    organization-wide budgets and, 233
    proposals and, 312–315
    types, 229–232
Incompetence, 142–147
Incremental budget, 228
Indemnification of board members, 412
Indirect costs, 231–232
Inequities in organizations, 166–168
Inflation tendency, 203
Informal communication, 376–377
Information flow
    pilot projects and, 65
    time management and, 106–107
Information referral as throughputs, 40
Initial outcomes for logic planning
    model, 44
In-kind matching funds, 230, 325–326

Innovative programs. *See also* Pilot
    projects
    block grants and, 338
Inputs and logic planning model,
    39, 45–46
Insubordination, 143
Insurance, 248, 278–279
Insurance companies, 53
Interactions. *See also* Meetings
Intermediate outcomes for logic
    planning model, 44–45
Internal case statement, 257–258
Internal Revenue Service (IRS), 232,
    283, 289, 302–303
    corporate foundations and, 326
    lobbying and, 339
    private foundations and, 325
    private inurement and, 412
Internet. *See also* Technology
    applying for funds via, 317. *See also*
        Foundations
    for consumer feedback, 51
Interviews
    employment, 114–119
    termination, 146–147
Intrapreneur, 67
Invitation for bids (IFB), 336
Irrevocable plan, 277
Isolation, 16

Job Accommodation Network, 138
Job analysis, 123–125
Job burnout. *See* Stress
Job classification system of
    compensation, 204–206
Job enrichment, 125–126
Job ownership, 152–154
Job rotation/enlargement, 125–126
Job sharing, 123
Job stress. *See* Stress
Job training as throughputs, 40
Job-needs analysis, 119
Joint issue promotions, 285
Joint planning, 397

Key informants, 29
Key realities of strategic planning,
    29, 32

Language in objective statements,
    59–60
Lawsuits. *See* Legal matters;
    Termination

Lead trust, 278
Leadership attributes, 153
    leadership styles and, 16
    tipping point leadership and, 64
    types of, 15–16
    v. managerial attributes, 3
Leadership competencies
    communication of significant
        messages and, 12
    dignity towards staff and, 11–12
    leaders as social entrepreneurs and,
        10–11
    leadership styles and, 16–17
    meetings and, 358–359
    performance inspiration and,
        13–15
    as seeking future trends, 9–10
    trust and, 12–13
Leadership styles
    diagnosing, 16–17
    flawed, 6–8
    types of, 4
Leasing equipment, 244, 247
Legacy programs, 281
Legal matters
    obligations of board of trustees as,
        412–413
    protection of employees as,
        135–139
Letters of interest, 316
Liabilities, 232
Licensing of names/logos, 285
Life income gifts, 278
Line-item budget, 226–227
Linkage-ability-interest principle of
    fundraising, 265
Lobbying, 339–341
Local funding. See Foundations
Logic planning model
    evaluation of outcome measures of,
        46–47
    outcome establishment for, 44–46
    outcome measures for, 43–44
    and pathway for client flowcharts,
        40–42
    social system analysis for, 39–41
Loner manager, 8
Long-term outcomes for logic
    planning model, 45

Managed care contracts, 337–338
Management by objectives (MBO),
    196–200

Managers. See also Supervision
    diversity and, 162
    executive director of board of
        trustees, 407–408
    and handling of stress, 157–158
    interactions with situations, 5–6
    interactions with staff/situations, 4
    leadership styles of, 4
    leading teams, 385
    response to conflict, 369–370
    and retaining staff, 128–129
    span of control of, 373
    time management and, 99–100
    v. leaders, 3
Market structural organization, 121–122
Marketing
    budgets, 283
    cause-related (CRM), 284–285
    fundraising events and, 292–295
Marketing planning model
    consumer feedback and, 51–52
    consumer service market
        determination and, 47–48
    external markets and, 52–55
    and outstanding service offering,
        48–50
    strategic marketing and, 54
Maslow's Need Hierarchy theory, 181
Matrix structural organization, 121–122
McClelland's Need for Achievement
    Theory, 181
McGregor's Theory X and
    Theory Y, 181
Media involvement, 379–380, 414
Medical conditions, 136–138
Meetings
    analogous thinking and, 355–356
    brainstorming and, 352–353
    creative questions and, 354–355
    decision to hold, 345–346
    facilitation of discussion at,
        350–351
    functions of, 348
    improving board of trustee, 415–416
    leading, 358–359
    nominal group technique (NGT)
        and, 353–354
    problems of, 348–350
    pro-con discussions and, 354
    reaching consensus at, 351–352, 390
    recording, 357–358
    scenarios and, 356–357
    time management and, 346–347

Mentors, 162
Micromanager, 7
Minorities. *See* Diversity
Misleading manager, 6–7
Mission drift, 53, 70
Mission interaction sessions, 415
Mission statement
  board of trustees and, 406
  external markets and, 53, 56
  search process for funding and, 328
  for strategic planning, 25–26, 31
  strategic resource development and,
    256, 271
Motivation
  applying theories of, 180–182
  appraisal methods and, 195
  as leadership attributes, 15
  pay for performance (PFP) as, 210
  planned giving programs (PGPs)
    and, 279
  problem people and, 133–135
  rewards and, 215

Narcissist manager, 7–8
*The National Directory of Corporate
  Giving*, 327, 329, 331
National Federation of Nonprofits, 248
Need for Achievement Theory, 181
Need Hierarchy theory, 181
Negative cash flow, 228–229
Net assets, 232
Net profits, 293
Networking, 378
Nominal group technique (NGT),
  353–354

Obesity, 138
Oblivious manager, 6
Online solicitations. *See* Electronic
  philanthropy
On-the-job training (OJT), 119–120
Operating budget, 226–227
Operating objectives, 307. *See also*
  Goals/objectives
Operational objectives, 59–60
Opportunistic thinking, 33
Organizational culture
  board of trustees and, 406
  capabilities and, 310
  coalition building and, 393–394
  complacency/stagnation in, 165–166
  conveying expectations and, 186–188
  creation of, 151–152

diversity and, 159–162
  importance of team building and,
    384–392
  inequities in, 166–168
  integrated fund plan development
    and, 255–256
  job ownership and, 152–154
  pay for performance (PFP) and, 212
  restructuring jobs in, 122–127
  strategic alliances and, 395
  stress and, 155–159
  structuring for productivity and,
    120–122
  Values Statement and, 154–155
Organization-wide budget, 233–234
Organization-wide pay plans, 214
Organized abandonment, 23
Outcome budget, 226–227
Outcome measures
  consumer-oriented programs and, 55
  evaluation of, 46–47
  initial/intermediate/long-term, 44–46
  logic planning model and, 43–44
  performance contracting and, 338
Outcomes and logic planning
  model, 39, 45
Outputs
  consumer-oriented programs and, 55
  logic planning model and, 39,
    43, 45–46
  performance contracting and,
    337–338
Outright gifts of appreciated
  property, 277
Outsourcing, 243
Overhead costs, 231
Overload/underload of work, 156

Part time working, 244, 246–247
Participative leadership, 4–5
Partnership arrangements, 285
Passive managers, 6
Pathways and logic planning model,
  40–42
Pay for performance (PFP)
  compensation system, 206–212
Performance appraisal. *See also*
  Compensation of work
  conducting conference of, 200–204
  methods of, 194–200
Performance budget, 226
Performance contracting, 215
Performance contracts, 337–338

Performance inspiration, 13–14
Performance standards. *See also* Staff
  age and, 135–136
  agency executive director
      performance review, 419
  appraisal methods and, 194
  dating policies and, 165
  informing staff of, 145
  organizational culture and, 152
  supervisors and, 175–176
  team building and, 386
Permanent endowments, 282
Peron-needs analysis, 119
Persecution of subordinates, 369
Personal feuds, 368
Personal life experiences and stress, 158
Perspectives, 80–81. *See also* Problem
  analysis
Persuasive communication, 371–373
Pilot programs, 64–67, 341
Pilot projects, 64–67
Planned giving programs (PGPs),
  276–282
Planning
  business ventures and, 287–288
  capital campaigns and, 263
  daily work plan and, 103–104
  decision to hold meetings and, 345
  detail management and, 71–74
  forward sequence, 73
  fundraising event, 291–294
  joint, 397
  persuasive communciation and, 371
  poor, 157
  reverse order, 72
Pledged income, 230
Policies/procedures
  board of trustees and, 404–405,
    410–411
  collective bargaining agreements,
    140–141
  dating, 165
  discipline and, 145–146
  diversity and, 161
  and harassment, 164–165
  media involvement and, 380
  organization-wide budgets and, 233
  personnel, 246–247
  policymakers and, 53
  poor employee performance
    and, 132
  for quality control, 92–93
  termination and, 144–145

Political endorsements/funding,
  338–339
Pooled income funds, 278
Positive cash flow, 228
Posteriority. *See* Priorities and time
  management
Pre-will programs, 281
Pride in one's work, 153–154, 363
Priorities and time management,
  101–103
Privacy and interviews, 118
Private foundations, 325–326
Private inurement, 412
Problem analysis, 77–82
Problem solving
  alternative solutions while, 82–84
  appraisal conference and, 201
  conflict and, 368–370
  decision-making while, 84–90
  making corrections while, 93–94
  problem analysis and, 77–82
  results monitoring and, 91–93
  staff involvement in, 184
  supervisors and, 175
  team building and, 386–387
Process objectives, 59
Pro-con discussions, 354
Procrastination, 110–111
Product objectives, 59–60, 307. *See
  also* Goals/objectives
Program budget, 226–227, 234–235
Program committee of board of
  trustees, 414
Program officers, 324
Promotions
  the passed-over employee and, 133
  restructuring jobs due to, 123
  transaction-based, 284–285
Proposals
  federal grant, 335–336
  funding foundations and,
    315–317, 326
  persuasive communciation as, 372
  preliminary assessments and,
    301–315
  success of, 317–320
Public information committee of
  board of trustees, 414
Public relations, 176, 409
Put-downer manager, 7

Quality control, 92–93
Quasi-endowments, 281–282

Recency tendency, 202
Recruitment process. *See* Interviews
Referral sources, 53
Relationships. *See also* Supervision
  between board of trustees and
    director, 402–404
  cause-related marketing (CRM) as,
    284–285
  coalition building and, 397
  for effective proposals, 317–320
  participative leadership and, 5
  and planned giving programs
    (PGPs), 279–280
  with prospective donors,
    270–271
  resource development and, 255
  with volunteers, 188–189
Reliability, 92
Requests for proposals (RFPs)
  The Foundation Center and, 326
  state/local government funding and,
    336–337
Reserves, 232, 249
Resistance to change
  dealing with, 67–69
  decision to hold meetings
    and, 346
  team building and, 387
Resource audit, 27–29
Resource development committee of
  board of trustees, 413–414
Resources. *See also* Strategic resource
  development
  board of trustees and, 413–414
  business ventures and, 286
  coalition building and, 393–395
  cost reduction considerations
    and, 248
  development of, 255
  external markets and, 52–55
  sharing of, 244
  supervisors and, 176
  web sites for human service
    managers, 425–428
Revenues. *See* Finance management
Reverse order planning, 72
Rewards, 214–218, 243. *See also*
  Compensation of work
Ridicule. *See* Harassment
Risk factors
  decision-making and, 84–86
  in new projects, 69–70
Role ambiguity, 156

Salary. *See also* Compensation of
  work
  bonuses and, 212–214
  cost allocation and, 231
  cost reduction considerations
    and, 244
  fundraising consultants and, 271
  and retaining staff, 128–129
Satisficing, 83
Scanning the environment, 28–29
Self-awareness as leadership
  attribute, 15
Self-regulation as leadership
  attribute, 15
Service customer
  consumer-oriented programs and, 55
  definition, 48
  quality control and, 93
Service objectives, 59, 307. *See also*
  Goals/objectives
Services and pilot projects, 65
Sexual harassment/assault, 163–165
Sexual harassment/assault, 143
Shared costs, 231
Silo mentality, 122
Situational scenarios, 120
Situations
  diagnosing leadership styles and,
    16–17
  managers interactions with, 5–6
  strategic planning and, 22–23
Skill-based pay system of
  compensation, 206
Social intrapreneur, 67
Social skills as leadership attributes, 16
Solicitations, 262, 265–269. *See also*
  Strategic resource development
Staff. *See also* Employees; Time
  management
  applying motivational theories to,
    180–182
  communication and, 363
  conduction of interviews for, 114–119
  decision-making and, 85
  decision-making and involvement
    of, 87–89
  delegation of assignments to, 178–180
  development of, 119–120
  dignity towards, 11–12
  dissatisfaction v. low morale, 167
  and leadership attributes, 15–16
  management by objectives (MBO)
    and, 198

managers interactions with, 4
micromanager and, 7
objectives and, 62
oblivious managers and, 6
performance inspiration and, 13–15
personnel coordination and, 398
physical environment and, 126–127
pilot projects and, 64–66
procrastination and, 111
program officers as, 324
reduction of turnover of, 126
resistance to change by, 68–69
risk factor assessment and, 69
roles of supervisor concerning,
 174–175
seeking other employment, 128–129
staffing patterns and, 121
strategic planning process and, 24
support, 158
and surveys as communication, 375
task forces and, 392–393
team building and, 386–387
Stagnation in organizations, 165–166
Strategic alliances, 394–396. *See also*
 Coalition building
Strategic marketing, 54
Strategic planning
 business fundamental questions for,
  26–27
 conduction of analysis for, 24–25
 conduction of SWOT process for,
  27–29
 drafting of, 31–33
 dynamic planning and, 33–35
 engaging staff in, 24
 examination of critical issues for,
  30–32
 external markets and, 53
 function of, 20–21
 integrated fund plan development
  and, 255
 mission statement development for,
  25–26
 resource development committee of
  board of trustees and, 413–414
 review for, 22–23
 search process for funding and, 328
Strategic resource development. *See
 also* Proposals
 annual campaign and, 258–262
 assessment of gifts program amd,
  271–273
 business ventures and, 286–289

capital campaigns principles and,
 262–264
case statements and, 257–258
corporate contributions and,
 283–285
and development of loyal donor
 base, 264–266
electronic philanthropy and,
 285–286
and evaluation of fundraising event,
 297–298
and expense reduction of
 fundraising event, 296–297
fundraising consultants and, 271
fundraising event considerations
 and, 289–290
fundraising event feasibility analysis
 and, 290–291
fundraising event objectives and, 291
integrated fund plan development
 and, 255–256
major gifts and, 266–270
and maximizing profits of
 fundraising event, 294–296
planned giving and, 276–282
and planning of fundraising event,
 291–294
and tax considerations of
 fundraising event, 297
Stress, 155–159, 211
Subsidiary funds, 283
Substance abuse problems, 136, 138,
 337–338
Suggestion systems, 375–376
Suits. *See* Legal matters
Summer intern programs, 161
Supervision
 constructive criticism and, 184–185
 and conveying expectations,
  186–188
 and delegating assignments,
  178–180
 differing perspectives and, 172–174
 and enhancing relationship with
  staff, 183–184
 handling multiple roles of, 177–178
 mistakes to avoid in, 185–186
 roles of, 174–178
 using motivational theories'
  application for, 180–182
 of volunteers, 188–189
Support service budget, 226
Surplus, 232

Surveys
  communication and, 375
  for consumer feedback, 49, 51
  discrimination, 161
  electronic philanthropy and, 286
SWOT (SCOT) process, 27–29, 31
Synergy of coalitions, 393

Task assignments, 72–73
Task conflict, 388
Task forces, 392–393
Tax savings, 248, 277. *See also*
  Income tax
Team building. *See also* Board of
  trustees
  coalition building and, 393–399
  exercises for, 390–391
  importance of, 384–392
  task forces and, 392–393
Team-based structural organization,
  121–122
Technology
  applying for funds via Internet, 317
  communication and, 379
  electronic philanthropy and,
    285–286
  resistance to, 133–134
  restructuring jobs due to, 122
  time management and, 106–108
  written communication and, 366
Telephone calls
  electronic philanthropy and, 286
  solicitation and, 262
  time management and, 109
Termination
  better jobs elsewhere and, 128–129
  funding reductions and, 127–128
  grounds for, 143–144
  of older employees, 135–136
  problem people and, 133–135
  progressive discipline and, 142
Theory X and Theory Y, 181
Throughputs, 39–40, 45–46
Time management
  blocking out time and, 104–106
  combating time waste for, 106–109
  daily work plan and, 103–104
  determination of priorities for,
    101–103
  factors affecting, 99–100
  leadership styles and, 5
  meetings and, 346–347
  procrastination and, 110–111

  quality control and, 92
  use of time log for, 199
  volunteers and, 189
Timeline chart
  action plans and, 73–74
  capital campaigns and, 262
  fundraising events and, 291, 298
  for management by objectives
    (MBO), 198–199
  for strategic planning, 31–32
Tipping point leadership, 64
Top-down communications, 373–374
Total indirect costs, 231
Training
  decision to hold meetings and, 346
  performance contracting and,
    337–338
  of staff, 119–120
  summer intern programs and, 161
  team building and, 386
  technophobes and, 133–134
  trainee assignments and, 133, 135
Transaction-based promotions, 284
Transparency, 412–413
Travel budgets, 247
True endowments, 282
Trust
  job ownership and, 153
  leadership competencies and,
    12–13
  quality control and, 92
  supervisory mistakes and, 185–186
  team building and, 386
Trustees. *See* Board of trustees
Trusts, 278, 287
Turf battles, 369
Turkey farm, 143

U.S. General Accounting Office, 335
Unions and PFP, 212
Unit budget, 234–235
United Black Fund, 53
United Way, 53–54
Unitrust, 278
Unit-wide pay plans, 214
Unjust dismissal, 146
Unrelated business income tax (UBIT),
  288–289
Unrestricted funds, 229

Values of organization
  appraisal methods and, 194
  decision-making and, 84

external markets and, 53
inequities in organization and,
    166–168
organizational culture and, 151
Values Statement, 154–155
Variable expenses, 231, 247, 293
Variable revenues, 231
Variance analysis,
    241–242, 247
Variance report, 242
Venture audit, 287
Venture committee, 287
Venture entrepreneur, 287
Verbal warnings, 141–142, 146
Violence, termination due to, 143
Vision statement
    dynamic planning and, 33–34
    for strategic planning, 26, 31
Vital signs report, 415

Volunteers
    coalition building and, 393
    fundraising events and, 289
    as in-kind contribution, 325–326
    reduction of costs and, 245–246
    as solicitors, 267, 272
    supervising, 188–189
Vroom's Expectancy Theory, 181

Web sites, 379, 425–428
Work plan, 103–104, 235–236
Work simplification, 125
Worker of the Month, 216
Working capital, 249–250
Workload analysis, 124–125
Workplace celebrations, 161
Writer's block, 363–366

Zero-bases budget (ZBB), 228, 245

About the Author

Ralph Brody, Ph.D., teaches courses on social service administration at Cleveland State University and has taught service delivery models (Ph.D. program) at Case Western Reserve University. He was the executive director of the Federation for Community Planning, an organization that provides research, planning, and advocacy on health and human services. His other managerial positions have included director of a job training program, director of five multiservice centers, and associate director of a college urban institute. He has provided consultation or training to more than 40 community agencies, including the Catholic Charities Services Corporation; the Council on International Programs, USA; the Ohio Bureau of Employment Services; Ohio Department of Health; the Ford Foundation; United Way Services; the YMCA of Kenya; the Ministry of Civil Affairs, People's Republic of China; the School of Social Welfare in Barcelona, Spain; agency directors in Kerala, India; community leaders in Nigeria; NGO directors in Ghana; the Alliance for Arab Women in Egypt; Madrasa Pre-School organizers in Mombasa, Kenya and Kumasi, Uganda; Forum on Street Children in Ethiopia; and sustaining Kenya community-based organizations for the International Partners in Mission.

He is the author of books on case management, the state legislative process, fundraising events, community problem solving, service learning, and macro practice. He has produced documentaries on supervision and drug free zones. For five years he chaired the Options Committee, which successfully planned and advocated for additional public funding for services for older persons in the Greater Cleveland area.